Organizational Behaviour

CANADIAN EDITION

WileyPLUS Learning Space

Includes **ORION**  Adaptive Practice

An easy way to help students learn, collaborate, and grow.

Designed to engage today's student, WileyPLUS Learning Space will transform any course into a vibrant, collaborative, learning community.

Identify which students are struggling early in the semester.

Educators assess the real-time engagement and performance of each student to inform teaching decisions. Students always know what they need to work on.

Facilitate student engagement both in and outside of class.

Educators can quickly organize learning activities, manage student collaboration, and customize their course.

Measure outcomes to promote continuous improvement.

With visual reports, it's easy for both students and educators to gauge problem areas and act on what's most important.

www.wileypluslearningspace.com

WILEY

Organizational Behaviour

CANADIAN EDITION

MITCHELL J. NEUBERT

Baylor University

BRUNO DYCK

University of Manitoba

MARY J. WALLER

Schulich School of Business, York University

THOMAS MEDCOF

Schulich School of Business, York University

WILEY

PRODUCTION CREDITS

EXECUTIVE EDITOR	Darren Lalonde
VICE PRESIDENT AND DIRECTOR, MARKET SOLUTIONS	Veronica Visentin
SENIOR MARKETING MANAGER	Anita Osborne
EDITORIAL MANAGER	Karen Staudinger
DEVELOPMENTAL EDITOR	Daleara Jamasji Hirjikaka
MEDIA EDITOR	Luisa Begani
ASSISTANT EDITOR	Ashley Patterson
PRODUCTION AND MEDIA SPECIALIST	Meaghan MacDonald
TYPESETTING	SPi Global
COVER AND INTERIOR DESIGN	Joanna Vieira
COVER PHOTO	Robert Churchill/Collection E +/ Getty
PRINTING AND BINDING	Quad Graphics

Library and Archives Canada Cataloguing in Publication

Neubert, Mitchell J., author
    Organizational behaviour / Mitchell J. Neubert (Baylor University), Bruno Dyck (University of Manitoba), Mary Waller (Schulich School of Business, York University), Thomas Medcof (York University). — Canadian edition.

Includes bibliographical references and indexes.
ISBN 978-1-119-19432-3 (binder ready version)

    1. Organizational behaviour. I. Dyck, Bruno, 1961-, author II. Waller, Mary, author III. Medcof, Thomas, author IV. Title.

HD58.7.N45 2016   658   C2015-907285-9

Printed and bound in the United States of America

1 2 3 4 5 QG 20 19 18 17 16

This book is dedicated to my mother and father, who believed in me; my family, who love and support me; and to my students, who motivate me to keep learning.

MITCH

This book is dedicated to my family, friends, colleagues, and students, who have challenged and helped me to think deeply about organizational behaviour and its place in the world.

BRUNO

To B.M.S. and our family—relatives, friends, colleagues, students, and four-footed.

MARY

about the authors

Canadian Edition

DR. MARY J. WALLER

Dr. Mary J. Waller is Professor of Organization Studies at York University's Schulich School of Business in Toronto. She earned her Ph.D. in Organization Science from the University of Texas at Austin, her M.Sc. degree in Information Systems from the University of Colorado, and her B.B.A. degree in Petroleum Land Management from the University of Oklahoma.

Before beginning her academic career, Dr. Waller worked in the petroleum, aviation, and software industries, which often involved collaborating in teams under time-pressured situations. Those experiences helped motivate her team dynamics research, resulting in over 20 years of research involving studies of flight crews, nuclear power crews, emergency medical teams, harbour management teams, mine rescue teams, and other teams, all working under real or simulated crisis situations. Dr. Waller's work has been published in numerous journals, including the *Academy of Management Journal, Academy of Management Review, Journal of Applied Psychology, Management Science, Journal of Organizational Behavior, Group & Organization Management,* and *Small Group Research,* and she has been quoted in *The New York Times* and *The Wall Street Journal.* She has twice been awarded the Schulich MBA Teaching Excellence Award and has developed workshops and simulations for numerous organizations on the topics of team dynamics and crisis management. She served on the Board of Governors of the Academy of Management from 2012 to 2015 and currently serves as Director of the Schulich Centre for Teaching Excellence at York University.

In her spare time, Dr. Waller enjoys learning German, playing the concertina and button accordion, and being herded by her three border collies.

DR. THOMAS MEDCOF

Dr. Thomas Medcof has extensive experience in business administration, having earned his MBA from the Anderson School of Management at the University of New Mexico and his Ph.D. in Management from York University's Schulich School of Business. He has taught at the University of Guelph's College of Business and Economics and at Ryerson's Ted Rogers School of Management, and he is currently teaching at the Schulich School of Business. Dr. Medcof was the recipient of the Seymour Schulich Award for Teaching Excellence in 2011 and 2014.

U.S. Edition

DR. MITCHELL NEUBERT

Dr. Mitchell Neubert's interest in organizations was initially stirred by observing the ups and downs of a parent in a small family business. He completed his Bachelor of Science in Business degree at the University of Minnesota and, after his own experiences with a regional bank, global manufacturing company, and non-profit organization, earned his Ph.D. in Business Administration at the University of Iowa, with emphases in human resource management and organizational behaviour.

Dr. Neubert now serves at Baylor University, where he is an Associate Professor of management and entrepreneurship and holds the Chavanne Chair of Christian Ethics in Business. In this role, Dr. Neubert provides leadership in a variety of ethics initiatives, including hosting an annual ethics forum and the National MBA Case Competition in Ethical Leadership. He teaches virtue-based leadership in both undergraduate and executive MBA programs and was awarded the Hankamer School of Business Teaching Excellence Award in 2013. Outside of the classroom, Dr. Neubert is a mentor and advisor to students in promoting personal leadership development and social entrepreneurship initiatives. He also learns from and consults with business leaders through his association with Leadership Trek Corporation (www. LTrek.com), an adventure-themed leadership development company.

Dr. Neubert's research is wide-ranging and practical in its orientation. His interests in leadership have been focused on ethical leadership and servant leadership, which are evident in his *Journal of Applied Psychology, Leadership Quarterly, Journal of Business Ethics*, and *Business Ethics Quarterly* articles. His research on personality, creativity, commitment, teams, and organizational change has resulted in publications in journals such as *Journal of Applied Psychology, Human Relations, Journal of Business and Psychology, Journal of Personnel Psychology, Leadership Quarterly, Business Horizons*, and *Journal of Business Venturing*.

DR. BRUNO DYCK

Growing up the son of an immigrant entrepreneur, Dr. Bruno Dyck has always been interested in how organizations are managed and how they can help to make the world a better place. He studied management as an undergraduate student in Manitoba and Virginia, and he earned a Ph.D. in Business from the University of Alberta in 1991. As an organizational theorist, Dr. Dyck has focused his research on organizational learning and change, on issues such as distributive justice and sustainable development, and especially on how people's beliefs and values influence what they do.

Dr. Dyck is now a professor in the I.H. Asper School of Business at the University of Manitoba, where he has won research and teaching awards. He teaches courses in management, organization theory, and corporate social and environmental responsibility. His students have encouraged him to write books that show how management is never value-neutral and which enable readers to think about how their character as persons can influence the kind of manager they want to become.

Dr. Dyck's work has been published in leading scholarly journals, such as *Administrative Science Quarterly, Academy of Management Review, Business Ethics Quarterly, Case Research Journal, Journal of Applied Behavioral Science, Journal of Business Venturing, Journal of Developmental Entrepreneurship, Nonprofit and Voluntary Sector Quarterly*, and *Journal of Management Studies* (Best Paper award winner). Dr. Dyck also has done consulting work for a variety of businesses and other organizations, and he spent a year doing voluntary service work overseas.

preface

Our Approach

This book is unique because it presents two approaches to organizational behaviour (OB), which we call "conventional OB" and "sustainable OB." Conventional OB refers to traditional research and practices that you might find in the best OB textbooks on the market today. Sustainable OB refers to emerging research and practices that are growing in importance and use in many organizations. The conventional approach emphasizes things like performance, commitment, short-term profits, predictability, and personal considerations. The sustainable approach also emphasizes performance and commitment, but it places greater emphasis on long-term consequences, creativity, and community considerations. The two approaches are related, with sustainable OB building upon but also being different from conventional OB. Compared to the conventional approach, sustainable OB places more emphasis on social and ecological concerns, consistent with a broad definition of sustainability promoted by many leading OB scholars and practitioners, such as Jeffrey Pfeffer, Stanford Professor of Organizational Behavior.[1]

By offering these two approaches to OB, the textbook has three important advantages. First, many OB instructors already see their course as serving as somewhat of a counterbalance to the primacy of focusing on short-term financial well-being and shareholder interests found in many business courses. A textbook like ours helps instructors to underscore and draw attention to the distinct contribution that OB can make toward providing a more holistic understanding of organizations and their place in the world, today and in the future. By exploring the reasoning for sustainable OB practices, students become more sensitive to how values and ethics influence decisions about OB practices, which is a goal of the leading accrediting association of business schools, the Association to Advance Collegiate Schools of Business (AACSB).

Second, offering two approaches promises to foster students' critical thinking, which is also a goal of the AACSB. As leading scholars recognize and lament, learning only one approach to business can become a self-fulfilling prophecy that shapes students' values and practices.[2] Presenting two approaches provides students with an opportunity to look at OB through two different "lenses." Just as our understanding of other phenomena has been enriched by similar typologies (e.g., our understanding of "personality" is enriched by thinking of where someone lies along an introversion–extraversion continuum), so also students' abilities to understand OB are improved when they understand complementary views. Our particular approach has been class-tested, and students were found to exhibit enhanced critical thinking as a result of being exposed to two lenses.[3]

Finally, a book like ours is timely. It reflects current trends in both popular media and scholarly literature. Susan Peters, who oversees General Electric's executive development initiatives, is among the many practitioners who are encouraging leaders to employ less hierarchy and more teamwork in contrast to the efficiency-oriented approaches of the industrial age.[4] Dominic Barton, Global Managing Director of McKinsey & Company, is imploring leaders to emphasize long-term thinking that recognizes the needs of a broad set of stakeholders.[5] Moreover, an increasing number of people are looking for ways to find greater meaning in their work and are asking organizations to be more attentive to long-term societal well-being.[6] A sustainable approach also is being increasingly advocated by OB and management scholars (e.g., Jeffrey Pfeffer, Henry Mintzberg, Gretchen Spreitzer, Gary

Hamel, Rosabeth Moss Kanter, and others)[7] and is becoming more evident among vanguard practitioners.

Other OB textbooks also address these emerging issues and literatures, but we believe ours is the most wide-ranging and extensive treatment of the OB literature from a sustainable perspective. Vivid and inspiring examples are offered across the range of OB approaches, offering students practical suggestions for how to live out their values in the context of both for-profit and non-profit organizations. According to one reviewer of drafts of this text, its pedagogy "brings my classroom and students into the 21st century."

Distinctive Features

In addition to presenting theory and examples of sustainable OB that extends and enhances conventional OB, our book contains many features that will give students an interesting, positive experience in their OB course.

Chapter Navigators

As preferred by students (based on in-class testing), we start each chapter with this navigation tool instead of a more traditional listing of learning goals. The chapter navigator provides the same essential information as learning goals, but it does so in a form that students have found to be more helpful. Each chapter navigator is designed to (1) help readers anticipate where the chapter is heading; (2) provide readers with a quick reference point to their location as they navigate the chapter; and (3) provide an overarching look at the chapter for review after reading it.

Global and Diverse Practitioner Examples

Textbook examples of practitioners can be somewhat mundane and U.S.-centric. One of the distinguishing features of this book is that it highlights examples from organizations across the globe that inspire students to make a lasting difference in the world. Because the book includes the best of proven OB practices as well as cutting-edge examples from a diverse group of organizational leaders, the reader will be introduced to a wide range of thought-provoking practitioners. In addition to commonly found examples drawn from Starbucks, Google, Disney, and SAS, a variety of novel examples are drawn from small and large organizations, for-profit and non-profit organizations (including NGOs), family-owned and publicly traded companies, top management and middle management, and national and international companies. For example, students will read about . . .

- David Labistour, CEO of Mountain Equipment Co-op, who leads the Canadian company's mission to offer exceptional products and customer service while incorporating sustainability throughout its business practices and helping to conserve the outdoors.
- Ricardo Semler, CEO of Semco, who took over his father's manufacturing company in Brazil at the age of 21 and created an innovative culture that treats people with dignity, fosters trust and participation, values experimentation, and remains sensitive to stakeholder interests.
- Angela Samuels, CEO of Voluptuous Clothing, a successful Toronto-based retail clothing chain for plus-size women, which began by Samuels selling fashion pieces out of her car trunk on the city streets.
- Tom Szaky, who immigrated from Hungary to Canada, started his own web-design firm at the age of 14, and later founded TerraCycle based on the practice of using worms to transform campus trash into organic fertilizer.

- Yoling Sevilla, CEO of The Leather Collection in the Philippines, who models in her small business a reflective style of leadership that weighs the concerns of a broad set of stakeholders.
- Thorkil Sonne, a Danish software executive who, after discovering that his son Lars had autism, set up a new business that hires and provides meaningful and dignified work for people with autism.

Practical Orientation

Perhaps the most outstanding feature of the book is that it is very practical. Two elements are of particular importance in contributing to its practicality, the first of which is captured in the Kurt Lewin adage that "there is nothing so practical as a good theory." This book is unique because it presents two approaches to OB and thereby provides students with the concepts and theoretical tools to help them make their own decisions as to what sorts of leaders they want to become. This provides a compelling conceptual framework for rich reflection and meaningful class discussion.

Second, beyond simply describing OB theory, each chapter contains features designed to encourage readers to "own" key OB principles by reflecting on how they would respond in real-world situations. **My OB** encourages students to think about their opinion or experience regarding an issue; reflect on examples from film, television, music, and other forms of media; or explore how the content fits with their major. Another feature, **OB in Action**, engages students to consider an in-depth example or intriguing research finding. Finally, the end-of-chapter **OB Activities** enhance self-awareness and reinforce learning by offering students opportunities to reflect on the content; receive feedback on their own tendencies, attitudes, and behaviour; participate in engaging group activities; and wrestle with unique cases. These features also are designed to facilitate class discussion.

Ethical Emphasis

Unlike other OB textbooks that set apart ethical thinking and discussion to a portion of a chapter or a sidebar, the premise of this textbook is that organizational behaviour is value-laden and that each thought, attitude, and action is influenced by a person's values. This textbook makes this process explicit and compels readers to consider how their values impact every aspect of OB. Ethics is directly addressed in chapter 4 as an important aspect of individuals that shapes behaviour. Additionally, throughout each chapter are included questions, examples, and research that directly invite students to think about ethics. Finally, a scenario drawn from ethics research is included in the OB Activities at the end of each chapter.

Engaging Writing Style

Students have commented that they have found the writing style in this textbook to be more engaging than that found in other textbooks: "I felt like you were writing to me," said one. We have tried hard to develop a reader-friendly writing style.[8] We wanted to avoid writing in "bland" textbook-ese, but we also wanted to avoid becoming too much like a "fluffy" popular press book that might be found in an airport bookstore. Our chapters are grounded in the scholarly literature and are highlighted by relevant and instructive examples and thoughtful questions. Moreover, in many cases our footnotes provide more background information for those students who are interested in exploring novel topics.

Students want their higher education to help them think about important things like the meaning and purpose of life, but the majority of students say that professors rarely, if ever, encourage such discussion.[9] When in-class testing this material, we found that students find the book engaging because it invites conversation about how OB addresses important issues of the day, such as meaningful work, social justice, and ecological sensitivity. It also appeals to students from a range of majors, including those outside the business school. The book compels readers to think about how they will put their own values into practice in the organizations that they will manage or belong to. This makes OB come alive and, after all, as Socrates put it: "The unexamined life is not worth living."

A Process-Based Framework

As we reviewed other textbooks, it became clear that there are both similarities and differences in how material is presented. Rather than present content in a "checklist" fashion to ensure that the key information is covered in each chapter, our chapters have been designed to draw attention to how the different ideas and theories in each chapter are related to each other. In particular, and consistent with models drawn from the larger literature, our book often presents the material in each chapter in terms of a four-step process model (the four stages of team development, the four steps in decision making, etc.).

Organization of the Book

The first chapter is critically important to this textbook as it introduces readers to the field of OB and explains the conventional and sustainable approaches to OB. The second chapter examines the landscape of OB, including its history, its evolution as a science, key stakeholders, and the global context in which OB occurs. The rest of the book proceeds by discussing OB from three levels: individual, interpersonal or group, and organizational. These three levels are linked together in Figure 1.3 in chapter 1.

The chapters focusing on the individual level of analysis describe the importance of individual attributes (diversity and surface characteristics, abilities and personality, core self-evaluations, and beliefs and values of individuals—chapter 3), individual states (ethics, attitudes and commitments, perceptions, and emotions—chapter 4), motivational processes (chapter 5), decision-making dynamics (chapter 6), and self-leadership principles (chapter 7).

The next main section of the book presents research and practices in OB at the interpersonal level. This section begins by discussing issues of politics, trust, fairness, and conflict and negotiation that influence relationships (chapter 8), then follows with chapters on leadership (chapter 9), leading groups and teams (chapter 10), and communication (chapter 11).

The final section of the book is devoted to organization-level factors. These chapters describe the basic features of organizational culture and structure (chapter 12) and explain how to develop appropriate organizational cultures and structures (chapter 13), align systems that affect motivation (chapter 14), change the organization (chapter 15), and, as needed or desired, create new organizations (chapter 16).

Teaching and Learning Resources

Organizational Behaviour is supported by a comprehensive learning package designed to aid both teaching and learning.

Companion Website   The text's website at http://www.wiley.com/go/neubertcanada contains myriad tools and links intended to facilitate both teaching and learning, including many of the student and instructor resources discussed here.

Instructor's Manual The Instructor's Manual offers helpful teaching ideas as well as chapter-by-chapter text highlights, learning objectives, lecture outlines, lecture notes, and tips on using the OB Activities located at the end of each chapter. This resource also includes a "sample exam" for each chapter featuring multiple-choice and short-answer questions.

Test Bank The Test Bank is comprehensive and includes true/false, multiple-choice, and short-essay questions that vary in their degree of difficulty. All of the questions are tagged to learning objectives, and the difficulty level is specified for each. The Computerized Test Bank allows instructors to modify and add questions to the master bank and customize their exams.

Practice Quizzes This online study tool, made up of quizzes of varying levels of difficulty, helps students evaluate their progress through each chapter. As they contain questions that are similar to those in the Test Bank, the Practice Quizzes can be used to help students prepare for their exams.

PowerPoint Presentation Slides This robust set of PowerPoint slides can be accessed on the instructor portion of the *Organizational Behaviour* website. Lecture notes accompany each slide. An Image Gallery, containing jpg files for all of the figures in the text, is also provided for instructor convenience.

Lecture Launcher Videos Short video clips developed from *CBC News* source materials provide an excellent starting point for lectures or for general class discussion. Teaching Notes accompany the clips, with video summaries and quiz and discussion questions.

WileyPLUS Learning Space with Orion

Learning experts have shown greater gains in outcomes and improved retention when students are able to read, interact with, discuss, and write about course content. Research also shows that when students collaborate with each other, they make deeper connections to the content. Typically, when students work together, they also feel part of a community. This sense of community helps them grow in areas beyond topics in the course—they are able to develop skills like critical thinking and teamwork that can be applied down the road in future careers and life.

WileyPLUS Learning Space will transform any course into a vibrant, collaborative, learning community. This exciting online platform invites students to experience learning activities, work through self-assessment, ask questions, and share insights. As they interact with the course content, their peers, and their instructor, *WileyPLUS Learning Space* creates a personalized study guide for each student.

Through a flexible course design, you can quickly organize learning activities, manage student collaboration, and customize your course—having full control over content as well as the amount of interactivity between students.

WileyPLUS Learning Space lets you:

- Assign activities and add your own materials
- Guide your students through what's important in the interactive e-textbook by easily assigning specific content
- Set up and monitor group learning
- Assess student engagement
- Gain immediate insights to help inform teaching

Defining a clear path to action, the visual reports in *WileyPLUS Learning Space* help both you and your students gauge problem areas and act on what's important.

With the visual reports, you can:

- See exactly where your students are struggling and intervene as needed
- Help students see what they don't know to better prepare for exams
- Give students insight into their strengths and weaknesses to succeed in the course

WileyPLUS Learning Space with ORION provides students with a personal, adaptive learning experience so they can build their proficiency on topics and use their study time most effectively. ORION helps students learn by learning about them.

- Unique to ORION, students **begin** by taking a quick diagnostic for any chapter. This will determine each student's baseline proficiency on each topic in the chapter. Students see their individual diagnostic report to help them decide what to do next with the help of ORION's recommendations.
- For each topic, students can either **Study** or **Practice**. Study directs students to the specific topic they choose in *WileyPLUS Learning Space,* where they can read from the e-textbook or use the variety of relevant resources available there. Students can also practice, using questions and feedback powered by ORION's adaptive learning engine. Based on the results of their diagnostic and ongoing practice, ORION presents students with questions appropriate for their current level of understanding. The system continuously adapts to each student so that he or she can build proficiency.
- WileyPLUS Learning Space with ORION includes a number of reports and ongoing recommendations for students to help them maintain their proficiency over time for each topic.

WileyPLUS Inside Leading Learning Management Systems

WileyPLUS is fully integrated with BlackBoard, D2L, Moodle, and other learning management systems, allowing instructors to create a unified learning experience for students. You will have everything you need for teaching and learning all in one place:

- Single sign-on provides faculty and students with direct access to all *WileyPLUS* content with the convenience of one log-in.
- Direct links to *WileyPLUS* readings and assignments give faculty greater control over how they deliver information and allow students to conveniently access their course work.
- Gradebook synchronization saves instructors time and increases student accountability.
- Student data privacy compliance means student data are always protected and secure.

acknowledgements

We want to acknowledge that this book was developed in a community of colleagues and students. As a result, we want to acknowledge that there are many people whose names could be mentioned here but are not. This includes colleagues, family members, and friends whose ongoing encouragement and support have inspired and sustained us.

We also want to thank the editorial staff at Wiley for their belief in the promise of this project and their commitment to bringing it to fruition.

Mary would like to gratefully acknowledge the hard work and dedication of research assistants Psalm Cheung and Vincent Ho.

Additionally, we are grateful to the following reviewers and supplement contributors who gave constructive and invaluable feedback at various stages of this book:

Sharon Archibald, *Fleming College*
Karen Hitchings, *Northern Alberta Institute of Technology*
Barbara Kelly, *Conestoga College*
Richard Michalski, *McMaster University*
Kyleen Myrah, *Okanagan College*
Selcuk Onay, *University of Waterloo*
Gursher Pannu, *Southern Alberta Institute of Technology*
Martha A. Reavley, *University of Windsor*
Sarah Jane Ross, *Western University*
Matthias Spitzmuller, *Queen's University*
Simon Taggar, *Wilfrid Laurier University*
Ken Yandeau, *Conestoga College*

Mary Waller
Thomas Medcof

Toronto, Ontario
January 2016

brief contents

Preface **xi**

(**CHAPTER 1**) Putting People First **2**

(**CHAPTER 2**) Exploring the Landscape of OB **20**

(**CHAPTER 3**) Understanding Individual Attributes **44**

(**CHAPTER 4**) Considering Individual States **66**

(**CHAPTER 5**) Motivating Individuals **90**

(**CHAPTER 6**) Making Decisions **112**

(**CHAPTER 7**) Leading Self **136**

(**CHAPTER 8**) Understanding Relationships **160**

(**CHAPTER 9**) Leading Others **184**

(**CHAPTER 10**) Leading Groups and Teams **210**

(**CHAPTER 11**) Communicating with Purpose **236**

(**CHAPTER 12**) Understanding Organizational Culture and Structure **258**

(**CHAPTER 13**) Developing Organizational Culture and Structures **284**

(**CHAPTER 14**) Motivating with Systems **308**

(**CHAPTER 15**) Leading Organizational Change **334**

(**CHAPTER 16**) Creating Organizations **358**

Glossary **A-1**

Endnotes **A-11**

Name Index **A-61**

Organization Index **A-67**

Subject Index **A-73**

contents

Preface xi

CHAPTER 1 Putting People First **2**

OPENING CASE: *Creating an Unparalleled Customer Experience* 4

Why Study Organizational Behaviour? 5

What Is *Effective* Organizational Behaviour? Two Approaches 6

■ My OB: Does Money Buy Happiness? 7
Description of Two Approaches 7
Implications of the Two Approaches 9

■ My OB: The Bottom Line(s) about Effectiveness 9

■ OB in Action: The Importance of Critical Thinking 10

Organizational Behaviour and Management 11
Planning 11

■ OB in Action: Moonshots for Management 2.0 12
Organizing 12
Leading 12
Controlling 13

What You Will Explore in This Book 13

CLOSING CASE: *The Forest and the Trees at Timberland* 15

Summary 16

Key Terms 16

Questions for Reflection and Discussion 16

OB ACTIVITIES 17
Self-Assessment Exercise: Are You Ready for this Adventure in Learning? 17
Self-Assessment Exercise: What Is Your View of Effective Leadership? 17
Ethics Scenario 18
Discussion Starter: Is it the People, or the Place? 18
Application Journal 19

CHAPTER 2 Exploring the Landscape of OB **20**

OPENING CASE: *Finding Strength in Community* 22

A Brief History of OB 23
The Scientific Management Era (1910 to 1930) 24
The Human Relations Era (1930 to 1950) 25
The Systems Era (1950 to 1970) 26

The Beliefs Era (1970 to 1990) 26
The Sustainability Era (1990 to present) 27

OB as a Science 28

■ OB in Action: Hungry for Evidence 29

Stakeholder Relationships 30

■ OB in Action: Growing with Your Suppliers and Competitors 33

Global Environment 34

CLOSING CASE: *The Bittersweet Story of Chocolate* 38

Summary 40

Key Terms 40

Questions for Reflection and Discussion 40

OB ACTIVITIES 41
Self-Assessment Exercise: What Are Your Views on the Natural Environment? 41
Ethics Scenario 41
Discussion Starter: Cultural Comparisons 42
Discussion Starter: A Case of Unusual Collaboration 42
Application Journal 42

CHAPTER 3 Understanding Individual Attributes **44**

OPENING CASE: *Understanding Angela Samuels* 46

Diversity and Surface Characteristics 47

■ My OB: Do Generational Differences Make a Difference? 49

Abilities and Personality 50
Abilities 50
Personality 50

■ OB in Action: Employee Candidacy Tests 51

Core Self-Evaluations 53

■ My OB: Humility or Hard Work? 55

Beliefs and Values 55
Beliefs 56
Values 56

■ OB in Action: Political Values and Geographic Differences 59

CLOSING CASE: *Life in the Fast Lane—Elon Musk* 60

Summary 61

Key Terms 61

Questions for Reflection and Discussion   62

OB ACTIVITIES   62

Self-Assessment Exercise: What Is Your Myers–Briggs Type?   62
Self-Assessment Exercise: What Are Your Values?   63
Ethics Scenario   65
Discussion Starter: Personalities on YouTube.com   65
Application Journal   65

CHAPTER 4   Considering Individual States   **66**

OPENING CASE: *Jack Dorsey*   68

Ethics   69

Individual Characteristics Affecting Ethical Behaviour   70
Organizational Characteristics Affecting Ethical Behaviour   73

■ **OB in Action: Business Ethics and Personal Standards of Honesty**   75
Attitudes and Commitments   75

Attitudes   75

■ **My OB: What Makes a Job Satisfying?**   77
Commitments   77
Perceptions   78

■ **OB in Action: Deceptive First Impressions**   81
Emotions   81

■ **My OB: When Managing Emotions Matters**   83
CLOSING CASE: *The Power of the Powerless*   84
Summary   85
Key Terms   85

Questions for Reflection and Discussion   86

OB ACTIVITIES   86

Self-Assessment Exercise: What Is Your Emotional Intelligence?   86
Self-Assessment Exercise: How Do You Act When No One Is Looking?   87
Ethics Scenario   87
Discussion Starter: YouTubing Ethical Challenges   88
Discussion Starter: Reflections from a U.S. Woman Working in a Filipino Garment Factory   88
Application Journal   89

CHAPTER 5   Motivating Individuals   **90**

OPENING CASE: *Brewing Motivation at Starbucks*   92

■ **My OB: Understanding Motivation Inside-Out**   93
Innate Needs   94

Desire for Achievement   97

Goal-Setting Theory   97

■ **OB in Action: Olympic-Sized Aspirations**   98
■ **OB in Action: Changing Vice to Virtuous Goals**   101
Expectancy Theory   101
■ **My OB: Is Your Motivation Intrinsic or Extrinsic?**   103
Desire for Fairness   104

Desire for Affiliation   106

Desire for Power   107

CLOSING CASE: *Indigo Bookmarked Values*   108
Summary   109
Key Terms   109

Questions for Reflection and Discussion   109

OB ACTIVITIES   110

Self-Assessment Exercise: What Is Your Approach to Motivation?   110
Ethics Scenario   110
Discussion Starter: SMART2 Goals Activity   111
Discussion Starter: Desire for Achievement Activity   111
Application Journal   111

CHAPTER 6   Making Decisions   **112**

OPENING CASE: *Recalling a Classic Example of Decision Making*   114

Step 1: Identify the Need for a Decision   115

■ **My OB: Neuroscience and Decision Making**   116
Step 2: Develop Alternative Responses   117

Step 3: Choose the Appropriate Alternative   119

Goal Consensus   119
Available Knowledge   120
■ **My OB: Networks That Promote Sustainable OB Decision Making**   123
■ **OB in Action: How Do Managers Actually Make Ethical Decisions?**   124
Step 4: Implement the Choice   125

■ **OB in Action: Culture and the Decision-Making Process**   127
CLOSING CASE: *How Decisions Can Lead to a $7 Billion Loss*   130
Summary   131
Key Terms   131

Questions for Reflection and Discussion   131

OB ACTIVITIES   132

Self-Assessment Exercise: How Courageous Are You in Making Decisions?   132
Self-Assessment Exercise: What Is Your Cognitive Style in Making Decisions?   132
Ethics Scenario   133
Discussion Starter: Ethics, Profits, and People   133

Discussion Starter: Factors That Influence the Quality of Decision Making 134

Application Journal 135

CHAPTER 7 Leading Self 136

OPENING CASE: *Following a Different Voice* 138

Authentic Leadership 139

Knowing Self 141

■ My OB: How Real Is Reality TV? 143

Living Intentionally 144

■ OB in Action: Conrad Black in the Red 144

Managing Stress and Roles 147

Workplace Stress 147
Role Conflict 148
Dealing with Stress 149

■ OB in Action: Is First Really the Worst? 149
■ OB in Action: Give Me a Break 151

Acting Creatively 151

The Creative Process 152
Characteristics of Creative Individuals 152
Improving Creativity in Organizations 153

CLOSING CASE: *Getting Paid to Have Fun* 154

Summary 156

Key Terms 156

Questions for Reflection and Discussion 156

OB ACTIVITIES 157

Self-Assessment Exercise: What Are Your Self-Leadership Behaviours? 157
Ethics Scenario 158
Discussion Starter: Debate: To Be or Not to Be Responsible 158
Discussion Starter: Authentic Leadership 158
Application Journal 159

CHAPTER 8 Understanding Relationships 160

OPENING CASE: *Conrad Black Guilty of Fraud* 162

Politics and Self-Interest 163

■ My OB: Machiavellianism in the Workplace 164

Trust 165

■ OB in Action: Keeping a Lid on Layoffs 167
■ My OB: Fair or Foul 170

Fairness 170

Negotiation 172

Influence Tactics 172
Approaches to Negotiation 173

■ My OB: How Skilled Are You at Understanding Others? 176

Conflict Styles 177

CLOSING CASE: *Transformational Relationships at Tata* 179

Summary 180

Key Terms 180

Questions for Reflection and Discussion 180

OB ACTIVITIES 181

Self-Assessment Exercise: How Do You React to People Who Act or Think Differently? 181
Self-Assessment Exercise: What Is Your Style in Dealing with Conflict? 181
Ethics Scenario 182
Discussion Starter: Trust Bank Activity 183
Discussion Starter: Norton Manufacturing 183
Application Journal 183

CHAPTER 9 Leading Others 184

OPENING CASE: *Creating Happiness: Passion and Purpose at G Adventures* 186

Leadership Traits 188

■ OB in Action: Rock Star Businessman 189
■ My OB: All for One or One for All? 190

Leadership Behaviour 191

Dimensions of Leadership Behaviour 192
The Leadership Grid 192

■ My OB: Gender and Leadership—Does One Size Fit All? 194

Servant Leadership 194

Contingency Theories 195

Fiedler's Contingency Theory 195
House's Path-Goal Theory 196
Leader-Member Exchange 197

Integrative Models 198

Situational Leadership Models 198
Integrated Conventional Leadership Model 199
Integrated Sustainable Leadership Model 201

■ OB in Action: "Krafting" a New Culture of Empowerment and Entrepreneurial Spirit 204

CLOSING CASE: *Sustainable Leadership at Work in the Philippines* 205

Summary 206

Key Terms 206

Questions for Reflection and Discussion 207

OB ACTIVITIES 207

Self-Assessment Exercise: What Type of Leader Are You? 207
Ethics Scenario 208

Discussion Starter: Debate: Are Leaders Born or Made? 208
Discussion Starter: What Are the Characteristics of an Outstanding Leader? 208
Application Journal 209

CHAPTER 10 Leading Groups and Teams **210**

OPENING CASE: *Taking WestJet to New Heights* 212
Groups and Teams 213
Forming 216
■ My OB: What Makes an Effective Student Team? 218
Storming 219
■ OB in Action: Groupthink 222
Norming 223
■ My OB: Stimulating Information Sharing 225
Performing 226
■ OB in Action: Front-Line Management Teams 228
CLOSING CASE: *LEGO Mindstorms* 229
Summary 230
Key Terms 231
Questions for Reflection and Discussion 231
OB ACTIVITIES 231
Self-Assessment Exercise: How Do You Lead Teams? 231
Ethics Scenario 232
Discussion Starter: Wilderness Survival 232
Discussion Starter: Avoiding Team Dysfunctions 234
Application Journal 234

CHAPTER 11 Communicating with Purpose **236**

OPENING CASE: *A Bay Worthy of the 21st Century* 238
The Four-Step Communication Process 239
Step 1: Identify Your Message 240
Step 2: Encode and Transmit the Message 242
Identify and Overcome Communication Barriers 242
■ OB in Action: Your Seat at the Table Sends a Message 243
■ My OB: Communicating across Cultures 244
Choose Communication Media and Channels 244
■ My OB: Impersonally Delivering What Is Personal 246
■ My OB: Trouble for Organizations When Members Text and Tweet? 247
Step 3: Receive and Decode the Message 248
Step 4: Confirm the Message with Feedback 250
CLOSING CASE: *Lessons in Teaching Abroad* 253

Summary 254
Key Terms 254
Questions for Reflection and Discussion 255
OB ACTIVITIES 255
Self-Assessment Exercise: Where Are You along the Conventional–Sustainable Continuum? 255
Ethics Scenario 256
Discussion Starter: Communicating Your Interests and Active Listening 256
Discussion Starter: The Empty Seat 256
Application Journal 257

CHAPTER 12 Understanding Organizational Culture and Structure **258**

OPENING CASE: *The Fundamentals of Organizing at Semco* 260
Basic Assumptions of Organizational Culture 262
■ My OB: What Is the Culture of Your Class? 263
Key Values that Shape Organizational Culture 263
The Competing Values Framework 263
■ OB in Action: Pounding the Rock 265
Artifacts of Organizational Culture 265
Fundamentals of Organizational Structure 266
■ OB in Action: Will a Spoonful of Efficiency Change the Culture of Starbucks? 269
■ My OB: What Brand of Shoes Are You Wearing? 277
CLOSING CASE: *New Ways of Organizing for New Needs* 279
Summary 280
Key Terms 280
Questions for Reflection and Discussion 281
OB ACTIVITIES 281
Self-Assessment Exercise: Where Are You along the Conventional–Sustainable Continuum? 281
Ethics Scenario 282
Discussion Starter: Organizational Assessment 282
Discussion Starter: Chief Sustainability Officers 282
Application Journal 283

CHAPTER 13 Developing Organizational Culture and Structures **284**

OPENING CASE: *Managing a Smile Factory* 286
Creating an Organizational Culture 287
■ OB in Action: Reddit Revolt 289
Prioritizing a Form of Organizational Culture 290
Clan Organizational Culture 290
Hierarchy Organizational Culture 291

Adhocracy Organizational Culture 291
Market Organizational Culture 292

■ **My OB: Culture at Your Workplace** 292

Aligning Organizational Culture with Structure, Technology, and Strategy 293

Organizational Structure 294

■ **OB in Action: Organizational Structure in the Global Marketplace** 296

Technology 296
Strategy 297

■ **OB in Action: Mission-Driven Organizations** 298

Combining the Pieces to Make Four Organizational Types 299

The Simple Type 300
The Defender Type 300

■ **OB in Action: Open-Source Philosophy at Tesla Motors Advances Industry** 301

The Prospector Type 301
The Analyzer Type 302

CLOSING CASE: *About Face at Interface* 303

Summary 304

Key Terms 305

Questions for Reflection and Discussion 305

OB ACTIVITIES 305

Self-Assessment Exercise: Where Are You along the Conventional–Sustainable Continuum? 305
Ethics Scenario 306
Discussion Starter: Introducing Sustainable Culture and Structures in the Classroom 306
Discussion Starter: Design for a Soup Kitchen 306
Application Journal 307

CHAPTER 14 Motivating with Systems **308**

OPENING CASE: *High-Tech Loyalty at SAS Institute* 310

Job Design 312

■ **My OB: Was Your Big Mac a Big Mistake?** 314

Performance Management 314

■ **OB in Action: Where Is the Motivation?** 316

Performance Appraisal 316

■ **My OB: Is Rank-and-Yank an Effective Motivational Method?** 319

Compensation 319

Training and Development 321

Training 322
Career Development 323

■ **OB in Action: Whataburger, Whatacompany** 323

Mission and Vision 325

■ **OB in Action: Kasasa against the World** 327

CLOSING CASE: *People, the Planet, and Profits at Herman Miller* 328

Summary 329

Key Terms 330

Questions for Reflection and Discussion 330

OB ACTIVITIES 330

Self-Assessment Exercise: Diagnosing Your Job 330
Self-Assessment Exercise: Personal Career SWOT Analysis 332
Ethics Scenario 332
Discussion Starter: Interview a Business Owner or Manager 332
Discussion Starter: Advertising a Mission (Group activity) 332
Application Journal 333

CHAPTER 15 Leading Organizational Change **334**

OPENING CASE: *Learning from the Journey* 336

Organizational Change 337

■ **OB in Action: Delivering Change** 339

Step 1: Recognize Need 340

Step 2: Unfreeze 341

■ **OB in Action: Diverging Thoughts at Harvard** 342
■ **OB in Action: Managing the Morning after the Merger** 344

Step 3: Change 345

■ **My OB: How Does Change Make You Feel?** 346

Members' Confidence in Organizational Leaders 347
Members' Confidence in Their Own Ability 348
Members' Attitudes toward the Change 349

Step 4: Refreeze 350

■ **OB in Action: TOMS Walks the Talk** 351

CLOSING CASE: *Calming the Waters* 353

Summary 354

Key Terms 354

Questions for Reflection and Discussion 354

OB ACTIVITIES 355

Self-Assessment Exercise: How Do You Cope with Change? 355
Self-Assessment Exercise: Where Are You along the Change Continuum? 355
Ethics Scenario 356
Discussion Starter: Balls of Fun 356
Discussion Starter: Engineering Change in Bangladesh 357
Application Journal 357

CHAPTER 16 Creating Organizations **358**

OPENING CASE: *One Person's Trash is Another Person's Treasure* **360**

Identify Opportunity   363

Take Initiative   364

■ My OB: When a Hobby Becomes a New
     Venture   366
■ OB in Action: From Failure to Fame   368
Develop Plans   368

■ OB in Action: Gourmet Just Got Better   371
Mobilize Resources   372

■ OB in Action: Can Entrepreneurs Take
     the Heat?   373
CLOSING CASE: *Googling Google*   375
Summary   376
Key Terms   377
Questions for Reflection and Discussion   377

OB ACTIVITIES   377
     Self-Assessment Exercise: What Kind of Entrepreneur
        Might You Be?   377
     Ethics Scenario   378
     Discussion Starter: Intrapreneurship in Academia   378
     Discussion Starter: U2 Can Be a Social Entrepreneur   378
     Application Journal   379

Glossary   A-1

Endnotes   A-11

Name Index   A-61

Organization Index   A-67

Subject Index   A-73

One

Putting People First

Before you embark on any long journey, it is always a good idea to have a guide to see where you're headed and to help you remember where you've been. Each chapter in this book begins with a Chapter navigator designed to help you anticipate where the chapter is heading; provide a quick reference point throughout the chapter in case you need to get your bearings; and offer an overarching look at how, from two perspectives introduced in this chapter (conventional and sustainable), the content can look different. We sincerely hope that you will enjoy your journey learning about organizational behaviour and how it applies to your present and future experiences in organizations.

Learning Objectives	Conventional OB	Shared	Sustainable OB

WHY STUDY ORGANIZATIONAL BEHAVIOUR (OB)

1. Discuss the three reasons to study organizational behaviour.	Enhance your self-awareness and capacity for self-improvement Enable you to understand, interact with, and influence others Equip you to serve in managerial roles within organizations	

WHAT IS EFFECTIVE OB: TWO APPROACHES

2. Explain the two effective approaches to organizational behaviour.	Value material or financial well-being and the interests of a narrow range of stakeholders (especially owners) Focus on performance, commitment, personal interests, predictability, and short-term profit	Value multiple forms of well-being (financial, social, ecological, spiritual) and the interests of a broad range of stakeholders Focus on performance, commitment, community interests, creativity, and long-term consequences

OB AND MANAGEMENT

3. Analyze the link between organizational behaviour and management.	Plan by identifying organizational resources and goals Organize by designing systems and structures to meet goals Lead by influencing others to meet goals Control by ensuring that members' actions are consistent with organizational goals	Plan by exercising practical wisdom Organize by demonstrating courage and experimentation Lead by encouraging self-control and treating members with dignity Control by promoting justice and ensuring that actions are consistent with organizational values

WHAT YOU WILL EXPLORE IN THIS BOOK

4. Illustrate the integration of organizational behaviour concepts.	Explore conventional ideas, research, and examples	Explore sustainable ideas, research, and examples

creating an unparalleled customer experience[1]

THE CANADIAN PRESS/Larry MacDougal

While organizations exist to reach goals and fulfill missions, the day-to-day pursuit of these goals and missions often becomes tedious work for the people who make up the organization. For several decades, society largely supported Nobel Prize laureate Milton Friedman's philosophy that "the social responsibility of business is to increase its profits." However, many organizations have started to shift away from this way of thinking and have started building organizations that remind people that there's more to a job than focusing narrowly on the bottom line. This was the case for Sport Chek, Canada's largest retailer of sporting goods and clothing, which in 2008 abandoned its profit-driven sales mentality because of increased consumer price sensitivity during the economic downturn.

In the past, sales associates at Sport Chek were paid on commission and therefore embraced a hard-sell mentality. But this began to change at the end of 2008, when Sport Chek's parent company, FGL Sports Ltd., started concentrating its efforts on "creating an unparalleled customer experience." Today, Sport Chek sales associates are paid a fixed wage and are trained, alongside all members of the organization, to make the customer experience their priority. This shift has created a people-centred organizational culture. Its secret is focusing on what Sport Chek calls the "Complete Experience." From day one, Sport Chek employees, or "team members," are trained to provide customers with the Complete Experience, which includes connecting with the customer through sport and activity and setting them up with everything they need, as well as with everything they need to know. Team members are encouraged to go the extra mile to provide customers with an unparalleled customer experience and to do what is right for the customer, even if it is costly. Unlike many organizations that train their employees to only highlight the positive aspects of the products on offer, Sport Chek encourages all of its team members to give honest, personalized, and informative advice to customers, just as if they were helping a friend or family member.

A real-life example of the Complete Experience philosophy involved a sales associate at one of Sport Chek's locations in Vancouver, British Columbia, when a customer called the store to put a pair of outdoor running shoes on hold. While the sales associate could have simply handed the customer the shoes for a quick sale when she came in to the store, he initiated a conversation and discovered that the specific shoes were not suitable for the customer, who was buying them for indoor volleyball. And so the associate found a more suitable, albeit less expensive, shoe. A few days later the customer called the store to ask if the same sales associate who'd helped her was working that day. Worried that the phone call meant something awful had happened, the associate was surprised when the customer showed up in person to thank him, even bringing her husband and daughter to get new shoes because she was so pleased with her customer experience earlier that week.

Sport Chek's people-centred culture goes beyond the customer and extends to its team members. In fact, two key components that FGL Sports includes within its leadership brand are serve others (make employees a priority so they will make our customers a priority), and recognize a job well done. As such, managers regularly recognize team members that provide exceptional customer service and the Complete Experience. From personally thanking team members to highlighting stories on the morning-huddle board to distributing sporting products to team members, managers make an effort to ensure that they publicly recognize and appreciate the work that everyone does. The result is an environment where team members regularly share positive customer stories among each other and thank their teammates, reinforcing the people-centred culture and the focus on providing an unparalleled customer experience.

After being acquired by Canadian Tire in 2011, FGL Sports, and subsequently Sport Chek, began executing a strategic initiative to "create powerful super-brands with unparalleled emotional connections" to their customers. Today, success at Sport Chek centres on the fulfillment of the company's mission "to help Canadians live active, healthy lives," and team members are always working with managers and providing input on how to create a better customer experience.

However, this approach does not guarantee that leaders won't still be faced with difficult decisions. For example, under the direction of Canadian Tire, FGL Sports closed or converted 115 of its underperforming stores, including Sport Mart and Athletes World, as a result of an aggressive expansion initiative launched in 2012. While the closures were part of a strategic effort to position FGL Sports, through Sport Chek, as the ultimate authority in sports in Canada, the required layoffs caused anxiety within the company. The decision was a difficult one given the consequences for employees; however, management reaffirmed

The "Complete Experience" … includes connecting with the customer through sport and activity and setting them up with everything they need.

their commitment to employees, stating that "For all store closures, the company will undertake efforts to retain as many employees as possible through transfers to converted or new stores." Additionally, FGL Sports' President Michael Medline emphasized that the company would be employing even more people the year after its closures and conversions.

This case illustrates the complexities involved in understanding organizational behaviour. The behaviour and the responses of members within organizations are influenced by the members' own individual characteristics as well as their interpersonal relationships with others, their organization's culture and structures, and the environment in which the organization operates.

Why Study Organizational Behaviour?

WHY OB | TWO APPROCHES | OB & MGMT | WHAT IS EXPLORED

LEARNING OBJECTIVE 1
Discuss the three reasons to study organizational behaviour.

Organizations are essential and dominant influences on life in our modern world. They are the principal means by which we achieve goals beyond the capability of individuals acting alone.[2] More formally, **organizations** are "social structures created by individuals to support the collaborative pursuit of specific goals."[3] These social structures come in many forms and serve to meet various goals: commodity wholesalers and grocery stores gather and distribute food; schools and universities educate and socialize children and adults; factories manufacture goods; hospitality and consulting businesses offer services; government agencies and hospitals dispense assistance; coffee houses and online bookstores sell products; and social networking and dating sites connect people. Yet, despite the fact that some organizations (such as corporations) are given legal status as persons, organizations do not exist, operate, or influence society without people. It is more accurate to say that *people acting collectively* can accomplish a great deal.

Organizations are "social structures created by individuals to support the collaborative pursuit of specific goals."

Organizational behaviour (OB) is the discipline that sets out to explain human behaviour in organizations by examining the behaviour of individuals, groups, or all the members of an organization as a whole. This examination relies on the science of identifying cause and effect relationships, making explicit the factors influencing decisions and behaviour, and taking into account the specifics of various situations.[4] It also calls upon developing theory that takes into account empirical research and that helps to set the agenda for future research. Together, OB theory and science explain what influences individual and collective behaviour, when these influences operate and have their greatest impact, and how people's behaviour shapes the internal and external organizational environment. Simply put, the focus of this book is on understanding people and their essential role in enabling organizations to serve society.

Organizational behaviour (OB) refers to explaining human behaviour in organizations, which includes examining the behaviour of individuals, groups, or all the members of an organization as a whole.

It is impossible to escape, avoid, or eliminate the influence of organizations. Given that organizations are part of our everyday life, every person reading this book either has experienced or will experience many of the principles and situations we will explore. You can thus expect to benefit in your daily life from understanding and applying the concepts discussed in this book. More specifically, there are at least three reasons to keep reading (see Figure 1.1).

First, studying OB will help you to understand yourself. By understanding OB, you can get a better sense of the values and forces that influence your attitudes, feelings, and behaviour. This will not only make your work experience less stressful and more enjoyable, it should also help you understand how people respond to you.

Second, understanding OB can improve the interactions you have with others by providing practical suggestions for influencing and collaborating with them, working in teams, and leading organizations. It also will help you understand the behaviour of your managers, the people you manage, and those who work alongside you in teams or on projects.

Third, having a strong grasp of OB will allow you to increase your contribution to an organization and prepare you to serve in a management or leadership role, a challenge to

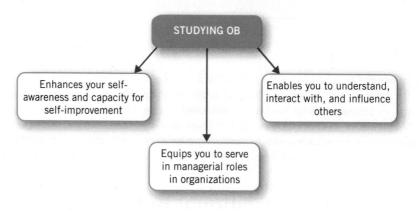

FIGURE 1.1 Three Reasons to Study OB

Figure content: STUDYING OB — Enhances your self-awareness and capacity for self-improvement — Equips you to serve in managerial roles in organizations — Enables you to understand, interact with, and influence others

Technical skills refer to expertise in a particular task or field.

Relational skills are talents for getting along with and motivating people.

Conceptual skills refer to the capability to understand complex issues and underlying causes and to solve problems with broad implications.

which we give particular attention throughout this book. According to prominent management philosopher and scholar Peter Drucker, the work of managers and leaders is a great responsibility because it "deals with people, their values, and their personal development . . . management is deeply involved in moral concerns."[5] Fulfilling this responsibility will require **technical skills** or expertise in areas like marketing, accounting, finance, or human resources; strong **relational skills** that help you get along with and motivate people; and strong **conceptual skills** that include the ability to understand complex issues, underlying causes, and problems with broad implications. Our discussion of OB in this book is primarily focused on improving your relational and conceptual skills.

LEARNING OBJECTIVE 2
Explain the two effective approaches to organizational behaviour.

What Is *Effective* Organizational Behaviour? Two Approaches

WHY OB   **TWO APPROACHES**   OB & MGMT   WHAT IS EXPLORED

In our journey through the theories and practices of organizational behaviour, we will explore behaviour at three interdependent levels of analysis: Individual, Interpersonal, and Organizational. Each level depends to some degree on the others, and each influences the others.

At each level, we'll investigate what is effective OB. *A behaviour or action is effective if it creates a desired effect or accomplishes a desired goal or outcome.* Your belief about whether a particular approach to OB is effective will depend on which effects or outcomes you value. This book thus challenges you to examine the underlying assumptions behind OB theory and practice and to decide for yourself what it means for a person, group, and organization to behave *effectively*. For example, what do you feel are key overarching goals that organizational members should strive to accomplish? What did Mike Duke, former CEO of Walmart, mean when he asserted, "More will be expected from market leaders and globally successful companies, and those companies who are most involved will be most successful, creating an upward spiral."[6] Did he mean more profits, or that there is more to being an effective organization than simply maximizing profits? Should the decisions and behaviours of organizational leaders and members reflect a concern for other outcomes, such as employee well-being or environmental impact?

To one person, behaviour that results in optimal task performance might be considered effective and behaviour that merely results in job satisfaction not effective, whereas someone else might consider the reverse to be true. Do team members believe their team is operating effectively when no one disagrees with anyone else, or when members are free to share their

When Paul James (P.J.) Phelan took over his family's business, Cara Operations Ltd., in the 1950s, he switched its focus from transportation to restaurants. During his tenure, Cara grew into a Canadian food service empire with over $1 billion in sales. Today Cara's brands include Harvey's, Swiss Chalet, Milestones, and East Side Mario's. While Phelan amassed a large family fortune before his passing in 2002, he faced challenging health and personal issues, and spent the later years of his life embroiled in a bitter succession battle with his family for control of the company.

Many believe that, while money may not actually buy happiness, it certainly can't hurt. The empirical evidence is unclear. Some research suggests that money is related to happiness for the very poor, and there is a small relationship between money and happiness among young and middle-age adults, but the relationship disappears for older adults. Other research indicates that money and materialism are associated with a decline in life satisfaction and personal well-being. A third body of research suggests that money can indeed buy happiness, but only if you give it away. A series of studies show that people are happier if they spend money on gifts or charities than on themselves, that workers who received a profit-sharing bonus were happier if they gave some of it to others instead of keeping it all for themselves, and that students who were given $5 to $20 and told to spend it on others were happier at the end of the day than students who were instructed to spend it on themselves.

QUESTIONS FOR REFLECTION

1. What is your experience with money and happiness?
2. Do you agree or disagree with the idea that money can buy happiness?
3. How can you personally apply the findings about giving money away?
4. How can organizations apply this finding?

diverse views? The meaning of effectiveness also may vary depending on the type of organization being considered. For a community-run soup kitchen, effectiveness may mean providing needy people with nourishing food in a way that enhances their dignity. A business might define effectiveness as maximizing profitability, while for a government agency it may mean serving the public in a timely fashion. In learning about OB, effectiveness is an important issue that deserves our attention.

Description of Two Approaches

This book presents two approaches to organizational behaviour (OB): the conventional approach with its rich history, and an emerging sustainable approach that builds upon and stretches the boundaries of the conventional approach. **Conventional OB** tends to emphasize what contributes to material or financial well-being and the interests of a narrow range of stakeholders in the immediate future, whereas **sustainable OB** emphasizes what contributes to multiple forms of well-being (e.g., financial, social, ecological, spiritual) for a broad range of stakeholders in the immediate as well as the distant future.

The work of German sociologist Max Weber provides a conceptual framework that helps us to think more carefully about what constitutes "effective" OB. As we've just learned, effective OB from a conventional perspective is primarily about maximizing material or financial benefits for ourselves or a narrow range of stakeholders. The logic behind this view is captured in the popular interpretation of Adam Smith's "invisible hand" metaphor, which suggests that the good of the community is assured when every individual is permitted to pursue his or her own self-interested goals.

Weber acknowledges that this conventional approach has contributed greatly to unprecedented productivity and the creation of financial wealth, but he argues that it ultimately renders a disservice to humankind.[7] In what has become one of the most famous metaphors in all the social sciences, Weber posits that this approach leaves humankind trapped in an "iron cage," focusing on a narrow set of materialist-individualist considerations that trump other forms of well-being. He laments that such a focus weakens the human spirit and limits human flourishing.

Conventional OB tends to emphasize material or financial well-being and the interests of a narrow range of stakeholders in the immediate future.

Sustainable OB tends to emphasize multiple forms of well-being (e.g., financial, social, ecological, spiritual) and the interests of a broad range of stakeholders in the immediate as well as the distant future.

Sustainable OB draws attention to Adam Smith's first (and lesser-known) published work, *The Theory of Moral Sentiments*.[8] When Smith says everyone should be "perfectly free to pursue his [or her] own interest," he assumes that this pursuit takes into account the virtues of concern for others (benevolence), practical wisdom (prudence), self-control (temperance), fairness (justice), and courage.[9] Put differently, Smith's "invisible hand" is effective only if it is attached to a "virtuous arm."

Sustainable theory and practice rest on several conceptual and philosophical bases.[10] We will ground them in Aristotle's **virtue theory**[11] because it is an appropriate and highly regarded perspective that has stood the test of time. From this perspective, the purpose of human behaviour is not simply to maximize individual material interests; rather, the purpose of human behaviour is to maximize people's *happiness*, which Aristotle called the "supreme good." Happiness is achieved by practising **virtues** *in community*.[12] From a virtue theory approach, sustainable OB is about demonstrating concern for others and facilitating organizational members' practice of four cardinal virtues: practical wisdom, self-control, justice, and courage. In short, sustainable OB seeks to nurture community and happiness by modelling and enabling the practice of virtues in financially viable organizations.

Table 1.1 provides an overview of the priorities associated with conventional OB and those associated with sustainable OB. The differences in priorities between the two approaches to OB are consistent with the differences in the philosophical assumptions described above. As we will see in the following pages, these priorities are important for understanding and practising OB.

The priorities in Table 1.1 indicate which outcomes are relatively more important for each of the two OB approaches. Of course, as illustrated in Figure 1.2, these approaches overlap to some extent. For example, performance and commitment are priorities that are important to both conventional OB and sustainable OB, but with subtle differences. Thus, performance may be defined more narrowly or specifically from a conventional point of view, whereas performance from a sustainable point of view may include a broader set of less specific and measurable contributions. Further, commitment based on obligations or shared values may be equally attractive from a conventional perspective, whereas a sustainable perspective decidedly favours commitment that is based on shared values.

While a conventional approach to OB has a long and rich history, as we will see in chapter 2, this history also includes research and practices consistent with a sustainable approach. Many scholars and practitioners have long placed a higher priority on improving the multidimensional well-being of humankind than on merely maximizing the financial wealth of their organizations.[13] Evidence suggests that the number of practitioners and scholars practising and promoting a sustainable approach to OB is growing to meet the complex challenges of the future.[14]

TABLE 1.1 **Understanding Key Priorities**

Conventional OB Priorities	Sustainable OB Priorities
Personal: focus on self-interest	**Community:** focus on community interests
Performance: focus on individual, group, and organizational performance	
Predictability: focus on what is stable and can be explained	**Creativity:** focus on what is dynamic and difficult to explain
Commitment: focus on bonds among people, actions, and organizations	
Short-term profits: focus on relatively immediate profits	**Long-term consequences:** focus on relatively long-term consequences

CONVENTIONAL   SUSTAINABLE

Personal   Community
Performance
Predictability   Creativity
Commitment
Short-term   Long-term
Profits   Consequences

FIGURE 1.2 Signs Highlighting Priorities for Organizational Behaviour

Implications of the Two Approaches

Both the conventional and the sustainable approach offer compelling ideas and examples worth careful consideration. Each is an **ideal type** (i.e., fundamental model or theoretical extreme), which does not mean they are the best or "ideal" way of managing or behaving, but rather that together they help us think critically about what OB means and how we can apply it. Throughout the chapters we will provide conceptual tools and examples, thus enabling you to compare conventional OB and sustainable OB and make up your own mind about what is effective. Discussing two "ideal types" has at least four key advantages.

First, allowing the sustainable and conventional approaches to act as two end points can help us better understand the position that we and others occupy on a continuum. Just as we would expect to find very few people to be examples of "pure" extraverts or introverts, we

Ideal types are fundamental models or theoretical extremes.

M**O**B | THE BOTTOM LINE(S) ABOUT EFFECTIVENESS

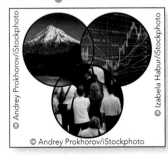

For many conventional managers, the bottom line is likely to focus primarily on profits or financial well-being, whereas sustainable managers are more likely to favour a "triple bottom line" approach that places importance on balancing three measures of effectiveness: profit, people, and planet. Research on organizations in 19 different countries suggests that emphasis on a "triple bottom line" approach results in enhanced well-being for people and the planet but is also associated with higher financial costs in the short term. Although a conventional approach may be less financially costly in the short term, it can have long-term drawbacks, such as reducing employee motivation and job satisfaction and harming the environment.

Learning two approaches to OB will provide you with a wealth of knowledge that will help you to think deeply about what is "effective" organizational behaviour and decide the bottom line(s) you will measure.

QUESTIONS FOR REFLECTION
1. Which approach do you personally think is more effective?
2. Will shareholders be willing to accept lower (short-term) profits if it means improved ecological well-being and a more motivated workforce?
3. Will sustainable organizations eventually go bankrupt due to competition from more profit-oriented firms? Or will firms that place primary emphasis on profits suffer as people grow less willing to work for them and buy goods and services from them?

would also expect to find very few "pure" examples of the conventional or sustainable approach. Recall FGL Sports President Michael Medline, who was mentioned in this chapter's opening case. Medline sometimes exhibits behaviour that is consistent with sustainable OB, and at other times his behaviour is more conventional. The same is true for other people we highlight in this book.

Second, understanding one ideal type helps us to better understand a second ideal type. For instance, we develop a richer understanding of extraversion when we contrast and compare it to introversion. We have a better understanding of "bitter" when we contrast and compare it to "sweet." Similarly, we have a deeper understanding of conventional OB if we contrast and compare it with sustainable OB, and vice versa.

Third, learning two ideal types of OB adds more complexity and can create tension, but mastering the ability to resist simple answers and explore and integrate opposing ideas or viewpoints is the mark of outstanding managers.[15] In other words, learning two approaches OB enhances **critical thinking**, an important skill for business students.[16] In practice, OB is complex and filled with challenges that require balancing different ideas and values. As is discussed in the OB in Action box, "The Importance of Critical Thinking," this book's approach will help you develop essential critical thinking skills that are highly valued in organizations.

Critical thinking involves actively questioning and evaluating assumptions and information.

OB in Action

The Importance of Critical Thinking

Everett Collection/Canadian Press Images

Filmed in Vancouver, the reboot of the science fiction television series *The X-Files* reunites FBI Special Agents Fox Mulder (David Duchovny) and Dana Scully (Gillian Anderson) to investigate paranormal phenomena. One of the secrets to the partners' success is that each person brings their own perspective to the problems they face. Mulder is a believer in the supernatural and a conspiracy theorist, while Scully is a skeptic. Their contrasting perspectives challenge each other's thinking, encouraging them both to explore alternatives they might not ordinarily consider.

An OB course is one of the main courses offered in business schools to facilitate critical thinking, precisely because its emphasis on people serves to counterbalance the primary emphasis on maximizing profits that characterizes many other business courses. While there is some debate on what exactly "critical thinking" means, most scholars agree that it has two components: (1) a technical component (being able to perform tasks in a logical, linear, and instrumental way) and (2) a philosophical component (being able recognize and evaluate the underlying assumptions that help to decide which tasks to perform). This echos Aristotle's idea that

critical thinking requires thinking about something deeply and from different perspectives.

An excellent way to improve critical thinking is to learn more than one approach to understanding a topic area. Research shows that students who learn two approaches to management—a conventional approach and a sustainable approach—improve their perceived and their actual critical thinking abilities. Put differently, learning two approaches helps to prevent dysfunctional self-fulfilling prophecies associated with teaching only one dominant approach. The benefit of exploring alternative approaches is being increasingly advocated by OB and management scholars (such as Jeffrey Pfeffer, Henry Mintzberg, Gretchen Spreitzer, Rosabeth Moss Kanter, and others) as well as by vanguard practitioners. For example, Dominic Barton, the global managing director of McKinsey & Company, is imploring leaders to explore alternatives that emphasize long-term thinking that recognizes the needs of a broad range of stakeholders, including employees, society, and the environment.

QUESTIONS FOR DISCUSSION

1. Do you agree that critical thinking is a key skill to be taught in university?
2. What courses have you taken that improve your ability to think outside the box and/or to challenge assumptions about "effectiveness" that are associated with general views on business?
3. What are some drawbacks to hearing only one perspective on a problem or organizational practice?

Fourth, exploring two approaches to OB shows that the actions and practices of organizational members are not value-neutral. It is, in fact, impossible to develop OB theory that is *not* based on some set of values. Thus, *both* the conventional and the sustainable ideal types are value-laden, though each is based on different assumptions about what is valuable. Learning the two approaches enables—even compels—you to think about what your own moral point of view is and about how it can be expressed in the workplace where you spend a significant portion of your life. Studying two ideal types of OB will help you to think about what kind of person or leader *you* want to become in the future and where on the continuum you fall. It will also help you understand and relate to people who favour a different approach than yours.

In sum, we hope that by exploring two approaches to OB you will understand a range of perspectives and practices that you can choose from to guide your experiences in organizations. You may end up favouring one approach over the other, or you may use the concepts and frameworks you learn in this course to form your own holistic approach. Heeding Socrates' observation that "the unexamined life is not worth living," we believe that learning about OB with critical reflection is of great worth.

Organizational Behaviour and Management

WHY OB | TWO APPROACHES | **OB & MGMT** | WHAT IS EXPLORED

LEARNING OBJECTIVE 3
Analyze the link between organizational behaviour and management.

The theories and practices of OB and management are intertwined. Managers rely upon and use their knowledge of OB in managing people, but even if you do not plan to be a manager, you are still likely to be influenced by the behaviour of managers in your workplace.

The most common definition of management has two components, one that focuses on what managers do, and the other on how they do it: **Management** is *the process of planning, organizing, leading, and controlling human and other organizational resources toward the achievement of organizational goals.* This definition and its conventional application to organizations arose during the Industrial Revolution, and they still remain dominant today.

Management is the process of planning, organizing, leading, and controlling human and other organizational resources toward the achievement of organizational goals.

Despite calls for a change in the way we do management from Gary Hamel and others (see "OB in Action: Moonshots for Management 2.0"), the basic functions of management continue to be planning, organizing, leading, and controlling. These four tasks were first identified by Henri Fayol almost a century ago.[17] We will look at them briefly and then suggest how conventional and sustainable perspectives might result in different organizational behaviours for each.

Planning

From a conventional perspective, planning focuses on how managers set goals and design strategies to achieve them; typically the focus is on how managers plan to improve productivity and profits. A sustainable approach emphasizes how managers *work alongside others* to set goals and design strategies. Moreover, sustainable managers reach for goals that go beyond profits and productivity, even when such goals are difficult to measure, such as those related to environmental sustainability, human dignity, and happiness. Sustainable OB emphasizes using **practical wisdom** (prudence), which is exercising foresight, reason, and discretion to achieve what is good for the community.[18] Because a sustainable approach to planning recognizes that individual and community well-being are closely related, members strive to make decisions that reflect the needs of multiple stakeholders (an organization's members, customers, owners, suppliers, and neighbours).

Practical wisdom (prudence) is exercising foresight, reason, and discretion to achieve what is good for the community.

Courtesy NASA

Gary Hamel is a Harvard Business School Research Fellow who is among those calling for organizations to dramatically improve the way they perform the four functions of management and achieve organizational goals. Hamel comments, "In a world in which economic value is increasingly the product of inspiration, mission, and the joy that people find in their work, the sorts of management innovation that will be most essential are precisely those whose benefits will be most difficult to measure." He goes so far as to say that if the discipline of management, which relies on OB theory and practice, does not innovate, some organizations would be better served by getting rid of their managers.

Hamel also reports on a meeting of leading practitioners and scholars in the organizational sciences who believe the time has come to "shoot for the moon" and develop a form of Management 2.0 that better meets the challenges that organizations face. Here are some examples of how these "moonshots" may be applied to OB 2.0:

- *Serve a higher purpose. Organizations should devote themselves to the achievement of noble, socially significant goals.*
- *Integrate the ideas of community and citizenship in organizational systems. Processes and practices should reflect the importance and interdependence of all stakeholder groups.*

- *Abandon the pathologies of formal hierarchy. Replace with natural hierarchies, where power flows up from the bottom and leaders emerge instead of being appointed.*
- *Decrease fear and increase trust. Mistrust and fear destroy innovation and engagement and must be replaced in tomorrow's organizational systems by trust.*
- *Refocus the source of control. To transcend the systems of monitoring and top-down control, systems will need to encourage self-control and peer accountability.*
- *Value and leverage diversity. Systems and practices must be created that value diversity, disagreement, and divergence as much as conformance, consensus, and cohesion.*
- *Redefine the role of leadership. The notion of the leader as a heroic decision maker is unsustainable. Leaders must re-invent themselves as social-systems architects who enable innovation and collaboration.*

QUESTIONS FOR DISCUSSION

1. Which moonshots do you think might be most important to the success of organizations in the future? Explain.
2. Which moonshots, if landed, would make an organization attractive to you as an employee? Why?
3. Which moonshots would make you nervous if you were a manager?

Organizing

From a conventional perspective, organizing is arranging human and other organizational resources in order to achieve planned goals and strategies. Basic organizing issues include concepts such as centralization (how much authority people at different organizational levels have), specialization (dividing large, complex tasks into a series of simpler tasks), and standardization (achieving coordination across organizational members). Sustainable organizing includes arranging resources but emphasizes a spirit of dignification, experimentation, and sensitivity to others' needs in the process. The virtue of **courage**, a hallmark of sustainable organizing, is evident when managers structure work to improve overall happiness even if it might reduce their own status or power. Courageous OB envisions and nurtures a sense of wholeness and integrity and promotes organizational structures that help employees flourish.

Courage is the willingness to take action to do what is good regardless of personal consequences.

Leading

From a conventional perspective, leading uses systems and interpersonal human skills to influence others to achieve organizational goals. Leadership styles or motivational techniques are valued for contributing to maximizing individual productivity. Sustainable leaders seek to develop workplaces in such a way that the emphasis on financial and productivity goals is balanced by an emphasis on sustainability and healthy social relationships. Self-control is necessary for fostering other corporate virtues such as caring, gentleness, and compassion.[19] **Self-control**, sometimes called temperance, relates to a person's emotional regulation and ability to overcome impulsive actions and greed. Leaders require self-control to use, but not abuse, their power when leading those around them. From a sustainable perspective, leaders take the role of a servant, focusing on the development of others and working together to meet mutually accepted organizational goals.

Self-control relates to a person's emotional regulation and ability to overcome impulsive actions and greed.

Controlling

From a conventional perspective, controlling ensures that organizational members do what they are supposed to be doing and that their performance meets expectations. Control can be achieved through the use of systems that monitor and encourage particular behaviours. For sustainable managers, control goes beyond simply ensuring that organizational directives are followed. It also involves ensuring that members' actions are just and consistent with the organization's values. **Justice**—a sense of fairness that ensures everyone connected with an organization gets his or her due—is an essential virtue that guides organizations and holds them together. Social justice, or a special sense of compassion for people ill-served by the status quo, is also a hallmark of some sustainable OB practices.

Justice is a sense of "fairness" that ensures that everyone connected with an organization gets his or her due.

What You Will Explore in This Book

`WHY OB` `TWO APPROACHES` `OB & MGMT` **`WHAT IS EXPLORED`**

This book will introduce you to key principles and theories in OB. An impressive and lengthy history of conventional OB shows how it can help to maximize the productivity, profitability, and competitiveness of organizations. The book will also introduce you to the growing body of literature that explores and supports many of the practices and concepts that are central to sustainable OB. Studies on servant leadership, corporate social responsibility, social entrepreneurship, positive scholarship, and stakeholder theory are examples of notable research advancing sustainable OB practices.

As you continue reading this text, you will be challenged to consider conventional and sustainable approaches to most OB concepts and practices. Following this chapter, you will examine the landscape of OB, including its history, its evolution as a science, the important stakeholders, and a few issues that arise in the global context of OB (chapter 2). Next, you will move into discussing OB on three levels: individual, interpersonal or group, and organizational.

Figure 1.3 illustrates how the concepts across these three levels form an integrated system of explanations for and influences on OB. First, represented by the circles in the centre of the figure, you will explore a set of chapters that focus on understanding individuals. These will introduce you to the importance of individual attributes (surface characteristics, abilities and personality, core self-evaluations, and beliefs and values of individuals—chapter 3), individual states (ethics, attitudes and commitments, perceptions, and emotions—chapter 4), motivational processes (chapter 5), decision-making dynamics (chapter 6), and self-leadership principles (chapter 7). These individual-level concepts are at the centre of our understanding of how individuals can influence and be influenced by their interpersonal relationships and organizational context.

The second main section of the book, represented by the rectangle in Figure 1.3, will help you to better understand OB at the interpersonal level. The section begins by discussing issues of politics, trust, conflict, and negotiation that influence relationships (chapter 8), then follows with chapters on leadership (chapter 9), groups and teams (chapter 10), and communication (chapter 11).

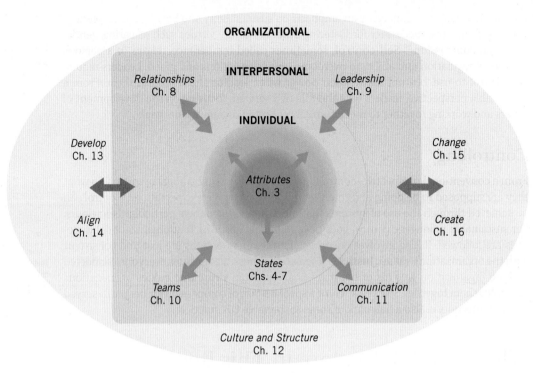

FIGURE 1.3 Illustrating the Integration of OB Concepts

The final section of this book, represented by the outer oval in Figure 1.3, is devoted to organization-level factors. These chapters will help to enhance your understanding of the basic features of organizational culture and structure (chapter 12), including an emphasis on developing appropriate organizational cultures and structures (chapter 13), aligning systems that affect motivation (chapter 14), changing the organization (chapter 15), and, as needed or desired, creating new organizations (chapter 16).

Enjoy the journey!

the forest and the trees at timberland[20]

Courtesy Timberland Asia Pacific Limited

Timberland is an outdoor shoe and apparel company known primarily for durable boots, although it is also known for its commendable environmental and societal footprint. Under the leadership of President and CEO Jeffrey Swartz, Timberland has become a pioneer in sustainability initiatives while following the mantra of "Doing Well by Doing Good."

As far back as the 1990s, Timberland believed in empowering its employees and providing them with opportunities to volunteer in the community. In one noteworthy example that combines employee empowerment and concern for the environment, Timberland and its employees partnered in working toward the goal of planting a million trees in China. The idea originated from Japanese employees who expressed concerns about deforestation in China and issues with air quality. A plan emerged to plant a few trees in the Horqin Desert of Northeast China. It began as a small employee community service project in 2000, six years before Timberland sold any shoes in China. The project grew, and the goal of a million trees being planted was reached in April 2010.

Swartz is the third generation from the Swartz family to serve at the helm of Timberland. His father, Sydney, was the CEO before him, and his grandfather started the company in 1952. Before taking on the role of CEO, Jeffrey was educated in the best schools and received training to prepare him to lead the large international retailer. Unexpectedly, one of the most significant training experiences occurred when he and a handful of employees volunteered to help troubled teens. One of the young men asked Swartz what he did for a living. He told the teenager he was the Chief Operating Officer of Timberland.

"He says, 'What do you really do?' I say, 'I'm responsible for the global execution of strategy.' Then I say, 'So what do you do?' He said, 'I work at getting well.' That was an answer that sort of trumped mine."

Swartz notes that the exchange made him feel like a trained seal that gave simple and shallow answers to important questions. The short, unassuming conversation was a critical influence on Swartz, inspiring him to reflect deeply on his fundamental beliefs and reasons for being in business. He became convinced that a meaningful and fulfilling life requires thinking beyond himself to the needs and concerns of others: "It wasn't frightening," he remembers. "It was, in fact, exalting and exhilarating."

Swartz carried this life lesson and the awakened sense of responsibility and purpose into his role as CEO. Even with his passion and sustainable perspective, he still has to balance these interests with the interests of shareholders in all of his decisions, including his decision to sell Timberland to VF Corporation. He believes Timberland's reputation of sustainability is part of the value that attracted VF Corporation to purchase the company, and he expects that Timberland will continue to do well, and do good, in the future.

QUESTIONS FOR DISCUSSION

1. If you were an employee at Timberland, how would you respond to the idea of planting trees in China? How would you respond as a shareholder?
2. What is your reaction to the conversation between Swartz and the troubled teen?
3. Have there been conversations in your life that have triggered deep introspection?
4. Do you think it was reasonable for Swartz to expect that Timberland would retain its priority on sustainability after being bought by another company?
5. Where might you place Timberland along a conventional-sustainable continuum? Explain your answer.

Summary

The study of OB is important because it enables you to have a better understanding of who you are and what your life ambitions are, it improves the working relationships you will have with co-workers, and it helps to increase your contribution to an organization and prepare you to serve in a management role. OB and management can be considered and practised from at least two perspectives: conventional OB and sustainable OB.

Learning Objectives	From a conventional OB perspective:	From a sustainable OB perspective:
• Explain the two effective approaches to organizational behaviour.	• Effectiveness emphasizes outcomes associated with personal interests, performance, commitment, predictability, and what will profit a narrow set of stakeholders in the short term.	• Effectiveness balances conventional outcomes while emphasizing community interests, creativity, and consequences for a broad set of stakeholders into the foreseeable future.
	• Planning is the process of deciding on an organization's goals and strategies.	• Planning happens through participation, practical wisdom, and higher-order goals.
• Analyze the link between organizational behaviour and management.	• Organizing means ensuring that tasks have been assigned and that the structure of organizational relationships facilitates the meeting of organizational goals.	• Organizing emphasizes courage and experimentation.
	• Leading means relating with others so that their work efforts help achieve organizational goals.	• Leading relies on relational self-control and treating members with dignity.
	• Controlling means ensuring that the actions of organizational members are consistent with organizational goals.	• Controlling involves promoting justice and ensuring that actions are consistent with organizational values.

Key Terms

Conceptual skills (p. 6)
Conventional OB (p. 7)
Courage (p. 12)
Critical thinking (p. 10)
Ideal types (p. 9)
Justice (p. 13)

Management (p. 11)
Organizational behaviour (p. 5)
Organizations (p. 5)
Practical wisdom (p. 11)
Relational skills (p. 6)
Self-control (p. 13)

Sustainable OB (p. 7)
Technical skills (p. 6)
Virtue theory (p. 8)
Virtues (p. 8)

Questions for Reflection and Discussion

1. What outcomes do you think represent effective OB? Why?
2. Think for a moment about a current or past manager you have worked for. Would you rate that person as a conventional or a sustainable manager? What factors did you take into account in choosing your answer?

3. The conventional approach to OB has been the dominant approach for well over a century. People like Max Weber and Gary Hamel have argued that is it not sustainable in the long term. Do you agree? Explain.

ob activities

Are You Ready for this Adventure in Learning?

Using a scale of 1 – Strongly Disagree (SD), 2 – Disagree (D), 3 – Neutral (N), 4 – Agree (A), and 5 – Strongly Agree (SA), indicate your level of agreement with each statement on the 5-point scale.

Typically, I . . .	SD	D	N	A	SA
1. Prefer variety to routine.	1	2	3	4	5
2. Like to visit new places.	1	2	3	4	5
3. Prefer to stick with things that I know.	1	2	3	4	5
4. Am interested in many things.	1	2	3	4	5
5. Don't like the idea of change.	1	2	3	4	5

Key: This is a short version of an adventurousness scale from the International Personality Item Pool (http://ipip.ori.org/). To calculate your total score, add the following:

_____ *(response to statement 1)*
+ _____ *(response to statement 2)*
+ _____ *(response to statement 3, subtracted from 6)*
+ _____ *(response to statement 4)*
+ _____ *(response to statement 5, subtracted from 6)*

= _____ *Total score*

The greater the score (out of 25 possible), the higher your self-rating on being adventurous. Being adventurous relates to being open to learning new ways of doing things and may indicate that you have the potential to succeed as an international business executive.[21]

What Is Your View of Effective Leadership?

Using a scale of 1 – Strongly Disagree (SD), 2 – Disagree (D), 3 – Neutral (N), 4 – Agree (A), and 5 – Strongly Agree (SA), indicate your level of agreement with each statement on the 5-point scale.

To be an effective leader, I should . . .	SD	D	N	A	SA
1. Maximize organizational profitability.	1	2	3	4	5
2. Maximize employee productivity.	1	2	3	4	5
3. Look after my own self-interests first.	1	2	3	4	5
4. Expect the people around me to be looking after their own interests first.	1	2	3	4	5
5. Focus on ensuring predictable behaviour and performance.	1	2	3	4	5
6. Emphasize short-term outcomes and organizational performance.	1	2	3	4	5

To be an effective leader, I should . . .

	SD	D	N	A	SA
7. Focus on promoting creativity and experimentation.	①	②	③	④	⑤
8. Emphasize long-term consequences and organizational viability.	①	②	③	④	⑤
9. Be someone who generously "goes the extra mile" for those around me.	①	②	③	④	⑤
10. Genuinely care for the people around me.	①	②	③	④	⑤
11. Maximize employee well-being.	①	②	③	④	⑤
12. Consider the interests of all stakeholders.	①	②	③	④	⑤

Key: This exercise is designed to see how your understanding of effectiveness compares to that of other students. Add together the scores for questions 1–6 to assess your orientation toward conventional OB and questions 7–12 to assess your orientation toward sustainable OB. Compare your scores on individual statements, or your total scores on items 1–6 versus items 7–12, with the scores of other students.

ETHICS SCENARIO

This is the first in a series of brief ethical scenarios that can be used for discussion. These scenarios have been used in previous research.[22]

A comptroller selected a legal method of financial reporting that concealed some embarrassing financial facts that would otherwise have become public knowledge.

Why might this scenario occur in organizations?

Use the following scale to indicate whether you feel this behaviour is ethically acceptable:

NEVER ACCEPTABLE		SOMETIMES ACCEPTABLE			ALWAYS ACCEPTABLE	
①	②	③	④	⑤	⑥	⑦

Explain the ideas you considered in arriving at your answer.

DISCUSSION STARTER

Is It the People, or the Place?

Life in prisons can be brutal and dehumanizing. There is some debate over whether this outcome is attributable to the individual characteristics of the inmates or to the organizational characteristics of prison. A famous experiment, dramatized in the recent film *The Stanford Prison Experiment*, was carried out with students at Stanford University to shed light on this debate.

Twenty-four male participants were chosen from a group of 75 volunteers based on tests that showed they were the most psychologically stable. The experiment, intended to last two weeks, took place in the basement of the building that housed Stanford's Psychology Department.

Half of the participants were assigned to be prisoners. Those in this group were intentionally not told what to expect or how to act, but they were assured that they would receive adequate food, clothing, and medical care. On the first day of the experiment, they were "arrested" by the local police department, blindfolded, taken to "prison" in the Psych building, and dressed in simple gowns and mandatory nylon caps. The remaining participants were assigned to be guards, and their assignment was also left deliberately vague: "to maintain a reasonable degree of order within the prison necessary for its effective functioning." They were given khaki uniforms and symbols of authority, such as silvered sunglasses.

The outcome of the experiment was dramatic and unexpected. "Guards" were aggressive and, on at least one occasion, abusive. Within 36 hours, one "prisoner" showed signs of severe psychosomatic disturbance and had to be released. Before the experiment was brought to a premature close, four more prisoners were released for similar reactions.

"At the end of only six days we had to close down our mock prison because what we saw was frightening," shared one of the students who ran the experiment. "It was no longer apparent to most of the subjects (or to us) where reality ended and their roles began. The majority had indeed become prisoners or guards, no longer able to clearly differentiate between role-playing and self. There were dramatic changes in virtually every aspect of their behavior, thinking and feeling. In less than a week the experience of imprisonment undid (temporarily) a lifetime of learning; human values were suspended, self-concepts were challenged, and the ugliest, most base, pathological side of human nature surfaced."[23]

In short, the results of the Stanford Prison Experiment suggested that the characteristics of a place—prison—and *the way it is organized* can have a great influence on the people within it. It can bring out the worst even in psychologically well-adjusted people. The influence of organizational "places" may be less dramatic in everyday organizations, but it may be every bit as real.[24]

QUESTIONS FOR DISCUSSION

1. How would you have acted if you were a guard?
2. What if you were a prisoner?
3. How do you explain the experiment's findings?
4. Are there places (e.g., classrooms, places of worship, sports stadiums) in which you act differently than you might at home?
5. What is it about certain places that make you act differently?

APPLICATION JOURNAL

This is the first in a series of journal entries that can be used for class discussion or be compiled and included in a self-reflection paper.

Based on this introduction to OB, what do you want to take away from your journey through the book? Create a series of goals for the course and explain why each is important to you.

Two

Exploring the Landscape of OB

Each generation takes a somewhat different path through the world of work and organizations, given different historical, scientific, and social conditions. These conditions make up the landscape of OB. In this chapter we explore four key characteristics that contribute to which theories of OB managers emphasize and which theories of OB they practice.

Learning Objectives	Conventional OB	Shared	Sustainable OB

A BRIEF HISTORY OF OB

Discuss the history of organizational behaviour.	Consider these eras: Scientific management era (1910–1930) Human relations era (1930–1950) Systems era (1950–1970) Beliefs era (1970–1990) Sustainability era (1990–present)

OB AS A SCIENCE

Recognize organizational behaviour as a science.	Emphasize objectivity and quantitative methods	Emphasize creativity and qualitative methods

STAKEHOLDER RELATIONSHIPS

Describe stakeholder relationships and management's responsibilities to stakeholders.	Manage key stakeholders' interests	Collaborate with multiple stakeholders

GLOBAL ENVIRONMENT

Discuss the influence of globalization on organizational behaviour.	Approach differences from an ethnocentric or polycentric view	Approach differences from an egalicentric view

finding strength in community[1]

Since its founding by a group of West coast mountaineers in 1971, Mountain Equipment Co-op (MEC) has taken an unconventional approach to operating a retail business, as well as to the challenges and opportunities it faces along the way. Today MEC is Canada's largest consumer retail co-operative by membership, with over 4.3 million members, and the country's largest supplier of outdoor equipment. Serving its members through 18 retail locations in six provinces and its online storefront, MEC generated CAD $336 million in sales in 2014. Its ambitious mission is to inspire and enable everyone to lead active outdoor lifestyles, offer incredible products and superlative service, embed sustainability practices throughout their business, and help conserve the outdoors. Guided by its values—quality, integrity, cooperation, creativity, leadership, sustainability, stewardship, humanity, and adventure—MEC topped the Corporate Knights ranking of the Best 50 Corporate Citizens in Canada in 2007 and 2014, and it has been recognized as one of Canada's Top 100 Employers on several occasions.

MEC's unconventional co-op model consisting of members, who are also shareholders, sets it apart from other retailers. That said, David Labistour, MEC's current CEO, knows that competition in the industry is stiff, with other companies offering high-quality products at better prices. Labistour attributes the organization's day-to-day success to its nearly 2,000 employees who serve as the touchpoints for the brand:

> We want people who share our passion; who are curious; energetic; who want to learn and grow. And without a doubt, they have to be great communicators. Business is so complex today, and so collaborative, that great team members have to excel in communication at every level.

In turn, MEC makes an effort to take care of its people by providing them with the environment, resources, and support they need to excel in their day-to-day work and to help members engage in active lifestyles. MEC's corporate headquarters in Vancouver is a LEED Platinum–certified building equipped with bike lockers, a bouldering room, a space for yoga and CrossFit, and views of the North Shore Mountains. It was designed to attract and retain the best people. MEC also offers its casual, part-time, and full-time retail employees hourly

wage rates that are higher than the national retail average and competitive benefits packages with access to tuition assistance and interest-free loans.

A deeper look into MEC reveals that its dedication to embedding sustainability into all aspects of its business over the years separates it from the crowd:

> *"[MEC's] dedication to embedding sustainability into all aspects of its business over the years separates it from the crowd."*

MEC outshines its retailing peers when it comes to areas such as carbon productivity, the percentage of women in senior management, and the ratio of the CEO's pay compared to that of the company's average worker.

For Labistour, embracing sustainability is smart business. Sustainable practices have become standard operating procedure for the organization and have been integrated into deliverables within everyone's job descriptions, from improving the supply chain to meeting customer expectations. Embracing a people-, planet-, product-, and performance-approach to sustainability, MEC strives to make great products that lessen its impact on the environment and improve the lives of people it touches.

MEC establishes long-term partnerships with suppliers built on transparency and mutual trust; it does not simply chase the lowest cost. These relationships focus on shared values and sourcing criteria between MEC and its factories: quality, skill, technology, price, service, ability to meet delivery timelines, and environmental and social performance. Its Social Compliance Program is dedicated to improving working conditions in factories that produce MEC-brand apparel and gear. It also requires its suppliers and wholesale brand partners to uphold the MEC Code of Conduct, which sets out minimum standards for workers' rights and for environmental responsibility. In 2008, MEC was the first retailer in Canada to publish a factory list, which is updated and published twice a year.

Aligned with its mission, MEC also extends its reach to benefit the communities in which it operates. In addition to partnering with national and regional outreach and advocacy programs, and product donation programs, MEC is a proud member of 1% for the Planet, investing 1 percent of annual revenue to environmental causes. To date, MEC has invested over CAD $29 million in Canada's environmental and outdoors communities through community involvement programs.

Locally, MEC also hosts events such as 5k races, triathlons, clinics, and festivals to help its members engage in active outdoor lifestyles. In 2014, the organization held 5,024 community events, with 88,000 attendees.

MEC strives to be an agent for change in the outdoor, apparel, and retail industries. Sustainability is a key consideration in the product design process, and MEC works to minimize its environmental impact by finding new innovative materials. To reduce its impact MEC follows a strict pattern: challenge the status quo, ask the hard questions, don't take no for an answer, and partner with like-minded industry peers to change the system. To keep itself accountable to its members, MEC sets multi-year goals that often stretch the bounds of current technology, and it reviews those goals each year. To further help it push the boundaries of what is possible, MEC collaborates with key players in the outdoor industry culture, including the Outdoor Industry Association, Sustainable Apparel Coalition, bluesign® system, and the Textile Exchange. Other MEC practices include offering products that are certified by Fairtrade International, an organization committed to increasing the earnings of factory workers; promoting the use of natural, organic, or recycled fibres; and advocating animal welfare. To minimize the environmental impact downstream, MEC also operates an online gear swap free of charge to its members who wish to buy, sell, or swap outdoor gear.

> Labistour believes one of the company's biggest sustainability achievements is also one of its least recognized, and that's the fact that more than half of its MEC-brand apparel materials are bluesign approved. The bluesign system looks at the use of sustainable ingredients and the production process in the textile industry and is based on five principles: resource productivity, consumer safety, water emission, air emission, and occupational health and safety.

Finally, MEC sets its goals, tracks its metrics, and publicly reports its performance in all key areas, including product performance, human rights and employee well-being, operations, members and community impact, employee engagement, and financials. Like many companies, MEC once reported its environmental and social performance in a stand-alone report separate from its financials; however, over time it has moved toward having one integrated year-end business and sustainability report. Labistour does not believe that you can run a business in silos and believes in breaking down barriers so that a company can run as an organic whole. To him and the organization, sustainability should work symbiotically with all aspects of a business, not separately.

Although MEC, like all corporate retail giants, carefully examines and employs market research in order to stay competitive in the market, the organization has learned to rely also on its grassroots foundation. Its principles of making things happen, dealing fairly, finding strength in community, and inspiring adventure have held up over time.

The example of MEC shows how OB is influenced, in part, by an organizational landscape that developed over time through organizations and their members engaging in various OB practices and through researchers testing ideas and relationships in organizations. This landscape continues to change as the context of OB increasingly includes a variety of stakeholders and connects to a global society. We will explore these characteristics of the organizational landscape further in this chapter as we take a quick trip through OB history and the development of OB as a science in order to set the stage for understanding the current challenges and opportunities in OB.

As described in chapter 1, many OB scholars and practitioners feel that the time is ripe to consider enhancing how we think about OB by upgrading from what we might call "OB 1.0" to "OB 2.0." This shift may include placing greater emphasis on sustainability in how we achieve profitability and how we affect people and our planet, while respecting and learning from the history and current practices of OB. To paraphrase a quote first made famous by Sir Isaac Newton, we can see a possible new future only by standing on the shoulders of giants. The goal in this chapter is to review some of the key developments in OB that have brought us to the present and to consider some of the main challenges facing organizations today. This will help set the stage for thinking about and improving OB going forward.

After reading the chapter, you will see that the meaning of OB has been constantly changing over time, that it will continue to do so in your lifetime, and that you have an opportunity to shape what it means.

A Brief History of OB

BRIEF HISTORY OF OB | OB AS A SCIENCE | STAKEHOLDERS | GLOBAL ENVIRONMENT

LEARNING OBJECTIVE 1
Discuss the history of organizational behaviour.

We'll now take a brief tour through the development of OB over the past century, looking at five key "eras" in that time. Ideas and theories about management and OB may be plentiful today, but research on these topics started to flourish only about 100 years ago. One reason is that, until the Industrial Revolution, there were very few large organizations of the type so common today. Workers and craftspeople had at times organized themselves into guilds,[2] but until recently most work took place in very small businesses, which were often called cottage industries because the work was literally done in cottages. There were many family firms, whose owner was personally related to most of the workers. Because organizations were small, workers knew how their work fit into the whole and there was a strong sense of community and interdependence in the workplace.[3]

A few centuries ago these small-scale organizations started to change in response to social, technological, and legal changes. Adam Smith's seminal *Wealth of Nations*, which was published in 1776, provides what is perhaps the best single example to help explain the shift that was occurring toward working in factories instead of in households. Using a pin factory as an example, Smith demonstrated the merits of specialization and "division of labour" by describing how four workers, each performing a specialized task, could produce 48,000 pins per day, instead of the 12 pins per day that each could produce by working independently and doing all the tasks. Smith's analysis was compelling and reflected how the Industrial Revolution was changing both where people worked and the type of work they did.

Modern management and OB would be very different today had there not been changes to the social and legal meaning of an organization. Traditionally, most businesses were seen as an extension of a household, but eventually organizations were given a life of their own and allowed to act as legal citizens with limited liability.[4] Citizenship status allowed organizations to enter into contracts, and limited liability provided protection for shareholders against the risks associated with new ventures and expanded commercial dealings. These privileges were granted with the understanding that organizations were supposed to enhance the common good and that their charter could be taken away if they failed to do so. Initially, an organization's responsibility was intended to extend beyond mere concern for the financial investments of owners and shareholders—it also included considering what is good for the community. It seems that some organizations today could use a reminder of this.

The Scientific Management Era (1910 to 1930)

Scientific management focuses on analyzing and improving the efficiency of work processes.

From about 1910 to 1930, in the era of **scientific management**, management scholars focused on studying human behaviour to maximize the efficiency and productivity of *individual jobs*, and on using bureaucracy to maximize the productivity of the *overall organization*. Frederick W. Taylor (1856–1915), who is often called the father of scientific management, explained: "In the past man [sic] has been first. In the future, the system must be first."[5] Taylor's most famous study helped increase the shovelling productivity at the Bethlehem Steel plant in Bethlehem, Pennsylvania. Rather than have workers bring their own shovels, as had been the custom at the time, Taylor carried out studies to determine the best-designed tool for each particular task, which proved to be different shovels for different types and weights of materials. In one study, after management provided optimally designed shovels to the workers, the average output per worker increased almost 350 percent, from 12.5 tonnes per day to 47.5 tonnes per day. At the same time, workers' pay was increased about 50 percent, from $1.15 per day to $1.85 per day. This was seen as a "win-win" situation, and Taylor's ideas and methods quickly spread throughout the industry.

Other important contributors to scientific management were Frank B. Gilbreth (1868–1924) and his wife, Lillian, who conducted studies identifying the most efficient way to organize work to reduce time and motion.[6] The Gilbreths were known for their quest to find the "one best way" to do work. Frank may be best known for his work with bricklayers, where his analysis resulted in simplifying the bricklaying process from 18 different motions down to 5, which resulted in a productivity increase of more than 200 percent. The Gilbreths' pioneering work in time and motion studies inspired such innovations as foot levers for garbage cans and contributed to the design of many ergonomic products and practices. They also applied their methods at home with their dozen children. For example, Frank would record video of his children washing dishes so that he could analyze the work and subdivide it into its basic steps in order to enable his children to proceed through the task more efficiently. He also placed record players in the bathrooms of the family home, playing foreign language lessons so that his children could learn new languages as they went about their daily business.[7]

Max Weber (1864–1920) described how the scientific management approach contributed to the rise of the "bureaucratic organization," wherein work was reorganized based on rules and procedures, and reporting relationships were designed to maximize efficiency. Henry Ford provides perhaps the most famous example of this. With his engineers, Ford pioneered the development of mass production manufacturing. By 1920, seven years after he opened the Model T–producing car-manufacturing plant in Highland Park, Michigan, the cost of a car had been reduced by two-thirds. Efficiency was enhanced by things like the use of conveyor belts to move the car to workers along a production line. Each worker did one job, like bolting the door to the frame or attaching the handle to the door. Each job was highly specialized and repetitive.[8]

In addition to studying the most efficient ways to organize work, some of the prominent researchers from this era, like Lillian Gilbreth, also foreshadowed the next era by concluding that Taylor's approach to scientific management must be supplemented by research on psychology to account for the human element in all work.[9]

The Human Relations Era (1930 to 1950)

If Frederick Taylor is the father of the scientific management era, then Mary Parker Follett (1868–1933) could be considered the mother of the **human relations** era, which focused on the social environment of work. Follett's approach was in stark contrast to that of the scientific management school, as evident in her advice: "Don't hug your blueprints."[10] Follett argued that authority should not always go to the person who formally holds the position of manager, but rather that power is fluid and should flow to the worker whose knowledge and experience makes him or her best able to serve the company at any given time. Follett viewed organizations as "communities" in which managers and workers work in harmony, neither dominates the other, and each has the freedom to discuss and resolve differences and conflicts.

Follett was far ahead of her time and drew from sociology and psychology to promote a human rather than a mechanistic approach to OB. Another important early proponent of the view that people are important in organizations was Chester Barnard (1886–1961), who was an executive with AT&T and the president of New Jersey Bell Telephone Company. Barnard drew attention to the importance of leadership and informal organization, pointing out that all organizations have social groups and cliques that form alongside the formal structures. In his view, organizations are not machines and cannot be managed effectively in the impersonal way implied by scientific management theory.

A critical finding from this era resulted from research that was conducted by Elton Mayo and Fritz Roethlisberger for a project originally sponsored by General Electric.[11] The company wanted to sell more light bulbs by demonstrating to potential business customers that factory workers' productivity would increase with improved lighting. The thing was though, the results from one particular research location, the Hawthorne plant of the Western Electric Company, were counterintuitive. Researchers had walked around and monitored workers in varying lighting conditions and, as expected, productivity increased when lighting was increased; however, productivity also increased when the lighting remained consistent and even when it was decreased. Only when the lighting was dimmed to the level of moonlight did productivity decrease. Not surprisingly, General Electric soon after withdrew its sponsorship of the study.

After further studies tried to account for these odd results, researchers concluded that *workers' productivity will increase whenever managers give them special attention*. In the case of the Hawthorne factory, workers did not want to disappoint the scientists who were monitoring their performance, so they worked extra hard in response to the special attention they were receiving. The results—labelled the **Hawthorne effect**—suggested that relationships are

Human relations focuses on how the social environment of work influences attitudes and behaviour.

Hawthorne effect is an improvement in work productivity resulting from people receiving attention from observers.

important in understanding behaviour in organizations.[12] To modern ears, these findings may sound pretty simple-minded, but, at the time, they served as the foundation for the human relations movement, which expanded our understanding of how the social environment of work influences people's attitudes and behaviour at work. This movement stimulated much of the OB research and practices described throughout this text.

The Systems Era (1950 to 1970)

Industrial productivity had to improve during World War II to aid the war effort, and new management techniques were needed as well. The British, for example, assembled mathematicians and physicists into operations research teams that analyzed the compositions, routes, probable location, and speed of Nazi submarines to help convoys of supply ships avoid being sunk by German subs. These teams developed an approach, later termed *systems analysis*, to analyze complex problems that could not be solved by intuition, straightforward mathematics, or simple experience. Lessons learned from these military situations were subsequently adapted and applied to managing civilian organizations. For example, managers at General Electric used lessons about troop deployment to decide where to assign employees, where to build plants, and how to design warehouses. This contributed to the development of **systems theory** in OB, which highlights the interdependencies between individuals, features of organizations, and the broader organizational context.

Systems theory highlights the complex interdependencies between individuals, features of organizations, and the broader organizational context.

The systems theory approach draws attention to the complexity of managing organizations and, in particular, the need to look beyond organizational boundaries.[13] In systems language terms, rather than look at an organization as a *closed system* and managing activities only within an organization's boundaries, managers should adopt an *open-systems* perspective. For example, a closed-system perspective of a pizza restaurant will focus attention on activities happening within the walls of the restaurant—friendly customer service, cleanliness in the kitchen, adequate staff training, and so on. An open-systems perspective will be more aware of where to recruit staff, how to advertise to specific target markets, which suppliers to choose, and so on.

Perhaps the best example of this movement is total quality management (TQM), an approach that emphasizes the importance of managers continuously improving organizational work systems so that products or services better meet the quality level customers desire. W. Edwards Deming, a founder of the quality movement, asserted that variability in quality of output is largely attributable to *organizational* systems and processes, not to the efforts of individual workers.[14] Individual workers being evaluated on their numerical output or quantified standards without consideration of system effects was an approach that Deming considered to be a disease that destroys the health of the work environment.

An emphasis on systems helped to expand the understanding of OB beyond theories focusing primarily on the individual. During the systems era scholars moved toward a contingency view, arguing that the best decisions or behaviours depend on the situation. As such, leadership theories featuring a situational or contingency approach became the dominant way of thinking about leadership during this era.

The Beliefs Era (1970 to 1990)

The 1960s were a time of phenomenal technological and large-scale organizational accomplishment, exemplified by the achievements of space travel and the first moonwalk. The following two decades were a time of cultural upheaval and questioning the meaning of the status quo. A heightened interest in the role of beliefs within organizations emerged at the beginning of this era. Scholars emphasized how people are controlled by social or cultural "scripts" they have learned in the course of their lives, scripts that are difficult to change. The unwritten scripts or informal norms that guide behaviour in organizations are an important part of an organization's culture.[15]

In studying the management practices at the Tennessee Valley Authority (TVA), Philip Selznick discovered how scripts may become dysfunctional over time.[16] Selznick found that many standard operating procedures (organizational scripts) at the TVA had been rational when they were initially developed but were no longer rational when he studied the organization. He called this change **institutionalization**, which means certain practices or rules have become valued in and of themselves, even though they may no longer be useful for the organization.[17] Institutionalized social norms and expectations control people's actions by setting up predefined patterns of behaviour, and these patterns in turn channel behaviour in one direction instead of in any of the many different directions that are theoretically possible.[18] Although research indicates that these routines and taken-for-granted norms often lie beneath the level of our consciousness, they can change when someone deliberately chooses to adopt a new script.[19]

A key concept from this era is the **social construction of reality**, the idea that what we experience as real and the meanings we attach to ideas, objects, and events have been socially constructed.[20] Consider the example of money, which seems very real and is the focus of much human activity. And yet for most of the history of humankind, there was no such thing as "money" as we know it. Up until several thousand years ago, goods and services were primarily exchanged via bartering. Indeed, although we place considerable value on a hundred-dollar bill, in reality it is just a piece of paper with some colours and lettering. There is nothing inherent in a hundred-dollar bill that makes it particularly valuable; the value people ascribe to money is socially constructed. A less abstract example is the way we view and treat men and women in society. Not so long ago it was considered normal to deny women equal treatment and equal rights. Although we still have a way to go in making equal treatment a reality, perceptions have changed and continue to change.

The experiences that members have in organizations are critical to their social construction of reality. For example, professors in our business schools introduce to students ways of thinking and concepts that shape the way students interpret behaviour in organizations.[21] Organizational leaders also have a powerful influence in constructing the meaning of reality for the organization's members.[22] In the beliefs era, OB found a deeper understanding of human behaviour by emphasizing the informal and unconscious beliefs that influence organizational life.

Institutionalization has occurred when organizational practices or rules are accepted and perpetuated without regard to instrumental rationality.

Social construction of reality is the idea that what we perceive to be real is influenced by the social environment

The Sustainability Era (1990 to present)

Questioning of the prevailing theories and practices of management and OB has been growing in the last generation. Indian organizational theorist Sumantra Ghoshal pointed out that all management theory is value-laden but felt that conventional management theory and practice has given too much emphasis to narrow self-regarding behaviour. Ghoshal argued that organizational scholars should help students build "delightful organizations" that positively affect their members and society for generations to come.[23] Other scholars have also called for more positive alternatives to prevailing theory and practice, which inform the sustainable approach described in this book.[24]

Business and community leaders also have recognized the need to think and act sustainably in such ways that profitability and progress in the present are not achieved at the expense of damage to future generations. For example, the World Business Council for Sustainable Development (WBCSD) is a CEO-led coalition of over 200 influential companies across the world that share a commitment to sustainable development through balancing economic, ecological, and social goals.[25]

New times call for a new way of thinking, but the challenges are great. Here are some of the major issues:

- *Ecological sustainability.* Consensus is building that managers, consumers, and investors must take greater account of their impact on the natural environment. Understanding and adopting practices that contribute to ecological sustainability may be critical for organizations to remain competitive and viable.[26] Further, more people are recognizing that there is little satisfaction in achieving financial wealth if future generations will suffer clean-up costs.[27]

- *Societal well-being.* The gap between rich and poor is growing within organizations as well as within and across countries. Even people from relatively wealthy countries are challenging systems they see as unjust, regardless of whether those systems serve their financial interests. A growing body of scholarly research indicates that the conventional obsession with materialism—that is, with maximizing productivity and profitability—results in significant physical and emotional costs, such as increased stress and decreased overall health and happiness.[28]

- *Holistic concerns.* Beyond material success, people are increasingly placing greater value on less tangible concerns, such as aesthetic quality and spirituality. For example, some communities are resisting the spreading marks of commercialism that they fear will decrease the beauty of their surroundings.[29] In light of the growing interest in spirituality and its relationship to organizations, the world's largest scholarly association of management, the Academy of Management, has established a "Management, Spirituality, and Religion" interest group.[30]

Research suggests that people around the world are increasingly more interested in quality of life and a sense of community and social equity than in material and economic rewards, prosperity, and control.[31] For example, in a nationally representative poll of 1,269 adults, 93 percent of U.S. adults said they felt that people are too focused on working and making money and not focused enough on family and community. Approximately half of the respondents claimed to have voluntarily opted not to maximize their material wealth in order to facilitate other forms of well-being.[32]

Each era in the history of OB has contributed unique insights and provided important components to the research that is the basis for the science of OB that guides current practices and stimulates further research. What we mean by "the science of OB" is discussed in the next section.

OB as a Science

LEARNING OBJECTIVE 2
Recognize organizational behaviour as a science.

| BRIEF HISTORY OF OB | **OB AS A SCIENCE** | STAKEHOLDERS | GLOBAL ENVIRONMENT |

The modern academic study of organizations and OB, which has developed over time, involves some common concepts and processes that will be referred to throughout the book and so are worth introducing here.

Overall, OB scholars examine factors that help to explain, predict, and ultimately influence behaviour. Researchers describe each factor as a *variable* because it varies across individuals (e.g., personality, self-confidence, and skills) and across contexts (e.g., organizations, industries, or countries). The variable a researcher wants to predict is called the *dependent variable* because it is proposed to "depend on" or be influenced by other variables that are *independent variables*. For example, consider the two variables "paylevel" and "job satisfaction." A number of studies have investigated the relationship of pay (independent variable) with job satisfaction as the dependent variable. Your own experience may suggest that these variables are closely related, but across a range of studies the findings indicate that they are only slightly related.[33]

After researchers identify the variables of interest, they must measure them by observation, assessment, interviews, surveying, or by compiling historical information. Then researchers analyze the *association* between the variables. A simple statistic that represents the association between two variables is a *correlation.* Two variables are perfectly associated if they correlate at 1.0, although most correlations are much lower. In fact, a correlation of .50 is considered to be quite strong. When two variables are *positively* correlated, they are related in the same direction—as one goes up or is higher, the other variable also goes up or is

Bill Aron/PhotoEdit

An interesting research experiment, conducted by Walter Mischel and his colleagues, involved putting preschoolers in a room and giving them two options: eating a marshmallow now, or waiting for a period of time (15–20 minutes) and then receiving two marshmallows to eat. The researchers were interested in learning more about willpower, or self-control. Search YouTube for "marshmallow test" and you'll find several variations of this experiment.

If researchers are interested in what explains willpower, willpower is the dependent variable and its explanations are independent variables. If researchers are interested in what willpower predicts, willpower is the independent variable and subsequent behaviour, or another variable, is the dependent variable. Incidentally, having more willpower is associated with higher educational achievement, better ability to cope with stress, and less drug use. Further, in organizations, willpower is positively related to work performance.

QUESTIONS FOR DISCUSSION

1. What else do you think willpower might predict?
2. Do you have any theories about what contributes to willpower?
3. Do you have any suggestions for how to go about testing willpower among adults?
4. Are you hungry?

higher. If two variables are *negatively* correlated, when one goes up the other goes down. In the previous example investigating pay and job satisfaction, the association across a range of studies was .15, which is positive but considered to be a relatively small association.

Although OB research employs more complex and rigorous analyses than simple correlations to draw conclusions, when this textbook refers to two things being related or associated, such as personality and job performance, the statements are based on research that has demonstrated there is evidence of the relationship. An interesting example of how the variable of willpower has been measured and how it relates to other variables is described in the OB in Action feature "Hungry for Evidence."

OB research generally adheres to the following basic process. It starts with a question, expressed in terms of a theory (a collection of assertions explaining what is likely to cause a particular behaviour and why), and the development of hypotheses that are specific predictions about the relationships between the variables of interest. These hypotheses are then tested in the context of organizations or in behavioural laboratories, which yields information and data that are analyzed to draw conclusions. In turn, these conclusions are confirmed or disconfirmed by additional studies.

As research studies accumulate around a specific question or set of associations, a *meta-analysis* can be conducted. A meta-analysis is a study that combines the evidence from numerous studies to draw general conclusions. This cumulative evidence can then be taught to leaders and organizational members so that they adopt the practices or behaviours that are most likely to result in the organizational variables that are important to organizations, such as performance, creativity, commitment, and collaboration. For example, some of the results presented in the "Hungry for Evidence" OB in Action feature are based on a meta-analysis of studies on self-control.

Conventional and sustainable OB researchers follow similar norms of scientific methods and rigour, but there are some different tendencies within each stream. For example, because conventional OB research questions tend to focus on factors that are easily quantifiable (like performance measures based on productivity or profitability) and have a long history of study that has created reliable survey instruments (like measurement scales for job satisfaction or different personality types), many conventional OB research designs have a quantitative or positivistic orientation. A positivistic approach to research insists on data that are directly available by sensory perception and are empirically verifiable.[34] These studies have specific variables that we can measure and analyze quantitatively. Indeed, its perceived objectivity makes this type of OB research very appealing and relatively easy to do.

In contrast, research in sustainable OB is more likely to engage in qualitative research designs. This is in part due to the kinds of questions that sustainable OB research asks. Measuring the views of multiple stakeholders on multiple dimensions of well-being is very challenging using traditional quantitative research methods. For example, consider the difficulties facing sustainable OB researchers who wish to measure the amount of "virtue" evident in organizations and the effect it has on members and other key stakeholders now and in the future. As a result of these challenges, sustainable OB research is more likely to explore a variety of research designs, many of which will likely be qualitative in nature. Of course, just as conventional OB research utilizes some qualitative research, sustainable OB is concerned also with quantitative research; indeed, we have already seen considerable improvement in empirical measurement of virtues and in aspects of the triple bottom line sustainability measure of profit, people, and planet.[35]

In sum, OB theories and research have proven to be beneficial, but there are always limitations. For example, sometimes interesting and potentially useful new theories can be difficult to get published because of their novelty.[36] Also, many important individual and organizational variables are difficult to measure or assess and, thus, are ignored in research. Further, OB deals with people and complex organizational contexts that offer specific challenges that make it difficult for OB scholars to draw broadly applicable conclusions.[37] Even so, OB has a growing body of evidence that serves as the foundation for the ideas discussed in this textbook.[38] Going forward, OB research needs to develop and test new or integrated theories and practices that will not only create successful organizations today but that will also contribute to a better world for future generations. This will require that OB research and practice take into account the emergence of important stakeholder and global influences on OB.

Stakeholder Relationships

BRIEF HISTORY OF OB | OB AS A SCIENCE | **STAKEHOLDERS** | GLOBAL ENVIRONMENT

LEARNING OBJECTIVE 3
Describe stakeholder relationships and management's responsibilities to stakeholders.

A **stakeholder** is any group within or outside an organization that is directly affected by the organization and has a stake in its performance.

The field of OB exists in a historical context and is built on accumulated wisdom and science, but no organization exists in a vacuum. Organizations have key stakeholders to whom they must pay attention. A **stakeholder** is any group within or outside an organization that is directly affected by the organization and has a stake in its performance. Stakeholders have many different expectations, but, with a few exceptions, they all want the organization to remain viable. For example:

- Customers want products and services that meet their needs and wants.
- Members want rewarding and meaningful work and interactions on the job.
- Owners want to receive an appropriate reward for their investment.
- Other organizations, such as suppliers, want predictable orders with on-time payments, and competitors expect fair and legal actions.
- Community members want organizations to operate in ways that benefit or at least do no harm to the community and the environment.

Organization-specific responsibility (OSR) is the responsibility of organizations to focus on the organization's owners and their financial interests.

Corporate social responsibility (CSR) is the responsibility of organizations to act in ways that protect and improve the welfare of multiple stakeholders.

Conventional OB is more consistent with the classical view of stakeholders that emphasizes the **organization-specific responsibility (OSR)** of organizations to focus on one particular stakeholder group and one particular form of well-being, namely the organization's owners and their financial interests. Sustainable OB is consistent with the growing interest in the **corporate social responsibility (CSR)** of organizations to act in ways that protect and improve the welfare of multiple stakeholders.[39] A sustainable approach recognizes OSR responsibilities but does not always act to *maximize* financial well-being. Rather, while recognizing that financial sustainability is clearly necessary, sustainable OB also actively seeks to consider the interests of other stakeholders, including the natural environment and future generations. Sustainable OB is based on the belief that with the considerable power that organizations have to affect other stakeholders, along with it comes considerable responsibility to these stakeholders. A similar sentiment about power and responsibility was expressed by French philosopher Voltaire, New Testament author Luke, and, more recently, Spider-Man's Uncle Ben. Table 2.1 highlights key differences between conventional versus sustainable OB assumptions about responsibilities to shareholders.

Conventional and sustainable OB must deal with the same key stakeholders, but their orientations toward the stakeholders differ. For example, both conventional and sustainable OB recognize that the customer stakeholder group provides financial resources that organizations require to be financially viable. However, whereas conventional OB seeks to manage customers to serve the financial interests of the organization, sustainable OB is characterized by its service and relationship-building orientation with customers. Similarly, instead of trying to maximize control over a supplier, sustainable managers seek to benefit from inviting suppliers' expertise into decisions. A sustainable approach is more likely to engage in co-creation, a collaborative process whereby multiple organizations work with customers to provide solutions to customers' needs,[40] and in joint ventures, whereby two organizations share the risk and gain for developing a new technology or delivering products or services.[41]

Sustainable OB is more likely to emphasize that serving others provides a sense of purpose for members. For example, two or three times each year, the management team of Tomasso Corporation—a successful food processing plant in Montreal, Quebec—serves food in a local soup kitchen. After the meal, they sit with the people they have served and get to know them.[42] Other workers from the plant may join the managers; they're allowed to go during work hours and are paid for their time. Rather than see stakeholders as outsiders who must be managed to maximize the organization's financial well-being, sustainable OB strives to enhance multiple forms of well-being for multiple stakeholders. In essence, the sustainable approach fosters a sense of community among stakeholders, even competitors, as the OB in Action feature "Growing with Your Suppliers and Competitors" describes.

TABLE 2.1 Assumptions about Responsibilities to Stakeholders

	Conventional OB (OSR)	Sustainable OB (CSR)
Management is ethically obligated to . . .	the organization's owners.	*all* organizational stakeholders.
The general public wants organizations . . .	that maximize profits.	that take care of economic and social goals.
Managers who pursue CSR actions . . .	tend to weaken financial performance.	enhance financial viability in the long term.
The costs of CSR are . . .	too high and threaten viability.	lower than long-run non-CSR costs.
Businesses . . .	know how to make money but lack CSR skills.	have resources that can uniquely benefit society.
Caring for the natural environment . . .	dilutes the purpose of organizations.	enhances organizations' long-term sustainability.
The power of organizations in society . . .	is too great already (and CSR would add to it).	obligates them to become more responsible.

In addition to stakeholders with names and faces, organizations also have relationships with the natural environment. The **natural environment** is composed of all living and non-living things that have not been created by human technology or human activity. Organizations depend on the natural environment for inputs like raw material, natural resources, minerals, water, and air, and to dispose of organizational outputs such as waste. Growing awareness of ecological problems like global warming and non-sustainable ecological footprints have prompted organizational members to become increasingly sensitive to the natural environment.

Many leading organizations have announced green initiatives, such as Walmart's promise to be "packaging neutral" by 2025, GE's "ecomagination" program that supports environmentally friendly products, and DuPont's goal to derive $6 billion in new revenues from operations that reduce harmful emissions or create energy efficiency.[43] As shown in Figure 2.1, the approach that organizational members take with respect to the natural environment varies along a continuum.

The *obstructionist stance* is the least sensitive to the natural environment. Organizational members taking this approach do as little as possible to address environmental problems. Instead, their focus is on narrowly defined economic priorities, and they resist any social demands lying outside the organization's perceived financial self-interests. This can sometimes lead to illegal activity, such as dumping toxic waste in low-income countries in an effort to avoid paying the high costs associated with proper cleanup.[44]

With a *defensive strategy* or *legal approach,* organizational members do only as much as is legally required and may even try to use the law to their own advantage. They will insist that their employees behave legally, but they will put the interests of shareholders above those of other stakeholders and the environment. For example, Willamette Industries of Portland, Oregon, agreed to install $7.4 million worth of pollution control equipment in its 13 factories in order to comply with U.S. Environmental Protection Agency requirements—but only after it was fined $11.2 million for violating emissions standards.[45]

With the *market approach*, organizational members show concern for environmental concerns in response to demands or opportunities in the marketplace. If customers are willing to pay for environmentally friendly products and services, then organizations will provide them. For example, Clorox introduced its Green Works environmentally sensitive cleaning line in 2008 and sold over $100 million of the products, but in the years following the recession sales dropped to $60 million, leading the organization to de-emphasize the Green Works brand.[46]

The *accommodation* or *stakeholder approach* goes beyond the market approach and responds to the environmental concerns of various stakeholder groups, including customers, the local community, business partners, and special-interest groups. Organizational members acknowledge the need to be socially responsible and want to make ecological choices that are reasonable in the eyes of society. They may agree to participate in specific programs they believe are worthy of support. For example, in response to data compiled by Ma Jun and other like-minded environmentalists that detailed the air, water, and hazardous waste pollution in China, Walmart began to actively access this data when evaluating factories in its supply chain and made changes that positively affected the environment.[47]

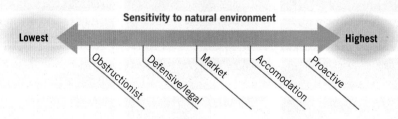

FIGURE 2.1 Five Options to Manage the Natural Environment

OB in Action

Growing with Your Suppliers and Competitors

Hakan Dere/iStockphoto

The Vancouver-based company 49th Parallel Coffee Roasters is billed as one of the top independent specialty coffee roasters and cafés in Canada. While the organization's dedication to offering the world's finest and highest quality coffee to its customers has been pivotal to its success, its approach to sourcing coffee is what separates it from the crowd.

Thanks to the passion of company founder Vince Piccolo and his team, 49th Parallel has earned a strong reputation for treating its stakeholders well. Starting with its suppliers, the organization is highly transparent about its sourcing process, publishing an annual Transparency Update that shares the prices of the coffee that it buys each year and breaks down the prices to show where the money goes. Included in the report are also the challenges faced by the company and how those challenges affect pricing.

To 49th Parallel, coffee is much more than a beverage. It is a representation of the regions the beans come from and of the dedication and commitment of those who produce them, whom the organization has great appreciation for. This is reflected by its setting an ethical standard with its direct relationship program and paying producers a special premium that is above the Fair Trade price standard:

The people we work with are up at the crack of dawn, tirelessly working towards a plentiful and sweet harvest. They are vibrant members of their communities. We love working with them.

Laura Perry, 49th Parallel's green coffee buyer, notes that the thing 49th Parallel cherishes most about its sourcing program is how the company maintains its relationships with its producers. While the organization recognizes that there are many ways to cultivate strong supply chains in the industry, it chooses to embrace an approach that is focused on facilitating positive changes in producers' harvests by "listening, providing feedback, then coming up with solutions together" as opposed to telling suppliers what to do. The organization takes a very active approach, visiting each of its producer partners on a regular basis.

By embracing such a collaborative approach with its suppliers, 49th Parallel has the opportunity to make positive changes throughout its supply chain that benefit all of its stakeholders. Take, for example, the case of Martir Fernandez. Fernandez had been working with 49th Parallel for over five years and wanted to improve the quality of his harvest, so in early 2015 the organization pre-financed a new production dryer for him. Fernandez, along with Perry, also proceeded to measure the moisture and water activities for Fernandez's 2014 drying cycle. Together they identified quick fixes that would improve both the working conditions at the coffee plantation and the shelf life of his future harvests. The result of this collaboration was a better harvest for Fernandez, which translated to better coffee for 49th Parallel and its customers.

Committed to supporting the coffee industry as a whole, and with all of its suppliers in mind, 49th Parallel takes the initiative to collaborate with smallholder farmers who are often unable to offer their harvests to the international market because of small harvest sizes. To address this ongoing issue, 49th Parallel offers its customers a Small Lots Series, which features exceptional coffees sourced from smallholder farmers. Customers pay a premium for the Small Lots Series and are given additional information about the farmers who have harvested the coffee.

Downstream, 49th Parallel also embraces a collaborative approach with its customers, and even its competitors. In addition to running its own coffee houses, the company operates as a wholesale coffee roaster, supplying its specialty coffees to cafés throughout Vancouver. Extending more than just a buy–sell relationship to other cafés, 49th Parallel also offers training to staff at competing cafés that purchase its coffees, education on choosing the right equipment, and installation and repair services for many brands of espresso machines and grinders.

Vancouver, ranked by the Matador Network as the third best city in the world for coffee lovers, is a highly competitive market. Although 49th Parallel is one of many coffee roasters and cafés in Vancouver, the organization has established a unique identity as a company that is passionate about and committed to its industry and all of its stakeholders.

QUESTIONS FOR DISCUSSION

1. Do you know of any instances when companies went out of their way to help out their suppliers or competitors?
2. Why would an organization make an effort to collaborate with its suppliers and competitors?
3. What do you think are key factors (independent variables) that help to explain such behaviour?
4. Do you think such companies are more, or less, vulnerable to being taken advantage of?

Organizational members exhibit a *proactive approach* when they take the initiative and actively seek out opportunities to enhance the natural environment. They go out of their way to learn about the needs of different stakeholder groups, and they are willing to use organizational resources to promote the interests of the community and the environment. TerraCycle was founded with the idea of eliminating waste by converting it into usable products.[48] Beginning with using worms to transform garbage into organic fertilizer, founder Tom Szaky set a precedent for working with partners to better the environment. His company collects trash in more than 20 countries and transforms it into over 1,500 different products sold through major retailers such as Whole Foods Market. In another example, and one that's closer to the classroom, 284 university presidents from some of the most prestigious U.S. schools pledged to make their campuses "carbon neutral": "We're saying that sustainability is no longer an elective," said Cornell University's president at the time, David Skorton.[49]

Sustainable OB tends to focus on the proactive end of the continuum in Figure 2.1. Moreover, it is interested in **sustainable development**—that is, "development that meets the needs of the present without compromising the ability of future generations to meet their own needs."[50]

National culture and laws also influence the approach that organizational members take with regard to the natural environment. For example, leaders in cultures that defer to those in authority face less pressure to attend to issues of environmental sustainability.[51] Stakeholders of an organization may span the globe, so in order to work in or partner with people and organizations in other countries, we need to recognize how OB is emphasized in different cultures, as the next section discusses.

Global Environment

| BRIEF HISTORY OF OB | OB AS A SCIENCE | STAKEHOLDERS | **GLOBAL ENVIRONMENT** |

Globalization has and will increasingly be an important factor influencing OB. **Globalization** refers to the increased interdependence and integration among people and organizations around the world.[52] According to a conventional approach, increasing global trade promises to improve economic conditions for everyone in the world, as captured in the motto: "A rising tide lifts all the boats"[53] The reason is relatively simple. Just as specialization helps to improve productivity *within* organizations, so too are there mutual advantages *among nations* when each develops and focuses on different strengths. For example, the weather in some countries is conducive to growing bananas, while the weather in other countries is conducive to growing wheat or rice. Some countries have expertise in growing flowers; other countries are good at making watches or cameras or computer components. Instead of every country having its own car companies, it is more efficient for fewer car companies to manufacture cars for use around the world. This creates a web of interdependence and integration across nations.

Even though it wasn't until the 1960s that multinational corporations became commonplace, they are now a dominant fixture on the organizational landscape. Although no official definition exists, a **multinational company (MNC)** is often defined as an organization that receives more than 25 percent of its total sales revenue from outside its home country. This description can include both large corporations, such as General Electric, and small businesses like Botanical PaperWorks, a Canadian company that produces handmade stationery that is sold online to markets outside Canada. According to the World Bank, MNCs hold about one-third of the world's productive assets, and they conduct approximately 70 percent of world trade. There are about 50,000 MNCs worldwide, which is considerably more than the 7,000 that the United Nations counted in the mid-1970s.[54] To some, the proliferation in number and power of multinationals is a concern, while others argue that it is beneficial. Either way, one clear result is that more people will be exposed to other cultures in their work.

Conventional OB typically follows one of two basic approaches to working in other cultures: polycentrism and ethnocentrism. **Polycentrism** assumes that organizational members in a host country know the best way to manage an organization in their country. Organizational members with a polycentric orientation believe that the best way to maximize their firms' profits is to adapt to the practices found in foreign countries.[55] For example, because of the emphasis in China on establishing interpersonal relationships among business partners, starting a new trade relationship there may require many more visits than is typically the case in, say, the United Kingdom.

Ethnocentrism is the belief that your own country offers the best way to manage in a foreign country. An ethnocentric approach may be especially likely when organizational members believe that their home country is more developed or more advanced than the foreign country in which they are working. Ethnocentrism has potential dangers. For example, after it opened to poor sales, many of the initial assumptions that had been made in operating the Euro Disney theme park in Paris (such as retaining the restriction on alcohol sales applied in U.S. parks) were changed in order to account for differences in cultures.

Rather than an ethnocentric or a polycentric approach, sustainable OB emphasizes an **egalicentric** approach, which recognizes that a key opportunity of cross-cultural relationships is the ability to learn from one another.[56] Egalicentrism is characterized by two-way, give-and-take communication that fosters mutual understanding and community. Sustainable OB does not assume a one-size-fits-all approach in foreign countries (ethnocentrism), nor does it simply assume that the locals know best (polycentrism). Rather, sustainable OB acknowledges that when people from different cultures interact with and learn from one another, the result is knowledge and practices that neither could imagine on their own. Egalicentrism is more a means of developing new practices than a process of picking and choosing the "best" of existing practices from around the world. Even so, a sustainable approach does not discount the impact of culture in shaping how people behave and respond to one another. The emphasis is not on arguing about which culture is best, however; the emphasis is on understanding the differences between the cultures and learning how to interact with each other to accomplish shared interests.

Today's international organizational members must be sensitive to social and cultural differences if they are to meet their organizational objectives. **National culture** includes the shared values, beliefs, knowledge, and general patterns of behaviour that characterize a country's citizens. People's beliefs about what is good, right, desirable, or beautiful are influenced by the national cultures in which they grow up. A variety of research frameworks exist to measure culture, including the World Values Survey and the GLOBE project.[57] Arguably the most influential research looking at cross-cultural differences and their implications for OB was done by Geert Hofstede, who gathered data between 1967 and 1973 from more than 100,000 IBM employees working in 64 different countries.[58] Hofstede began with four dimensions of national culture but later added a fifth, time orientation, to account for cultural differences in Asia.[59]

As shown in Figure 2.2, Hofstede's five dimensions can be described as individualism, materialism, short-term time orientation, power distance, and uncertainty avoidance. Low levels of each dimension can be described alternatively as collectivism (low individualism), quality of life (low materialism), long-term time orientation (low short-term time orientation), challenge to authority (low power distance), and comfort with uncertainty (low uncertainty avoidance). Even though Hofstede's research is still widely used,[60] many cultural and economic changes have occurred, such as in China and South Korea, since he first collected his data. Also, just as there tend to be differences *between* countries, so too is there variation *within* countries, so not everyone from the same country shares the same cultural values. We'll look at each of Hofstede's dimensions next.

Individualism   Some cultures place a strong emphasis on individualism, which makes individuality and individual rights paramount and encourages people to act in their own

Polycentrism is the assumption that members in a host country know the best way to manage an organization in their country.

Ethnocentrism is the assumption that members of one's own home country offer the best way to manage in a host country.

Egalicentrism is the assumption that people from different cultures working together in a manner characterized by two-way, give-and-take communication fosters deeper mutual understanding, community, and new insights.

National culture includes the shared values, beliefs, knowledge, and general patterns of behaviour that characterize a country's citizens.

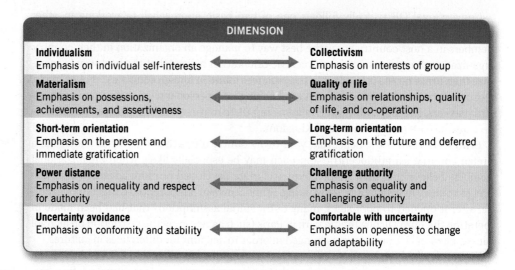

DIMENSION

Individualism Emphasis on individual self-interests	**Collectivism** Emphasis on interests of group
Materialism Emphasis on possessions, achievements, and assertiveness	**Quality of life** Emphasis on relationships, quality of life, and co-operation
Short-term orientation Emphasis on the present and immediate gratification	**Long-term orientation** Emphasis on the future and deferred gratification
Power distance Emphasis on inequality and respect for authority	**Challenge authority** Emphasis on equality and challenging authority
Uncertainty avoidance Emphasis on conformity and stability	**Comfortable with uncertainty** Emphasis on openness to change and adaptability

FIGURE 2.2 Overview of Hofstede's Five Dimensions of National Culture

self-interest. Members of these cultures tend to be motivated by opportunities to achieve personal gain and to look out for themselves or their immediate family. In countries with high levels of individualism, effective ways to increase workers' productivity may include using piece-rate systems and basing promotions and salary on workers' *individual* performance rather than on the length of time they have worked in an organization. In contrast, other cultures emphasize collectivism, whereby the interests of the group take precedence, people look out for one another, and loyalty to the group is higher. These societies emphasize extended families and groups in which everyone takes responsibility for the general well-being of all. For example, in Japan, everyone in an office might stay at work until a colleague who must work overtime is finished, and promotions may be based on seniority rather than on individual performance.

Materialism   Cultures that emphasize materialism place high value on assertiveness and achievements, such as acquiring better-paying jobs, material possessions, or money.[61] Members of high materialism cultures tend to be motivated by competition for extrinsic rewards—for example, higher salaries, bonuses, and being identified as number one. By contrast, cultures that emphasize quality of life tend to place high value on co-operation, relationships, and overall well-being. People may be more interested in aesthetic and spiritual concerns and the intrinsic satisfaction of meaningful work and be less motivated by financial rewards and status symbols.[62] It follows that members of these cultures emphasize personal relationships, camaraderie in the workplace, and the welfare of others.

Time Orientation   The concept of time orientation differentiates between cultures that have a short-term view and those that take a long-term perspective. Cultures with a short-term orientation (such as Pakistan, the Philippines, the United Kingdom, and the United States) emphasize living for the present. Members tend to prefer immediate rewards to delayed gratification, and they may cut corners now that won't get noticed until much later. Such countries may provide greater opportunities for organizations that offer quick fixes, such as fast food and instant credit. By comparison, cultures with a long-term orientation (such as China and Japan) have a greater concern for the future, are more likely to persevere patiently in the face of short-term setbacks, and are more likely to save for purchases than to buy on credit. Members tend to make decisions that consider and respect the future. For example, some First Nation cultures try to keep in mind how their decisions will affect people living seven generations into the future.

Power Distance   The relative emphasis placed on power differences in a culture is called power distance (or deference to authority). In cultures with high power distance (such as Mexico, the Philippines, and China), it is considered entirely appropriate that power is distributed unevenly throughout society. Managers are expected to make decisions, and lower-level employees will hesitate to voice disagreement. In addition, subordinates will react negatively if they are asked to do work that is traditionally part of managers' jobs (e.g., participation in decision making). In some cases, high power distance is found in countries with totalitarian governments and distinct social class systems. In cultures characterized by low power distance, people are willing to challenge authority, and power differences across different positions are less readily evident. In these cultures, many people are involved in decision making—not just the manager. Thus, in countries such as Israel (which had one of the lowest scores on this dimension), managers may have relatively little authority over other members, especially when others have greater knowledge and experience. In Israeli *kibbutzim*, for example, leadership is often rotated on a cyclical basis so that everyone gets a turn at various jobs in the organization.

Uncertainty Avoidance   Cultures with high uncertainty avoidance scores prefer predictable rules and regulations to ambiguity and risk. When working in these countries (such as Greece and Japan), managers should expect members to respond well to stable and predictable structures and systems, to have a heightened appreciation for conformity, and to become anxious when routines are disrupted. People in these cultures prefer to make only small improvements to the "tried-and-true" traditions that have served society well in the past. By comparison, in cultures characterized by low uncertainty avoidance (such as Singapore and Denmark), members are more likely to value and to be comfortable with risk taking and innovativeness.[63] Managers expect members to be relatively adaptable and willing to try new things. Organizations in countries with low uncertainty avoidance are likely to reinforce risk taking by recognizing and rewarding members who take reasonable chances that result in benefits for the organization. Furthermore, a culture with low uncertainty avoidance is likely to encourage investments in novel research and development.

Understanding cultural differences can be useful to all organizational members, regardless of where their perspective lies on the continuum between conventional and sustainable approaches. It is apparent that the national cultural descriptions of materialism and individualism are similar to values that characterize conventional versus sustainable thinking and action. As we might expect, countries that rate high in both materialism and individualism—such as the United States, the United Kingdom, Germany, Australia, and Ireland—are precisely the ones where conventional OB theory and practice have been most thoroughly developed. Conversely, we would expect that countries such as Costa Rica, Peru, and South Korea, which are low on individualism and materialism, may have ideas to offer regarding developing sustainable OB. Figure 2.3 shows where select countries rank in terms of their relative emphases on materialism and individualism (low, medium, or high).[64]

The differences between Costa Rica and the United States make for an interesting comparison. The United States is a prime example of a culture associated with conventional OB. Indeed, its emphasis on individualism is greater than that found for any other country in Hofstede's study, and it is considered high in materialism, although it is not one of the highest in this group. By contrast, Costa Rica is a clear opposite. No other country in Hofstede's study had a lower overall score in terms of Hofstede's individualism and materialism data.[65] Per capita, the U.S. gross domestic product is almost four times greater than that of Costa Rica. Further, whereas it takes approximately 269 acres to support the consumption of the average U.S. adult, it takes only 35 acres to support the average Costa Rican.[66] Perhaps the most striking finding is that the two countries' scores for overall life satisfaction and life expectancy are virtually identical.[67]

		High	Medium	Low
Materialism	Low	Sweden, Norway, Denmark, France, Netherlands, Finland	Spain, Portugal, Uruguay, Iran	Costa Rica, Peru, El Salvador, Thailand, Chile, South Korea, Guatemala
	Medium	Belgium, New Zealand, Canada	India, Israel, Greece, Czech Republic, Turkey, Brazil, Argentina	China, Hong Kong, Panama, Malaysia, Indonesia, Taiwan, Singapore, Pakistan
	High	Germany, Switzerland, Australia, South Africa, United Kingdom, Italy, United States, Ireland	Japan, Jamaica, Mexico, Philippines, Austria, Hungary, Poland	Ecuador, Colombia, Venezuela
		High	Medium	Low

Individualism

FIGURE 2.3 Examples of Countries' Scores on Hofstede's Materialism/Individualism Dimensions

the bittersweet story of chocolate[68]

Gosphotodesign/Shutterstock

Chocolate may be the favourite flavour for many of us, but most people know little about how the chocolate industry has developed over time or how current chocolate companies are managed (it is one of the most secretive of industries). The first people to make use of cocoa were the Mayans, who lived in the Yucatan Peninsula as long ago as 600 A.D. Chocolate became an item for the masses thanks to the efforts of businesspeople and inventors such as C. J. van Houten, a Dutch chocolate master whose invention of the cocoa press helped to make the product more affordable. Many pioneers in the chocolate industry were Quakers, whose motivation for getting into the business included a desire to persuade the poor to give up alcohol in favour of the healthier chocolate drink.

One such Quaker was John Cadbury, who started Cadbury Limited in 1831. An important turning point for the company occurred in 1866, when it introduced a process for pressing cocoa butter from the cocoa bean. By 1879 the firm had grown so successful that the Cadbury family was able to build what became known as the "factory in a garden" on a park-like property in Bournville, England. Cadbury's Bournville factory set a standard for other companies in sustainable industrial relations. For example, Cadbury was the first firm to introduce the Saturday half-day holiday, promote the idea of workers continuing their education while working, offer medical and dental departments, and provide workers with a kitchen where they could heat up their dinners (a forerunner of modern staff dining rooms).

Wanting to offer wage earners affordable housing in pleasant surroundings, in 1895 George Cadbury (son of founder John Cadbury) purchased another 120 acres near the Bournville plant and began to establish a community consistent with the then-popular Garden City movement. In 1903, the estate had grown to include 330 acres of land and 313 cottages, and George Cadbury decided to turn it into a charitable trust for future generations to enjoy. He handed over the land and houses to the Bournville Village Trust with the proviso that revenues be devoted to the extension of the estate and the promotion of housing reform. Today, the Bournville Estate covers 1,000 acres and has 8,000 dwellings.

In addition to instituting employee-friendly policies, Cadbury emphasized the value of diversity by attracting the best talent to the company and, in doing so, reflected the diversity of the communities in which it operated and of the customers it served. The company's approach to diversity created a culture of inclusiveness in which diverse members trusted each other, were inspired to do their best, and took pride in their company. Cadbury's 2007–2008 Corporate Responsibility and Sustainability report described inclusiveness as "a workplace climate where all colleagues feel empowered to bring a rich variety of approaches to achieve business results." Cadbury's Equal Employment Opportunities & Diversity policy also encouraged implementing these values in a way that honours local laws and cultural norms.

As a mass-consumption item, chocolate is big business. In Canada, chocolate sales now exceed $3 billion per year with the average Canadian consuming 5.5 kg of chocolate every year. Globally, about 60 percent of all chocolate is consumed in North America and the European Union. As the industry has grown, it has become dominated by three very large firms: Cadbury, Mars, and Nestlé. Unfortunately, the farmers who grow the 3.5 million tonnes of cocoa beans produced every year experience the bitter taste of an industry structure where so much power is concentrated in the hands of just a few major players. Over the past decades, the price of cocoa (corrected for inflation) has declined almost steadily; in the 2003–2004 cocoa year, real prices were less than half what they were in 1970–1971.

Recognizing some of the problems especially facing small producers in an economic system where large-scale companies are trying to maximize their profits, "fair trade" companies, such as the Day Chocolate Company, started with the intention of mixing social and business goals. Fair trade is a system of international trade based on dialogue, transparency, and respect that benefits producers in poorer countries, consumers in richer countries, and the earth. Companies such as Day Chocolate that abide by the highest standards of this system receive Fair Trade certification by Fairtrade International and its members, including Fairtrade Canada.

Attributable to Day Chocolate's success were the facts that cocoa farmers in Africa owned one-third of the shares in the company, had a direct say in how it was run, and received a share of its profits. Consider that there are approximately 2 million cocoa farmers in Ghana, each of whom earns about USD $350 per year. Fair trade chocolate companies like Day Chocolate promise to pay farmers a fair price that ensures a living wage (say, a floor price of $1,600 per tonne) and to give back to their communities (such as by paying an extra $150 per tonne to spend on community projects chosen by the farmers, like new drinking wells and toilets). Globally, around 3.5 million tonnes of cocoa are produced each year. Fair trade certified production represents just a fraction of this amount.

Since the 1990s, the chocolate industry has been working to expand sustainable cocoa farming efforts. The World Cocoa Foundation, formed in 2000, has helped to increase farm incomes by teaching cocoa farmers how to reduce costs and crop losses and how to diversify the crops grown for family income. The foundation also helps farmers organize themselves into co-operatives to sell their cocoa. Farm families participating in such programs have seen their income rise by as much as 24 percent (Ivory Coast) or even 55 percent (Cameroon). Initiatives like the Cadbury Cocoa Partnership—designed to improve the wages and working conditions of its cocoa farmer stakeholders—helped to secure the economic, social, and environmental sustainability of around a million cocoa farmers. In addition to working with farmers to improve yields, the partnership directed funds toward community development, such as educational and environmental projects that enhance biodiversity and ensure clean water for residents.

Through the initial efforts of Cadbury (now owned by Mondelēz International) and Day Chocolate Company (now named Divine Chocolate), the pleasing effect of chocolate is increasingly extending to the stakeholders who produce it.

QUESTIONS FOR DISCUSSION

1. What are key research questions and issues within the chocolate industry from a conventional OB perspective?
2. How about from a sustainable OB perspective?
3. What sorts of research methods would each perspective use to examine those questions and issues?
4. Who are the key stakeholders in the chocolate industry?
5. Why do you think companies like Cadbury are taking steps to enhance the welfare of cocoa growers? Why didn't they do this sooner?
6. Do you think the ethical issues facing the chocolate industry have parallels in other global industries?
7. Why are wages and living conditions so poor in many of the factories in low-income countries that produce goods consumed in high-income countries?
8. What are some of the implications for OB?

Summary

◆ **Learning Objectives**

- Discuss the history of organizational behaviour.

- Recognize organizational behaviour as a science.

- Describe stakeholder relationships and management's responsibilities to stakeholders.
- Discuss the influence of globalization on organizational behaviour.

◆ **From a conventional OB perspective:**

- Learn from and build on the past to fine-tune our understanding of how to improve the productivity and profitability of organizational members.
- Focus on research questions that lend themselves to objective, quantitative methods.
- Manage key stakeholders' interests.

- Approach cross-cultural differences from an ethnocentric or polycentric view.

◆ **From a sustainable OB perspective:**

- Learn from and build on the past to expand our understanding of how to improve multiple stakeholders.

- Welcome research questions that may require creative, qualitative methods.
- Collaborate with stakeholders for mutual benefit.

- Approach differences from an egalicentric view.

Key Terms

Corporate social responsibility (CSR) (p. 30)
Egalicentrism (p. 35)
Ethnocentrism (p. 35)
Globalization (p. 34)
Hawthorne effect (p. 25)
Human relations (p. 25)

Institutionalization (p. 27)
Multinational company (MNC) (p. 34)
National culture (p. 35)
Natural environment (p. 32)
Organization-specific responsibility (OSR) (p. 30)

Polycentrism (p. 35)
Scientific management (p. 24)
Social construction of reality (p. 27)
Stakeholder (p. 30)
Sustainable development (p. 34)
Systems theory (p. 26)

Questions for Reflection and Discussion

1. History can teach us lessons about how to act in the present. Is there a specific lesson or era in OB history that seems particularly important to your current understanding of OB?

2. OB research is the basis of some OB practices in organizations, but many OB research findings are ignored. Why do you think this is the case? What can be done to improve the use of OB research?

3. The conventional and sustainable approaches to stakeholders differ in a number of ways. Describe how the approaches are different.

4. Identify a set of stakeholders for a particular organization and discuss the relative importance of addressing the needs of each.

5. Hofstede found that there is a strong relationship (correlation = 0.67) between a country's power distance score and its gross national product (GNP) per capita. In particular, he found that countries with the highest GNP per capita were more likely to challenge authority. What are some plausible explanations for this relationship?

ob activities

What Are Your Views on the Natural Environment?

Using a scale of 1 - Strongly Disagree (SD), 2 - Disagree (D), 3 - Neutral (N), 4 - Agree (A), and 5 - Strongly Agree (SA), indicate your level of agreement with each statement on the 5-point scale.

	SD	D	N	A	SA
1. The ecological crisis facing humankind has been greatly exaggerated.	1	2	3	4	5
2. The earth is like a spaceship with limited room and resources.	1	2	3	4	5
3. If things continue on their present course, we will soon experience a major ecological catastrophe.	1	2	3	4	5
4. The balance of nature is strong enough to cope with the impact of modern industrial nations.	1	2	3	4	5
5. Humans are severely abusing the environment.	1	2	3	4	5

Key: The preceding five statements are taken from a "New Ecological Paradigm" scale that researchers have developed to measure people's attitudes toward the natural environment, and in particular whether humans have a substantial adverse effect on the natural environment.[69] To calculate your total score, add the following:

___ *(response to statement 1, subtracted from 6)*

+ ___ *(response to statement 2)*

+ ___ *(response to statement 3)*

+ ___ *(response to statement 4, subtracted from 6)*

+ ___ *(response to statement 5)*

= ___ *Total score*

Higher scores (16–20) on this scale indicate a greater concern for the environment, which has been linked to more environmentally sensitive behaviour by students.[70] Compare your views with those of your classmates.

A publicly held company decides to install new systems in order to voluntarily reduce water consumption in its facilities at a considerable cost to the organization that will not likely be recouped.

Why might this scenario occur in organizations?

Use the following scale to indicate whether this behaviour is ethically acceptable:

NEVER ACCEPTABLE			SOMETIMES ACCEPTABLE			ALWAYS ACCEPTABLE	
				5		6	7

Explain the ideas you considered in arriving at your answer.

Cultural Comparisons

If you have visited another country, Geert Hofstede and his colleagues' research on cultural values can help explain your experiences in that culture. Go to their website (http://geert-hofstede. com) and click on the "compare countries" link. Now select the country you visited from the Select a Country pull-down list, and then select your native country (where you grew up) from the Comparison Country drop-down list. The website should show a comparison of the two countries based on the five dimensions of national culture.

QUESTIONS FOR DISCUSSION

1. How does this information explain your experiences in the country you visited?

2. How might these cultural values affect how you would do business in the country you visited?

A Case of Unusual Collaboration[71]

In Kalundborg, Denmark, a set of uncommon relationships exists among a diverse community of businesses, wherein one organization helps another and, in most cases, by doing so helps itself. In essence, these relationships involve taking the "waste" produced by one organization and turning it into valuable inputs for another organization.

This synergetic co-operation started when the coal-fired Asnæs Power Plant stopped pouring its waste heat into a nearby fjord as condensed water. Instead, Asnæs began selling the heat directly to the Statoil refinery and the Novo Nordisk pharmaceutical firm. Shortly thereafter, the Statoil refinery installed a process to remove sulphur from its waste gas. It then sold the extracted sulphur to the Kemira chemical company and sold the cleaner-burning gas to both the Gyproc sheetrock factory and Asnæs (thereby saving roughly 30,000 tonnes of coal). When Asnæs began to remove the sulphur from its smokestacks, it produced calcium sulphate, which it sold to Gyproc, where it was used in place of mined gypsum. Waste fly ash from Asnæs coal generation was also used for road construction and concrete production. In time, Asnæs began to provide surplus heat to greenhouses, a fish farm, and residents of Kalundborg (who were then able to shut off 3,500 oil-burning heating systems). Soon waste heat from Statoil also went to the fish farm, which produces about 200 tonnes of turbot and trout that is sold in the French market. Sludge from the fish farm is used as fertilizer by farmers, who also receive sludge from the Novo Nordisk pharmaceutical company.

All of these relationships happened spontaneously, based on shared interests and without direct government regulation. Over time the co-operation among stakeholders has yielded both ecological and financial benefits.

QUESTIONS FOR DISCUSSION

1. What do you think is necessary to form and maintain these relationships?

2. What problems might arise in these collaborative relationships?

3. Do you know of any other organizations that might work together to reap mutual benefits?

This is a personal journal entry that can be used for class discussion or be compiled and included in a self-reflection paper.

Based on this discussion of the landscape of OB, what are some of the key inputs that have helped to "socially construct" the reality you live in? Your response will likely include family, friends, media, and past jobs. Focus your journal reflections on how your current academic studies are influencing what you perceive to be "objective" facts. For example, you are likely learning about new concepts and theory and terms that you did not know previously. Is this influencing how you see other people, organizations, or yourself? Explain. In what ways might this be a good thing, and what ways might it be undesirable?

Three

Understanding Individual Attributes

Individuals are complex and unpredictable, some perhaps more than others. Understanding and explaining the actions of even those we know best can be challenging, because beyond the surface of what we see are important attributes of their inner selves. In this chapter, we investigate both surface and deeper attributes of individuals that explain behaviour.

Learning Objectives	Conventional OB	Sustainable OB
DIVERSITY AND SURFACE CHARACTERISTICS		
1. Identify diversity and surface characteristics and their value to achieving organizational goals.	Reinforce differences between individuals and maximize benefits from this diversity	Recognize differences and similarities between individuals and explore synergies from diversity
ABILITIES AND PERSONALITY		
2. Discuss abilities and personality and their effect on achievement and performance in organizational roles.	Match individual differences in abilities and personality to demands of individual jobs	Consider individual differences in abilities and personality in light of broader organizational needs
CORE SELF-EVALUATIONS		
3. Explain what core self-evaluations are and how they help to understand organizational behaviours and attitudes.	Emphasize the self-evaluation attributes that improve productivity	Acknowledge the influence of both self-evaluation attributes and collective evaluations
BELIEFS AND VALUES		
4. Discuss beliefs and values and how they develop and guide behaviour in relationships and organizations.	Attend to beliefs and values that explain individual behaviour and affiliations	Encourage beliefs and values that promote mutual benefits and trust

understanding angela samuels

ANGELA SAMUELS, CEO, Voluptuous Clothing

Angela Samuels' decision to create her Toronto-based retail chain, Voluptuous Clothing, was inspired by her own experience as a plus-sized woman and model. Growing up in Calgary, Alberta, Samuels faced intense criticism due to her weight even though her Jamaican heritage traditionally celebrated fuller figures. She found it difficult to find trendy and fashionable pieces that fit her body shape. In her words, "All the stuff I wanted to wear didn't look good on me."

After moving to Toronto in the 1990s as a young adult, she noticed a very different vibe in Ontario's capital. Not only was the Caribbean culture much more prominent, thus giving Samuels a greater sense of belonging, she also observed a growing plus-sized fashion industry there. She began working as a plus-sized model while pursuing her studies in child and youth care at Centennial College and subsequently George Brown College. She has posed in catalogues and other marketing materials for massive retail chains including Walmart, Hudson's Bay Company, and Kmart.

Still, even as a model, Samuels noticed that clothing options for plus-sized women were limited and often consisted of "matronly" or "frumpy" clothing that was simply unflattering. As a result, in 2000 she was inspired to establish Voluptuous Clothing, which she specifically geared toward plus-sized women like herself. She wanted to empower women to feel sexy and confident by providing them with fashionable options regardless of body size.

Samuels recognizes the value of outside advice.

As with most businesses, the early years were tough. Samuels bought plus-sized fashion pieces from the United States and sold them out of the trunk of her car. She would approach women on their way to the club, asking them if they would be interested in viewing her products. In 2001, Samuels opened her first retail location at the North York Sheridan Mall in Toronto, and she has since moved her flagship store to downtown Toronto's revered Queen Street West neighbourhood and expanded into online retailing. Annual sales have reached into the millions, and Samuels and her company are frequently featured in local newspaper and magazine articles discussing fashion and/or entrepreneurship.

Yet, even with all of her success, Samuels recognizes the value of outside advice. In one particular interview, she recalled a difficult conversation she had with her creative director back in 2012. She said that he'd advised her to change the company's business strategy, claiming that "[Voluptuous Clothing] had to grow up because their customers grew up." Although initially reluctant, Samuels eventually realized that in order to survive, her company did indeed need to cater to the changing needs of her clientele, who now have children and professional lives. Today, she credits this one piece of advice with saving her company and is thankful that she was smart enough and open enough to listen.[1]

Respect for multicultural diversity is a fundamental value included in the Canadian Charter of Rights and Freedoms, but what does diversity mean on an individual level? What we see of people on the outside is important, yet it is just one small part of what explains a person's behaviour. As we move through this chapter, we will discuss diversity and the surface characteristics that are noticeable from the outside, but we will spend more time peeling back the layers of the individual's inner self, from more stable and enduring attributes to the beliefs and values that lie under the surface of those we work with in organizations. These attributes are illustrated in Figure 3.1.

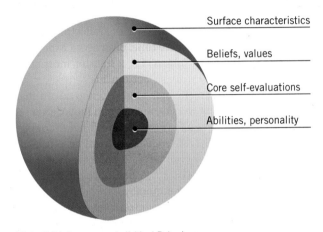

FIGURE 3.1 Layers of Potential Influences on Individual Behaviour

Diversity and Surface Characteristics

DIVERSITY | ABILITIES & PERSONALITY | CORE SELF-EVALUATIONS | BELIEFS & VALUES

The organizations in which we work and interact include a variety of people. Each person has unique attributes, such as the surface-level characteristics of race, ethnicity, age, gender, and physical abilities, as well as deep-level or internal characteristics like abilities, personality, self-evaluations, and beliefs and values.[2] **Diversity** is a state of having or being composed of differing attributes.

Diversity is a state of having or being composed of differing attributes.

Diversity among people in an organization can cause problems and it can also present opportunities.[3] On the one hand, differences can contribute to misunderstandings, discomfort, poor communication, and conflict. The theory that best supports this point of view is **social categorization theory.** It proposes that we use characteristics to categorize others into groups, and that the more different the group is from ourselves, the less we like, identify with, trust, or feel comfortable with people from that group, and the more likely that diversity will contribute to performance problems and absenteeism or turnover within an organization.[4] People generally feel more comfortable with and are drawn to people who are similar to themselves.

Social categorization theory proposes that we use characteristics to categorize others into groups, and this shapes our attitudes and behaviour toward them.

On the other hand, we find the positive potential of diversity in theories about information processing and decision making,[5] which propose that diversity offers more and different types of information, perspectives, experiences, and social networks to aid in the decision-making process. This diversity of resources contributes to a better understanding of the issues related to a problem or challenge, a greater number of ideas generated during brainstorming, and broader support for the decision that is made. Consistent with these opposing effects of diversity, the research on diversity is inconclusive.[6] Some studies indicate that it contributes to negative attitudes and issues with work group performance, while others suggest that it can contribute to positive experiences such as better decision making and long-term performance.

Whereas conventional OB increasingly recognizes the value of diversity in contributing to organizational goals, sustainable OB is more likely to celebrate diversity and emphasize the uniqueness of people regardless of their instrumental value. From a sustainable perspective, treating all people from diverse backgrounds with dignity is an inherent characteristic of true community, achieved not by focusing on members as individuals apart from the group but rather by valuing and embracing one another's differences as part of the group. The Toronto-Dominion Bank (TD), one of Canada's banking giants, consistently ranks among the nation's top diversity employers. Valuing diversity is entrenched in the organizational culture of the company, whereby, according to its *2014 Corporate Responsibility Report*, "achieving [TD's] mission depends on understanding and reflecting the people, cultures and communities where [it] operates. At the same time, diversity of expertise and perspectives in [its] boardrooms, branches and stores makes [TD] a smarter, more creative organization, leader to better decision-making and a stronger bottom line."[7]

The visible surface characteristics of the individuals around us can shape our initial perceptions of them. For example, as a university student you may view a professor with grey hair as a wise person who has been through your stage of life before, or perhaps as someone out of touch and behind the times. **Stereotypes** are general perceptions about a group of people with similar characteristics. They can result in potential biases surfacing, for example, in decisions about whom to hire or promote. A similar-to-me bias is one explanation for the "glass ceiling" situation that can arise for employees who are in the minority, when an unseen bias blocks minority advancement in organizations run by a visible majority. Surface characteristics also contribute to the formation of subgroups, as similar folks "flock together" for the psychological safety and affirmation that similarity provides. Many organizations encourage "affinity groups" based on specific characteristics so that people in the minority have a group of people to identify with and draw support from.

While many surface characteristics are qualities we are born with, like skin colour, some are chosen, such as tattoos, hairstyle or hair colour, and body piercings. Mark Zuckerberg created a stir by wearing a hoodie to Wall Street when courting would-be investors for the initial public offering of Facebook. Some were offended that he did not match the business dress code of the financial district, while others wondered whether Zuckerberg's chosen surface characteristic was part of his personal branding, similar to how CBC hockey commentator Don Cherry is known for wearing flamboyant suits.[8]

Some research shows that the effects of internal characteristics in explaining behaviour persist and may even strengthen over time, but the effects of external or surface characteristics can diminish over time as diverse group members get to know each other.[9] A large study of bank branches found that if members of the majority racial group (in this case, whites) and members of the minority group both believe the work environment is open to input and learning from a variety of perspectives, the diversity–performance relationship is positive.[10] A work environment that values diversity does not always occur naturally; it must be fostered through the intentional efforts of organizational members, particularly leaders.

Valuing diversity helps minimize the negative effects of our natural tendency to categorize people based on their characteristics. When people value diversity, they are less likely to experience discomfort or have biased judgments, both of which can result from interacting in a diverse group.[11] The power of valuing diversity becomes particularly significant in situations involving people with special challenges. For example, Tim Harris was born with Down's syndrome and no doubt has faced innumerable challenges, some of which were likely related to

Stereotypes are general perceptions about a group of people with similar characteristics.

people questioning his abilities. Thankfully, Tim's parents and the co-workers who knew him from his work experiences in the restaurant industry looked deeper than Tim's disability and recognized his innate love for people and his ability to make others feel comfortable and loved.[12] They partnered with him in starting a restaurant called Tim's Place in Albuquerque, New Mexico. It serves up comfort food with a hug from Tim—19,000 hugs and counting.[13]

Sustainable OB balances valuing uniqueness with honouring community. Affirming the uniqueness of individuals is clearly important from a sustainable point of view, but emphasizing differences can also lead to problems. For example, supporting affinity groups and connecting individuals with others who share the same characteristics, such as pairing women with women in mentoring relationships, can have the unintended consequences of creating subgroups and furthering stereotypes. These subgroups can then engage in a harmful process of promoting their identity by finding faults with others, which creates greater divisiveness and animosity toward others outside their group. Instead of inadvertently reinforcing categories, a sustainable approach attempts to break down categories, emphasizing that, as human beings, we have many basic similarities—such as common needs, shared interests, and group goals—that can form the basis for identifying with each other and building trust. This approach practices inclusiveness by including all types of people in decision making and encouraging broad participation in organizational activities such as picnics and softball teams. In other words, it invites all people to share in building a whole community instead of defending their own neighbourhood.

Sustainable OB typically looks beyond individuals' surface characteristics to discover what internal attributes might connect to needs within the organization. For example, Tim Hortons recently revised its dress code policies to permit some visible tattoos. In a Canadian Press article that appears on CTVnews.ca, Stephanie Hardman, Vice-President of Organizational Development and Team Tim Hortons, is quoted as saying, "We want to be sure we're attracting from the greatest pool of applicants that we can so that we can, in fact, attract the best to serve our guests that we possibly can. And one of those constraints we felt was our policy on tattoos." Furthermore, the change coincides with Canada's evolving

M⊘B | DO GENERATIONAL DIFFERENCES MAKE A DIFFERENCE?

MGM/Photofest

In the movie *Antitrust*, Ryan Phillippe and Tim Robbins face off in a battle partly about generational differences and partly about greed. The movie portrays young idealistic programmers working for a large corporation. Despite being a progressive software company, generational differences regarding which outcomes from work should be more highly valued creates tension. Of course, the real intrigue comes in the fictional plotline involving death and betrayal.

In real life, as the workforce ages and older workers choose to work longer, workers of all ages need to understand the differences between generations. In a 2012 study that included more than 3,000 Canadians, researchers found significant differences in workplace attitudes, preferences, and levels of satisfaction when they compared employees with their counterparts from different generations: Millennials (born in 1980 or later), Matures (born prior to 1945), Baby Boomers (born between 1946 and 1964), and Generation Xers (born between 1965 and 1979). More specifically, it was discovered that Millennial employees involved in the study valued autonomy and independence as well as entrepreneurial creativity more than did their counterparts when it came to career-related decision making. The study results also suggest that Millennials and Generation Xers change employers more often than do the Baby Boomers and Matures, due to the former's search for continual development opportunities and greater work–life balance.

QUESTIONS FOR REFLECTION

1. What thoughts do you have about younger or older workers?
2. How might your perceptions about different age groups or generations influence your motivation to work?
3. How might the findings above, if present in your workplace, create problems or opportunities?

societal preferences, as tattoos are no longer uncommon, especially among today's youth, thus tattoos no longer carry the same degree of risk in offending potential customers. This point is underscored by employment lawyer Danny Kastner, who is quoted in the article as saying that "a company would be unnecessarily limiting its talent pool [and] causing potential conflict with current employees [by prohibiting tattoos.]"[14]

The less-visible internal attributes of individuals are discussed in the following sections.

Abilities and Personality

| DIVERSITY | **ABILITIES & PERSONALITY** | CORE SELF-EVALUATIONS | BELIEFS & VALUES |

The innermost layer of a person includes the abilities and personality attributes that, in comparison to other attributes, tend to change little and consistently explain behaviour throughout life and work as adults.

Abilities

Abilities are innate capabilities to perform a specific task.

Abilities are innate capabilities to perform a specific task. Although particular abilities can be developed and honed to be more effective in specific circumstances, people are either born with them or not. Unlike skills that can be learned or acquired, abilities are stable traits that are evident early in life and predict important life outcomes, such as occupational achievement.[15]

Consider physical abilities as an example. Some people are naturally strong or coordinated and have an advantage in being able to excel at sports; others can make very precise movements such as those used by a surgeon or craftsperson; and still others can see, hear, or sense things, such as precise pitches in music, that others cannot. Another way to look at abilities is to think of them as the hardware that provides the basic capabilities for running the software we use in daily life. You've probably used a computer that was not able to run a specific software program or ran it much slower than you would like. We may not be able to upgrade our natural abilities, but we can make sure we are fully utilizing them through learning and practice.

Cognitive abilities are less visible than physical ones, but they are generally more important in organizations. Cognitive abilities are characteristics of a person's intellect and its functioning; they include reasoning, verbal and quantitative processing and comprehension, memory, and spatial and perceptual recognition.[16] What some might refer to as "book smarts" is not intelligence gained from books but rather cognitive ability that predicts both academic and career success.[17] Recall Angela Samuels from the chapter's opening case: she no doubt benefited from her experience as a model, but she is also blessed with cognitive abilities that have contributed to her success. Cognitive ability is among the strongest predictors of job performance, in part because it contributes to learning, skill development, and adaptation to changing conditions.[18]

Higher cognitive ability is also linked to lower counterproductive behaviours, such as stealing or destroying property and verbally or physically abusing others.[19] One interpretation of this research finding is that smarter people avoid behaving counterproductively because they are more aware of possible negative consequences. Research supports developing selection tests that assess cognitive ability; results are more valid for complex jobs that require processing and learning a great deal of information and that require critical thinking, such as higher levels of management.[20]

Personality

Personality is the unique and relatively stable pattern of behaviours, thoughts, and emotions shown by individuals.

Although it may sometimes seem like your roommate or co-worker "doesn't have a personality," at the core of everyone's inner self is a set of personality traits. **Personality** is the unique and relatively stable pattern of behaviours, thoughts, and emotions shown by individuals. It shapes what they are motivated to do and how they perform in organizational roles.[21] Individuals' personalities are rooted much more deeply in their biological makeup than in their background or upbringing. As a demonstration, consider how members of one family can be very different—one sibling can be organized and the other messy; one can be talkative while the other is shy.

Personalities can vary greatly among people. There are those with a Type A personality who strive for achievement but can burn out themselves and others;[22] those with an optimistic personality who have positive beliefs about the future but potentially harmful unrealistic expectations;[23] and those with a Machiavellian personality who selfishly manipulate others but typically perform poorly on the job and alienate co-workers.[24] In the last few decades, researchers have described personality traits as falling into broad categories called the "Big Five":[25]

- **Extraversion:** sociable, talkative, assertive, adventurous
- **Agreeableness:** good-natured, cooperative, trustful, not jealous
- **Conscientiousness:** achievement-oriented, responsible, persevering, dependable
- **Openness to experience:** intellectual, original, creative, imaginative, cultured
- **Emotional stability:** calm, placid, poised, not neurotic

Research based on the Big Five shows that personality can predict individual behaviour and performance.[26] For example, the personality trait of *conscientiousness* has been shown to be a good predictor of job performance as well as **organizational citizenship behaviour (OCB)**, which is work behaviour that goes above and beyond normal role or job expectations to help others or benefit the organization.[27] Why? Well, at least one reason is that conscientious individuals are more likely to set goals that lead to high levels of performance.[28] Conscientious people also are more likely to be dependable and to strive for accomplishments, which are valuable characteristics across a variety of jobs.

Emotional stability also tends to be important across most jobs because a person high in emotional stability is typically able to remain calm and perform in stressful situations without feeling emotionally exhausted or acting inconsiderately toward others.[29] In contrast, a person low in emotional stability (highly neurotic) is likely to be anxious, nervous, moody, and self-absorbed. A neurotic personality is synonymous with **negative affect**, which is a

Extraversion is a personality trait associated with being sociable, talkative, assertive, and adventurous.

Agreeableness is a personality trait associated with being good-natured, cooperative, trustful, and not jealous.

Conscientiousness is a personality trait associated with being achievement-oriented, responsible, persevering, and dependable.

Openness to experience is a personality trait associated with being intellectual, original, imaginative, and cultured.

Emotional stability is a personality trait associated with being calm, placid, poised, and not neurotic.

Organizational citizenship behaviour (OCB) is work behaviour that goes above and beyond normal role or job expectations to help others or benefit the organization.

Negative affect describes a person who is generally angry, anxious, and pessimistic.

 **B in Action** Employee Candidacy Tests

Getty Images/lina aidukaite

An example of a personality test is The Attentional and Interpersonal Style (TAIS) assessment, which can be used by employers to determine a candidate's personality, on a scale of "sociable" to "analytical," after they've decided what kind of individual they are looking for. This test is often used by smaller organizations that are more concerned about, and potentially impacted by, a new member's fit with the existing team. The evaluation adds an interesting dimension to a candidate's traditional job hunt and offers a more data-driven approach for employers. The TAIS test is used to evaluate candidates at David Aplin Group, a Canadian headhunting and recruitment firm based out of 11 offices across the country.

QUESTIONS FOR DISCUSSION

1. What do you think about organizations using a test like TAIS in evaluating job applicants?
2. Does your opinion about these tests change if you are the owner or part of the management team?
3. Are there cognitive abilities not easily measured on a paper and pencil test that may be important for new hires?
4. What are the benefits for organizations using tests like TAIS to aid in selection?
5. What are the drawbacks for organizations using these tests?

state of being angry, anxious, and pessimistic that has been shown to relate to dissatisfaction with jobs and life.[30] On the other hand, individuals with **positive affect** tend to be happy, enthused, and optimistic, which are characteristics linked to extraversion.

Extraversion is one of the most easily identifiable personality traits and is particularly helpful for predicting success in jobs with a great deal of social interaction, such as sales jobs or customer service positions.[31] Extraverts are sociable and assertive; they initiate actions and often emerge as leaders.[32] Extraverts also can dominate conversations or fail to listen to their employees, which can result in not being perceived as a servant leader.[33]

Openness to experience would seem to be a valuable trait in organizations given that most organizations are seeking innovations in their products, processes, and services. Angela Samuels likely scores high in this trait due to her orientation toward innovation, ability to adopt new ideas, and willingness to take risks. Research indicates that openness to experience alone generally does not contribute to performance in most jobs, unless the job specifically requires creativity and offers support for creative behaviour.[34] In such cases, openness is clearly beneficial. Openness to experience is also notable in that high levels relate to more positive attitudes toward diversity.[35] This is likely to be particularly important for people working in diverse teams that are often used to address complex problems or provide suggestions for improvement. Diversity within a team is a potential source of unique input, but it also can generate problems if it leads to stereotyping and divisive subgroups. A team that is highly open to experience is more likely to capitalize on members' differences and perform better.[36]

Agreeableness might be undervalued because it does not tend to predict performance in most jobs, but having more agreeable members on a team contributes to higher levels of cohesion, less conflict, and better overall performance.[37] Agreeable workers are also willing to abide by work rules and contribute to the organization positively outside of what is formally expected by their job description.[38] It is easy to imagine that having a kind and agreeable waiter or customer service representative is also likely to influence your satisfaction as a customer. Evidence even suggests that people who are agreeable may not be perceived as leaders but may actually be effective in leadership roles.[39] Honestly, does anyone really respond well to a disagreeable boss?

Conventional OB is particularly interested in understanding how the Big Five personality traits predict individuals' behaviour and enhance their productivity. Although sustainable OB is interested in this as well, it is just as interested in how personality traits can nurture a sense of collaboration and community.[40] For example, those who value willing participation and service may be encouraged by research that links conscientiousness to consistent effort in groups of volunteers.[41] Similarly, research identifies agreeableness as perhaps the most critical factor in helping a team bond and in reducing conflict.[42] Personality also is interesting from a sustainable perspective because it offers insight into the tasks and activities that are intrinsically motivating for various members of the organization and it can promote self-understanding and workplace harmony, whether or not it can be directly linked to individual performance.

Table 3.1 summarizes behaviours that the Big Five personality traits predict and gives examples of possible applications in the workplace based on either a conventional or sustainable perspective.

Although the Big Five are helpful for research and selection decisions, many people find other personality categories more useful for thinking about personality differences among the people at work. One popular and user-friendly personality inventory is the **Myers–Briggs Type Indicator (MBTI),** based on Carl Jung's work on psychological types.[43] The MBTI was developed by Isabel Briggs Myers and her mother, Katharine Briggs, to make the insights of type theory broadly accessible. It is less evaluative in terms of "good" and "bad" and more focused on description and understanding. Nonetheless,

Positive affect describes a person who is generally happy, enthused, and optimistic.

Myers–Briggs Type Indicator (MBTI) is a personality inventory based on Carl Jung's work on psychological types.

TABLE 3.1 Same Traits, Different Applications

Big Five Personality Traits	Conventional Applications	Sustainable Applications
#1 Extraversion	Valuable for being assertive, engaging customers, and initiating actions	Valuable for being sociable, encouraging community, and leading collective actions
#2 Agreeableness	Conducive to agreeing with top-down rules and supporting management	Conducive to agreeing with team members and developing mutual trust with co-workers
#3 Conscientiousness	Contributes to productivity across a variety of individual jobs and tasks	Contributes to consistent effort in group work and helping others beyond what is required
#4 Openness to experience	Useful in adapting to change and profitable innovations	Useful in promoting creativity and learning from diverse stakeholders
#5 Emotional stability	Necessary in order to be hired and to handle job pressures	Necessary to remain calm and considerate in working with a diversity of people

Table 3.2 illustrates that the MBTI includes four psychological types that are roughly similar to four of the Big Five personality types.[44] Missing from the MBTI is a set of types corresponding to emotional stability; perhaps this is because it's hard to put a positive spin on the label "emotionally unstable." To learn more about the MBTI and to discover your unique personality type, see the end-of-chapter Self-Assessment Exercise on assessing your personality with the MBTI.

TABLE 3.2 Comparing the Big Five and the MBTI

Big Five Trait	Myers–Briggs Dimension
Extraversion	Extraversion–Introversion
Agreeableness	Feeling–Thinking
Conscientiousness	Judging–Perceiving
Openness to experience	Intuiting–Sensing
Emotional stability	(Not applicable)

Core Self-Evaluations

DIVERSITY | ABILITIES & PERSONALITY | **CORE SELF-EVALUATIONS** | BELIEFS & VALUES

Growing out of the innate abilities and personality traits of an individual, and perhaps influenced by early life experiences, are another set of individual attributes, which together make up a person's sense of self. **Core self-evaluation** is a broad trait that integrates an individual's sense of self-esteem, generalized self-efficacy (self-confidence), emotional stability, and locus of control.[45] Emotional stability was explained earlier in the chapter, but the other components may be less familiar.

Locus of control is a person's consistent belief about the sources of success and failure. A person with an internal locus (source) of control believes that his or her own behaviour and effort are the primary reasons for success or failure, whereas people with an external locus of control point to circumstances or sources outside themselves to explain life's outcomes. As a result, internals tend to be self-starters who perform better in most activities, including work.[46] Generally it makes sense to hire or promote those who score as "internals" because they are likely to demonstrate determination to perform and personal responsibil-

LEARNING OBJECTIVE 3
Explain what core self-evaluations are and how they help to understand organizational behaviours and attitudes.

Core self-evaluation is a broad trait that integrates an individual's sense of self-esteem, generalized self-efficacy, level of emotional stability, and locus of control.

Locus of control is a person's consistent belief about the sources of success and failure.

ity to improve, whereas externals may lack persistence because they believe the outcome is related to fate, luck, or forces beyond their control. Internal locus of control is related to higher job performance and satisfaction and lower job stress in both Western and non-Western contexts.[47] See the My OB feature "Humility or Hard Work" for a further explanation of locus of control and an example.

Self-esteem is an individual's self-evaluation of worth.[48] Although feelings of worth can fluctuate, self-esteem as a component of core self-evaluations is relatively stable after a person's childhood.[49] Individuals with low self-esteem may be motivated to prove themselves worthy or to perform in order to make up for their sense of inadequacy, but generally the outcomes of poor self-esteem are negative for the person and the organization. In contrast, a healthy self-esteem is associated with greater enjoyment of work, job performance, and career satisfaction, and less psychological strain and motivation to work out of guilt or anxiety.[50]

Self-efficacy is a person's belief that he or she will be able to complete a task successfully.[51] A high level of self-efficacy or confidence in completing a task or performing a job positively relates to performance at work, but it is less important than general mental ability, conscientiousness, and work experience.[52] Further, task- or job-specific self-efficacy has its greatest effect on simple tasks where confidence may be more important than past experience or mental ability. Research suggests that task-specific self-efficacy can be increased by coaching, training, ample or new resources, clear expectations, and other influences under managers' control.[53] **Generalized self-efficacy** is a person's belief or confidence in their capability to cope with and perform in a variety of situations.[54] This more general and stable form of self-efficacy is included in a person's core self-evaluation.[55] Individuals with higher levels of generalized self-efficacy set high goals, exert more effort, adapt their behaviour to succeed, and persist in the face of difficulties.[56]

People who demonstrate confidence can get ahead of those with less confidence even when capabilities are equal, in part by drawing attention to themselves and using this attention for self-promotion.[57] Of course, over time confidence that is not coupled with competence can be exposed and hinder a person's career.

Although the separate characteristics on their own may be of help in explaining some organizational behaviours and attitudes, together these core self-evaluations have been shown to explain a range of individual work outcomes, such as performance, career success, job satisfaction, stress, conflict, and coping behaviour.[58] Generally, a higher or more positive sense of self results in better or more positive work outcomes in Asia, Europe, and North America.[59] The relationship between strong core self-evaluations and positive work behaviour is even stronger when individuals are not simply focused on themselves but are also sensitive to the concerns of others.[60]

Organizations must determine how to deal with core self-evaluations considering that they are relatively stable in adulthood, or at least difficult to change. Core self-evaluations could be useful for selection, given that generally people with a low sense of self will not perform as well as those with a more positive view of themselves. A sustainable approach does not deny these general findings, but it has a hopeful view of how people with low core self-evaluations may prosper in specific contexts and with positive organizational support. The hope is that, in the right context, those who have been dealt a difficult hand consisting of less positive traits and a less-than-ideal childhood development environment may see themselves more positively over time. One example to support this perspective is research showing that self-sacrificing leadership behaviour (risking or experiencing a meaningful loss of personal reward or prestige to maintain values and integrity) positively influences follower self-esteem.[61]

Another way core self-evaluations may be viewed differently from a sustainable perspective is in focusing on evaluations of self as part of a group. For example, collective efficacy is an assessment of the group's abilities and likelihood of succeeding. In a large-scale study conducted in China, when leaders were able to build the group's confidence in their abilities, group creativity increased.[62]

Self-esteem is an individual's self-evaluation of worth.

Self-efficacy is a person's belief that he or she will be able to complete a task successfully.

Generalized self-efficacy is a person's belief or confidence in his or her capability to cope with and perform in a variety of situations.

M⊘B | HUMILITY OR HARD WORK?

© Krista Kennell/ZUMA Press/Corbis

After achieving something significant, you may have been asked to say a word about your success. What did you say?

When Virginia "Ginni" Rometty assumed the role of CEO of IBM and was elevated by *Fortune* magazine to the top spot in their annual ranking of "Most Powerful Women in Business," she was given frequent opportunities to talk about her success. When doing so she often deflected credit to her family, mentors, and business associates who supported her. Others, including past IBM CEO Sam Palmisano, give credit to her hard work and her personal capabilities.

When business leaders, political figures, or even students step to the podium to receive recognition for their achievements, many defer to others in thanking their family, friends, colleagues, or even God. Although a humble approach may be well received in public statements and is worth commending, it is not received as well on work-related selection instruments.

Some selection instruments assess if an individual has an external or an internal locus of control. If individuals generally perceive personal outcomes to be related to factors outside themselves (such as help from others, destiny, or fate), they are likely to have an external locus of control, whereas those who attribute personal outcomes to their own hard work or skills are likely to have an internal locus of control. Generally, "internals" perform better and exercise the personal initiative that organizations value.

QUESTIONS FOR REFLECTION

1. To whom might you give credit for your success on a selection test?
2. What do you think about using locus of control to make hiring decisions?
3. What might bother you about schools using locus of control to make admissions decisions?
4. Can you imagine specific people or whole cultures that might respond in a sincerely humble fashion to a test but still have a strong work ethic?

Hootsuite is a rapidly growing Vancouver start-up that has helped thousands of companies better manage their social media marketing. The company recently opened a new office called the "HQ2." It's an example of a workplace configuration that incorporates modern trends in workplace design. Not only is the physical layout flexible to the demands of a changing and growing company, employees are free to configure their workstations however they wish, including standing desks or creating their own quiet space. Throughout the day, team members can leave their desks and relax in collaborative settings, including kitchen areas, libraries, lounges, and even an area with ping pong tables. These creative spaces allow for the facilitation of collective efficacy, and they foster spontaneous staff innovation. In addition to the beneficial effects that the unique character and functionality of Hootsuite's workspace has on its staff, immediate effects included a more collaborative work culture and improved productivity for the company as a whole.[63]

Beliefs and Values

| DIVERSITY | ABILITIES & PERSONALITY | CORE SELF-EVALUATIONS | **BELIEFS & VALUES** |

> **LEARNING OBJECTIVE 4**
> Discuss beliefs and values and how they develop and guide behaviour in relationships and organizations.

Beliefs and values develop over the course of our lives and become relatively deep-seated and important guides for behaviour in our relationships and in the organizations in which we work. For example, the cultural values described in Chapter 2 help explain some of the unique ways in which people from different parts of the globe act. Beliefs and values are generally slow to change but can evolve through personal experience or exposure to compelling evidence that contradicts what we believe to be true or important.[64]

Beliefs

Beliefs are ideas or opinions we hold to be true.

Beliefs are ideas or opinions that we hold to be true, but in most cases we do not have undeniable evidence that they are true. Renowned management theorist Douglas McGregor argued that "every managerial act rests on assumptions, generalizations, and hypotheses—that is to say, theory."[65] These theories are beliefs that grow out of our experiences and observations as well as our upbringing and education. Beliefs differ across individuals, although certainly some other people share our beliefs, and we are typically attracted to like-minded people.

McGregor identified two contrasting key beliefs about the human nature of workers within organizations that he called Theory X and Theory Y.[66] **Theory X** states that managers assume that people are inherently lazy, dislike work, will avoid working hard unless forced to do so, and prefer to be directed rather than accept responsibility for getting their work done. As a consequence, Theory X managers design structures and systems that will ensure people work hard. These measures usually take the form of control systems that set specific and narrow rules for behaviour, monitor employee performance, reward compliance, and punish those who break the rules or fail to work hard enough. In McGregor's view, Theory X assumptions reflected the "classical" approach to management.

Theory X states that managers assume people are inherently lazy, dislike work, will avoid working hard unless forced to do so, and prefer to be directed rather than accepting responsibility.

McGregor proposed that some managers adopt Theory Y assumptions because these beliefs are a more humanistic (and realistic) approach to management practice. **Theory Y** states that managers assume that work is as natural as play, that people are inherently motivated to work, and that they will feel unfulfilled if they do not have the opportunity to work and thereby make a contribution to society. Under Theory Y, workers are not seen as merely hired hands, nor are managers seen as the brains of an organization. Instead, managers design systems and structures that encourage creativity and discretion by employees and that allow them to use their full selves in doing their work.

Theory Y states that managers assume that people are inherently motivated to work and will feel unfulfilled if they do not have the opportunity to work and make a contribution to society.

American professor and author William Ouchi subsequently presented Theory Z as an alternative theory that emphasizes the belief that people like to be members of a group and will work most productively in stable groups.[67] This belief is associated with more traditional Japanese management practices such as working in teams, providing long-term employment, and investing in training.[68]

McGregor's ideas and subsequent research point to the importance of the assumptions we make about human nature. More recently, the discussion of human nature has resurfaced in the work of evolutionary psychology, in which some scholars have ascribed to humans the characteristics of evolved mammals with purely selfish instincts.[69] Proponents of this theory argue that selfishness explains it all, which is consistent with classic Theory X thinking. Others offer alternatives by giving examples of altruistic acts that range from aiding Jewish people during the Holocaust to helping co-workers in organizations.[70] Regardless of which side you favour, whatever you believe is likely to shape how you act toward or manage others. In research related to an individual's beliefs regarding whether it's possible for people to change, studies have been able to demonstrate that if leaders believe people can change, they are more likely to make investments in developing employees and give them credit for changes in behaviour.[71]

A sustainable perspective is more likely to favour positive beliefs about human nature rather than McGregor's Theory X or negative views of people's potential. Sustainable OB would suggest that other members of the organization are motivated to contribute not only to the material output of the organization but also to other aspects, such as the organization's social and spiritual nature. Moreover, those who have a sustainable perspective are likely to embrace the potential for change in others and to create organizations that promote their growth.

Values

Values are a set of personal tenets that guide a person's actions in evaluating and adapting to his or her world.

The list of possible beliefs people may hold is immeasurable, as is the list of possible values. **Values** are a set of personal tenets that guide a person's actions in evaluating and adapting to his or her world.[72] One general system for categorizing values was provided by

TABLE 3.3 Examples of Values Emphasized Across Approaches

	Conventional OB	Sustainable OB
Terminal values	Financial wealth, individual status, power	Multiple forms of well-being for multiple stakeholders
Instrumental values	Efficiency, control, formalization	Participation, experimentation, sustainability

Polish-American social psychologist Milton Rokeach. He classified values as either "terminal" or "instrumental." According to Rokeach's classification, **terminal values** relate to desirable ends (what a person values achieving in life) and **instrumental values** are desirable means to achieve end states (the way a person goes about living).[73] Terminal values include outcomes related to financial wealth, individual status and well-being, peace, health, and performance, while instrumental values include love, adventure, service, charity, efficiency, control, and independence.

As noted in Table 3.3, conventional and sustainable perspectives are likely to emphasize different terminal values as well as the instrumental values to achieve those ends.

An organization's values will nurture and attract members with similar values.[74] For example, a sustainable organization will emphasize values that promote the well-being of a range of stakeholders, including organizational members, community members, and the environment. German shoe and sports lifestyle company PUMA is a leader in creating an organization that is committed to promoting its values of environmental sustainability, peace, and creativity within and outside of the organization.[75] The company doesn't just talk the talk by using flashy slogans and publicity campaigns, it walks the walk and was recently recognized with an international sustainability award for its pioneering work in assessing the costs a business has on the environment, across its entire supply chain.[76] No doubt this is a source of pride for employees who hold these shared values and is an important factor in attracting employees to PUMA.

Other research on values has identified 10 values that, in differing combinations, are helpful to describe different cultures and to differentiate one group of people from another.[77] This research suggests that there will be disparity across cultures in terms of how much value is placed on the following:

- Power—exerting control or dominance for the sake of status or prestige
- Achievement—demonstrating competence and capability to achieve personal success
- Hedonism—pursuing self-gratification and pleasure
- Stimulation—seeking excitement and challenge for the sake of stimulation and experience
- Self-direction—choosing autonomy and freedom to ensure personal independence
- Universalism—seeking equal treatment and justice among all people and the environment
- Benevolence—acting to promote and preserve the welfare of others
- Tradition—demonstrating respect for the customs and traditions of others
- Conformity—living in accordance with established norms and expectations
- Security—ensuring harmony, stability, and order in relationships and society

As illustrated in Figure 3.2, these 10 values can be characterized along continua based on their relative emphasis on self-interest or others' interests and on maintaining or changing the status quo. Further, the more similar values are closer together, whereas more different or conflicting values are farther apart. For example, conformity and tradition are close

Terminal values are related to desirable ends (what a person values achieving in life).

Instrumental values are desirable means to achieve end states.

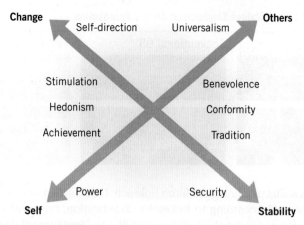

FIGURE 3.2 Ten Values along Two Dimensions

Adapted from Schwartz, S. H., Melech, G., Lehmann, A., Burgess, S., Harris, M., & Owens, V. (2001). Extending the cross-cultural validity of the theory of basic human values with a different method of measurement. *Journal of Cross-Cultural Psychology*, 32(5), 519–542.

together and similar in honouring established norms and customs, but the two values are situated on the opposite side of the figure from stimulation, which relates to seeking new and challenging experiences. As a result, it would be challenging for a culture to simultaneously place a high value on both "stimulation" and "tradition," and yet people need both of these to thrive in the long term.

When we make a choice between several possible actions, the relative emphasis we place on particular values will influence the action we choose to take. For example, a person who values self-enhancement (hedonism, achievement, power) may act differently than someone who values self-transcendence (benevolence, universalism, tradition) when faced with a request to sacrifice personal time to help a co-worker or to participate in a volunteer community service initiative. Or a person who values openness to change (stimulation, self-direction) may respond differently to an organizational change initiative than someone who values conserving the status quo (conformity, security).

Values are particularly important in influencing which organizations individuals choose to work for and whether they will choose to continue working in a particular organization.[78] We'll discuss organizational values later in the text when we explain organizational culture (see Chapters 12 and 13). For now, it is enough to say that *value fit* means individuals tend to be attracted to and feel comfortable in organizations that have the same values. Perceptions of value fit also come into play when recruiters make decisions about who they think might be a good fit for their organizations.[79]

People's values also can have a significant impact on the organizations they create and the way those organizations evolve over time. The business of social change and the integration of people's values with business objectives have evolved immensely throughout the past few decades. When determining where charity funds are directed, for example, Canadian telecommunications giant TELUS International engages the expertise and networks of community leaders to ensure that the corporation's funding is allocated in the most impactful way. To facilitate this, the company asks community leaders to serve on TELUS Community Boards. For instance, in 2014 the company's Community Board in the Philippines contributed $100,000 to fund a variety of community-focused projects, including helping the Kythe Foundation, a Philippine-based organization that provides psychosocial care to chronically ill children and improves the delivery of health services in the Philippine Children's Medical Center. The Telus International program is a good example of effective corporate philanthropy as managed in partnership with experts from the community.[80]

OB in Action

Political Values and Geographic Differences

Although the residents of each province and territory and the supporters and members of each political party in Canada share distinctive opinions on policy, the political culture of Canada transcends provincial boundaries. For example, Canadians are largely committed voters, but at the same time they do not participate widely in the political process. This unique feature to Canadian political culture is often described as a "spectator–participant" characteristic. As well, research indicates that Canadians strongly support political authority and widely accept the role of elites in leadership. Unlike Americans, Canadians often prefer to rely on government intervention (e.g., through public ownership) rather than the private sector to solve economic problems.

Another feature of Canadian political culture is Canada's "approach and avoidance" relationship with the United States. Despite the fact that the United States is Canada's greatest trading partner, and a country with which Canadians share a large number of common interests, many Canadians have been frustrated by the way in which their culture (especially in English Canada) and their businesses have been dominated by American interests. As a consequence, Canadians have attempted to regulate this relationship by creating a number of government institutions designed to promote Canadian culture or to restrict the flow of foreign investment into Canada. These contradictory sentiments toward the United States have occasionally helped to unite Canadians as well as helped the development of their political and popular culture.

Finally, a belief system known as "regionalism" exists in Canada, whereby the political climate contains attitudes that are uniquely Canadian while, at the same time, distinguish Canadians from one another. There may be several different belief systems existing simultaneously, including one involving French–English differences and another based on notions of economic development and geographical diversity.

In summary, although members of different regions and political affiliations have differing views on culture and policy, a majority of Canadians share a similar view on the role of government and have shared values toward multiculturalism. Although the ends to which policy is determined may differ, the means through which policy is implemented may be fundamentally similar to most Canadians.

QUESTIONS FOR DISCUSSION

1. What values do you think most Canadians believe differ the most between Canada and the United States?
2. How might different values affect the priorities of businesses in both countries in dealing with various stakeholders—employees, customers, shareholders, community members, or the environment?
3. Offer specific examples of how values differ across regions of Canada.

life in the fast lane—elon musk[81]

On any given day, you might find Elon Musk at Tesla Motors examining the detail in an electric automobile, or at SpaceX observing the test launch of a Dragon spacecraft, or at SolarCity exploring ways to expand the use of solar panels and other services to enhance energy efficiency. He is the CEO of the first two organizations and Chair of the Board for the other, but he is not your typical executive. You could call him an engineer, an explorer, an inventor, and an entrepreneur—but none of these titles does justice to Musk. His colleague from PayPal, Peter Thiel, describes him as a combination of John D. Rockefeller, Steve Jobs, and Howard Hughes. His friend, actor, and director, Jon Favreau, is said to have based the Tony Stark character from the *Iron Man* film franchise on Musk.

Musk was born in South Africa to an engineer and a nutritionist who later divorced. He and his brother enjoyed a great deal of independence growing up and gained confidence by having the freedom to pursue their ideas. Musk got an early taste of success at the age of 12 when he coded and sold his own video game, called Blastar. From an early age he read a great deal and also liked to experiment with rockets and explosives—interests that have not faded over time.

As a teenager, Musk spent time travelling through Canada, moving from place to place, bunking with distant relatives, or working various jobs on farms. He eventually made his way to Queen's University in Ontario, where he spent two years before transferring to the University of Pennsylvania. There, he earned two separate bachelor's degrees, one in physics and the other in economics. He then ventured out to California, where he began his Ph.D. studies at Stanford University. However, only two days into the program, Musk dropped out to pursue a business venture with his brother, Kimbal, in Internet mapping and directory services. The program was called Zip2, and a mere four years later Compaq Computer Corporation purchased the program for around $300 million. Musk also benefited from launching another innovative project, X.com, which became PayPal and sold for $1.5 billion in 2002.

Musk has an intense, curious, and driven personality. He has an insatiable hunger to learn and innovate, which can be unnerving for those who move at a different pace. His insistence on excellence and his attention to detail can make him difficult to please, but he gets results. Those who have worked for him describe him as autocratic and "blunt to the point of offensive." Similar to Steve Jobs, who also had a reputation for being difficult to work with, Musk expects the best from every

© Bob Daemmrich/Bob Daemmrich Photography, Inc./Corbis

person he hires. Steve Jurvetson, a board member for SpaceX and a true believer (and investor) in Musk's visions, described him like this: "Like Jobs, Elon [Musk] does not tolerate C or D players, but I'd say he's nicer than Jobs and a bit more refined than Bill Gates." Some leave Musk's companies on a sour note, but others love working in his companies because they offer employees the opportunity to change the world.

Musk's combination of unique attributes and past successes make him supremely confident in projects that others consider impossible. With his successful resupply of the International Space Station with a SpaceX rocket, he accomplished something that to this point in history only sovereign nations have achieved in space flights. Some people set stretch goals for themselves; Musk sets stretch goals for the human race. Musk believes humans can be a multi-planet species and has set his sights on living on Mars. His dissatisfaction with the status quo has made him a maverick in many industries. He is in the fast lane, driving a transformation of the energy we use, how we travel on earth, and, perhaps, where we live in the future.

QUESTIONS FOR DISCUSSION

1. What abilities make Elon Musk successful?
2. What personality traits characterize Musk? How might these traits affect your ability to work with him?
3. How do you explain Musk's supreme confidence in projects that others don't think are feasible?
4. What beliefs does Musk hold about human beings and their potential?

Summary

Individuals can be understood, in part, by examining layers of individual attributes. From visible surface characteristics to less-visible internal attributes, individual differences can help explain behaviour in organizations.

 Learning Objectives

- Identify diversity and surface characteristics and their value to achieving organizational goals.
- Discuss abilities and personality and their effect on achievement and performance in organizational roles.
- Explain what core self-evaluations are and how they help to understand organizational behaviours and attitudes.
- Discuss beliefs and values and how they develop and guide behaviour in relationships and organizations.

From a conventional OB perspective:

- Diversity and surface characteristics offer potential benefits for organizations that should be maximized.
- Abilities and personality can be helpful in explaining performance in individual jobs.
- Core self-evaluations can help explain productive behaviour.
- Beliefs and values can explain individual behaviour and affiliations that are useful to the organization.

From a sustainable OB perspective:

- Diversity and surface characteristics can provide the basis for connections and synergies.
- Abilities and personality can be helpful in addressing broader organizational needs.
- Core self-evaluations and evaluations of the group can influence individual behaviour.
- Beliefs and values can promote mutual benefits and trust.

Key Terms

Abilities (p. 50)

Agreeableness (p. 51)

Beliefs (p. 56)

Conscientiousness (p. 51)

Core self-evaluation (p. 53)

Diversity (p. 47)

Emotional stability (p. 51)

Extraversion (p. 51)

Generalized self-efficacy (p. 54)

Instrumental values (p. 57)

Locus of control (p. 53)

Myers–Briggs Type Indicator (MBTI) (p. 52)

Negative affect (p. 51)

Openness to experience (p. 51)

Organizational citizenship behaviour (OCB) (p. 51)

Personality (p. 50)

Positive affect (p. 52)

Self-efficacy (p. 54)

Self-esteem (p. 54)

Social categorization theory (p. 47)

Stereotypes (p. 48)

Terminal values (p. 57)

Theory X (p. 56)

Theory Y (p. 56)

Values (p. 56)

Questions for Reflection and Discussion

1. Provide a list of reasons that organizations should devote time and energy to understanding diversity issues. Which are the most compelling for you personally, and which might be most compelling as a manager?

2. How does diversity within a classroom help or hinder learning? Provide examples of both. What suggestions do you have for maximizing the helpful aspects of diversity and minimizing the hindering aspects of diversity?

3. How does your personality affect your behaviour? List some things you naturally like to do. Is there an underlying pattern in these activities that hints at your personality?

4. Which of the core self-evaluation components seem most relevant to behaviour in organizational settings? Explain. What, if anything, might be done to enhance these components?

5. Where do your beliefs about human nature come from? Are they rooted in religious beliefs, your upbringing, media messages, or your schooling? To what extent have your work experiences shaped or changed your beliefs about human nature?

6. Organizational behaviour research shows how the personality that someone is born with is related to different aspects of job performance. This information can be used by managers and human resources professionals to make hiring decisions. Is this ethical? How would you answer this question as a shareholder of a business? How would you answer it as someone who was born with a personality that is not optimal for organizational performance? What would happen if we had a society (or an organization) composed only of people with "performance-optimizing" personalities? What sort of dependent variables might OB researchers want to examine other than "job performance"?

ob activities

SELF-ASSESSMENT EXERCISE

What Is Your Myers–Briggs Type?

Several MBTI questionnaires are available, including some that are administered and interpreted by certified MBTI consultants. To get a relatively short but reasonably accurate assessment using the Internet, visit www.humanmetrics.com/. After you identify your type, read the short summaries below.

ISTJ	ISFJ	INFJ	INTJ
Process ideas through reflection; focus on the present and ensure that facts and details are considered; value objectivity and thorough analysis; prefer specific procedures and formal methods.	Process ideas through reflection; focus on the present and ensure facts and details are considered; value relationships and group harmony; prefer specific procedures and formal methods.	Process ideas through reflection; focus on the future and take a broad perspective on issues; value relationships and group harmony; prefer specific procedures and formal methods.	Process ideas through reflection; focus on the future and take a broad perspective on issues; value objectivity and thorough analysis; prefer specific procedures and formal methods.
ISTP	**ISFP**	**INFP**	**INTP**
Process ideas through reflection; focus on the present and ensure that facts and details are considered; value objectivity and thorough analysis; prefer flexibility and are open to change.	Process ideas through reflection; focus on the present and ensure facts and details are considered; value relationships and group harmony; prefer flexibility and are open to change.	Process ideas through reflection; focus on the future and take a broad perspective on issues; value relationships and group harmony; prefer flexibility and are open to change.	Process ideas through reflection; focus on the future and take a broad perspective on issues; value objectivity and thorough analysis; prefer flexibility and are open to change.

ESTP	ESFP	ENFP	ENTP
Process ideas through interaction; focus on the present and ensure that facts and details are considered; value objectivity and thorough analysis; prefer flexibility and are open to change.	Process ideas through interaction; focus on the present and ensure facts and details are considered; value relationships and group harmony; prefer flexibility and are open to change.	Process ideas through interaction; focus on the future and take a broad perspective on issues; value relationships and group harmony; prefer flexibility and are open to change.	Process ideas through interaction; focus on the future and take a broad perspective on issues; value objectivity and thorough analysis; prefer flexibility and are open to change.
ESTJ	ESFJ	ENFJ	ENTJ
Process ideas through interaction; focus on the present and ensure that facts and details are considered; value objectivity and thorough analysis; prefer specific procedures and formal methods.	Process ideas through interaction; focus on the present and ensure facts and details are considered; value relationships and group harmony; prefer specific procedures and formal methods.	Process ideas through interaction; focus on the future and take a broad perspective on issues; value relationships and group harmony; prefer specific procedures and formal methods.	Process ideas through interaction; focus on the future and take a broad perspective on issues; value objectivity and thorough analysis; prefer specific procedures and formal methods.

E = extraverted, **I** = introverted, **S** = sensing, **N** = intuitive, **F** = feeling, **T** = thinking, **P** = perceiving, **J** = judging

How well does your type, as described in the table above, fit your view of yourself? How does your type explain where you perform well or what you are motivated to do?

SELF-ASSESSMENT EXERCISE

What Are Your Values?

Please read each of the 20 statements below and in each case think about how much the person described is or is not like you. Put an X in the box to the right that shows how much the person in the description is like you.

HOW MUCH LIKE YOU IS THIS PERSON?

	very much like me	like me	some-what like me	a little like me	not like me	not like me at all
1. Thinking up new ideas and being creative is important to him/her. He/she likes to do things in his/her own original way.	☐	☐	☐	☐	☐	☐
2. It is important to her/him to be rich. She/he wants to have a lot of money and expensive things.	☐	☐	☐	☐	☐	☐
3. He/she thinks it is important that every person in the world be treated equally. He/she believes everyone should have equal opportunities in life.	☐	☐	☐	☐	☐	☐
4. It's very important to her/him to show others her/his abilities. She/he wants people to admire what she/he does.	☐	☐	☐	☐	☐	☐
5. It is important to him/her to live in secure surroundings. He/she avoids anything that might endanger his/her safety.	☐	☐	☐	☐	☐	☐
6. She/he thinks it is important to do lots of different things in life. She/he always looks for new things to try.	☐	☐	☐	☐	☐	☐
7. He/she believes that people should do what they're told. He/she thinks people should follow rules at all times, even when no one is watching.	☐	☐	☐	☐	☐	☐

HOW MUCH LIKE YOU IS THIS PERSON?

	very much like me	like me	some- what like me	a little like me	not like me	not like me at all
8. She/he believes she/he should always show respect to her/his parents and to older people. It is important to her/him to be obedient.	☐	☐	☐	☐	☐	☐
9. It's very important to him/her to help the people around him/her. He/she wants to care for others' well-being.	☐	☐	☐	☐	☐	☐
10. She/he seeks every chance she/he can to have fun. It is important to her/him to do things that give her/him pleasure.	☐	☐	☐	☐	☐	☐
11. It is important to him/her to make his/her own decisions about what he/she does. He/she likes to be free to plan and choose his/her activities for him/herself.	☐	☐	☐	☐	☐	☐
12. Enjoying life's pleasures is important to her/him. She/he likes to "spoil" her/himself.	☐	☐	☐	☐	☐	☐
13. Being very successful is important to him/her. He/she likes to impress other people.	☐	☐	☐	☐	☐	☐
14. It is very important to her/him that her/his country be safe. She/he thinks the state must be on watch against threats from within and without.	☐	☐	☐	☐	☐	☐
15. He/she likes to take risks. He/she is always looking for adventures.	☐	☐	☐	☐	☐	☐
16. It is important to her/him always to behave properly. She/he wants to avoid doing anything people would say is wrong.	☐	☐	☐	☐	☐	☐
17. It is important to him/her to be in charge and tell others what to do. He/she wants people to do what he/she says.	☐	☐	☐	☐	☐	☐
18. It is important to her/him to be loyal to her/his friends. She/he wants to devote her/himself to people close to her/him.	☐	☐	☐	☐	☐	☐
19. He/she strongly believes that people should care for nature. Looking after the environment is important to him/her.	☐	☐	☐	☐	☐	☐
20. She/he thinks it is best to do things in traditional ways. It is important to her/him to keep up the customs she/he has learned.	☐	☐	☐	☐	☐	☐

Key: This is a shortened version of the Schwartz Portrait Values Questionnaire (PVQ) that has been adapted to be gender-neutral.[82] *Each value is followed by the items that measure the value in parentheses: Conformity (7,16), Tradition (8,20), Benevolence (9,18), Universalism (3,19), Self-Direction (1,11), Stimulation (6,15), Hedonism (10,12), Achievement (4,13), Power (2,17), Security (5,14). How are these values reflected in your choice of a university major or a job? How are these values reflected in what you do outside of work (check your schedule)?*

An employer received applications for a supervisor's position from two equally qualified applicants but hired the male applicant because he thought that some employees might resent being supervised by a female.

Why might this scenario occur in organizations?

Use the following scale to indicate whether this behaviour is ethically acceptable:

NEVER ACCEPTABLE		SOMETIMES ACCEPTABLE		ALWAYS ACCEPTABLE	
①	②	③	④	⑤	⑥	⑦

Explain the ideas you considered in arriving at your answer.

DISCUSSION STARTER

Personalities on YouTube.com

YouTube is a cultural phenomenon that some say also exemplifies a new culture of exhibitionism. Pick a homemade YouTube video from among the "most viewed" or "favourites" of the day that focuses on regular people, not celebrities.

QUESTIONS FOR DISCUSSION

1. What personality traits are evident in the video participant(s)?
2. What does the video communicate about the participants' beliefs or values?
3. If you have ever posted a video on the Internet, why did you do it?

4. What does the video say about you? Consider what others might think—particularly a potential employer—if they were to find the video online.

APPLICATION JOURNAL

This is a personal journal entry that can be used for class discussion or compiled as input into a self-reflection paper.

Based on this discussion of individual attributes, what would you say are the attributes that contribute most to explaining your behaviour? Some of these behaviours you would like to continue doing while others you would like to discontinue. Although changing your abilities may not be possible, you can manage your behaviour. Make a list of your key attributes and your past behaviours that may be explained by each attribute. Pick one or more behaviours you want to continue, or even increase, and state one action that will help achieve that goal. Pick one or more of the behaviours you want to discontinue or decrease, and state one action that will help you achieve that goal. Your action may be, for example, to get help from someone with more experience or different attributes.

Four

Considering Individual States

The challenge of explaining behaviour in organizations is that you must take into consideration the stable attributes as well as the more dynamic states of individuals. These dynamic states—the way a person acts, thinks, or feels—can be a result of individual attributes, but they also are influenced by contexts such as relationships and the workplace. This makes understanding individuals both complex and interesting. This chapter will consider a handful of important individual states that are related to OB.

Learning Objectives	Conventional OB	Sustainable OB
ETHICS		
1. Describe ethics and how organizational characteristics affect ethical behaviour.	Base ethics on consequential utilitarianism (seek the greatest material well-being for the greatest number of people)	Base ethics on virtue theory (practice character in order to nurture happiness in the community)
ATTITUDES AND COMMITMENTS		
2. Explain attitudes and commitments and their influence on performance and turnover.	Encourage attitudes and commitments that contribute to individual and organizational performance	Encourage attitudes and commitments that contribute to individual and community well-being
PERCEPTION		
3. Discuss perceptions and their effect on information received in an organization.	Develop accurate perceptions to enhance predictability and decision making	Invite dissonance and diverse perceptions to enhance creativity and information sharing
EMOTIONS		
4. Discuss emotions, how they determine behaviour, and their importance in an organization.	Manage emotions to meet organizational goals	Value emotions and treat members with dignity

jack dorsey

BILLIONAIRE BAD BOY OR BAD BOSS?[1]

Stephen Lam/REUTERS/NewsCom

When he was in his late 20s, Jack Dorsey co-founded Twitter, the groundbreaking social communications platform that surpassed 200 million users by its fifth birthday. Despite co-founding the company and serving as the initial CEO in Twitter's early years of explosive growth, Dorsey was forced out of daily operations and ultimately left the company after only a few years. He describes the move to depose him as feeling like a punch in the gut. After a few years, he recovered from the emotional bruise to his ego and returned to the company to oversee design and product development initiatives, but again he saw his role diminished and eventually turned his attention to pursuits outside the company.

Opinions differ about Dorsey's rocky experience at Twitter. Dorsey himself admitted he wasn't a good manager in his original experience as an executive, but word of employee dissatisfaction also emerged during his second stint. Employees were said to complain about the difficulties of working with Dorsey and the stress caused by his frequent changes in direction regarding product features.

Others, including Dorsey, assert that his most recent transition out of operations at Twitter had more to do with his commitment to Square, Inc., and his enthusiasm about its prospects. Square, the company Dorsey co-founded in 2009, produces the small card-swiping device that can be connected to a smartphone to collect payments from customers.

At the core of his being, he really wants to make the world a better place.

Dorsey may have a bold tattoo on his forearm and a reputation as an intense leader, but he still begins each day with a text to his mother. In his role as CEO at Square, he has attempted to change his management style, striving to communicate more clearly with employees and hosting a "town square" meeting each Friday to share information. Although even with this improvement, there is still evidence of low job satisfaction at Square due to its pressure-filled environment. These persistent attitudes may be related to real issues with Dorsey's leadership style or perhaps some employees' perceptions that his perfectionism and attention to detail don't fit their idea of what makes a good boss.

Despite his faults, Dorsey's supporters say that all of his innovations are aimed at contributing to a more humane and efficient society. A mentor of his, Ray Chambers, is the UN Secretary-General's special envoy for malaria. Said Chambers of Dorsey, "At the core of his being, he really wants to make the world a better place." Peter Fenton, an investor in Twitter, said of him, "We dream about backing people who have that kind of character—purity, authenticity, but just deep optimism." Most likely Dorsey is neither a "bad boy" nor a "bad boss," but like many young, idealistic innovators who are thrust into leadership roles by their success, he is still learning lessons about himself as well as about organizational leadership.

As the example of Jack Dorsey makes clear, leaders have a significant influence on the way that other members of the organization experience their work. The current experience of an individual is a state of being. As used in this chapter, states are dynamic conditions of a person evident in what he or she thinks, feels, or acts. Factors that influence these states include the attributes of organizational members themselves, their interactions with others, and the organization's culture and structures.

Figure 4.1 includes a subset of the components from the more comprehensive figure introduced in chapter 1. In this chapter, the emphasis of the figure is on a set of key states in the outer ring of the circle that lie below surface characteristics and are influenced by a person's stable attributes, which are described in the previous chapter. Although states are not directly visible, they often show themselves through words, expressions, and behaviours. What is not illustrated is that these states are also shaped by interpersonal and organizational influences. This will become clear in this chapter and discussed in more detail in following chapters.

The states of individuals we will consider in this chapter are ethics, attitudes and commitments, perceptions, and emotions. Given their importance to OB, we discuss motivation, decision making, and self-leadership separately in following chapters.

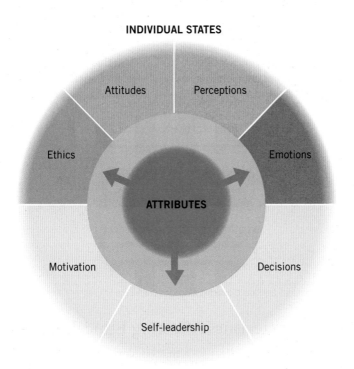

INDIVIDUAL STATES

Attitudes
Perceptions
Ethics
Emotions
ATTRIBUTES
Motivation
Decisions
Self-leadership

FIGURE 4.1 Key Individual States in the Context of Organizations

Ethics

ETHICS   ATTITUDES   PERCEPTIONS   EMOTIONS

The past decade has seen a surge of interest in ethics within organizations, due in part to an unfortunate worldwide outbreak of ethical scandals. Consider these examples: accounting fraud at Enron, Nortel,[2] and Sino-Forest[3]; bribery allegations associated with Avon, Samsung, and SNC-Lavalin[4]; financial misdealing at AIG, Lehman Brothers, and Portus[5]; dubious decisions at energy companies such as British Petroleum; and a rash of insider trading and Ponzi schemes from the likes of Raj Rajaratnam, Bernie Madoff, and Gary Sorenson.[6] The destructive effects of unethical behaviour can have personal as well as societal implications. For example, dishonesty can destroy a person's career,[7] and an abusive supervisor who berates, embarrasses, lies to, and insults employees at work ends up hindering the work performance of those employees as well as creating stress in their home lives.[8]

As explained earlier, **states** are dynamic conditions of a person evident in what he or she thinks, feels, or acts. What do we mean by ethics? **Ethics** are a set of principles or moral standards that differentiate right from wrong. The state of an individual's ethics is perceptible in his or her behaviour. When we observe unethical behaviour in organizations, is it due to a few bad individuals, or is a bad organization influencing otherwise good people? Research indicates that ethical and unethical behaviour are influenced by individual attributes *and* by the organizational context in which the individual works.[9]

LEARNING OBJECTIVE 1
Describe ethics and how organizational characteristics affect ethical behaviour.

States are dynamic conditions of a person evident in what he or she thinks, feels, or acts.

Ethics are a set of principles or standards that differentiate right from wrong.

Some contexts can be more ethical than others, but each presents challenges to maintaining and demonstrating ethical behaviour. This may be particularly true if you are a business school student. Compared to other students, those in business school self-report a greater frequency of cheating, which could mean that many business students personally don't believe that cheating is wrong or they perceive that in their environment "everyone is doing it."[10]

Without a doubt, there will be no shortage of ethical challenges in your future. Successfully addressing those challenges will require having a deeper understanding of what contributes to ethical and unethical behaviour. As Figure 4.2 shows, in this section we will take a look at both individual and organizational influences on ethical and unethical behaviour.

FIGURE 4.2   Individual and Organizational Characteristics Both Contribute to Unethical Behaviour

Individual Characteristics Affecting Ethical Behaviour

Among the many individual characteristics that employees bring to the workplace, a few characteristics have particular importance when it comes to understanding their ethical behaviour. Two of these are the employees' level of moral development and their particular moral point of view.[11]

Moral development is the state or level of a person's moral reasoning.

Level of moral development. Although our ethics have been influenced by prior experiences in our upbringing,[12] each of us is still maturing in our **moral development**, which American psychologist Lawrence Kohlberg suggested can be at one of three levels at a given time, as shown in Figure 4.3:[13]

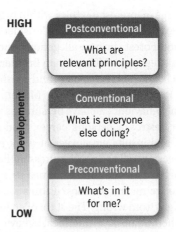

FIGURE 4.3   Levels of Moral Development

- The lowest level of moral development is *preconventional*. For a manager at this level, right and wrong are determined by what is rewarded and punished. In other words, ethics is determined by self-interest: "What's in it for me?"
- The next level is *conventional*. Here right and wrong are determined by social norms or external standards. In other words, "What is everyone else doing?"
- The final level of moral development is *postconventional,* where right and wrong are determined by transcendent universal principles established through conscience and reason: "What are the relevant principles?" Philosopher Immanuel Kant's categorical imperatives—such as never stealing or deceiving others—are examples of universal principles or duties that he argued could be arrived at by reason.[14] The Golden Rule found in leading world religions—do to others as you would have them do to you—is another example.[15]

Not everyone is at the same stage of moral development, nor does everyone proceed through all of the stages Kohlberg described. Research indicates that higher levels of moral development are associated with less unethical behaviour.[16] Organizational members at higher levels of moral development also are more likely to courageously challenge organizations that condone unethical behaviour.[17]

Moral point of view. What one person sees as ethical behaviour, another may see as unethical. This can make it difficult to argue that one choice is "more ethical" than another; however, adopting a relativistic perspective, which says what is right depends only on the situation instead of universal principles, is dangerous because it is often associated with unethical behaviour.[18] The ethicality of an action or decision is usually more apparent after we have observed the long-term effects of the action or decision,[19] but in the meantime, different people will have different moral points of view.

A **moral point of view** is a framework of values we use to develop our internally consistent and logically justified principles and standards of right and wrong. It acts as a sort of lens that influences the way we view the process of making ethical decisions and the way we act ethically in the workplace. For example, a rights-based moral point of view, which stems from the teachings of John Locke and Thomas Jefferson, emphasizes maintaining and protecting the fundamental rights and privileges of individuals.[20] Obviously an OB textbook cannot possibly represent all the different moral points of view that exist, but it can help you develop an understanding of the way a moral point of view influences ethics so that you'll be able to think about ethics from your own moral point of view, whatever it is. In short, our purpose here is not to convince you that one moral point of view is more ethical than others. Instead, the goal is to examine the assumptions and implications associated with different moral points of view that may characterize conventional and sustainable OB.

In terms of moral philosophy, the conventional moral point of view draws from **consequentialist theory**, which considers the consequences of an action when determining what is ethical. In other words, an action that results in beneficial outcomes, be they financial or social, is deemed ethical, whereas an action that results in harmful outcomes (costs) is deemed unethical.

Perhaps the best-known consequentialist theory is utilitarianism. Espoused by the nineteenth-century philosophers Jeremy Bentham and John Stuart Mill, **utilitarianism** holds that what is ethical produces "the greatest good for the greatest number." It is a results-oriented moral point of view that assesses decisions in terms of their consequences. In other words, the "utility" of an option is its benefits minus its costs. To be ethical, a person is expected to consider the effect of each alternative on all parties and select the one that benefits the greatest number of people. Another consequentialist approach is **egoism**, a point of view in which the utility of the option depends on the consequences for the

Moral point of view is a framework of values we use to develop our internally consistent and logically justified principles and standards of right and wrong.

Consequentialist theory considers the consequences of an action when determining what is ethical.

Utilitarianism is a moral philosophy that holds that ethical managers strive to produce "the greatest good for the greatest number."

Egoism is a moral philosophy based on what "benefits me the most."

individual decision maker. Simply stated, this approach amounts to deciding which option benefits "me" the most.

Over time, a variation of consequentialism has developed that represents a moral point of view associated with conventional OB. This conventional perspective depends on two assumptions, the first of which answers the question of how we measure "good" when different people value different consequences. This perspective assumes that the best generic measure of good is wealth or money. Because different people have different preferences for basic human needs like food, clothing, and shelter, and because money can buy each of these resources, the best way to maximize the greatest good is to create individual financial wealth, which people can then use according to their own preferences for what constitutes a "good life."

The second assumption is about how to maximize wealth. From a conventional perspective, the answer is to embrace and encourage individualism, as exemplified by the interpretation of Adam Smith's (1776) concept of the "invisible hand" that says collective good and the wealth of nations can be maximized by elevating individual self-interest.[21] Nobel Prize laureate Milton Friedman is the best-known advocate of this conventional perspective, which suggests that what is ethical for an organization is the course of action that is most profitable for its shareholders, within legal bounds. Maximizing the financial return for an organization's owners expands the economy, which in turn maximizes the "good" of the larger community.

Sustainable OB, in contrast, draws from virtue theory as the basis of its moral point of view. Recall from chapter 1 that virtue theory focuses on character and the ways in which people practice virtues in community, thereby facilitating happiness, which Aristotle called the "supreme good."[22] **Virtues** are ways of acting that are noble or have value *regardless* of the end result or consequences. From a virtue theory perspective, therefore, the purpose of OB is not to maximize financial well-being or self-interest but, rather, to maximize people's happiness by practising virtues in the community. Virtue theory, as applied to organizations, focuses on the character of leaders and organizational members instead of on utility.[23] Having a focus on character offers guidance and constraints, but it avoids legalistic rules. It asks questions such as, "Is this action consistent with who I am or aspire to be?"[24] Although a sustainable moral point of view can be characterized by many virtues, perhaps it is best exemplified by service and balance.

First, sustainable OB suggests that organizational leaders should be concerned for the welfare of others and be committed to serving them in their work. In this view, the organization exists to serve its employees (and society at large), rather than the other way around.[25] The focus is on achieving not just self-interest but also mutual interest, particularly the growth and development of organizational members.[26] Those whose moral philosophy focuses on the welfare of others in this way are less likely to act unethically.[27]

Second, sustainable OB values balance. More specifically, it promotes **sustaincentrism,**[28] which seeks to balance human and ecological concerns, avoiding the extremes of disregarding the environment on the one hand and putting the environment over human needs on the other. It recognizes the interconnectedness between humankind and the environment and the complexity of that relationship.[29]

Although an individual's moral point of view is shaped by family and to some extent by friends, organizational experiences also influence a person's related ethics and ethical behaviour. For example, what we are taught in class and observe among our classmates contributes to our ethical beliefs about cheating, competition, and respecting others and the natural environment. Research suggests that a materialist-individualist orientation can be taught and learned, and that economics and business students do tend to become more materialist-individualist during their time in college.[30] In light of this, it only makes sense that people can also be influenced by the organizational context in which most of them will spend a significant portion of their lives; that is, their workplace.

Virtues are good ways of acting that are noble or have value regardless of the end result or consequences.

Sustaincentrism is a perspective promoting balance between human and ecological concerns in organizational endeavours.

Organizational Characteristics Affecting Ethical Behaviour

Research has shown that experiences in the work context influence attitudes toward ethical behaviour.[31] **Ethical climate** describes the informal shared perceptions of what are appropriate practices and procedures.[32] An ethical climate can be characterized as primarily promoting egoism (self-interest), benevolence (concern for others), or principles (laws and policies). Unethical behaviour abounds when the ethical climate is focused on self-interest. Alternatively, unethical behaviour is constrained by benevolent and principled ethical organizational climates.[33]

Ethical culture consists of the formal and informal systems aimed at influencing the ethical behaviour of organizational members.[34] A common feature of formal systems is an organization's **code of ethics**, a formal written statement of the primary values and ethical rules that employees are expected to follow. Not surprisingly, enforcing the codes of ethics discourages unethical behaviour.[35] To this end, in a study of four of Canada's largest companies, involving employees at all levels of the organization (managerial, non-managerial, and executive-level), researchers sought to identify why and how codes of ethics impacted behaviour. They found that some employees viewed the code as a "rulebook" that dictates acceptable and unacceptable behaviour. Others perceived the code as a "mirror" that validates and/or reinforces individual beliefs of right and wrong. Additional interpretations included that the code is a "shield" that serves as backup to justify resisting unethical behaviours and that it's a "club" to articulate consequences for non-compliance. Better understanding the ways in which these formal systems impact actions and decision making within an organization is critical to their effectiveness.[36]

Other features of formal systems to reinforce ethical behaviour include organizational training, hotlines for reporting ethical breaches, and effective monitoring and sanctioning systems that communicate and reinforce the ethics code.[37] Another way to formally signal the importance of ethics is to create a position within the organizational hierarchy that is devoted to it. For example, French cosmetics company L'Oréal has a Chief Ethics Officer position. Currently in this role is Emmanuel Lulin, who works to ensure that employees stay true to L'Oréal's values to "earn and retain the trust of our stakeholders so that together we can grow and contribute usefully to the society in which we live."[38] To be effective, such a position mustn't just be window dressing; it must have access to and the support of top management.

In addition to creating specific ethics positions such as the one at L'Oréal, organizations should also create a clear ethics program or framework that is consistent with their codes of ethics. For example, SAI Global, an international risk management firm, recommended the following to the Canadian Centre for Ethics and Corporate Policy as an effective ethical compliance program: (1) set clear, long-term program goals; (2) make critical program requirements mandatory and follow through on them; (3) treat ethical compliance education as both a cultural initiative and professional development, rather than as "training"; (4) continually assess risk and employee attitudes using multiple vehicles; and (5) utilize shorter, more frequent compliance periods to maintain a continuous level of awareness.[39]

It is important to note that people may ignore the official values in formal organizational programs or codes if the reward systems reinforce something else.[40] Enron is a well-known example of an organization whose corporate statements espoused the value of ethics but whose financial reward systems contributed to performance pressures that encouraged unethical behaviour. The firm's human resources management system had a practice of ranking employees based on performance and then "yanking" or firing the lowest-ranking employees.[41] Ironically, lucrative rewards for performance and innovation were keys to Enron's early success and growth, before excesses in pursuit of these goals contributed to the ethical failures that ultimately destroyed the company. Managers need to be attentive to precisely which behaviours their organization's reward systems reinforce. Sometimes the unintended consequences of a seemingly reasonable reward system can undermine the ethical behaviour of employees.

Ethical climate describes the informal shared perceptions of what are appropriate practices and procedures.

Ethical culture consists of the formal and informal systems aimed at influencing the ethical behaviour of organizational members.

Code of ethics is a formal written statement of an organization's primary values and the ethical rules it expects its members to follow.

Organizational leaders shape the formal system that supports ethical behaviour, but their influence as role models is especially important in communicating *informal* expectations.[42] If they model ethical behaviour, they are ethical leaders who demonstrate "normatively appropriate conduct through personal actions and interpersonal relationships."[43] That is, ethical leadership is more than talk; it is the walk of leaders. The ethical behaviour of top leaders is particularly important because their influence trickles down throughout the organization and ultimately influences all members.[44]

Within both large and small organizations, employees are acutely aware of their bosses' ethical strengths and lapses. SNC-Lavalin, a construction and engineering services firm, is still recovering from a number of ethical scandals and regulatory and criminal investigations stemming from actions taken over the past several years. Unethical behaviour such as bribery had become commonplace within the organization and was frequently rationalized as simply "part of doing business." In an attempt to turn around the company's reputation. Andreas Pohlmann was hired as the new Chief Compliance Officer, not only to ensure that SNC-Lavalin's decisions erred on the right side of the law, but also to reintroduce ethical business practices and decision making to the organization.[45] Ultimately, the importance of trust and maintaining a good track record are the foundations for conducting business where consistently rewarding ethical behaviour, disciplining unethical conduct at all levels, and setting realistic performance goals for others are crucial components of ethical leadership.

The conventional approach to ethics often focuses on creating systems that identify and punish unethical behaviour, after giving fair warning of the consequences. It assumes that a person's misconduct comes from rational calculations about the likelihood of getting caught and the severity of the punishment compared to the potential "benefits" of misconduct.[46] Focusing on deterrence can simply draw attention to opportunities for unethical behaviour, however. For example, what are you tempted to do when a sign says "Do not touch" or a package label states "Do not open"? Sometimes surveillance systems and threats of punishment can turn employees against the company because they do not feel they are trusted, or it can cause them to base a decision on how likely they are to get caught and not on whether their behaviour is ethical.[47]

A sustainable approach also involves deterring unethical behaviour, but it tends to focus more on promoting positive behaviour than on prevention and punishment. This difference between sustainable and conventional ethics is evident in the way sustainable companies run their ethics training. Whereas conventional training primarily focuses on what *not* to do, sustainable training points to positive role models of ethical behaviour and shared values in order to guide behaviour.[48] This positive training creates a self-fulfilling prophecy, focusing attention on and influencing the desirable ways people act.[49]

Sustainable companies celebrate ethical behaviour, even if it may cause loss of sales or profits in the short term. For example, the manager of a Brazilian medical supply business that emphasizes treating stakeholders, including competitors, with dignity, tells the following story:

> Our competitors are shocked by the fact that we are happy to show them how we work—and they try to do the same. They don't manage to copy our way of working, however, because it is not a formula that says "do this," "do that" . . . it is a way of being, a way of acting.
>
> Last year there was a competitor who tried to attack us on every corner . . . creating a very difficult situation for our business. At a certain point, the law in Brazil changed and it was a very important change. In order to help this other business, we faxed the news to them. The business owner was so struck by our gesture that he not only wanted to reestablish his friendship with us, but he offered to help us in areas that we find difficult. It was through him that we had the idea of getting in a consultancy—the best decision that we ever made. That consultant was so impressed by how we run our business that he goes out of his way to help us in whatever way he can. This all started through responding to the aggression of our competitors with a different attitude.[50]

●●●● ●B in Action

Business Ethics and Personal Standards of Honesty

©Zorani/iStockphoto

In a series of studies that involved tempting participants to cheat on a task that required solving math problems for pay, a majority of participants were dishonest in reporting their results. Adjusting the risk of being caught had little effect on the results, but when people were asked to consider their own standards of honesty before beginning the task, cheating was completely eliminated.

People's standards of honesty come from a variety of sources, including their family of origin and their personal philosophies. Religion has also shown itself to be a primary source of standards for some people. Even though a study of 1,522 Canadians found that only 42 percent deemed religion to be an important aspect of their lives, for these individuals, religious beliefs can influence their workplace ethics. For example, most major religions include the values of avoiding harm to others and acting honestly, which research has linked to ethical intentions and actions. On the flip side, other studies point to particular religious beliefs as being associated with discriminating against others in the workplace. Some scholars argue that failing to consider the influence of religion and the appropriate expression of religious views in the workplace does a disservice to our understanding of ethics in organizations.

QUESTIONS FOR DISCUSSION

1. What is your primary source of ethics?
2. Do you think that religious beliefs have an influence on ethical behaviour in organizations?
3. Do you think the study of organizational ethics should include religious beliefs?

Finally, sustainable OB promotes a broader set of ethical behaviours for multiple stakeholders, to counter the narrow focus on promoting financial well-being for shareholders. Kenneth Goodpaster claims that having an excessive focus on one primary goal is evidence of **teleopathy**, a disease *(pathy)* that entails an addiction to the unbalanced pursuit of a single purpose *(teleo)*.[51] Employees who fixate on financial goals are prone to rationalize the supreme worth of these goals over others and, ultimately, are likely to detach themselves from their normal ethical inclinations. A person with teleopathy may indeed be loyal, driven, dedicated, and enthusiastic, but encouraging such traits in excess can be detrimental to the individual and the organization.[52] A sustainable perspective considers goals that support relationships with a broad range of its stakeholders instead. For example, the German shoe company Adidas-Salomon has rigorous standards for working conditions and environmental sustainability that it contractually requires its suppliers to meet.[53]

Teleopathy is an addiction to the unbalanced pursuit of a single purpose or goal.

Attitudes and Commitments

ETHICS **ATTITUDES** PERCEPTIONS EMOTIONS

> **LEARNING OBJECTIVE 2**
> Explain attitudes and commitments and their influence on performance and turnover.

Attitudes and commitments are some of the most studied states of individuals. Who or what we like and feel attached to are important predictors of organizational behaviours such as performance and turnover.

Attitudes

Attitudes are summary evaluations of a particular object or person.[54] For example, some people are in the state of having a bad attitude toward or are dissatisfied with their experience in their job, while others have a good attitude or are satisfied with their job. Some early

Attitudes are summary evaluations of a particular object or person.

descriptions of attitudes used an **ABC framework** in which attitudes toward an object consist of *A*ffect (how you feel about it), *B*ehavioural intentions (what you plan to do), and *C*ognitions (what you think about it).[55] Others have argued that these ABC factors are instead the *result* of an attitude. In any case, job attitudes are very important to organizations because they help explain job performance, organizational citizenship behaviour, turnover, and who shows up late for work or not at all.[56]

Unlike values and beliefs, which apply more broadly to a variety of situations, attitudes are directed toward something or someone specific. We may like one boss but not another, or we may be satisfied with one job and dissatisfied with a different one. That's not to say that attitudes are not influenced by our disposition or personal characteristics, because they are to some degree,[57] but they are also influenced by the characteristics of the object in question. In other words, you can be generally very cheerful and optimistic but still take issue with and dislike a boss because of that person's characteristics and your experiences with him or her. Perhaps you have experienced a boss like the late Ted Rogers, the media mogul who founded Rogers Communications, where he was the self-proclaimed head of the "department of discontent."[58] He felt that his criticisms and high standards pushed his employees and, by extension, his company forward. Rogers became well-known for his 24/7 work ethic and for expecting the same of his senior management team, to the point where he would call them even at odd hours of the night. At one point at the company's head office, there was even a dartboard with Rogers's face on it.[59] Clearly, some employees had developed negative feelings toward their boss.

Job satisfaction is a person's general attitude toward his or her job or job experiences. It is an important attitude in organizations because of its positive relationship with performance and its negative relationship with withdrawal behaviours like laziness, absenteeism, and turnover.[60] As the adage goes, "A happy employee is a productive employee." Research also has shown that a satisfied employee makes customers happy.[61] It is no wonder that leaders of organizations invest time and money in conducting employee satisfaction surveys. The influence of job satisfaction on work behaviour can depend on the importance of the job to the person. **Job involvement** is the extent to which a person thinks about, is immersed in, and is concerned about his or her job.[62] The relationship between job satisfaction and job involvement is discussed further in the My OB feature—What Makes a Job Satisfying?

A sustainable perspective views job satisfaction as valuable beyond its benefits to the organization. For example, job satisfaction is a key contributor to overall life satisfaction for employees.[63] The sustainable approach seeks to improve job satisfaction not only or even primarily because it increases productivity, but also because providing satisfying and meaningful work enhances the life of organizational members and improves community well-being. Think of a world where people are less stressed by their work, where they come home at the end of their shift more satisfied with their jobs. What effect would these attitudes have on customers, neighbourhoods, families, and individual employees' physical and mental health? Promoting positive attitudes creates a virtuous cycle of positive benefits for the bottom line and beyond.[64]

What contributes to job satisfaction? It could be pay, the potential for promotion, the characteristics of the job, your boss or co-workers, or the attitude you bring into the job. Being rewarded for your performance and having opportunities to be promoted do positively influence job satisfaction.[65] Although it seems reasonable to think that pay and promotions are the top concerns for employees, it turns out that the characteristics of the job itself are even bigger contributors. Is the job interesting, challenging, and meaningful, and does it offer variety, autonomy, and feedback? If so, job satisfaction is likely to be high.[66] Fitting well with a sustainable perspective, higher levels of teamwork, training, and participation are strong contributors to job satisfaction.[67] Opportunities to live out one's calling, serve the community, or preserve the environment can also contribute to job satisfaction.[68]

M⊘B | WHAT MAKES A JOB SATISFYING?

Discovery Channel/Photofest

Mike Rowe, host of Discovery Channel's *Dirty Jobs*, made an interesting discovery. After years of viewing work as just the stuff between vacations, he learned through rubbing shoulders with those who do the dirty work of society that those employees are often "happier than the rest of us." This may be hard to believe, looking at the work these folks do, but it also points to the possibility that there may be more to certain jobs than meets the eye.

Research indicates that the characteristics of a job are the strongest determinant of job satisfaction across different positions and countries. More specifically, these are the factors that are classically viewed as being critical to employee motivation and, by extension, job satisfaction: the extent to which the job utilizes an employee's skills and abilities, how much the employee is able to identify with the final output, whether the job contributes to a broader purpose, the ability of the employee to carry out the work as he or she sees fit, and the employee's awareness of the results of his or her work.

QUESTIONS FOR REFLECTION

1. Have you ever had a job that you felt that anyone, no matter how unskilled, could do? How satisfied were you with that job? What changes would have been necessary to make the job more satisfying for you?
2. What have been some of the main reasons you decided to stay in a particular job in the past? Was it based solely on pay, your co-workers, or any other factors?

Leaders also play an important role in employees' job satisfaction, beyond the policies and employment practices they promote in the workplace. Leaders who act ethically, treat others with respect, and are inclusive and fair contribute to employee satisfaction.[69] Finally, the attributes a person brings to the workplace also make a difference. When people bring to their job a strong sense of hope, optimism, efficacy, and resiliency, they are more likely to report experiencing high levels of job satisfaction, organizational commitment, and psychological well-being.[70]

Commitments

Workplace commitments are sometimes referred to as work attitudes, and they share similarities in predicting behaviours such as absenteeism, turnover, performance, perseverance, and willingness to go the extra mile.[71] Yet commitments are distinct from attitudes when you go beyond a summary evaluation. **Commitments** are attachments or bonds to people, actions, or organizations.[72] Individuals can have a variety of commitments within a work environment, some strong and others weak. For example, people can be committed to their co-workers but not to their organization, or they can be committed to the organization but not to a particular organizational change. Commitments also form for different reasons.

> **Commitments** are attachments or bonds to people, actions, or organizations.

One popular and well-researched model describes workplace commitment as originating from three main sources:

- Attitudes (affective commitments—I want to)
- Obligations (normative commitments—I ought to)
- Limited alternatives (continuance commitments—I have to)[73]

Organizational commitment is an attachment or bond to a particular organization.[74] Commitment to an organization can result in lower turnover costs and increased personal and group productivity.[75] Members with *affective commitment* are the most motivated to contribute positively to the organization by willingly exerting effort, helping others, and

> **Organizational commitment** is an attachment or bond to a particular organization.

making creative contributions.[76] This bond is likely to form when members feel that the organization's values fit with their own personal values. Also, offering opportunities to participate in decisions, support for growth and advancement, fair rewards, and interesting jobs are among the top organizational practices that contribute to affective commitment.[77]

If an organization can create a sense of obligation by providing fair exchanges of pay for performance, the resulting *normative commitment* can motivate extra effort, helping, and creativity, but not to the extent that affective commitment does. Enhancing commitment by reducing employees' *alternatives,* say by offering attractive benefit packages or entering into non-compete contracts with employees, does little to motivate behaviour beyond what's needed to meet minimal expectations, but it does reduce turnover.[78] Indeed, it has been suggested that a bond based on being stuck in a situation is not a commitment at all but instead may be closer to coercion.[79]

A sustainable approach to organizational commitment involves building bonds by emphasizing values associated with building community and having a long-term positive effect on society. Research affirms that building community through teamwork positively influences organizational commitment.[80] The consulting firm Accenture promotes the value of community by investing in cutting-edge technologies that allow employees to connect with each other and still maintain flexibility in their work and travel schedules, leaving more time for their personal interests and needs.[81] Accenture has also embarked on a broad program of collaboration outside the company that provides job skills and business development expertise to community members. Showing this kind of support for community within and beyond the organization is likely to increase affective organizational commitment among the company's workforce.

Perceptions are the subjective interpretations we give to information and messages we receive from sensory inputs.

Perceptions

The state of what individuals are thinking about what they are experiencing in organizations is their perceptions. Perceptions are what you think about the information you see, hear, and experience, whereas emotions, which are described in the next section, are the ways you feel about those inputs. Perceptions are relatively dynamic because, as information and experiences change, so do perceptions. Still, we know that some perceptions can be hard to change (e.g., your first impression of a person who was a jerk) and some emotions can have lingering effects (e.g., when a person "blows up" in anger over something that turns out to be a misunderstanding).

Perceptions are the subjective interpretations we give to information and messages we receive from sensory inputs. For example, what do you see in Figure 4.4?

One person sees a white vase while another sees the profiles of two faces looking at each other. If you only saw one initially, the additional information can help you change your perception. Similarly, perceptions are relatively dynamic in that they can change based on more information, new experiences, or training. Our perception of something is shaped by our own unique perspective, the characteristics of the target, and other influences that can help or hinder the perceptual process, such as time to observe or motivation to make an accurate interpretation. For example, the power or status of a person can influence interpretations, with more powerful people being less accurate in their interpretations of the social network within a group.[82] One possible

FIGURE 4.4 The Pictures We Perceive

explanation is that those with more power don't need to understand the social relationships as much as others do to get what they want.

In perceptions about people (person perceptions), two main influences on interpretations are the way the perceiver categorizes the person (called the "target actor") and the way the target actor behaves. It is generally reasonable to assume that more time observing the person could make perceptions more accurate, but that is not necessarily the case.[83] In the Jane Austen novel *Sense and Sensibility,* sisters Marianne and Elinor argue over their interpretation of a suitor named Willoughby. Elinor asserts the traditional view that the character of Willoughby cannot be accurately determined because they have not known him for very long. Marianne disagrees, saying that despite only a few encounters with him, she feels she knows him well. Marianne's interpretation is likely influenced by her categorizing Willoughby as similar to someone she knows very well. If indeed the two are similar, her interpretation may be accurate. As a way of making sense of all the input we receive that we must base our interpretations on, we use this kind of categorization as a cognitive shortcut. If, in our initial impression, a person seems similar to a category of people we have in our minds, we associate that person with the characteristics of the category.

Person perceptions related to interpreting behaviour are **attributions**, our explanations of the causes of behaviours or performance. For example, research suggests that most people make their attributions and react to a co-worker who is performing poorly by answering two unspoken questions.[84] The first question, as noted previously, is whether the poor performance is the fault of the person in question; that is, whether it's due to an internal factor or an external factor. If the person seems to be the source, a second question comes into play, asking whether the behaviour is controllable (it springs from motivation) or not controllable (it results from a lack of ability). If the problem is a lack of ability, team members are more willing to help, whereas if motivation is considered to be the problem, team members will seek to punish the poor performer.[85]

<aside>**Attributions** are people's explanations of the causes of behaviours or performance.</aside>

The person being perceived (that is, the target actor) can also try to influence the perception process in others through **impression management**, which is an active attempt to limit or influence the information that the perceiver receives. Common impression management techniques include self-promotion tactics like talking about personal accomplishments and claiming responsibility for positive events, or agreeing with and flattering the perceiver. Impression management can contribute to higher performance ratings and positive emotions toward the actor, but it also can backfire if it includes deception.[86] Cultural differences, described in chapter 2, may influence the use of impression management tactics. There is some evidence that workers from cultural backgrounds with high power distance view impression management as more appropriate and necessary to earn the approval of those above them in the organization.[87] Yet willingness to use impression management may not extend to telling lies. Students with high power distance were less willing to lie to earn a positive impression than were students from a culture with low power distance.[88]

<aside>**Impression management** is an actor's active attempt to limit or influence the information that the perceiver receives.</aside>

Often people's perceptions of a target actor or an issue differ, and when this happens it can create conflict and contribute to misunderstandings. In groups, differing perceptions can cause conflict, destroy confidence in the group's ability to function, and reduce members' desire to work with each other.[89] One reason people's perceptions can disagree is that our perceptions are not as accurate as we may like to believe. Here are some perceptual errors or biases most people commit at one time or other:

- Representativeness: assessing something based on its similarity to a typical (representative) person or experience instead of on the unique characteristics of the current situation

- Anchoring and adjustment: failing to sufficiently adjust a judgment from an initial impression (an anchor), even in the face of contrary evidence

- Halo/horn effects: using one piece of known information—good or bad—to influence general perceptions
- Availability: relying on memorable information—dramatic or recent—to make judgments
- Selective perception: screening out information that contradicts an existing perception
- Fundamental attribution error: attributing the source of another's behaviour or performance to personal factors instead of to the situation itself

Relying on *representativeness* can be helpful when what is being judged is similar to a representative person or experience that comes to mind, but it also can bias perceptions. For example, when we judge a person from a particular culture based on the typical person we have experienced in the past who is from that culture or the cultural categories described in chapter 2, this can be helpful to aid understanding, but it also can distort reality by inaccurately stereotyping people and deemphasizing their individuality. As we noted in our discussion of diversity, stereotyping people can dramatically influence our behaviour toward them. Stereotypes also strongly influence first impressions. The perceptual error of *anchoring and adjustment* comes into play when people get stuck on their first impression and are slow to make the appropriate adjustments in their thinking, even after getting more information.

Halo/horn effects and *availability* biases are rooted in limitations in the information we possess or our memory. When we make judgments about others, we rely upon the information we have available or what we can remember. If what we know about a person happens to be positive, even if the only interaction we've had with them is a friendly conversation in the hallway, the "halo" of this positive impression carries over to the areas where we lack information. If we know something negative about a person, such as his or her poor performance on a school project, we often apply the "horn" of this negative impression when forming our overall impression of the person. Additionally, our perceptions are shaped by what we remember. People tend to remember something because it recently occurred or the experience was particularly positive or negative, but overemphasizing this information when making a judgment is an availability bias.[90] Some students have figured this out and try to increase their participation in class near the end of semester in order to make a positive impression right before grades for class participation are decided. In the workplace, a variety of situations call for judgments that may be influenced by these biases. In chapter 6, we consider the potential of these biases and others to influence decisions in performance appraisals.

Selective perception occurs across a variety of situations. Although it can help us navigate the constant bombardment of information we all face, only attending to select information can blind us to important information. Selection perception is driven by our general desire to avoid **cognitive dissonance**, the uncomfortable mental state we experience if a current perception, belief, or behaviour conflicts with a past perception, deeply held belief, or previous behaviour.[91] A surefire, though not always wise, way to avoid this tension is to consider or focus only on information that is consistent with what we already believe. This is why faulty perceptions, particularly if held by the majority of organizational members, can persist despite contradictory evidence. Unfortunately, the drive to maintain consistency is the reason for many poor decisions.

The *fundamental attribution error* is the bias of attributing others' behaviour or performance to personal factors, like personality or effort, instead of to the situation in which it occurred.[92] People also tend to make this error by attributing their success to their own actions, but when it comes to their failures they tend to take situational factors into consideration. The tendency to alter attributions based on whether a person is judging herself or someone else is called the *actor-observer bias*.[93] You might make an internal attribution when a team member turns in a portion of a group project late (poor work ethic), but if you

Cognitive dissonance is the uncomfortable mental state we experience if a current perception, belief, or behaviour conflicts with a past perception, deeply held belief, or previous behaviour.

OB in Action — Deceptive First Impressions

Jeff J Mitchell/Getty Images

When Susan Boyle first stepped onto the stage to compete in *Britain's Got Talent*, she was derided by the audience and judges because their first impressions were based on Boyle's old-fashioned appearance, quirky comments onstage, and lofty aspirations. Thankfully, instead of being dismissed, as often occurs in organizations, she was given an opportunity to sing and immediately wowed the audience with her fantastic voice.

Boyle went on to record the strongest debut album ever for a female artist, selling 8.3 million copies of *I Dreamed a Dream*. As her incredible talent and top spot in global album sales for 2009 attest, it can be a big mistake to judge a book by its cover.

QUESTIONS FOR DISCUSSION

1. Do you have an example of making an initial judgment about a person that was proven inaccurate?
2. What contributed to your first impression?
3. When are first impressions harmful to an organization or its members?
4. How might first impressions be helpful to an organization or its members?

have to turn in your part late you might attribute it to an external cause (you were assigned a more difficult part of the project).

The likelihood of a perceptual bias or error affecting a person's judgment is also influenced by cultural factors. For example, in a study comparing Asian and American managers' attributions of others, Asians were more likely to make external attributions because their thinking process took into account a broader amount of information and considered interdependencies in the work environment.[94]

A sustainable OB approach to perception has several notable characteristics. First, it is more likely to consider diverse perspectives and sources of information. A person with a sustainable perspective may not avoid all the pitfalls of perceptual biases, but he or she can minimize the negative use of stereotypes and selective perception by seeking out more information about individual people, including the relatively quiet voices of marginalized members within a community. Second, a sustainable perspective may help to loosen perceptual anchors and appropriately adjust perceptions of others based on new information. In fact, while inviting cognitive dissonance by seeking new information can make for a life lived in greater tension, it also makes us better able to understand others and come up with creative ideas.[95]

Emotions

ETHICS | ATTITUDES | PERCEPTIONS | **EMOTIONS**

> **LEARNING OBJECTIVE 4**
> Discuss emotions, how they determine behaviour, and their importance in an organization.

Emotions are another important state people experience that influences their behaviour. The state of what a person feels is often more important in determining his or her behaviour than what the person thinks.[96] For example, when team members have to work together, anger and sympathy are more important than rational factors in predicting how they will respond to poor performers.[97]

Emotions are affective states that arise in response to information or messages a person receives from specific sensory inputs. Affective states can be linked to specific targets or they can be more general, without clear ties to a person or circumstance. Your frustration with your roommate for eating all of your home-baked goodies is an emotion, for instance. A *mood* is more general, such as the feeling of being generally annoyed. Consistent with the saying about "waking up on the wrong side of the bed," moods at the start of the day do influence how a person perceives interactions and acts toward others.[98] Emotions are usually more intense than moods, while moods tend to last a bit longer and are influenced to some degree by personality. A person who is often or generally in a happy and optimistic mood likely has the personality trait of positive affect, and a person who is generally in an unhappy or cynical mood likely has the personality trait of negative affect.[99]

One of the reasons that emotions and moods are important in organizations is that they are contagious.[100] For example, a leader's mood can influence the performance of a group of sales representatives who are under his or her supervision.[101] Negative emotion can spread like a disease, creating an unhealthy and energy-sapping work environment, but positive emotion can feel like a breath of fresh air that invigorates the work environment with energy and optimism.

Your own displays of emotion influence how others react to you. For example, showing anger can make men seem more authoritative, whereas it can cause women to be perceived as incompetent and out of control.[102] The mismanagement of emotions can create a toxic work environment of stress, burnout, as well as low levels of job performance and employees' sense of personal well-being.[103] It can be tempting to avoid, ignore, or remove those who contribute to these situations; however, from a sustainable perspective, toxic emotions may be a sign of an underlying issue that requires attention. The following actions can help to detoxify undesirable work situations:[104]

- Focused listening—Give others your undivided attention and hear them out.
- Create breathing room—Provide others with a temporary reduced workload or time off or away from stressful conditions in order to work through their emotions.
- Buffer the pain—Intercept toxic messages and translate them into less inflammatory or accusatory language.
- Remove the problem—Relieve people from emotionally toxic positions or relationships.
- Transform the problem—Commit to helping others learn from and change a toxic situation.

The capability to display and manage positive emotions is essential for those who occupy the large number of service-oriented jobs in many organizations. **Emotional labour** is a term given to the display and management of appropriate emotion as part of fulfilling job responsibilities.[105] Most of us have had the experience of working in a job where it is important to be positive and express concern for customers. For example, salespeople are directed to smile, offer a warm "hello," and say "thank you" because these positive expressions increase customers' satisfaction and the likelihood of their returning to the store and recommending it to others (see Disney opening case, Chapter 13).[106] The dark side of this emotional expectation is that if being positive is required when a person actually feels negative, the resulting emotional dissonance can be exhausting and may lead to a sense of depersonalization whereby the employee treats customers as objects instead of people.[107]

Some people are clearly better at recognizing and managing emotions than others. **Emotional intelligence (EI)** is the innate or developed capability to recognize, manage, and exercise emotions in relationships.[108] EI is generally described as having four main components:

- Self-awareness
- Self-management
- Empathy
- Use of emotion (internal motivation and social skills)

Emotional *self-awareness* is the ability to recognize when emotional responses are triggered and what triggers them. *Self-management* of emotions is the skill of harnessing emotions to positively influence interactions with others. *Empathy* allows us to read non-verbal messages and to understand the emotional content of others' communications. The *use of emotion* can be broken down into at least two areas. Internal motivation lets us summon emotional energy to get something started and persevere through difficulties, and social skills help us use emotion to establish strong connections with and influence others.

People with high EI are generally more satisfied with their jobs and perform better across a variety of jobs. The influence of EI on performance is particularly important when the job includes emotional labour.[109] In those cases, having higher levels of EI positively influences performance, enhances commitment, and reduces turnover.[110] And a leader with high EI contributes to followers experiencing higher levels of satisfaction and indicating a greater willingness to go beyond their job descriptions to fulfill organizational goals. We'll discuss the important role of EI in leaders again in chapter 9. For now, consider how managing emotions is portrayed in the next My OB feature.

A sustainable perspective is more likely to value emotions that may not seem to enhance productivity or that are messy and difficult to quantify. It's a perspective that believes people are more than the sum of their job-related abilities and skills. In particular, a sustainable approach is much less likely to promote the emotional labour practice of faking positive emotion. Acting out emotions that are not truly felt contributes to dissatisfaction and emotional burnout, particularly among employees who believe in expressing authentic emotions and who question their ability to fake.[111] Rather than telling employees what emotions to exhibit, a sustainable approach will work toward creating a work environment in which the desired emotions develop naturally and are genuinely expressed. Taking a more holistic approach to individuals in organizations is a hallmark of sustainable thinking.

M♡B | WHEN MANAGING EMOTIONS MATTERS

Samuel Goldwyn/Photofest

In the 2008 movie *Management*, Mike Flux (Steve Zahn) has a difficult time controlling his emotions toward Sue Claussen (Jennifer Aniston), who is a guest at his parents' motel. Mike is the night manager and, after meeting Sue, he makes several impulsive decisions, some of which are better received than others. Ultimately, after Mike travels a long distance to pursue Sue, she sends him away because she doesn't want to have a relationship with someone who is impulsive. In this sense, Mike wasn't a good "manager" of his emotions.

Managing your emotions can have a number of benefits personally and professionally, including contributing to your own performance and to the job satisfaction of those you lead.

QUESTIONS FOR REFLECTION

1. How have emotions influenced your relationships with other students, friends, or co-workers?
2. In what tasks or jobs has managing your emotions been the most important to your success?

the power of the powerless[112]

Odd Anderson/AFP/Getty Images

Leymah Gbowee had a relatively pleasant childhood growing up in Liberia, Africa, and was looking forward to her first year in university. Then the First Liberian Civil War started, throwing her country into chaos and bloodshed. For a while, Gbowee lived as a homeless refugee in Ghana, and because she was almost starving, she experienced a "crippling hopelessness" that was destroying herself and her family. Her attitude and perceptions changed thanks to a comment from her 5-year-old son, prompting her to become an active agent for peace and social change. She decided to return to Liberia with her three young children.

Soon Gbowee was holding several jobs in organizations related to aspects of peacebuilding. She would attend related conferences and had developed a network of colleagues and mentors in this area. Although there had already been fragmented and uncoordinated attempts by women to promote peace in Liberia starting in the early 1990s, this changed "when women became completely exasperated with the situation and decided to take more coordinated and systemic action with clearly defined objectives."[113] In 2001, Gbowee and several other women founded WIPNET (Women in Peacebuilding Network), the only organization in Africa that focused only on peace and only on women.

WIPNET had humble beginnings and lacked resources, and Gbowee became its unpaid leader. An early success was establishing a presence at an outdoor fish market, where women wore white T-shirts (symbolizing peace) with the WIPNET logo and handed out emotion-provoking flyers that said: "We are tired! We are tired of our children being killed! We are tired of being raped! Women, wake up—you have a voice in the peace process!"[114]

In a very risky move, the group (illegally) occupied a large soccer field that Liberia's ruthless president at the time, Charles Taylor, passed by twice daily. Eventually it provoked him to meet with them and hear their message. That meeting helped lead President Taylor to agree to attend 2003 peace talks with representatives from the rebel groups he was at war with.

Those peace talks showed little progress in the first few months, even though Gbowee and a delegation of several hundred women gathered daily outside the hotel to hold the negotiators accountable. As violence was continuing in Liberia, Gbowee sent a message to the lead mediator informing him that the women were intending to hold negotiators "hostage" in their meeting room until a peace agreement was reached inside. To achieve this, the women remained seated in the hallways outside of the room, arms interlocked. When the men tried to leave the meeting room, Leymah and other women threatened to take their clothes off in protest. Realizing the seriousness of this threat, the negotiators agreed to complete the peace process within two weeks, and they did so.

When one of the rebel warlords was asked about the role the women played in bringing peace, he said, "Those women? Those women were nothing—they were only our conscience." When asked why Gbowee's threat to disrobe could have such an effect, he answered:

> Because they were our mothers. . . . You have to imagine what would drive your mother to do such a thing, to strip, to offer to cast off her last shred of dignity like that. When they did that there was not one man in that room who did not ask himself, no matter what he had done during the conflict, "What have I done to bring us to this place?"[115]

But Gbowee and the other women were not naïve enough to believe that their work was finished; many peace treaties have been signed only to fail. And so they made great efforts to ensure that Liberia would have a democratic election and that women would register to vote. For example, at one point,

two hundred women were deployed in teams of 20 to the ten counties to encourage women to register. To facilitate this, the women volunteered to baby sit, undertake domestic chores, and assist with selling at the market. Five days later . . . the total number of registered female voters [had risen] to 51%. The women then mobilized support for Ellen Johnson-Sirleaf, who . . . was elected as President of the Republic of Liberia in November 2005.[116]

By 2011, Liberia had moved up 13 places from the bottom of the UN Human Development Index, and the country's females had begun to catch up to men in terms of access to education. Also that year, President Sirleaf was re-elected and she, Leymah Gbowee, and Twawkkul Karman (of Yemen) were awarded the Nobel Peace Prize.

QUESTIONS FOR DISCUSSION

1. How does this case demonstrate states of ethics? What do you think are the ethics of the various people in this case? Use concepts from this chapter to defend your answers.

2. In this case there are many commitments expressed. Identify what you think are the key commitments and their bases.

3. What are some of the important perceptions in the case? Which, if any, changed and how?

4. There had been many peacemaking attempts in Liberia before WIPNET was created. Why was WIPNET so influential?

5. What was the role of emotions in this case? Which expressions of emotion were appropriate, and which were inappropriate? How did you decide?

Summary

At least four states are helpful for understanding individuals.

 Learning Objectives

- Describe ethics and how organizational characteristics affect ethical behaviour.
- Explain attitudes and commitments and their influence on performance and turnover.

- Discuss perceptions and their effect on information received in an organization.

- Discuss emotions, how they determine behaviour, and their importance in an organization.

From a conventional OB perspective:

- Ethics emphasizes focusing on the greatest financial outcomes for the most stakeholders.
- Attitudes and commitments are important to understand because they contribute to individual and organizational performance.
- Perceptions that are accurate can be beneficial, but welcoming dissonance and diverse perceptions may enhance creativity.
- Emotions need to be controlled to avoid negative outcomes and achieve positive outcomes in the workplace.

From a sustainable OB perspective:

- Ethics emphasizes focusing on being of virtuous character and on benefits for multiple stakeholders.
- Attitudes and commitments are important to understand because they contribute to individual and community well-being.
- Perceptions should be accurate to improve predictability and ensure optimal decisions.

- Emotions need to be authentic and should arise naturally from a work environment that values emotion.

Key Terms

ABC framework (p. 76)
Attitudes (p. 75)
Attributions (p. 79)
Code of ethics (p. 73)
Cognitive dissonance (p. 80)
Commitments (p. 77)
Consequentialist theory (p. 71)
Egoism (p. 71)
Emotional intelligence (EI) (p. 82)

Emotional labour (p. 82)
Emotions (p. 82)
Ethical climate (p. 73)
Ethical culture (p. 73)
Ethics (p. 69)
Impression management (p. 79)
Job involvement (p. 76)
Job satisfaction (p. 76)
Moral development (p. 70)

Moral point of view (p. 71)
Organizational commitment (p. 77)
Perceptions (p. 78)
States (p. 69)
Sustaincentrism (p. 72)
Teleopathy (p. 75)
Utilitarianism (p. 71)
Virtues (p. 72)

Questions for Reflection and Discussion

1. Failing to articulate your own moral point of view leaves you vulnerable to wrongly believing that how you behave in organizations has nothing to do with your nature as a moral person.[117] Can you describe the main components of your moral point of view? To whom or to what do you attribute your moral point of view and ethics?

2. Whose responsibility is it to teach ethics? Do you think ethics can and should be taught in school? How about in organizations? Explain your answers.

3. Do you enjoy getting your hands dirty while doing a task? What is satisfying about the kind of work that requires jeans instead of a suit and often results in getting dirty?

4. What have been the most common perceptual errors or biases you have experienced? What were the consequences of these errors or biases?

5. Displaying emotions can be harmful or helpful in a work context. Drawing from your own experience, describe examples showing when it was helpful or harmful for a person to share emotions in a work context. Why was it so?

ob activities

What Is Your Emotional Intelligence?

For each item below, rate how well you are able to display the ability described. Try to think of actual situations in which you have had the opportunity to exercise the ability.

Very Slight Ability		Moderate Ability		Very Large Ability
1	**2**	**3**	**4**	**5**

_____ 1. Understand why you are feeling what you are feeling

_____ 2. Relax when under pressure in situations

_____ 3. "Gear up" at will for a task

_____ 4. Know the impact that your behaviour has on others

_____ 5. Initiate successful resolution of conflict with others

_____ 6. Know when you are becoming angry

_____ 7. Calm yourself quickly when angry

_____ 8. Regroup quickly after a setback

_____ 9. Recognize when others are distressed

_____ 10. Build consensus with others

_____ 11. Know what senses you are currently using

_____ 12. Use internal "talk" to change your emotional state

_____ 13. Enjoy completing challenging tasks

_____ 14. Understand where others' emotions are coming from

_____ 15. Make others feel comfortable around you

_____ 16. Identify when you experience mood shifts

_____ 17. Stay calm when you are the target of anger from others

_____ 18. Stop or change an ineffective habit

_____ 19. Show empathy to others

_____ 20. Provide advice and emotional support to others as needed

_____ 21. Know when you become defensive

_____ 22. Suppress your emotions when they might interfere with work

_____ 23. Follow your words with actions

_____ 24. Accurately reflect people's feelings back to them

_____ 25. Engage in intimate conversations with others

Key: This questionnaire provides some indication of your emotional intelligence. Your score for self-awareness is the total of questions 1, 6, 11, 16, and 21. Your score for emotional self-management is the total of questions 2, 7, 12, 17, and 22. Your score for self-motivation is the total of questions 3, 8, 13, 18, and 23. Your score for empathy is the total of questions 4, 9, 14, 19, and 24. Your score for social skill is the total of questions 5, 10, 15, 20, and 25. Add up your responses to the 25 questions to obtain your overall emotional intelligence score. If you received a total score of 100 or more, you are most certainly a person with high emotional intelligence. A score from 50 to 100 means you have a good platform of emotional intelligence from which to develop your leadership capability. A score below 50 indicates that you realize that you are probably below average in emotional intelligence. Similarly, on the individual levels—self-awareness, managing emotions, motivating one's self, empathy, and social skill—a score above 20 is considered high, while a score below 10 is considered low.

Source: Adapted from Weisinger, H. (1998). Emotional intelligence at work. San Francisco: Jossey-Bass, 214–215.

How Do You Act When No One Is Looking?

Using a scale of 1 – Strongly Disagree (SD), 2 – Disagree (D), 3 – Neutral (N), 4 – Agree (A), and 5 – Strongly Agree (SA), indicate your level of agreement with each statement on the 5-point scale.

Typically, I . . .	SD	D	N	A	SA
1. Am trusted to keep secrets.	1	2	3	4	5
2. Keep my promises.	1	2	3	4	5
3. Lie to get myself out of trouble.	1	2	3	4	5
4. Can be trusted to keep my promises.	1	2	3	4	5
5. Am true to my own values.	1	2	3	4	5

Key: This is a short version of an integrity scale from the International Personality Item Pool (http://ipip.ori.org/). To calculate your total score, add the following:

_____ *(response to statement 1)*

+ _____ *(response to statement 2)*

+ _____ *(response to statement 3, subtracted from 6)*

+ _____ *(response to statement 4)*

+ _____ *(response to statement 5)*

= _____ *Total score*

The greater the score (out of 25 possible), the higher your self-rating on integrity. Although lengthier tests have been used in research and conclusions across studies vary, the general finding is that higher levels of integrity relate to better work performance and lower frequency of counterproductive behaviour such as stealing, lack of effort, substance abuse, or harm to others.[118]

A company paid a $350,000 "consulting" fee to an official in a foreign country. In return, the official promised to assist in obtaining a contract that should produce $10 million in profit for the contracting company.

Why might this scenario occur in organizations?

Use the following scale to indicate whether this behaviour is ethically acceptable:

NEVER ACCEPTABLE		SOMETIMES ACCEPTABLE			ALWAYS ACCEPTABLE	
1	2	3	4	5	6	7

Explain the ideas you considered in arriving at your answer.

DISCUSSION STARTER

YouTubing Ethical Challenges

Have teams create original short videos capturing an ethical challenge. Each video must be between 30 seconds and three minutes. Videos can focus on a workplace or academic ethical dilemma relating to either (1) personal or professional ethics, or (2) an opportunity to act socially responsible or virtuous. The focus could also be narrowed to a specific business discipline such as Information Systems or Accounting. Share your videos with your colleagues.

This could be used as a competition. On a specified day, show all the videos and have students rate each video on (1) relevance to focal topic (the use of information, technology, or media in student life or the workplace); (2) ethicality; and (3) quality, clarity, and creativity. These ratings can contribute to a score on the assignment or be used to identify a winning video. Bring some popcorn to add to the fun!

QUESTIONS FOR DISCUSSION

1. Were there common types of ethical challenges?

2. Which videos captured your attention? Why? Who was the best actor?

DISCUSSION STARTER

Reflections from a U.S. Woman Working in a Filipino Garment Factory[119]

When we put on a shirt, we don't think or feel much about those who made it. When we read a story about poor conditions in a garment factory on the other side of the world, we may take a few moments to feel pity for the workers, no more. But if we experience those conditions firsthand, it can fundamentally affect our ethics, attitudes, perceptions, and emotions. To get this firsthand experience, researchers sometimes use a method called "participant observation."

Patty Wagner, an American who worked on non-governmental democracy projects in the Philippines, conducted a study while working in a factory there. She and her co-workers were creating clothing samples for buyers. She was excited at first to try something new. She made many mistakes with her sewing, and the employer was patient as she ripped out her stitches. Suddenly, though, she realized that the factory was expecting perfection but was paying "slave wages." "If they expect artistry, they should pay for it," she thought.

Wagner and her co-workers worked long hours, up to almost 80 hours a week, without the protection of labour laws or unions. Employees worked what the market demanded. They worked Monday to Friday from 6 a.m. to 6 p.m. On Saturday, they worked from 6 a.m. to 3 p.m. Sundays they started at 6 and finished at 2.

She continually heard stories from the workers that whenever they asked for fair wages and better working conditions, the factories shut down. They earned just $3 to $4 a day for 12 hours of work. Employees would literally never see daylight, spending those hours in the factories. The employees, mostly women, would rarely see their children or husbands, who were also working long hours.

Wagner was touched by the story of a co-worker, Julie. One day, Julie removed her foot from her sewing machine foot pedal while she took out some stitches. She took the opportunity to cross her feet and stretch her ankle. Her supervisor reprimanded her for it. Her supervisor also yelled at her when she laughed or spoke to others nearby. She had to work seven nights a week unless there was a special reason. Julie told Wagner that she was exhausted after just a week of work. Telling Wagner her story, Julie choked up with anger and fatigue, sobbing. Wagner recalled, "I sat beside this woman, holding a pillow to her face to catch the tears, a woman I had never known to weep, and thought, 'I want to remember this moment for the rest of my life.'" She noted that Julie made clothes for Western women that were supposed to make them feel free, but she herself was crying from the pain of work and couldn't even cross her ankles.

QUESTIONS FOR DISCUSSION

1. Do you think operating such factories is ethical? Explain.

2. Reflect on the forms of affective, normative, and continuance organizational commitment that were mentioned in the chapter. How might the workers in the factory differ across these forms?

3. What emotions surfaced when you read this case?

4. Strong emotions can influence behaviour, but what prevents your emotional reaction from turning into action?

APPLICATION JOURNAL

This is a personal journal entry that can be used for class discussion or be compiled and included in a self-reflection paper.

Each of the individual states discussed in this chapter likely influence your behaviour, although perhaps some more than others. Identify the states that you believe strongly contribute to your behaviour and indicate what actions you can take to enhance how each state influences your behaviour.

Five

Motivating
Individuals

Just as some people want to climb mountains, others prefer to hike through rainforests. Still others like to walk along beaches. In the same way, people respond to different motivators in organizations. These differences may exist due to innate needs that people are born with, or they may reflect what individuals have experienced and learned in life. In this chapter, we explore the various influences that motivate people in organizations.

Learning Objectives	Conventional OB	Sustainable OB
INNATE NEEDS		
1. Identify the innate needs of people in organizations.	Satisfy physiological, safety, social, esteem, and self-actualization needs Focus on individual needs	Satisfy a balance of material, social, spiritual, aesthetic, and ecological needs Focus on community needs
DESIRE FOR ACHIEVEMENT		
2. Discuss the need for achievement and how it is satisfied by productivity and accomplishing goals.	Set goals that are specific, measurable, achievable, results-based, and time specific Motivate by increasing a person's sense that "I can do it," "There's something in it for me," and "I value my desired outcomes"	Set goals that are significant, meaningful, agreed upon, relevant, and timely - Motivate by increasing a person's sense that "We can do it," "There's something in it for us," and "We value balanced outcomes"
DESIRE FOR FAIRNESS		
3. Discuss the desire for fairness and how it influences interactions with others in the workplace.	Treat members equitably	Treat stakeholders justly
DESIRE FOR AFFILIATION		
4. Explain the desire for affiliation and its impact on motivation and commitment to an organization.	Promote opportunities to receive affirmation from others and network with others	Promote opportunities to develop shared values and caring relationships
DESIRE FOR POWER		
5. Identify the sources of power and its importance for motivation.	Seek to acquire legitimate, reward, coercive, referent, or expert power	Seek to trust and share power with others

OPENING CASE

brewing motivation at Starbucks[1]

Bloomberg/Getty Images

Starbucks works hard to identify means of unleashing employee enthusiasm. There is plenty of energy at Starbucks, and it's not all due to the caffeine. From its strong benefits program that is made available even to part-time employees to the extensive training it provides, Starbucks very deliberately tries to understand what it takes to ensure its "partners" (as employees are called) are happy and motivated. Sure, partners appreciate receiving the occasional M.U.G. Award (acknowledging Moves of Uncommon Greatness) and Spirit of Starbucks Award for passionate service, but Starbucks has realized that the keys to motivating its partners are ensuring competence, promoting social responsibility, and encouraging ownership. If these conditions are in place, partners tend to work harder and stick around longer.

The long-term value of Starbucks was best served by creating value for employees.

Before stepping into their roles, managers experience 8 to 10 weeks of training, including a course called Coffee Knowledge 101. Following their training, managers, in turn, ensure that all employees are fully trained. Starbucks partners complete 24 hours of training at one of the company's regional training centres before serving up their first cup of coffee. They also learn by observing their managers, who model positive attitudes and superb customer service.

Partners and customers alike find motivation in Starbucks's emphasis on corporate social responsibility. The company's annual Global Responsibility Report sets forth impressive progress in reaching its aspirations to source 100 percent of its coffee from growers who either are Fair Trade Certified or committed to Coffee and Farmer Equity Practices, increase the community service hours of partners to a million hours annually, and engage in a variety of environmentally sensitive initiatives, such as decreasing store usage of water and energy by 25 percent over a seven-year span and increasing store and customer use of recycling. An initiative begun in recent years that is a source of pride to Starbucks partners is a program designed to promote and provide resources for local small businesses that, in turn, can create jobs.

Partners who work at least 20 hours per week are eligible for the company's Your Special Blend benefits program, which is tailored to each employee and can include supplemental health care coverage (which, in Canada, goes beyond the basic government-funded coverage), tuition reimbursements, and stock options, known as "Bean Stock," that give partners an ownership stake in the company's success. Ownership enhances the desire to provide input and promote Starbucks's mission "to inspire and nurture the human spirit—one person, one cup and one neighbourhood at a time." It is a mission based on treating one another with respect and dignity, embracing diversity, enthusiastically satisfying customers, and contributing positively to the community and the environment. If partners sense that the company is drifting away from its mission, the Mission Review program allows them to raise questions, express concerns, and receive answers from managers.

Beginning in 2007, Starbucks experienced a significant downturn in sales during the recession and faced increased competition and other challenges that led some people to forecast its demise. Founder Howard Schultz returned as CEO after eight years serving in the background as chairman of the board, and he redoubled his commitment to living out Starbucks's values. Although he did end up laying off some employees as a result of several hundred store closures, he met with employees throughout the company to explain the long-term plan for the future. At one critical point, when Starbucks was still struggling, a trusted advisor suggested that the company scale back its benefits program, particularly for part-time employees, in order to achieve automatic savings, but Schultz refused. He believed that the long-term value of Starbucks was best served by creating value for employees. So instead, Schultz focused on improving efficiencies and reviving the spirit of innovation within Starbucks.

Starbucks is reaping the benefits of having motivated partners. Like many organizations, it relies heavily on repeat customers to drive its business. In fact, some return as often as 20 times per month. Customers often comment that the partners at Starbucks are always happy and having fun. Regular customers also appreciate that, in comparison to other organizations in the same industry, there is relatively low turnover. (Starbucks's turnover rate is 60 percent, which drops to 10 percent if only voluntary turnover is counted, compared to the industry average of 300 percent.)

You don't need to go to Starbucks to find someone who is motivated. You may know someone who works tirelessly to earn good grades, another person who spends hours tinkering with some new technology just to figure out how it works, another who spends countless hours mentoring kids in the community, and still another who stays up all night playing video games to beat his or her past high score. These people are highly motivated. People who are highly motivated will persist in behaving a certain way. In this chapter, we consider why people behave the way they do, with particular attention given to what they do in organizations.

The study of motivation helps managers better understand what prompts their employees to initiate action, how much effort they exert, and why their effort persists over time. One or more of the theories in this chapter is likely also to help you understand why you are interested in and energized by certain tasks and why you are disinterested in and avoid others. Ideally this understanding will shed some light on why you feel and act the way you do and will provide some ideas for managing your motivation. Although we share basic motivations with others, each of us is unique and our behaviour may not be explained equally well by each theory. Thus we cover a diversity of theories and examples to give you more information and offer ideas to consider in exploring your motivation and others' motivation.

Understanding and managing a person's motivation can be quite challenging because it requires considering a variety of characteristics about the person and the situation. It is similar to how doctors working to diagnose a mysterious condition can see physical symptoms, but the symptoms are caused by a combination of internal characteristics (e.g., a person's unique DNA, body chemistry) and a person's reaction to external influences (e.g., germs exposed to, food consumed). Motivational theories developed to diagnose behaviour have tended to focus on either innate and unconscious needs (the "what" of motivation) or learned and conscious processes (the "why" of motivation).[2] Although most recent theories of motivation are a complex combination of both,[3] for the sake of discussion, our overview of the central theories of motivation begins with innate needs (natural and unconscious) and then moves into developed desires (learned and conscious).

M**Ø**B | UNDERSTANDING MOTIVATION INSIDE-OUT

PETER BROOKER/REX FEATURES

Canadian-born Harley Pasternak is the go-to personal trainer for Hollywood's elite, often being referenced as the "person behind so-and-so's body." But after years of working with celebrities such as Katy Perry, Rihanna, and Megan Fox, as well as CEOs and average clients, Pasternak has learned that he can't motivate his clients in a sustainable way. He cannot (and does not want to) be the one to drag his clients out of bed to a workout or force vegetables down their throats. Ultimately, their motivation must come from within. Pasternak has learned that his main job is to guide his clients through tailored exercise and eating recommendations that will help them achieve *their* goals.

QUESTIONS FOR REFLECTION

1. Consider a time when you were highly motivated to do a job or achieve a goal. Why were you so motivated?
2. Think about a time when you were not motivated. Why were you not motivated? What changes, if made, would have motivated you more?
3. Do you think others would have experienced similar levels of motivation in these two situations? Why or why not?

Innate Needs

| INNATE NEEDS | ACHIEVEMENT | FAIRNESS | AFFILIATION | POWER |

Motivation is a psychological force that helps to explain what arouses, directs, and maintains human behaviour.

Maslow's hierarchy of needs is the theory that people are motivated to satisfy five need levels: physiological, safety, social, esteem, and self-actualization.

ERG theory describes three universal categories of needs: existence, relatedness, and growth.

Motivation is a psychological force that helps explain what arouses, directs, and maintains human behaviour. One of the best-known theories of motivation is **Maslow's hierarchy of needs**. Abraham Maslow argued that people are motivated to satisfy five levels of needs: physiological, safety, social, esteem, and self-actualization needs. He suggested that these constitute a hierarchy, as illustrated in Figure 5.1. The most basic or compelling needs—physical and safety needs—are at the bottom of this hierarchy, and esteem and self-actualization needs are at the top. Although it is no longer highly regarded in academic circles because research has offered little support for it,[4] Maslow's work is worth reviewing, as it has served as a foundation for subsequent theories of motivation.

Maslow believed that people are motivated by unmet needs that are activated in a particular order: lower-order needs always take priority and must be substantially satisfied before higher-order needs are activated. Later research challenged the assumption that needs are satisfied in sequence and found that other factors can explain why needs are activated. For example, the importance of both safety and self-actualization increases with a person's age, while esteem becomes less critical.[5] An additional problem with Maslow's hierarchy is that people from different cultures are likely to have different need categories and hierarchies.[6] Although researchers have questioned the details of Maslow's theory, it provided an initial framework for the types of innate needs that might motivate people.

Clayton Alderfer built on Maslow's work to construct his **ERG theory**,[7] which collapsed the five needs into three universal categories: existence, relatedness, and growth. *Existence* needs correspond to physiological and safety needs. *Relatedness* needs focus on how people relate to their social environment; in Maslow's hierarchy these needs correspond to social needs and the need to earn others' esteem. *Growth* needs—the highest level in the ERG system—are desires for continued psychological growth and development, including the need for self-esteem and for self-actualization.

Self-Actualization needs reflect the desire to realize one's full potential.

Esteem needs reflect the desire for recognition and respect from others.

Social needs reflect the desire to be accepted by peers or part of a group.

Safety needs reflect the desire for security, stability, and protection from physical and emotional harm.

Physiological needs reflect the desire for food, clothing, drink, shelter, and other physical necessities.

FIGURE 5.1 Maslow's Hierarchy of Needs

Alderfer's ERG theory also differs from Maslow's theory in that it does not assume lower-level needs must be satisfied first. According to ERG theory, any or all needs can influence individual behaviour at any given time. Alderfer also introduced the **frustration-regression principle**, which suggests that people who are unable to satisfy higher-order needs will compensate by oversatisfying lower-order needs. For example, a worker who cannot fulfill a need for personal growth may turn his or her attention to deepening relationships at work.

Frederick Herzberg developed his theory of motivation by interviewing employees and asking them to recall occasions on the job when they had been satisfied and motivated and occasions when they had been dissatisfied and unmotivated. Herzberg's findings suggested that the work characteristics associated with dissatisfaction were quite different from those pertaining to satisfaction. That is, two sets of characteristics relating to different needs emerged: hygiene and motivator factors. **Hygiene factors** refer to the presence or absence of sources of *job dissatisfaction*, such as working conditions, pay, company policies, and interpersonal relationships. Generally, these factors relate to the lower-level needs described by Maslow and Alderfer. When hygiene factors are absent, work is dissatisfying. However, the presence of hygiene factors simply removes the dissatisfaction; they do not in and of themselves cause people to become highly satisfied and motivated in their work. **Motivator factors** refer to the presence or absence of sources of *job satisfaction*, such as interesting work, autonomy, responsibility, opportunities to grow and develop on the job, and a sense of accomplishment and achievement. Generally, these factors relate to the higher-order needs described by Maslow and Alderfer.

Although many factors influence both satisfaction and dissatisfaction to some degree, Herzberg's most prominent contribution to management theory was his challenge to the prevailing assumption that pay is the most important motivator. In his research, opportunities for growth and autonomy prevailed over pay.[8] For example, before taking on the role of CEO at Luvo Inc., a young start-up company looking to provide consumers with healthy frozen meals, Christine Day had already built an impressive resumé. She had previously headed up Lululemon Athletica Inc. in her home province of British Columbia, and prior to that she served as a vice-president at Starbucks. Nevertheless, Day stepped down from her role as CEO of Lululemon and joined the much smaller Luvo because she was craving a challenge. She wanted the opportunity to build the organization and its brand, culture, and business model from the ground up.[9] The energy and excitement at start-ups are like no other, and for many people those elements do not compare to pay as a motivator. The excitement at start-ups tends to drive employees and leaders alike to persevere and overcome the numerous challenges that face new businesses. Even though Herzberg's theory and findings continue to be contested and refined, managers can draw on his work to consider the influence of a variety of factors—beyond simply pay—in motivating workers.

Despite concerns about the lack of research support for specific needs-based theories, we can usefully draw a few general conclusions from these theories:

- People have needs and seek to meet those needs, in part, in the context of organizations. Leaders in organizations should consider how to create a work environment that reasonably accommodates these needs.
- Low-level needs are important to people, but higher-level needs are powerful sources of intrinsic motivation. Thus, leaders should not only consider how to create a work environment that provides sufficient pay, safety, and respect, they should also focus on appealing to employees' needs to grow and contribute.

From a sustainable perspective, it is no surprise that empirical research provides limited support for motivation theories like Maslow's hierarchy of needs that emphasize materialist-individualist assumptions such as "self-actualization." This view stands in contrast to the sustainable perspective, which argues for the motivational potential of balancing a

Frustration-regression principle suggests that people who are unable to satisfy higher-order needs will compensate by focusing on oversatisfying lower-order needs.

Hygiene factors refer to the presence or absence of sources of job dissatisfaction.

Motivator factors refer to the presence or absence of sources of job satisfaction.

variety of needs and sees long-term meaningful relationships as more sustainable sources of motivation. Evidence exists to support the assertion that we all have a natural need or innate motivation to contribute to group goals, but this tendency is often overridden or displaced by an organizational focus on individual interests or rewards.[10]

Recall from chapter 1 that, from Aristotle's perspective, true happiness cannot be achieved at the individual level of analysis (via self-actualization). Rather, it comes from practising the four cardinal virtues of practical wisdom, justice, courage, and self-control in community. Put in terms of motivation, Aristotle's theory essentially argues that people will be motivated when they participate in an organization in which members practise and experience the four virtues. Extending the argument a bit further, from a sustainable perspective, everyone has an innate need to practise and experience the following virtues:

- *Practical wisdom*—evident in foresight and actions in the interests of the community
- *Justice*—evident when all stakeholders connected with an organization get their due
- *Courage*—evident when actions improve overall happiness, even at a threat to self
- *Self-control*—evident when members overcome impulsive actions and the self-serving use of power

This is quite different from Maslow's idea of satisfying one need before other needs are activated; likewise, it differs from Alderfer's frustration-regression principle that people unable to satisfy higher-order needs will oversatisfy lower-order ones. A sustainable approach also recognizes and supports motivating people through meaningful work and opportunities to grow, but it favours a balance of hygiene factors and motivators, recognizing that hygiene factors make contributions toward building community and dignifying members even if these factors do not seem to have a direct link to the organization's performance.[11] For example, a program at eBay allows employees to meet with a company chef during work hours to plan a week's worth of take-home meals.[12] This is intended to de-stress employees by making nutritious meals simpler and more available.

McClelland's acquired needs theory states that certain types of needs or desires are acquired during an individual's lifetime.

A well-known conceptual framework for understanding motivation, and the one that we will use as a basis to organize the remainder of our chapter, comes from **McClelland's acquired needs theory**. According to David McClelland, we may be born with needs, but we also develop certain types of needs during our lifetime through our experiences and interactions with the surrounding environment. McClelland described acquired needs associated with achievement, affiliation, and power. Another need we include in our framework, the need for fairness, is also considered an important source of motivation at work.

To make the distinction more clear between innate needs and developed needs, we will discuss developed needs as "desires" in our framework motivation:

- The *desire for achievement* is the extent to which an individual has a desire to perform challenging tasks well and to meet personal standards for accomplishment.
- The *desire for fairness* is the desire to be treated fairly compared to how others are treated.
- The *desire for affiliation* is the desire to form satisfying relationships and experience a sense of belonging.
- The *desire for power* is the desire to control other people, to influence their behaviour, or to be responsible for them.

Because each of these desires is thought to be present within most people to varying degrees, you are likely to identify to some extent with each of the motivational theories discussed within this framework.

Compared to the conventional emphasis of these developed needs, a sustainable emphasis is less individualistic and less materialistic. These different emphases are represented in different titles given to the needs and the different descriptions that follow in Table 5.1.

TABLE 5.1 Four Developed Desires from Each Perspective

Developed Desire	Conventional Emphasis	Sustainable Emphasis
Achievement	Personal accomplishment	Significance
Fairness	Equity	Justice
Affiliation	Satisfying relationships	Community
Power	Individual power	Shared power

Desire for Achievement

| INNATE NEEDS | **ACHIEVEMENT** | FAIRNESS | AFFILIATION | POWER |

LEARNING OBJECTIVE 2
Discuss the need for achievement and how it is satisfied by productivity and accomplishing goals.

Most people have a desire or need to accomplish something at work. Of the four main "needs," the need for achievement has received the most research attention, presumably because it has a direct impact on productivity. Research suggests that, from a conventional approach, "ideally motivated employees" are characterized by a high sense of achievement coupled with a low sense of anxiety.[13] According to McClelland, the need for achievement is satisfied by being productive and accomplishing goals. Further, those individuals with a high need for achievement will pursue *goals* that they can reasonably *expect* to achieve and that will be rewarded or recognized as important—that is, *reinforced*. This achievement focus is central to two important process theories of motivation: (1) goal-setting theory and (2) expectancy theory.

Goal-Setting Theory

One of the most studied of all management theories, with arguably some of the strongest research support, is **goal-setting theory**. A great deal of research indicates that goals must be both difficult and specific if they are to motivate high levels of productivity.[14] Specific and difficult goals produce higher levels of output than do easy goals or the general goal of "Do your best." Specific and difficult goals are most effective when people receive feedback about their progress toward achieving them. Feedback helps people learn and regulate their behaviour. It is not surprising, then, that adding feedback to goals dramatically improves performance.[15] And, of course, people must have the capability to achieve the goals. Yet perhaps the single most important lesson is this: The more committed that employees are to reaching a goal, the more motivated they will be to reach it.[16]

Goal-setting theory states that goals direct and motivate behaviour.

Conventional goal-setting research has found that performance is maximized when goals have certain characteristics. Companies such as Microsoft use the acronym SMART to summarize these characteristics, which are described below. They may seem like common sense, but an audit of SMART goals at Microsoft revealed that nearly 25 percent of employees' goals were not specific, and more than half were not measurable.[17]

Consider the characteristics of SMART goals. First, they are *specific*. According to researcher Gary Latham, having a specific goal clarifies expectations and improves performance.[18] For example, rather than simply asking salespeople to do their best to increase sales revenues at Microsoft, a specific goal could be identified by asking them to increase the sales of Microsoft Office software to small business owners in the United Kingdom by 30 percent in the next fiscal year. The more specific the goal is, the more likely it is to be accomplished.

OB in Action   Olympic-Sized Aspirations

Interviews with Olympic athletes seem to have at least one thing in common regardless of the athlete's nationality: a childhood dream. Commitment and endless practice are necessary to achieve high-level performance in any sport or discipline, but what about the other resources that are necessary along the way? Jennifer Heil, a Canadian Olympic gold medallist in moguls events, credits her parents' ongoing support and willingness to shuttle her back and forth from practice and competitions as being critical to her success. Even though Heil had a goal in mind and was prepared to dedicate the required time and effort to reach it, she still needed help along the way from other sources. Without this support, she may have never been able to realize her dreams and fulfill her potential.

QUESTIONS FOR DISCUSSION

1. Consider a time when you were working with or for someone to achieve a goal. What kind of help or information did you need to succeed?
2. How did (or would) a lack of access to these resources impact your motivation?
3. What would you have changed in the situation, if anything, in order to be more motivated to attain the goal?

Second, SMART goals are *measurable*. This allows organizational members to monitor how well goals are being met. This may mean using existing data (for example, total sales revenues for Microsoft Office software in the United Kingdom) or setting up systems to collect it. Managers at Microsoft knew they had a problem when an audit showed that only 40 percent of their employees' goals could reasonably be measured.[19] Measuring goals provides feedback so that people can evaluate whether their behaviour is helping to meet the goal or whether their actions should change.

Third, SMART goals are *achievable* or attainable. This is not to say they should be easy. In fact, research clearly shows that people perform better if they are given challenging goals rather than easy goals or are told to "do your best." For example, a "C" student who sets the goal of earning a C+ is likely to succeed (a little bit challenging and readily achievable), but a "C" student who sets the goal of earning a B is also likely to succeed (more challenging, yet still attainable). However, a "C" student who sets the goal of getting an A+ may quit halfway through a course upon realizing that the quest for an A+ is too challenging and not attainable.

A **stretch goal** is one so difficult that people do not immediately know how to reach it. Matthew Rendall, Ryan Gariepy, Patrick Martinson, and Bryan Webb co-founded

A **stretch goal** is one so difficult that people do not immediately know how to reach it.

Clearpath Robotics in Kitchener, Ontario, based on a singular idea: building robots to do jobs too dangerous for humans. Even though the "how" behind this objective was puzzling at first, the four co-founders persevered and wound up creating a multi-million dollar company whose clients include the Canadian Space Agency and the Massachusetts Institute of Technology.[20] For established or mature firms, stretch goals may be called for when conditions demand dramatic improvements to productivity, efficiency, and profitability.[21]

Fourth, SMART goals are *results-based* in that they focus on specific outcomes, not on activities. Results-based goal setting is effective because it focuses attention on goal-relevant behaviour. Rewarding employees with financial incentives for achieving the desired results also enhances motivation and achievement.[22] Yet, this enhanced drive to earn the reward can also have a dark side of encouraging taking shortcuts, such as sacrificing quality to meet quantity goals or engaging in unethical behaviour to achieve results.[23]

Finally, SMART goals are *time specific*. Having a deadline provides a sense of urgency and helps managers reconsider goals on a regular basis. It makes a big difference whether Microsoft's goal to achieve a 30 percent increase in sales of Office software is set at six months or six years. Once the time allotted to achieve a specific goal has passed, managers are armed with information they can then use to set the goals for the next round.

Conventional goal setting yields worthwhile results; however, goal setting from a sustainable perspective also has benefits. We will call the sustainable approach to goal setting SMART2. The two approaches are compared in Table 5.2.

Some of the characteristics of SMART2 goals are consistent with SMART goals, including the merit seen in setting achievable yet challenging goals. Even so, a sustainable perspective does not fully embrace some of the SMART criteria. For example, while a focus on specific and measurable goals does, in fact, increase productivity, at the same time it can decrease organizational citizenship behaviour, which includes positive activities such as helping co-workers.[24] This is an example of **goal displacement**, which happens when people become so focused on specific goals that they lose sight of more important overarching goals. In this case, the overall organizational goal of working together co-operatively is sacrificed or displaced by a focus on specific individual goals.

Goal displacement occurs when important overarching goals are displaced by other specific goals.

TABLE 5.2 **SMART and SMART2 Goals**

The five characteristics of conventional or SMART goals:

Specific	The goal is precise on what is to be accomplished.
Measurable	The goal to be accomplished can be assessed objectively.
Achievable	The goal is within reach yet also challenging.
Results-based	The goal has clear, demonstrable outcomes (not just activities).
Time specific	The goal has a specific time by which it is to be accomplished.

The five characteristics of sustainable or SMART2 goals:

Significant	The goal is challenging and important.
Meaningful	The goal has meaning beyond its objective value.
Agreed upon	Members participate in developing their own goals.
Relevant	The goal is linked to important issues for a variety of stakeholders.
Timely	The goal is appropriate for the present situation and the future.

A sustainable perspective emphasizes different goal characteristics. First, SMART2 goals are *significant*, meaning they are challenging (consistent with conventional SMART goals), but they also acknowledge the long-term impact on the employee and on others. For example, when Bill and Melinda Gates set goals for their foundation related to reducing disease and poverty, they took the advice of their friend Warren Buffett who suggested, "Don't just go for safe projects; take on the really tough problems."[25] Goals that are both significant and motivated by a focus on others energize people and result in high levels of creativity.[26] In essence, significant goals invite members to think about both their work and themselves in a broader way.[27]

Second, SMART2 goals are *meaningful* because they seem worthwhile to pursue even if we cannot always measure them objectively. For instance, employees of domestic home-builders Mattamy Homes can be inspired by the company's stated values, one of which includes the objective of making a positive impact in all of the communities that they serve.[28] SMART2 goals that benefit others in need may be particularly meaningful even if their achievement is difficult to quantify.

Third, SMART2 goals are *agreed upon* by the people who are expected to implement them. Whereas a conventional approach advocates participation in goal setting in some circumstances (such as when there are multiple goals and participation helps to avoid goal conflict),[29] a sustainable approach welcomes participation even if it does not provide immediate or obvious benefits to the organization. Participation is likely to increase motivation, but it also ensures that participating members will be more sensitive to the need for changing or fine-tuning goals. For example, MEC (Mountain Equipment Co-op) frequently seeks feedback from its key stakeholder groups such as members (i.e., customers), employees, and industry experts to help develop the company's strategy. Amy Roberts, the company's Director of Sustainability, refers to this process as gaining "sweat equity," which has the ability to greatly impact organizational commitment and the acceptance of company goals.[30]

Fourth, SMART2 goals are *relevant*, both to the organization's mission and vision and to the aspirations of members and other stakeholders. Despite the presence of countless energy companies who are hungry for employee talent in Alberta, Vermilion Energy Inc. manages to attract and retain its employees thanks to its strong corporate values of respect and responsibility. What truly differentiates Vermilion from not only its competitors but from other businesses as well is its commitment to investing in its people and in important causes, even when times are tough. This consistent demonstration of care and concern is what keeps employees sticking around.[31]

Finally, SMART2 goals are *timely*. The timely goals of the sustainable approach contrast with having a singular focus on materialist short-term goals, such as favourable quarterly financial reports, which often results in other kinds of goals being overlooked. Consider the tradition of some First Nation communities, who think about how current actions will affect their descendants seven generations later.[32] While this very long-term view may seem extreme, it does point to the possibility of thinking beyond a five-year time period. What if organizational members placed as much emphasis on the implications of their goals for their children as they do for the next quarterly report? No doubt some goals for short-term material riches may suffer, but perhaps everyone would enjoy a more sustainable lifestyle.

SMART2 goals may be more intrinsically motivating than conventional goals, but it is possible they may translate into relatively lower levels of material output and financial wealth in the short term. On the other hand, they promote community commitment, creativity, and long-term thinking, which are likely to contribute to relatively high amounts of spiritual, social, ecological, aesthetic, and intellectual "well*th*."

OB in Action
Changing Vice to Virtuous Goals

Mohandas Karamchand Gandhi, more commonly known as Mahatma Gandhi, identified seven blunders of the world: (1) wealth without work; (2) pleasure without conscience; (3) commerce without morality; (4) science without humanity; (5) knowledge without character; (6) worship without sacrifice; and (7) politics without principles. For each blunder,

Gandhi's grandson Arun notes that seven noble goals are created when we replace the word "without" with the word "with," and he challenges people to live accordingly.

QUESTION FOR DISCUSSION

1. Does the transformation of these blunders or vices into virtuous goals appear somewhat incomplete or too general to guide your actions? Consider the transformed goals and craft a subgoal for each that follows the SMART or SMART2 framework. Share the goals with others or, better yet, commit yourself to pursuing one.

Expectancy Theory

Another motivational theory that emphasizes achievement is **expectancy theory**, which was originally proposed by Victor Vroom. According to this theory, motivation depends on individuals' learned expectations about their ability to perform certain tasks and receive desired rewards. In particular, motivation is seen as a function of mental calculations related to three separate questions illustrated in Figure 5.2.

Expectancy is the probability perceived by an individual that exerting a given amount of effort will lead to a certain level of performance ("Can I achieve the goal?"). Expectancy is similar to the task-specific self-efficacy discussed in chapter 2. High expectancy contributes to high levels of effort and persistence. Expectancy is more likely if the individual has the appropriate capability, experience, and resources (e.g., time, machinery, tools). For example, a student may be motivated to earn an A in a class if he or she believes that with hard work getting this grade is possible. However, if the student believes that earning an

Expectancy theory states that motivation depends on an individual's learned expectations about his or her ability to perform certain tasks and receive desired rewards.

Expectancy is the probability perceived by an individual that exerting a given amount of effort will lead to a certain level of performance.

Expectancy x Instrumentality x Valence = Motivation

FIGURE 5.2 Expectancy Theory Questions

A is not possible given his or her limited capability or available time to study, then the student is likely to have low expectancy.

Interestingly, others' expectations about our performance can also influence our confidence. Research on the **self-fulfilling prophecy effect** indicates that subordinates often live up (or down) to the expectations of their managers.[33] In other words, a simple word of encouragement—for example, "I believe you can do it"—can go a long way toward building someone's confidence.

Rather than an "I can do it" view of *expectancy*, the sustainable approach is more likely to take a "We can do it" view, with possibly profound implications for managing motivation. Instead of primarily focusing on and building self-efficacy, a sustainable perspective focuses on pursuing goals in the context of community and building **group efficacy**, a collective belief (expectancy) in the group's performance capability. Not only do groups with high levels of efficacy perform well over time, but members are also likely to be motivated to engage in participative decision making, co-operative problem solving, and workload sharing.[34]

You might expect that group efficacy is possible only among a group of people who are similar and familiar to each other, but research among branches of an international bank demonstrated otherwise. The study found that culturally diverse groups developed higher levels of group efficacy in comparison to less diverse groups and earned higher group reputation ratings from customers.[35] Although diversity may initially hinder the development of group efficacy, when group members take the time to understand one another, their differences are likely to be seen as a source of strength that translates into expecting that "We can do it."

Instrumentality refers to the perceived probability that successfully performing at a certain level will result in attaining a desired outcome ("Will I get something for achieving the goal?"). Employees will be motivated to perform at high levels only if they think their high performance will serve as a means to certain ends or outcomes such as pay, job security, interesting job assignments, bonuses, or feelings of accomplishment. For example, a student may be motivated to earn an A in a class if he or she is believes this grade will be instrumental in gaining entrance into a professional program or in securing a job. If an A grade is not perceived to be linked to any foreseeable outcome, the student's motivation is likely to be low.

In terms of *instrumentality*, while the conventional approach answers "What's in it for me?" with individual extrinsic motivators such as money, a sustainable approach is likely to also seek to answer "What are the effects on others, especially those at the margins of society?" A sustainable approach thus broadens the outcomes to include such rewards as a group bonus, the group's learning, or community well-being. Research shows that the more people are given individual goals and incentives, the less effort or attention they direct toward organizational citizenship behaviour,[36] which includes helping others and going above and beyond normal practices to serve organizational stakeholders. By asking "What's in it for others?" and encouraging more collective thinking, a sustainable approach encourages organizational citizenship behaviour.[37]

Valence is the value an individual attaches to an outcome. To motivate organizational members, the outcomes that are provided when each member performs at high levels must be highly valued (have high valence). Simply put, the higher the value of the outcome to the employee, the greater the motivation. Returning to the student example, the more the student values the outcome of entrance into a professional program ("I've always wanted to be a lawyer"), the more motivated he or she might be to earn a high grade. Conversely, if being a lawyer was Mom or Dad's dream for the student and not his or her own, then this outcome is not likely to be as highly motivating. In organizations, some outcomes are likely to please most employees, but not every person values the same thing.

The sustainable approach to *valence* takes a less individualistic and less materialistic approach in determining what is valuable. It favours exploring motivators that, for example, emphasize outcomes that benefit others, contribute to ecological sustainability, or enhance schedule flexibility, which is likely to be particularly valued by people who balance family and

Self-fulfilling prophecy effect is the idea that people often live up (or down) to the expectations of others.

Group efficacy is the collective belief about the group's performance capability.

Instrumentality refers to the perceived probability that successfully performing at a certain level will result in attaining a desired outcome.

Valence is the value an individual attaches to an outcome.

work roles.[38] This view of *valence* is perhaps best exemplified by volunteer firefighting programs, which are especially prominent in small, rural communities.[39] Volunteer firefighters often have other jobs (either full-time or part-time) but still dedicate a portion of their free time to serving their local communities in emergency situations despite not receiving a paycheque. Even though there may be no financial benefit derived from the action (aside from possibly an income tax credit), these individuals' actions benefit the community at large.

Motivation can be extrinsic or intrinsic. **Extrinsic motivators** come from factors outside the task itself and are usually given by a supervisor or higher-level manager. They include promotions, pay increases, time off, special assignments, awards, and verbal praise. **Intrinsic motivators** come from doing the activity or work itself. For example, we experience satisfaction from demonstrating competency or making decisions, feel pride in achievement, and enjoy learning and growing. A common approach to using expectancy theory focuses on extrinsic motivators as the valued outcomes linked to performance. An alternative approach would be to link performance with more decision-making authority or opportunities to learn. The My OB in Action feature describes why organizations would do well to consider how intrinsic motivators can be integrated into the workplace.

To illustrate how all the elements of expectancy theory work together, think about the following example. Imagine that a sales representative at a Canadian clothing retailer believes the company's products to be superior to competitors' products and she is well-trained in how to point out the benefits of the materials her company uses, its manufacturing process, and its quality designs. Here, expectancy is high. Further, if she has been told that achieving a certain sales target will lead to an all-expenses-paid ski trip to Whistler, British Columbia, and a $5,000 cash prize, instrumentality is high. Lastly, if the salesperson places a high value on both the trip and the cash prize, valence is high and she will be highly motivated. However, if she believes any one of the expectancy theory components to be low, such as having no interest in travelling to Whistler (low valence), her motivation to reach that goal will be limited.

The bottom line is that expectancy theory is very practical: Managers can ensure that employees believe they can achieve goals, that goals are linked to clear outcomes, and that the outcomes are valued by employees. Research supports the idea that expectancy, instrumentality, and valence each have an effect on motivation, though there is less support for the assertion that motivation is the multiplicative effect of all three thought processes.

Extrinsic motivation is a source of motivation that comes from factors outside the task itself.

Intrinsic motivation is a source of motivation that comes from doing the activity or work itself.

MOB | Is Your Motivation Intrinsic or Extrinsic?

Tara Moore/Getty Images

Extrinsic motivators are sometimes referred to as carrots. Extrinsic motivators come from factors outside the task itself, whereas intrinsic motivators come from doing the activity or work. Although businesses tend to focus primarily on extrinsic motivators, particularly pay, other sources of motivation may be more powerful and lasting. If both extrinsic and intrinsic factors are present in a job or task, extrinsic motivators can diminish the motivation level of an individual. For instance, if children are offered excessive rewards for playing with a toy that they already enjoy playing with, their interest in the toy will diminish. Moreover,

extrinsic motivation is not sustainable. If the reward is taken away, the motivation disappears.

QUESTIONS FOR REFLECTION

1. Is your motivation as a student more intrinsic or extrinsic?
2. Think about your current or most recent job. Is/was your motivation there primarily extrinsic or intrinsic?
3. Can you think of something you used to do for the sheer fun of it (intrinsic motivator) that you later started to get paid for (extrinsic motivator)? How did the addition of pay affect your motivation? What would happen to your motivation if you were no longer paid for that behaviour?
4. What possible drawbacks are there to relying on the extrinsic motivator of pay in organizations?

Desire for Fairness

LEARNING OBJECTIVE 3
Discuss the desire for fairness and how it influences interactions with others in the workplace.

| INNATE NEEDS | ACHIEVEMENT | **FAIRNESS** | AFFILIATION | POWER |

People want to be treated fairly. In particular, from a conventional perspective, people typically want to get what they think they deserve. We all have an inherent sense of fairness that influences our thinking about interactions with others, particularly in regard to the outcomes we receive for our performance compared to what others in the workplace receive. For example, workers who feel underpaid compared to their co-workers are likely to be demotivated due to a perceived lack of fairness.

Equity theory developed from John Stacey Adams's work on people's responses to inequity.[40] This theory, based on the logic of social comparisons, assumes that people are motivated to seek and preserve social equity in the rewards they expect for performance. In particular, perceived inequity has been shown to relate to decreased performance and increased turnover and absenteeism.[41] People evaluate equity by calculating a ratio of inputs to outcomes. Inputs to a job include education, experience, effort, and ability; outcomes from a job include pay, recognition, benefits, and promotions. Employees may compare their input-outcome ratio to that of another person in the work group or to a perceived group average. If an employee perceives his or her ratio as equal to those of relevant others, then a state of equity exists, as shown in Figure 5.3. In other words, the employee perceives that the situation is fair.

> **Equity theory** is based on the logic of social comparisons, and it assumes that people are motivated to seek and preserve social equity in the rewards they expect for performance.

Both the formulation of the ratios and the comparisons between them can be very subjective and are based on individual perceptions. As a result of the comparison, one of three conditions may result:

- The individual may feel equitably rewarded.
- The individual may feel under-rewarded.
- The individual may feel over-rewarded.

The equity question is this: "In comparison with others, how fairly am I being compensated for the work that I do?" Individuals may feel *equitably rewarded* if, for example, they feel that they are being paid fairly compared to their co-workers. This situation may occur even though another person's outcomes are greater than an individual's own outcomes—provided that the other person's inputs are also proportionally higher. Suppose one employee has a high school education and earns $30,000. He may still feel equitably treated relative to another employee who earns $45,000 because she has a university degree.

Workers may feel *under-rewarded* when, for example, they have a high level of education or experience but receive the same salary as a new, less educated employee. Equity theory predicts that when individuals perceive they are being treated unfairly in comparison to

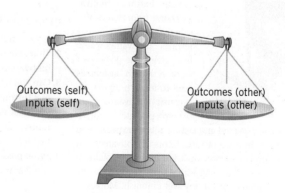

FIGURE 5.3 Equity Theory: The Comparison Process

others, they will be motivated to act in ways that reduce the perceived inequity. For example, employees may:

- Put less effort into the job, thereby lowering inputs (self).
- Ask for a pay raise or some other higher outcomes (self).
- Pressure others to provide more inputs (others).
- Attempt to limit or reduce others' outcomes (others).
- Rationalize the differences as explainable by some other means.
- Change the situation by leaving the job.

It should come as no surprise, however, that wages are not the only factor that contribute to perceived equity or inequity. Other rewards for performance, such as supplemental health care benefits, flexible working hours, and vacation time, can also impact how an individual perceives his or her own input-output ratio and that of others.[42] Therefore, even if an employee earns the same salary as one of his or her colleagues, he or she may still feel under-rewarded if the latter receives additional benefits for the same amount and quality of work.

Lastly, an individual may feel *over-rewarded* relative to another person. This situation is not likely to be terribly disturbing to most people, but equity theory suggests that some people who experience inequity under these conditions are somewhat motivated to reduce it. They might (1) increase their inputs by exerting more effort, (2) reduce their outcomes (say, take a voluntary pay cut), or (3) rationalize the situation by comparing themselves to a different person (such as when CEOs compare their salaries to those of top paid athletes).

The conventional approach to fairness focuses on the motivation that comes when someone is treated equitably compared to how others are treated in similar jobs. In contrast, the sustainable approach to fairness focuses attention on the motivation that can result when people enable others on the margins of society to be treated more justly. The question is not so much "Am I getting my fair share?" as it is "What can I do to help others who are not getting their fair share?" A sustainable approach does not argue that everyone should get the same outcomes regardless of contribution, but it does suggest that others' needs are also worth consideration. If given an opportunity to participate in creating fair distribution rules, most people prefer rules that take into account *both* the needs of members (the poorest-paid members should not be in poverty) and their performance (highly productive people should be paid more).[43] Research also suggests that those within the group who receive rewards based on both need *and* contributions tend to be more motivated than those whose rewards are based only on need *or* contributions.

From a sustainable perspective, people may be motivated to distribute resources more justly, especially if managers provide opportunities and examples of doing so. Some sustainable leaders set an example by insisting on reasonable salaries, removing unnecessary perks such as executive dining areas and parking spots, and focusing some of the organization's resources (time or money) on addressing community needs. One such example can be found at Gildan Activewear Inc., a prominent clothing manufacturer headquartered in Montreal, Quebec, where they have taken a very decided stance against the use of Uzbek cotton due to ongoing concerns related to child labour. Moreover, the company has since implemented cotton traceability assessment procedures to ensure that all of its suppliers adhere to its strict requirements for the sourcing of raw materials.[44] Despite the added costs stemming from the company's position on Uzbek cotton, Gildan executives have decided that the pursuit of ethical practices as well as the riddance of unethical practices are simply more important.

The sustainable approach of considering the just treatment of stakeholders in our mental calculations of fairness, as discussed in this chapter, is not the only use of the term *justice* in organizational research. In chapter 8, we will discuss perceptions of justice as it relates to the distribution of outcomes, the process by which outcomes are achieved or decided, and interpersonal behaviour.[45]

LEARNING OBJECTIVE 4
Explain the desire for affiliation
and its impact on motivation
and commitment to an
organization.

Desire for Affiliation

INNATE NEEDS | ACHIEVEMENT | FAIRNESS | **AFFILIATION** | POWER

Relationships are not only a source of social comparisons; people also tend to look to relationships for affirmation. That is, they seek to identify or affiliate with those who make them feel good about themselves. Like the innate social needs noted in our discussion of motivation at the beginning of the chapter, the need for affiliation implies that people can be motivated by receiving affirmation from others, especially if they think highly of those who are providing the affirmation. For some people, this need for affiliation is a strong motivational driver.

These affiliations are usually worth promoting because they can be a source of commitment to the organization that can lower turnover costs and increase motivation.[46] Some organizations try to encourage affiliation among their members and with their organization by hosting picnics, sponsoring softball teams, and providing a fun environment in which to work. WestJet Airlines, for example, has a designated care team responsible for organizing internal events such as ski days and wine tastings. The company further promotes affiliation between employees and the company by encouraging them to become owners through its profit-sharing program, which includes a dollar-for-dollar matching of up to 20 percent of an employee's salary.[47]

Early research on managerial effectiveness indicated that having a strong need for affiliation with the members of an organization was a weakness for managers because they favoured pleasing others over making decisions that others may not like.[48] Although this could be a case of too much of a good thing, particularly in older command and control bureaucracies, affiliations with members of an organization are generally a positive thing. If employees feel a bond with their leaders, supervisors, or team members within an organization, they are more helpful toward others, comply with expectations, demonstrate loyalty, and even provide better customer service.[49] In contrast, when there is relational conflict between members of a work group, helping and participation decline.[50]

The principle of exchange is central to the conventional perspective on affiliation. People will be especially motivated by affiliations if they receive benefits that are in their self-interests. For example, knowing the right people can pay off in gaining promotions or prized assignments. Those who spend a great deal of time networking or building relationships with powerful people in their organization typically receive more promotions. In this sense, the need for affiliation is not an end in itself so much as it is a means to getting something of value.

A sustainable approach to affiliation extends beyond simple exchanges, however, and emphasizes identifying with the values and goals of others in a community. Relationships are motivating not only because of a personal need for acceptance and affirmation, but also because of the deep connection with others that emerges when we adopt their values and goals as our own.[51] This orientation of "we" over "me" also benefits organizations by contributing to motivation within teams, which enhances team performance.[52] It is inherently motivating to belong to a community and to use your gifts, time, and resources to serve common needs or the needs of others. A good example of this is Lululemon Athletica Inc. Founded in Vancouver in 1998, it is a company that has a very strong corporate social responsibility focus with a sustainability vision separate from its corporate mission. Employees have the liberty to pursue projects and initiatives that contribute to the vision.[53] Additionally, the company works to ensure that its suppliers share its values and are held to the same standards of excellence and sustainability by hosting an annual Vendor Summit as well as developing a Vendor Code of Ethics.[54] Lululemon also provides funds to its stores, district managers, suppliers, and ambassadors to promote the development of local communities.[55]

A sustainable approach begins with a profound respect for all people within and outside the organization regardless of the benefits that might result from the association. John Beckett, President of the American company R.W. Beckett Corporation, knows this to be true and is quoted as saying, "I must place a high value on each person and never look down on another, regardless of their station and situation in life ... there is something sacred about every individual."[56]

Desire for Power

INNATE NEEDS ACHIEVEMENT FAIRNESS AFFILIATION **POWER**

People can desire power for a variety of reasons. Conventional theories of power have tended to focus on the desire of an individual to gain and exercise control over organizational resources and members, or over his or her own job. Not surprisingly, a high need for power is often associated with successful attainment of top levels in the organizational hierarchy. Power is important for motivation in two ways. First, people who have a desire for power will be motivated to work hard to acquire it. Second, people who have power can use it to motivate others. Power can be based on a position (legitimate, reward, coercive) or personal factors (expert, referent), with personal factors being most effective in influencing others. French and Raven identified at least five sources of power, which are described in Table 5.3.[57]

Whereas a conventional perspective focuses on gaining more power to shape others' behaviour, a sustainable perspective focuses on sharing power with others and facilitating mutual motivation. Research indicates that consulting with co-workers and seeking their input increases their motivation and performance.[58] Employees who have autonomy, responsibility, and opportunities to participate, in conjunction with having appropriate levels of authority and resources, are generally more motivated because they feel more ownership. Empowerment of this kind also translates into the organization performing better.[59]

A sustainable approach favours the shared power that comes from open access to information while trusting employees to do the right thing with the information they receive. In environments characterized by high levels of shared power, people are motivated to spot problems, solve problems, engage customers, and satisfy customers because they own the work. Organizational members who see themselves as empowered are generally more innovative, less resistant to change, more satisfied, less stressed, and judged as more effective by others.[60] Research indicates that empowered people also have a stronger bond with the organization, greater confidence in their abilities, and a clear sense of being able to make a difference.[61] In contrast are those who seek to gain and hold power in organizations through an emphasis on controlling information and reinforcements. They create a sense of powerlessness and helplessness that demoralizes their co-workers.

Canadian steakhouse chain Keg Restaurants Ltd. has managed to overcome challenges, such as high employee turnover and low engagement, which tend to plague the restaurant industry. Keg managers at both the restaurant-level and the corporate-level emphasize the importance of every employee's role in the overall customer experience. As CEO David Aisenstat says, "there are no second-class citizens here. You can't serve a dish without a dishwasher and you can't seat a customer without a busboy." Every employee actively contributes to the restaurant's impeccable customer service—even managers, who can be found washing dishes or bartending when staff members need an extra hand. Moreover, employees are empowered to provide anonymous feedback on management, and they have the liberty to make decisions such as last-minute schedule changes. This ensures that no

TABLE 5.3 Sources of Power

✓ Legitimate power **is based on the power of the position that someone holds in an organization's hierarchy.**

✓ Reward power **is based on the capability to give or withhold positive benefits or rewards.**

✓ Coercive power **is based on the capability to motivate others' behaviour through threat of punishment.**

✓ Expert power **is based on the special knowledge, skills, and expertise that someone possesses.**

✓ Referent power **is based on the capability to motivate through identification with or by association.**

one comes to work distracted or ill-equipped, which would ultimately impact the quality of customer service.[62] Sustainable managers share power, and in the end they often receive more than they give up in terms of measurable and immeasurable rewards.

indigo bookmarked values[63]

Fernando Morales/The Globe and Mail

Heather Reisman has been a book enthusiast since childhood, although she didn't transform this passion into a career until after nearly two decades of working in consulting and executive capacities at various Canadian companies. In 1996, Reisman founded Indigo Books & Music, opening its first retail location in Burlington, Ontario, the following year. She envisioned Indigo as being the booklover's cultural department store that would combine the comfort and familiarity of a small independent bookshop with an impressive emporium-level selection. Since then, Indigo merged with Chapters Inc. to form the largest book retailer in Canada, launched an e-reading service that evolved into the company known today as Kobo Inc., and partnered with American Girl to launch the brand's dolls in Canada.

One attribute that has really set Reisman and Indigo apart over the years is Reisman's vocalness. She is quoted as saying, "Indigo has a policy created on Day 1. To the best of our knowledge, we will not sell child pornography or material with detailed instructions on how to build weapons of mass destruction. And we will not sell any material that has as its sole intent the incitement of society toward the annihilation of any group." Reisman is also a diehard supporter of "caring capitalism"; in every business decision, careful consideration is given to the impact it will have on stakeholders as well as on customers, employees, the environment, and society as a whole.

Reisman freely shares her belief that the ability to attract and build relationships with great talent is the cornerstone for success in business. In her view, leadership is about understanding how to inspire employees to work toward a shared vision while also enabling them to achieve their own dreams. Not only must employees and executives alike move together in the same direction, every person must feel as if he or she is doing what he or she wants. Everyone has to want to be there.

Reisman has also developed a special relationship with her customers. For starters, she formed a community that encourages interaction among customers themselves as well as with the company through the Indigo Ideas Facebook application. In doing this, she has provided a platform through which customers have a voice in Indigo's operations and initiatives. Furthermore, Reisman consistently demonstrates her genuine care for her customers. Following the announcement of the impending closure of Indigo's iconic Runnymede location in the west end of Toronto, Reisman held a town-hall-style meeting at that store to "mourn" the closure and to explain why Indigo was leaving. Her openness and the informal nature of the meeting were very well-received by locals, despite the sad premise.

To this day, Reisman continues to run her company based on the same values with which she began it, and outside of her corporate life she remains dedicated to the betterment of society. In 2010, she launched an online petition that garnered widespread media attention around the globe to save an Iranian woman who was sentenced to death by stoning. Through Indigo's Love of Reading Foundation, Reisman works to improve the functional literacy of children and instill her own childhood passion for reading in others. Her love of books and clear emphasis on people, whether they be employees, customers, or simply members of the global community, are the driving forces behind Indigo and the reasons for Reisman's success.

QUESTIONS FOR DISCUSSION

1. The careful reader will note that the word "motivation" is not used once in this case, and yet the case is fundamentally linked to motivation in the workplace. Use the previously discussed theories to explain how Heather Reisman motivates others at Indigo.
2. Is conventional motivation theory or sustainable motivation theory used at Indigo? How?
3. Would you be motivated to work for Heather Reisman? Why or why not?

Summary

Learning Objectives	From a conventional OB perspective, motivation can be influenced by satisfying people's	From a sustainable OB perspective, motivation can be influenced by satisfying people's
• Identify the innate needs of people in organizations.	• Innate needs by addressing physiological, safety, social, esteem, and self-actualization needs individually.	• Innate needs by balancing material, social, spiritual, aesthetic, and ecological needs in the community.
• Discuss the need for achievement and how it is satisfied by productivity and accomplishing goals.	• Desire for achievement by providing goals that are specific, measurable, attainable, results-oriented, and time specific; and by increasing individual expectancy, instrumentality, and valence.	• Desire for significance by promoting goals that are significant, meaningful, agreed upon, relevant, and timely; and by facilitating collective expectancy, instrumentality, and valence.
• Discuss the desire for fairness and how it influences interactions with others in the workplace.	• Desire for fairness by treating people equitably compared to others working in similar positions.	• Desire for justice by providing opportunities to treat stakeholders justly, especially people who are on the margins.
• Explain the desire for affiliation and its impact on motivation and commitment to an organization.	• Desire for affiliation by providing people with affirmation and opportunities to build productive networks.	• Desire for community by providing opportunities to develop shared values and caring relationships.
• Identify the sources of power and its importance for motivation.	• Desire for individual power by seeking to gain legitimate, reward, coercive, expert, and referent power.	• Desire for shared power by seeking to develop a sense of shared ownership.

Key Terms

Equity theory (p. 104)
ERG theory (p. 94)
Expectancy (p. 101)
Expectancy theory (p. 101)
Extrinsic motivation (p. 103)
Frustration-regression principle (p. 95)

Goal displacement (p. 99)
Goal-setting theory (p. 97)
Group efficacy (p. 102)
Hygiene factors (p. 95)
Instrumentality (p. 102)
Intrinsic motivation (p. 103)
Maslow's hierarchy of needs (p. 94)

McClelland's acquired needs theory (p. 96)
Motivation (p. 94)
Motivator factors (p. 95)
Self-fulfilling prophecy effect (p. 102)
Stretch goal (p. 98)
Valence (p. 102)

Questions for Reflection and Discussion

1. Maslow's hierarchy of needs theory is a well-known theory. What about it do you think fits with your motivational experiences? What about it does not?

2. Goal setting is a well-established means to improve performance. What is your experience with goal setting? When did it work or not work well for you?

3. Discuss why two people with similar abilities might have very different expectancies for performing at a high level. What could you do as a manager to increase workers' expectancies?

4. Compare and contrast sustainable and conventional views on the need for fairness. How is equity different from justice?

5. Explain how conventional and sustainable perspectives on affiliation differ. Is one necessarily better than the other?

6. Many organizational leaders have been accused of abusing power in organizations. How can you make use of power without abusing it?

ob activities

What Is Your Approach to Motivation?

Indicate the extent to which the two comparison statements fit you best. Rankings of 1 or 5 indicate strong agreement with the statement closest to the number, 2 or 4 indicates slightly less agreement in either case, and 3 indicates you are undecided or neutral.

To be an effective leader, I should . . .

Implement goals that are SMART (specific, measurable, achievable, results-based, and time specific).	① ② ③ ④ ⑤	Implement goals that are SMART2 (significant, meaningful, agreed upon, relevant, and timely).
Ensure an equitable distribution of outcomes based on the contributions of individuals.	① ② ③ ④ ⑤	Ensure a just distribution of outcomes based on the needs and contributions of stakeholders.
Build relationships based on exchanges and mutual benefits.	① ② ③ ④ ⑤	Build community based on considering the benefits for others.
Seek to increase my personal and position power to influence others.	① ② ③ ④ ⑤	Seek to share power with others and engage in mutual influence.

Key: These questions measure your views about how to motivate. The 1s and 2s reflect conventional tendencies, and the 4s and 5s represent sustainable tendencies. Add up your scores. A sum of 12 means you do not tend to favour one approach over the other, a sum of 11 and lower suggests you prefer a conventional approach, and a sum of 13 and higher suggests you tend to favour a sustainable approach. Your score gives a sense of the kind of motivational approach you might use as a leader.

A corporate executive promoted a loyal friend and competent manager to the position of divisional vice-president and, in doing so, passed over a better-qualified manager with whom he had no close ties.

Why might this scenario occur in organizations?

Use the following scale to indicate whether this behaviour is ethically acceptable:

NEVER ACCEPTABLE	SOMETIMES ACCEPTABLE	ALWAYS ACCEPTABLE
① ②	③ ④ ⑤	⑥ ⑦

Explain the ideas you considered in arriving at your answer.

SMART2 Goals Activity

SMART2 goals are goals that are significant, meaningful, agreed upon, relevant, and timely. Develop one or two goals for your academic pursuits or professional career. To foster an inspirational mindset, read the following quotes:

"Nobody can make you feel inferior without your consent."
- Eleanor Roosevelt

"If you really put a small value upon yourself, rest assured that the world will not raise your price."
- Author Unknown

"A successful person is one who can lay a firm foundation with the bricks that others throw at him or her."
- David Brinkley

This activity can be an individual activity in which participants are encouraged to draft one or two personal SMART2 goals to share, or it can be a group activity in which the group is challenged to develop SMART2 goals for the university or for an existing business.

QUESTIONS FOR DISCUSSION

1. What was your reaction to the quote by David Brinkley?
2. Do you think it applies to businesses or organizations?
3. Did you find it difficult to develop SMART2 goals? Explain.
4. Which SMART2 goals seemed most compelling to you?

Desire for Achievement Activity

This activity is an adaptation of an activity used in early research on the need for achievement. You can do this activity as a class or pick a handful of participants. The activity involves trying to maximize the participants' points in a series of five tosses.

The original activity involved tossing rings onto small posts, but this can work tossing quarters or small balls into three cans or small containers. Position the first can three feet from the tossing line; the second, six feet; and the third, nine feet. Landing an object in the first can is worth 1 point, the second can is worth 2 points, and the third is worth 3 points. The intention is that the first can is an easy goal, the second a moderately difficult goal, and the third is a goal that is not easily achieved. *Adjust the cans if necessary to ensure these levels of difficulty.* The object is for each participant to maximize his or her points to win the overall best score.

QUESTIONS FOR DISCUSSION

1. How do the choices that the participants make demonstrate different levels of need for achievement?
2. Primarily aiming at the second can demonstrates the highest need for achievement because it is an achievable option of earning a high amount of points, whereas aiming at the first is too easy and not likely to win, and aiming at the third is too difficult and therefore also not likely to win. Why might this activity not be an accurate assessment of need for achievement?
3. What other factors might explain the choices participants made?

This is a personal journal entry that can be used for class discussion or be compiled and included in a self-reflection paper.

Which motivation principles discussed in this chapter seem to explain your motivation the best? Consider an area of your life in which you lack motivation but it is important for you to perform well. Describe the situation and indicate what you can do to improve your motivation.

Six

Making
Decisions

M aking decisions is a critical task for most organizational members. It requires us to know when decisions are needed, to develop alternative responses, to select
the most appropriate response, and, ultimately, to implement our chosen course of action. As this chapter's navigator indicates, conventional and sustainable OB both offer a
range of ideas to consider for each of these four steps.

Learning Objectives	Conventional OB	Sustainable OB
STEP 1: IDENTIFY THE NEED FOR A DECISION		
1. Describe the importance of identifying the need to make a decision.	Identify problems or opportunities, especially those that may help to improve the bottom line	Identify problems or opportunities together with other stakeholders, to improve various forms of well-being
STEP 2: DEVELOP ALTERNATIVE RESPONSES		
2. Recognize the alternative responses decision makers can follow once a need for a decision has been identified.	Develop alternatives with an eye to ensuring that financial benefits outweigh costs	Develop alternatives that enhance overall well-being
STEP 3: CHOOSE THE APPROPRIATE ALTERNATIVE		
3. Discuss the key factors in choosing the appropriate alternative decision.	Seek conformity Emphasize explicit knowledge and avoid uncertainty	Celebrate diversity Balance tacit knowledge and explicit knowledge
STEP 4: IMPLEMENT THE CHOICE		
4. Describe how decisions are implemented.	Use selective participation Favour staying the course	Use ongoing participation Favour experimentation

recalling a classic example of decision making[1]

© Bettmann/Corbis Corp

Product recalls have been in the news with increasing frequency. Faulty products can be the result of flawed decision making in the design or during production stages. Either way, poor decisions can cost a firm greatly in terms of repair expenses and loss of reputation, as Mattel and Toyota and other firms have experienced. In addition to poor decisions that create the faulty product in the first place, there is the decision as to whether to admit the mistake and recall the product. A classic and instructive example of a recall decision-making process gone awry is what doomed the Ford Pinto.

Imagine it is the early 1970s and Ford Motor Company is working hard to develop its Pinto, which the company hopes will compete effectively against the popular low-priced Volkswagen Beetle. To lower production costs so that they can price the Pinto at $2,000, Ford engineers decide to locate the car's gas tank behind the rear axle, just in front of the rear bumper, where it is vulnerable to being ruptured in an accident.

Now imagine that it is a few years later, Pintos are on the road, and you are Ford's Field Recall Coordinator. You have just received data showing that the Pinto's design makes it prone to explosions when the car is rear-ended. You recognize that a decision needs to be made, so you gather data and develop two options. The first option is to recall all 12.5 million Pintos on the road and install an $11 baffle plate between the fuel tank and the axle housing. The estimated cost of this option is $137.5 million. The second option is to not recall the vehicles but instead be prepared to pay the damages that arise from lawsuits. Using data provided by the U.S. National Highway Traffic Safety Administration, you estimate that the total cost of this option will be $49.5 million ($200,000 for each of the 180 anticipated burn deaths, $67,000 for each of the 180 anticipated burn injuries, and $700 for each of the 2,100 anticipated burned vehicles).

The numbers send a clear message, so senior managers at Ford choose the second, lower-cost, option, thereby saving the company an estimated $88 million. However, the public is outraged when it finds out about the cost-benefit analysis that was used to make this decision. In February 1978, a California jury awards a Pinto accident victim $125 million in punitive damages (subsequently lowered to $3.5 million by the judge). Later that year Ford finally upgrades the Pinto's fuel system, and in 1980 it stopped making the car altogether.

Many people today are shocked by this true story, but if they were to find themselves in a similar situation, most would likely at least be tempted to make a similar choice. To understand why, consider the experiences of Dennis Gioia, Ford's Field Recall Coordinator at the time the problems with the Pinto were first noticed. When he was an MBA student, Gioia had often been critical of business, so his classmates were surprised when he accepted a job at Ford. Gioia explained to them that he hoped to influence social change from within the company to prod it into socially responsible action.

Soon after starting his job at Ford, however, Gioia became resocialized in the process of competing for attention with other MBAs who had recently joined the company: "The psychic rewards of working and succeeding in a major corporation proved unexpectedly seductive," he recalls. As Field Recall Coordinator, the basic routines Gioia inherited—the "scripts" that decision makers learn and follow—became second nature to him, along with the organizational culture and unspoken norms.

The psychic rewards of working and succeeding in a major corporation proved unexpectedly seductive.

Gioia was no longer the Field Recall Coordinator in 1978, but if he had voted earlier to recommend a recall when the Pinto problems had first surfaced, perhaps future damage could have been avoided. He recalls his failure to do so: "To do the job 'well' there was little room for emotion. Allowing it to surface was potentially paralyzing and prevented rational analysis about which cases to recommend for recall."

The routines, or programmed decisions, that he acquired in his position seemed practical and rational. They provided Gioia with ways of behaving and making decisions, and he lacked well-developed scripts to enact his countercultural values.

In retrospect, I know that in the context of the times my actions were legal (they were all well within the framework of the law); they were probably also ethical according to most prevailing definitions (they were in accord with accepted professional standards and codes of conduct); the major concern for me was whether they were moral (in the sense of adhering to some higher standards of inner conscience about the "right" actions to take).

In short, organizational scripts and routines can have a powerful effect on how we make decisions. Decisions that are rational according to one perspective may seem immoral from another perspective, and vice versa. Although in hindsight the Pinto story is disturbing, at the time some may have considered a recall to be unethical because of the $88 million cost it would have imposed on shareholders.

In both our personal and our professional lives, all of us make many decisions every day. A decision is a choice among a number of available alternatives, such as when decision makers at Ford chose to pay damages from anticipated lawsuits rather than to recall the flawed Pinto. Figure 6.1 provides an overview of the four-step decision-making process, which we'll examine in this chapter from both the conventional and the sustainable perspective.

The test of time has shown that the relatively simple four-phase model depicted in Figure 6.1 is useful for teaching and practising the fundamentals of decision making. Even so, as you might guess, actual decision-making processes in organizations and in your personal life are often not as linear as depicted here. In the messiness of real life, there is a lot more back and forth within the model, with steps being skipped and returned to. Of course, these realities only serve to make the model more valuable, because it serves as an elegant overarching framework that captures a lot of this messiness and allows decision makers to think about the decision-making process as a whole as they navigate their way between the various steps of the model.

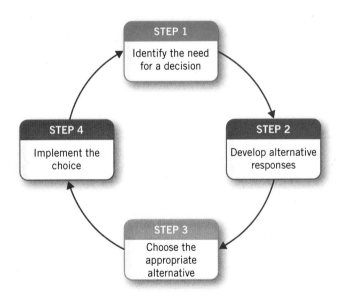

FIGURE 6.1　The Four-Step Decision-Making Model

Step 1: Identify the Need for a Decision

IDENTIFY NEEDS | DEVELOP ALTERNATIVES | CHOOSE ALTERNATIVE | IMPLEMENT DECISION

We may face many problems and opportunities at any given time, some that require a decision now and some that we can delay or even ignore. Examples of problems in which a **decision** should be made include situations in which a person's or an organization's reputation is at stake, or when organizational members receive negative feedback from disgruntled customers. Recognizing that there is a problem or an opportunity is Step 1 of the decision process.

Just as a movie script helps actors know what to do and say in specific scenes, the scripts we use in decision making help us identify which situations require decisions and, often (as in the case of the Ford Pinto), what those decisions should be. Think of these **scripts** as learned guidelines or procedures that help people interpret and respond to what is happening around them.[2] Organizational decision makers learn to pay attention to scripts associated with key financial reports, productivity reports, and consumer trends. Schools teach scripts (e.g., certain theories or concepts about OB) that students can apply in their personal and professional lives. Of course, as described in My OB: Neuroscience and Decision Making, people's innate abilities influence how well they process "scripts" and the four steps of the decision-making process more generally.

An important part of identifying the need for a decision is defining the *underlying* issues and relevant stakeholders. Consider how you might react if your doctor made a decision about your back pain based on a speedy examination and a few questions. Would you have much confidence in the diagnosis? If the doctor gave you a thorough exam and took the time to ask you several detailed questions about your symptoms and their possible causes, you probably would be more confident based on this in-depth investigation. The same applies to organizational decisions.

If an employee arrives late for work, the supervisor should find out whether the person has a sick child, is fearful of a conflict with a co-worker, or is simply irresponsible. Likewise, if, due to a recent surge in sales, an organization's members are faced with a decision about whether to invest in increased production, they should find out whether the sales increase is due to an improved product, a new advertising campaign, or a general economic upturn. The more

Scripts are learned frameworks that provide direction for people by helping them to interpret and respond to what is happening around them.

M͟OB | Neuroscience and Decision Making

Rogue Pictures/Photofest

In the movie *Limitless*, Bradley Cooper plays struggling writer Eddie Morra. After he takes a drug offered by his former brother-in-law, Eddie's cognitive functioning dramatically increases, allowing him to rapidly formulate his thoughts, analyze data, and connect seemingly insignificant pieces of information to make decisions and predictions. The movie depicts the brain as a powerful and underutilized key to exceptional decision making.

Our decision making is influenced by physical and chemical characteristics of our brains. Contrary to the assumption that humankind is predisposed to be competitive, research suggests that our biological make-up has a built-in tendency to reciprocate altruism and that competitiveness requires cognitive effort to override this ingrained co-operative nature. The naturally occurring chemicals in our brains are also associated with what sorts of things we perceive to be opportunities or threats, the kinds of alternatives we develop, the criteria we use to make choices, and how we implement decisions. For example, the neuropeptide oxytocin increases behavioural expressions of trust, generosity, and altruism; and serotonin increases empathy and mutual co-operation.

Can people change the way their brains work? Not to the extremes presented in *Limitless*, but drugs do alter brain functioning. For example, drugs are prescribed to help people with attention deficit hyperactivity disorder (ADHD) focus their attention. Sometimes such drugs are used illegally by people, particularly students, who do not have the disorder. Like the dangers of misusing brain-altering drugs presented in the movie, the use of such drugs can be addictive and contribute to other mental health issues like depression. Additional research suggests that while some of these drugs can promote focus, they dull creativity.

Another way to change our thinking is simply to pay attention to and learn from others who model the behaviours we wish to exhibit. Research also shows that carbohydrate-rich meals increase serotonin levels and that the flow of oxytocin is stimulated by physical touch through things like hugging, getting a massage, or even petting a dog. Other research shows that physical activity can improve the functioning of the brain.

QUESTIONS FOR REFLECTION

1. What sorts of things do you do to keep your brain in top decision-making shape?
2. What can organizations do to help with this?
3. Do you think that loving relationships, large helpings of fettuccine alfredo, and good role models would make the world a more altruistic place? Perhaps it's worth a try.

time and resources that decision makers devote to thoroughly understanding and defining the problem or opportunity, the greater the likelihood that they will make a good decision.[3]

A complicating factor in identifying the need to make a decision is that people often interpret the same event in different ways, depending on the scripts they use. Politicians are very familiar with this challenge. For example, during an economic recession, should the government lower taxes to stimulate the economy, keep taxes at the current level to minimize the deficit, or increase spending to create new jobs?

Sustainable decision making considers long-term problems and opportunities in the context of a broad group of stakeholders. The merit of a long-range perspective may seem obvious, especially if you consider that a focus on immediate goals can sway people to forego short-term sacrifices that might enhance long-lasting viability. For example, a plant manager can arrange her production schedule and workforce to put forth a maximum number of products, but if at the same time she fails to account for preventive maintenance needed on the machinery, it will hurt long-term organizational performance.[4]

Despite the unfavourable economic backdrop of the past few years, Canadian Tire executives have made some good decisions. They vigorously increased the efficiency of the company's back-end operations to help reduce costs and, as a result, have fared decently well for a mature retailer. However, as competition continued to stiffen, Canadian Tire needed to find a new way to differentiate itself in the market in order to survive. Former CEO and current Deputy Chairman Stephen Wetmore knew that revenue growth would be the key. Yet, rather than simply creating new revenue streams for Canadian Tire, Wetmore focused on strengthening relationships with dealers (store-level owner/operators) to achieve a strong buy-in for strategic changes and ensure the long-term viability of the company.[5]

A sustainable decision-making process can also be triggered by other stakeholders. Sustainable decision makers adopt a "listening" posture, which involves being sensitive to the needs of other stakeholders and putting those needs, such as the need for environmentally friendlier practices or social justice, on the decision-making agenda.[6] For example, in light of exploitive working conditions in low-income countries, a growing number of organizations have voluntarily chosen to adopt an international standard of social accountability—SA8000—and have agreed to pay wages that cover basic needs (not just the legislated minimums), not to employ children younger than 15 years of age, and not to use forced labour. Some large retailers have committed themselves to choosing suppliers that follow the same standards, even if they are not the lowest-price option. For instance, decision makers at the large European retailer C&A chose to stop dealing with 19 suppliers who had not been following the company's code of conduct.[7]

Step 2: Develop Alternative Responses

| IDENTIFY NEEDS | **DEVELOP ALTERNATIVES** | CHOOSE ALTERNATIVE | IMPLEMENT DECISION |

LEARNING OBJECTIVE 2
Recognize the alternative responses decision makers can follow once a need for a decision has been identified.

When the need for a decision has been identified, decision makers can develop or follow three basic kinds of alternative responses:

1. Do nothing.
2. Follow a programmed response.
3. Develop a nonprogrammed response.

The first alternative—to do nothing—requires no effort to develop, which is a welcome feature when decision makers do not have much time or many resources to invest. Doing nothing is actually an appropriate response for all those situations in which doing something else is not worth the effort. For example, it is often not worth the effort to respond to most unsolicited mail or emails. Doing nothing can also be appropriate when the overall cost of doing something exceeds the benefits.

The second alternative is to follow a routine response, such as simply adhering to standard operating procedures. This response is consistent with **programmed decisions**—or routine decisions—in which we choose standard alternatives in response to recurring organizational problems or opportunities. For example, an organization may have routines for responding to employees who arrive late to work, or for dealing with irate customers who do not receive their orders on time. Over time, decision rules and policies are typically developed to handle situations that recur frequently. For example, when an employee arrives late to work, the manager can ask for an explanation and may have several programmed alternative responses from which to choose:

1. Excuse the employee if he or she provides an acceptable explanation.
2. Reduce the employee's pay.
3. Provide the employee with a professional development course on time management.
4. Fire the employee if the person has a long history of tardiness and has been warned that dismissal is the next step.

These programmed decisions are shortcuts that help decision makers avoid going through all four steps in the decision-making process. Dennis Gioia (featured in the opening case) inherited such programmed decision "scripts" when he worked as the Field Recall Coordinator at Ford. Research suggests that it takes less than a month for newcomers to adopt the attitudes and decision-making scripts of the organization into which they are hired.[8] In other words, within a month of joining an organization, you are likely to adopt its decision-making scripts, whether they are conventional or sustainable. Of course, scripts should be reviewed occasionally to ensure that they have not become obsolete or dysfunctional.[9] For example, human resources policies developed for a previous generation of workers are not likely to apply well to employees who today have flexible work schedules or who work from home.

Decision makers must guard against the temptation to limit themselves to programmed decision making when the situation actually calls for developing nonprogrammed alternatives. BlackBerry (which formerly operated under the name Research In Motion) was once on top of the mobile universe. After having practically invented the smartphone market, then co-CEOs Mike Lazaridis and Jim Balsillie were extremely dismissive of the emergence of Apple's iPhone and Google's Android devices. The BlackBerry leaders assumed that their company could do no wrong and that consumers would continue to demand whatever it produced. Needless to say, BlackBerry's lack of awareness of the changing market and inability (or perhaps refusal) to adapt resulted in the company's fall from grace.[10]

The third option is for decision makers to develop nonprogrammed alternatives. **Nonprogrammed decisions** call for discovering and choosing new alternatives when programmed alternatives have not yet been developed or are not appropriate. The quality of the nonprogrammed alternatives depends on the amount of time and resources that decision makers invest in developing them. The best alternatives are often those that are based on input from a variety of sources, including other organizational members, customers, and suppliers. The process of generating alternatives can benefit from consulting with experts, brainstorming, or using a variety of group-oriented creativity techniques, as we will see in subsequent chapters.

Sustainable decision makers have the same three basic options for developing alternatives that conventional decision makers have, but with two qualitative differences. First, because their emphasis is more likely to go beyond maximizing owners' short-term financial well-being, sustainable decision makers often develop a comparatively broader range of alternatives.[11] For example, despite warnings about limited oil supplies and global warming, in the 1980s and 1990s it may have been in the best short-term financial interest for car manufacturers to promote the sale of larger vehicles (e.g., SUVs) rather than to invest heavily in alternative fuels and fuel efficiency, and indeed, many manufacturers did exactly that.

But improved long-term viability—and the lion's share of the environmentalist market segment—went to automobile manufacturers like Toyota, which decided to develop technology perceived to be ecologically friendly, such as can be found in hybrid cars like the Toyota Prius.[12]

Second, a sustainable approach to decision making is likely to involve a greater variety of stakeholders when developing alternatives. This often improves the chance for innovation.[13] For example, rather than give them explicit product specifications, Japanese car manufacturers such as Toyota, Honda, and Nissan have drawn on their *suppliers'* expertise and asked them to help identify appropriate specifications for automobile components. Sustainable managers take into consideration even stakeholders who seem quite distant from the organization, such as the communities in which the company operates in other countries.[14]

Step 3: Choose the Appropriate Alternative

LEARNING OBJECTIVE 3
Discuss the key factors in choosing the appropriate alternative decision.

The third step—choosing the best alternative—lies at the heart of the decision-making process. The way this choice is made often depends on two key factors:

- Goal consensus
- Available knowledge

As shown in Figure 6.2, combining these two dimensions creates a simple conceptual framework that helps to describe five basic methods that decision makers use to make choices. We'll first discuss the two dimensions and then the five methods.

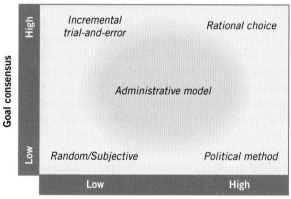

FIGURE 6.2 Five Basic Methods for Choosing an Option

Goal Consensus

The level of agreement among members about which goals the organization should pursue is **goal consensus**. When goal consensus is high, the criteria for making the decision—whether long-term or short-term, related to quality or quantity, focused on people or performance—are clear and agreed upon. Low goal consensus means that there is considerable debate about what the organization's goals should be, and therefore the criteria for a decision are not as clear. For example, the Scouts organization faces a problem related to goal consensus when some of its members argue for the continuation of the Scouts's traditional emphasis on camping and woods lore, while others argue that the organization should move

Goal consensus is the level of agreement among members about which goals the organization should pursue.

away from this traditional emphasis because most boys attending Scouts programs today live in the inner city. Even within organizations where there is widespread agreement, for example, that maximizing shareholder financial well-being is the ultimate goal, there may be considerable disagreement about which subgoals will help achieve that ultimate goal.

Available Knowledge

Even if there is widespread consensus on *which* goals to pursue and *which* criteria to use in decision making, there may be a lack of information about *how* to achieve the desired goals. Imagine that the decision makers at an online video game company agree to pursue the goal of maximizing the number of people that can play a particular game. Even with this consensus, significant debate may arise about how this goal can be achieved. Should the company offer its game for free, advertise the game in virtual media or during TV gaming shows, develop the latest graphics that only the newest hardware can handle, or invest in developing multiple game-playing experiences? In many cases, decision makers have historical data to help them make such a decision, but if the external environment is rapidly changing, such data may not be very useful.

The amount of available knowledge helps decision makers reduce their uncertainty and risk.[15] **Uncertainty** is evident when decision makers do not know what outcomes to expect as a result of choosing a particular alternative. For example, based on past experience, decision makers in a hotel may be quite certain that about 90 percent of customers whose room is not ready when they arrive will be satisfied if they are given a voucher for a complimentary breakfast. However, the decision makers may not know whether or how much the percentage would increase if the voucher were for a free night at the hotel.

As indicated in Figure 6.2, the decision-making method that is most likely or appropriate in a situation is determined in part by the circumstances facing the decision makers. The classic **rational choice** method is evident when goal consensus is high and there is adequate time to collect all of the required information. This analytical approach—which is fitting when the problem is clearly understood—focuses on using tools such as decision trees, break-even analysis, and other analytical models to identify the right decision. However, despite the ready availability of so many tools, only a few organizational decisions use full-fledged rational decision-making techniques because decision makers rarely have complete information at their disposal.[16] Even when they think they have all of the information they require to make a rational decision, poor decisions can still result, as the opening case about the Pinto illustrates.

The **political method** may apply when there is much debate about which goal to pursue, even though a lot of knowledge is available. Debate can be intense, even when there is consensus that the overarching goal is to maximize the financial interests of shareholders. For example, marketing managers might argue for maximizing sales revenue, manufacturing managers might argue for minimizing production costs, and research and development (R&D) managers might argue for developing the most technologically advanced product on the market. Often these competing goals are mutually exclusive, or the organization lacks the resources to pursue them all at the same time. This can lead to a politicized decision-making process, in which decision makers trade favours, bargain, compromise, and form coalitions—techniques discussed in chapter 8.

The **incremental trial-and-error method** is found in situations with a high agreement on goals but a low level of technical knowledge. For example, decision makers may agree on the need to increase unit sales of their key product through advertising, but they may not know whether to use television, radio, computer, or print media for this purpose because they have little knowledge about the relative effectiveness of each. Through trial and error, they may be able to fine-tune existing strategies, make small changes, or test-pilot a decision with a small group of employees or customers.

Uncertainty is evident when decision makers do not know what outcomes to expect as a result of choosing a particular alternative.

Rational choice as a method of decision making is evident when goal consensus is high and there is adequate time to collect all of the required information.

Political method of decision making is evident when there is much debate about which goal to pursue, even though a lot of knowledge is available.

Incremental trial-and-error method of decision making is evident when decision makers have a high agreement on goals but a low level of technical knowledge.

The random or **subjective method** occurs when there is little or no agreement on goals and there is limited information. This is generally not an ideal approach in organizations that favour rational methods, but it is perhaps more likely to yield breakthrough decision making than other approaches because people may rely on intuition or inspiration to make decisions.[17] **Intuition** is tacit knowledge, experience, insight, hunches, or "gut" feelings. Intuition often plays an important role in the way experts make decisions.[18] Intuitive decision making is especially striking when it goes against the rational analysis of the information at hand. Before Ray Kroc purchased McDonald's, his accountant advised against the deal, but Kroc had a "gut feeling" that the investment would turn out to be a winner.[19] Intuitive decision makers often rely on **tacit knowledge**, which is information people possess that is difficult to articulate or codify. It is hard to put into words how to ride a bicycle, for instance, even if you know how to do it. Tacit knowledge, for example, helps art experts distinguish between authentic and counterfeit works of art.[20]

Finally, the **administrative model method** at the centre of Figure 6.2 may be the most commonly used, because decision makers usually have *some* knowledge and at least *partial* goal consensus. Herbert Simon argued that even the best management decision-making process is constrained by a lack of complete information and by our limited ability to process information.[21] Simon called this set of constraints *bounded rationality*. As a result of having incomplete information and a lack of complete goal consensus, decision makers tend to **satisfice**, collecting information and developing alternatives until they are able to identify one that will adequately meet specific criteria rather than attempting to develop an optimal solution. For example, they may choose an alternative because it fits the budgeted amount for a project.

When we lack complete information, subtle factors can influence our decisions. For example, researchers have found patterns in the way that the **framing** or presentation of information affects decision making.[22] In particular, people's choices are influenced by whether a goal is framed in terms of (1) securing gains or (2) avoiding losses.[23] Generally, when faced with opportunities for gain, we tend to be risk adverse, whereas when faced with losses, we are more likely to take risks. In one experiment, participants in an investment simulation who were experiencing losses made riskier choices, as predicted by the framing effect.[24]

Given that human beings have limited cognitive processing capacities, subjective factors can also influence decisions, such as may be evident when appraising an employee's work performance, as described in Table 6.1.[25]

Subjective method of decision making is evident when there is little or no agreement on goals and there is limited information.

Intuition refers to making decisions based on tacit knowledge, which can be based on experience, insight, hunches, or "gut" feelings.

Tacit knowledge is information people possess that is difficult to articulate or codify.

Administrative method of decision making is evident when decision makers have *some* knowledge and at least *partial* goal consensus.

Satisficing is evident when managers choose an *adequate* response to a problem or opportunity, rather than make the effort to develop an *optimal* response.

Framing refers to presenting ideas and alternatives in a way that has an influence on the choices that people make.

TABLE 6.1 Subjective Effects on Employee Appraisals

Anchoring and adjustment bias	is evident when an appraiser places too much emphasis on his or her first impression of an employee (i.e., an anchor), which does not change even after being presented with conflicting information; this may result, for example, in an initial poor impression being weighed too highly in an appraisal.
Availability bias	is evident when an appraiser relies too much on memorable information—for example, a dramatic or recent event—to make judgments, and ignores other fuller information; this may result, for example, in things like the latest sales numbers or a particular incident with a customer having too much influence in an appraisal.
Halo/Horn bias	is evident when appraisers use one piece of known information—good or bad—to generalize about an employee's performance on matters where no information is available; this may result, for example, in an employee who did well on an observed task being credited for doing well in other instances of unobserved performance.
Representativeness	is evident when appraisers make judgments about an employee in comparison to a typical (representative) employee from past experience; this may result, for example, in an employee receiving a critical review because he or she doesn't fit well with the image of a successful employee.

Sustainable OB emphasizes multiple goals, multiple forms of well-being, and multiple criteria in seeking the best decisions. Sustainable decision makers *expect* to encounter a variety of goals among the various members of the organization. Furthermore, they respect those differences and do not feel threatened by lack of consensus. For example, at HCL Technologies, a global IT services firm based in India, executives are required to post their business plans online to be rated and reviewed by the company's 15,000 employees. Former CEO Vineet Nayar said that this approach has yielded more valuable feedback than would have been possible using more traditional methods. The initiative mirrors the sustainable OB approach, as it takes into account the perspectives, experiences, and objectives of the company's diverse workforce ranging from administrative to front-line staff.[26] The process of encouraging feedback from individuals at all levels of the organization and sharing responsibility has enabled HCL to accomplish more and to devote the necessary attention to each proposal.

When we are aware of and sensitive to the competing goals among an organization's stakeholders, we are more likely to make choices that work to everyone's benefit.[27] Decision makers who take into account a range of forms of well-being, rather than focus primarily on financial well-being, tend to engender more respect and more effort from followers.[28] Support for sustainable decision making is evident among business schools and managers who participate in initiatives like the MBA Oath (see My OB: Networks That Promote Sustainable OB Decision Making). It's also evident among the more than 400 business schools who participate in "The Principles of Responsible Management Education" initiative, including York University, Dalhousie University, and the University of British Columbia. Note the initiative's emphasis on sustainability, as evidenced by its Six Principles:[29]

Principle 1 | Purpose: *We will develop the capabilities of students to be future generators of sustainable value for business and society at large and to work for an inclusive and sustainable global economy.*

Principle 2 | Values: *We will incorporate into our academic activities and curricula the values of global social responsibility as portrayed in international initiatives such as the United Nations Global Compact.*

Principle 3 | Method: *We will create educational frameworks, materials, processes and environments that enable effective learning experiences for responsible leadership.*

Principle 4 | Research: *We will engage in conceptual and empirical research that advances our understanding about the role, dynamics and impact of corporations in the creation of sustainable social, environmental and economic value.*

Principle 5 | Partnership: *We will interact with managers of business corporations to extend our knowledge of their challenges in meeting social and environmental responsibilities and to explore jointly effective approaches to meeting these challenges.*

Principle 6 | Dialogue: *We will facilitate and support dialogue and debate among educators, students, business, government, consumers, media, civil society organizations and other interested groups and stakeholders on critical issues related to global social responsibility and sustainability.*

Explicit knowledge is information that can be articulated or codified.

Sustainable decision makers pay attention to a combination of both explicit *and* tacit knowledge, perhaps more than do conventional decision makers. **Explicit knowledge** is information that can be articulated or codified, such as that which is found in an organization's standard operating procedures, blueprints, mission statements, and so on. A sustainable approach goes beyond written guidelines and is more likely to also take into account concerns that are difficult to quantify, such as environmental sustainability, neighbourliness, and social justice. Some research suggests that the more decision makers rely on quantifiable information rather than following their intuition, the less ethical their decisions tend

© Yuri/iStockphoto

The values and principles that underpin a sustainable OB approach to decision making are becoming increasingly institutionalized among managers and business schools. For example, students and graduates from over 300 institutions around the world have embraced the MBA Oath, including the Harvard Business School, London School of Business and Finance Canada, and McGill-HEC School of Management. The MBA Oath deliberately de-emphasizes the blind pursuit of profits and individual self-interests.

THE MBA OATH

As a business leader I recognize my role in society. My purpose is to lead people and manage resources to create value that no single individual can create alone. My decisions affect the well-being of individuals inside and outside my enterprise, today and tomorrow. Therefore, I promise that:

- *I will manage my enterprise with loyalty and care, and will not advance my personal interests at the expense of my enterprise or society.*
- *I will understand and uphold, in letter and spirit, the laws and contracts governing my conduct and that of my enterprise.*
- *I will refrain from corruption, unfair competition, or business practices harmful to society.*
- *I will protect the human rights and dignity of all people affected by my enterprise, and I will oppose discrimination and exploitation.*

- *I will protect the right of future generations to advance their standard of living and enjoy a healthy planet.*
- *I will report the performance and risks of my enterprise accurately and honestly.*
- *I will invest in developing myself and others, helping the management profession continue to advance and create sustainable and inclusive prosperity.*

In exercising my professional duties according to these principles, I recognize that my behavior must set an example of integrity, eliciting trust and esteem from those I serve. I will remain accountable to my peers and to society for my actions and for upholding these standards. This oath I make freely, and upon my honor.

Some argue that this oath is a violation of managers' fiduciary responsibility to maximize the wealth of shareholders and that "externalities"—such as the consequences of business decisions on the ecological and social environment—should be dealt with by governments rather than by businesses. Others argue that the oath's emphasis on the greater good is timely for our hyperlinked economy with its increasingly interdependent businesses, wherein "old school thinking" about competitive relationships and (merely) maximizing profits is obsolete.

QUESTIONS FOR REFLECTION

1. Would you be willing to take this oath?
2. Do you think all managers should take such an oath? Why or why not?
3. Which of these promises do you think would be the most difficult to keep?

---

to be.[30] An intuitive approach is consistent with research showing that we often make decisions using factors that are difficult to quantify. For example, people often rely on intuition when making choices on the basis of hard-to-measure outcomes (like "happiness") that they hope to achieve.[31] A sustainable approach encourages these considerations in decision making.[32]

Lee Roy Beach's **image theory** describes decisions as being made not "by the numbers," but rather in comparison with ideal states or ideal images of self or outcomes.[33] Image theory assumes that people choose alternatives using a relatively simple two-step process. First the decision maker uses a *compatibility* test to determine how well a particular alternative fits his or her self-image in terms of values, goals, and plans. If the alternative is not compatible, it is rejected. If the alternative is compatible, the decision maker moves to the second step, applying a *profitability* (pro-fit-ability) test that will show which of the compatible alternatives best *fits* with his or her principles, values, goals, and plans.

Image theory describes decisions as being made not "by the numbers," but rather in comparison with ideal states or ideal images of self or outcomes.

This comparison of possible alternatives to our ideal self is consistent with the use of virtue theory to make decisions regarding ethical dilemmas. Beyond considering what is legal or allowed by company policy or even what is fair for everyone involved, virtue theory considers whether the decision reflects noble character. Ethical decisions can mean going beyond what is required by the law. For individuals, making ethical decisions according to the standard of virtue may mean considering what someone whom they respect or admire (say, their grandmother) would do in a similar situation, or it may mean considering how they would feel if their actions were shared with others, perhaps via a "tweet" or Facebook status update. In other words, it requires people considering whether they would be ashamed of their behaviour or proud of it (for more on this, see OB in Action: How Do Managers Actually Make Ethical Decisions?)

Despite Air Canada's tumultuous relationship with its employees in recent years, there was a time when the company and its staff shared a sense of common purpose that propelled it forward. Back in 2003 when the airline declared bankruptcy, Air Canada's unions agreed to take significant pay cuts, ranging from 10 to 30 percent, in order to help the company overcome the period of financial difficulty. If the employees had been purely or even mostly self-serving and cared only about themselves, they could have easily voted against the pay cut and thus would have probably caused some of their colleagues to be laid off. Air Canada's leadership team could have done the same and simply laid off a portion of its workforce to reduce costs quickly. Yet, even under such distressing circumstances, both parties reached a compromise which, to the credit of them both, certainly helped cause members of the public to view the organization and its employees more favourably.[34]

OB in Action

How Do Managers Actually Make Ethical Decisions?

© Josh Blake/iStockphoto

To study how newly graduated managers actually make ethical decisions in the workplace, researchers interviewed managers one year after they had graduated from the Harvard MBA program. All interviewees had taken a course on business ethics and many now worked in organizations that had an explicit code of ethics, offered ethics training, and had top management teams who communicated the importance of ethics. Even with all of this support, the young managers participating in the study stated that their most important external source for determining the ethicality of the decisions was their family. The managers would ask themselves, "Can I comfortably tell my parents what I did?" They also considered their own moral code, invoking what might be called the Sleep Test: "If I do this, can I fall asleep at night? When I look at myself in the mirror in the morning, will I see the kind of person I want to be?"

In addition, the researchers identified four rules of thumb that managers had learned on the job to help them make ethical decisions:

1. Performance is what really counts, so make your numbers.
2. Be loyal and demonstrate that you are a team player.
3. Don't break the law.
4. Don't *over*-invest in ethical behaviour.

The research also pointed out that once a manager starts acting unethically, his or her behaviour will worsen. Perhaps the most discouraging finding was that managers said that fear of punishment motivated them to do the *wrong* thing! A similar finding from another study concluded that ethical decision making is often fraught with pressures from powerful people in the organization. In the minds of many managers, "What is right is what the guy above you wants you to do." Other research found that the more performance-oriented students were, the more likely they were to cheat, including when they were assigned goals to out-perform others.

QUESTIONS FOR DISCUSSION

1. Who are your personal "go to" people when considering what would be the ethical choice of action?
2. Have you ever feared being punished for doing the right thing? If so, when and why?
3. Do you agree that seeking to out-perform others can increase the likelihood of unethical behaviour?

Step 4: Implement the Choice

IDENTIFY NEEDS | DEVELOP ALTERNATIVES | CHOOSE ALTERNATIVE | **IMPLEMENT DECISION**

LEARNING OBJECTIVE 4
Describe how decisions are implemented.

Some decisions may be relatively easy to implement, especially if they are consistent with and improve upon an organization's existing way of doing things. The most difficult decisions to implement are the ones that challenge an organization's basic ways of operating. Even a technically brilliant decision along these lines will fail if it is not implemented in such a way that members will embrace it. A key challenge for decision makers, therefore, is to overcome resistance to implementation.

There are several ways to overcome resistance, including removing barriers to implementation, offering various incentives for implementation (e.g., financial bonuses, opportunities for career advancement), and introducing various forms of punishment (e.g., demotion) for members who do not support implementation (see chapter 15 on organizational change). Perhaps the best way to overcome resistance is to involve other members in earlier steps of the decision-making process. From a conventional perspective, this practice can be costly and is not necessary for *most* decisions, but it may be cost-effective in *particular* situations. Researchers have developed a model to identify specific situations when participation is warranted, which represent less than 20 percent of all types of decisions.[35]

Figure 6.3 shows five levels of organizational member involvement in decision making and suggests key questions that can be asked to determine whether more or less participation is appropriate, including: How much time is available? Does the decision maker have sufficient information necessary for a successful implementation? Is commitment of other members critical? Are the goals of the decision maker aligned with the goals of those who will implement the decision? When considered together, answers to these questions can provide general guidance for the appropriate level of participation in decision making and implementation, but for a more definitive recommendation, answers to additional questions are necessary.[36]

An important aspect of implementation is to monitor the outcomes of the decision. Has the problem or opportunity that was originally identified in Step 1 been addressed? Have unanticipated new problems or unexpected opportunities been created? Research suggests that about half of all decisions fail.[37] The key is to learn from these mistakes and then apply that knowledge to future decision-making processes.

Many poor decisions persist for longer than they should because decision makers are reluctant to admit that they made a mistake. **Escalation of commitment** is evident when a decision maker perseveres with the implementation of a poor decision despite evidence that

Escalation of commitment occurs when a decision maker perseveres with the implementation of a poor decision despite evidence that it is not working.

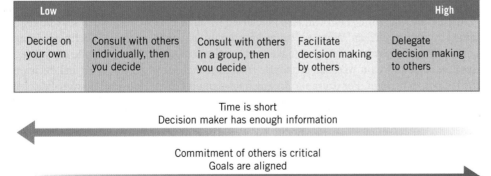

Level of participation

Low				High
Decide on your own	Consult with others individually, then you decide	Consult with others in a group, then you decide	Facilitate decision making by others	Delegate decision making to others

Time is short
Decision maker has enough information
←

Commitment of others is critical
Goals are aligned
→

FIGURE 6.3 Factors That Influence the Appropriate Level of Participation in Decision Making and Implementation
Source: Adapted from Vroom, V. H. (2003). Educating managers for decision making and leadership. *Management Decision, 41*(10), 968–978.

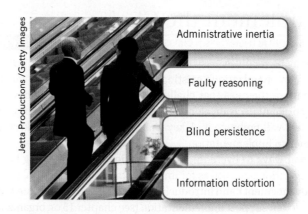

FIGURE 6.4 Factors That Contribute to Escalation of Commitment

Information distortion refers to the tendency to overlook or downplay feedback that makes a decision look bad and focus instead on feedback that makes it look good.

it is not working. As shown in Figure 6.4, the most basic reason for escalation of commitment is due to **information distortion**, which is the tendency to overlook or downplay feedback that makes a decision look bad and focus instead on feedback that makes it look good. Ashley Good, the founder and CEO of consulting firm Fail Forward, actually specializes in helping organizations prepare for failure by providing them with the necessary tools to subsequently bounce back. In her words, "the symptom of not being able or willing to talk about what's not working, regardless of the cause, creates a serious challenge to moving forward." In order to diagnose and overcome failure, Good recommends the following:[38]

1. **Lose your ego**—recognize that just because you failed doesn't mean that you're a failure. It was something you did. You have to look at it objectively and separate yourself from what happened. Great, smart people make mistakes and fail all the time.

2. **Do a deep-tissue post-mortem**—try to figure out why the failure happened. What assumptions were made? What experiences led to it? Also, listen to other perspectives on what happened.

3. **Share your story**—separate yourself from the shame and the other negative emotions that go along with it. Sharing the story and getting other people's perspectives helps you to see it objectively.

4. **Try again or move forward**—Maybe you've learned that you weren't on the route you should have been on, and that's fine. But whatever your decision, it's important to have something lined up that's a step forward.

Escalation of commitment can also be caused by blind persistence, which may be reinforced by sayings such as "When the going gets tough, the tough get going." Such sayings are bolstered by stories about decision makers who refused to admit failure despite early negative feedback and who were subsequently treated as heroes when their original decision turned out to be right. For example, an engineer named Chuck House at Hewlett-Packard received a "Medal of Defiance" because, even though David Packard himself had told him to quit working on a particular project, House persisted using organizational resources to develop what eventually became a highly successful new product.[39] In this case, not listening to the boss garnered praise and a medal; in other cases, however, it may be "rewarded" with a pink slip indicating termination of employment. Perhaps comedian W. C. Fields got it right when he said, "If at first you don't succeed, try, try, again. Then quit."

Escalation of commitment can also occur due to faulty reasoning, such as when decision makers inappropriately repeat the same process they used for an earlier successful decision. Recall the previous discussion about the downfall of Research In Motion (now BlackBerry).

Former co-CEOs Jim Balsillie and Mike Lazaridis fell victim to overconfidence, mistakenly believing that because they had essentially monopolized the smartphone market and had been so successful up until 2007, they would continue along the same path for years to come and consumers would be generally happy with whatever the company produced. But as we now know, even the company's first foray into the touchscreen devices that have made iPhone and Android phones so popular was disappointing. Simply put, RIM failed to provide the right mix of features that consumers demanded. When Thorsten Heins finally stepped in as CEO in 2012, he prepared to refocus the company and actually follow market trends; however, many believed that this reform was coming too late. Even though the company has managed to rebound slightly from its all-time stock price low in September 2012, BlackBerry can hardly be considered to have recovered from the problems that stemmed from an unwillingness or inability to adapt.[40]

Finally, escalation of commitment can result from **administrative inertia**, which is the tendency of existing structures and systems to persist even though they may not be useful. For

> **Administrative inertia** describes what happens when existing organizational structures and systems persist simply because they are already in place.

OB in Action

Culture and the Decision-Making Process

Roberto Machado Noa/Getty Images

Quintessentially Canadian coffee chain Tim Hortons has set its sights on expansion into the United States for years now, but it continues to struggle to gain a strong foothold there. In 2010, the company was actually forced to close some of its stores in the New England region, and it and has since opened fewer stores south of the border than it has in Canada. Why has Tim Hortons struggled so much to penetrate the American market?

Culture experts and Canadians themselves often caution against the misconception that Canadians and Americans are the same. Despite the high degree of similarity between the two cultures, the subtle differences in etiquette, preferences, values, and communication styles are equally noteworthy. These differences are likely to influence the way leaders, managers, and employees make decisions, possibly rendering existing organizational scripts obsolete. Also, these cultural differences lead consumers to make decisions differently, and therefore products that resonate well with Canadians may not have the same effect on other individuals—even our American neighbours.

More striking cultural differences can be observed between countries and/or regions that are more geographically distant from one another. In Western cultures, for instance, formal rationality and individualism are highly valued, which is consistent with a centralized approach to decision making whereby managers (1) identify problems, (2) generate solutions, (3) rationally evaluate and choose the best solution, and (4) implement the solution by telling others what to do.

In contrast, Japanese managers are more likely to follow the *ringi* decision-making process, whereby (1) the need for a decision can be informally presented by any member of the organization; (2) once it has been discussed informally, it is written in a memo and formally circulated; (3) further discussion takes place as the memo is circulated and approved by each member; and (4) the final decision is formally recorded and "stamped" as approved by members.

This approach is based on a value system wherein the group reigns supreme and there exists a cooperative ethic that places a high value on maintaining interpersonal peace and harmony is key. Even though the *ringi* process may take longer and seem less efficient than a conventional approach, its emphasis on group consensus and collective responsibility means that once the process has been completed, implementation of a decision is virtually assured.

Just as they vary across societies, so also decision scripts vary across organizations. One way to recognize the scripts or thought patterns that an organization or culture reinforces is to be mindful of the values that influence decision making. To be "mindful" means to be aware of and attentive to values in each of the four steps of the decision-making process. Mindfulness is enhanced when you are able to contrast and compare two different approaches to the four-step decision-making process, as described in this chapter. It can also help you overcome mindlessly enacting scripts that are inconsistent with values you aspire toward.

QUESTIONS FOR DISCUSSION

1. Describe some new "scripts" you learned when you started a new job or a new school, or when you lived in a different culture.
2. When is it good to learn new scripts, and when might it be dysfunctional?
3. How mindful are you about the scripts you learn at work, school, or in society at large?

instance, if millions of dollars have been spent on a merger that is clearly not working, managers will have a difficult time deciding to "un-merge." The business press publishes more stories about business mergers and acquisitions than it does stories about companies selling off businesses, even though one study showed that 61 percent of the largest mergers and acquisitions over a two-year period actually destroyed shareholder wealth, and only 17 percent created positive returns.[41]

What can decision makers do to reduce the likelihood that escalation of commitment will occur? One tactic is to simply view the results of previous decisions as important information rather than as a legacy that must be continued. Decision makers need to ask themselves what they have learned during the decision-making process that will inform future decisions.[42] In addition, they must be bold enough to use what they have learned to undo poor decisions. Recognizing a past flawed decision is often easier for people who did not themselves make the decisions. For example, newly appointed managers are 100 times more likely to sell a business unit that was acquired as the result of a poor decision than are the managers who made the decision in the first place.[43]

The sustainable approach has some inherent advantages in overcoming resistance to implementing challenging decisions, and also in overcoming problems associated with the escalation of commitment. First, whereas the conventional approach encourages the *selective* use of participation in order to overcome resistance to the implementation of decisions, the sustainable approach is less likely to meet resistance because of its ongoing emphasis on participation in all four steps of the decision-making process. In the sustainable approach, participation influences the kinds of decisions considered (Step 1), the types of alternatives developed (Step 2), the alternatives chosen (Step 3), and the process by which decisions are implemented (Step 4).

Second, because sustainable decision makers tend to view decisions as experiments, they are more likely to look for feedback that will help them *improve* their decisions rather than *defend* them. In this way, a sustainable approach reduces the likelihood of escalation of commitment, information distortion, inappropriate persistence, and administrative inertia. In addition, it increases the likelihood that decision makers will learn from poor decisions.

For an example of sustainable decision making, consider what happened when Robert Greenleaf noticed that African-American employees were underrepresented at the higher managerial levels at AT&T (Step 1). He met with a group of managers and invited them to participate in developing alternatives that might improve the situation (Step 2). Group members suggested recruiting more African-American employees for management training programs and providing African-American specialists with job experiences that would better prepare them for managerial positions (Step 3). Managers were invited to implement both, one, or neither of these options. Those who did implement either option or both did so in a spirit of experimentation and out of a desire to learn from and improve upon practices based on the feedback they received. In time, an increasing number of managers began to adopt the new "scripts," and over a nine-year period these activities helped increase the proportion of African-American managers at AT&T almost tenfold (Step 4).[44] A similar sustainable decision-making approach would be of benefit in Canada, given that in 2013 visible minorities were found to hold only 2 percent of the seats on Canadian corporate boards of directors, a number that falls well short of representing the increasingly diverse Canadian population. A sustainable approach to rectifying this disparity would include calling on boards to replace a certain percentage of retiring directors with a diversity candidate—precisely what the Canadian Board Diversity Council is doing, in addition to asking boards to also include a minimum number of "diverse" people in its pool of candidates for open board seats.[45]

Finally, the decisions that result from a sustainable approach may counter conventional wisdom and require courage to implement. In a world characterized by an increasing gap between the rich and the poor, implementing decisions that consider the interests of a broad set of stakeholders—some powerful and others not—is the road less travelled. This sentiment is captured in the following observations by a manager who had worked his way to the top of a large national organization before spending 10 years working in various inner-city organizations trying to facilitate economic development among the urban poor:

> I think often, when we say that we want a nice life, we mean an easy life. Sure, there's a little more tension when you are accountable to a team rather than to only a manager, but I think that there is a whole mix of relationships happening there that makes life richer, even if it makes it a little more complicated.[46]

The courage to deliver counter-cultural decisions can result from having followed a thorough decision-making process that gives you confidence you have chosen the best alternative, but it also arises from a participative sustainable decision-making process that, by its nature, provides a supportive circle of co-workers and other stakeholders. Members of this circle have ownership of the decision, which can go a long way in overcoming the uncertainty inherent in most decisions.

how decisions can lead to a $7 billion loss[47]

© Pierre Merimee/Corbis

The 144-year-old French bank Société Générale was known as a world leader in derivatives (a type of financial investment) when it lost more than USD $7 billion in January 2008. How could an organization with a reputation of making good investment decisions suddenly lose so much money? There may have been a variety of factors at play, but the story centres on decisions made by Jérôme Kerviel, a then 31-year-old bank employee accused of circumventing bank controls and rules in his trades.

An early signal that something was amiss occurred the previous November 7, when compliance officers at Société Générale received an email from Eurex, one of Europe's biggest exchanges, stating that over a period of seven months Kerviel had engaged in several transactions that raised red flags. Société Générale receives about 15 to 20 such queries from exchanges like Eurex each year. The compliance officer at Société Générale looked into the problems, and Kerviel's supervisor indicated that there was no anomaly. Société Générale responded with a memo to Eurex describing how the increase in volatility in the European and U.S. markets explained the need for Kerviel's after-hours trading.

Eurex sent a follow-up email toward the end of November asking for more information. Société Générale provided more

details on December 10, and the issue seemed settled. Kerviel reported that by the end of December his trades had resulted in a profit of about $2 billion for the bank, and he was rewarded with a $400,000 bonus for the year.

Unfortunately, a few weeks later, when Kerviel set off the next alarm, it was too late. Kerviel had exposed Société Générale to over USD $70 billion in risk—more than the bank's market value. After his trades were unwound, the result was $7 billion in trading losses within a week.

How could this happen? Various explanations have been offered. First, Société Générale had a culture that rewarded risk and encouraged its employees to engage in "proprietary trading," which involves using the bank's money to make bets on the market. As a result, to get bigger rewards, managers would be tempted to take larger risks, and in a complex industry, a bank's internal controls cannot always keep up with the clever actions of its members. In Kerviel's case, thanks to his earlier job experience working in the bank's back office, he knew what time its reconciliation for each day's trades took place, and he was able to use this information to delete his unauthorized transactions and then re-enter them.

Another explanation points to the fact that specific challenges in maintaining self-control may be inherent in a trader's job. Research in neuroeconomics indicates that the brain images of drug addicts about to take another hit are identical to the brain images of traders who are making money and about to make another trade. Put differently, making money is similar to a chemical addiction.

For his part, Kerviel accepted a share of the responsibility for his decisions, but he refused to become the scapegoat, insisting that his managers had been aware of his unusually large trades and had received warnings about his activities several months earlier.

QUESTIONS FOR DISCUSSION

1. What step or steps in the decision-making process are problematic in this case?
2. How might framing theory help to explain what happened at Société Générale?
3. Does escalation of commitment help explain what happened? How?
4. In light of your analysis, what advice about employee decision making would you give to Société Générale?

Summary

Both conventional OB and sustainable OB describe decision makers following the same basic four-step decision-making process, but there are differences in how the process unfolds.

 Learning Objectives

- Step 1: Describe the importance of identifying the need to make a decision.
- Step 2: Recognize the alternative responses decision makers can follow once a need for a decision has been identified.
- Step 3: Discuss the key factors in choosing the appropriate alternative decision.

- Step 4: Describe how decisions are implemented.

 In the conventional OB approach:

- First, decision makers identify problems and opportunities for the organization, with a particular emphasis on maximizing shareholder wealth.
- Second, decision makers develop alternative ways to respond to those problems or opportunities, with an eye toward ensuring that the financial benefits of an alternative outweigh its financial costs.
- Third, decision makers choose one of the alternatives, using an appropriate method based on the level of goal consensus and available knowledge.

- Fourth, decision makers implement the chosen alternative, using a participative approach if necessary to overcome resistance.

In the sustainable OB approach:

- First, decision makers and other stakeholders identify problems and opportunities for the organization that will improve a variety of forms of well-being over time.
- Second, decision makers and other stakeholders develop alternative ways to respond to those problems or opportunities, with an eye toward ensuring that overall well-being is enhanced long-term.

- Third, decision makers and other stakeholders choose one of the alternatives that have been developed, appreciating the healthy tension among various goals and drawing on both explicit and tacit knowledge.
- Fourth, decision makers and other stakeholders implement the chosen alternative, using an experimental approach that nurtures continuous learning.

Key Terms

Administrative inertia (p. 127)

Administrative method (p. 121)

Decision (p. 115)

Escalation of commitment (p. 125)

Explicit knowledge (p. 122)

Framing (p. 121)

Goal consensus (p. 119)

Image theory (p. 123)

Incremental trial-and-error method (p. 120)

Information distortion (p. 126)

Intuition (p. 121)

Nonprogrammed decisions (p. 118)

Political method (p. 120)

Programmed decisions (p. 118)

Rational choice (p. 120)

Satisficing (p. 121)

Scripts (p. 116)

Subjective method (p. 121)

Tacit knowledge (p. 121)

Uncertainty (p. 120)

Questions for Reflection and Discussion

1. Identify and briefly describe each of the four steps in the decision-making process.
2. Which of the four steps do you think is the most challenging for decision makers? Why do you think so?
3. What advice do you have for students in your class who, like Dennis Gioia in the chapter opening case, aspire to bring corporate socially responsible decision making to an organization that does not have a reputation for making such decisions?
4. Explain how you decided which post-secondary school to attend or which major to choose. Did your decision-making process follow the four-step process described in the chapter? Which steps were most important? Why?
5. From what you know of the major you have chosen (e.g., marketing, accounting, finance), what are the most common criteria used in decision making by practitioners in this field? Can you imagine some unintended negative consequences of using these criteria exclusively in decisions?

ob activities

How Courageous Are You in Making Decisions?

Using a scale of 1 - Strongly Disagree (SD), 2 - Disagree (D), 3 - Neutral (N), 4 - Agree (A), and 5 - Strongly Agree (SA), indicate your level of agreement with each statement on the 5-point scale.

Typically, I . . .

	SD	D	N	A	SA
Don't hesitate to express an unpopular opinion.	1	2	3	4	5
Call for action while others talk.	1	2	3	4	5
Do not stand up for my beliefs.	1	2	3	4	5
Speak up in protest when I hear someone say mean things.	1	2	3	4	5
Don't speak my mind freely when there might be negative results.	1	2	3	4	5

Key: This is a short version of a courage scale from the International Personality Item Pool (http://ipip.ori.org/). To calculate your total score, add the following:

_____ *(response to statement 1)*

+ _____ *(response to statement 2)*

+ _____ *(response to statement 3, subtracted from 6)*

+ _____ *(response to statement 4)*

+ _____ *(response to statement 5, subtracted from 6)*

= _____ *Total score*

The greater the score (out of 25 possible), the higher your self-rating on being courageous. Having higher levels of courage has been shown to be positively related to decisions and actions that are ethical and that benefit others.[48]

What Is Your Cognitive Style in Making Decisions?

In each pair of statements of this simplified questionnaire, circle the number of the one that best describes your style of decision making.

1 - I primarily rely on logic when making career decisions.
2 - I primarily rely on my feelings when making career decisions.

1 - I primarily weigh quantitative factors, such as my age, budget needs, or future earnings, when making a decision about a large purchase or investment.
2 - I primarily weigh qualitative factors, such as my gut feelings or a sense that the decision is right for me, when making a decision about a large purchase or investment.

1 - When making important decisions, I pay close attention when a number of people with well-justified expertise give me the same advice.
2 - When making important decisions, I pay close attention when I experience a "knowing in my bones," chills, tingling, or other physical sensations.

1 - The most important factor in making life-altering changes is knowing that the change is based on objective, verifiable facts.
2 - The most important factor in making life-altering changes is feeling it is right for me.

1 - When my analysis and intuition are in conflict, I give precedence to my analytical reasoning.
2 - When my analysis and intuition are in conflict, I give precedence to my intuitive insights.

Key: Total the circled numbers. A score of 5 or 6 suggests that your style is to make decisions in a linear, logical, or analytical fashion. A score of 9 or 10 suggests that your style is to make decisions in a nonlinear, creative, or intuitive fashion. A score of 7 or 8 suggests that you do not seem to have a dominant style or that your style is flexible, using both approaches to making decisions. Analytical thinking is positively associated with grade point average of undergraduate students, but intuitive thinking is considered critical to new breakthroughs that are the lifeblood of organizations.[49] These items are a shortened version of a more comprehensive research instrument.

Source: Vance, C. M., Groves, K. S., Paik, Y., & Kindler, H. (2007). Understanding and measuring linear-nonlinear thinking style for enhanced management education and professional practice. *Academy of Management Learning and Education, 6*(2), 167–185.

ETHICS SCENARIO

A highway building contractor deplored the chaotic bidding situation and cutthroat competition in his industry. The contractor therefore reached an understanding with other major contractors to permit bidding that would provide a reasonable profit.

Why might this scenario occur in organizations?

Use the following scale to indicate whether this behaviour is ethically acceptable:

NEVER ACCEPTABLE		SOMETIMES ACCEPTABLE			ALWAYS ACCEPTABLE	
①	②	③	④	⑤	⑥	⑦

Explain the ideas you considered in arriving at your answer.

DISCUSSION STARTER

Ethics, Profits, and People[50]

Aaron Feuerstein, previous owner and CEO of Malden Mills Industries in Lawrence, Massachusetts, has become a classic example of a sustainable manager. When most of the Malden Mills factory, which made Polartec fleece products, burned to the ground in December 1995, the 70-year-old Feuerstein could have taken the $300 million insurance money and enjoyed retirement. He could have also followed the lead of others in his industry and used the money to rebuild the factory in the American South, where labour costs were lower than in the Northeast.

Instead, Feuerstein decided to remain loyal to his economically depressed community. He rebuilt the factory on the same site, even though the insurance covered only three-fourths of the reconstruction costs. He also voluntarily kept all 3,000 employees on the payroll during the long reconstruction process. Clearly Feuerstein, who found guidance in Jewish moral law and tradition, placed a high value on community: "I simply felt an obligation to the entire community that relies on our presence here in Lawrence; it would have been unconscionable to put 3,000 people out on the streets." His willingness to use his financial resources to nurture community in a counter-cultural way attracted much media attention: "I got a lot of publicity. And I don't think it speaks well for our

times. . . . At the time in America of our greatest prosperity, the god of money has taken over to an extreme."

Feuerstein's actions generated much good will. When the factory reopened, customers sought out his product. Suppliers, buyers, and employees all went the extra mile to support the company through tough times after the new factory began operations. Even so, a series of warm winters and cheaper overseas goods conspired to reduce the sales of the firm's fleece products, and its furniture upholstery customers, who turned to other suppliers after the fire, never returned. Despite its state-of-the-art mill and its popular products, these unforeseen market challenges forced Malden Mills to operate under bankruptcy between 2001 and 2003.

Although the company emerged from that crisis, Feuerstein left the company's board in 2004 (he still owned about 5 percent of the company). By 2006, its annual revenue was around $160 million, including $25 million that came from producing high-tech clothing for the U.S. military. Ultimately, heavy debts forced the firm to declare bankruptcy again, and it sold its assets to Chrysalis Capital Partners. In 2007, the company re-emerged as Polartec LLC and continued to sell its patented products.

QUESTIONS FOR DISCUSSION

1. What criteria did Aaron Feurerstein use in his decision making?
2. Was Feuerstein an effective decision maker?
3. Refer back to the discussion about moral points of views found in chapter 4, and explain whether you think Feuerstein's decisions were ethical in terms of (a) consequential utilitarianism and (b) virtue theory. Would it have been more ethical for him to decide to relocate to the South?
4. Do you think, in hindsight, he has regrets about not deciding to relocate to the South?
5. What decision-making criteria would each of Malden Mills's key stakeholders (employees, customers, suppliers, competitors, and neighbours) have preferred?

DISCUSSION STARTER

Factors That Influence the Quality of Decision Making[51]

Imagine that you are part of an organization's executive committee and that you must make a choice among several alternatives developed by the marketing department to promote a new product. Indicate the effect you believe each of the following possible actions would have on the overall quality of the decision your executive committee makes.

Possible Actions

Overall Effect on Decision Making

Possible Actions	Negative	Neutral	Positive
1. The marketing committee recommends the alternative that strengthens its relative power within the company.	1	2	3
2. When the president of a company indicates her preference, everyone provides his or her support for it.	1	2	3
3. Members of the committee describe how the preferred option is very similar to a previous highly successful event in the company's history.	1	2	3
4. Before making the decision, the executive committee agrees not to consider any additional information that was not included in the marketing team's analysis.	1	2	3
5. Decision makers consider the information in a holistic sense (i.e., they do not get lost in whether some details are based on past facts or future projections).	1	2	3
6. One of the options is favoured because it is thought to be consistent with the successes enjoyed by an industry leader.	1	2	3
7. One of the options is favoured because it helps to take advantage of previous investments that the company has made, especially because those investments would not likely be made today.	1	2	3
8. The choice is made primarily based on internal conditions, with little emphasis on external factors that you have little control over (e.g., like guessing how competitors might react).	1	2	3
9. Alternatives are considered that offer modest worst-case scenarios, rather than extreme worst-case scenarios.	1	2	3
10. The choice of the executive committee is influenced by knowing that it is the alternative the marketing department has fallen in love with.	1	2	3

QUESTION FOR DISCUSSION

1. Discuss each possible action with a small group of classmates and provide a group answer. Defend your answer by referring to relevant research in the chapter. Suggested answers will be provided in the Instructor's Manual.

APPLICATION JOURNAL

This is a personal journal entry that can be used for class discussion or be compiled and included in a self-reflection paper.

Reflect on some of the "scripts" you use when you make decisions. Think about possible differences in how you make big decisions versus everyday decisions. Who "wrote" these scripts, and when did you learn them? Now reflect on some of the new scripts you are learning in your studies. Have you had a chance to put them into practice in your own life or in the workplace? Which of the OB scripts that you are learning do you think will be most useful in your career?

Seven

Leading Self

Our experiences in organizations are coloured by interactions with interesting individuals who are motivated in sometimes familiar ways and who make decisions that influence us. Yet to focus on the choices of others in some ways diminishes the essential role that our own choices make in determining our path. This chapter concludes our focus on individual OB by turning our attention to how we lead ourselves.

Learning Objectives	Conventional OB	Sustainable OB
AUTHENTIC LEADERSHIP		
1. Identify the components and outcomes of leading self in organizations.	Focus on choosing which portions of self to reveal in organizational settings	Focus on developing and presenting self holistically and honestly to others
KNOWING SELF		
2. Describe the process of gaining self-knowledge.	Focus on understanding self to build confidence	Focus on understanding self to promote humility
LIVING INTENTIONALLY		
3. Discuss self-leadership and how it can determine whether an individual performs well or fails in organizations.	Emphasize personal, tangible outcomes	Emphasize relational, intangible outcomes
MANAGING STRESS AND ROLES		
4. Discuss stress and role conflict in the workplace.	Care for self and secure financial resources	Care for both self and others and secure social resources
ACTING CREATIVELY		
5. Explain the creative process, characteristics of creative individuals, and strategies for improving creativity in organizations.	Highlight self-expression and profits	Highlight self-expression and organizational authenticity

following a different voice[1]

Todd Plit/Contour by Getty Images

Cynthia Cooper was moving forward in her accounting career, having become the vice-president of Internal Audit at WorldCom after rising through the ranks during nearly a decade at the telecommunications company. She was looking forward to the challenge of new responsibilities. WorldCom was a darling of the stock market, once the fifth most widely held stock in the United States, and was growing at breakneck speed.

In a review of the financial books she inherited, Cooper uncovered what appeared to be unusual transactions. Her first response was to approach the company's financial executives about these items. Upon doing so, she was assured that a previous audit had reviewed them and that she should assume any questionable transactions were appropriate and not her concern. Cooper then discussed the issues with one of WorldCom's external auditors, who did not seem alarmed. CFO Scott Sullivan, who was widely admired in the company and industry and was once the highest-paid CFO in the United States, also dismissed her concerns. Still, the transactions bothered Cooper, so she approached other executives with her concerns, but no one was interested in pursuing the issue further. The message was clear: she was to stop wasting time on her investigations and do her job.

Cooper believed that it was her business to look into the problem, even if it did not occur on her watch and others were discouraging her inquiries. She continued to investigate the dubious accounting transactions in the secrecy of late evenings, telling her small team of auditors to keep digging. She and her team also pored over the external auditor's working files. She eventually uncovered massive fraud at WorldCom. Ultimately, Cooper went public with the fraud—which amounted to a whopping USD $9 billion and resulted in the company's collapse and the imprison-

It's important to be able to dig down and find your courage, which isn't always so easy.

ment of five executives, including Sullivan and CEO Bernie Ebbers, who received a 25-year sentence.

Cooper faced opposition in her attempts to do what she knew in her heart was the right thing. The leaders above her insisted that she let go of her concerns, sending a clear message to be loyal to the company, which was facing difficulties in a troubled industry, rather than follow up on her personal reservations. Cooper likely also felt considerable pressure knowing that exposing problems at WorldCom could hurt friends and neighbours who worked at the corporate headquarters nestled in the small town of Clinton, Mississippi. Even so, to be true to herself, she had to blow the whistle.

Cooper attributed her tenacity to her training and experience in accounting, auditing, and fraud examination, plus the obligation she felt to the WorldCom shareholders to ensure that the company's accounting was accurate and legal. She also has a psychologically tested personality type of people who are strong-willed and natural leaders—a type found in fewer than 1% of the population. But Cooper said that during her investigations, she did not always feel strong. "There were times when I was scared, when my hands were shaking and my heart was pounding. I certainly knew there was a very real possibility I would lose my job, and I also worried at times that I was overreacting."

In further reflecting on her decision, Cooper asserted, "It's important to be able to dig down and find your courage, which isn't always so easy. My mother would say, 'Don't ever allow yourself to be intimidated.' That was really ingrained in me, and I think that helped." No doubt it did. When everything outside her called for compromising her values just this once, Cooper turned to the lessons and values she had learned growing up, and she acted with integrity.

Authentic Leadership

| AUTHENTIC LEADERSHIP | KNOWING SELF | LIVING INTENTIONALLY | MANAGING STRESS | ACTING CREATIVELY |

LEARNING OBJECTIVE 1
Identify the components and outcomes of leading self in organizations.

Leading yourself means being authentic in your roles—inside and outside of organizations—and acting with integrity. **Authenticity** is the state of being true to oneself; it is a way of living in which your outward actions match up with your inner self because you know who you are and what you want to be. It takes courage and intentionality to live according to this sense of self, regardless of circumstances and challenges. Authenticity allows us to act with integrity.

Authenticity is the state of being true to oneself; it is a way of living in which your outward actions match up with your inner self because you know who you are and what you want to be.

The call to be authentic has a rich history dating back to Ancient Greece and the adage "Know thyself.'"[2] Research on authenticity and authentic leadership has confirmed that authentic living contributes to psychological well-being and self-esteem regardless of a person's circumstances.[3] When you are authentic, you are being true to yourself and therefore will be less prone to the stress and tension that come from feeling the need to please others. Authenticity creates a reservoir of personal health and strength that grows from a sense of purposeful living, personal mastery, meaningful connections with others, and living above circumstances.[4] In the long run, being authentic is better for you and, as an attractive side benefit, has many positive benefits for organizational life. Alternatively, as shown in the opening case, it can also have negative outcomes for your organization or your career. Although many government regulations do exist to protect whistleblowers, acting with authenticity can lead to losing your job.[5]

Authenticity in organizational leadership roles is called authentic leadership. There are various descriptions of **authentic leadership**, but most have in common being self-aware, staying true to an internal sense of what is right, relating to others transparently, and objectively balancing all relevant data in decision making.[6] It's important to note that consistency with one's values and motives does not necessarily imply authentic leadership. People with integrity are typically viewed as self-aware and often regulate their behaviour to be consistent with their best self—but that doesn't mean that they have strong, authentic relationships with others or that they try to achieve balanced decision making.[7]

Authentic leadership is authenticity in organizational leadership roles.

Authentic leaders influence individuals, the work environment, and organizational performance because others perceive them as having integrity and acting in predictable and consistent ways. These leaders earn higher levels of trust and contribute to the existence of positive emotions and higher levels of psychological capital.[8] Psychological capital has been described as the sum of psychological resources represented by self-efficacy, hope, optimism, and resilience that motivate an individual to persevere toward goals despite adversity.[9] Taken together, these results offer even further benefits for a leader's co-workers. In particular, research shows that people who work with a leader who is authentic tend to experience[10]

- greater work engagement, a sense of empowerment, and job satisfaction;
- less burnout and worries about status within the work setting;
- higher levels of job performance, organizational citizenship behaviour, and commitment to the organization; and
- enhanced trust in, identification with, and satisfaction with the leader.

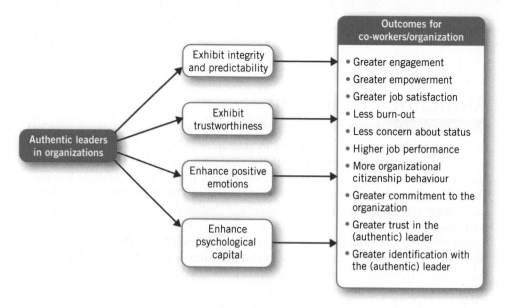

FIGURE 7.1 Outcomes Associated with Leading Self in Organizations

Figure 7.1 describes some of the workplace outcomes associated with authentic leadership.

David W. Hill is an investment banker and consultant in the restaurant, real estate, banking, and entertainment industries.[11] Hill has extensive experience as a deal maker in major mergers and acquisitions. He indicates that getting the financial matters figured out is relatively easy, but what is most challenging is understanding the people. In his experience, most deals fall through after information is discovered that points to a lack of authenticity. Hill is committed to practising authentic behaviour in his business dealings, and he promotes the principle of being real in all his dealings. For him, authenticity is paramount. "If you have trust, you have everything," he says. He asserts that being real is efficient; if you are the same person in your personal and professional dealings, you don't have to manage dual lives.

Authentic leadership also promotes the creativity that is critical for innovating and adapting to organizational challenges.[12] At Taiwanese real estate offices, authentic leadership was associated with a positive mood and high-quality relationships that encouraged employees to speak out when problems arose or changes were necessary.[13] In new businesses that are just starting out, when the top management teams act authentically, the firm performs better.[14] Authenticity also has been positively linked to the financial performance of existing firms.[15]

As shown in Figure 7.2, two hallmarks of authenticity—self-awareness and self-regulation—can be further broken down into four separate components, which we will focus on in this chapter. We will start with research and practice related to *Knowing Self* before moving on to self-regulation as evident in *Living Intentionally, Managing Roles and Stress,* and *Acting Creatively.* Figure 7.2 also shows what people can do to strengthen these four components and thus improve their authenticity in the workplace.

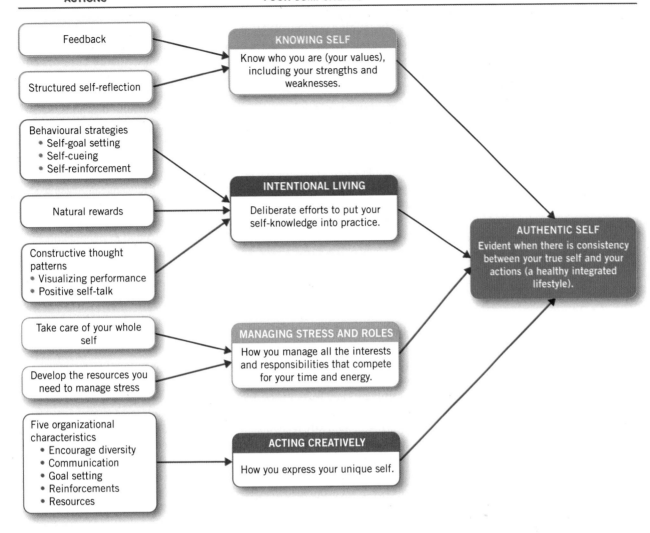

FIGURE 7.2 Actions and Components of Leading Self

Knowing Self

AUTHENTIC LEADERSHIP | **KNOWING SELF** | LIVING INTENTIONALLY | MANAGING STRESS | ACTING CREATIVELY

Self-awareness arises from our life experiences, our successes, and our failures. Some lessons about ourselves are obvious to us; others we learn from conscious personal reflection or from feedback we receive from others. We can improve our self-awareness by adopting an ongoing process of discovery and reflection that provides insight into our strengths and weaknesses, our values, and the sources of our feelings.[16] One result of increased self-awareness is greater self-confidence and trust in our ability to successfully transform situations.[17] Other results include higher self-esteem, more positive emotions, and reduced anxiety and depression.[18] Understanding ourselves is a prerequisite for being authentic and for exercising authentic leadership.[19]

The process of gaining self-knowledge can begin with gathering information about your behaviour at work.[20] First, how do you work with others inside your organization? Do you emphasize hierarchy and authority or participation and collegiality? Second, what goals do you emphasize? Is your energy primarily directed toward maximizing financial well-being,

> **LEARNING OBJECTIVE 2**
> Describe the process of gaining self-knowledge.

or do you also pursue social, spiritual, and ecological well-being? Third, how do you relate to people outside your organization? Do you treat others as competitors or as collaborators?

The process of acquiring self-knowledge is fraught with dangers and the possibility of self-delusion. On the one hand, some people have an inclination to think too little of themselves, which can lead to self-defeating behaviours and poor performance.[21] On the other hand, some people think too highly of themselves. This tendency results in **hubris**, a "grandiose sense of self" evident in excessive confidence and narcissism.[22] Organizational leaders with hubris might persist in implementing their own questionable decisions, such as overpaying for acquisitions; such actions are particularly damaging when the leader is surrounded by a weak board of directors and is given broad decision-making authority.[23]

Hubris at the upper levels of an organization can keep a firm from questioning such persistence. Bombardier Inc., an aerospace and transportation company headquartered in Montreal, Quebec, was extremely successful back in the 1990s with its Canadair Regional Jets.[24] Since then, though, the company has struggled after placing all of its figurative eggs in one basket with the C Series jets. Seemingly endless cost overruns and delays continued to threaten Bombardier's existence, yet general managerial stubbornness resulted in minimal organizational or strategic change to improve the company's performance.[25] Despite a February 2015 announcement regarding the appointment of a new CEO,[26] industry analysts question whether this change will be enough, as almost all other major players in the firm's decision-making and leadership process remain on board. At this point, only time will tell whether Bombardier's C Series jets will provide the comeback that the company desperately needs. Whether or not hubris is the ultimate culprit, the firm's persistence is definitely under scrutiny.

While a conventional approach to self-knowledge focuses on how much people know about themselves, a sustainable approach is likely to include the humility to recognize that "the more you know, the more you know you don't know."[27] Humility is a proper sense of self, an awareness of strengths and weaknesses, and an appreciation of knowledge outside yourself.[28] Humility can be thought of as a sense of self that lies "between arrogance and lowliness."[29] Humble people inherently recognize that they are part of a greater and mutually interdependent whole. Consistent with a sustainable perspective, humility is associated with "self-awareness, valuing others' opinions, willing to learn and change, sharing power, having the ability to hear the truth and admit mistakes, and working to create a culture of openness where dissent is encouraged in an environment of mutual trust and respect."[30]

People with greater emotional awareness are more likely to be humble, and those who lead with humility are more likely to support others, encourage participation, and act with others to accomplish shared goals.[31] Humility can contribute to job performance, particularly when being empathetic and demonstrating concern for others are important aspects of the job.[32] A humble person asks, "Who" am I in my relationships, and how can I foster community?[33] This is borne out in research that shows that humble people are more likely to help others.[34]

Two factors in particular are crucial for enhancing self-awareness: feedback and structured self-reflection.

1. Feedback. Unfortunately, it can be challenging to truly know yourself because self-assessments are based on incomplete or biased information processing that is prone to self-deception and positive bias.[35] These self-serving biases are prevalent and particularly damaging for leaders in organizations who fail to get adequate corrective feedback.[36] Given their power and perceived expertise, leaders are often not provided with personal feedback, especially negative feedback, from those who report to them. Very few people are willing to tell their boss that he or she is acting like a jerk.

Feedback from others is a means to reduce blind spots that can hinder being authentic, and it helps organizational members and leaders better understand their behaviour and make adjustments as necessary to act authentically.[37] The Johari window, pictured in Figure 7.3,[38] is a tool that illustrates the idea that some information about us is known to ourselves and to others; it is public information. Other information is private in that it is known to ourselves but

Hubris is a "grandiose sense of self" evident in excessive confidence and narcissism.

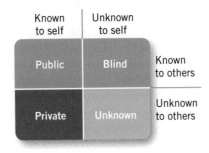

FIGURE 7.3 A View of Self-Awareness through the Johari Window

not to others, and some information is unknowable both to us as well as to others. The fourth type of information, our blind spot, is what others know about us that we do not.

An important occasion to provide and receive feedback in organizations occurs during the formal performance appraisal process (described in more detail in chapter 14; see also the discussion of feedback in communication in chapter 11). But as has already been noted, complete feedback is not always forthcoming, perhaps especially for leaders whose actions are creating negative effects in the workplace. As a result, it is important for people who aspire to be authentic to actively seek out feedback from others. **Feedback-seeking behaviour** involves asking for feedback or collecting information from the work environment to better understand how you are performing.[39] This behaviour contributes to improved performance, and it promotes creativity by increasing the quality and quantity of information available.[40] Receiving such feedback is important for all members in an organization, though the nature of the feedback being sought may differ from a conventional versus a sustainable approach. From a conventional approach, the feedback sought will focus on instrumental concerns, such as how to improve the financial performance or power of the person and the organization. A sustainable approach will also seek feedback on more relational concerns, such as how to create positive feelings and satisfy interpersonal relationships in the workplace.

> **Feedback-seeking behaviour** is asking for feedback or collecting information from the work environment to better understand how you are performing.

M**O**B | HOW REAL IS REALITY TV?

DARRYL DYCK/ CP Images

For years, television audiences have questioned the truth behind reality TV shows. Both format-driven shows like *Big Brother Canada* and lifestyle-based shows like *The Real Housewives of Vancouver* have been plagued by ongoing skepticism. Are certain characters really that rude, direct, or kind in their everyday lives, or is it all staged to achieve high ratings? Additionally, how much do editors and producers manipulate the footage in order to fit certain individuals into specific character profiles such as "the girl next door," "the self-absorbed one," "the jerk," etc.?

As one of the stars of *Shark Tank* as well as a former star of the Canadian equivalent *Dragons' Den*, Kevin O'Leary is well-known for his direct and often harsh commentary. His co-stars refer to him sarcastically as "Mr. Wonderful" due to his frequent insensitivity toward the show's featured entrepreneurs who come seeking investment partnership. O'Leary has never been afraid to tell these people that their ideas are stupid, even going so far as to say that he would "take them behind the barn and shoot them." He even sometimes speaks to his fellow Sharks and Dragons in the same manner. But are these behaviours authentic or simply part of a persona, similar to the notion of a stage name, in order to make the show more interesting and marketable?

This leads to the question, how often do we change our own behaviours either at home, at work, at school, or while engaging in extracurricular activities, where what we portray to others does not match how we really feel? And why do we do it? Are there external pressures that make us feel as if we need to act or feel a certain way?

QUESTIONS FOR REFLECTION

1. When do you feel the most pressure to be someone you are not?
2. How do you feel when you have to put on a face for others?
3. Are there situations where "just being yourself" may be better or more appropriate than behaving in an unauthentic manner?

2. Structured self-reflection. Another method to increase self-awareness and improve authenticity is structured self-reflection.[41] Knowledge of the inner self is not easily accessible without the help of a thoughtful reflective process. Such deliberate examination does not come naturally to some, nor does the hectic pace of life and business facilitate it. However, many people believe that the busier you are, the more you need to find time for reflection.

The process can begin with a conscious examination of the critical experiences in your life and the memory, feelings, and lessons you've drawn from them.[42] It can be as simple as spending half an hour every evening recalling the events of the day, including anything you may wish you had done differently, and reflecting on what your actions tell you about yourself. Or you may spend some time every morning anticipating the events of the day and thinking about how to respond to them. Many people find keeping a journal to be an effective means of acquiring self-knowledge. This may mean, for example, spending a little time on the weekend reflecting on the events of the past week, anticipating those of the coming week, and thinking about what it all means to you.[43]

Living Intentionally

| AUTHENTIC LEADERSHIP | KNOWING SELF | **LIVING INTENTIONALLY** | MANAGING STRESS | ACTING CREATIVELY |

LEARNING OBJECTIVE 3
Discuss self-leadership and how it can determine whether an individual performs well or fails in organizations.

Self-leadership practices are self-regulatory actions that help us manage and motivate ourselves.

Living intentionally, also known as applying self-leadership, means exercising self-discipline or self-influence. From a sustainable perspective, living intentionally also involves temperance—the exercise of self-control to avoid excess and achieve balance. **Self-leadership practices** are self-regulatory actions that help us manage and motivate ourselves. These practices rely on behavioural strategies, the use of natural rewards, and constructive thinking.[44]

OB in Action — Conrad Black in the Red

Darren Calabrese/CP Images

Conrad Black is the famous (or perhaps more appropriately, the infamous) former newspaper magnate who controlled Hollinger International. He was convicted of criminal fraud and obstruction of justice in the United States as a result of diverting millions of dollars from Hollinger to himself through various business transactions. Black served 37 months in prison and has since been stripped of his Order of Canada title and his honorary position on the Queen's Privy Council for Canada.

Prior to 2007 when his actions were revealed, there was little doubt about Black's leadership abilities. In fact, at the time of his appointment to the Order, he was described as "a distinguished Toronto entrepreneur and publisher . . . a man of diverse achievements within the realms of Canadian commerce, education, literature and the arts." Of course, in hindsight, many now perceive the trust and acclaim he once received as having been misplaced.

Digging deeper, we can identify Black's lack of intentional living from a sustainable perspective. Clearly he was motivated by a goal—achieving continued wealth and power—but it was defined by excess and self-interest. Sure, Black was extremely successful for a long time; however, his inability to exercise self-discipline and refrain from questionable behaviours ultimately led to his own and his company's ruin.

QUESTIONS FOR DISCUSSION

1. Think about a time when you had an important goal in mind. What were some of the temptations that came up while you worked to achieve that goal?
2. Did you manage to overcome those temptations? If so, how?
3. Was there a time when you had to consider others' interests and/or preferences while you were working to achieve that goal?

Another avenue to self-knowledge is to think of your life as a story or a journey, consider where you have been and where you are heading, and then compare how this path fits with your character, your values, and the things that motivate you.[45] You may find that you've gotten off track. Acting consistently requires self-awareness combined with self-regulation, which is the focus of the following sections.

In organizations, self-leadership can determine whether an individual performs well or fails.[46] It is related to higher levels of job satisfaction and lower levels of absenteeism,[47] and it contributes to career progression and success.[48] It also can reduce the stress and strain that individuals experience in the workplace.[49] In an extensive study of over 300 organizations across 22 years, increasing self-leadership was a stronger approach for improving worker productivity than were systems-oriented management strategies, such as lean production.[50] The benefits of self-leadership even extend across cultures. In China, self-leadership behaviours are associated with higher levels of job performance and creativity.[51] Given these benefits, it is helpful to know that self-leadership can be learned through training in organizations.[52] Research suggests that there are three types of activities that can help people in organizations to live intentionally: behavioural strategies, natural rewards, and constructive thought patterns. Let's look at each.

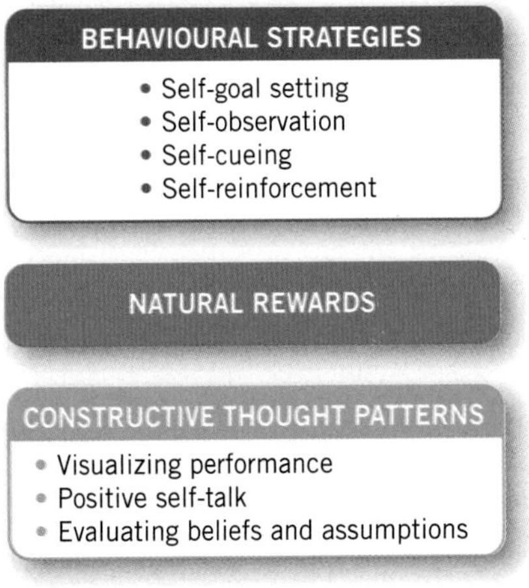

1. *Behavioural strategies.* As illustrated in Figure 7.4, living intentionally through self-leadership includes the behavioural strategies of:

   - Self-goal setting—Building on the motivational power of setting specific and difficult goals to direct attention and enhance perseverance, self-goal setting involves setting individual goals for behaviour. These goals may focus on behaviour that benefits the organization, or they may focus on setting aside time to learn to play the guitar or on losing weight to improve health. Sustainable self-goal setting is likely to also include goals that extend beyond benefiting one's self. Such goals may consist of committing a certain amount of time to serving others through mentoring or of using products from companies that are environmentally sensitive or that provide benefits to the community. Of course, the conventional and sustainable perspectives can complement one another.

BEHAVIOURAL STRATEGIES
- Self-goal setting
- Self-observation
- Self-cueing
- Self-reinforcement

NATURAL REWARDS

CONSTRUCTIVE THOUGHT PATTERNS
- Visualizing performance
- Positive self-talk
- Evaluating beliefs and assumptions

FIGURE 7.4 Living Intentionally: Self-Leadership Practices

   - Self-observation—This practice is linked to self-awareness as well as to living intentionally. It consists not only of intentional self-reflection and assessment but also of asking, "How can I improve?" The purpose is to pause, reflect, and assess how our behaviour fits our goals and aspirations, and then make plans to improve.

   - Self-cueing—Self-cueing uses pictures, Post-it notes, a screensaver, or even voice prompts as a tangible means to point us to something important we want to think about during the course of the day. Typically these cues are related to specific goals, but from a sustainable perspective they could also include reminders such as "stop and smell the flowers," "ask your colleague about his daughter's weekend basketball tournament," or "walk around the firm's neighbourhood and look for people whom your firm might be able to help."

   - Self-reinforcement—Reinforcement theory describes ways to encourage certain behaviours and to discourage others by following each behaviour with a particular outcome, either a reward or a punishment. You can use this strategy on yourself. If you complete your homework on time, for example, celebrate by going out for dinner with friends. If you have been procrastinating doing homework, eat in your residence by yourself instead. With self-reinforcement, it is up to you to administer the outcome. You can even give yourself a proverbial pat on the back by saying to yourself "well done" or, in contrast, you can challenge yourself to do better if necessary.[53]

From a sustainable perspective, a self-reward may be to do something nice for someone else. Recall (from chapter 1) that people who spend a windfall $20 on themselves are less happy than people who give it away to someone who needs it.

2. *Natural rewards.* Self-leadership includes coupling these behavioural strategies with natural rewards to enhance intrinsic motivation. Natural rewards are personally preferred or satisfying outcomes. In other words, a task that is unpleasant or not naturally motivating can become more motivating if connected to a natural reward. An assignment to complete a research report could be naturally motivating if you pick a topic that interests you, but if the topic is assigned and not very interesting, you could make the overall experience more positive by working on it with friends or while at a coffee shop. In the work environment, an unpleasant task such as bathing patients in a hospital can be made more meaningful by focusing on their inherent dignity or the added comfort they will have as a result.[54]

3. *Constructive thought patterns.* Lastly, self-leadership employs methods of thinking constructively. These include:

   - Visualizing performance—Visualizing performance often occurs in sports, such as when a baseball player mentally rehearses successfully fielding a ground ball or getting a hit. In organizational terms, the technique can involve thinking about delivering a successful presentation or sales pitch. It is a mental rehearsal that walks you through all the steps that will lead to the successful performance of a task. From a sustainable perspective, important interpersonal interactions may be worth practising, such as apologies. They aren't always easy to deliver, particularly for a leader, but communicating a sincere apology contributes to your being perceived more positively.[55]

   - Positive self-talk—A skit on *Saturday Night Live* had Stuart Smalley (played by Al Franken) speaking to a mirror, asserting that "I'm good enough, I'm smart enough, and doggone it, people like me!"[56] Humour aside, talking positively to yourself does boost confidence and perseverance and improve attitudes.[57] In the conventional view, the self-talk may consist of words that focus on winning or beating the competition (as it was for former General Electric CEO Jack Welch, for example[58]), while the sustainable view may focus on affirming your self-esteem and worth regardless of your performance.

   - Examining individual beliefs and assumptions—This self-leadership practice evaluates personal beliefs and assumptions, identifying those that may be hindering performance and replacing them with more functional or helpful thoughts.[59] It can involve the critical-thinking process of exposing yourself to competing ideas. This book's basic framework of including the conventional and sustainable approaches, for instance, has been employed to help you thoughtfully consider your assumptions.[60]

The story of Milan Heger, an architect in Seattle, Washington, demonstrates how these constructive thought patterns can work together to manage a stressful situation. Heger had ventured out on his own in a furniture design business.[61] Initially his business grew and he was able to expand it to five employees; however, when the economy tanked, he had to lay them off and cut back across the board to make sure he could pay his bills. He worked through these stressful times by envisioning an optimistic end to what he was experiencing, practising positive self-talk, and refusing to give in to irrational fears. Heger found that it also helped to resist the entrepreneurial temptation to constantly work; instead, he set goals of taking breaks to exercise, engage in hobbies, meditate, and stretch frequently.[62]

Finally, although self-leadership and "living intentionally" can be motivated by a desire to achieve immediate and tangible individual benefits, it is also motivated by a sense of calling and the less tangible purpose of contributing to community happiness and well-being.[63] Although the term *calling* has connections to religious beliefs, it also can be rooted in a sense of meaning apart from a particular religious tradition.[64] In general terms, a **calling** is an experienced passion and sense of meaning toward work or a career.[65] People who feel a calling toward their work experience a zest or excitement, higher levels of satisfaction, and greater commitment to their organizations; in addition, they are less likely to consider leaving.[66] If you don't feel called to your work, you can change jobs or improve your sense of being called by identifying meaningful tasks in your current job and the positive effects your work has on others.[67]

A **calling** is an experienced passion and sense of meaning toward work or a career.

Managing Stress and Roles

| AUTHENTIC LEADERSHIP | KNOWING SELF | LIVING INTENTIONALLY | **MANAGING STRESS** | ACTING CREATIVELY |

LEARNING OBJECTIVE 4
Discuss stress and role conflict in the workplace.

Everyone lacks enough time to do all the things that he or she wants to do. We are pulled in many different directions and have competing responsibilities, at work (urgent deadlines, long-term priorities) and beyond (family commitments, friendships). Finding effective ways to manage everything in your life is crucial to becoming an authentic person who chooses actions consistent with who you are.

The busyness of work and life contributes to stress. **Stress** is the body's state of heightened readiness for action in response to challenges or pressures in the environment. Sometimes stress is welcome in the workplace, such as when it motivates us to meet a deadline. Often, however, sress is dysfunctional, such as when it wears on us over time to the point that it decreases work performance, contributes to absenteeism and burnout, or even damages health. Indeed, researchers differentiate between *eustress,* a good kind of stress, like the extra adrenalin charge that makes athletes more likely to break world records, and *distress,* the bad kind of stress.[68]

Stress is the body's state of heightened readiness for action in response to challenges or pressures in the environment.

Workplace Stress

Unfortunately, the workplace is full of sources of stress. **Stressors** can be situations, events, people, or perceptions that contribute to experiencing stress. Common stressors include long hours, heavy workloads, constraints on time or decision-making authority, role ambiguity and role conflict, interpersonal conflict, and a perceived lack of control.[69] Bad bosses are a "major source of misery" for many employees, with 75 percent of working adults in the United States pointing to their boss as the biggest source of stress in their job.[70] While some organizations are more stressful than others, even so almost half of working Canadians identify work as the most stressful part of their lives. Even more concerning is the fact that many associate work with anxiety and depression.[71]

Stressors can be situations, events, people, or perceptions that contribute to experiencing stress.

Excessive amounts of strain can lead to burnout in the form of emotional exhaustion or depersonalization. Emotional exhaustion is the feeling of being overwhelmed, overextended, and out of emotional and physical energy,[72] whereas depersonalization is a psychological detachment from and distancing of yourself from others.[73] Although everyone may experience this to some degree when under excessive and lasting stress, women are more likely to experience emotional exhaustion, whereas men tend to depersonalize under stress.[74] Neither is good for the stressed individuals or the organizations that employ them.

For the individual, the persistence of work stressors can result in significant immediate and long-term health problems.[75] Difficulty sleeping and a range of uncomfortable gastrointestinal problems seem to emerge most often in the presence of stress. For employers, stress reduces productivity and can even increase expenses due to accumulating disability claims. According to 2010 data collected by Statistics Canada, mental health problems cost organizations $20 billion annually.[76] To lead self, organizational members—and perhaps leaders in particular—should consider what they can do to reduce stress on themselves and within the organization.

Role Conflict

A major source of stress in need of self-leadership is role conflict. Anyone who works knows you cannot be in two places at once. Spending 40 to 60 hours or more a week on a job limits the time and energy available for other roles, such as family member, parent, friend, student, and community member. As a student, you probably have experienced some level of tension trying to balance the demands of school with the expectations of family and possibly also the responsibilities of working.[77] Having multiple roles not only eats away at the time in a day and drains energy, it can also contribute to stress and poor performance in those roles due to conflicting expectations and incompatible behaviours.[78]

Work–life conflict occurs when work role demands interfere with life role demands, such as running errands, exercising, pursuing hobbies, developing relationships, or participating in community activities.[79] The clash of roles creates stress and reduces satisfaction with work and life.[80] The conflict can be time-based if the time demanded in one role conflicts with the time demands of the other; it can be strain-based if the pressure or stress of one role overflows into another; or it can be behaviour-based if actions transferred from one role to another create problems, such as when assertive behaviour in the workplace is demonstrated outside the workplace and damages relationships.[81]

A vast majority of employees report experiencing difficulty balancing work and personal demands, with 90 percent specifically identifying concerns about not spending enough time with family.[82] **Work–family conflict** is role conflict that results from the incompatibilities and pressures of work and family roles.[83] Juggling the demands of work and family is becoming increasingly challenging as more workers are part of families in which either both spouses work or a single parent is providing for the needs of other family members.[84] Work–family conflict arises for a number of reasons.[85] If role expectations at home or at work are ambiguous, it can lead to misunderstandings and disagreements that create stress across roles. If a demanding home or work role requires excessive hours, it can hinder the performance of other roles. In the absence of support from the organization, supervisors, co-workers, or family members, conflict emerges and persists. Finally, having an external locus of control and a negative disposition (affect) also increases conflict, whereas having a positive disposition (affect) and self-efficacy reduces it (see chapter 3).

As illustrated in Figure 7.5, work–family conflict has many detrimental effects in the workplace, including poor work performance, lower career satisfaction, and limited advancement.[86] At home, role performance, satisfaction, and relationships suffer from role

Work–life conflict exists when work role demands interfere with life role demands.

Work–family conflict is role conflict that results from the incompatibilities and pressures of work and family roles.

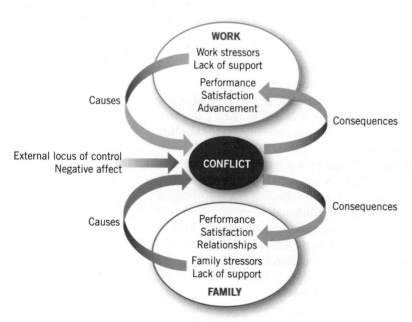

FIGURE 7.5 Work–Family Conflict: Causes and Consequences

conflict. For working mothers, the interference between work and family roles contributes to role dissatisfaction, distress and tension, poor health, and turnover.[87]

Dealing with Stress

People who find effective ways to deal with (potential) stressors are able to live more authentically than others who become overwhelmed by stress. In light of her challenging experience at WorldCom, Cynthia Cooper observed that the way people respond to a potentially stressful situation is determined only in small part by the situation (10 percent) and in large part by the individual's choices (90 percent).[88] Although people may not always be able to make choices that minimize 90 percent of the stressors facing them, research suggests that there are two keys to managing stress: (1) taking care of your whole person, and (2) developing the resources required for the situation.

1. *Managing stress by looking after the whole person.* To be authentic means to consider who you are as a whole person, finding a healthy balance between your work life and your personal life, and balancing a variety of forms of well-being. When it comes to stress, research suggests that it is particularly important to take care of your physical self. Physically fit people are more resistant to stress and more resilient when they experience it. Health Canada recommends that people exercise and undertake hobbies to

OB in Action   Is First Really the Worst?

michaeljung/Shutterstock

At first glance, many may assume that the "top dog" of any organization is the one who experiences the most stress and is most likely to burn out. However, contrary to popular myth, CEOs are not necessarily the most stressed, or at least are not the most negatively impacted by stress, within a company. Of course, leaders face challenges like greater responsibilities and difficult decisions that are unique to their high-ranking positions, but they also have much more control over their jobs and their work environment than do other employees in a company. The sense of control and power can help to compensate for the various stressors that company leaders encounter at work.

It's actually mid-level managers who are at a greater risk of burnout, because while they have some degree of responsibility, it may not be accompanied by having sufficient autonomy or resources to meet, much less exceed, expectations. According to Michael Leiter, Director of the Centre for Organizational Research and Development at Acadia University in Wolfville, Nova Scotia,

employees and managers who are of middle age are also more vulnerable to burnout as they perceive future opportunities for promotion and/or growth becoming increasingly limited.

Young adults just entering the workforce are also more likely to burn out than the top dog as a result of becoming shocked and disappointed with the reality of the work environment. Either their day-to-day work is not what they had envisioned or wanted for themselves or they are struggling financially more than they had anticipated.

To address these stress-related issues, managers and employees must both recognize that working less will not solve the problem. Even though breaks can be helpful by providing individuals with a fresh perspective and some rejuvenation, it's of more use pairing the time off with a critical analysis of stressors and developing next steps to address the problem now in order to prevent future reoccurrences.

QUESTIONS FOR DISCUSSION

1. Where do you feel the most stress?
2. How much control do you feel in those situations?
3. Is there any way to gain more control in your stressful situations?
4. Do you ever eat when stressed?

cope with stress, as such things provide a "mental holiday." These activities help individuals take their minds off their problems and create distance from them so that the problems become easier to solve. The risk of losing one's freedom and livelihood is probably one of the most stressful situations a person might encounter, regardless of one's innocence or guilt.[89] When Conrad Black was faced with criminal charges and the prospect of jail time, he turned to exercise, reading, and writing to help him cope with the stress. He spent so much time on these activities during this period that when he was released from prison he had amassed enough content for a book over 1,000 pages in length (that would later be published).[90]

2. *Develop the resources required to manage the stress.* Stress often arrives when we lack the time, money, or emotional energy to meet the demands that we are faced with. The idea of reducing stress by managing resources draws from **conservation of resources theory**, which proposes that people strive to gain and maintain resources that help them achieve goals.[91] Resources can be physical, such as money; social, such as support from others; and psychological, such as self-efficacy.

Conservation of resources theory proposes that people strive to gain and maintain resources that help them achieve goals.

Loss of resources can result in a vicious cycle where, for example, people deplete their psychological resources due to role conflict, which reduces their workplace performance, which in turn causes further deterioration in their personal life.[92] One solution involves thinking about the nature of the stress, identifying resources that might help alleviate it, and then assembling those resources. The process starts with heightening your awareness of stressors through the processes of structured self-reflection and self-observation, which were discussed earlier in the chapter.[93] Consider where, when, and why you feel stressed. Do you feel stressed in certain contexts or around certain people? Are there times when you consistently feel stressed during the day or month? Why do these situations cause you stress? Answering these questions might help you find a way to reduce your stressors, such as by avoiding certain people or enrolling in training to improve your time management skills.

Another strategy is to identify situations in which you can reduce the use of your own resources and draw on the help of others. For example, you may be able to arrange with a parent, sibling, or spouse to prepare meals, check on older relatives, or chauffeur children. Or perhaps you can negotiate to have the part of your job that you find stressful assigned to someone else. If priorities are ambiguous at work or home, making you unsure where you should focus your resources, rank them through proactive and honest conversation.

When considering any of these suggested strategies, be aware of who you are, what you enjoy doing and do well, what you would like to improve on, and what you would like someone to take over (and how, in return, you can help them). Identifying and making helpful changes can create a virtuous cycle in which you gain more energy, perform at a higher level, and improve your self-confidence, which in turn gives you new energy. Increasing your confidence to handle stress and employing a variety of practices to cope with stress are proven prescriptions for decreasing strain.[94]

A simple approach to reduce stress and improve your capacity to handle stress is to take breaks from your work. Taking a vacation or having a relaxing weekend during which time you don't think about work restores energy, improves attitudes, and even enhances creativity.[95] As featured in OB in Action: Give Me a Break, one CEO believes breaks are so important that he pays people to take them.

A conventional OB perspective on managing stress might favour financial remedies. Having more money can be a resource to buffer stress, such as when employees are asked to work evenings and need to hire babysitters or order in food. Yet financial solutions may only treat a symptom. A sustainable perspective takes a broader perspective and is more likely to

emphasize that an individual won't last long as a lone ranger; people function best when they can rely upon and learn from others. With this in mind, sustainable managers might set up a wide variety of organizational social supports, which could include enabling members to seek the help of co-workers or direct reports through collaboration or delegation, to work remotely or on a flex-time schedule, or to call upon organizational resources such as employee assistance programs for child care or elder care.[96]

Finally, not all stress is bad. For example, a small amount of stress resulting from being evaluated can improve creativity, but too much pressure suppresses creativity.[97] The next section discusses more effective ways to spur creativity. Generally, conventional and sustainable OB approaches share a commitment to reducing stress and, in particular, to encouraging organizational support for employees who are balancing multiple roles. However, a sustainable perspective may be more likely to resist the temptation to keep roles separate and instead recognize that resources from one role may enrich the other. In fact, research supports this holistic approach; skills, confidence, and encouragement from one role can be significant sources of satisfaction and overall well-being in other roles.[98]

> **LEARNING OBJECTIVE 5**
> Explain the creative process, characteristics of creative individuals, and strategies for improving creativity in organizations.

Acting Creatively

| AUTHENTIC LEADERSHIP | KNOWING SELF | LIVING INTENTIONALLY | MANAGING STRESS | **ACTING CREATIVELY** |

To be authentic calls for acting creatively, expressing your unique self in the situations you face. **Creativity** is the process of coming up with novel and useful ideas for solving a problem or developing an opportunity. It is related to but distinct from **innovation**, which takes a creative idea and puts it into practice. Both creativity and innovation are necessary when the prevailing ways of acting in an organization conflict with being true to oneself.

Creativity is the process of coming up with novel and useful ideas for solving a problem or developing an opportunity.

Innovation takes a creative idea and puts it into practice.

In the most general terms, creativity is facilitated by **divergent thinking**, which means looking at a problem in a unique way. In contrast, **convergent thinking** means looking at a problem from a traditional perspective and then trying to find the best solution by thinking logically. Divergent thinking can lead to creative breakthroughs, because we sometimes find alternative solutions when we view the problem in a non-traditional way. Of course, the link between divergent thinking and authenticity is quite clear; divergent thinking is enhanced by people's genuine uniqueness.

The Creative Process

One way to act creatively is to spontaneously generate many unusual or crazy ideas, but often the best ideas are the result of engaging in a creative process involving the following four stages:[99]

1. *Preparation*—The popular view that creativity just "happens" is not supported by research. Creativity requires preparation in the form of hard work and a high level of intentionality in order to assemble relevant information about the problem to be solved.

2. *Incubation*—In the incubation stage, the decision maker stops thinking intensively about the problem and simply allows it to exist in the back of his or her mind. It may appear that he or she is doing little or no work on the problem, but in the subconscious work is being done that will become evident in the next stage.

3. *Inspiration*—Inspiration can consist of either a flash of insight (the so-called *Eureka!* moment) or a gradual awareness of a solution to the problem. This is the most satisfying and most visible phase of the creative process, in which ideas unique to each individual are born; but without the work of the first two stages, it would likely not occur.

4. *Validation*—The final step is to test the creative solution to see whether it actually works. This may take a considerable amount of time. If the idea doesn't work, the decision maker returns to the preparation stage. If the idea does work, it can be adopted as an expression of the person's unique self while maintaining authenticity in his or her work.

Consider how these four stages are evident in the work of Steve Jobs, founder of Apple, who was able to create ideas for products that represented an expression of his authentic self. For example, his early interest and unique training in calligraphy (preparation), while probably not top of mind while he was developing computer software (incubation), nevertheless led to the revolutionary design of different fonts and properly spaced lettering for word processing (inspiration), which became a symbol of his intense attention to stylistic detail (validation).[100]

Characteristics of Creative Individuals

What makes a person creative? Research on this issue reveals that three key elements need to be in place.[101] First, creative people generally have a *deep knowledge* of the problem area they are working on. That means, for example, that a well-trained chemist is far more likely to come up with a novel discovery than is a person who simply dabbles in chemistry. A base of knowledge is a foundation for self-awareness that can stimulate creativity.

Simply having deep knowledge about an area is not sufficient to guarantee creative ideas, however. A second requirement is *creativity-relevant skills*. These skills—such as not leaping to premature conclusions, being able to see situations in new ways, and being comfortable with ambiguity—facilitate the creative process because they free the decision maker from old ways of doing things. Creativity-relevant skills are like the skills of "living intentionally" we described earlier in the chapter; both require discipline.

Third, creative people are *intrinsically motivated* to come up with new ideas. They are actually fascinated with the problem or opportunity they are working on. Without a high level of intrinsic motivation, the hard work required to come up with new ideas is not likely to be done. Creative people have managed to find the eustress in problems, rather than the distress (as discussed earlier in this chapter).

Creative people have additional characteristics that set them apart.[102] They are *nonconformists* who have and pursue their own view of the world; they value *thinking* and get satisfaction from using their mental abilities to solve difficult problems; they are *persistent* and do not give up easily; and they function best in environments that afford them a great deal of *autonomy* and freedom to act on ideas. Although creativity often manifests itself early and can last a lifetime, the most creative time for most people is between 30 and 40 years of age.

Improving Creativity in Organizations

A conventional OB perspective values employee creativity for its positive effect on the organization's competitiveness and profitability. Sustainable managers recognize these benefits but also value creativity in and of itself because it can facilitate authenticity in the workplace. Regardless of the perspective, encouraging creativity in organizations is beneficial because it helps members find win-win ideas that enhance multiple forms of well-being for multiple stakeholders.

The following five strategies are useful for improving creativity in organizations.[103] Note how they not only help employees to be creative and find and develop their authentic selves, but they also reflect some of the key elements in Figure 7.1 at an organizational level. Thus they enable the organization as a whole to discover its authentic "organizational self."

1. *Encourage diversity.* When organizations are staffed with individuals of different ethnic, cultural, and educational backgrounds, it is easier to uncover many different ways of approaching problems and to let divergent thinking flourish.[104] Multiple perspectives are valuable not only because they provide a richer storehouse of unique ideas to, say, improve profits, but also because they contribute to the authentic practice of critically examining personal beliefs and assumptions about others and organizational issues.

2. *Encourage interdepartmental communication.* When employees from different functional areas interact with each other, the flow of information increases and new perspectives on problems are more likely to develop.[105] Research is clear that such broad organizational participation can yield creative insights that could not have been developed by any one individual. Today, cross-functional teams (teams composed of individuals from different departments or divisions within an organization) have become a popular buzzword in business, appearing in job descriptions and resumés alike. Various companies have instituted these formal structures to promote consistent interdepartmental communication and collaboration with the belief that it will enable the organization to provide customers with the best product or service. PricewaterhouseCoopers Canada, for example, frequently uses cross-functional teams, especially when providing services related to mergers and acquisitions, in order to help its clients formulate a strategy that integrates financial, commercial, and operational perspectives and considerations.[106]

   Note how encouraging diversity and interdepartmental communication is in some ways the organizational equivalent of "knowing thyself." Organizations that deliberately seek to diversify their workforce and stimulate cross-departmental communication are in a sense deliberately growing their organizational "self," providing opportunities for richer and more broadly informed reflection.

3. *Set goals and deadlines.* Although many people think goals and schedules go against the notion of freewheeling creativity, the establishment of realistic deadlines actually facilitates creativity because goals can stimulate motivation and help focus attention and effort on making abstract ideas more concrete.

4. *Offer positive reinforcement.* Applying positive reinforcement to creativity means rewarding new ideas and creative decisions instead of being suspicious of them. Positive reinforcement may involve a cash bonus, a humorous symbolic award, or a simple public "thank you," as long as the message to employees is clear—creativity is recognized as valuable.

5. *Provide appropriate resource support.* Employees must have the resources necessary to facilitate creativity; for example, a well-equipped lab for scientific research, a meeting room equipped with white boards for brainstorming sessions, or an information system that allows team members to share information and ideas. Most importantly, employees need the resource of time to be creative. 3M, the inventor of Post-it notes, Thinsulate insulation, and Scotch tape, owes the success of these products to allowing time for employees during the week to work on their own novel ideas and projects.

Many of these recommendations are evident at Hallmark Cards, Inc., a company that depends on creative ideas from employees. Its Shoebox division is expected to develop 70 new greeting cards each week, which means coming up with about 150 ideas. Teams of writers and editors facilitate creativity by watching videotapes of popular television shows, looking at magazines, and doing physical exercises. At the end of each day, new greeting card ideas are screened at a meeting led by the senior editor. Each idea is read aloud, and the group decides which to reject and which to accept. Sales of each card that makes it to market are tracked so that each employee knows how well his or her card ideas are selling.[107]

getting paid to have fun[108]

John Lehmann/Globe and Mail

Elaine "Lainey" Lui is a self-proclaimed gossip maven who currently co-hosts the daytime talk show *The Social*, maintains a full-time celebrity gossip blog, and serves as an entertainment reporter for *etalk*. She's managed to take a hobby she once shared with a couple of co-workers and transform it into multiple jobs. She earns her living being her honest, opinionated, and apologetic self, but how did she get so lucky?

Lui was born in Toronto, Ontario, to Chinese immigrant parents who worked multiple jobs in order to provide her with every opportunity possible and enroll her in the prestigious Toronto French School. Subsequently, Lui pursued a bachelor's degree in French and history at the University of Western Ontario. She would work as a trainer for Rogers Communications and as a development consultant at non-profit organization Covenant House before taking her first official job in the entertainment industry in 2006. Still, the roots of her popular gossip blog LaineyGossip.com date back to 2002.

Lui was living in Vancouver when she returned to Toronto in order to care for her mother, who was in need of a kidney transplant. While away, she promised to provide a daily digest of celebrity gossip via email to her colleagues in Vancouver who shared her fascination. As her co-workers began sharing her emails with their friends, Lui's distribution list soon grew to hundreds and eventually thousands. In late 2004, she transferred her opinions to a blog format to improve accessibility without crashing her email server (which was happening on a daily basis by that point). Today, her blog boasts more than one million monthly readers and followers spanning the globe. But to those who attribute all of her success to good fortune, Lui offers some important thoughts on the notion of following one's dreams.

When asked in an interview about turning hobbies into a full-time job, she said "be prepared to work hard at something for a long time without the promise of making any money," and this certainly rang true for herself. "When I started LaineyGossip. com, I was working full time and then coming home and putting in another eight hours on the blog. Nobody was paying me, and I didn't have any expectations." Even after she established herself and "made it" in the entertainment scene, her fans and followers never wavered. She continues to publish anywhere between 2,000 to 4,500 words per day, five days a week, on her blog, and this sometimes skyrockets to upwards of 10,000 words during ultra-buzzworthy days like those surrounding the Oscars. Might we add that this is all on top of her other jobs on The Social and etalk? She also somehow found time to write a memoir in between.

Lui's success boils down to passion, commitment, and hard work. She loves what she does. In her view, celebrity gossip offers yet another window into the behaviours and values of society. How we interpret this information about celebrities is a reflection of our own beliefs. That's what keeps her job interesting and what drives her to put in the seemingly endless hours of work. In her words, "world leaders survive all the time on three-to-four hours of sleep and they are running the world. So [I] can survive on three-to-four hours of sleep and . . . do [my] job, see [my] friends, watch TV, catch up on pop culture, read and write. [I] can do that." This can-do attitude and willingness to put in the time and effort required to achieve her dreams is the real story.

QUESTIONS FOR DISCUSSION

1. In what ways did Elaine Lui demonstrate behaving authentically in her life and her work?
2. Why might it have been difficult for her to be authentic?
3. What aspects of self-leadership are evident in Elaine Lui's life? How did self-leadership contribute to her success?

Summary

Leading self describes how people can get in touch with and express their authentic selves in their organizations.

 Learning Objectives

- Identify the components and outcomes of leading self in organizations.
- Describe the process of gaining self-knowledge.
- Discuss self-leadership and how it can determine whether an individual performs well or fails in organizations.
- Discuss stress and role conflict in the workplace.

- Explain the creative process, characteristics of creative individuals, and strategies for improving creativity in organizations.

From a conventional OB perspective, the four components of leading self emphasize how:

- Choosing which portions of self to reveal in organizational settings can result in more influence.
- Knowing yourself is related to enhancing self-confidence.
- Intentional living can help contribute to achieving tangible, personal outcomes.

- We can manage stress by taking care of ourselves and ensuring we have access to adequate financial resources.

- Creativity can enhance self-expression and organizational profits.

From a sustainable OB perspective, the four components of leading self emphasize how:

- Developing and presenting self holistically and honestly to others enhances relational connections.
- Knowing yourself is related to enhancing humility.
- Intentional living can help contribute to achieving less tangible, relational outcomes.

- We can manage stress by taking care of our larger community and by making sure we have access to adequate social resources.
- Creativity can enhance self-expression and organizational authenticity.

Key Terms

Authenticity (p.139)
Authentic leadership (p.139)
Calling (p.147)
Conservation of resources theory (p.150)
Convergent thinking (p.152)

Creativity (p.151)
Divergent thinking (p.152)
Feedback-seeking behaviour (p.143)
Hubris (p.142)
Innovation (p.151)

Self-leadership practices (p.144)
Stress (p.147)
Stressors (p.147)
Work–family conflict (p.148)
Work–life conflict (p.148)

Questions for Reflection and Discussion

1. Who do you know that you would consider to be an authentic leader? What has he or she done to earn your respect?
2. What are the main barriers to you improving your self-awareness? How should you act toward others to ensure you receive appropriate feedback?
3. Describe each of the practices associated with living intentionally and describe situations in which you have practised each. What specific practices do you need to more consistently practise to help you in your career?

4. Compare and contrast sustainable and conventional views on managing stress. What are the advantages or disadvantages of each approach?
5. Why is acting creatively important for you? Are there any organizational practices that you can apply to yourself that may enhance your creative behaviour?

ob activities

What Are Your Self-Leadership Behaviours?

Using a scale of 1 - Strongly Disagree (SD), 2 - Disagree (D), 3 - Neutral (N), 4 - Agree (A), and 5 - Strongly Agree (SA), indicate your level of agreement with each statement on the 5-point scale.

Typically . . .

	SD	D	N	A	SA
1. I think about the goals that I intend to achieve in the future.	1	2	3	4	5
2. I try to surround myself with the objects and people that bring out my desirable behaviours.	1	2	3	4	5
3. I talk to myself (out loud or in my head) to work through difficult situations.	1	2	3	4	5
4. When I have successfully completed a task, I reward myself with something I like.	1	2	3	4	5
5. I think about and evaluate the beliefs and assumptions I hold.	1	2	3	4	5
6. I use my imagination to picture myself performing well on important tasks.	1	2	3	4	5
7. I tend to be tough on myself in my thinking when I have not done well on a task.	1	2	3	4	5
8. I work toward specific goals I have set for myself.	1	2	3	4	5
9. I focus my thinking on the pleasant rather than the unpleasant aspects of my job activities.	1	2	3	4	5
10. I purposefully visualize myself overcoming the challenges I face.	1	2	3	4	5
11. When I do something well, I reward myself with a special event such as a good dinner, movie, or a shopping trip.	1	2	3	4	5
12. I openly articulate and evaluate my assumptions when I disagree with someone.	1	2	3	4	5
13. I deny myself something I value when I have performed poorly.	1	2	3	4	5
14. When I'm in a challenging situation, I talk to myself (out loud or in my head) to help me get through it.	1	2	3	4	5

Key: Add the item scores for each component to determine strengths (high scores, 8–10) and weaknesses (low scores, 1–4) in practising self-leadership. *Self-Goal Setting = Items 1 + 8; Self-Reward = Items 4 + 11; Self-Punishment = Items 7 + 13; Focusing on Natural Rewards = Items 2 + 9; Visualizing Success = Items 6 + 10; Self-Talk = Items 3 + 14; Examining Beliefs and Assumptions = Items 5 + 12.*

Source: Items were selected from or adapted from Houghton, J. D., & Neck, C. P. (2002). The revised self-leadership questionnaire: Testing a hierarchical factor structure for self-leadership. *Journal of Managerial Psychology, 17,* 672–691.

An owner of a small business obtained a free copy of a copyrighted computer software program from a business friend rather than spending $500 to obtain his own program from the software dealer.

Why might this scenario occur in organizations?

Use the following scale to indicate whether this behaviour is ethically acceptable:

NEVER ACCEPTABLE			SOMETIMES ACCEPTABLE		ALWAYS ACCEPTABLE	
1	**2**	**3**	**4**	**5**	**6**	**7**

Explain the ideas you considered in arriving at your answer.

DISCUSSION STARTER

Debate: To Be or Not to Be Responsible

Divide the class into two sides and have one argue in support of the following quote and the other argue against it:

"In the long run, we shape our lives, and we shape ourselves. The process never ends until we die. And the choices we make are ultimately our own responsibility."— Eleanor Roosevelt

QUESTIONS FOR DISCUSSION

1. What were the most compelling arguments offered for each perspective?

2. Do you think the arguments would change if this quote were from a popular business leader?

DISCUSSION STARTER

Authentic Leadership

Consider leaders with whom you interact regularly—a fellow student, co-worker, or anyone else—one that you respect and one that you don't. Using a scale of 1 - Strongly Disagree (SD), 2 - Disagree (D), 3 - Neutral (N), 4 - Agree (A), and 5 - Strongly Agree (SA), indicate your level of agreement with each statement on the 5-point scale twice—once for each of the two leaders you choose.

Typically . . .	SD	D	N	A	SA
1. He/she solicits feedback for improving his/her dealings with others.	1	2	3	4	5
2. He/she clearly states what he/she means.	1	2	3	4	5
3. He/she shows consistency between his/her beliefs and actions.	1	2	3	4	5
4. He/she asks for ideas that challenge his/her core beliefs.	1	2	3	4	5
5. He/she describes accurately the way that others view his/her abilities.	1	2	3	4	5
6. He/she admits mistakes when they occur.	1	2	3	4	5
7. He/she uses his/her core beliefs to make decisions.	1	2	3	4	5
8. He/she carefully listens to alternative perspectives before reaching a conclusion.	1	2	3	4	5

Key: Add the item scores for each component to determine strengths (high scores) and weaknesses (low scores) in practising authentic leadership. Self-Awareness = Items 1 + 5; Relational Transparency = Items 2 + 6; Internalized Moral Perspective = Items 3 + 7; Balanced Processing = items 4 + 8.

Source: These statements come from a scale in Neider, L. L., & Schriesheim, C. A. (2011). The Authentic Leadership Inventory (ALI): Development and empirical tests. *The Leadership Quarterly, 22*(6), 1146–1164.

QUESTIONS FOR DISCUSSION

1. How do the scores on these authentic leadership behaviours explain those who you respect and those who you don't?

2. Which dimensions or questions seem most important to you?

APPLICATION JOURNAL

This is a personal journal entry that can be used for class discussion or be compiled and included in a self-reflection paper.

Writing brief journal entries on a consistent basis is an important self-leadership practice that can increase your self-awareness, critical thinking, and learning.[109] Reflect on four components of self-leadership and identify one practice from each component that you need to improve or begin practising. Describe the practice and set a goal for using it. Assess your progress daily or weekly.

Eight

Understanding Relationships

The dynamics of relationships in organizations are in many ways similar to those of relationships outside organizations, with perhaps one major exception; that is, organizational relationships are often influenced by organizational politics and challenging performance goals. In a sometimes treacherous sea of political motives and performance pressure, we can still build and nurture relationships when guided by trust, fair exchanges, and sound negotiation practices.

Learning Objectives | Conventional OB | Sustainable OB

POLITICS AND SELF-INTEREST

Learning Objectives	Conventional OB	Sustainable OB
1. Discuss organizational politics and its effects on an organization.	Recognize that political behaviours are inevitable, are necessary for success in organizations, and, therefore, must be practised	Question whether political behaviours are inevitable, are necessary for success in organizations, and therefore, can be minimized

TRUST

2. Explain the importance of trust in the workplace and ways to build trust in the workplace.	Develop a reputation of trustworthiness and be willing to extend trust in important workplace relationships	Develop a reputation of trustworthiness and be willing to extend trust in all stakeholder relationships

FAIRNESS

3. Recognize how fairness promotes positive feelings, improves satisfaction, promotes organizational citizenship behaviour, and reduces turnover.	Focus on tangible factors in determining distributive, procedural, and interactional justice	Focus on tangible and intangible factors in determining distributive, procedural, and interactional justice

NEGOTIATION

4. Discuss negotiation as an everyday occurrence in organizational relationships.	Bargain to secure self-interest and short-term financial interests of the organization (distributive bargaining)	Negotiate to improve the holistic interests of all negotiators and other stakeholders (integrative negotiation)

conrad black guilty of fraud[1]

Darren Calabrese/CP Images

As touched upon in the previous chapter, Conrad Black is a Canadian-born former media baron who was CEO of Hollinger International Inc., a holding company through which he once controlled one of the world's largest English-language media empires, including the Daily Telegraph, Chicago Sun-Times, Jerusalem Post, and National Post. Black was known to the world as a distinguished entrepreneur and publisher with a diverse range of achievements in commerce, education, and literature. He was awarded the Order of Canada in 1990, and in 2001 he was appointed to the United Kingdom's House of Lords after giving up his Canadian citizenship.

However, in 2003, Black's reputation started its downward spiral when Hollinger International opened an internal investigation into USD $74 million in unauthorized non-compete fees that were paid to Black and other executives and directors. The matter had come to light the year before at Hollinger's annual general meeting, when some shareholders questioned Black over the payments. He denied that the non-compete fees were "back-door" payoffs to himself and other officers. Hollinger announced in 2003 that its past earnings had been overstated by USD $17 million because of these non-compete fees.

Over the next few years, Black would lose his position and control of Hollinger International; face multiple counts of fraud as well as racketeering, money laundering, and obstruction of justice; be convicted of one count of obstruction of justice and three counts of mail fraud in the United States; and be sentenced to six and a half years in prison.

Among the many allegations against Black were those from the U.S. Securities and Exchange Commission. The SEC had sought sanctions in 2004 against Black and former Hollinger Deputy

Black and another director of Hollinger International Inc. "treated it as their personal piggy bank," U.S. authorities alleged.

Chairman and Chief Operating Officer F. David Radler. "Black and Radler abused their control of a public company and treated it as their personal piggy bank," Stephen M. Cutler, the SEC's Director of the Division of Enforcement, said at the time. "Instead of carrying out their responsibilities to protect the interest of public shareholders, the defendants cheated and defrauded these shareholders through a series of deceptive schemes and misstatements." Radler later pled guilty to mail fraud and received a 29-month sentence in return for cooperating with U.S. authorities.

In the end, most of the U.S. charges against Black were dropped and most of his convictions were overturned after his many appeals. His sentence was shortened to 42 months. He was released in 2012, having served 37 months in a Florida prison. After his release, Black was stripped of his Order of Canada and permanently banned by the Ontario Securities Commission from serving as an officer, director, investment fund manager, or promoter of any public or private company that issues securities in Ontario. In the U.K., he retained his title of Lord Black of Crossharbour because a peerage is awarded for life.

In Canada and the United States, a director has the fiduciary duty to act in the best interest of the corporation. This fiduciary duty is divided into two major categories: duty of care and duty of loyalty. In short, directors are required to exercise a standard of care, diligence, and skill and to act honestly and in good faith in the best interests of the corporation. Directors who do not meet their fiduciary duties are legally liable for their actions. When a director engages in fraud (deliberate deception in order to obtain unlawful or unfair gains), it is a breach of his or her fiduciary duties to the corporation. Black is one of the many examples of a director who has been convicted of fraud. By paying himself, in addition to other associates, an unauthorized salary, Black acted dishonestly and not in the best interest of the corporation.

KPMG's 2013 integrity survey, based on interviews of 3,500 U.S. workers, reports that approximately two-thirds of employees believe that their chief executive officer and other senior executives exhibit characteristics attributable to personal integrity and ethical leadership and that they set the right tone regarding the importance of ethics and integrity. However, in an analysis of global trends in fraud, KPMG found that a large proportion of those who engage in fraud hold managerial or executive positions and that CEOs are the fastest-growing group of fraudsters.

Described as a highly self-confident and ruthless individual by many, Conrad Black engaged in deceptive, dishonest, and insensitive behaviours that violated the trust of Hollinger International and its stakeholders. Fortunately Black's excessive self-interest and destructive use of relationships is uncommon, but most work environments produce at least some challenges that come from working with or for others. This chapter introduces our discussion of interpersonal aspects of OB and is devoted to foundational issues that shape workplace relationships. We will discuss the causes and consequences of political and self-interested interpersonal behaviour as well as the counterbalancing relational concepts of trust, fairness, and integrative negotiation (see Figure 8.1).

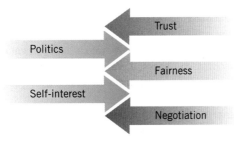

FIGURE 8.1 Political and Relational Factors

Politics and Self-Interest

POLITICS | TRUST | FAIRNESS | NEGOTIATION

Organizational politics refers to the activities that individuals in organizations pursue to reach their own desired outcomes (which may or may not be in the interests of the organization).[2] Organizational politics may be both universal and inevitable, because most people look out for their own self-interest and because organizations have limited resources and opportunities. People with strong political skills are able to assess social situations, adapt their behaviour to appear genuine, and, ultimately, influence others to gain an advantage.[3] Political behaviour—which includes bargaining, networking, compromise, coalition formation, and sometimes deception—may be most evident when there is much debate about which goal to pursue and no clear decision rules to follow because the situation is complex or ambiguous. Political behaviour can be used to benefit the organization or to advance the cause of a team or department, but it also can harm the organization when it interferes with organizational goals, undermines authority, or hinders effective decision making.[4] Politicized decision makers do things such as:

- Trading "favours" with each other in their own long-term self-interests
- Withholding information that will weaken their own position
- Forming coalitions and sharing information within exclusive "cliques"

LEARNING OBJECTIVE 1
Discuss organizational politics and its effects on an organization.

Organizational politics refers to the activities that individuals in organizations pursue to reach their own desired outcomes.

MOB | MACHIAVELLIANISM IN THE WORKPLACE

P_Wei/iStockphoto

Machiavellianism, briefly mentioned in chapter 3, is a personality trait that was identified in the 1960s by researchers Richard Christie and Florence Geis. The trait is named for Niccolò Machiavelli and his political treatise, *The Prince*, which advises rulers to use fear, cruelty, and deceit to gain and maintain power. Power remains a central aspect of modern corporate life, and Christie and Geis's research demonstrates that some people are particularly likely to engage in political behaviour in order to seize and maintain power and advance their own interests within any organizational context.

QUESTIONS FOR REFLECTION

1. Have you experienced political behaviour? Do you think that political behaviour is common at your university or college?
2. Do you think there are certain environments or industries in which politics are more or less likely to occur?

- Blaming others for failure
- Breaking promises if it serves their interests

When organizational politics increase, the strain and anxiety felt by organizational members increases, job satisfaction and organizational commitment decrease, and employees leave the organization more often.[5] Broken promises combined with a political workplace communicate to employees that they are not cared for or valued by the organization.[6] Sometimes members become so obsessed with managing the day-to-day political battles that they fail to devote the necessary time to tasks that serve the interests of the organization.

Leaders aren't immune; in addition to suffering some of the same stress from politics as others do, leaders receive lower effectiveness ratings if politics occur on their watch.[7]

What do managers in the trenches think about organizational politics? Consider the results of just two studies. In one, 428 managers were given a series of statements and asked to agree or disagree with them:[8]

- 70 percent felt that politics were common in their organization.
- 60 percent agreed that most casual talk at work was political in nature.
- 84 percent indicated that politics are irrational.

Even so, more than 70 percent of the study participants felt that successful and powerful executives acted in a political fashion, and most felt that they needed to be good politicians to get ahead.

Another study examined the experience of 149 managers in a manufacturing firm over a five-year period. The findings of this study showed that managers who were promoted realized that (1) it was more important to get along with their peers than with their subordinates, (2) good performance was not automatically rewarded, and (3) it was important to become known rather than to just do a good job and hope for recognition.[9]

These and other studies generally show that people are keenly aware of the importance of organizational politics but that they wish politics weren't so important. When asked whether organizational politics are good or bad, managers often say that they are bad. Unfortunately, political behaviour is very common in organizations and is perceived as being important to success. Perhaps it is not surprising that political behaviour is as widespread as it is, given that organizational contexts in which power and information are centralized and the rewards of personal success are high are fertile grounds for politics.[10]

A sustainable approach to organizational politics is not likely to assume that these behaviours are inevitable, nor would it necessarily value them. Although it may be difficult to eliminate politics completely, a sustainable approach to OB emphasizes proactive attempts to minimize the perceived need for political behaviours. Leaders who model ethical behaviour and contribute to an ethical work environment can reduce organizational politics.[11] For example, politics are less potent in an environment that is transparent and open, where there is less need to secure or withhold information. The necessity for political behaviour decreases when trust and fairness flourish and when leaders are very inclusive, welcome participation, emphasize co-operation, and develop opportunities for others.[12] These qualities encourage members to collaborate and help others as well as to share information and creative suggestions instead of acting primarily from self-interest.[13]

For example, in the highly competitive environment of financial services, you might think it unwise for a woman to refuse a promotion in order to take time off to adopt a baby. After all, it might not look good to the boss, the opportunity would go to someone else, and if she were gone too long, other representatives might steal her clients. Not so at Edward Jones, where Darcy Beeman was able to voice her family priorities and follow through without repercussions.[14] In response, leaders at Edward Jones sent someone to Beeman's office to cover for her during her leave of absence, they allowed her to gradually transition into a new position upon her return, and they even provided adoption reimbursement benefits.

A sustainable approach can also reduce interorganizational politics. A study of the fashion industry in New York City found that interorganizational relationships were characterized by trust and responsiveness to the concerns of suppliers and customers, rather than by simply maximizing short-term economic gain.[15] For example, because the process of contract negotiation left them with less time for quickly responding to the marketplace and for making changes on the fly, some companies would place or deliver orders before any prices had been set. Both the supplier and the buyer trusted that, at the end of the day, they would agree upon a fair price. They also tried to accommodate each other in other ways. For example, during slow times, one partner in the relationship might place orders sooner than usual so as to create work for the other. Unfortunately, this trusting community was fractured when some of its members were purchased by large corporations that insisted on establishing and adhering to binding contracts. An unintended consequence of this trend was that fashion became more of a commodity, with less emphasis on working collaboratively and less time spent on ensuring its aesthetic beauty.

Safe passage through the perfect storm of organizational politics may be aided by a sustainable approach, but the relational counterforces of trust, fairness, and integrative negotiation skills are also critical to healthy and effective organizational relationships. We look at these counterforces next.

Trust

POLITICS **TRUST** FAIRNESS NEGOTIATION

A trusting relationship includes a mutual willingness to be vulnerable and to have faith in the other person's intentions and actions. **Interpersonal trust** consists of the "expectations, assumptions, or beliefs about the likelihood that another's future actions will be beneficial, favourable, or at least not detrimental to one's interests."[16] The question of whether we can count on someone or believe what he or she says is answered in our interactions and experiences with the person. Within an organization, employees also develop expectations about how the organization will treat them. This unwritten expectation about the exchanges that will take place between an employee and the organization is a **psychological contract**.[17] If this contract is fulfilled, employees trust the organization; if these expectations are not fulfilled, employees can feel as though the organization does not value their efforts or care for

Interpersonal trust consists of the expectations, assumptions, or beliefs about the likelihood that another's future actions will be beneficial, favourable, or at least not detrimental to one's interests.

A **psychological contract** is an unwritten expectation about the exchanges that will take place between an employee and the organization.

them.[18] Left unchecked, this violation of trust results in lower levels of performance, job satisfaction, and organizational commitment.[19]

Trust is an important factor in establishing and maintaining the social networks that workers rely on to perform their jobs. **Social networks** are patterns of repeated interactions that influence the flow of resources, information, and support among organizational members.[20] Organizational members who demonstrate consistent (1) competence, (2) character, and (3) goodwill in their interactions are deemed trustworthy, and they establish strong networks of interpersonal relationships.[21] Those who do not demonstrate these characteristics are not trusted.

In organizations, where completing work often requires relying on others, competence is an important factor that influences trust. Trusting others requires believing that the other person has the relevant knowledge, skills, and abilities to direct, guide, or assist in the completion of a task or project. Lacking trust in another person's competencies decreases the likelihood that you will include that person in the network of people you talk to for advice or help.[22] In interactions that include people from different cultures, the skill of being mindful of and adapting to cultural differences contributes to trusting relationships.[23]

Character is critical to trust, because trustworthiness depends on the consistency and qualities we observe in a person's actions. Does this person persist in the face of difficulties, can she keep something in confidence, does she work hard and give her best effort, is she forthright and truthful, does she demonstrate respect for others, and will she do what is right despite possible negative consequences to herself? Trust also is related to being authentic or real, having a clear sense of self and values, acting consistently with those values, and being transparent about who you are and what you value.[24] In organizations, authentic leadership and perceived trust allow members to become more committed and perform well.[25]

Finally, a person's intentions influence our perceptions of trust. If you believe someone has others' best interests in mind and generally exhibits goodwill toward others, this belief enhances his trustworthiness. Goodwill expressed by offering compliments, listening to problems, engaging in good-hearted joking, and providing gentle encouragement enhances positive feelings and trust in relationships.[26]

Competence, character, and expressions of goodwill each provide unique contributions to trust, but all are necessary for the highest levels of trust. For example, a boss at work may be an expert in a particular technology or process but may not be completely trusted because he or she is not perceived to be someone who will persist in doing the right thing or considering others' interests.

Trust is vital in organizations. Without it, organizational members can be distracted by worries and become self-protective, immobilized, and unwilling to take any risks. In an environment of trust, however, members are able to focus on their work responsibilities; build a strong commitment to the organization; and develop the confidence to take risks, be creative, and help others.[27] The model illustrated in Figure 8.2 incorporates these findings. More

Social networks are patterns of repeated interactions that influence the flow of resources, information, and support among organizational members.

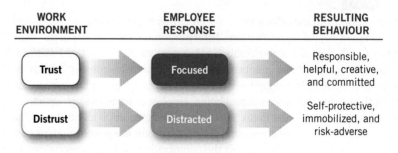

FIGURE 8.2   A Model of Trust

specifically, having trust in the leaders of an organization is related to members having more confidence in information that is shared, more of a willingness to go outside of their formal roles to do what is best for the organization and its members, a higher level of satisfaction with their leaders, more of a commitment to the organization, and lower turnover intentions.[28]

From a sustainable perspective, trust not only results in tangible benefits to the person and the organization but also is an expression of virtuous character. The presence of trust promotes the dignity of others by limiting the necessity of controls and policies, excessive formalization, and centralization of authority and decision making. Building sustainable trust means treating other people with dignity, whether or not it improves the organization's bottom line. The long-term (prudent) perspective of a sustainable approach is evident when managers are willing to sacrifice short-term gains and avoid laying off employees during times of lower sales or economic struggles in order to maintain trust with employees. This approach is reflected in the comments of Delta Hotels and Resorts employee Janice Smith provided in the next OB in Action feature.

A sustainable perspective establishes trusting relationships with stakeholders outside the organization in addition to doing so internally with shareholders, board members, and employees. Outsiders include customers, suppliers, community members, and even competitors. Trust is established and grows when you and your organization stand behind your products and services, are clear and collaborative in dealing with your suppliers, consistently demonstrate a concern for and commitment to the community's well-being, and honestly and ethically deal with competitors. Demonstrating a balanced concern for stakeholders outside the organization generates goodwill that contributes in the long term to co-operative relationships that yield mutual benefits and lower transaction costs for monitoring, double-checking, and legally defending information or actions. Long-term investments in trust building can make the organization an attractive employer or customer, yield collaborative partnerships or strategic alliances, and enhance customers' loyalty and their willingness to recommend the company to others.[29] But in all cases such investments represent the organization's (or its members') values and are therefore worthwhile regardless of the end result.

Consider The Dannon Company and its venture into community development partnerships to produce yogurt in poor and underdeveloped communities.[30] Acting in a socially

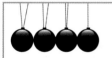

OB in Action   Keeping a Lid on Layoffs

Sandy Jones/Getty Images

Delta Hotels and Resorts is consistently recognized as one of the companies on Aon Hewitt's list of the 50 Best Employers in Canada. At the centre of the ratings process is an assessment of the level of trust that employees have in their company. No doubt the high ratings for the Toronto-based company are attributable, in part, to its "no-layoff" philosophy as well as to its empowering and innovative culture and generous reward and recognition programs when the organization is prospering.

In difficult financial times, companies often attempt to improve short-term results by downsizing in an attempt to reduce costs. However, Janice Smith, Delta's Director of People & Organizational

Performance, says that looking for alternatives to layoffs is "thinking long-term." Smith believes that the negative long-term consequences on morale and productivity outweigh the temporary windfall from cutting staff, and she says that Delta "will always look for alternatives" to layoffs.

Research indicates that the negative effects of layoffs are even worse if the work environment and the relationships between employees and management were characterized by high-involvement work practices based on trust.

QUESTIONS FOR DISCUSSION
1. How do layoffs destroy trust?
2. How do you restore the trust of employees who remain?
3. Are there cases were you can lay off employees and maintain trust?

responsible manner to make the world a better place is part of Dannon's values as a company. Yogurt is a healthy source of nutrients that can be produced relatively inexpensively in small facilities appropriate for the villages and rural settings of many poor communities. An investment in these production facilities may have the potential to earn attractive profit margins for Dannon in the future, but the company's overall "profit" is measured in more than dollars and cents. Dannon is living out its values by adding value to the broader global community. When he was still CEO of Dannon's parent company, Groupe Danone, Inc., a role he held for 18 years until stepping down in 2014, Franck Riboud described his approach: "My job is to create balance between the expectations of the shareholders, the expectations of the people working for the company, and on top of that, the expectations of the community around the company."[31]

Conventional and sustainable approaches to building trust are very similar. Competence-based trust will follow from a commitment to increase and expand your knowledge, skills, and abilities and an honest admission when a customer request falls outside your current capabilities. In today's rapidly changing work environments, this requires that organizational members demonstrate a willingness to continuously improve themselves and learn new skills. Character-based trust grows when communication is honest and open, when people demonstrate sensitivity to others' needs, and when courageous decisions are made to do what is right rather than what is convenient or self-serving. We discuss the relationship between communication and trust in more depth in chapter 11, but at this point it cannot be overemphasized. It is a management myth that information is best shared only on a need-to-know basis: that is, unless you have a specific reason to pass along information to others, don't do it. This approach is destructive to trust because it implies that only certain people can be trusted with information. Secretiveness also arouses suspicion that leaders are withholding information to protect their interests, preserve their power, and promote a hidden agenda. Table 8.1 provides a list of practical suggestions for building trust.

Trust is a two-way street; you need to be trustworthy and you need to trust others. Some people have a natural propensity to trust others, a tendency captured in part by Theory Y discussed in chapter 3. From a conventional perspective, trust is necessary to distribute work efficiently in order to accomplish more. A sustainable perspective recognizes the value of sharing the load, but it also may extend trust when there is little or no clear benefit to the organization.

Delegation is the process through which a person trusts another person with the authority to accomplish a task or make decisions.

Regardless of the approach, we may best describe the behaviours related to trusting others by talking about delegating. **Delegation** is the process through which a person, usually an organizational leader, trusts direct reports, followers, or even peers with the authority to accomplish a task or make decisions. At least five basic steps occur in conventional delegation:[32]

1. *Select a qualified person.* Competence is the key qualification here, because you should not hold a person responsible for something he or she is not capable of doing. Character also is important to ensure responsible behaviour.

2. *Assign the tasks or goal.* The critical skill here relates to communicating clear expectations about what is to be accomplished.

TABLE 8.1 Six Suggestions for Building Trust

---

1. Tell the truth, even when it does not serve you well.
2. Never make promises you cannot reasonably expect to keep.
3. Commit firmly to values that respect the interests and rights of others.
4. Be known for having high standards of integrity, for doing the right thing because it is right—even if your company and society are willing to accept a lower standard.
5. Don't let personal ambition interfere with being honest and fair.
6. Consistently remind yourself that it is not in your self-interest to be selfish.

Source: These suggestions are found in Williams, C. (2007). *Effective Leadership* (7th ed.). LTrek Corporation.

3. *Provide the necessary resources.* Necessary resources may include access to certain people and information; the right to control specified budgets, facilities, equipment, and technologies; and authority over personnel.

4. *Affirm the person's acceptance of responsibility.* Delegation is incomplete if it consists of one-way communication. Make sure the person assuming the responsibility understands and accepts it.

5. *Hold the person accountable for the results.* Delegating does not end with the transfer of responsibility; it requires follow-up to assess and recognize progress and to adapt when improvements are necessary.

These steps are deceptively simple to describe but far more difficult to implement. Some people avoid delegating, while others resist accepting delegated responsibility. Delegation occurs more frequently when those who are delegating view an employee as competent, when they believe the employee shares similar goals, and when the delegating supervisor or manager has a heavy workload. Delegation occurs less frequently if the task or decision is viewed as very important or the employee has been on the job for a short time.[33]

In interviews with managers about their decision whether to delegate a task to a particular employee or not, 95 percent indicated employee dependability was a critical factor. Other considerations were the relevant expertise of the employee (88 percent), the relationship of the task to other responsibilities (85 percent), the need to develop employee skills (76 percent), the available time to complete the task (73 percent), and the employee's receptivity to delegation (70 percent).[34] Ego also may play a role in that some bosses or experts want it done their way, they may want the praise for completing the task, or they may even be worried about someone else's success threatening their own position.

Of course, employees or others may resist receiving delegation if they work in a political environment where people claim others' success or blame others for failures. Resistance also may come from reasonable concerns about a lack of capability, resources, or even time. Organizations should be interested in promoting delegation because when employees are willing and competent to receive delegation, they perform better.[35] From a sustainable perspective, delegation is worth engaging in even if an employee is not yet fully competent because it communicates that development is a priority and prepares the employee for future responsibilities.

From a sustainable perspective, delegation need not follow lines of authority nor need it be necessarily top-down. For example, upward delegation is implicit in servant leadership (when a subordinate asks a boss for help, the subordinate is in one sense delegating work to the boss). Delegation can also take place among peers or even stakeholders (such as asking a customer or supplier to complete a task for the sake of the larger enterprise). Once you break out of authority-based linear thinking, the meaning and practice of trusting others changes. Consider this sustainable adaptation of the steps in delegation:

1. *Partner with another person.* This step recognizes and affirms others and their potential, regardless of their position or power.

2. *Mutually agree on the tasks or goal.* A collaborative discussion is likely to result in the most appropriate fit between tasks or goals and the partners' capabilities, and result in high levels of commitment.[36]

3. *Creatively acquire the necessary resources.* Although the person initiating the partnership may have more resources, the search for relevant resources should be a joint one to which both parties contribute.

4. *Mutually affirm each person's responsibilities.* Clear communication is essential to ensure that both parties understand their commitments.

5. *Share accountability for the results.* Feedback on progress should be frequently and broadly communicated, and all partners should share in the results.

MOB | FAIR OR FOUL

Universal Pictures/Photofest

Tom Hanks in the movie *Larry Crowne* experiences a surprising outcome when he is fired after years of faithful service and frequent recognition as "employee of the month" at a big box retailer. The news is delivered by a group of inconsiderate managers who spend more time joking around than providing Larry with helpful information. He finds out for the first time at his firing—when it is too late—that he was not seen as having promotion potential because he was not college educated.

Unfortunately, it is fairly common for managers to fail to provide information or feedback that can help workers understand why decisions were made and how to change to improve their outcomes such as a raise, a promotion, or keeping their jobs. It is a problem that affects perceptions of fairness in workplaces across the world.

When feedback is offered, it often focuses on the person rather than the behaviour, is vague or general, and does not clearly provide suggestions for specific actions to address shortcomings. To be perceived as fair and improve the response from those to whom you provide feedback, be specific, focus on behaviours instead of personalities, and provide information regarding how the person can improve.

QUESTIONS FOR REFLECTION

1. Have you been in a situation where the outcome for you—your amount of playing time on a team, your shot at a promotion, your grade on a project or paper—did not seem to match what you put into it? How did you react?

2. If you were put in the position of deciding the outcome, what would you have done differently?

In hospital trauma centres, a style of delegation that mirrors aspects of the sustainable approach has proven effective in addressing the urgent and long-term needs of the work environment.[37] In tending to the critical needs of trauma patients, there is a recognized line of authority that begins with the attending surgeon, then goes to the surgical fellow, then to the chief resident, and then to residents and interns. But at any moment the active responsibility for meeting a patient's needs may be trusted to any person at any level. The key to this dynamic process is clear two-way communication and the expectation that all team members can make critical contributions. Teaching and monitoring by senior team members ensures that patients receive the proper treatment, while delegating responsibilities to junior members ensures the development of skills necessary for assuming greater responsibility in the future.

LEARNING OBJECTIVE 3
Recognize how fairness promotes positive feelings, improves satisfaction, promotes organizational citizenship behaviour, and reduces turnover.

Fairness is a judgment about whether treatment has been just, equitable, and impartial.

Fairness

| POLITICS | TRUST | **FAIRNESS** | NEGOTIATION |

Fairness is a judgment about whether treatment has been just, equitable, and impartial. According to our description of organizational politics in this chapter, fairness is an obvious counterforce to politics. That is, in political work environments, people may not get what they deserve or may not understand how a decision was made because it was made in secrecy without broad input from organizational members. In contrast, when fair behaviour becomes the norm because leaders or members make it a priority, the frustrations and stress of the political environment are reduced. Fair behaviour promotes positive feelings, improves satisfaction and commitment, promotes other-centred organizational citizenship behaviour, and reduces turnover.[38]

Perceptions of fairness also affect relationships; they influence whether a person is trusted or not.[39] In addition, employees' perceptions of how fairly they are treated affects the way they treat customers and the way customers, in turn, perceive the organization.[40] Being fair goes a long way . . . and so does fair treatment.

All cries of "It's not fair" don't have the same meaning. In organizations, perceptions of injustice can relate to at least three issues: the distribution of outcomes, the process by which outcomes are achieved or decided, and interpersonal behaviour.[41] First, **distributive justice** compares the individual's inputs and outcomes to other members' inputs and outcomes. For example, an employee may not think a small raise is a fair outcome for his efforts when others are given larger raises for doing the same work. Second, **procedural justice** looks at the extent to which policies and rules are transparent, developed in consultation, and fairly administered without bias or favouritism. For example, another employee may not take issue with the size of her raise once she understands how it was decided, but she may think it was unfair that she didn't know in advance how the decision would be made. Finally, **interactional justice** is the interpersonal form of justice concerned with the behaviour of leaders in their relationship to followers or direct reports. Two aspects of **interactional justice** relate to the extent to which a leader provides relevant, reasonable, and timely information, and the extent to which a leader treats followers with respect, dignity, and sensitivity in their interactions.[42]

Although all of these justice perceptions are important, research suggests that procedural justice has a stronger positive influence than distributive justice on organizational commitment, job satisfaction, and positive organizational citizenship behaviour.[43] In other words, if people understand the process to be fair, they can usually live with not receiving the outcomes they'd hoped for. Procedural justice in team operations such as organizing and completing team tasks and rewarding team members also is important. Perceptions of procedural justice will be high if team members believe that all team members have acted consistently, accurately, and ethically and that all have been allowed a say in team decisions. Greater procedural justice within a team is positively related to better team performance and fewer instances of absenteeism.[44]

Whereas distributive justice and procedural justice involve perceptions of what the organization is doing to its members, interactional justice relates to personal interactions that can buffer or reduce the negative impact of unjust actions by the organization. In other words, a person can feel that the organization or its top leaders are acting unfairly but still feel that he or she is being treated fairly by a supervisor who takes the time to listen to concerns and provide reasonable explanations. Interactional justice plays a critical role in developing trust in organizations. For example, amid the stress of organizational change, just treatment by immediate supervisors or leaders is critical to avoiding or reducing the cynicism and distrust that usually accompanies a major workplace change.[45] Overall, demonstrating distributive, procedural, and interpersonal forms of justice builds trust between people and within the organization.[46]

Organizational politics often result in special treatment that can violate all three forms of organizational justice. *Nepotism* is the political behaviour of granting relatives special treatment or favouritism. Typically, this behaviour is frowned upon and companies go to great lengths to avoid perceived injustice related to this type of favouritism. In other cultures, it is more common and accepted. For example, Chinese food products firm Lee Kum Kee Ltd. (LKK) is a family-owned company that employs close to 4,000 workers and sells products in 80 countries.[47] Its leadership has passed from its founder, Lee Kum Sheung, through to family members, who also are planning for family members to be future leaders. In his role as LKK Group Chairman, Lee's grandson Man Tat gave preference to his sons for positions as division CEOs, but he also recruited non-family board members and managers who were "culturally attuned to the firm, and to family as CEOs of its divisions." In being clear about his plans for nepotism, Man Tat was being procedurally just, even if outsiders may have questioned whether he was being distributively just.

A sustainable perspective values all forms of justice but favours procedural justice—not because it necessarily yields the most positive outcomes, but because it is consistent with the sustainable principles of collaboration and transparency. A fair process is one in which organizational members understand beforehand how decisions are going to made and are invited to ask questions about, or even participate in, changes that might make things fairer or more consistent. A sustainable perspective on distributive justice might look a bit different from a conventional one; it might argue that the inputs weighed in determining outputs should be broader and take into account less-tangible factors. For example, in determining a merit-based bonus for individuals, a sustainable approach might consider the role that the person played in helping others. Did she participate within a team, train or mentor others, put together a community engagement event, or offer suggestions for reducing environmentally harmful waste? Each of these activities may have taken time away from her individual performance, but from a long-term perspective they add value to the organization.

LEARNING OBJECTIVE 4
Discuss negotiation as an everyday occurrence in organizational relationships.

Negotiation is a social interaction between two (or more) parties who attempt to persuade or influence each other regarding some end.

Negotiation

POLITICS | TRUST | FAIRNESS | **NEGOTIATION**

Successfully responding to the political and self-interested behaviour of organizational members requires knowing how agreements and decisions are made and using appropriate skills and behaviours. **Negotiation** is a social interaction between two (or more) parties who attempt to persuade or influence each other regarding some end.[48] It is central to contracts but is also an everyday occurrence in organizational relationships. The outcome of a negotiation might be an agreement about how to divide a resource or accomplish a task, an idea for solving a problem, or a new creation.[49] According to James Sebenius, "Negotiation matters wherever parties with different interests and perceptions depend on each other for results."[50] In every case, the choice of influence tactics, the approach to framing the negotiation, and the parties' own conflict styles can shape the outcome.

Influence Tactics

Influence tactics are specific behaviours exercised to achieve an outcome, particularly getting personal interests satisfied.

Influence tactics are specific behaviours exercised to achieve an outcome, particularly getting personal interests satisfied.[51] They can range from pressuring someone into an agreement to inviting others to discuss or consult about a decision. A list of common influence tactics appears in Table 8.2.

TABLE 8.2 Influence Tactics

Influence Tactic	How to Use the Tactic
Rational persuasion	Use logical arguments and factual evidence.
Inspirational appeal	Arouse enthusiasm by appealing to values, ideals, aspirations.
Consultation	Involve others in planning or formulating an idea or strategy.
Ingratiation	Use praise, flattery, or friendly behaviour before making a request.
Personal appeal	Appeal to feelings of loyalty or friendship.
Exchange	Indicate willingness to reciprocate or share benefits.
Coalition tactics	Note the support of others in attempting to persuade.
Legitimizing tactics	Appeal to an agreed-upon authority such as a vision, mission, or goal.
Pressure	Introduce or suggest threats or negative consequences.

Source: Adapted from Yukl, G. (2013, p. 202). *Leadership in Organizations.* (8th ed.). Upper Saddle River, NJ: Prentice Hall.

Research confirms that the use of influence tactics, especially ingratiation and rational persuasion, are positively related to performance ratings and success as measured by promotions and salary level.[52] From a conventional perspective, using influence tactics to accomplish goals is appropriate, but from a sustainable perspective the long-term health of the relationship and the other parties' commitment to the agreement is more relevant. Although rational persuasion does work well—after all, most people appreciate facts and logic—consultation and inspirational appeal are most likely to gain the commitment of others.[53] Coalition tactics, legitimizing tactics, and pressure are the least likely to promote such commitment; and exchange, personal appeal, and ingratiation are only moderately effective.[54]

Approaches to Negotiation

There are two broad approaches to negotiation. The first assumes there is a limited amount of money, resources, or opportunities that must be divided through negotiation because people have competing interests. That is, everyone wants his or her interests satisfied, and satisfying one person's interests often means that someone else is less satisfied. This approach is **distributive bargaining**. If a pumpkin pie is set on the table in front of a hungry family with growing teenagers, conflict can break out in the course of deciding who gets how much. An integrative approach assumes that more might be added to the negotiation and considers that the parties' interests are not always competing. Perhaps if hunger is the issue, one could add brownies or ice cream to the dessert offering in order to satisfy everyone.

> **Distributive bargaining** is a negotiation behaviour that assumes there is a limited amount of money, resources, or opportunities that must be divided because people have competing interests.

In practice, most negotiations include both the challenge of dividing up the available resources and a search for more. Of course, cultural differences do exist. For example, one study demonstrated that Indian negotiators were less trustful of the motives of others than were U.S. negotiators, with the unfortunate result that less trust related to worse outcomes for everyone involved.[55] Even so, there are principles and practices for negotiation that generally work across cultures to improve negotiation outcomes. We will begin with some that are relevant to distributive bargaining. In essence, these ideas can help you ensure that you or your organization will get an adequate portion of the pie.

Perhaps the simplest and most effective practice in distributive negotiation is to make the first offer. An offer is a statement of who will get what and other relevant details necessary for an agreement. Research affirms that the first offer sets the tone for the negotiation and is a strong determinant of the final agreement.[56] How does something so simple work so effectively? It is the perceptional influence of anchoring and adjustment (discussed in chapter 4) at work again. Once an offer has been put on the table, it serves as an anchor against which all other offers are adjusted; the farther away these offers are from the original anchor, the more tension or cognitive dissonance that is created. In other words, psychologically we all seem bound to the first offer as a reference point, and it can seem uncomfortable to move far from it.

The power of this effect—even with seemingly irrelevant anchors—is illustrated in Table 8.3. Imagine a *Price Is Right*–type of game show or a friendly competition. The object of the game is to guess the right price for a product. In this case, two products are presented to several participants. Before estimating the price of the cordless keyboard and Belgian chocolates, the participants are asked to think of the last two digits of their social security number. Do you notice anything about the value of the social security number digits and the relative prices the participants guessed? A correlation between the numbers indicates there is a relationship between the social security number in a person's head and the prices he or she guesses for the products. The seemingly random act of asking about a social security number influenced the participants' price estimates; it is anchoring and adjustment at work.

Obviously, it is critical to make sure you are prepared for and intentional about your first offer and that you have thought through two issues: your aspiration point and your

Last 2 Digits of SS#	Cordless Keyboard	Belgian Chocolates
00–19	$16.09	$9.55
20–39	$26.82	$10.64
40–59	$29.27	$12.45
60–79	$34.55	$13.27
80–99	$55.64	$20.64

Source: Ariely, D., Lowewenstein, G., & Prelec, D. (2003). Coherent arbitrariness: Stable demand curves without stable preferences. *The Quarterly Journal of Economics, 118*(1), 73–105.

Aspiration point is what you hope for in a given situation; it is your preferred result.

Reservation point is the bottom-line offer you would accept.

Zone of possible agreements (ZOPA) is a range of possible offers you and the other party are willing to accept.

reservation point. Your **aspiration point** is what you hope for in a given situation; it is your preferred result. In the case of a job offer, it might be a high salary and comprehensive benefits, whereas for someone else it might be a flexible schedule and a particular location. The key is that you need to know your aspiration and state it first, if possible. Your **reservation point** is the bottom-line offer you would accept. It might represent the lowest salary you are willing to take, given your living expenses, or the maximum amount of responsibilities you can accept, given your limited time. Many people have made an agreement without considering their reservation point, due to either lack of preparation or poor information in the negotiation process.

Together, your aspiration and reservation points make up the range of possible offers you are willing to accept. This range and the other party's range together make up a **zone of possible agreements (ZOPA)**; see Figure 8.3. Where in this zone the final agreement lies depends in part on your negotiation skills and the skills of the other party. When one person's range of acceptable agreements does not overlap with another's, there is no ZOPA and each person should go elsewhere to find an acceptable deal.

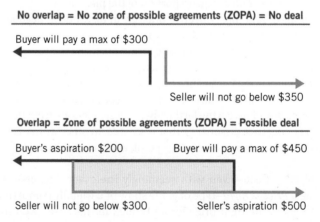

No overlap = No zone of possible agreements (ZOPA) = No deal

Buyer will pay a max of $300

Seller will not go below $350

Overlap = Zone of possible agreements (ZOPA) = Possible deal

Buyer's aspiration $200   Buyer will pay a max of $450

Seller will not go below $300   Seller's aspiration $500

FIGURE 8.3 Zone of Possible Agreements (ZOPA)

Even given a ZOPA, agreement is not guaranteed. The way each party treats the other can influence the likelihood of reaching a deal. A *concession* is a revision of an offer whereby one party moves away from his or her aspiration and gives up or adds something of value. Most often concessions are reciprocal, such as "I will give you A, if you will include B." It is a common myth that in an exchange of concessions a person should start out by offering a significant move away from their aspiration as a gesture of goodwill, such as dropping your price on the bike you are selling by 30 percent. Although this makes some sense, research actually supports the opposite tactic. An agreement is more likely if you proceed with caution, starting with small concessions and then closing with a more substantial one if possible.[57]

A key to negotiating power is having other alternatives than what is being offered to you. The most attractive option available to you outside of the current negotiations is your **best alternative to a negotiated agreement (BATNA)**.[58] In fact, whether you should accept a deal with another person depends upon your BATNA. Having an attractive alternative to the result you are attempting to negotiate, such as holding a job when you are interviewing for a new one, reduces your dependence on the other party and your need to reach an agreement.[59] Lacking an alternative can force you to accept an agreement that violates your reservation point and leaves you with an outcome that you cannot afford or that you believe to be unacceptable.

Integrative negotiation is an alternative to distributive bargaining that seeks to achieve a win-win result for both parties. Instead of allowing one person to gain at the other's expense, the integrative approach encourages the parties to gain more information about each other's underlying interests and to generate more options that will satisfy the most important goals of both. A win-lose "fixed pie" approach results in suboptimal agreements.[60] For example, if satisfaction could be quantified, in a win-lose situation the winner might end up with 100 satisfaction points, whereas the loser might end up with 50 points or less and may be frustrated enough to not want to deal with the other party in the future. In contrast, in a win-win approach each party would end up with 100 points or more—if the pie was expanded. The overall immediate satisfaction is higher and so is the likelihood that the parties will work together again in the future.

The steps in integrative negotiation are (1) building a relationship of understanding and respect; (2) collaborating to generate creative solutions, explore options, and evaluate them against objective or agreed-upon standards; and (3) choosing the alternative that best satisfies the interests of all parties in the negotiation.[61] These steps are illustrated in Figure 8.4.

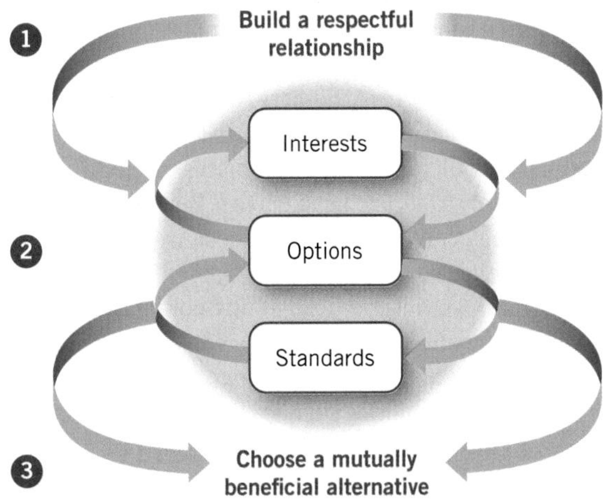

The **best alternative to a negotiated agreement (BATNA)** is the most attractive option available to you outside of the current negotiations.

Integrative negotiation is an alternative to distributive bargaining that seeks to achieve a win-win result for both parties.

FIGURE 8.4 Integrative Negotiation
Source: Adapted from Patton, B. (2004). Building relationships and the bottom line: The circle of value approach to negotiation. *Negotiation,* 7(4), 4–7.

Building a respectful relationship is primarily a matter of demonstrating a sincere concern for the other party and an appreciation of his or her situation. This foundation of trust sets the stage for the next step—asking questions and listening in order to understand the other person's underlying interests. Initial negotiating positions or offers seldom accurately or completely represent a person's underlying interest. For example, a person who resists a change in the way work is done in an organization might say, "This new way isn't going to work. I've tried it before and it's a waste of time." But his actual interest might be in remaining

In his book *The 7 Habits of Highly Effective People*, Stephen Covey popularized the advice, "Seek first to understand, then to be understood." This is easier said than done.

Social awareness is the ability to focus on others and their words and reactions instead of on yourself. How well do you turn your attention outward to others? Think of a specific situation in which you were negotiating something of importance to you.

In that situation, to what extent did you do the following? Grade yourself, giving an A (4 points), B (3 points), C (2 points), D (1 point), or F (no points, of course):

_____Did you take note of the situation and how it might affect the conversation?

_____Did you notice body language and interpret its meaning?

_____Did you focus on listening to the person—not interrupting or daydreaming?

_____Did you consider what it might be like to be in the other person's shoes?

QUESTIONS FOR REFLECTION

1. What grade, on average, did you give yourself?
2. How did your actions relate to the negotiation outcomes?
3. What grade would you give the other party that was involved in the situation?

---

competent at doing his work, which the proposed change threatens. He isn't likely to commit to the change unless his underlying interest is satisfied. Usually these interests can be uncovered through asking questions in a non-threatening manner. In the My OB feature, a popular book by Stephen Covey suggests that effectiveness in influencing others can be enhanced by seeking first to understand, then to be understood.

Consider for a moment this adaptation of a classic story. Two chefs who are roommates are in the kitchen, each preparing a tasty dessert to impress their guests. When they both reach for the last remaining orange, their positions are the same— "I need the orange for my dessert for our guests." They could argue (as roommates often do) about who has the right to the orange, but this isn't likely to satisfy both parties. But if one of them were to ask, "What do you need?" that would make all the difference, because one chef needs the peel to add orange zest to her dessert while the other needs the juice.

As this story demonstrates, sometimes apparently conflicting interests are not actually in conflict. But even when they are, brainstorming creative alternatives can add more value or "grow the pie" by introducing options. Perhaps two employees are at an impasse about distributing the work and responsibilities of a co-worker who is transferring to a different part of the organization. Although the two employees may not want to add more work to their already full schedules, they could sit down over coffee and lay out the responsibilities of the three jobs, divide up specific tasks based on their personal strengths or preferences, and then jointly approach their manager about covering the least-appealing task with temporary help. In the end, each is maximizing his or her satisfaction by doing the work that he or she is more motivated to do or more capable of doing, and by acting co-operatively they're also improving their chance of receiving additional help from their boss. Even if after discussion and collaboration the decision does not fully satisfy each party's interests, agreed-upon standards or principles can ensure the fairness of the outcome.

Integrative negotiation is by nature a sustainable approach. It goes beyond simply dividing up resources or outcomes, and it intentionally dignifies the other party or parties by getting to know and understand them, the value of which is hard to quantify but is nonetheless meaningful. It invites participation and the sharing of information, both of which contribute to a spirit of collaboration, creative solutions, and commitment to an ongoing work relationship. Finally, it seeks to maximize the holistic benefit to all parties by considering others' interests and the overall well-being of the partnership, not simply one person's interests or gain.[62]

A sustainable approach also extends integrative negotiations to parties who might be unlikely to benefit from a conventional approach. For example, Dan and Wilma Wiens established and operated a community-shared agricultural farm in a community just south of Winnipeg, Manitoba. It was set up such that customers who bought shares were entitled to fresh, locally grown organic vegetables. The first year Dan Weins set the share price, but the second year he invited the sharers (customers) to set the price. Having seen how much work the farming involved, the sharers increased the price they paid by approximately 50 percent. In the following years, when drought or flooding reduced the yield of vegetables, some sharers voluntarily gave Wiens a bonus cheque.

Integrative negotiation has great potential to improve outcomes for all parties, but that's not to say that there is no role for distributive bargaining. The two approaches can sometimes work well together. A negotiation could begin with distributing certain items but then reach an impasse and need to become integrative in order for an agreement to be reached.[63] For example, in a negotiation about who is going to do what on a team, having team members state their preferences may result in the assignment of most tasks, but an integrative approach may be necessary to determine the designation of the remaining tasks.

Conflict Styles

When people have different interests, real or apparent conflict is possible. The way people handle conflict—their **conflict style**—is based on how much they value their own interests relative to the interests of others.[64] (See the OB Activities section at the end of the chapter for an assessment of interpersonal conflict styles.) A high concern for your own interests tends to result in assertive behaviour, whereas a high concern for others' interests tends to result in co-operative behaviour. Five conflict styles are typically identified that represent unique combinations of assertive and co-operative behaviour. These styles are avoiding, accommodating, competing, compromising, and integrating; see Figure 8.5.

Conflict style is the way people handle conflict.

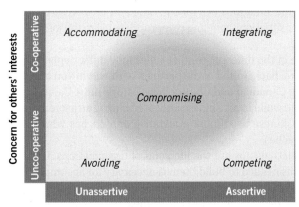

FIGURE 8.5 Conflict Styles

The avoiding style, which is a passive response to conflicts, is both unco-operative and unassertive. It is characterized by withdrawal from the conflict or suppression of the reasons that the conflict occurred. It may be effective when the conflict is too costly to resolve or when the issue is trivial. Drawbacks include missed opportunities to provide input and results that leave both parties frustrated.

The accommodating style—sometimes referred to as obliging—focuses on satisfying others' interests with a high level of co-operativeness and a low level of assertiveness. It may be useful when harmony is desired, when the goal is building a relationship, or when the issue is more important to the other party. Drawbacks include the possibility that legitimate interests will be left unresolved and the feeling of being used or taken advantage of over time.

The competing style—sometimes referred to as dominating—reflects a high level of assertiveness and a low level of co-operation designed to satisfy your own needs. This style, concerned with "winning" the conflict, may be useful against another competitor or when a quick decision is needed. Drawbacks include the possibility that competitors will burn bridges or harm relationships.

The compromising style has moderate levels of both co-operativeness and assertiveness and requires each side to give up and receive something of importance. This style may be effective if both sides are equally powerful, if a temporary solution is acceptable, or if all options for a win-win solution have been tried without reaching agreement. Drawbacks include a possible short-circuiting of creativity and dissatisfaction for both parties.

The integrating style—sometimes referred to as collaborating—implies a high level of co-operation and a high level of assertiveness. It seeks to find maximum benefits for all parties, creating a win-win situation. It may be useful when all interests in the conflict are too important to compromise and when consensus is needed. One drawback is that integrators may make a simple decision very complex by taking too much time to talk through every issue.

Research indicates that a person's natural conflict style, which is rooted in his or her personality or shaped by his or her culture, will dominate as a conflict endures. For example, people with collectivistic orientations are more likely to prefer the integrating and compromising styles than are people with individualistic orientations.[65] Even so, organizational members can learn other styles, and their relationships will benefit from using the style that is most appropriate to what the situation calls for. Sometimes, an accommodating style is necessary to build goodwill, whereas in other situations competing may be necessary to stand up for an idea that serves not only your own interests but also those of the organization. Moreover, some situations call for the time and creativity required in the integrative style, while in other situations avoiding is appropriate given the insignificance of the issue or due to lack of time.

The prevalence of the different conflict styles may differ depending on the country you are in or the cultural background of the partners with whom you negotiate. For example, in a study comparing Canadian and Chinese negotiators, most Canadians indicated having a compromising style while most Chinese indicated having an avoiding style.[66] When engaged in a negotiation, Chinese used more integrative approaches while Canadians used more distributive approaches.

In summary, relationships are the lifeblood of organizations. Understanding them and developing the skills needed to build them is necessary for accomplishing self-interests and organizational goals. From a sustainable perspective, however, relationships are inherently valuable and worth developing regardless of their "return" in meeting personal or professional interests. Building relationships may be a low priority for some organizations, perhaps because "business isn't personal" and organizational members aren't paid to make friends. Still, it seems short-sighted to consider the value of relationships only in terms of their contribution to organizational outcomes. Relationships are fundamental to human life and essential to our long-term personal, and perhaps also organizational, well-being, happiness, and ability to flourish. In this sense, relationships are of immeasurable worth and merit our understanding in more depth.

transformational relationships at tata[67]

Sam Panthaky/AFP/Getty Images

The Tata Group, India's largest conglomerate and perhaps its most pervasive and valuable brand, makes products Indians use from morning to night. The alarm clock that wakes them, the tea they drink with breakfast, the clothes they put on, the car they drive to work, the phone and computer they use, and even the lights they turn off when they go to bed all come from companies owned in part by the Tata Group.[68]

From its founding, Tata has seen itself as more than a profit-making enterprise; it also wants to be a force in modernizing and improving India. It not only markets products and services and provides jobs through its for-profit businesses, Tata also provides generous support—more than the equivalent of USD $150 million annually—for non-profit organizations committed to community development, education, emergency aid, and the arts.

The Tata Group invests in the country and the community, sometimes sacrificing short-term profits to do so. When faced with tight financial markets and cost-cutting mandates in 2007, Tata's companies were challenged to maintain their current approach to charitable giving. In response, the chairman at the time, Ratan Tata, said: "I can't ensure this [level of social spending] will survive . . . [We] could turn it into a more conventional company. But you would have great discontent."[69] People have come to expect Tata to act differently.

Tata has an impressive track record of building positive relationships with its employees. For example, since the 1930s Tata Steel has had policies in place supporting an eight-hour workday, maternity leave, free medical care, and disability and retirement benefits. When layoffs are necessary due to modernization or depressed markets, Tata transfers employees to other plants or provides those who lose their jobs with severance packages, including full salaries until employees turn 60. At Tata Consultancy Services, offering the personal touch of inviting families of employees to cultural events and providing best-in-industry health care benefits prompted one employee to say, "Why leave a Tata company?"[70] Most don't.

The Tata Group's investment in building positive community relationships included contributing substantial money and resources to developing a model city around the enterprise's first steel mill. That city, Jamshedpur, received support from Tata in the form of funding for public water, trash pickup, and health care and education services. Similar subsidies to education and health care have been given in other communities, such as Kerala, even after Tata ceased its operations there.

In an initiative that reached beyond the communities in which its companies operate, Tata invested in an anti-bribery ad campaign. Concerned about a report from Transparency International that bribery was rampant in India, the Tata Group paid for numerous ads that challenged Indians to "wake up" and stop accepting bribes. In the enterprise's own business dealings, bribes were refused and partnerships with companies reputed to be corrupt were ended. These efforts contributed to improved rankings from Transparency International that now list India as surpassing most of the neighbouring countries in ethical business practices. Tata's actions were consistent with its long-held values emphasizing honesty and social responsibility and its motto, "Leadership with Trust."

Altogether, the efforts and initiatives of the Tata Group have resulted in its being rated the most trustworthy company in all India and many of its companies, such as Tata Consultancy Services, being rated as the best places to work.[71]

QUESTIONS FOR DISCUSSION

1. From what you've learned about the Tata Group, what characteristics might limit organizational politics?
2. How would you describe the quality of relationships Tata has with its stakeholders?
3. What specific behaviours contribute to the quality of those relationships?
4. What are some unique relationship challenges in India?
5. How is Tata addressing those challenges?

Summary

Learning Objectives	From a conventional OB perspective, relationships are best explained by people seeking their own self-interests and the financial interests of their organizations.	From a sustainable OB perspective, relationships can be enhanced to include stakeholders seeking to improve their mutual (holistic) interests and those of their organization.
• Discuss organizational politics and its effects on an organization.	• Political behaviours are perceived to be inevitable, are important for success in organizations, and, therefore, must be practised.	• Political behaviours are not assumed to be inevitable, are not considered necessary for success in organizations, and, therefore, can be minimized.
• Explain the importance of trust in the workplace and ways to build trust in the workplace.	• There are many benefits for organizations and individuals in being trustworthy and extending trust in important workplace relationships.	• There are many benefits for organizations and individuals in being trustworthy and extending trust in all stakeholder relationships.
• Recognize how fairness promotes positive feelings, improves satisfaction, promotes organizational citizenship behaviour, and reduces turnover.	• Fairness in relationships focuses on tangible factors in determining distributive, procedural, and interactional justice.	• Fairness in relationships focuses on tangible and intangible factors in determining distributive, procedural, and interactional justice.
• Discuss negotiation as an everyday occurrence in organizational relationships.	• Distributive bargaining serves to secure self-interest and short-term financial interests of the organization.	• Integrative negotiating serves to improve the mutual holistic interests of the negotiators and other stakeholders.

Key Terms

Aspiration point (p. 174)
Best alternative to a negotiated agreement (BATNA) (p. 175)
Conflict style (p. 177)
Delegation (p. 168)
Distributive bargaining (p. 173)
Distributive justice (p. 171)

Fairness (p. 170)
Influence tactics (p. 172)
Integrative negotiation (p. 175)
Interactional justice (p. 171)
Interpersonal trust (p. 165)
Negotiation (p. 172)

Organizational politics (p. 163)
Procedural justice (p. 171)
Psychological contract (p. 165)
Reservation point (p. 174)
Social networks (p. 166)
Zone of possible agreements (ZOPA) (p. 174)

Questions for Reflection and Discussion

1. Have you worked in an organization where politics was prevalent? How did it affect behaviour? What do you think caused it?
2. Trust can be earned. Which of the main factors influencing trust—competence, character, and goodwill—do you think is most important to earning and maintaining trust?
3. Describe the three types of fairness discussed in the chapter. What are some examples of violations of each type that you have experienced?

4. What are the main components of successful integrative negotiation? How do these differ from the main components of a distributive bargaining approach?
5. The chapter mentioned that culture can affect conflict styles. What might be other factors that influence conflict styles?

ob activities

How Do You React to People Who Act or Think Differently?

Using a scale of 1 - Strongly Disagree (SD), 2 - Disagree (D), 3 - Neutral (N), 4 - Agree (A), and 5 - Strongly Agree (SA), indicate your level of agreement with each statement on the 5-point scale.

Typically, I . . .

	SD	D	N	A	SA
1. Accept people as they are.	1	2	3	4	5
2. Treat people as inferiors.	1	2	3	4	5
3. Believe there are many sides to most issues.	1	2	3	4	5
4. Believe that others have good intentions.	1	2	3	4	5
5. Am quick to judge others.	1	2	3	4	5

Key: This is a short version of an integrity scale from the International Personality Item Pool (http://ipip.ori.org/). To calculate your total score, add the following:

____ *(response to statement 1)*

+ ____ *(response to statement 2, subtracted from 6)*

+ ____ *(response to statement 3)*

+ ____ *(response to statement 4)*

+ ____ *(response to statement 5, subtracted from 6)*

= ____ *Total score*

The greater the score (out of 25 possible), the higher your self-rating on tolerance for others. Tolerance for diversity has the potential to improve satisfaction with teamwork and contribute to a sense of belonging and closeness in a team or work group.[72]

What Is Your Style in Dealing with Conflict?

Using the scale of 1 - Strongly Disagree (SD), 2 - Disagree (D), 3 - Neutral (N), 4 - Agree (A), and 5 - Strongly Agree (SA), indicate your level of agreement with each statement on the 5-point scale.

Typically . . .

	SD	D	N	A	SA
1. I argue my case with others to show the merits of my position.	1	2	3	4	5
2. I negotiate with others so that a compromise can be reached.	1	2	3	4	5
3. I try to satisfy the expectations of others.	1	2	3	4	5
4. I try to investigate an issue with others to find a solution acceptable to both of us.	1	2	3	4	5

Typically . . .

	SD	D	N	A	SA
5. I am firm in pursuing my side of the issue.	1	2	3	4	5
6. I attempt to avoid being "put on the spot" and try to keep my conflict with others to myself.	1	2	3	4	5
7. I hold on to my solution to a problem.	1	2	3	4	5
8. I use "give and take" so that a compromise can be made.	1	2	3	4	5
9. I exchange accurate information with others in order to solve a problem together.	1	2	3	4	5
10. I avoid open discussion of my differences with others.	1	2	3	4	5
11. I accommodate the wishes of others.	1	2	3	4	5
12. I try to bring all our concerns out in the open so that the issues can be resolved in the best possible way.	1	2	3	4	5
13. I propose a middle ground for breaking deadlocks.	1	2	3	4	5
14. I go along with the suggestions of others.	1	2	3	4	5
15. I try to keep my disagreements with others to myself to avoid hard feelings.	1	2	3	4	5

Key: To determine your score for each conflict style, sum up the response values from the questions associated with each category. The highest score is your dominant style.

Questions Representing Category	Category Score
Avoiding (6, 10, 15)	_____
Accommodating (3, 11, 14)	_____
Competing (1, 5, 7)	_____
Compromising (2, 8, 13)	_____
Collaborating (4, 9, 12)	_____

Source: Adapted from Rahim's original measure: Rahim, M. A. (1983). A measure of styles of handling interpersonal conflict. *Academy of Management Journal, 26*(2), 368–376.

ETHICS SCENARIO

Despite not having a lower bid, a purchasing representative for a company tells a supplier during a negotiation to reduce its price because the company can purchase the product at a lower cost from someone else.

Why might this scenario occur in organizations?

Use the following scale to indicate whether this behaviour is ethically acceptable:

NEVER ACCEPTABLE   **SOMETIMES ACCEPTABLE**   **ALWAYS ACCEPTABLE**

1   2   3   4   5   6   7

Explain the ideas you considered in arriving at your answer.

Trust Bank Activity

You can think of each relationship in your work environment as having a "Trust Bank," the balance of which is the sum of all your relational deposits (that is, behaviours that build trust) and withdrawals (behaviours that reduce trust). Create a list of your recent deposits and withdrawals. Be specific about the behaviours, but don't name names.

After everyone has created his or her own list, have each person share examples of their deposits and withdrawals. Listen to the ideas of others and add them to your list—this is the most critical step in the process. After all, to be a trust builder you have to be interested in what *others* believe builds trust.

QUESTIONS FOR DISCUSSION

1. Which deposits and withdrawals were mentioned most often?

2. Which deposits and withdrawals were surprising?

3. What is one deposit you intend to make in the future and one withdrawal you will try to avoid?

Norton Manufacturing[73]

Rick Douglas is the sales manager for the industrial products division of Norton Manufacturing. He has held this position for nearly two years. Most orders from clients are for the standard version of the division's products, but customized versions are becoming increasingly important as a source of profits. A few months ago one of Rick's sales representatives obtained an order from a new client for some customized products. Now the client wants to speed up delivery of the order by three weeks. It is a very lucrative order, and the client will pay extra for early delivery. Rick's sales representative has asked him to expedite the order. Rick knows that two things are necessary to get faster delivery to the customer.

First, Rick must influence Carl Miller, the product design manager, to finish developing the specifications and testing the samples. Carl needs to run some more tests on the products, but he could be ready for production next week. Rick has a friendly working relationship with Carl, and they occasionally play golf together. When he first came to Norton, Rick spent several months working in product design as part of the company's management training program. He understands the technical specifications of the products and works closely with Carl in determining how to satisfy the specialized needs of industrial clients.

The other thing Rick must do to expedite the order is influence Ken Williams, the plant manager, to change his production schedule.

Ken has been trying to complete work on a large production run for one of the company's regular products. Interrupting this work to shift production to Rick's order would cause delays and make more work for Ken than if he just finished the current run first. The production equipment must be adjusted for Rick's customized products, then readjusted afterward for the regular products. In addition, special materials must be obtained quickly to make the customized items. Ken is loyal to the company, but he has complained that the industrial salespeople seem to favour the customized products with lots of "bells and whistles" over the basic products that have kept the company going through the years. Ken is still a little distrustful of people in sales due to some conflicts he had with the person who formerly held Rick's position.

Rick is confident that the profits from his special order would more than compensate the company for any delays or costs of changing production schedules. Moreover, if this client is pleased with the product quality and customer service on the initial order, the client could become one of the division's most important clients in future years. The new business would provide justification to purchase some new equipment that Ken wants for the production department. Ken requested the new equipment last year, but the funds were not approved by top management.

QUESTIONS FOR DISCUSSION

1. Describe the characteristics of the relationships in this case.

2. Which influence tactics might be most useful in Rick's negotiations with Carl, and which ones might be most useful in his negotiations with Ken?

This is a personal journal entry that can be used for class discussion or be compiled and included in a self-reflection paper.

Consider the most satisfying and productive relationships you have experienced in the workplace. What made these relationships satisfying and productive? Were some relationships satisfying but not productive or productive but not satisfying? List specific behaviours that were important in shaping these relationships, and indicate a relationship that might benefit from your engaging in more of each behaviour.

Nine

Leading Others

Leadership may be the most frequently researched topic in all the social sciences—but there is still much to learn. In this chapter, we begin by briefly describing different ways to think about leadership in comparison to management. We then consider how studies of leadership have explored leaders' traits, their behaviours, and the influence of situations. We will examine these issues from both a conventional and a sustainable point of view.

Learning Objectives	Conventional OB	Sustainable OB
LEADERSHIP TRAITS		
1. Describe the personal characteristics of leaders.	Leverage traits for personal gain, to get ahead, and to accomplish what serves the interests of a few	Leverage traits for others' gain, to make a difference, and to accomplish what serves the interests of many
LEADERSHIP BEHAVIOURS		
2. Identify the ways or manners in which leaders act.	Utilize consideration and/or initiating structure behaviours	Utilize socioemotional and/or infrastructural behaviours
CONTINGENCY THEORIES		
3. Analyze the contingency theories of leadership and their importance in explaining and guiding leadership behaviour.	Adapt leadership behaviour to promote individual performance	Adapt leadership behaviour to promote individual and community well-being
INTEGRATED MODELS		
4. Discuss the value of integrative leadership models.	Employ directing, coaching, supporting, or delegating based on the needs of the situation	Encourage enabling, equipping, engaging, or empowering based on the needs of the situation

creating happiness: passion and purpose at g adventures[1]

Rick Madonik/Getty Images

Bruce Poon Tip is the founder of G Adventures (formerly GAP Adventures), the world's largest small-group, outdoor adventure travel company that offers socially and environmentally conscious travel with a grassroots approach. Poon Tip's revolutionary vision and leadership style have led G Adventures to remarkable success in the travel industry. He has built his company to focus on outcomes beyond the conventional measure of profit and even beyond the triple bottom line of people, planet, and profit—the goal of his business is to make people's lives better and enable them to achieve sustained happiness.

Headquartered in Toronto, G Adventures was founded in 1990 as a one-man operation but has grown to employ over 1,350 people worldwide and serve over 100,000 travellers annually. Specializing in sustainable tourism, the company is active in over 100 countries, offering more than 1,000 small-group experiences that embrace "authentic accommodation, exotic cuisine and local transport to put travellers on a first-name basis with the planet's people, culture, landscape and wildlife." As a company, G Adventures strives to preserve cultural heritage and conserve and replenish the natural environment while improving the lives of local people.

Poon Tip's vision for his business is to create happiness and make people's lives better. From his perspective, the most successful and sustainable businesses are those that go beyond the triple bottom line and infuse their organization with passion and purpose. In his book, *Looptail: How One Company Changed the World by Reinventing Business*, Poon Tip says that this is the key to engaging people internally, who in turn will engage people and customers externally. On his company's website, the core values are explained in this way:

> *At G Adventures, changing people's lives isn't just a mantra, it's the very core of our company culture, the essence of who we are, and the driving force behind everything we do. The way we see it, change is the key to innovation, and people are the key to change.*

In today's increasingly complex business environment, Poon Tip suggests that leaders need to create and manage an environment and culture in which people can create happiness,

Poon Tip's vision for his business is to create happiness and make people's lives better.

because happiness drives performance. For him, this requires having a team that believes in and lives by the company values. Poon Tip has built G Adventures on four pillars: (1) the ability to grow and develop, (2) being connected to people and the company, (3) being united and a part of something bigger than yourself, and (4) freedom. According to Poon Tip, an environment that embraces all four elements gives people the opportunity to find their passion and purpose. While it does not guarantee that people will be happy, it gives them the potential to achieve happiness if they truly desire it. The company describes itself as a "work hard/play hard" company that is dedicated to the entrepreneurial spirit.

As well as pursuing its passion to show people the world, G Adventures provides people with an opportunity to be a part of a community that truly makes people's live better. The company is known for its international philanthropic efforts: It has backed more than 40 projects, including a women's weaving co-operative and a home for street children in Peru, safe drinking-water programs in Tanzania and Kenya, and a training centre for former sex workers in Cambodia.

Empowering and trusting his employees are hallmarks of Poon Tip's management style—so much so that he took the controversial steps of renouncing his title of CEO and eliminating the company's human resources (HR) department. In lieu of having himself serve as Chief Executive Officer, he appointed his 700 tour leaders and salespeople as Chief *Experience* Officers. As it is they who are directly responsible for the experience of G Adventures's customers, Poon Tip wanted to convey that they have the freedom and ability to think for themselves to improve the travel experience. His thinking behind eliminating the HR department was that its policies were overly bureaucratic, restrictive, and aimed at the bottom 10 percent of employees. As he saw it, these policies were created to take away people's freedom and ability to think for themselves, which resulted in high achievers being punished and overall happiness in the organization being restricted. Poon Tip transferred HR's administrative functions to the finance department, where he felt they would be more effectively performed, and he created two new departments: the Talent Agency, which is aimed at hiring and evaluating talent, and the Culture Club, whose members are responsible for promoting the company's culture.

Although happiness is the company's main focus, Poon Tip still recognizes the importance of profit, performance, and overall excellence. Every year, employees whose performance is in the bottom 10 percent of the organization are identified and then managed either "up or out." He also acknowledges that while his philanthropic initiatives help the local people, many of the initiatives also create experiences for G Adventure travellers that help to differentiate the company from its competitors.

Poon Tip advises business leaders who wish to build a successful and sustainable business to use passion and purpose to engage people internally and externally. In his own organization, having built a culture that allows members to pursue happiness and to make the lives of others better, Poon Tip has consistently made decisions and taken actions that affirm and perpetuate the organization's values.

Leadership is the purposeful and relational process of influencing others.[2] In organizations, the primary purpose of the leadership process is to influence members to achieve organizational goals. Although leadership is sometimes associated with formal positions of authority, there are also many informal leaders within any organization. For scholars such as Henri Fayol, "leading" is one of the main functions of management (alongside planning, organizing, and controlling). From this point of view, leading is a subset of a manager's activities. In a competing view, management is a subset of leading, because leading includes both transactional (managing) and transformational behaviour.[3]

> **Leadership** is the purposeful and relational process of influencing others.

Transactional leaders focus on having fair exchanges with organizational members to motivate them to achieve established goals. These leaders clarify role or task requirements, set up structures, provide appropriate rewards, and try to be considerate of the needs of employees. They take pride in keeping things running smoothly and efficiently, have a sense of commitment to the organization, and encourage conformity to organizational norms and values.

> **Transactional leaders** focus on having fair exchanges with organizational members to motivate them to achieve established goals.

Transformational leaders focus on inspiring change in members and the organization. These leaders unite others in seeking extraordinary performance accomplishments. They take pride in challenging the status quo and stimulating change in their organization's mission, strategy, structure, and culture. Transformational leaders create change in employees and the organization in four ways:[4]

> **Transformational leaders** focus on inspiring change in members and the organization.

- They identify with followers, creating personal loyalty.
- They articulate a clear vision that serves to motivate employees to transcend individual goals for the sake of a team or organization.
- They pay personal attention to followers' needs by supporting and encouraging them in their attempts to work toward the vision.
- They challenge followers to be innovative, model new behaviours, and exhibit a high moral standard in their actions.

Ken Chenault, CEO of American Express, is a transformational leader. He lives out his conviction that leaders can help to define reality and give hope. For example, in the post–September 11 turbulence that threatened the travel industry, Chenault was able to draw upon his reputation as a gentleman, innovator, and problem solver to communicate a credible message to his employees. He talked about how the company had reinvented itself in the aftermath of past crises and emerged stronger, and he assured members of his organization that this crisis too would make them better. Chenault delivered this message in person to employees in New York City one week after the attack. He presented a realistic road map that acknowledged current challenges and difficult decisions (including reductions in staff) but offered hope for the future. His transformational leadership galvanized members of the organization and prepared them for three subsequent years of solid growth.[5]

Chenault also leads by example. In the wake of the expected economic downturn in 2008, he agreed to a new personal incentive package that included stock options he could exercise only if he met challenging goals for company performance.[6] This action modelled a high standard of accountability and demonstrated that he had a stake in making the whole organization successful. When speaking in 2013 about how to lead when there are challenges in the economy, Chenault offered this advice: "People want to see the leader. You need to communicate constantly. Don't assume that people are seeing what you are seeing. And, you've got to act. Never let events freeze you up."[7]

Leadership Traits

| LEADERSHIP TRAITS | LEADERSHIP BEHAVIOURS | CONTINGENCY THEORIES | INTEGRATIVE MODELS |

In the quest to understand what differentiates leaders from non-leaders, researchers initially focused on leaders' **traits**, personal characteristics that are relatively stable. The goal was to analyze great leaders, find out what made them great, and then use the traits they had in common to identify future leaders.

Charisma, a special ability or "gift" to attract and inspire others, is one trait commonly thought to make great leaders. Charismatic leaders exude the enthusiasm and self-confidence that establish interpersonal connections and motivate people to do more than they normally do, especially in the face of obstacles and personal sacrifice. Typically, these leaders are visionaries who persuasively communicate their vision, demonstrate a willingness to take risks to achieve it, are sensitive to how their vision meets follower needs, and display extraordinary behaviour in pursuit of it. In many ways, this behaviour is similar to that of transformational leaders. If there is a difference between the two kinds of leaders, it may be that a charismatic leader's influence tends to be tied to the force of his or her personality.

Despite the popularity of the idea of charismatic leadership, it sometimes raises ethical issues.[8] Notorious leaders such as Adolf Hitler used their personal charisma to encourage followers to engage in behaviour they might otherwise have rejected. In the business world, former CEOs Bernie Ebbers of WorldCom and Jeffrey Skilling of Enron also have been described as having charismatic personalities. Under Ebbers's leadership, WorldCom was forced into bankruptcy after it defrauded investors, while during Skilling's tenure, Enron collapsed from the weight of its culture of greed and fraud. Both men were sentenced to prison.

Over the years, instead of finding traits that are *always* present within a leader, scholars have found many traits that are *likely*, but not certain, to be associated with leadership. For example, conventional leaders are likely to enjoy having influence over others (desire to lead), demonstrate a strong ambition to get ahead (drive), believe in their abilities to achieve organizational goals (self-confidence), recognize the value of being truthful and keeping their word (honesty and integrity), and have excellent conceptual skills for understanding how the organizational structures and systems work together to achieve overall goals (intelligence and knowledge).[9] Recently, the general personality traits of extraversion, conscientiousness, and openness to experience also were found to influence who becomes the leader within a group and to influence leaders' performance ratings.[10]

In many ways, the traits that characterize a sustainable leader are similar to those that distinguish a conventional leader. However, sustainable leaders apply these traits to more relational, and less materialistic, causes. For example, when Winifred Mitchell Baker, the chairperson and former CEO of Mozilla Corporation, works tirelessly to promote open-source development of the Internet, she is working for the benefit of a larger community of Internet users. Throughout her career at Netscape and Mozilla, Mitchell Baker has served a cause broader than promoting her own career or padding her paycheque.

In scholarly terms, this motivation to lead for the sake of serving others is called a "socialized power motive," in contrast with a "personalized power motive," which is a desire to lead

for personal gain. Academic terms aside, employees easily recognize the difference in their workplaces. Although leaders with a personalized power motive may get promoted and gain status, often their career stalls or derails as other people resist their self-centred motives and insensitivity.[11]

Sustainable leaders also have a sense of *drive*, but it is different from the type of drive demonstrated by conventional leaders. Whereas conventional leaders are often propelled by a sense of competitiveness and a desire to get ahead financially, sustainable leaders are driven by a desire to nurture community and foster a variety of forms of well-being. In other words, their drive is not simply to get ahead but, rather, to make a positive difference. For example, Bruce Poon Tip's desire to create happiness is apparent in the many philanthropic projects he oversees through G Adventures. Although Poon Tip is also competitive and driven to succeed financially, his drive is tempered by his commitment to preserving the natural habitat and improving the situation of others around the globe.

Evidence is mounting that while self-centred drive can have short-term benefits, it ultimately destroys the collective capability and morale of a department or organization.[12] Jim Collins's research on good- and great-performing companies indicates that leaders who instead combine humility with a strong will to succeed—whom he calls Level 5 leaders—are critical to the long-term profitability and success of great companies.[13]

The humility and the strong will of sustainable leaders also affect their expressions of *self-confidence*. Collins describes the Level 5 leaders from his research as attributing their success to others rather than to their own abilities or decisions. Their confidence does not come from the attitude that they are somehow better or smarter than others; rather, it is rooted in their beliefs about the capability of the members of their organization. These leaders believe in the potential of collaboration, and they draw confidence from the power of people working together to solve problems. Cecilia Ochoa Levine is a business owner who provides Level 5 leadership to manufacturing operations in border towns of Mexico and the United States.[14] She is also a leader in addressing business and societal challenges related to drugs and violence along the border. Although Levine has counselled political leaders from across the globe and rubbed elbows with Pope John Paul II, her confidence is rooted in the

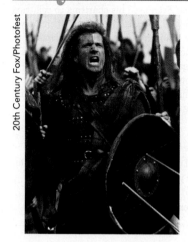

MOB | ALL FOR ONE OR ONE FOR ALL?

20th Century Fox/Photofest

In the Academy Award–winning movie *Braveheart*, Mel Gibson portrays William Wallace, a notable leader in Scotland's historic fight for independence from English rule at the close of the 13th century. Wallace is depicted as rallying the ragtag Scottish troops by appealing to a common vision of freedom that would benefit all the people, not just the ruling Scottish noblemen. While the noblemen demonstrate a personalized power motive, Wallace demonstrates a socialized power motive by orienting his words and actions around this compelling vision.

QUESTIONS FOR REFLECTION

1. Can you think of any recent movies in which a main character demonstrates a similar example of socialized power orientation?
2. From your experience, what have been the power motives of leaders you have worked for?

---

broad collaboration she has nurtured between U.S. and Mexican politicians and business leaders.[15]

For both conventional and sustainable leaders, "honesty is the best policy." Sustainable leaders see honesty and integrity as not only valued by others and good for business but as good or right regardless of the circumstances. When employees of The AES Corporation, one of the largest energy companies in the world, falsified reports to the Environmental Protection Agency, then-CEO Dennis Bakke wrote an open letter to everyone in the company acknowledging the misdeed and committing to redoubling efforts to teach company values. He did not try to hide the wrongdoing, nor did he take the company lawyer's advice to fire the employees in order to solve the problem. When the letter became public, AES's share price dropped temporarily, but Bakke had no regrets.[16]

Finally, sustainable leaders also score high in terms of *intelligence* and *job-relevant knowledge,* but their intelligence and knowledge extend beyond the traditional bounds of the organization. Compared to conventional leaders, sustainable leaders are more likely to apply their intellect toward acquiring knowledge about how their organization affects a wider variety of stakeholders along a wider array of dimensions. They educate themselves broadly regarding the opinions and interests of their stakeholders. For example, at Whole Foods Market, managers are expected to build connections with and promote the practices of local organic farmers. According to Ram Charan, author of the book *Know-How: The 8 Skills that Separate People Who Perform from Those Who Don't,* this application of intellect to understanding the broader organizational context helps leaders avoid emerging threats, and it allows them to seize opportunities for growth or innovation.[17] Of course, intellectual and technical knowledge and skills are necessary for all leaders, but those who perform best may excel at utilizing their intelligence differently or at using other forms such as emotional intelligence.

Everyone seems to know a leader who is "book smart" but clueless when it comes to emotional and interpersonal skills. In chapter 4, we described *emotional intelligence (EI)* as the capability to recognize, manage, and exercise emotions in relationships. Leaders with emotional *self-awareness* are in tune with their own emotions and know when they may arise in certain situations. *Self-management* of emotions is required when a leader may need to maintain his or her cool in a conflict, whereas in another situation revealing a certain level of frustration may be useful in emphasizing an idea or point of view. A leader with *empathy* has a strong sense of what others are feeling or experiencing. *Internal motivation* allows a leader to harness emotions in order to tackle challenging tasks or push through difficulties. Finally, a leader with emotional *social skills* is able to gain the commitment of followers and excels at collaborating with others.

Sometimes leaders who lack EI have risen to management positions thanks to their technical expertise or short-term accomplishments. Yet, in his research on leadership Daniel Goleman has asserted that EI is one of the most important factors that influences the success of leaders.[18] In his review of 188 leadership competency models—used by such organizations as British Airlines and Lucent Technologies—Goleman found EI to be at least twice as important as intellectual or technical skills in predicting leadership performance.[19] Follow-up research indicates that across a range of workplace contexts, EI consistently contributes to leadership effectiveness.[20] Part of the reason EI is so valuable is that followers of leaders with EI are more satisfied with their jobs and more willing to do whatever it takes to satisfy organizational goals.

Emotional intelligence is critical in a variety of situations. The rational approach of stating facts and figures can be ineffective in motivating change, for example, whereas an emotional appeal can resound deeply and compel action.[21] In a study of restaurants in the United Kingdom, the EI of managers was strongly associated with profit and customer satisfaction.[22] In addition, EI is particularly important for fulfilling the relational and motivational aspects of effective team leadership.[23] Finally, when coupled with cultural awareness, EI is a crucial factor in determining leadership success in foreign cultures.[24]

Whether their approach is conventional or sustainable, EI is beneficial for leaders. Even though EI has some basis in personality traits, leaders can improve their emotional intelligence somewhat with coaching, feedback, and consistent practice.[25] In elementary and secondary school programs, training students to improve their social and emotional competencies associated with EI enhanced prosocial behaviour and improved attendance and grades while it decreased antisocial and aggressive behaviour.[26] From a sustainable perspective, this research suggests that the development of EI is worthwhile given its potential to contribute to positive interactions both inside and outside of the workplace.

While possessing certain traits makes it more likely that an individual will emerge as a leader and be successful in accomplishing organizational goals, this outcome is not guaranteed. Some effective leaders do not have all of these traits, and some who do possess them are not effective in leadership roles. Clearly, traits alone are not sufficient for explaining the emergence of and the influence exerted by leaders. Nonetheless, organizations can use traits that are more stable, such as intelligence, as criteria in hiring and promoting people into leadership positions.

Although traits may be helpful for understanding what types of people are more likely to become leaders, traits are relatively difficult to change in order to improve leadership. Behaviours, on the other hand, can be learned or developed. With this in mind, in the middle part of the 20th century researchers shifted their focus to behavioural styles and examined whether there is something unique about what the best leaders *do*.

Leadership Behaviour

| LEADERSHIP TRAITS | **LEADERSHIP BEHAVIOURS** | CONTINGENCY THEORIES | INTEGRATIVE MODELS |

LEARNING OBJECTIVE 2
Identify the ways or manners in which leaders act.

Moving from trait theory to behavioural theory shifts our attention from who leaders *are* to what they *do*. **Behaviours** are the ways or manner in which people act. If some leader behaviours are associated with highly productive workers, then any leader could maximize worker productivity simply by adopting the correct behaviour through appropriate training.

Behaviours are the ways or manner in which people act.

Dimensions of Leadership Behaviour

Revealing research studies on leadership behaviour were conducted at the University of Michigan and Ohio State University in the 1940s and 1950s. The Michigan studies described two basic kinds of leadership behaviour: employee-centred and production-centred. Similarly, the Ohio State studies identified two general sets of leadership behaviours—consideration and initiating structure[27]—and found them to be independent of each other. Practically, this means that a leader can engage in one set of behaviours but not the other, or a leader can engage in both. Combining these research studies, we can describe two types of behaviour as such:

- **Consideration** behaviours are supportive, relationship-oriented, and/or employee-centred. Leaders engage in consideration behaviour when they show concern for employees and attempt to establish a friendly and supportive climate where job relationships are defined by mutual trust and respect for group members' ideas and feelings. Examples of consideration behaviour are listening, showing support, expressing appreciation, and asking for input.

- **Initiating structure** behaviours are directive, task-oriented, and/or production-centred. Leaders engage in initiating structure when they take action directed toward followers to ensure that work gets done, that employees perform their jobs in a specific way, and that efficiency is optimized. Leaders do this by clarifying roles, explaining tasks, providing direction, and communicating procedures.

Sometimes productivity is enhanced when leaders rate high in both consideration and initiating structure behaviours. In general, however, initiating structure is more strongly related to productivity, whereas consideration is more strongly related to employee satisfaction.[28]

Dina Dwyer-Owens is the chairwoman and CEO of The Dwyer Group, a services-based franchise group that includes Mr. Rooter, Glass Doctor, and five other worldwide franchises. Dwyer-Owens engages in initiating structure when she establishes challenging goals for her employees and when she starts each meeting with a discussion of The Dwyer Group's code of values.[29] She also initiates structure when she teaches the Group's service expectations to franchisees and sets up programs that provide training and incentives for women and U.S. military veterans to work in and own franchises. Dwyer-Owens demonstrates consideration when she shows her commitment to employees' well-being, expresses confidence in their abilities to solve challenging problems, offers encouragement, and celebrates employee and franchisee achievements.[30]

The Leadership Grid

Robert Blake and Jane Mouton developed the **Leadership Grid** (initially known as the Managerial Grid) as a two-dimensional management development framework.[31] The Leadership Grid identifies five leadership styles that combine different degrees of concern for production (initiating structure) and concern for people (consideration). These behaviours are ranked on a scale of 1 (low) to 9 (high). As shown in Figure 9.1, a leader's behavioural style can fall into one of 81 categories. Among these many possibilities, there are five basic styles:

- *Impoverished style* (1 in concern for production, 1 in concern for people): Exhibits a low concern for both people and production. Leaders who use this style tend to avoid engagement in the work environment in hopes of avoiding trouble by "going with the flow." This lack of engagement tends to promote neither a trusting work environment nor high productivity.

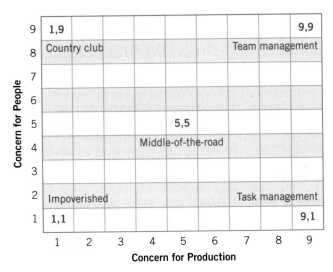

FIGURE 9.1 The Leadership Grid

Source: Adapted from Blake, R. R., & Mouton, J. (1982). A comparative analysis of situationalism and 9,9 management by principle. *Organizational Dynamics, 10*(4), 20–43.

- *Country club style* (1,9): Exhibits a high concern for people and a low concern for production. Leaders who use this style try to create a secure, comfortable atmosphere of trust with their employees based on friendship. This style will generally lead to a very friendly work environment but not necessarily to high productivity.

- *Task management style* (9,1): Exhibits a high concern for production and a low concern for people. Leaders who use this style are very directive, emphasize organizational productivity and compliance, and show little regard for employees' personal needs. They tend to promote performance but not a trusting work environment.

- *Middle-of-the-road style* (5,5): Exhibits both relational and task behaviours in either an insufficient or an underdeveloped manner. This style tends to result in adequate organizational performance but falls short of producing high levels of commitment or achievement.

- *Team style* (9,9): Exhibits a high level of concern for both people and production. Leaders who use this style emphasize common productivity goals and use participative or team-oriented processes that value individuals' opinions and concerns. This style tends to yield high levels of productivity and feelings of commitment and trust.

Training associated with the Leadership Grid typically engages leaders in a series of leaderless group activities and stressful interactions, over the course of which each person's "real" leadership style will become evident. Behavioural training is then provided to move the leader toward the optimal *team* style.

According to the research of Blake and Mouton, leaders perform best when using the team management style (9,9).[32] However, most researchers and managers agree that leading is more complex than suggested by that theory. An unlimited number of personal and situational factors interact to determine why leaders lead the way they do and why followers respond in the ways they do.

Paralleling this conventional dual emphasis on consideration and initiating structure, the sustainable approach emphasizes **socioemotional behaviour** and **infrastructural behaviour**. A key difference is that, whereas the conventional approach tends to focus on leadership behaviours that are directed at and visible to followers, the sustainable approach includes behaviours that are invisible to followers. Thus, *visible* socioemotional behaviour

Socioemotional behaviour is a category of leadership behaviours, which may or may not be visible to followers, that are supportive, relationship-oriented, employee-centred, and promote personal and collective well-being.

Infrastructural behaviour is a category of leadership behaviours, which may or may not be visible to followers, that are directive, task-oriented, production-centred, and promote information exchange and learning.

Male and female leaders share many similarities. Nevertheless, research indicates that women leaders tend to be more participative and nurturing, whereas male leaders tend to make decisions more independently and be more assertive in leading. When women make up the majority of the managers in an organization, supportive behaviour (consideration) is more common while directive behaviour (initiating structure) is less common.

Some research points to there being certain behavioural differences in the way men and women communicate. In an article she wrote for the *Harvard Business Review* called "The Power of Talk: Who Gets Heard and Why," linguist Deborah Tannen argued that women use language that is more inclusive and participative, going so far as to frame opinions as questions and assertions as suggestions. Whereas in the past this tendency may have been perceived as a weakness and not a good fit for leadership, a leadership style that places a greater emphasis on shared power, communication, co-operation, and participation seems to be an excellent fit with the demands of a diverse workforce and team-oriented environments.

Just because men and women may have somewhat different leadership styles, we should not assume that leaders of one gender are preferable or that men and women should be held to different standards of behaviour. Both male and female leaders can adjust their behaviours to fit a situation and can be equally effective in leadership roles. Gender differences simply point to behavioural tendencies that may influence their approach to leadership.

QUESTIONS FOR REFLECTION

1. In your experience, are behaviours that characterize successful male leaders the same as those that characterize successful female leaders?
2. Are there differences?
3. How has the gender makeup of the management teams you have worked for shaped the work environment?
4. Do you act differently as a leader when surrounded by others of your same gender than when you are in the minority?

---

is akin to the conventional idea of consideration, and it may be illustrated by a leader offering a follower words of encouragement or empathy. An example of *invisible* socioemotional behaviour is evident when, without the follower's knowing, a leader gives credit for and supports the follower's idea to upper management. Similarly, infrastructural behaviour is *visible* when the leader organizes and leads a training session (akin to initiating structure), and it is *invisible* when the leader works behind the scenes to provide the resources employees need to experiment with new ideas.

Additionally, socioemotional behaviours include but go beyond consideration behaviour to promote personal and collective well-being;[33] infrastructural behaviours include but go beyond initiating structure to promote information exchange and learning across the organization.[34] These sustainable behaviours are evident in the idea of servant leadership.

Servant Leadership

Servant leadership is an active approach to leadership that promotes the interests of others.

The idea of servant leadership is essentially what distinguishes the behaviours of sustainable leaders from those of their conventional counterparts. **Servant leadership** is an active approach to leadership that promotes the interests of others.[35] Often the behaviours of servant leaders are behind the scenes and essentially invisible to followers. According to Robert Greenleaf,[36] who is credited with coining the term, servant leadership has three interrelated components:

- Servant leaders help others to "grow as persons." This focus on personal development goes beyond narrow organizational concerns and includes growing through service to the community. In response, employees are motivated to act creatively and collaboratively.[37]

- Servant leaders want others to become "healthier, wiser, freer, more autonomous, [and] more likely to themselves become servants." Servant leaders model service, treat employees and others with dignity, and encourage them to do likewise.[38]

- Servant leaders seek to have a positive effect on the stakeholders who are "the least privileged in society," never a negative effect. They especially seek to improve the situation for people disadvantaged by the status quo, whether they are within or outside the organization's boundaries.

Many influential leaders such as Jesus Christ, Confucius, and Gandhi were servant leaders who emphasized putting the collective interest of others ahead of their own. However, Greenleaf built his concept of a servant leader on an example he had read in Hermann Hesse's novel *Journey to the East*. In this story, a group of travellers enjoy success and good cheer along their journey without taking much notice of a faithful servant, named Leo, who does the menial but necessary tasks and encourages the others with his positive spirit and song. After he leaves the party, however, Leo's leadership role becomes obvious to everyone when the group falls into disarray and the journey is forsaken. One of the travellers, after years of wandering aimlessly, meets up with Leo again, only to find that although Leo had taken on the role of a servant to the travellers, among his own people he is recognized as a great and noble leader.

Greenleaf tested out and refined his theory of servant leadership as a manager at AT&T, where he worked behind the scenes to promote the equitable treatment of women and ethnic minorities. William Pollard, former CEO and Chairman of ServiceMaster, says he learned about servant leadership through the "school of hard knocks."[39] He was recruited to head legal and financial affairs at ServiceMaster, but he almost lost the job in his final interview by pressing for information regarding the possibility of becoming CEO in the future. Ken Hansen, who was Chairman at the time, explained that if Pollard wanted the job because of its prospects for delivering impressive titles and power, he would be disappointed, because at ServiceMaster leaders have to learn how to put the interests of others ahead of their own. To reinforce this principle, upon accepting the position, Pollard was assigned six weeks of cleaning floors and doing the custodial work that is the core business of ServiceMaster. Pollard believes that these early lessons about service to others were critical to shaping his leadership style.

Just as studies of leadership *traits* were incomplete in their explanation of leadership, so too did studies of leadership *behaviours* fall short of providing a full explanation of what constitutes effective leadership. Taking up where those studies left off, the next stream of leadership research examined the impact of different leadership styles in different situations.

Contingency Theories

| LEADERSHIP TRAITS | LEADERSHIP BEHAVIOURS | **CONTINGENCY THEORIES** | INTEGRATIVE MODELS |

LEARNING OBJECTIVE 3
Analyze the contingency theories of leadership and their importance in explaining and guiding leadership behaviour.

According to **contingency theories** of leadership, the *situation* determines which leadership style is most effective at maximizing productivity. Given the wide variety of situations in which leadership occurs, an effective style in one set of circumstances will not necessarily work in another. For example, a directive style that is effective in leading new hospital nurses might be ineffective in leading seasoned financial planners. The goal of contingency theories is to identify key situational factors that help determine which leadership behaviours best meet organizational goals under different conditions.

Contingency theories assert that the *situation* determines which leadership style is most effective at maximizing productivity.

Fiedler's Contingency Theory

Fred **Fiedler's contingency theory of leadership** is based on the premise that effective leadership depends on there being a match between leadership style and situational demands. At the heart of his theory is the assumption that a leader's style is predominantly

Fiedler's contingency theory of leadership is based on matching a person's leadership style with the appropriate situation.

either *relationship-oriented* or *task-oriented*, and that this style is *fixed*. This idea suggests that a leader will need to seek out or be assigned to positions that fit his or her style.

Fiedler and his colleagues examined three basic "contingencies" they thought would help determine the best type of leader for a given situation. The first contingency, which they called *Leader-member relations,* looks at whether or not followers have trust in or respect for their leader. The second contingency, *Task structure,* looks at whether followers know what needs to be accomplished and how to go about doing it. And the third, *Position power,* looks at whether the leader has power to reward and punish employees. In general, Fiedler's theory suggests that when situational contingencies are either all very favourable or very unfavourable, a task-oriented leader will be most successful, and when situational contingencies are moderately favourable, a relationship-oriented leader will be most successful.

Fiedler's theory was important because it highlighted the impact of situational factors on leadership effectiveness. Later, his specific model came under criticism, particularly his assumption that leadership styles were fixed. Nonetheless, the idea of leaders identifying and working in their areas of strength has considerable merit. In their popular book *First, Break All the Rules: What the World's Greatest Managers Do Differently,* Buckingham and Coffman offer convincing evidence, based on extensive data collected by the Gallup Organization, that working in your areas of strength has many benefits.[40] For example, if an organizational change requires a leader to cut costs and change well-liked structures or systems, a task-oriented leader may be best suited for the job. Conversely, if organizational change requires a leader to get input from workers, a relationship-oriented leader may be most successful.

House's Path-Goal Theory

Path-goal theory focuses on what leaders can do to motivate and align their followers' behaviour to achieve organizational goals.

One of the most respected leadership theories among researchers is **path-goal theory**. Developed by Robert House, it focuses on what leaders can do to motivate and align their employees' or followers' behaviour to achieve organizational goals.[41] House based his theory on the idea that a leader's behaviour is motivational to the extent that he or she is successful in clarifying the *path* to employees' payoffs and in making it easier for them to travel that path by providing support, reducing roadblocks, and ensuring that employees are rewarded for performance that results in *goal* attainment.

In path-goal theory, a leader's behaviour is considered acceptable to a follower to the degree that it satisfies a follower's needs. What a follower needs depends on two factors: characteristics of the follower and characteristics of the workplace. House identifies four leadership styles:

- *Directive leadership* occurs when a leader tells employees exactly what is expected of them by giving guidance, setting goals, and scheduling work. This kind of behaviour is similar to the initiating structure leadership style. Directive behaviours are advisable when job assignments are unclear and followers need to know how the reward structures work.

- *Supportive leadership* occurs when a leader shows concern for employees' well-being and personal needs. It means treating employees as equals and being friendly and approachable. This kind of behaviour is similar to consideration leadership behaviour. Supportive behaviours are advisable when followers are experiencing a high level of stress or anxiety or when their jobs are boring or tedious.

- *Participative leadership* occurs when a leader consults with employees about decisions and engages them in a workplace setting to encourage group discussion and hear suggestions. Participative behaviours may increase motivation when employees' support of a decision is required or when their self-confidence needs a boost.

- *Achievement-oriented leadership* occurs when a leader sets clear and challenging goals for employees, showing confidence in their abilities and an expectation that they can perform at high levels. Achievement-oriented behaviours can motivate highly capable employees who are bored because they have too few challenges and who would thrive if given new responsibilities and decision-making authority.

Although path-goal theory focuses on only a few prominent situational factors, it acknowledges that a vast number of situational factors influence whether a particular leadership behaviour is appropriate. In one example of related research that was more narrowly focused on participative decision making, Vroom and colleagues described 12 situational factors—ranging from decision importance to time constraints—that a leader should consider in determining the appropriate level of follower participation in a particular decision.[42]

According to path-goal theory, leadership styles should fit the needs of the situation. In other words, the leader adds value by contributing things that are missing from the situation or that need strengthening. In contrast to Fiedler's view that leaders cannot change their behaviour, path-goal theory assumes that leaders are flexible and can display any or all leadership styles as needed. Most evidence supports the logic underlying this theory—namely, that employee performance and satisfaction are likely to be positively influenced when the leader adjusts to situational factors related to the employee and the work setting.[43]

Leader-Member Exchange

Another theory with a particular focus on the relationship between the leader and his or her followers is **Leader-Member Exchange (LMX)** theory.[44] LMX is a measure of the quality of exchanges between a leader and a follower. Although this is not typically a contingency theory, it explains why leaders end up treating one employee differently than another. Based on similarities, shared interests, or the follower's competence or likeability, different relationships form that lead to different treatment.[45] High-quality exchange relationships are characterized by mutual trust, inclusion, and frequent interactions, whereas low-quality exchange relationships are characterized by distrust, exclusion, and infrequent interactions. As a result, employees in high-quality relationships perform better and have more positive attitudes in both individual jobs and in team contexts.[46]

Leader-Member Exchange (LMX) is a measure of the quality of exchanges between a leader and a follower.

Although leaders should attempt to establish with all employees a high-quality relationship that is mutually satisfying and that contributes to productivity, not all relationships are of this quality.[47] Over time, leader-member relationships can evolve into two general groups, with members in the "in group" receiving greater attention and influence than those in the "out group." Although this result may occur due either to intentional decisions or unintentional biases, leaders should be aware that perceived favouritism can create resentment and resistance from followers.[48]

Conventional and sustainable perspectives both recognize the importance of contingencies in explaining and guiding leadership behaviour. One difference is the relative importance given to particular factors in prescribing changes in leadership behaviour. From a conventional perspective, factors that do not contribute to immediate workplace productivity are not likely to merit much attention, but from a sustainable perspective that is holistic, community focused, and long-term oriented, they might. Recall that the hallmark of servant leadership is its focus on contingencies that contribute to others' personal growth and well-being. For example, Carewest, a continuing care services provider located in Calgary, is recognized as being one of Alberta's top employers.[49] To help its employees balance work and personal concerns, the company has numerous family-friendly policies, including flexible hours, shortened and compressed workweek options, and paid personal days off. Carewest also believes in continuous education and is open to employee feedback and employee-driven initiatives. Recent surveys show that the vast majority of Carewest staff say that their job allows them to effectively balance their work and family/personal life, and there are high levels of overall job satisfaction.[50]

Integrative Models

LEADERSHIP TRAITS | LEADERSHIP BEHAVIOURS | CONTINGENCY THEORIES | **INTEGRATIVE MODELS**

Integrative models are combinations of various leadership theories, research findings, and leaders' experiences with a focus on practical application. The intent of these models is to build on the best ideas from research and practice to provide a framework for leading others.

Integrative models are combinations of various leadership theories, research findings, and leaders' experiences with a focus on practical application.

Situational Leadership Models

Paul Hersey and Ken Blanchard developed situational leadership models that continue to receive strong support from practitioners. Their approach focuses a great deal of attention on the characteristics of followers in determining appropriate leadership behaviour. This way of thinking is in line with that of Marcus Buckingham, who, in his *Harvard Business Review* article "What Great Managers Do," shared his belief that great managers understand and adapt to the uniqueness of individual followers.[51]

In their original leadership model, Hersey and Blanchard argued that leaders can and should adjust their style of leadership depending on the "readiness" of the follower to perform in a given situation. "Readiness" was based on how (1) able and (2) willing or confident followers are to perform required tasks. Organizational members have varying degrees of readiness, depending on their maturity, expertise, and experience in relation to the specific tasks that they undertake.

Situational Leadership II describes four leadership situations and the appropriate leadership styles based on the development level of followers.

After experience using situational leadership with business leaders, Blanchard modified the original model. His **Situational Leadership II** model describes four leadership situations and the appropriate leadership styles for each based on the "development level" of employees or followers (instead of "readiness"). Development level includes two components:

- Competence (instead of "ability")
- Commitment (instead of "willingness")[52]

At the lowest level of employee development, which may be evident with a newly hired employee, an employee is eager and committed to performing the task but not competent or fully trained. In the next level of development, competency has increased somewhat, but the challenges of mastering the task can discourage the employee or reduce commitment. Next, competency at a task is evident, but the employee's confidence may still be lacking. At the final stage of development, the employee is both competent and committed. The Situational Leadership II model suggests that leaders need to change their style over time according to how their followers develop. As followers' needs change, the leadership style that best fits their needs also changes:

Directing is a high-direction, low-support leadership style.

- A **directing** style is appropriate when organizational members lack technical knowledge yet are enthusiastically committed to learning the new task or position. This might be the case, for example, when a new, enthusiastic, but untrained employee joins a department. In response, the leader defines roles and tells the new employee how, when, and where to do various tasks in a high-direction, low-support style.

Coaching is a high-direction, high-support leadership style.

- A **coaching** style is appropriate when organizational members lack technical knowledge and their motivation or commitment is waning. For example, consider a new employee, faced with a long training period or adjustment to an organizational change, who begins to lose heart. In response, the leader uses a high-direction, high-support style, providing task direction and feedback in a supportive and convincing way.

- A **supporting** style is appropriate when organizational members have the competence but not the confidence necessary to perform the job. For example, an employee who has been micromanaged or led by a dictatorial leader may have the skills but not the confidence to take on more responsibilities and act independently. In response, the leader encourages this person by expressing confidence in the person's abilities, offering praise or recognition, and sharing decision-making authority in a low-direction, high-support style.

Supporting is a low-direction, high-support leadership style.

- A **delegating** style is appropriate when organizational members have the appropriate job-related competence and are highly committed to perform independently. For example, this style might be appropriate for an employee with a lot of experience, skills, and loyalty. In response, the leader provides little direction or support, allowing this person to make and take responsibility for task decisions in a low-direction, low-support style.

Delegating is a low-direction, low-support leadership style.

Leaders using a Situational Leadership II model must be able to implement the alternative leadership styles as needed on a case-by-case basis. As a leader helps followers to become more independent, his or her leadership style also needs to adapt. For example, Canadians John and David Temple, owners of Temple and Temple Tours, use different leadership styles depending on each employee's development level. When interacting with new tour guides, they give them specific instructions on processes for running tours and interacting with clients (*directing*). As employees advance through the learning process, the Temples continue to provide specific and detailed *coaching* to ensure that employees understand the nuances of the different tours, but they do so in a highly encouraging manner. As employees improve their competence yet still lack confidence, the leaders shift to a supporting style that affirms the employees' competence and encourages them to bring their own personal flair to the tours. Ultimately, the Temples hope to move employees to a level of competency and commitment that will allow each to accept the *delegation* of most tasks and responsibilities.

Despite the popularity and intuitive appeal of situational leadership models, research has not been as supportive as expected; this is due, in part, to the complexity of testing the models as well as failures to account for other factors that affect the situation.[53] The strongest support is related to providing high levels of direction for those who are new to a task, coupling direction with support for those at moderate levels of both competence and commitment, and providing more autonomy as employees gain more experience.[54]

Integrated Conventional Leadership Model

The integrated conventional leadership model in Figure 9.2 includes four basic leadership styles, each of which is associated with a particular combination of consideration and initiating structure behaviours; but in this model, other combinations of behaviours may exist to form other styles not pictured. For example, a "middle-of-the-road" approach may be useful when information about a follower is limited and no clear leadership style seems initially appropriate. Akin to situational leadership models, the arrows in the model point to a progression of leadership styles, suggesting which style of leadership may be most appropriate as a follower develops over time.[55]

In summary, this integrated conventional model of leadership combines behavioural and contingency theories:

- From a behavioural perspective, a leader's style should combine consideration (supportive, relationship-oriented) and initiating structure (directive, task-oriented) behaviours to meet the needs of followers.
- The appropriate or best-fitting leadership style depends on contingencies, particularly a member's or follower's commitment and capability, but also other factors such as those described by substitutes-for-leadership theory.

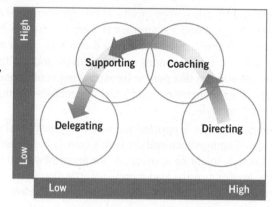

Consideration, supportive, and relationship-oriented behaviour
—to improve follower's commitment

High

Low

Supporting **Coaching**

Delegating **Directing**

Low High

Initiating structure, directive, and task-oriented behaviour
—to improve follower's capability

FIGURE 9.2 Integrated Conventional Leadership Model

Substitutes-for-leadership theory argues that characteristics of the task and work environment may

- substitute for the influence of leaders,
- neutralize the influence of leaders, or
- enhance the influence of leaders.[56]

Specifically, when a task is highly structured or highly formalized according to specific policies and procedural rules, the leader does not need to initiate as much structure. Similarly, when highly cohesive teams are at work or when followers perform tasks they find intrinsically interesting, the leader does not need to provide as much consideration. For example, John and David of Temple and Temple Tours might not need to provide one of their guides with as much direction for a museum tour if the museum has specific guidelines governing the order in which the exhibits should be seen. This is not to suggest that leaders are not necessary but, rather, that the need for specific leadership behaviours may be reduced in certain situations.[57]

Sometimes leadership behaviour becomes irrelevant or is hindered because the task or the work environment neutralizes the leader's influence. Examples of "neutralizers" include a chronic indifference on the part of the follower, a low position of power for the leader, and a geographically dispersed work environment. This suggests that project managers in matrix organizations, for instance, where employees have multiple bosses, may find their normal leadership behaviour ineffective. Sometimes situational factors can enhance the impact of certain behaviours. For example, a leader's team-oriented behaviour is particularly likely to enhance productivity in collectivistic or group-oriented cultures.[58]

Substitutes-for-leadership theory provides a helpful reminder that the effectiveness of leadership is often influenced by factors beyond follower characteristics and leader behaviours. Leaders must find the right mix of behaviours—in some cases refraining from those that might be counterproductive or a waste of effort—to focus leadership energy in other places. For example, if directions for a specific task (such as how to work a cash register) are clearly spelled out in documents, then task-oriented leadership behaviour can be concentrated on areas (such as responding to angry customers) in which the ideal action is not as straightforward. In practice, having an awareness of possible leadership substitutes can help leaders diagnose followers' needs and adapt their behaviour to help followers perform well in a variety of work settings.

The integrated model of conventional leadership (combining behaviour and contingencies) has value in explaining which leadership behaviour might work best given certain assumptions and conditions. Even so, it may be difficult for leaders to apply the model when they experience pressure to meet short-term organizational goals, perhaps without being given adequate time or resources to provide special attention to all of their employees.

Integrated Sustainable Leadership Model

An integrated sustainable leadership model shares several features with the conventional model but includes several fundamental differences. First, a sustainable model is based on the principles of servant leadership that foster growth, autonomy, and concern for others in the community. Second, a sustainable approach also draws on relational and follower-centric theories of leadership that emphasize the responsibility of leaders to engage in dialogue, pursue mutual gain, and ensure the development of long-term follower and organizational capabilities.[59] Recent theory and research indicate that leaders with this emphasis nurture in followers an eagerness to learn, take risks, and be creative.[60] This sustainable approach also promotes helping behaviour: Organizational members go beyond their specific job expectations to listen to others and assist them with their work.[61] Finally, a sustainable perspective recognizes that it is rarely helpful for the leader to provide no or very low consideration or initiating structure behaviour, even for highly capable and committed followers.[62] Instead of eliminating these types of leadership behaviours, they become less visible in the sustainable approach.

Figure 9.3 highlights four basic styles of leadership. However, these four sustainable leadership styles differ from their conventional parallels and are based on somewhat different x- and y-axes. From a conventional perspective, the *frequency or amount* of consideration and initiating structure that leaders should provide depends on the follower's needs and on other situational factors. Alternatively, from a sustainable perspective, having the backing and assistance of leaders is almost always helpful to followers, so it is the *visibility,* not the level, of leadership behaviour that varies according to the situation.[63] Thus, a sustainable leader may exhibit socioemotional and infrastructural behaviour in a way that is visible to followers (e.g., face to face) or in a way that is invisible (e.g., behind the scenes). Recall Hesse's servant leader, Leo. He chose to work invisibly behind the scenes to help others be successful, and it was only after he left the group that the value of his sustainable leadership became obvious to others.

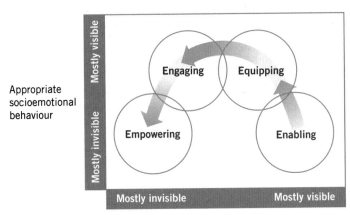

FIGURE 9.3 Integrated Sustainable Leadership Model

As summarized in Table 9.1, four sustainable leadership styles of enabling, equipping, engaging, and empowering run parallel to the four conventional styles of directing, coaching, supporting, and delegating, respectively; but they differ in their purposes and practices. The remainder of the chapter will briefly describe these four leadership styles.

TABLE 9.1 Comparing Conventional and Sustainable Leadership

Need for Support	Need for Direction	Four Styles of Conventional Leading	Four Styles of Sustainable Leading
Low	High	**Directing**	**Enabling**
		Telling followers what their job is and describing how the job or a task is to be completed most efficiently. Used when followers lack capability. *Goal:* Improve immediate productive capability	Emphasizing learning, providing general information, and allowing experimentation without performance pressure. Used when followers lack capability. *Goal:* Improve learning capability
High	High	**Coaching**	**Equipping**
		Providing training and specific feedback. Used when followers lack both capability and commitment. *Goal:* Address weaknesses and develop capability	Creating an environment for continuous learning. Used when followers lack both capability and commitment. *Goal:* Develop strengths and group capability
High	Low	**Supporting**	**Engaging**
		Motivating through praising and extrinsic motivators. Used when followers are capable but lack commitment or confidence. *Goal:* Enhance productivity	Appealing to intrinsic motivators and a sense of community. Used when followers are capable but lack commitment or confidence. *Goal:* Enhance meaning and affiliation
Low	Low	**Delegating**	**Empowering**
		Assigning tasks and responsibilities. Used when followers are capable and committed. *Goal:* Facilitate efficient division of labour	Freeing people to be responsible. Used when followers are capable and committed. *Goal:* Facilitate ownership and responsiveness

Enabling The primary focus of conventional directing is to make immediate improvements in productivity. In contrast, sustainable enabling is primarily concerned with having others learn the necessary skills for long-term performance. **Enabling** is the process of sharing or explaining information related to a job and its context. Like their conventional counterparts, sustainable leaders are *visibly* involved in providing information, guidelines, and structures to facilitate learning. This approach is also an *invisible* source of socioemotional support, in that it is patient and accepting of the time that learning requires. What leaders emphasize in their words and actions greatly influences whether followers focus on learning or focus on productivity.[64] Although under a sustainable approach followers may take longer to produce output, the focus on learning ultimately makes them more adaptable by helping them perform well on tasks of increasing complexity and variety.[65]

Darren Avrea and Dave Foster are the co-founders of AvreaFoster, a brand and marketing agency in Dallas, Texas. They enable their new employees by explaining the broad expectations for advertising

Enabling is sharing or explaining information related to a job and its context.

projects, providing the relevant information about resources and time constraints, and encouraging a variety of approaches to completing the project. This mastery orientation improves in-depth understanding, minimizes productivity-related stress, and fosters long-term performance.[66] In contrast, emphasizing short-term task performance tends to evoke a performance orientation that can lead to superficial learning or learning just enough to reach productivity goals.

Equipping   The conventional coaching style focuses on responding to followers' needs for both direction and support. This approach can have an implicit top-down bias in that the coach is the "brain" of the organization, develops the strategies and game plans, and provides the necessary instruction and training. In contrast, sustainable **equipping** responds to similar needs but with an emphasis on continuous and collaborative learning. Equipping creates an environment where employees are encouraged to learn from one another.

Equipping is creating an environment for continuous and collaborative learning.

American Express CEO Ken Chenault, referred to earlier in the chapter, illustrates equipping in the way he champions mentoring as a means to develop leaders within his company. He insists that you need to encourage people to invest in relationships both formally and informally.[67] Under Chenault's leadership, American Express also committed $25 million to develop leaders in non-profit organizations who can positively influence the community.[68] The American Express Leadership Academy has equipped over 1,200 emerging leaders in non-profit organizations by pairing them with mentoring executives from American Express and by providing skill-building activities that help enable them to operate in increasingly complex environments.

As this example demonstrates, sustainable leadership involves creating an environment where opportunities for learning are frequent, even if the learning has little relevance for the specific task an employee is doing and even if the source of learning is a not a direct manager. While the goal of conventional coaching is to ensure that followers address areas of weakness or shortcomings in specific areas, the goal of sustainable equipping is to ensure that others are encouraged to build on their successes, try new approaches, and learn transferable and adaptable skills for a range of work challenges.

Engaging   The conventional style responds to the followers' need for support by offering praise or extrinsic motivators to improve their commitment. In contrast, sustainable engaging focuses on intrinsic motivators that increase employees' self-respect and joy in coming to work because they perceive themselves to be fulfilling a meaningful role as part of a team or group. **Engaging** is the process of encouraging community and enhancing the intrinsic meaningfulness of work. Although the conventional approach of supporting includes participation, engaging is more than asking for input from others or sharing decision making. It means addressing the intrinsic motivations of meaning, purpose, and community. It *visibly* affirms employees' worth to the organization by giving them a voice, and it *invisibly* sets up systems and structures that create a sense of shared purpose and community.

Engaging is encouraging community and enhancing intrinsic motivators.

While CEO of HCL Technologies, Vineet Nayar attempted to replace a culture of hierarchical commands and restrictions on information by inverting the traditional pyramid to focus on making managers accountable to front-line employees.[69] This employee-first philosophy was made evident by the company's "Employee First Councils," collaborative platforms that were created to connect employees and to facilitate the sharing of information about job-related and personal interests. Three years after the launch of these online communities, 20 percent of the company's revenue was linked in some way to ideas that had originated by connecting people in order to facilitate learning and innovation. In sum, whereas the goal of conventional supporting is primarily to enhance productivity, the goal of sustainable engaging is to enhance employees' sense of meaning and connection.

Empowering   The conventional delegating style is similar to the sustainable empowering style in that it acknowledges that followers' needs for support and direction are low. However, conventional delegating often has an implicit connotation of managerial control, assigning specific tasks to increase efficiency through the division of labour. In contrast, sustainable **empowering** is more deliberate in freeing others to be responsible to carry out their tasks as they see fit.[70] Sustainable leaders expect followers who are performing the tasks and roles about which they are most knowledgeable to do things differently—and possibly better—than the leader might suggest. Sustainable leaders thus work behind the scenes to champion followers' independence and to provide them with resources and decision-making freedom within the scope of the organization's mission.

Gary Keller of Keller Williams Realty, Inc.—the fastest-growing consumer realty business and one of the largest in the world—made a profound discovery when he recognized that agents did not work for him; rather, *he* worked for *them*. At Keller Williams, this leadership approach means that employees bear some of the risks and expenses of operating independently, but they also reap a larger portion of the rewards of profit and personal satisfaction. Beyond providing increased autonomy for local agents, Keller has continuously worked to make organizational systems more democratic. For example, the wildly popular employee profit-sharing program was adopted after it was brought to a vote among the agents. Although Keller Williams is privately owned, Keller's empowering style has created an organization in which agents have a significant say in decision making at all levels.[71]

Empowering is freeing people to be responsible for their work.

⬤B in Action

"Krafting" a New Culture of Empowerment and Entrepreneurial Spirit

Tim Boyle/Bloomberg/Getty Images

During her time as a leader at food and beverage conglomerate Kraft Foods (now named Mondelēz International), Irene Rosenfeld was described as hard-nosed, determined, and competitive. It may be surprising, then, to hear that Rosenfeld describes herself as a servant leader: "I believe very strongly in the concept of servant leadership, and I would tell you that the people [who] work with me understand that I am there to help them, not for them to help me." She notes that, as a servant leader "you can engage the hearts and minds of your followers, and they're able to deliver the kind of results you are looking for!"

Rosenfeld believes that the workforce of today "is not interested in command-and-control leadership. They don't want to do things because I said so; they want to do things because they want to do them. The captain of industry who continues to run his business in a militaristic, 'siloed' way cannot compete in this global economy." In some of her first moves as CEO at Kraft, Rosenfeld decentralized decision making and let go of those who resisted the change in philosophy, which amounted to approximately 50 percent of the top two levels of management. In rebuilding her leadership team, Rosenfeld looked for those with an entrepreneurial spirit. Looking for entrepreneurs in a huge organization with over 100,000 employees may seem odd, but she was convinced it was necessary to remain competitive.

As Chair and CEO of what's now called Mondelēz International, Rosenfeld sees her main role as twofold: inspiring and facilitating. First, she seeks to inspire leaders with a clear vision and then release them to inspire their own people and implement the vision in ways that make sense in their locations. "The single biggest role I play is in communication and talking about where we are going, why we are going there and what it is I need the organization to do. Then I really need the leaders to grab that and translate that mess into what it means for their folks on the ground." Second, Rosenfeld commits her energy to identifying and securing the resources her people require. She spends over half of her time travelling to meet with employees in order to find out what they need to succeed.

QUESTIONS FOR DISCUSSION

1. Do you think the characteristics of being hard-nosed, determined, and competitive conflict with being a servant leader? Why or why not?
2. Which of Rosenfeld's leadership behaviours seem to be sustainable leader behaviours?
3. Do you think replacing people is inconsistent with being a servant leader?
4. How might replacing people who don't fit with the organization's culture be an act of service?

sustainable leadership at work in the philippines[72]

Courtesy of The Leather Collection, Inc.

Ms. Yoling Sevilla is President and CEO of The Leather Collection Inc., a firm of about 30 people that has positioned itself as corporate gift specialists in Manila, Philippines. Yoling and her husband, Federico, co-founded the company in 1991. The company designs, manufactures, and distributes business gifts and accessories, such as bags, briefcases, organizers, folders, and small leather goods like wallets. They are dedicated to using "Green–Earth Friendly" products and processes, which means using metal-free leathers and minimizing waste. Moreover, The Leather Collection's use of sea snake (*Lapemis hardwickii*), converting it into exotically beautiful products, augments fisherpeople's income and utilizes what would otherwise be a waste product in the local fishing industry.

Sevilla believes that a successful business is one "that has contributed in a positive way to the well-being of all stakeholders. So that goes beyond shareholder value. So you're talking about employees, you're talking about customers, you are talking about creditors, you're talking about society in general, you're talking about the environment." In her mind, successful business leaders "influence change in the direction of business being in service" to society. In a business environment often characterized by a narrow focus on the bottom line, she believes this requires a great amount of courage; as she puts it, "good business leaders need to be Bravehearts."

Sevilla suggests that a critical behaviour for business leaders is to be "contemplative in action." For her this requires being aware of two things. First is to know "what is driving you toward a particular decision." Second is to be "aware of the

environment in which we are leading, in which we are in business . . . aware of the impact of each option on the stakeholders." She describes how people may have a clear understanding of their personal values at any point in time, but then adds that such self-awareness should continue to develop over a lifetime:

> If one does not maintain a contemplative attitude, if one does not constantly examine one's self and one's motivations, one's values could change in directions one does not wish. And one might wake up one day to find that you are [a] person you do not like. And so I think it is important for everyone, whether you are a business leader or not, to develop self-awareness and other awareness—the impact of decisions one makes not just on one's self, but on . . . society.

In regard to the importance of relationships (as discussed in chapter 8), for Sevilla business is clearly much more about people than it is about things. Work is about people bringing out the best in one another and ultimately fostering something that she calls "the common good":

> All of us who work here consider ourselves . . . comrades in the efforts to enjoy life in its fullness, to be able to put all our time, our talents and our resources into this enterprise to be able to contribute to the common good . . . That effort cannot be done by me alone, it cannot be done by management alone, it cannot be done by labor alone. It can only be done by all of us working together, and by all of us collaborating with our suppliers, with our customers, all our other stakeholders.

Sevilla believes that work provides an opportunity to be a part of a community that nurtures concern for one another and that encourages each person to develop and use his or her talents to make unique contributions in service to others. As a leader, she plays an important role in creating and maintaining this type of work environment. She communicates a desire to lead not for self-promotion but to benefit her employees and others who belong to her community of relationships. She demonstrates the drive to make a difference and exudes confidence in the collective efficacy of the group to deliver excellent products and services. For Sevilla, the purpose of business leadership is broader and more holistic than to simply make money or even to earn a livelihood. Rather, business is all about "living life in its fullness, developing your talents to the full, and putting them in the service of humankind." To that end she enables, equips, engages, and empowers others in service to this common good.

QUESTIONS FOR DISCUSSION

1. In what ways does Yoling Sevilla exhibit the characteristics of sustainable leadership?

2. Sevilla readily admits that she is guided by a concern for stakeholders inside and outside of her business. What are the advantages and disadvantages of considering such diverse stakeholders in leadership decisions?

3. Similar to most businesses, as Sevilla's business grows, it needs investments of capital to expand its operations. Would you be inclined to invest in this business? Explain your answer.

Summary

Leadership was described by discussing traits, behaviours, contingencies, and integrated models.

 Learning Objectives:

- Describe the personal characteristics of leaders.

- Identify the ways or manners in which leaders act.

- Analyze the contingency theories of leadership and their importance in explaining and guiding leadership behaviour.

- Discuss the value of integrative leadership models.

In conventional OB, leadership is characterized by:

- Leadership traits include the desire to lead for personal gain, the drive to get ahead, self-confidence, honesty and integrity as a means to an end, intelligence and knowledge that is relevant to the workplace, and emotional intelligence that can benefit the leader.

- Leadership behaviour is of two general types: consideration (supportive, relationship-oriented, employee-centred) and initiating structure (directive, task-oriented, production-centred).

- Contingency theories provide prescriptions for how to adapt leadership behaviour to best promote individual performance.

- The integrated conventional model of leadership involves directing, coaching, supporting, or delegating, depending on the performance needs of individuals.

In sustainable OB, leadership is characterized by:

- Leadership traits include the desire to lead for others' gain, the drive to make a difference, collective confidence, honesty and integrity as ends, intelligence and knowledge that has broad relevance, and emotional intelligence that benefits all relationships.

- Leadership behaviour is of two general types: socioemotional (consideration plus promotion of personal and collective well-being) and infrastructural (initiating structure plus promoting information exchange and learning).

- Contingency theories provide prescriptions for how to adapt leadership behaviour to best promote holistic individual and community well-being.

- The integrated sustainable model of leadership involves enabling, equipping, engaging, or empowering, depending on the development needs of individuals and capabilities of the work group.

Key Terms

Behaviours (p. 191)

Charisma (p. 188)

Coaching (p. 198)

Consideration (p. 192)

Contingency theories (p. 195)

Delegating (p. 199)

Directing (p. 198)

Empowering (p. 204)

Enabling (p. 202)

Engaging (p. 203)

Equipping (p. 203)

Fiedler's contingency theory of leadership (p. 195)

Infrastructural behaviour (p. 193)

Initiating structure (p. 192)

Integrative models (p. 198)

Leadership Grid (p. 192)

Leader-Member Exchange (LMX) (p. 197)

Leadership (p. 187)

Path-goal theory (p. 196)

Servant leadership (p. 194)

Situational Leadership II (p. 198)

Socioemotional behaviour (p. 193)

Substitutes-for-leadership theory (p. 200)

Supporting (p. 199)

Traits (p. 188)

Transactional leaders (p. 187)

Transformational leaders (p. 187)

Questions for Reflection and Discussion

1. Do you think most leaders have a fixed, "one size fits all" leadership style, or are they flexible as appropriate to the situation? Give examples to support your view.

2. Consider the best boss for whom you have worked. Which characteristics define his or her leadership style? Are these characteristics predominantly traits or behaviours?

3. Is it possible to be a servant leader in a for-profit organization? Why or why not?

4. Identify a strength of a leader you know. When could this strength also be a weakness? Is this an example of contingencies in leadership?

5. Which contingency theory best explains your experience as a follower or employee?

6. What do you see as being the main differences among the four conventional leadership styles (directing, coaching, supporting, delegating) and the four sustainable leadership styles (enabling, equipping, engaging, empowering)? As a follower or organizational member, how would you respond to each style?

ob activities

SELF-ASSESSMENT EXERCISE

What Type of Leader Are You?

Indicate the extent to which the two comparison statements fit you best. Rankings of 1 or 5 indicate strong agreement with the statement closest to the number, whereas a 3 indicates you are undecided or neutral.

Part A. I tend to . . .

Desire to become a leader to influence others.	❶	❷	❸	❹	❺	Desire to become a leader to serve others.
Want to get ahead.	❶	❷	❸	❹	❺	Want to make a difference.
Have confidence in my capabilities.	❶	❷	❸	❹	❺	Have confidence in the group's capabilities.
See honesty and integrity as good for business.	❶	❷	❸	❹	❺	See honesty and integrity as always good.
Value the "know-how" that enhances our organization's interests.	❶	❷	❸	❹	❺	Value the "know-how" that enhances all our stakeholders' interests.

Part B. In my leadership, I . . .

Like to call the shots and make the decisions.	❶	❷	❸	❹	❺	Want input from followers to influence decisions.
Focus on my followers' at-work responsibilities.	❶	❷	❸	❹	❺	Am sensitive to followers' outside-work responsibilities.
Believe employees' development is their responsibility.	❶	❷	❸	❹	❺	Believe employees' development is my responsibility.
Emphasize the importance of seizing opportunities in the environment.	❶	❷	❸	❹	❺	Emphasize the importance of providing service to the community.
Try to create healthy competition among employees.	❶	❷	❸	❹	❺	Try to create a sense of collaboration among employees.

Key: For Parts A and B, make a simple count of the number of 1s and 2s selected and a separate count of the number of 4s and 5s selected. For Part A, the 1s and 2s reflect conventional tendencies and the 4s and 5s represent sustainable tendencies. Another approach would be to add all the selected numbers together and divide by the number of questions (i.e., 5). This may give you a better sense of the strength of your tendency, with strong conventional tendencies falling in the range of 1–2 and strong sustainable tendencies falling in the range of 4–5. For Part B, take a similar approach to scoring the items. Overall, a higher number indicates a servant leadership orientation, which research indicates is related to being agreeable and introverted.[73] Servant leadership also is related to higher levels of creativity and helping and lower turnover among followers.[74]

Sources: Items in Part B were adapted from Ehrhart, M. (2004). Leadership and procedural justice climate as antecedents of unit-level organizational citizenship behavior. *Personnel Psychology, 57*(1), 61–94.

ETHICS SCENARIO

A company president recognized that sending expensive Christmas gifts to purchasing agents might compromise their positions. However, he continued the policy because it was common practice and changing it might result in loss of business.

Why might this scenario occur in organizations?

Use the following scale to indicate whether this behaviour is ethically acceptable:

NEVER ACCEPTABLE   **SOMETIMES ACCEPTABLE**   **ALWAYS ACCEPTABLE**

(1)   **(2)**   **(3)**   **(4)**   **(5)**   **(6)**   **(7)**

Explain the ideas you considered in arriving at your answer.

DISCUSSION STARTER

Debate: Are Leaders Born or Made?

Divide the classroom into two groups. One group will argue that leaders are born not made, and the other will argue that leaders are made not born. Both groups will develop arguments in support of their assigned position regardless of what they currently think about the question. Invite each side to provide examples based on popular business leaders or on those with whom they have personal experience.

QUESTIONS FOR DISCUSSION

1. What are the main differences between the two points of view?
2. Which arguments were most compelling?

3. What other positions could be argued about the source of leadership?
4. How might answers differ in a different culture?

DISCUSSION STARTER

What Are the Characteristics of an Outstanding Leader?

Option 1: Think of three outstanding leaders from your own experience observing leaders in organizations. Focus on one leader at a time and list the characteristics that make each person outstanding in your mind.

Option 2: Interview three leaders whom you respect and ask them to list the characteristics of outstanding leaders. If you choose this option, pick leaders who work in organizations or industries that interest you. Most will be more than willing to share their advice with an eager university student. Prepare an additional set

of questions about leadership (What are your greatest challenges as a leader? What have been your most valuable developmental experiences?) and about each leader's specific organization (What do you like most about working here? What are the core values of this organization?).

Regardless of the option you choose, this is your data! Like some of the early researchers on leadership, you have gathered data about leadership characteristics through either observation or interviews.

QUESTIONS FOR DISCUSSION

1. How do the characteristics you identified compare across the three leaders—what is similar and what is different?

2. Are the characteristics primarily traits or behaviours?

3. How do the characteristics fit with the conventional and sustainable approaches discussed in the chapter?

4. Do the characteristics of outstanding leadership differ based on gender?

Group Activity: After gathering the responses from either option 1 or option 2, have each person list each "outstanding leader" characteristic from his or her research on a separate Post-it note. Then, in small groups, gather the Post-its in one location such as a desk and, working without talking, begin sorting the characteristics according to themes such as communication, integrity, or consideration. Finish by discussing any remaining characteristics that are difficult to sort. In a group discussion, ask "What are the benefits of learning about leadership from a larger sample of leaders instead of just one?"

APPLICATION JOURNAL

This is the next in a series of journal entries that can be used for class discussion or be compiled and included in a self-reflection paper.

Consider the leadership styles represented in the integrated conventional model of leadership—directing, coaching, supporting, and delegating. Which style do you tend to use most in the opportunities you have to lead others? Why do you use it? Why don't you use the other styles? Can you identify relationships in which a different style may be more effective? If so, set specific goals for adapting your behaviour in those relationships.

Ten

Leading Groups and Teams

This chapter discusses the differences between groups and teams and then focuses more directly on teams and their development. Whitewater rafting can serve as a familiar metaphor for those who work in teams. Teams and their members often experience the thrill and challenge of working in turbulent situations when the team must develop into a high-performing and cohesive unit in order to be successful. We offer a look at the conventional and sustainable perspectives for different aspects of team development, with a discussion of the differences that are highlighted in the Chapter Navigator.

Learning Objectives	Conventional OB	Shared	Sustainable OB
GROUPS AND TEAMS			
1. Identify the characteristics of and differences between groups and teams.	Permanent Hierarchical Functional On-site	Project Self-managed Cross-functional Virtual	
FORMING			
2. Discuss forming, the first category of team development behaviour, and how it clarifies goals and builds relationships.	Set direction and create cohesion	Foster a sense of purpose and identity	
STORMING			
3. Discuss storming, the second category of team development behaviour, and how it appeals to shared goals, encourages helping, and resolves conflicts.	Resolve conflict and stay on task	Transform conflict; refine roles	
NORMING			
4. Discuss norming, the third category of team development behaviour, when performance norms are affirmed and accountability is ensured.	Affirm performance norms and ensure accountability	Emphasize interdependencies and collaboration	
PERFORMING			
5. Discuss performing, the fourth category of team development behaviour, when feedback is provided and new goals are identified.	Provide feedback and recognition	Diffuse learning	

taking WestJet to new heights[1]

Roberto Machado Noa/Getty Images

WestJet is one of Canada's most beloved brands. The company boasts exceptional customer service stories, such as the time flight staff bought a new wedding dress for a bride after finding out that her original dress had never been loaded by the baggage handlers. Another time, as viral online videos attest, a WestJet Santa handed out presents to surprised customers. Amidst frequent consumer complaints about its rivals' substandard service and high prices, WestJet has seemingly come out on top, receiving glowing reviews and continued praise from the country's top marketing scholars. So how did the company get to where it is today?

WestJet is a relatively young company. Founded in 1996 by Clive Beddoe, Mark Hill, Tim Morgan, and Donald Bell and based on the belief that cheaper airfare should not imply inferior service, the company started off with only three planes operating between five destinations in Western Canada. Since then, WestJet has grown to service more than 88 destinations around the world, with almost $4 billion in annual revenue and more than 9,700 employees. Yet throughout its many years of growth and success, WestJet has continued to focus on its team-driven and empowerment-oriented corporate culture. In fact, one executive position is completely dedicated to maintaining and enhancing the firm's people and culture.

Every employee, regardless of title or salary, is a member of the WestJet team and contributes to the organization's many accomplishments.

From the beginning, WestJet has promoted a "people-first" mentality, not only in relation to its customer service but to its human resources management as well. Employees at all levels of the organization are granted the power to act as they see fit in order to maximize the customers' (known as "guests") experience. The company's generous employee share-purchasing plan further reinforces the sense of community that links individual with organizational success. The entire WestJet organization really does operate like a giant team devoted to exceeding customer expectations.

Even the top dogs at WestJet view themselves as no different from the rest and are not afraid to get "down and dirty" to understand what employees face every day. For example, one former vice-president of Corporate Culture would take a round-trip flight on average once per week in order to get feedback from his staff and to experience their challenges for himself. Current CEO Gregg Saretsky makes it a point to help employees clean the plane after every flight on which he is a passenger. Every employee, regardless of title or salary, is a member of the WestJet team and contributes to the organization's many accomplishments. This mutual understanding that employees have of each other's roles and the support they provide each other when facing challenges not only makes WestJet a happier place to work, it is what has enabled the company to continually transcend aviation industry norms.

Groups and Teams

GROUPS & TEAMS FORMING STORMING NORMING PERFORMING

LEARNING OBJECTIVE 1
Identify the characteristics of and differences between groups and teams.

The terms *group* and *team* are often used interchangeably, which in many cases is appropriate. Both terms refer to the interplay between two or more members within an organization. However, there are significant differences between them, as shown in Table 10.1. Whereas a **group** is a collection of two or more people who share a common interest or association, a **team** is a collection of people who work interdependently as a unit. Teams are *task oriented,* and their members share common goals, work toward those goals interdependently, and are accountable to one another to achieve those goals.

A **group** is a collection of two or more people who share a common interest or association.

A **team** is a task-oriented collection of people who work interdependently as a unit to achieve common goals and are accountable to one another to achieve those goals.

Teams have great potential for organizations. They can improve the quality of decision making, enhance creativity, increase motivation, and help facilitate organizational change. Implementing teams also can allow leaders to reduce their direct supervision of organizational members and reassign some job duties from supervisors to team members.[2] Teams are a good way to respond to the movement toward high-involvement work cultures and flatter and more flexible organizational structures.[3]

Whereas the notion of teams focuses on how members achieve tasks, the notion of groups focuses more on affiliation or the nature of the interpersonal relationships among members. Not all groups are teams. For example, members of the same department may be formally designated as a group, but they aren't considered a team if they do not work interdependently to complete their tasks. Organizations may have many informal groups, such as members who eat lunch together regularly, that are not teams. Other kinds of informal groups, such as "interest groups," are typically not created with organizational performance goals in mind but, rather, created to help individuals achieve personal goals and meet their mutual needs. For example, a number of organizations, such as Dell, support affinity groups based on race or religion by offering the use of company facilities for meetings and by allowing publicity for group events to appear in the organization's communication infrastructure.

Groups are typically more concerned with a common interest and the benefits of the interpersonal relationships among their members, whereas teams are generally more concerned with task and goal achievement. That is not to say that groups don't work together to accomplish things; nevertheless, group members typically carry out their tasks without having to rely on the work of other members. In teams, members rely on other members' work or contributions to successfully complete tasks.

TABLE 10.1 Typical Characteristics of Groups and Teams

Group	Team
Informal or formal	Formal
Share common goals	Work interdependently toward common goals
Affiliation oriented	Achievement oriented
Small or large in size	Generally small in size

Groups may range in size from a few people to a thousand or more. Teams are generally smaller in size, owing to limitations on how many people can work together interdependently. However, a large team may be possible if work is divided among subteams consisting of members who work interdependently. While subteams may increase team productivity, it is important that the collective maintain a strong common team identity.[4] A **team identity** is the collective sense of identification and loyalty that team members feel toward the team.[5]

Although the differences between groups and teams are important, some of what we will say in this chapter does apply to both. Unless otherwise noted, however, we will focus primarily on teams, in part because organizations make greater use of teams due to their task and goal orientation.

The following are types of teams you are likely to encounter in organizations:

- *Permanent Teams and Project Teams.* Permanent teams are relatively stable and ongoing, while project teams are intended to meet for a limited time, achieve short-term goals, or solve a particular problem. Project team members typically are chosen for their expertise and can include both managers and non-managers who represent various departments.[6] Healthy interpersonal relationships are more important for permanent teams, because their members will have to work together on an ongoing basis.

- *Hierarchical Teams and Self-Managed Teams.* In a hierarchical team one person has the responsibility and legitimate authority. In recent years, however, there has been a steady increase in the use of self-managed work teams across a range of workplaces.[7] A self-managed work team typically consists of a small number of employees who are collectively given primary responsibility to schedule work, assign tasks or job responsibilities, and make decisions in their daily work.[8] Members of self-managed teams tend to enjoy their enhanced decision-making responsibility and control over their jobs.[9]

- *Functional Teams and Cross-Functional Teams.* A functional team consists of a team of members in a particular area or department, such as finance or marketing. Because members have similar expertise and experiences, they are more likely to get along well as a group. In contrast, cross-functional teams bring together people with a variety of expertise and experiences who provide a diversity of perspectives and information but may hinder collaboration.

- *On-site Teams and Virtual Teams.* Most team members work alongside one another in the same building or factory. On-site members see each other regularly, often many times a day. A virtual team is composed of members who live in geographically diverse settings and who may even belong to different organizations. Members rarely if ever meet face-to-face; instead, they interact by computer, video, and/or telephone. In multinational organizations, team members may be spread across the globe.[10]

Regardless of the type, teams can improve productivity and performance, but this is not the defining motive for teamwork from a sustainable perspective. Team-based work environments can also dignify organizational members, contribute to meaningful work and creative expression, and promote individual and collective well-being. For example, when team members treat one another fairly and with respect, absenteeism decreases and team performance is likely to increase.[11]

The potential benefits of teamwork can be enticing to organizational leaders, but they can also be detrimental to members if teams are not managed in a way that draws out their benefits and minimizes their drawbacks. Leaders and team members need to learn to manage team processes in order to avoid some common problems. This is particularly important when stakes are high. An extreme example is a team that is formed to climb Mount Everest; in that challenging environment, poor team leadership and a lack of learning and teamwork can cost team members their lives.[12]

Although no two teams are the same, classic group development research suggests that most teams progress through a series of predictable developmental stages: forming, storming, norming, performing, and, sometimes, adjourning.[13] Although these developmental stages are well-known and easy to remember, there is little research evidence to suggest that all teams pass through all of them or that teams pass through them in this particular sequence. Other more recent studies suggest that the progress of the team has more to do with the pressure of meeting deadlines;[14] nevertheless, these stages describe important processes common to many teams regardless of the time spent in each stage or the sequencing of them.[15]

Although we may think of the stages as one following the other, team development is also an iterative process. Thus, while forming may be especially important in the early stages of a team's life cycle, team members must also engage in "re-forming" when new members join or when the teams' responsibilities change. Overall, given the countless external influences on teams (such as resource and membership changes, interruptions, task changes, and so on), while the activities associated with the group development stages may occur at some point during the life of a team, it would be unrealistic to expect most teams in organizations to progress through them sequentially in lock-step fashion. Because of these issues regarding their sequencing, and because the word "stages" tends to refer to a particular sequence, we refer to forming, storming, and so forth as *categories* here.

The first four categories are common to all teams, while the fifth occurs only when a team disbands. Adjourning is, in many ways, really the opposite of forming. As a team disbands, members may bask in the glow of their individual and team achievements and be saddened by the loss of friendship and camaraderie. In the rest of this section, we discuss the first four categories, noting important inputs (team diversity, structure, resources) and key processes (leadership, conflict management, information sharing, workload sharing, feedback, and recognition) that influence team outputs (member satisfaction and commitment, team performance).[16]

Like leadership in the integrative leadership models we discussed in chapter 9, the development process for teams in some ways mirrors the development process for individuals, suggesting that at different times a different set of behaviours is critical to managing a team (see Figure 10.1). A team leader may provide those behaviours directly if he or she is a member of the team. If the leader is not a member of the team, then he or she must find ways to support the team leader in providing what is necessary for the team's development.

To navigate team members' feelings and issues during the categories of team development and apply appropriate management techniques, we use the acronym FIT—that is,

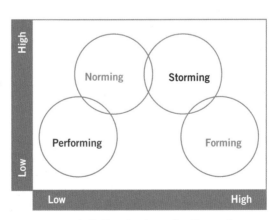

FIGURE 10.1 Four Basic Categories of Team Development and Leader Behaviour

Category Description	Feelings Members Are Experiencing	Issues Members Are Dealing With	Techniques Leaders Can Use
Category 1 – Forming: Team is created	Anticipation Apprehension	What will the team do? Why is it important?	Set goals Clarify roles and rules Build relationships
Category 2 – Storming: Obstacles emerge	Frustration Discouragement	Can we achieve our goals? How long will this last?	Appeal to shared goals Remove barriers Manage conflict
Category 3 – Norming: Habits are established	Optimism Acceptance	Will we continue to progress? Or will we regress?	Reinforce positive norms Ensure accountability
Category 4 – Performing: Team excels	Pride Confidence	Will we be recognized? What is our next challenge?	Provide feedback and rewards Identify new goals

Feelings, Issues, and Techniques. Table 10.2 shows the FIT typical for each category of team development. Although these can apply to more than one category, our exploration here is intended to help leaders "fit" specific techniques with specific categories of team development. We will explain the techniques in more detail as we discuss each category. We begin with the forming category.

Forming

GROUPS & TEAMS | **FORMING** | STORMING | NORMING | PERFORMING

LEARNING OBJECTIVE 2
Discuss forming, the first category of team development behaviour, and how it clarifies goals and builds relationships.

Team diversity is the extent to which member characteristics differ within the team.

The first category of team development is forming. Members may volunteer to join a team or they may be selected for their task-specific experience or perspectives. If a leader has the opportunity to select team members, conventional wisdom suggests that selection should maximize **team diversity**. Team diversity is the extent to which member characteristics differ within the team. Team members may differ in the function of their jobs, tenure within the organization, or their age, ethnicity, education, and even personality. More diversity allows the team to draw on a variety of perspectives and experiences in performing its tasks. Functional diversity and diversity in educational backgrounds have the strongest relationships with team performance and creativity.[17]

Despite the potential for diversity to contribute to a team, it also can cause significant problems in the quality of interactions, leading to lower team performance, less communication, more conflict, and the withdrawal of team members from the group.[18] The effect of diversity on a team can be influenced by the way the team is led. It has been shown that if leaders take proactive measures, such as setting timelines, coordinating members' efforts, and managing the schedule, the potential for negative results can be reduced among members who are diverse in their preferences for managing time.[19]

Now that many organizations operate globally, often with members working virtually, ethnic diversity and cultural diversity are becoming more important. Multinational corporations, such as Danish food and bio products company Danisco, form diverse teams.[20] Danisco teams have included members from across Europe, but since its acquisition by DuPont, the company's team members now come from almost every continent. Cultural differences may create problems early in a team's formation because members tend to be less satisfied and feel less connected in culturally diverse teams than members do in teams who all share similar cultural backgrounds.[21] This can be an even bigger problem if only one or two members are from a different culture than are the majority. They are bound to feel out of place and marginalized, or the team may divide into subgroups. If a team is to be culturally diverse, it is probably better that it be multicultural, with members representing a number of cultures.[22] An increase in diversity may minimize the tendency for subgroups to form and may prevent any one culture from being a minority. Without a dominant subgroup, all members will recognize the need to spend time working on communication and developing relationships.

While engaging in forming behaviours, members typically have *feelings* of anticipation and apprehension. There is excitement about being part of something new and potentially important, but there is also uncertainty about how the team members will work together and whether the team will be successful. The main *issues* in members' minds tend to be questions about what the team will be doing and why it is important. Because these feelings and issues reflect generally high levels of commitment but low levels of competency working in the team, the team may require more structure and directive behaviour from the leader. During this period, the team's goals are set and members begin to get to know one another while starting to see themselves as part of the team. Team members also begin to test each other for relationship potential and to determine what sorts of behaviours are acceptable. During forming activities, the leader's *techniques* should include setting goals for the team, clarifying roles and ground rules for interaction, and building a foundation for productive relationships.

While the team is forming, the leader helps team members to understand the meaning and importance of the team's goals in meeting larger organizational objectives. During forming, a team may benefit from bringing a sponsoring manager into its meetings—that is, someone who supports the team's goal and is willing to publicly affirm it. Teams can benefit from creating an informal or formal charter that states the goal of the project;[23] this document takes on more weight when it is signed by the leader and the team members.

Roles may relate to team facilitation, such as the role of note taker, scribe, or timekeeper. Or they may relate to a role or function, such as project manager, department liaison, analyst, or team spokesperson. Of the many team-building activities available, role clarification has perhaps the greatest impact on team performance.[24]

Ground rules are explicit agreements among team members regarding how to behave in such matters as being on time, communicating, and resolving conflict. For example, at Aecon Group, Canada's largest construction and infrastructure development company, all teams and individuals operating out of project sites as well as out of company offices understand that safety comes first. This ground rule guides all decision making at the company so that there is no confusion when tough decisions need to be made.[25] Ground rules may be instituted by the leader or agreed upon as a group.

Leadership techniques for goals, roles, and ground rules contribute to task cohesion within the team. **Task cohesion** is members' shared commitment to achieving a goal. Leaders can foster it by ensuring that team members have a voice in decision making and by inviting members to participate in establishing the group's goals and ground rules. Moreover, task cohesion will be high when the rewards for team success are clear and compelling. For example, an elite team of clinicians and scientists at the Campbell Family Institute for Breast Cancer Research at Princess Margaret Hospital in Toronto, Ontario, is dedicated to goals related to finding cures for breast cancer.[26]

Although task cohesion is more important than social cohesion in contributing to team performance, **social cohesion**, the attachment and attraction of team members to one another, is also important to "grease the wheels"—that is, to decrease friction and help the team run smoothly.[27] Typically, it arises from similarities within the group, time spent together, shared positive experiences, and shared goals. Social cohesiveness is fostered when team members build mutual trust, which was discussed in chapter 8. Members can speed up the process of achieving social cohesiveness by modelling trustworthiness in their relationships and encouraging open communication about themselves. For example, a leader might

Task cohesion is the shared commitment among members to achieving a goal.

Social cohesion is the attachment and attraction of team members to one another.

M💡B | WHAT MAKES AN EFFECTIVE STUDENT TEAM?

Konstantin Chagin/Shutterstock

As a student, you no doubt have worked in a number of "teams" to complete work for class projects on which you are judged based on the final product that is presented to your instructor (either in the form of a paper or a presentation or both).

Like students at many business schools across the country, students at York University's Schulich School of Business in Toronto, Ontario, frequently compete as teams in case competitions outside of the classroom. Depending on the specifics of the competition itself, these teams may be tasked with developing new products to satisfy a particular need, formulating a marketing strategy, outlining a new corporate strategy, and so on. However, one thing is certain: Regardless of the specific competition, all teams inevitably commit significant time and effort to researching the topic or industry, preparing reports, and building presentations to impress judges.

Ultimately, winning teams provide strong deliverables as a result of excellent teamwork and high levels of motivation throughout the preparation process.

QUESTIONS FOR REFLECTION

1. As a team member, what were the characteristics of your more effective team experiences?
2. What were the characteristics of your ineffective team experiences?
3. In future teams, which characteristics or behaviours could you model or promote to improve your chances of having an effective team experience?

---

start meetings with warm-up questions such as, "If you had the day off, what would you do?" Learning about other members' interests in this way personalizes the team members and enhances their relationships with each other. Members also can encourage interaction outside formal meeting times by hosting meals or organizing a fun night out. They might consider investing in team-building experiences, such as solving a mystery, navigating a ropes course, or making decisions to survive a simulated plane crash in the wilderness. Such activities simulate important team dynamics in a fun and memorable environment. Finally, social cohesiveness can be facilitated by something as simple as managing the team's size. Teams that are smaller tend to be more cohesive. If a department or team has many members, then it may be wise to subdivide it.

The forming process within team development from a sustainable perspective also includes developing a shared understanding of the team's sense of place and purpose in the organization. The emphasis is on building a shared team identity grounded in its organizational context. The heart of a team's identity comes not from its goals, nor even from how it fits with improving organizational performance, but rather from how it relates to other groups and the mission of the organization. Put differently, connecting with other individuals and teams, and with the overarching purpose of the organization, is the focal point of activities in this category.

A designated leader may be the one to identify and originate the team in a sustainable organizational culture, but teams may also emerge when an organizational member identifies a need or hot button and proposes it as a possible team focus. Companies such as German multinational engineering and electronics conglomerate Siemens have begun encouraging employees to submit ideas for improvement and to form their own teams to be part of change in the company. At Siemens's office in Mumbai, a group of employees initiated a yoga class to promote health and fitness as well as general employee interaction.[28]

The techniques associated with the sustainable approach are much more participative, even in the development of team goals and structures. The role of a leader in the team is to ask the right questions. For example, a leader might ask, "Given the mission of the organization and our understanding of our current needs, what should be the purpose and goals of this team?" Once members have agreed on the goals, a leader might then ask them to come up with ground rules for working together to meet the goals.

Another question to ask is who should be welcome to join the team. From a conventional perspective, the answer may be someone who has the expertise to help the team achieve its goals; from a sustainable perspective, the answer is more about who might add meaning through their participation or find it meaningful to be a part of the team. Sustainable teams are more inclusive of organizational members as well as of suppliers, customers, and possibly even community members. Membership also is more fluid during forming, as members move in and out of the meetings to explore the team's purpose and to provide input. The emphasis for sustainable team members during forming is exploring potential roles instead of defining specific roles. Eventually, a core of committed team members emerges over time.

Storming

GROUPS & TEAMS | FORMING | **STORMING** | NORMING | PERFORMING

LEARNING OBJECTIVE 3
Discuss storming, the second category of team development behaviour, and how it appeals to shared goals, encourages helping, and resolves conflicts.

The hallmarks of the second category of team development behaviours—storming—are conflict and discouragement. **Team conflict** is a real or perceived difference in interests between two or more team members. Relational conflict can detract from the performance of the team and contribute to dissatisfaction within the team, whereas task conflict can sometimes improve performance if it enhances information sharing.[29] Yet, how the team members work through their conflict is a more important factor in determining how the team performs and how team members feel.[30]

During storming, there is emphasis on managing conflict, as members sort out what it means to retain and express their individuality in the context of their membership in the group. In some cases, it may appear as though the team is going in circles, making little or no progress during storming. *Feelings* tend to be those of discouragement and frustration, opening up the possibility of withdrawal or even angry outbursts. The central underlying *issues* for team members are whether the team will get through this, whether the team will achieve its goals, and when the conflict will be resolved. A leader can address these feelings and issues through *techniques* such as reminding members of shared goals and of the value of all team members, removing barriers to progress, and managing conflict.

While storming, progress can be made by pointing to shared goals and by encouraging team members to take on more responsibility to support and help each other.[31] Participating in solving problems develops a sense of shared identity and trust among members. Deliberately modelling helping others can create a virtuous cycle in which this positive behaviour is embraced by more members.[32] A focus on others also makes it easier for members to exhibit self-control over their own self-interests and thereby better serve the interests of the team. When barriers such as a lack of time or information, poor communication, or the physical distance between members halt progress, the leader and team members need to negotiate for more resources, seek out the necessary information, explore using technology to improve communication, or schedule more frequent meetings.[33]

Applying proper techniques for managing conflict requires a deeper understanding of the source of conflict. Sometimes conflict may be healthy, such as when it motivates members to rally around their cause and work harder or when the discussion of diverse opinions and perspectives raises the quality of resulting decisions. At other times, conflict can be dysfunctional, such as when members' work efforts are undermined by others, communication becomes defensive and accusatory, or the most productive members leave the organization to find more harmonious environments in which to work. In one interesting study, conflict was found to be dysfunctional in that it decreased individual performance but functional in that it increased group performance.[34]

Team conflict is a real or perceived difference in interests between two or more team members.

When there is too much conflict, performance suffers because members are uncooperative and chaos erupts. When there is too little conflict, performance suffers because members become complacent and fail to respond to new ideas, and they avoid discussing differences of opinion that might provide useful information for the team.[35] Moderate amounts of conflict can improve performance because members constantly question and improve work practices, pushing one another to innovate, and there is a healthy tension in the organization. Research is unclear about whether an optimal amount of conflict exists in every team, but it is clear that extreme conflict is stressful and often counterproductive and that little or no conflict can be a sign of complacency.

Conflict can occur for a variety of reasons. First, group members must sometimes compete against one another for key scarce resources like money, information, or supplies. This competition undermines any attempts to develop a positive group identity, because members have to worry that a colleague will get more of something than they will. Competitive interactions, in most cases, decrease team performance and create bad feelings among team members.[36]

Conflict is also likely when someone's ability to achieve goals or objectives is connected to—and hampered by—the actions of another team member. **Team task interdependence** refers to the extent to which team members require resources or support from other team members to complete their tasks.[37] For example, in student team projects, each member of the team is typically expected to complete a different part of the team's assignment. Conflict is likely to arise if one member fails to complete his or her part of the assignment in an adequate manner, which would frustrate other members' ability to complete their parts of the project.

Another source of conflict arises from team members having different goals. For example, manufacturing production employees usually concentrate on efficiency and cost cutting; they have a relatively short time horizon and focus on producing high-quality goods or services in a timely and efficient manner. In contrast, marketing employees focus on sales and responsiveness to customers. When a team consists of members from different departments, this increases the potential for conflict within the team, as individual members promote agendas that put the interests of their department above the interests of the team.

Conflict also may arise when individual group members do not get along with one another based on their personal characteristics. The problem may be as simple as having personality traits that irk co-workers.[38] For example, a smart team member with a low level of conscientiousness can anger other team members.[39] Although some level of personal differences is almost inevitable, it can be disruptive if it gets in the way of members' everyday functioning.

Techniques to resolve conflict from a conventional perspective typically take one of four approaches, as shown in Table 10.3.

First, an obvious way to resolve conflict when there is a real or perceived lack of resources is to increase the resources available to the team. To do so, leaders can engage in boundary-spanning activities such as lobbying or bargaining with other departments and upper

Team task interdependence refers to the extent to which team members require resources or support from other team members to complete their tasks.

TABLE 10.3 Conflict: Causes and Cures

Causes	Cures (Techniques)
Scarce resources	Increase resources
Task interdependence	Redesign structures and systems
Conflicting goals	Appeal to superordinate goal
Personal conflicts	Help members work through issues

management for resources. Although boundary spanning can improve team performance, too much attention looking outward for scarce resources can detract from team members attending to and working collaboratively toward their common goals.[40] Another approach a leader can take is to rearrange resources within the team itself. For example, if conflict is occurring because a team member does not have enough time to adequately track the progress of customer orders, perhaps some of those responsibilities could be moved to someone who has skills to automate the process.

Second, conflict from task interdependence can sometimes be resolved by redesigning and improving the underlying structures and systems that caused the problem in the first place. For example, a leader can reduce conflict and enhance team performance by adjusting inconsistencies in workloads, clarifying expectations, improving communication systems, or creating a team identity. If team members feel a loyalty to the team, it encourages them to act co-operatively instead of competitively.[41]

A third approach to resolving conflict, especially when goals clash, is to appeal to a **superordinate goal**—that is, a higher-level goal recognized as important by team members—that may be jeopardized if the issue remains unresolved. For example, a running back or receiver on a football team may argue about who should get the ball, but a wise quarterback will focus his or her attention on the superordinate goal of winning the game. For a work team, a superordinate goal might be completing work by a certain deadline or delivering a certain level of performance improvement to earn a bonus.

A **superordinate goal** is a higher-level goal recognized as important by team members.

Finally, leaders with strong interpersonal and behavioural skills may be able to help other members overcome interpersonal conflict with their colleagues. For example, they might sit down to work things out between members, model and practise active interpersonal listening skills, or encourage training in diversity awareness that makes individuals more sensitive to cultural and gender differences. Teams that have higher levels of emotional stability and openness to experience are more likely to succeed at transforming conflict into something positive for the team; but if these personality traits are lacking within the team, attempts to resolve interpersonal conflict may backfire.[42] In some situations, it may be more prudent for a leader to remove a member or members from the team.

Conflict may be inevitable in most teams, but from a sustainable perspective it is not necessarily something to be avoided or quickly solved. In fact, research suggests that conflict can *contribute* to team performance. If it occurs early in the team's development, it can counteract premature confidence that can hinder team performance.[43] Conflict can contribute to a healthy exchange of ideas if team members are convinced that they are able to disagree and discuss differences in an environment of safety.[44]

A sustainable approach welcomes different perspectives as an opportunity for members to broaden their own understanding and build relationships. By simultaneously considering multiple views, a source of conflict in a team is transformed into a source of deeper understanding and greater appreciation of diverse perspectives. Instead of debating positions or issues, the sustainable approach—like transformational conflict resolution—emphasizes dialogue or conversation to help each person understand the other's perspective and be mindful of the person behind the perspective. By reframing the conflict as a search for deeper understanding, participants become more self-aware, empathetic, and open to mutually beneficial alternative solutions.[45]

Useful techniques during storming include facilitating and reframing conflict from something negative to something positive, thereby minimizing discouragement and frustration. Encouraging diversity of opinion is important because having different perspectives increases a team's creativity.[46] Using a transformative approach, a sustainable team member addresses conflict by asking questions and offering suggestions that prompt other members to see matters from a higher level of abstraction, changing their perspective from specific positions to more general goals, from parts of an issue to a broader view, and from individual concerns to system concerns.[47]

For example, a video game development team might be at odds about how much the game software emphasizes the specific dimensions of speed or dexterity; however, at a higher level of abstraction, speed and dexterity are both related to *motion*. Thus, a leader can direct the team's conversation toward the way motion is captured in the video game software and, in turn, how this motion combines with the hardware to shape the overall gaming experience. The focus on more abstract ideas helps dissenting members concentrate on common interests and challenges that can stimulate creative or transformative solutions that might not have been under discussion before.

Leaders need to be sensitive to the possibility that team members may tire of working through challenging conflict, however. With this in mind, leaders should look for opportunities for the team to take a break from the stress of working through problems and thinking about the task. Consider cancelling a meeting in order to allow frustrations to dissipate or replacing a meeting with an opportunity to refresh relationships—perhaps by scheduling a lunch together. If team members grow weary of conflict, they may lapse into conformity or fatigue-related consensus. **Groupthink** is an omnibus term that describes the tendency of group members to strive for and maintain consensus on a decision rather than disrupt the group.[48] The behaviours associated with groupthink short-circuit the critical examination of ideas in order to keep the peace and, as described in OB in Action: Groupthink, such behaviours can have dire consequences.

Groupthink is a term describing behaviours that encourage group members to strive for and maintain consensus on a decision rather than disrupt the group.

OB in Action   Groupthink

NASA

It's been suggested that the phenomenon of *groupthink* contributed to a number of tragedies throughout history, including the space shuttle disasters at the National Aeronautics and Space Administration (NASA). Problems in team decision processes were cited as contributing factors in both the destruction of the *Challenger* space shuttle shortly after its liftoff and in the disintegration of the *Columbia* shuttle at re-entry into the earth's atmosphere. American research psychologist Irving Janis, the originator of the term groupthink, regarded it as a "disease" that can afflict previously healthy teams. Symptoms include censoring dissent within the group, suppressing or discrediting information from other sources, acting decisively with overconfidence, and avoiding questioning the ethics of the group's decision.

The causes of groupthink include overblown social cohesion; pressures for team members to conform to the majority; rationalizations that highlight the positive aspects and discount the negative aspects of an issue; isolation or an insular group that has minimal contact with outsiders; stressful working conditions that promote quick decisions; the desire to avoid conflict; and leaders who are controlling and dominating, intentionally or otherwise. A vigorous debate among researchers focuses on whether the groupthink phenomenon actually exists, or whether it is simply a combination of group factors such as conformity and conflict avoidance; however, whatever its origins, "groupthink" is widely used as a shorthand term to describe combinations of these group behaviours.

To prevent groupthink's associated behaviours, team members must thoroughly examine a wide range of issues and alternatives. To ensure that this happens, a leader must refrain from stating personal opinions at the outset of the discussion, require a full analysis of each issue regardless of presumed consensus, invite criticism of ideas and suggestions, and use information-sharing and decision-making techniques that maximize input and minimize concerns about retribution for disagreement with the majority.

One simple technique is to assign someone within the team, perhaps on a rotating basis, to openly play the role of the critic or devil's advocate. This person is required to raise issues, call premature decisions into question, and demand justification for assertions made by team members. Another provocative technique, *dialectical inquiry*, is a staged debate between a dominant perspective or opinion and a counter-argument that represents an opposing point of view. A variation is to assign debate participants positions that are contrary to their expressed opinions but which they must defend for the sake of open discussion.

In sum, the strengths of teams—the attraction of social cohesion and the motivation of task cohesion—can leave a team open to the negative outcomes resulting from the behaviours associated with groupthink if not managed correctly.

QUESTIONS FOR DISCUSSION

1. Have you ever worked in a team that fell victim to the behaviours linked to groupthink? What was the end result?
2. What are some practical suggestions for combating these types of outcomes?

Norming

LEARNING OBJECTIVE 4
Discuss norming, the third category of team development behaviour, when performance norms are affirmed and accountability is ensured.

Another category of team development behaviour is referred to as norming. **Norms** are shared beliefs about social and task behaviours in a group.[49] Team norms can be informal, such as dress codes and whether members work overtime to help one another meet deadlines, or formal, such as standardized operating procedures governing the frequency of group meetings and processes for sharing information. In one sense, norming is "getting on track." After members resolve points of conflict and confusion, they develop shared mental models of the best ways to complete tasks and the appropriate ways to interact with one another.[50] These norms can promote group performance because they indicate common expectations, guide informal practices, help the group avoid interpersonal problems, and define the group's identity.[51] Behaviours as simple as offering justifications for ideas or confirming the ideas of others, when practised frequently in team discussions, can contribute to team performance.[52] Of course, team norms can be dysfunctional, such as when it is the norm to engage in groupthink or allow absenteeism.[53]

Norms are shared beliefs about social and task behaviours in a group.

Team members engaged in norming tend to experience *feelings* of optimism and acceptance of one another and the task. In other words, if the team emerges from the storm clouds, its progress contributes to the formation of a positive attitude toward the team and its goals. The main *issue* in the minds of members is whether the team will now work together effectively or spiral back into conflict. *Techniques* for leading the team through the norming activities include making functional norms explicit by "driving a stake in the ground." This can be as simple as saying to the team, "We're really making progress because everyone is going the extra mile to get tasks done on time." Another strategy is to plan a time during or outside team meetings for celebrating progress and positive contributions. Other examples include providing symbolic but tangible rewards, such as a smoothie for someone who helped defuse tensions in the team or lunch for the whole team when they have worked overtime.

Leaders play a critical role in establishing and promoting team norms that help improve team performance.[54] Two norms critical to team performance that require a team leader's attention are workload sharing and information sharing.

A functional workload-sharing norm is when each team member is contributing equally to achieve the team's task. Team members' contributions may not be the same, as team members perform different roles, but they may be equal in the amount of effort required. When workload sharing is equal, teams perform better than when workload is distributed unequally within the team.[55] Another functional workload-sharing norm is backing up or helping other team members who have a heavy workload. This norm can contribute to team performance by balancing the workload within the team, but it also can be harmful to the team if the helper's tasks go undone or the team member being helped reduces his or her effort.[56]

A typical dysfunctional norm relating to workload sharing is evident when one or more team members engage in **free riding**—doing less than their best or contributing less than their fair share to reach the team's goal. Free riders may lack commitment to the team's goals or reduce their contributions because they believe the team can achieve the goal without their full participation.[57] Free riding is most common when individual contributions are difficult to monitor or measure, when the team is perceived to be highly capable, and when team members are low in conscientiousness.[58]

Free riding is doing less than your best or contributing less than your fair share to reach the team's goal.

Free riding may make it necessary for the leader to intervene. Just one free rider can create a downward spiral of anger, retribution, and reduced effort if he or she is judged to have the ability to perform but not the motivation.[59] To avoid the "sucker effect"—which is evident when other team members reduce their effort to avoid being the sucker who does more than his or her fair share of the work—a leader needs to be aware of and address issues of motivation within the team.[60] Techniques to reduce free riding include monitoring team members' contributions, making members accountable for their work, and training members to constructively manage their emotional responses to free riders. Instead of getting back at a poor performer, team members can be guided to address issues face-to-face and arrive at a better solution.

Another set of norms governs information sharing. Information sharing is necessary for teams to benefit from the knowledge, creativity, and unique perspectives of team members. Finding successful solutions to complex organizational problems and making critical decisions requires information sharing. Indeed, the potential for teams to outperform individuals is linked to a team's capacity for information sharing. Teams perform better when they share more information, but this is particularly true when team processes encourage team members to exchange unique information.[61] In virtual teams, technology can facilitate sharing unique information, but it sometimes hinders the quantity of information that is shared. In order to build the trust and social cohesion that contributes to the performance of virtual teams, leaders of virtual teams should encourage both a high quality (unique information) and a high quantity of information sharing.[62]

Team members can withhold information for a variety of conscious and subconscious reasons. A dominant team member could discourage input from others, who might hold back in deference to the passion or expertise of the dominant member or to avoid the stress of conflict. Another reason could be that team members may have an introverted personality or may lack confidence in their ideas. Or they might intentionally withhold information to speed up the decision-making process once a satisfactory option has been presented. *Satisficing* describes a decision process in which an adequate option—one that meets the minimum criteria for a solution—is chosen instead of the best possible option (see chapter 6).[63] Satisficing may result in suboptimal team decisions, unless the decision is relatively unimportant and the cost of investing more time and energy to determine a better option would be greater than the benefit that would result from the better option. Team members also can unconsciously withhold information that is easy to forget because it represents a unique perspective and is not brought up in team discussions.

Withholding information, intentionally or not, is a dysfunctional norm that the leader of the team should address. Techniques for doing so include (1) **brainstorming**, (2) the **nominal group technique**, and (3) the **Delphi technique**, all of which are discussed in My OB: Stimulating Information Sharing.

From a sustainable perspective, team norms are important, but there also must be a spirit of freedom to preserve creative expression and counteract tendencies to conform.[64] The norm of workload sharing is still important, but the approach to dealing with it is different. Whereas conventional theory focuses on limiting the negative effects of free riders through monitoring and accountability, a sustainable approach tries to promote the positive effects of **consistent contributors**.[65] According to the sustainable view, there are three kinds of team members:

- Free riders—those who do as little as possible.
- Conditional contributors—those whose contribution depends on the situation.
- Consistent contributors—those who contribute regardless of how little their teammates do.

Research shows that, over the long term, teams with consistent contributors generally outperform teams without them. A sustainable approach to norming involves paying particular attention to recognizing, reinforcing, and, sometimes, even rewarding team members who consistently contribute to the tasks and goals of the team.

The consistent-contributor effect holds for both high- and low-status team members, although the influence of the high-status members is more likely to be recognized by others. One reason for this outcome is that the behaviour of consistent contributors influences the norms of the group by modelling service to the team. When the source of consistent contribution is an agreeable or co-operative personality, having more

Brainstorming is an unstructured process of sharing ideas.

Nominal group technique is an information-sharing technique in which the leader asks participants to silently and individually write down all of their ideas related to a specific question.

Delphi technique is a technique in which questions are posed to team members remotely and responses are returned to the leader.

A **consistent contributor** is someone who contributes regardless of how little his or her teammates contribute.

NBC/Getty Images

Have you been in a meeting where you or other members were disengaged? Sometimes this happens because, as was often depicted in both the British and the American versions of the television sitcom *The Office,* members recognize that the leader is going to decide what they want regardless of their input. Another reason could be that the norm is to keep quiet in order to get the meeting over quickly. Whatever the reason, there isn't a whole lot of information being shared at such meetings. Yet leaders and members of teams have a number of tools at their disposal to facilitate effective information sharing. Here are a few.

Brainstorming is typically an unstructured process for providing spontaneous ideas—a kind of "thought shower"—while at the same time not criticizing others' ideas. The purpose is to encourage free thinking and creative, even wild, suggestions. The focus is on the quantity and the novelty of ideas. Ideas may be captured on a flipchart, computer, or whiteboard by someone who serves as a scribe. Only after the shower of ideas is over does the group evaluate the quality of the ideas in relationship to the issue at hand. Brainstorming solves some of the issues related to a lack of information sharing, but it doesn't solve others, such as the fear of conflicting with a dominant or powerful team member.

Another tool is the *nominal group technique* whereby members are asked to individually and silently write down all their ideas or suggestions related to a specific question, problem, or possibility. This technique minimizes the impact of dominant team members or prevailing opinions on the generation of ideas. It produces a large quantity of unfiltered input that the leader or facilitator should incorporate into a group discussion. Capturing all team members' information and then sharing it in a systematic or even anonymous fashion serves to make more information available. Information also can be gathered electronically, with members sending or posting ideas anonymously. After all of the information is available, the group can clarify suggestions and prioritize ideas.

A tool that is similar and employs technology is the *Delphi technique.* Questions are posed to team members remotely and their responses are returned to the leader. The leader compiles all of the ideas and, without attaching names to them, sends the list back to team members for further consideration and response. This process typically goes through several rounds, and then individual members are asked to rank or vote on the ideas. Anonymity encourages information sharing from less assertive or less powerful people and from introverted team members who may be more comfortable taking time to contemplate their responses before submitting them.

QUESTIONS FOR REFLECTION

1. Which of these tools have you used? Have they facilitated the sharing of information?
2. Are there other techniques or tools that you have used in the past? Which have worked best?

---

consistent contributors on a team can increase performance, cohesion, and workload sharing while reducing conflict.[66]

Unfortunately, the servant orientation of consistent contributors can make them vulnerable to being exploited by other members of the team. Furthermore, to make more competitive team members aware of and influenced by persistent co-operation, a consistent contributor may need to relentlessly co-operate (and suffer, in relative terms) for a long time. Yet even then the co-operation of others is not guaranteed. Indeed, it is precisely this fear of exploitation and the potential for being a sucker that makes being a consistent contributor seem irrational from a conventional point of view. In the face of this vulnerability, sustainable team members provide socioemotional support by recognizing, encouraging, and drawing attention to the behaviour of consistent contributors.

From a sustainable perspective, information sharing is an important norm not only because it enhances team performance but also because it contributes to social cohesion, co-operation, team member satisfaction, and learning.[67] Information sharing is a form of collaboration that a leader can particularly influence through his or her example and encouragement.[68] Leaders as well as members can promote and reinforce a sustainable norm of collaboration when they take the initiative to communicate with stakeholders outside the team. At Google Canada, for example, the Toronto office is purposely designed to encourage collaboration by mixing work spaces and social spaces to promote as much interaction between employees as possible. The company also provides free snacks, meals, and beverages so that all employees, including the managing director, can eat (and work) together as opposed to eating by themselves at their desks. All employees are also equipped with a laptop so that they can easily move around and work with others.[69]

During norming, sustainable leaders provide a bird's-eye view of the forest—a systems view—that team members engaged in the detailed work of planting or cultivating one tree at a time might lose sight of. The leader works as a servant outside the team to smooth the road on which the team is travelling. Furthermore, the leader's focus is on encouraging but not dictating linkages both inside and outside the team and on empowering members to collaborate. With the trust built during other areas of team development, increasing levels of empowerment dignify the team and its members and contribute to high performance.[70]

Norming in a group is solidified when the team members have developed a shared set of expectations for workload, information sharing, and other norms for guiding team member behaviour.

Performing

GROUPS & TEAMS | FORMING | STORMING | NORMING | **PERFORMING**

LEARNING OBJECTIVE 5
Discuss performing, the fourth category of team development behaviour, when feedback is provided and new goals are identified.

Performing behaviours in a group occur when members have had experience working alongside one another. They have improved and fine-tuned their social as well as their task-oriented interrelationships. As a result, such teams are often more mature, are better organized, and function more effectively in performing their tasks. Members are likely to have a clearer understanding of team goals and, consequently, are better motivated to achieve them.

During performing activities, team members tend to experience *feelings* of pride and confidence in their ability to reach the goals of the team. The main *issues* in their minds are how others think the team is doing and what might be the next challenge for the team to conquer. The team seeks recognition of its performance and desires feedback to meet the challenges of improving performance and meeting new goals. In addition, team members are usually willing to assume more responsibility for team management. If the manager or leader is not already outside the team, performing presents the opportunity to delegate leadership responsibility to another team member.

Techniques for leaders during performing include maintaining and improving team performance by managing motivation through feedback and rewards. In moving from norming to performing, the leader's task changes from affirming progress to addressing deficiencies, and from recognizing behaviours to rewarding results. The leader also needs to encourage new challenging goals to avoid complacency.

Focusing on team goals, feedback, and rewards will unite individuals, encourage co-operative behaviour, and increase collective effort and performance.[71] It draws upon the motivational power of outcome interdependence—a situation in which "team members share a common fate."[72] Feedback alone may be sufficient to motivate employees in the short run, but financial incentives may be necessary to sustain motivation.[73] Individual goals within a team can detract from performance if they encourage maximizing individual performance, but they can be helpful if they encourage individual contributions to the group goal.[74]

Another advantage of using group systems of feedback and rewards is that group performance measurements may be more readily available and easier to use than individual performance measurements. Also, from a practical standpoint, it is often impossible to separate the contributions of each individual when members work interdependently.

With this in mind, in 2010 Rogers Communications set up an experimental call centre in Kitchener, Ontario, to try out new customer service techniques as well as management approaches, including performance evaluation and compensation based on team results. The company discovered that not only were employees less competitive with each other and less stressed when compared to an approach based mostly on individual results, sales remained strong and turnover decreased dramatically.[75]

Concerns about free riders can steer leaders to provide feedback and rewards to individual team members, but they need to approach this delicate situation carefully. Most team members acknowledge that leaders with formal authority (that is, managers) have a legitimate right to provide individual ratings, and they believe managers to be less biased than fellow team members. However, when managers are outside the team or don't spend much time with the team, they are viewed as having less information with which to rate individuals accurately.[76]

A sustainable leader will naturally focus on team-level rewards to reinforce a sense of community, and there are practical reasons for doing so—for example, to promote co-operation, reinforce interdependency, and increase collective motivation. If individual recognition or rewards are deemed necessary, a sustainable leader will be inclined to have teams decide how these rewards should be awarded. The American company W. L. Gore & Associates, Inc. (the inventors of Gore-Tex) uses compensation teams to decide how individuals are rewarded for work that was done as part of a team as well as for work that spanned several teams or, in cases of coaching and mentoring, that helped others to succeed.[77]

A sustainable leader is not likely to directly deliver feedback or prescribe solutions during behaviours in the performing category. Instead the leader can recommend that the team reflect on its performance and develop its own actions to improve performance. Teams that take time to evaluate their team functioning and past performance enhance their learning and future performance.[78] Although the team itself functions as the main source of learning and accountability, a leader can also seek out and provide sources of information that team members can use to enhance team learning. If a leader can subtly reframe failures or shortcomings as problem-solving opportunities, even negative feedback has the potential to stimulate co-operative behaviour within the team.[79]

From a sustainable perspective, during performing information about what the team has accomplished and learned should be diffused throughout the organization and beyond to benefit others. The leader serves the team by connecting the team to resources and opportunities within the broader organization or community. Promoting the success of the team and its expertise becomes a primary activity for the leader to enhance organizational learning. Yet even with a high-performing team, the leader should not step away from the team entirely. In a study of nuclear plants, leaders who remained integrated within their teams were better able to help the teams disseminate their learning throughout the organization.[80] The service of these teams outside conventional boundaries is an important part of the organizational learning process. A team's engagement with other teams or organizations is of benefit to others, but it also accelerates the learning within the team itself.

In summary, the inputs, processes, and outputs associated with each of these categories of team development can differ somewhat based on whether the approach the leader takes to team development is conventional or sustainable. So, too, might team development look different in self-managed, virtual, or other types of teams discussed earlier in the chapter. The OB in Action feature "Front-Line Management Teams" illustrates what team development challenges and practices might look like for front-line management teams.

 **OB in Action** Front-Line Management Teams

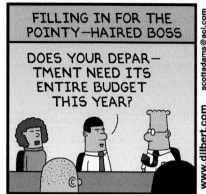

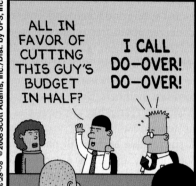

Some middle- to lower-level managers can talk a good game about the importance of teamwork but then fail miserably when they become members of a team with other managers. As the Dilbert comic illustrates, communication can break down and political activity can escalate.

In a study that investigated this issue, more than 200 practising managers shared their thoughts about teamwork among front-line managers. *Front-line managers* work closely with those on the production line, in the office, on the sales floor, and so on. The managers in the study discussed reasons for poor teamwork among front-line managers and offered suggestions for improving co-operation. Their responses are listed below (with the percentage of respondents who mentioned each).

One general prescription for the ills of front-line management teams is to build a shared team identity. When team members see themselves as part of the team, they act more collaboratively.

QUESTIONS FOR DISCUSSION

1. Which reasons for poor teamwork have you observed in your own work experience?
2. The suggestions for improving teamwork here are primarily conventional suggestions. What suggestions can you offer from a sustainable perspective?

Category	Reasons for Lack of Front-Line Management Teamwork	Ways to Improve Front-Line Management Teamwork
Forming	• Lack of unifying vision (35%) • Conflicting goals (37%)	• Develop a common vision and superordinate goals (36%)
Storming	• Personality conflicts (42%) • Poor teamwork skills (30%)	• Promote team skills development at all levels (28%)
Norming	• Deficient top management modelling and emphasis on the importance of teamwork (33%) • Personal agendas and organizational politics (24%)	• Ensure top management communicates the importance of teamwork in word and deed (31%) • Involve front-line managers in decision making (21%)
Performing	• Rewards based on individual performance (36%) • System and structural barriers to co-operation (29%)	• Implement team-based performance feedback and reward system (33%)

LEGO Mindstorms[81]

Joe Klamar/AFP/Getty Images

The LEGO Group was established in 1932 and for a long time was one of the most successful and well-known toy companies in the world. The company functioned in a traditional hierarchical fashion that focused on efficiency, encouraged incremental improvement, and counted on predictable product life cycles. In the mid-1990s, LEGO began experiencing struggles as increased competition, Internet-based games, and changing customer preferences led to reduced profits and concerns about the company's long-term viability. In response, LEGO launched the Mindstorms product development team, consisting of Ben Smith, a recent addition to the company who had experience managing an information technology company, and Thomas Atkinson, a long-time product manager. Essentially, they were to create a robotic LEGO toy. Working with a limited budget, the team had the following charge: take some partially developed programmable LEGO brick technology, develop an original product based on this technology, and bring it to market.

The Mindstorms team was placed in the company's low-profile Educational Division and allowed to create a novel product development process in which they could experiment more freely and act like a new business, working collaboratively and acting with agility. "We threw away most of the rulebook, and operated like a small, entrepreneurial business," said Atkinson.

Given that it had only limited funding, the Mindstorms team had to borrow people from within the existing system, which contributed to a great deal of conflict because the borrowed team members were expected to maintain their current jobs while contributing to the Mindstorms project. Beginning with only two members, facing a challenging charge, and getting help on borrowed time, the Mindstorms team intentionally engaged customers and embarked on cultivating an Internet community that would help shape the product's design and features. The team developed a large network of partnerships and alliances—a computer manufacturer, a museum, a software company, and a children's learning organization among them. In contrast to the typical LEGO way, Mindstorms team members set out to work with their partners as equals. Atkinson noted, "It is not like we can just say, 'This is the way it is going to work; this is the way to do it' . . . [the partner] would just say, 'stop.'"

During storming behaviours, the new way of working and the extended partnerships led to conflict or, in some cases, a lack of conflict. Smith said, "People weren't confronting each other with their differences of opinion. We had to make people talk directly to each other about this." Team members seemed to be looking for more clarity about working relationships, so Smith devised an organizational chart and talked to a few people about it. Ultimately, however, he ended up throwing out the chart. He realized that the Mindstorms process would suffer if it was formalized. Instead, Smith increased his communication, making it a point to chat with team members and ask questions, sometimes about work but many times not. He also encouraged the same behaviour from other team members, explaining his reasoning for investing in relationships as, "Employees are like bank accounts: If you just deposit money regularly, they grow like crazy!"

Collaborative norms emerged as the team adopted a form of parallel processing whereby the development and the implementation of ideas occurred at the same time. Often implementation issues surfaced that resulted in real-time adjustments in the design, thereby saving time and resources. The benefits were numerous, but so were the challenges. It was an exhausting, fast-paced environment in which feedback was almost immediate. At one point a marketing consultant concluded that the Mindstorms product was too complex for kids and would not sell. Smith called a two-week "time out" that excluded partners and even people from the parent company from discussions with the core team. Instead of making knee-jerk adjustments during this time, the team reaffirmed a vision for itself to "establish the LEGO company as the leading supplier of child-centered robotics in the . . . mass consumer market" and redoubled its efforts to position its emerging product as unique and distinct from existing LEGO products.

As word of the progress and potential of the Mindstorms team spread throughout the LEGO organization, the company's top managers decided to put resources behind another product, called TechToy, which was to be based on the same underlying technology. TechToy received a commitment from top management of four times the resources that Mindstorms received. The TechToy team operated like traditional product teams at LEGO—more hierarchical, slower, more sequential. The differences were obvious to outsiders: "The guy from Mindstorms . . . did all he could for that product, his heart was in it. The engineer working on TechToy took a holiday right in the middle of a very critical phase!"

Even with all of the challenges, the efforts of the Mindstorms team paid off. Despite enduring a dual launch with TechToy (a decision imposed by top management), the Mindstorms team received most of the publicity, in part due to support from its extensive network of partners. In fact, the Mindstorms debut was considered one of the most successful LEGO new product launches ever. Sticking with its partnership approach to development, LEGO Mindstorms evolved into the widely acclaimed microprocessor-based NXT system.

The Mindstorms robot kits have ended up being wildly popular beyond the target audience of children and educational markets; they often show up in computer labs and other settings where techies gather. LEGO Mindstorms has become the best-selling product in LEGO history—and without any advertising. Mindstorms also is at the root of an important social initiative to get children excited about science and technology. The FIRST LEGO League program engages teams of 9- to 16-year-olds in robotics competitions that improve science and technology skills and teach participants valuable team, employment, and life skills.

QUESTIONS FOR DISCUSSION

1. If you were asked to be one of the original members of the Mindstorms team, what would excite you about it? What would keep you up at night as the team developed?
2. What were the benefits and drawbacks of including a variety of stakeholders in the Mindstorms team's discussions?
3. Why do you think LEGO managers supported the TechToy team more than the Mindstorms team?

Summary

Organizations include both groups and teams. A group is a collection of two or more people who share a common interest or association. A team is a collection of people with shared goals who work interdependently as a unit and are accountable to one another to achieve those goals. Teams, and most groups, experience behaviours in a number of developmental categories. The behaviours in these categories include important processes that are common to teams and are critical for their success.

◆ Learning Objectives	◆ From a conventional OB perspective, team development requires leaders to exhibit the following behaviours to reap the material benefits of teams:	◆ From a sustainable OB perspective, team development requires leaders to exhibit the following behaviours to benefit the organization and community:
• Identify the characteristics of and differences between groups and teams.		
• Discuss forming, the first category of team development behaviour, and how it clarifies goals and builds relationships.	• Forming: Clarify goals and expectations and build relationships.	• Forming: Foster a sense of purpose/identity.
• Discuss storming, the second category of team development behaviour, and how it appeals to shared goals, encourages helping, and resolves conflicts.	• Storming: Appeal to shared goals, encourage helping, and resolve conflict.	• Storming: Transform conflict and refine roles.
• Discuss norming, the third category of team development behaviour, when performance norms are affirmed and accountability is ensured.	• Norming: Affirm performance norms and ensure accountability.	• Norming: Emphasize interdependencies and collaboration.
• Discuss performing, the fourth category of team development behaviour, when feedback is provided and new goals are identified.	• Performing: Provide feedback and recognition and identify new goals.	• Performing: Diffuse learning throughout the organization.

Key Terms

Brainstorming (p. 224)
Consistent contributors (p. 224)
Delphi technique (p. 224)
Free riding (p. 223)
Group (p. 213)
Groupthink (p. 222)

Nominal group technique (p. 224)
Norms (p. 223)
Social cohesion (p. 217)
Superordinate goal (p. 221)
Task cohesion (p. 217)
Team (p. 213)

Team conflict (p. 219)
Team diversity (p. 216)
Team identity (p. 214)
Team task interdependence (p. 220)

Questions for Reflection and Discussion

1. What is a group? What is a team? Provide an example of each.

2. Reflect back on your experiences as part of a school team. In what ways did your team experience the developmental behaviours described in this chapter? In what ways did your experience differ?

3. As a team leader, what approaches would you take to improve team task cohesion and social cohesion?

4. Suppose you are asked to head up a problem-solving team. Identify and explain information-sharing techniques that would reduce the likelihood of the behaviours associated with groupthink and that would improve the team's decision making.

5. How do you typically respond to free riders in teams? Do the perceived causes of free riding influence your response?

6. Have you ever been on a team with a consistent contributor? What effect did that person have on the rest of the members? Was he or she treated like a "sucker"?

7. Explain your experience of having team members evaluate your performance. If you have no experience in this area, how do you think you would respond to team members giving and receiving feedback that influences grades?

ob activities

SELF-ASSESSMENT EXERCISE

How Do You Lead Teams?

Using a scale of 1 - Strongly Disagree (SD), 2 - Disagree (D), 3 - Neutral (N), 4 - Agree (A), and 5 - Strongly Agree (SA), indicate your level of agreement with each statement on the 5-point scale.

In my team experiences, I . . .	SD	D	N	A	SA
1. Clarify the task or goal.	①	②	③	④	⑤
2. Expand goals to include new opportunities.	①	②	③	④	⑤
3. Seek to remove barriers to success.	①	②	③	④	⑤
4. Encourage team members to get to know each other.	①	②	③	④	⑤
5. Ensure that expectations are clarified.	①	②	③	④	⑤
6. Address sources of conflict within the team.	①	②	③	④	⑤
7. Explain the specific roles and responsibilities of team members.	①	②	③	④	⑤
8. Ensure accountability and follow-through for all members.	①	②	③	④	⑤
9. Provide recognition for results.	①	②	③	④	⑤

In my team experiences, I . . .

	SD	D	N	A	SA
10. Praise behaviours that are worth repeating.	①	②	③	④	⑤
11. Assess team effectiveness and adjust for better results.	①	②	③	④	⑤
12. Remind the team, when appropriate, that this is a normal phase that the team will get through.	①	②	③	④	⑤
13. Review and acknowledge progress.	①	②	③	④	⑤
14. Encourage sharing of information to avoid premature decisions.	①	②	③	④	⑤
15. Encourage team members to reflect on their strengths and weaknesses.	①	②	③	④	⑤
16. Discuss the importance of the goal and of each person in achieving it.	①	②	③	④	⑤

Key: Each statement represents a behaviour appropriate for a particular category of team development. Using the table below, assign points for each question. Add up your points for behaviours in each category. The maximum score for each category is 20. Higher scores indicate you tend to lead effectively when your team is engaged in that category's behaviours.

Questions Representing Categories

Q1, Q4, Q5, Q7: Forming

Q3, Q6, Q12, Q16: Storming

Q8, Q10, Q13, Q14: Norming

Q2, Q9, Q11, Q15: Performing

Source: This assessment is adapted from resources developed by LTrek, Inc. http://www.LTrek.com.

ETHICS SCENARIO

A publicly held software company donated software to a local school and allowed employees to serve as volunteers in teaching the use of the software to students while being paid by the company.

Why might this scenario occur in organizations?

Use the following scale to indicate whether this behaviour is ethically acceptable:

NEVER ACCEPTABLE		SOMETIMES ACCEPTABLE		ALWAYS ACCEPTABLE	
①	②	③	④	⑤	⑥	⑦

Explain the ideas you considered in arriving at your answer.

DISCUSSION STARTER

Wilderness Survival

Following are 10 questions concerning personal survival in the wilderness. Try to imagine yourself in the situation described. You are alone and have minimal equipment except where specified. The season is fall. The days are generally warm and dry, but the nights are cold. Your first task for this exercise is to individually select what you believe is the best of the three answers given under each item. Next, you will consider each question again, but this time as a member of a small group selecting the best answers by consensus. Do not change your individual answers even if you change your mind in the group discussion.

QUESTIONS

1. You have strayed from your party in trackless timber. You have no special signalling equipment. The best way to contact your friends is to:
   a. Call "help" loudly but in a low register.
   b. Yell or scream as loudly as you can.
   c. Whistle loudly and shrilly.
   Your answer_____ Group answer_____

2. You are in snake country. Your best action to avoid snakes is to:
   a. Make a lot of noise with your feet.
   b. Walk softly and quietly.
   c. Travel at night.
   Your answer_____ Group answer_____

3. You are hungry and lost in wild country. The best rule for determining which plants are safe to eat (among those you do not recognize) is to:
   a. Try anything you see the birds eat.
   b. Eat anything except plants with bright red berries.
   c. Put a bit of the plant on your lower lip for five minutes; if it seems all right, try a little.
   Your answer_____ Group answer_____

4. The day becomes dry and hot. You have a full bottle of water (about two pints) with you. You should:
   a. Ration it—about a cupful a day.
   b. Not drink till you stop for the night; then drink what you think you need.
   c. Drink as much as you think you need when you need it.
   Your answer_____ Group answer_____

5. Your water is gone. You finally come to a dried-up watercourse. Your best chance to find water is to:
   a. Dig anywhere on the stream bed.
   b. Dig up plant and tree roots near the bank.
   c. Dig in the stream bed at the outside of a bend.
   Your answer_____ Group answer_____

6. You decide to walk out of the wild country by following a series of ravines where a water supply is available. Night is coming on. The best place to make camp is:
   a. Next to the water supply in the ravine.
   b. High on a ridge.
   c. Midway up the slope.
   Your answer_____ Group answer_____

7. Your flashlight glows dimly as you are about to make your way back to the campsite after a brief trip looking for food. Darkness comes quickly in the woods and the surroundings are unfamiliar. You should:
   a. Head back at once, keeping the light on, hoping the light will last long enough.
   b. Put the batteries under your armpit to warm them and then replace them in the flashlight.
   c. Shine the light for a few seconds, get the scene in mind, move a distance, and repeat.
   Your answer_____ Group answer_____

8. An early snow confines you to your small tent. You doze with your small stove going. There is danger if the flame is:
   a. Yellow
   b. Blue
   c. Red
   Your answer_____ Group answer_____

9. You must cross a river that has a strong current, large rocks, and some white water. After carefully selecting your crossing spot, you should:
   a. Leave your boots and pack on.
   b. Take your boots and pack off.
   c. Take off your pack but leave your boots on.
   Your answer_____ Group answer_____

10. Unarmed and unsuspecting, you surprise a large bear prowling around your campsite. As the bear rears up about 10 yards away, you should:
    a. Run.
    b. Climb the nearest tree.
    c. Freeze, but be ready to back away slowly.
    Your answer_____ Group answer_____

Now compare your individual and group answers with the correct answers provided in the Instructor's Manual.

Total Answers Correct: Yours_____ Group's_____

Source: The Wilderness Survival, Interpretive Service: Annual Handbook for Group Facilitators (5th ed.). New York: Monroe County Parks Department, 1976.

QUESTIONS FOR DISCUSSION

1. How many individuals had more correct answers than their group?
2. What might explain the superior performance of those individuals?
3. How many individuals had fewer correct answers than their group? What explains the group's superior performance?
4. This is a task that involves choosing the best option out of more than one possible right answer. Groups can be faced with tasks that are more complex, when the right answers are not always as clear. What conclusions can you draw about the use of groups in certain types of tasks?

Avoiding Team Dysfunctions

The ability of managers and other organizational members to create, maintain, and lead teams is essential to maximizing the performance of an organization in the rapidly changing environment that most organizations face today. According to Patrick M. Lencioni, author of *The Five Dysfunctions of a Team,* effective teams within an organization represent a competitive advantage because they are so powerful and yet so rare. He argues that effective teams are rare because of the following common dysfunctions:

Absence of trust—the lack of open and transparent discussion of opinions, weaknesses, and failures due to distrust of team members.

Fear of conflict—the avoidance or suppression of honest and straightforward differences of opinion due to fear of conflict among team members.

Lack of commitment—the existence of superficial agreement and limited buy-in to a decision due to team members not having a fair say in the process.

Avoidance of accountability—the absence of a willingness to be responsible and hold others accountable due to team members not being clear about goals and expectations.

Inattention to results—the lack of attention to and energy directed to team needs and goals due to team members focusing on their own interests or goals.

Sources: Longenecker, C., et al. (2007). Causes and consequences of managerial failure in rapidly changing organizations. Business Horizons, 50(2), 145–155; Lencioni, P. M. (2002). The Five Dysfunctions of a Team. San Francisco, CA: Jossey-Bass.

QUESTIONS FOR DISCUSSION

1. Using team development techniques and your own experience in teams, provide suggestions for actions you can take in student teams to avoid these dysfunctions.

2. Describe how your suggestions address one or more dysfunctions.

This is the next in a series of journal entries that can be used for class discussion or be compiled and included as input in a self-reflection paper.

Consider your experiences in teams. What leader or team practices contributed to your best experiences? What leader or team practices contributed to your worst experiences? During which developmental behaviours did these experiences occur? List the top three practices to implement in your next team and the top three to avoid.

Eleven

Communicating with Purpose

Communication is a critical part of organizational life. In this chapter, we provide an overview of communication within organizations and describe the four basic steps of the communication process from both a conventional and a sustainable perspective.

Learning Objectives	Conventional OB	Sustainable OB
FOUR-STEP COMMUNICATION PROCESS		
1. Explain the four-step communication process from a conventional and sustainable perspective.	Focuses on how messages are drafted, transmitted, and understood. The emphasis is on efficient communication	Focuses on broader issues of communicating within a community
STEP 1: IDENTIFY YOUR MESSAGE		
2. Explain how a message is identified.	Focus on ideas that will enhance productivity "Sell" ideas and transfer task-based knowledge	Focus on ideas that serve various forms of well-being "Seek" divergent ideas and enhance relational identity formation
STEP 2: ENCODE AND TRANSMIT THE MESSAGE		
3. Describe how a message is encoded and transmitted.	Reduce "noise," choose lean media for routine messages, and emphasize top-down communication	Embrace diversity, facilitate rich messages and media, and emphasize multidirectional communication
STEP 3: RECEIVE AND DECODE THE MESSAGE		
4. Discuss how a message is received and decoded.	Overcome limitations of media and channels "Tune out" non-instrumental ideas and listen as individuals	Emphasize listening "Tune in" diversity and listen as a collective
STEP 4: CONFIRM THE MESSAGE WITH FEEDBACK		
5. Explain how to ensure that the receiver has understood the message.	Feedback: Confirm whether the message has been understood as intended	Feedforward: Seek divergent and reflective feedback

A Bay Worthy of the 21st Century[1]

THE CANADIAN PRESS IMAGES/Rachel Verbin

In Canada, there are only a handful of companies that most of us associate with our past, and Hudson's Bay Company (HBC) is one of them. HBC is a conglomerate that, in addition to the Hudson's Bay department store and its offshoot Home Outfitters in Canada, owns Lord & Taylor and Saks Fifth Avenue in the United States and Galeria Kaufhof in Germany. The company actually has a longer history than our nation, dating back to the 17th century when European settlers traded their manufactured goods for furs from First Nations peoples. From those humble beginnings, the company grew into the nationwide department store we know today as "The Bay," with its huge selection of products ranging from clothing to household items. Nevertheless, The Bay's road to success has definitely included some bumpy patches, and new ones continue to emerge that are reflective of the challenges specific to the 21st century and its increasingly globalized environment. However, with retail guru Liz Rodbell now at the helm, the department store is deep in a revitalization process; consequently, The Bay has finally begun to show promise of regaining its status as a Canadian corporate success story.

The first decade of the new millennium was certainly not the finest for Hudson's Bay, as revenues continually decreased and some retail specialists doubted the company's ability to remain afloat. Industry experts and consumers alike often joked (or lamented) that one could never find someone to help you at a Bay store. Yet in 2008, at the outset of the global recession, American real estate mogul Richard Baker acquired a majority share of the company and began implementing a turnaround strategy. His first order of business: hiring the right people to lead the charge and communicate the change, including Bonnie Brooks, who previously worked at upscale retailer Holt Renfrew, and Rodbell.

The Bay's road to success has definitely included some bumpy patches, and new ones continue to emerge

Today, as Hudson's Bay continues to face increased competition, especially from American retailers such as Nordstrom, Rodbell isn't necessarily concerned with how the department store can "improve." Rather, she approaches the existing retail landscape as an opportunity to evolve, creating and communicating an "exciting" environment for the consumer. This mentality is the driving force behind the many changes The Bay has recently undergone, including the introduction of Topshop and Kleinfeld Bridal, store renovations, and overall re-branding—all of which have proven quite successful thus far in communicating a fresh new image for the organization. Same-store sales have grown substantially since 2010, and retail consultants indicate that this growth is largely due to market share gains as opposed to simply industry growth. Finally, it seems as if Hudson's Bay is back on track and in a position that will make Canadians proud.

The Four-Step Communication Process

| THE 4-STEP PROCESS | IDENTIFY | ENCODE & TRANSMIT | RECEIVE & DECODE | CONFIRM |

Communication is the process of transferring information by using meaningful symbols so that a message is understood by others. In this chapter, we focus on communication among organizational members.

Communication takes place throughout organizations and at all different levels. Most organizational communication occurs when co-workers confer with one another; this is lateral, or horizontal, communication. Other times communication crosses hierarchical levels, such as when managers assign tasks to people in their departments using downward communication, or when members provide information to managers using upward communication. To illustrate how important communication is, consider the fact that managers spend about 75 percent of their time communicating with others in some way or another.[2]

The communication process has four basic steps, as shown in Figure 11.1.[3] In the first step, the sender identifies an idea or a message that is to be communicated. In the second step, the sender transmits the message after deciding how to express it (that is, which medium to use and how to encode the message). In the third step, the receiver receives the message and interprets it. The process by which the receiver attributes meaning to a message is called **decoding**. In the fourth step, information travels from the receiver to the sender, completing the communication cycle and indicating that the message has been understood or that more clarification is needed.

LEARNING OBJECTIVE 1
Explain the four-step communication process from a conventional and sustainable perspective.

Communication is the process of transferring information by using meaningful symbols so that a message is understood by others.

Decoding is the process by which the receiver attributes meaning to a message.

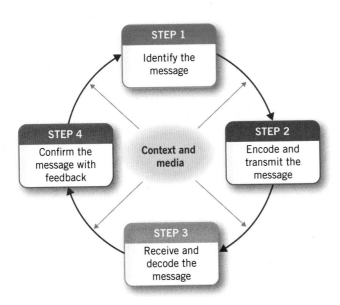

FIGURE 11.1 The Four-Step Communication Process
Source: Adapted from Shannon, C. E., & Weaver, W. (1949). *The mathematical theory of communication.* Urbana-Champaign: University of Illinois Press.

Communication is challenging because moving from one step to the next can be hampered by two factors:

- The *context* in which the communication takes place (for example, a noisy room can make it hard to hear a verbal message).
- The *media* through which the message is transmitted (for example, an email message does not usually convey as much information as a face-to-face conversation).

A conventional approach to communication focuses on how messages are drafted, transmitted, and understood by others. The intent is to ensure that ideas and information travel efficiently from the sender to the receiver in order to enhance overall productivity. From this perspective, communication is considered effective if receivers understand and do what the sender wants them to do.

A sustainable approach, while recognizing the importance of productivity, also focuses on broader issues, such as celebrating diversity, recognizing the context of people's struggles, nurturing interpersonal relationships, and building community (note that the word *community* shares the same root as the word communication).[4] Community is an important contributor to our overall well-being, and it is of particular relevance for OB because organizations are increasingly replacing the neighbourhood as the primary place where social connections occur.[5] According to James Autry, a former *Fortune* 500 executive,

by invoking the metaphor of community, we imply that we in business are bound by a fellowship of endeavor in which we commit to mutual goals, in which we contribute to the best of our abilities, in which there is a forum for all voices to be heard, in which our success contributes to the success of others, in which we can disagree and hold different viewpoints without withdrawing from community, in which we are free to express what we feel as well as what we think, in which our value to society is directly related to the quality of commitment and effort, and in which we all take care of one another.[6]

LEARNING OBJECTIVE 2
Explain how a message is identified.

Step 1: Identify Your Message

| THE 4-STEP PROCESS | **IDENTIFY** | ENCODE & TRANSMIT | RECEIVE & DECODE | CONFIRM |

A **message** is a specific idea or general information that a sender wants to convey to receivers.

The communication process typically begins when a sender (which may be an individual or a group) has a **message**—a specific idea or general information—that needs to be communicated to others. Of special interest to conventional OB are messages that improve an organization's productivity, profitability, or service capacity. Senders must decide which messages are worth communicating and which are not. Because time is a limited organizational resource, organizational members must be selective in the information they communicate.[7]

Filtering occurs when information is withheld or not communicated to others.

Filtering occurs when information is withheld or not communicated to others. It can have either positive or negative outcomes. Filtering is positive if the withheld information is not relevant to the other person. For example, a worker is filtering in a positive way when he does not tell his boss which brand of coffee spilled and ruined his laptop computer. Filtering is negative if the withheld information could help the organization but may harm the sender's self-interest. For example, the worker whose computer was ruined by coffee is filtering in a negative way if he fails to mention that he spilled the coffee on purpose in hope of getting a new computer. As shown in Figure 11.2, it is helpful to think about five different approaches to filtering information, ranging from "spray and pray," in which there is very little filtering, to "withhold and uphold," which uses the most amount of filtering.[8]

- *Spray and Pray*. In this approach, a sender showers co-workers with data, expecting them to sort out the important information. This tactic can overwhelm and confuse those on the receiving end—if they actually take the time to read the information.

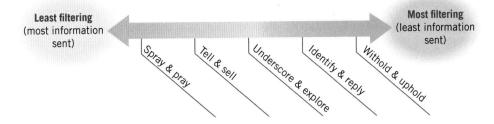

FIGURE 11.2 Approaches to Filtering Information
Source: Adapted from Clampitt, P. G., DeKoch, R. J., & Cashman, T. (2000). A strategy for communicating about uncertainty. *Academy of Management Executive*, *14*(4), 41–57.

- *Tell and Sell.* In this approach a sender tells others what the main issues are and then tries to sell them his or her own preferred solution. Tell-and-sell senders generally aren't interested in getting feedback and input from others. Their communications may take the form of a talking head video presentation or a one-way webcast by a top executive.

- *Underscore and Explore.* This approach is similar to "tell and sell" except that senders explicitly listen to feedback so that they can be aware of potential misunderstandings and address people's concerns. A "town hall" meeting in which executives ask for questions fits this style, but a *preferred* approach is for front-line managers and supervisors to discuss issues in small groups. Of the five approaches, "underscore and explore" is conventionally thought to be the most effective.

- *Identify and Reply.* In this approach, a person holding relevant information sends it to others only when they *explicitly* ask for it. This is a reactive style that puts fires out as they emerge.

- *Withhold and Uphold.* In this approach, the person holding relevant information sends very little of it to others, even when pressed to do so, perhaps in the belief that others will misuse the information or are not capable of understanding it, or because the person fears losing power over others by giving them information. You can recognize this approach when the communicator simply repeats the same message over and over without adding any more information.

To ensure that their messages are not haphazard or random, members sending a message should think about what their organization's overall strategy is and then develop messages consistent with the organization's "micro-stories" and "narrative."[9] For example, to foster a culture of innovation at 3M, employees routinely record and tell stories about breakthrough ideas, processes, and products.[10] At the same time, everyone must be aware of the potential for unintended messages, such as might occur if a manager's message that "mistakes will not be tolerated" inadvertently stifles innovation.[11]

Whereas conventional OB focuses on developing messages that enhance organizational productivity, sustainable OB welcomes messages that go beyond instrumental concerns and give external stakeholders a voice in choosing topics, messages, language, and symbols.[12] For example, sustainable international development agencies welcome the perspective of the people whom they are trying to help. Such agencies recognize that addressing poverty is not at its core a financial issue that is solved by providing poor people with money but, rather, by giving them voice and opportunity. Open-ended interviews with 20,000 poor people from over 40 countries showed that, "Poor people don't talk much about income … While [conventional] poverty measures that focus primarily on consumption and expenditures, education and health are important, they miss important dimensions of poverty, particularly voice and power."[13] This larger idea of communicating with a wide range of stakeholders can also include giving voice to the natural environment as a way to foster ecological sustainability.[14]

In general, sustainable communication is less about "selling" one's preferred ideas to others and more about seeking and welcoming divergent ideas and views. Its receptivity to diversity is consistent with the goal of fostering a healthy community by nurturing an ongoing sense of curiosity, trust, and openness to change. Sustainable managers see nothing wrong with changing their mind.[15] From a sustainable perspective, trying to develop a singular message in which you "think you have it" closes the door to deeper understanding that comes from incorporating insights held by others.[16] This view reflects a paradox: What might seem to be conflicting ideas can be enhanced "if they are held together, like two sides of a coin."[17] Thus, sustainable OB is not simply about reconciling competing views but, rather, about enriching them.

The sustainable emphasis on trust and nurturing long-term relationships in turn contributes to organizational commitment.[18] Peter Aceto, the president and CEO who helped ING Direct weather the storm that began with it being acquired by Scotiabank and continued through it being rebranded as Tangerine Bank, cites trust as one of the most important features within an organization:

> One of the most important lessons I'll take away is how important trust and flexibility within your team is [especially] during periods of change and uncertainty. You can have an ironclad business strategy in place, but when it comes time to meet the immediate needs of the business and get the job done, these are the traits that need to shine through.

As the changes were unfolding, Aceto and his executive team were physically unable to do or even oversee everything; they needed the help and support of their employees across various roles and departments in order to manage the huge volumes of work that were building up in certain functions, such as the contact centre. Even though not all staff members who lent an extra hand during that period had contact centre experience, managers needed to trust that the employees' understanding of the basic organizational values would carry them through, which it did.[19]

<table>
<tr><td>

LEARNING OBJECTIVE 3
Describe how a message is encoded and transmitted.

</td></tr>
</table>

Step 2: Encode and Transmit the Message

| THE 4-STEP PROCESS | IDENTIFY | **ENCODE & TRANSMIT** | RECEIVE & DECODE | CONFIRM |

After identifying the message they want to communicate, senders must decide *how* to communicate it. Senders encode their message when they use symbols and media to transmit it. As described in the OB in Action feature, sometimes messages are encoded and sent, whether intentionally or not, without uttering a word. When **encoding**, senders must perform two tasks:

Encoding is putting a message in understandable terms by using symbols and media.

1. Identify any communication barriers that must be overcome.
2. Choose the medium and channel to transmit the message.

Identify and Overcome Communication Barriers

Noise refers to potential barriers that may impede communication at all four steps of the communication process.

When choosing how to encode a message, the sender must be aware of potential barriers that could cause the message to be misunderstood—sometimes called **noise**—and may impede communication at any of the four steps of the process. Sometimes noise can be literal, such as when workers are trying to talk over the rumble of machinery or when there is a poor cell phone connection. At other times, noise is more figurative, such as when the receiver is being distracted by something else or when the sender's choice of wording causes the receiver to question the sender's intentions. For example, a Vancouver television news anchor picked up a word, "canoodling," from an interview and used it to unknowingly

Your Seat at the Table Sends a Message

© Squaredpixels/iStockphoto

The importance of some communication media is not always obvious, but an organization's processes, culture, structures, and systems are all communication media. Organizations send messages simply by the way they are designed.

Proxemics is the study of the way physical space conveys messages. For example, seating arrangements around a table influence the nature of the communication that takes place between participants. Sitting next to a person signals collaboration, sitting in a corner with someone is associated with conversation, sitting directly across from someone can be perceived as either conversational or confrontational, and sitting diagonally across a table is the preferred position if two people need to share the same space but do not wish to interact.

Informal rules suggest that in business meetings, the most powerful seat—reserved for the manager or perhaps an important client—is at the head of the table facing the entrance to the room. However, if the goal of the meeting is team building, the boss will symbolically step down from power and sit in a middle chair. People seated at either side are strong supporters of the boss, especially the person seated at the boss's right; people in the middle tend to be those who listen to all points of view; and the person at the foot of the table is often the one who voices concerns that challenge the leader. Given all of these nuances with seating location around a rectangular table, perhaps it is not surprising that people prefer round tables when in negotiations because they believe round tables ease tension.

QUESTIONS FOR DISCUSSION

1. Do you have a favourite seat in the classroom or lunch cafeteria or at your family dinner table?
2. What might your seating patterns say about you and your friends and family?
3. Predict what would happen if you were to sit in a different position than you normally do. Try it out and see if your prediction was right.

---

proposition the weather anchor. He thought canoodling meant "chatting," but the meaning is closer to "kissing and caressing."[20]

Noise may also occur when there are personality differences or ongoing conflicts between the sender and the receiver or when there is a history of mistrust among members of the organization. Of course, communication is made easier when the relationship between the sender and the receiver is friendly.[21]

Time is another general barrier to communication, including both the time needed to prepare a message and the time needed for a receiver to interpret it. Senders often underestimate how long it takes to fully communicate a major message, which in some cases can be a year or more.[22] Senders must work hard at finding ways to take complex ideas and present them as succinct messages. This insight is captured by an executive who described how at the end of a long letter someone had apologized, saying, "If I had had more time, I would've written a shorter letter."[23]

Ambiguous words and symbols can also be a barrier to communication. Consider the mixed message sent when the speaker's body language does not fit the words, such as an executive frowning while giving a well-deserved bonus to an employee. Sometimes people forget how significant non-verbal cues can be. Research shows that smiling at others makes the person who is doing the smiling feel happier (even if it is a forced smile), causes people who see the smile to feel happier and smile more, and increases the interpersonal connectedness between both parties.[24] Displays of happiness by leaders promotes co-operation and prosocial behaviour in organizations, and displays of happiness by front-line workers is associated with higher levels of customer satisfaction and perceptions of quality service.[25]

As evident in the My OB feature "Communicating across Cultures," problems relating to ambiguous words and symbols become magnified when communicating from one culture to another, because similar gestures or actions may be interpreted very differently in different

Focus Features/Photofest

Bill Murray and Scarlett Johansson earned acclaim for their roles in *Lost in Translation*. The movie illustrates the stress that is caused by cross-cultural living and communication, and the difficulties of decoding meanings across cultures. These challenges can lead employees of multinational organizations to communicate mostly with others who belong to their own culture. For example, in a study that looked at Danish managers who were working at a Saudi Arabian subsidiary of their company, the managers communicated primarily among themselves. This resulted in increased segregation, discrimination, and negative emotions between the different nationalities in the organization.

Researchers have identified several ways to help people working overseas to improve their ability to communicate in their new setting. First, attempts should be made to intentionally integrate people from the different cultures working together. Second, as language differences are a significant barrier to communication, expatriate employees (those working outside their home country) should be provided with the time and training to learn the local language where they are working. And third, efforts should be made to select employees who have the predisposition and attitudes to excel in an overseas assignment.

QUESTIONS FOR REFLECTION

1. Do you know students or others who have worked and lived in a foreign country for an extended period of time? What were some challenges and joys for them when they were communicating overseas?
2. Do you have a friend or classmate from another country or culture? What lessons have you learned about cross-cultural communication from interacting with his or her?
3. What can people do to improve cross-cultural communication within organizations?

---

cultures. Challenges related to cross-cultural communication may be especially noticeable in job interviews or other forms of negotiation, which can be stressful enough even in your first language and your home culture. A study conducted by professors at the University of Waterloo examined the differences between Canadians and Chinese students in their use and interpretation of body language in negotiation settings. The researchers noted some definite similarities in the usage and interpretation of certain actions, such as smiling and leaning forward. However, the differences between the two groups' usage and interpretation of some actions were found to be even more telling.

According to these researchers, in Canada we tend to communicate liking and engagement through the use of eye contact, while in Chinese cultures direct eye contact is used to communicate negative feelings. Another example of cultural differences and expectations concerns gazes. The Canadian students tended to look away from their negotiating partner whenever they felt uncomfortable or negatively about the person. Conversely, when the Chinese students lowered their gaze it was taken as a show of respect for their negotiating partner.[26]

Semantic problems arise when words have different meanings for people who are from different demographic groups or who have had different experiences.

Even people who speak the same language may not always understand one another. **Semantic problems** arise when words have different meanings for people who are from different demographic groups or who have had different experiences. For example, after reading this book you will be able to talk with your classmates about the differences between conventional OB and sustainable OB, but your co-workers who have not studied OB or read this book may not know what you mean by these terms when you use them, say, in reference to your boss's approach to communicating.

Choose Communication Media and Channels

Medium is the vehicle that is used to carry a message from the sender to the receiver.

The communication **medium** is the vehicle that carries a message from the sender to the receiver. Deciding on the appropriate medium to use is an important consideration for organizations. For example, should an employee who has accomplished a noteworthy achievement be sent a letter of congratulations from the CEO, be presented with a plaque at a departmental meeting, be featured in an organizational newsletter, or be praised in an organization-wide email? What sorts of media should an organization invest in—should all employees be provided with iPads, or should workspaces be designed to increase opportunities for informal face-to-face chats around the "water cooler"? Should members be encouraged to travel and meet clients in person, or should the organization invest in videoconferencing technology? These are meaningful decisions because the medium becomes part of the message, as described in the My OB feature "Impersonally Delivering What Is Personal."

A quality that is helpful to consider when choosing a communication medium is **media richness**, a medium's ability to resolve ambiguity. The richer a medium, the greater its capacity to provide quick responses (email is faster than regular mail), facilitate emotional connection (face-to-face is richer than video), and express a variety of cues (videophone is richer than regular phone).[27] Research suggests that managers generally prefer richer media when communicating non-routine information and prefer leaner media when communicating routine information.[28]

As shown in Figure 11.3, face-to-face communication is the richest medium because it allows participants not only to hear the content of each other's messages and their tone of voice, but also to see subtle body language. Face-to-face communication can take place one-on-one or within a group, where it can serve to facilitate the formation of a group identity. Because this medium also allows for instant feedback—such as a puzzled expression—it provides much more information than, say, memos.

Research suggests that in a face-to-face exchange, the actual words spoken may account for less than 20 percent of the information communicated.[29] Another 30 percent is accounted for by the vocal characteristics of the message, and approximately 50 percent is attributed to facial expressions and body language. Given this richness it is not surprising that, when considering relationship-building opportunities with their bosses, about 90 percent of employees prefer face-to-face communication over other media. Managers report that about 70 percent of their interaction time with subordinates is face-to-face. Despite these preferences, about 40 percent of both managers and employees say they have seen an increase in the use of email.[30] Of course, face-to-face communication also has its shortcomings, and organizational members often prefer written messages that can be more efficiently transmitted to many people at once.[31]

> **Media richness** refers to a communication medium's ability to resolve ambiguity.

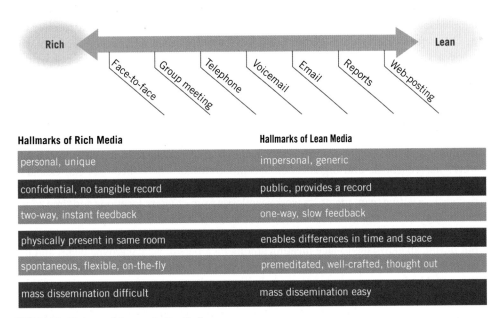

FIGURE 11.3 Richness of Communication Media
Source: Adapted from Daft, R. L., Lengel, R. H., & Trevino, L. K. (1987). Message equivocality, media selection, and manager performance: Implications for information systems. *MIS Quarterly, 11*(3), 355–366.

MOB | IMPERSONALLY DELIVERING WHAT IS PERSONAL

Paramount Pictures/ Photofest

Communicating negative feedback can be stressful for both the sender and the recipient. Research shows that people generally prefer to send negative feedback impersonally, such as via email, and that an impersonal medium is often more accurate and honest. Even so, social norms in organizations still favour delivering negative feedback face-to-face, perhaps because face-to-face communication helps to improve understanding and co-operation.

Using the movie *Up in the Air* as an example again, the character Natalie (played by Anna Kendrick) promotes the use of videoconference technology to deliver remotely the bad news of getting fired. Ironically, while on a business trip to experience the in-person method of delivering a firing with her client Ryan (played by George Clooney), Natalie receives a text message from her boyfriend saying he is breaking up with her. Ultimately, although delivering the bad news face-to-face proves difficult, extreme negative reactions to the impersonal method of delivery forces Ryan's company to abandon the idea of adopting the proposed videoconferencing program.

QUESTIONS FOR REFLECTION

1. Think about experiences you have had in the workplace or in the classroom when you received or provided bad news. Was the news communicated face-to-face, by telephone, or electronically?
2. In what situations would you find the in-person approach to be the most appropriate, and when would you prefer another method?
3. What relevant advantages and disadvantages did you consider?

Telephone calls are also quite rich, because the participants receive many verbal cues, although they don't receive visual cues. A voice mail is even leaner than a telephone conversation because it offers even fewer cues and no immediate feedback.

Media that emphasize the written word—such as texts, emails, intranets, and regular memos and letters—are leaner still, because they offer neither verbal nor visual cues, and they do not allow for immediate feedback. Some people try to add emotional richness to written messages by using a combination of punctuation symbols called emoticons. For example, the emoticon ;-) represents a wink. Written communication is useful when a lot of detailed information needs to be transmitted, especially if it is information the receiver will need to refer to in the future. Emails are also effective between senders and receivers who enjoy a strong working relationship and trust each other.[32] Impersonal formal written documents—including unaddressed bulletins, mass emails, and numeric reports—may offer detailed data but are considered very lean communication media because they do not build on known interpersonal relationships and understandings.

Computer-mediated communication is becoming increasingly prevalent in organizations. Some commentators have even suggested that email may soon be as obsolete as fax machines and that employees will prefer faster alternatives like text messages, social networks like Facebook, and organization-specific networks where members can exchange messages, pictures, and documents.[33] Computer-mediated media offer tantalizing possibilities, such as letting team members work seamlessly from different locations and time zones, but they also have some shortcomings. Trust is more difficult to develop without face-to-face communication, and a lack of trust can limit the sharing of information and knowledge. But having an early face-to-face meeting among members of virtual groups helps, and it is easier to build trust in a collaborative context than in a competitive organizational context. Video and audioconferencing may also help develop trust, although more slowly, and these media can result in a fragile trust that is vulnerable to opportunistic behaviour.

In any case, new technologies in communication media in the past two decades have contributed to explosive growth in the amount of information that is transmitted in organizations. This has resulted in several problems (see My OB: Trouble for Organizations When Members Text and Tweet?), including a phenomenon known as "information overload." As one manager feeling overwhelmed by email put it: "Previously I did not know what I was missing, and I was really happy in that ignorance. Now I get information, and I think 'I really should read this,' and I can't, I really don't have the time, and I feel really inadequate."[34] Of course, rather than seeing emails and text messages as *interruptions* to daily work, we can see them as the new way of communicating and performing on the job.[35]

We should also consider the strengths and the preferences of senders and receivers when we choose the medium. Some senders are gifted at writing reports, others at telling stories that capture the essence of their message, others at presenting engaging figures and charts, and so on. Similarly, some receivers prefer emails; others, the telephone; and others, face-to-face meetings. Communication works best when there is a match between the preferred media of the sender and that of the receiver. Often it is a good idea to send a message using various media and various messengers to cover all the bases.

Once the sender has selected the medium, he or she completes the encoding process by choosing a **channel**—the pathway the message travels to communicate the message. The channels can be direct or indirect. For example, a CEO might send a message about an impending organizational change directly to front-line workers, or she might use an indirect chain-like approach and send the message to managers, who in turn talk to supervisors,

> A **channel** is the pathway along which a message travels through a medium.

M⦻B | TROUBLE FOR ORGANIZATIONS WHEN MEMBERS TEXT AND TWEET?

© Squaredpixels/ iStockphoto

Ever since computers and access to the Internet became commonplace in offices, organizations have tried to control the amount of personal emailing and web surfing that goes on in the workplace. The same goes for newer social media like tweeting and texting. The main concerns are that employees are spending company time on personal pursuits, or that they may inadvertently provide "secret" information to competitors. Another area of concern is the possibility of employees making statements that are potentially harmful to an organization's image and/or reputation.

For example, players in the National Hockey League are not permitted to use Twitter from two hours before game time until after their post-game interviews. Other professional sports leagues, such as the NFL and NBA, impose similar restrictions on their players with the intent of preventing them from (inadvertently) making statements in the heat of the moment that they might regret later, or from saying things that their opposition could potentially use against them during the game. Major League Baseball takes these prohibitions one step further and has even developed a social media policy for its athletes, which includes not posting racial, sexist, homophobic, antireligious, or other potentially offensive or harmful content. This includes a ban on criticizing umpires!

In a business context, inappropriate tweets that reveal sensitive information can definitely get you in trouble, as a CFO for American

fashion retailer Francesca's Holdings Corp. discovered. The CFO tweeted and posted on Facebook light-hearted comments about board meetings, but the company did not think that passing on insider information was a laughing matter, so they fired him. In another example, a 22-year-old waitress was fired from the Brixx restaurant in Charlotte, North Carolina, for posting a derogatory comment on her personal Facebook account that complained about unnamed customers, a couple, who, after having occupied a table for three hours, left a mere $5 tip.

If you're still not convinced that what you post to your personal social media account may affect you professionally, consider that a recent survey by the Society of Human Resource Management revealed that a third of companies with social media policies took disciplinary actions in the span of one year for employee violations.

QUESTIONS FOR REFLECTION

1. Without giving specific examples, how many times have you sent an impulsive message that you regretted later?
2. How frequently do you check your email or texts? Do you do so at work or in class?
3. Do you think the frequency with which you do so has a negative influence on your job or the classroom?
4. What suggestions do you have for employers (and classroom instructors) regarding this issue?

who in turn tell the front-line workers about it. The direct approach is faster, but research suggests that employees prefer receiving information from their immediate supervisor rather than from senior managers.[36] However, indirect channels can result in poor communication, because each step in the channel usually results in a loss of information.

The **grapevine** is the information network along which unofficial information flows. The grapevine can carry both organizational information (such as rumours about an impending merger) and personal information (such as details about who gets along with whom). It provides a valuable window into what is important to organizational members. The grapevine helps employees meet their needs for social interaction, and it is a fast and efficient channel of communication. Sometimes the grapevine passes inaccurate information, but rumours in organizational settings have consistently had accuracy rates around 80 percent or higher.[37]

Sustainable and conventional encoding processes are similar but have two important differences. First, many of the barriers seen as "noise" in the conventional approach are viewed as opportunities for improvement in the sustainable approach. A sustainable approach accepts that differences and diversity among stakeholders can never be overcome—because people *are* different and diverse—and it also recognizes that this multiplicity of views can be a source of strength and insight. Thus, any effort to create a communication system that circumvents or suppresses these differences misses out on a chance to enrich community in the organization.

This approach is evident among CEOs who deliberately choose people for their top management team who have strengths that are different from their own; they recognize such diversity as a key to the company's success.[38] Sustainable OB not only welcomes diverse noise within the organization, it is also more likely to embrace such noise from outside by deliberately communicating collaboratively with external stakeholders.[39] This approach emphasizes **deliberative dialogue**, multi-way communication that allows stakeholders to learn from one another what is best for the overall community.[40] For example, one study showed that it was much more productive for everyone concerned when various stakeholders in a community met in a structured setting to deliberately discuss their ecological concerns about a local river than it was when stakeholders discussed these issues in a less deliberately structured way.[41]

The second difference is that, while sustainable OB and conventional OB may use identical media and channels, each approach has different intentions and outcomes. For example, in some organizations the use of email and other technology has resulted in a greater concentration of power and control in the hands of managers who use them to micromanage employees. In other organizations, the same media and channels enhance participative management, such as when decision-making opportunities increase for front-line employees thanks to the additional information they can easily access.[42]

Whereas a conventional emphasis on efficiency may favour impersonal media or channels, a sustainable approach generally favours face-to-face communication to foster collaboration and stronger relationships.[43] One study of friendships among young people suggests that the choice of medium may determine the quality of interpersonal relationships. Online friendships seem to be weaker than off-line relationships, include a narrower range of shared topics, and be less personal.[44] Other research suggests that once online friendships are well established, they can be just as strong and, for some people, more intimate than off-line relationships.[45]

Step 3: Receive and Decode the Message

THE 4-STEP PROCESS | IDENTIFY | ENCODE & TRANSMIT | **RECEIVE & DECODE** | CONFIRM

In the third step, the receiver attributes meaning to the message through a process called decoding. The decoding process mirrors the encoding process and thus has two similar components. First, like senders, receivers must be aware of the potential for noise and barriers to communication that may impede their understanding of the message. For example, if a receiver does not trust a sender, then the receiver will tend to have a skeptical interpretation of the message. Second, the communication medium and the channel can affect the richness and meaning of a message. A personalized "thank you" for a job well done from the CEO is decoded quite differently than is a form letter sent from an unknown staffer in the human resources department.

The most important decoding skill is being a good listener. The simple act of listening contributes to understanding and helps to create general positive feelings. Being a good listener is hard work, and it is much more difficult than speaking. We often confuse simply "hearing" a message with truly "receiving" it. Good listeners are able to focus and absorb what another person is trying to communicate.[46] They focus on the words and other messages being communicated—including the sender's tone, body language, and word choice—as well as what is *not* being said. Non-verbal communication is especially important in this regard, although people are generally poor at detecting deception,[47] despite the existence of research suggesting that some non-verbal indicators (like touching the hair or covering the mouth) increase in frequency among deceptive senders, while others (like simple hand gestures) decrease.[48] Table 11.1 describes the characteristics of active and poor listeners.

Active listening requires the ability to block out noise and distractions, but what are considered "distractions" from a conventional perspective may be viewed as valuable messages from a sustainable perspective, and vice versa. Consider the example of the renowned violinist Joshua Bell, who accepted an invitation from the *Washington Post* to dress up like a common street entertainer and play his $3.5 million Stradivarius violin in a subway station during rush hour. Hardly anyone took time to "decode" Bell's beautiful message. Indeed, of the 1,097 people who passed by him during his 43-minute concert, only 7 stopped to listen for more than a minute. When watching the video of his performance afterward, the feedback that Bell found particularly painful was what happened right after each musical piece ended—*nothing* happened; no applause, no acknowledgement. He said of the experience, "I'm surprised at the number of people who don't pay attention at all, as if I'm invisible. Because, you know what? I'm makin' a lot of noise!"[49]

We often admire people who focus so well on a task that they can tune out distractions. Joshua Bell was able to tune out the distractions while playing violin in a busy subway station (which is good), but the unreceptive commuters were also able to tune out Bell's beautiful music (which may not be so good). This example draws attention to the huge role of context in receiving and decoding messages. What some people think of as the most beautiful music ever composed in one context is considered "noise" in another. Context is equally important in organizations, and members must ensure that the context promotes the messages they encode and send, or decode and receive. In a conventional approach, the context or "frame" of organizational communication is focused on achieving results and competing with others.[50] In a sustainable approach, the larger frame or context emphasizes balancing and enhancing multiple forms of well-being.

TABLE 11.1 Hallmarks of Active and Poor Listening

Active Listening	Poor Listening
– Concentrating on verbal and non-verbal messages	– Letting the mind wander, thinking of what to say next
– Keeping an open mind, assimilating information	– Anticipating and prejudging what the person will say, showing impatience
– Providing feedback, paraphrasing, clarifying	– Assuming the message was understood as intended
– Making eye contact, nodding, mirroring body language	– Being easily distracted (such as by texting or multi-tasking)

Another difference between the conventional approach and the sustainable approach in this communication step is that, whereas conventional decoding tends to occur at the individual level, sustainable decoding occurs more often at the group level.[51] The sustainable tendency to embrace diverse voices and multiple forms of well-being influences the very nature of listening.[52] Whereas the conventional approach emphasizes listening to acquire knowledge, sustainable decoding highlights how listening contributes to the formation of a group's identity. Sustainable listening is not about filling our minds with thoughts about what to *do;* rather, it is about who we *are* and what we do *in relation to others.* Decoding is therefore oriented toward achieving mutual understanding, which is more than simply the linear transfer of knowledge from one person to the next.[53]

Consider what happened when Larry Mauws, then CEO of Winnipeg-based Westward Industries, announced to his employees that the company was going to completely redesign its main product, a three-wheeled car used by parking patrol officers throughout the United States. This major change, based largely on customer feedback, created a time of collective decoding. **Collective decoding** occurs when a message is interpreted by a group of two or more people, with the result that each member learns more than any one member could learn alone (and typically more than the sender could have put into the original message). On a basic level, everyone in the organization understood Mauws's message: they needed to redesign the car so that it had specific additional features. On a deeper level, however, the decoding took weeks and months of work because it required members to reconsider their overall work and the identity of the organization. At this deeper level, the message could not be fully decoded by any one person, not even by Mauws himself. Rather, to understand what it meant to make a new car required members to relearn their own tasks in the context of their interrelationships with the work of the people around them.[54]

The notion of collective decoding is important in the larger process of organizational learning because developing a shared language is a prerequisite for shared understanding.[55] Organizational members have many good ideas, but most of those ideas are never implemented because they haven't been collectively decoded. If the group does not understand the implications of new ideas, it cannot implement them.[56]

When collective decoding occurs, members understand ideas more fully and are less likely to resist them. If all members have their voices heard, they are more likely to accept decisions—even decisions not in their own self-interest—because they understand how the change benefits the whole. This kind of decoding involves not only hearing the words and content of the message being sent, it also involves a deeper relational acknowledgement of the sender as a person. Collective decoding recognizes and respects the unique knowledge that each member brings to the organization, thereby providing the opportunity to create new meanings that are richer than either the sender or a single receiver could come up with on their own.[57]

In sum, decoding a message can be challenging. The more we understand about the context and history of a situation, the more deeply we are able to understand the message. Thus, one person or group may decode a message quite differently from another. This is why feedback (Step 4) is so important.

Collective decoding occurs when a message is interpreted by a group of two or more people with the result that each member learns more than any one member could alone (and typically more than the sender could have put into the original message).

Step 4: Confirm the Message with Feedback

THE 4-STEP PROCESS | IDENTIFY | ENCODE & TRANSMIT | RECEIVE & DECODE | **CONFIRM**

This final step of the communication process involves the receiver using **feedback** to let the sender know whether the message has been received as intended. This step is essentially a repeat of the first three steps, except that the roles of sender and receiver are reversed.

LEARNING OBJECTIVE 5
Explain how to ensure that the receiver has understood the message.

Feedback lets the sender know whether the message has been received as intended.

Sometimes feedback is as simple as clicking "Reply" and writing a brief note to confirm that an email message was received and that a request has been fulfilled as instructed. At other times confirmation is more complicated, especially when the receiver does not fully understand what the message means or how to respond to it. In such cases, it is often helpful for the receiver to choose a richer medium for feedback than the medium in which the original message was sent. For example, a worker who is unclear about how to interpret a written policy regarding sick days should talk to his or her manager or, if appropriate, call someone from the human resources department and get clarification.

Feedback has several benefits. First, it provides the chance to confirm that the original message was received as intended. Sometimes feedback is evident in the receiver's non-verbal behaviour; a puzzled look makes it clear that additional information is needed, while non-compliance suggests that a request may not have been understood. Face-to-face communication provides immediate feedback, making it easier to paraphrase messages and ask clarifying questions. In this way feedback is similar to active listening.

The second benefit of feedback is that it provides an opportunity for the original sender to learn something new that will help create a new and improved message. For example, if a salesperson often receives a blank look when describing a certain feature of the product he or she is promoting, then it may be time to rethink how that feature is presented or reconsider whether it's valuable enough to be worth presenting at all.

Perhaps the most important aspect of feedback is the constructive criticism that it can provide. **Constructive criticism** is a serious examination or judgement delivered in a way that is intended to help the receiver to improve.[58] Constructive criticism works best if it seeks to help the person to whom it is being given (versus seeking to promote the relative status of the person sending it); deals with issues the receiver can change; is provided in manageable doses; and is descriptive and specific. Research suggests that most organizational members are hesitant to provide critical upward communication. In one survey, 85 percent of respondents indicated that they had been unable to raise an issue or concern with their manager even though they thought it was important.[59] This is consistent with the finding that managers tend not only to fail to accept criticism but that they also often denounce those who provide it (the "shoot the messenger" effect).[60] Indeed, the design of organizational communication systems often keeps decision makers "blind" to potentially helpful but challenging information.[61]

After Bill Gates's sales managers at Microsoft received market feedback that the promotional events for the company's new product launches were too technical and boring, they decided to stage a Broadway-style musical in a New York City theatre. But this idea didn't work well either and very little product information got through, which resulted in even more negative feedback from the market. Gates sent the sales managers an email that essentially said, "Better to have tried to do something interesting and failed than to do the same old event still one more time. It was a fiasco, sure. Now, learn from the mistakes we made and move on."[62]

Both conventional and sustainable approaches to communication seek to ensure that messages are received accurately, but a sustainable approach places greater emphasis on seeking out constructive upward feedback to enhance future communications. Research indicates that, in organizations where leaders welcome such feedback, they also tend to value differences; work well with people who hold different points of view; are open to new ideas and ways of doing things; and are perceived as friendly, approachable, and empathetic.[63]

A sustainable approach to communication also places greater emphasis on creating positive **feedforward communication**, the combination of relationships and prior communication that influences subsequent messages.[64] Feedforward communication can be negative and perpetuate a vicious cycle, or it can be positive and reinforce a virtuous cycle. At Omega, a 400-employee organization that provides residential care in Ireland, mid-level

Constructive criticism is a serious examination or judgement delivered in a way that is intended to help the receiver to improve.

Feedforward communication is the combination of relationships and prior communication that influences subsequent messages.

managers felt ignored by senior managers, who had a history of ignoring feedback from others below. After one frustrating encounter with the head office, a mid-level manager described whose voices were heard at meetings:

> There had been maybe 20 people at the previous meeting. But the only people that had [been recorded in the] minutes or made points were the head office staff. In eight pages there was nothing that I would have said, that anyone [other than top management] would have said. It was as if we weren't there. [65]

When top managers clearly—even if unintentionally—suggest in their feedforward communication that they have no interest in building community with mid-level managers, then mid-level managers will subsequently limit the sorts of messages and feedback they communicate to the head office. This may have certain short-term efficiencies, but it will minimize long-term organizational learning.

In contrast, consider James Despain's experience as the manager of Caterpillar Inc.'s 3,000-employee Track-Type Tractors Division. Despain's decision to make himself vulnerable by trusting everyone in the organization created the context for employees to engage in critical upward communication, consistent with the motto "Share information in all directions, both good news and bad news." As Despain described it,

> Instead of being forceful or loud in an effort to get our individual ways, we started to listen, really listen, to what others were trying to say. Instead of hurting feelings as sensitive issues surfaced, we began to practice real respect. We lost our need for ownership of ideas and began giving meaningful recognition to others. Our collective ideas were more innovative and powerful. [66]

Despain's feedforward communication helped to undo antagonistic union–management dynamics, and soon hourly and salaried members began to treat one another with more respect and dignity. Everyone at Caterpillar changed, from top managers to hourly workers, thanks to the growing influence of its virtuous cycle of communication. Employees' approval of management rose by more than 30 percent; there was a 25 percent increase in employee participation, satisfaction, and accountability; and workers' identification with the organization's goals jumped by 40 percent. Before long the division, which had been losing tens of millions of dollars a year, was again profitable. [67]

lessons in teaching abroad[68]

Courtesy of Bruno Dyck

Every year, numerous organizations facilitate international job placements for thousands of people to work abroad as teachers. Perhaps the most common of these jobs is to provide English language instruction in China, which is certainly a job that comes with high demands in terms of communication skills.

Based on the conventional four-step communication model described in this chapter, it would seem to make sense for these teachers to (1) begin by preparing their curriculum (message) before their departure to their overseas assignment (this might include gathering books on grammar or assembling resources on written and oral language exercises); (2) familiarize themselves with their overseas school's facilities and the available media (whiteboards, projectors, etc.) for teaching in creative ways to deliver their message; (3) minimize distractions for their students and ensure that they can focus on and listen to the teacher; and (4) develop feedback systems by asking questions and providing quizzes and tests to ensure that the knowledge is being adequately received by the students.

Although these four steps seem logical and rational, it turns out that many teachers who go abroad actually describe their work very differently. In particular, they say the key to their communication success starts at the fourth step, with an emphasis on feedforward knowledge. They describe the need to get to know the context and norms of the people they are teaching in order to communicate effectively. Moreover, as is evident in the following quote from an overseas teacher, those who teach abroad say they learn a lot more than they are able to teach:

> As an international person going somewhere, you will quite probably learn more than you will ever share. So it's a reverse knowledge transfer. You may think that you are going to teach things, when in fact you are going to learn more than you will ever teach.

This sensitivity to feedforward knowledge in turn has an effect on the content of what is taught (Step 1). For example, teachers of English learn that their grammar books often fail to capture the style of the English language as it is spoken, and that they themselves do not speak "proper" English. As another overseas teacher noted:

> According to the grammar books we should not be saying, "What are you doing tomorrow?" We should say, "What will you do tomorrow?" or "What are you going to do tomorrow?" . . . But that isn't the way we speak, and so when you teach the students . . . you learn much more about how you use the language.

In addition to shaping the content of the message that teachers identify as important (Step 1), feedforward communication also influences the way teachers encode and transmit the message (Step 2). In particular, rather than consider a face-to-face interaction that does not unfold as expected to be a distraction or consider it as "noise" to be overcome, these teachers see it as an opportunity to understand how to improve subsequent communication. The key, they say, is to see themselves as learners rather than as teachers:

> The most successful person cross-culturally, I think, is one who goes in as a learner. If they have the attitude that they have to "learn from the people I'm with," they will succeed. Be flexible, open to new ideas, new ways of doing, be willing to try things, always with the attitude of being a learner.

And finally, feedforward communication also has an effect on the process of receiving and decoding the message (Step 3). The emphasis is on building trust, respect, and relationships, and this bridge in turn facilitates the subsequent teaching of task-based knowledge. One overseas teacher put it this way:

> [You won't be very effective in your job] if you go in and say, "I'm going to help these people," and "I'm going to teach them so much." [Rather, you will be much more effective] if you go in saying, "What can they teach you?" "What can I learn?" Then you learn from each other and you build the respect, the relationships.

QUESTIONS FOR DISCUSSION

1. In our shrinking global village, international job postings are becoming increasingly commonplace. Sending people to work abroad is a way for knowledge to travel both ways across borders and cultures. Do you agree that people going overseas should expect to learn more than they will teach?
2. Do you think the emphasis on feedforward communication is more important in cross-cultural settings than it is when communicating with people who share a common culture and language? Explain.
3. What do you think should be selection criteria used by organizations that place teachers abroad? What are the key personality traits they should be looking for?

Summary

Communication can be understood as a four-step process that includes choosing a message, encoding and transmitting the message, receiving and decoding the message, and providing feedback to confirm and enhance the communication process.

 Learning Objectives

- Explain the four-step communication process from a conventional and sustainable perspective.

- Explain how a message is identified.

- Describe how a message is encoded and transmitted.

- Discuss how a message is received and decoded.

- Explain how to ensure that the receiver has understood the message.

From a conventional OB perspective, the four-step communication process proceeds as follows:

- Send messages that enhance productivity; use top-down communication; filter out non-instrumental messages; verify understanding of messages.
- First, messages consistent with improving organizational performance are crafted.
- Second, messages are encoded and transmitted based on an attempt to reduce "noise," with a bias toward choosing (efficient) large-scale and written communication media and channels for routine messages.
- Third, receivers decode messages individually, tuning out distractions so as to maximize the amount of knowledge being acquired.
- Fourth, receivers provide feedback to the sender to confirm that the message was understood as intended.

From a sustainable OB perspective, the four-step communication process proceeds as follows:

- Send messages that enhance well-being, and seek divergent ideas; use multidirectional communication; emphasize listening; feedforward.
- First, messages consistent with a wide variety of perspectives about how to enhance collective well-being are crafted.
- Second, messages are encoded and transmitted based on an attempt to embrace diversity, with a bias toward choosing face-to-face communication media and channels for multi-layered messages.
- Third, receivers decode messages collectively, paying attention to the meaning messages have for their co-workers so as to enhance relational understanding in the organization.
- Fourth, receivers provide feedback to the sender and use feedforward information previously received from others to enhance the meaning of messages.

Key Terms

Channel (p. 247)

Collective decoding (p. 250)

Communication (p. 239)

Constructive criticism (p. 251)

Decoding (p. 239)

Deliberative dialogue (p. 248)

Encoding (p. 242)

Feedback (p. 250)

Feedforward communication (p. 251)

Filtering (p. 240)

Grapevine (p. 248)

Media richness (p. 245)

Medium (p. 244)

Message (p. 240

Noise (p. 242)

Semantic problems (p. 244)

Questions for Reflection and Discussion

1. Identify and briefly describe the four steps of the communication process. What are the key similarities and differences between a conventional and a sustainable approach to the communication process? Explain.

2. Explain why upward constructive criticism seems to be such a challenge in the conventional approach.

3. Why is context important in decoding a message? Give an example.

4. What is the difference between treating contextual features as "noise" that *hampers* the communication process versus thinking of them as "diversity" that *enhances* the communication process?

5. Think of a time when you experienced "collective decoding"— that is, when your own understanding of a message was enhanced because you were interpreting it with others. Was the sender of the message part of the process of decoding it? Do you think the message you understood after this process was clearer and more complete than the original message sent? Explain your answer. (Hint: Think of communications you have experienced in study groups.)

6. Explain the difference between rich and lean communication media. Which criteria should be used to select a medium for a given message?

ob activities

SELF-ASSESSMENT EXERCISE

Where Are You along the Conventional–Sustainable Continuum?

Checking off the appropriate box in each case, indicate the extent to which the two comparison statements fit you best. Rankings of 1 or 5 indicate strong agreement with the statement closest to the number, whereas a 3 indicates you are undecided or neutral.

To communicate effectively in organizations, I should:

Focus on messages that will enhance productivity.	① ② ③ ④ ⑤	Welcome messages related to any facet of organizational well-being.
Focus on messages that are consistent with my own view.	① ② ③ ④ ⑤	Welcome messages that represent diverging views.
Choose media and channels that reduce noise and expense.	① ② ③ ④ ⑤	Choose media and channels that embrace diversity and richness.
Decode messages in a way that tunes out non-instrumental distractions.	① ② ③ ④ ⑤	Decode messages in a way that looks for hidden differences and opportunities.
Focus on the content of messages.	① ② ③ ④ ⑤	Focus on the relational implications of messages.
Seek confirmation that messages were received.	① ② ③ ④ ⑤	Decode messages collectively as intended.
Expect critical upward communication to be poorly received.	① ② ③ ④ ⑤	Expect critical upward communication to be well-received.

Key: These questions measure your views about the four mains steps of the communication process. The 1s & 2s reflect conventional tendencies, and the 4s & 5s represent sustainable tendencies. Add up your scores. A sum of 21 means you do not tend to favour one approach over the other, a sum of 20 or lower suggests you prefer a conventional approach, and a sum of 22 or higher suggests you tend to favour a sustainable approach. Your score gives you a sense of the kind of communicator you want to become as well as a sense of the kind of organization you would prefer to work in.

As part of the marketing strategy for a product, the producer changed its colour and marketed it as "new and improved," even though the product's other characteristics were unchanged.

Why might this scenario occur in organizations?

Use the following scale to indicate whether this behaviour is ethically acceptable:

NEVER ACCEPTABLE		SOMETIMES ACCEPTABLE			ALWAYS ACCEPTABLE	
①	②	③	④	⑤	⑥	⑦

Explain the ideas you considered in arriving at your answer.

DISCUSSION STARTER

Communicating Your Interests and Active Listening

In this exercise you will be paired with a classmate who will spend two minutes telling you about a topic that he or she is very interested in (perhaps a favourite course, a hobby, a travel experience, or a favourite sport). You may take written notes while listening. After the person has finished, you will repeat back to your classmate what he or she said, trying to capture the depth of the person's knowledge and interest. Once you've done this, reverse your roles and repeat the exercise.

QUESTIONS FOR DISCUSSION

1. Which role was easier to play: that of active listener or the person sending the message?
2. How did you feel when the person listening to you showed understanding or misunderstood you?
3. What did your classmate's feedback help you to learn about how to communicate better in the future?
4. What could you do to become a better listener?

DISCUSSION STARTER

The Empty Seat[69]

Staff in a retirement home for seniors have developed an interesting way to give a "voice" to the elderly clients whom they serve. At every staff meeting, there is an empty chair set aside for "Grace," the name they have given to an imaginary typical client. During every discussion, and before making any decision, the staff deliberately take time to listen to what "Grace" would say. Participants take turns expressing what they think Grace might say. This practice has allowed staff to make better decisions that are in the interests of both themselves and clients.

Consider a group of people with whom you meet regularly. It may be your family, a particular circle of friends, the people in your dorm, or your colleagues at work. Invite them to participate in the following experiment. Add a figurative empty chair to your times together.

Designate the chair to be filled by a particular stakeholder whom your group members believe to be important but whom you seldom hear from or whose voice is seldom considered. This stakeholder might be "Mother Nature," "impoverished people in Africa," or "unwed mothers." Once your group has agreed upon a stakeholder, represent that stakeholder with a person's name (for example, Grace) and describe some of his or her general characteristics. Then, during your times together as a group, make a point of asking what "Grace" might contribute to your discussions. Do this for several days or meetings.

Variation: This could be done in the classroom, where the chair might be filled by a "CEO" or "nature" or "taxpayers" or the "unemployed." Do this for several classes, or the entire term, and reflect on your experience.

QUESTIONS FOR DISCUSSION

1. How did the presence of the empty chair influence discussion?
2. How did the practice of deliberately hearing the stakeholder's voice change the group's views or your views on the topics being discussed?

This is the next in a series of journal entries that can be used for class discussion or be compiled and included in a self-reflection paper.

Which part of this chapter did you find the most thought-provoking? Describe why it captured your imagination. Identify the aspect of communication in which you think you have the greatest room for improvement. List three things you could do to improve how well you communicate.

Twelve

Understanding Organizational Culture and Structure

Our journey through OB so far has led us through examples and research related to individuals and groups. The final five chapters of the textbook examine OB at the organizational and interorganizational level. In this chapter, we describe basic elements of organizational culture and structure.

Learning Objectives	Conventional OB	Sustainable OB
BASIC ASSUMPTIONS		
1. Identify the basic assumptions of organizational culture.	Focus primarily on the financial bottom line. Give precedence to shareholder interests, and assume that everyone pursues his or her self-interests	Focus on a triple bottom line of financial, social, and ecological well-being. Consider the interests of multiple stakeholders, and encourage everyone to pursue the common good
KEY VALUES		
2. Recognize the key values that shape organizational behaviour.	Place appropriate emphasis on a relatively instrumental and individual-level understanding of flexibility versus predictability, internal versus external focus	Place appropriate emphasis on a more holistic understanding of flexibility versus predictability, internal versus external focus
CULTURAL ARTIFACTS		
3. Discuss cultural artifacts and how they shape an organization's culture.	Emphasize symbols of material and individual success, developed by top managers and introduced in a deliberate top-down fashion	Emphasize symbols of community and service, developed by organizational members from a variety of hierarchical levels and introduced in an emergent bottom-up fashion
ORGANIZATIONAL STRUCTURE		
4. Identify the four fundamentals of organizational structure.	Standardization: Specify desired behaviours Specialization: Provide job descriptions Centralization: Create authority structures Departmentalization: Create formal job groupings	Experimentation: Encourage constant improvement Sensitization: Seek and respond to needs and opportunities of the whole Dignification: Respect everyone Participation: Encourage mutual discernment

the fundamentals of organizing at semco[1]

© James Leynse/Corbis

Ricardo Semler was 21 years old when he took over his father's company, Semco, a São Paulo–based firm that generated $4 million in annual revenues by producing marine pumps for Brazil's shipping industry. At the time, the company employed about 100 people and was managed in a traditional manner according to well-developed operating standards, formal rules, and detailed job descriptions that indicated the training and experience required for each position. It also had a fairly centralized authority structure and an established departmental structure. In short, Semco's structures and systems were developed fully enough for the father to hand over the reins of power to his young son.

Ricardo Semler was not fond of the organizational culture, however, nor of the way that things were organized at Semco. He had worked in the company's purchasing department for a summer and had asked himself: "How can I spend the rest of my life doing this? How can I stomach years of babysitting people to make sure they clock in on time? Why is this worth doing?" So, when he became CEO, Semler threw out all of the books of rules and regulations that had been created during the previous years of standardization and formalization. As he explains it, "I'd come from having fun in rock bands . . . and I'd seen that there were ways to make people enthusiastic if they were involved entirely."

Although Semco has since grown to employ more than 5,000 employees and generate $1 billion in annual revenues, its employee manual has been reduced to 20 pages, complete with cartoons. The company doesn't even have a written mission statement, preferring instead to foster experimentation. Workers seldom take minutes during meetings at Semco, because writing things down can constrain future experimentation. Semler wants the standards that guide activity at Semco to be fluid and constantly (re)constructed by its members.

Specialization is also downplayed at Semco: There are no job descriptions. The company's "Lost in Space" program assumes that its young recruits often don't know what they want to do with their lives, so it allows them to roam through the company for a year, doing what they want to do and moving to a different unit whenever they want. This approach enables employees at Semco to be sensitized to needs and opportunities that might otherwise

I can honestly say that our growth, profit, and the number of people we employ are secondary concerns.

be overlooked. Semler himself spends little time at work (he doesn't even have his own office), preferring instead to expose himself to a wide variety of inputs and stimuli, such as implementing his ideas in schools and developing ecologically sustainable communities.

Semler is also not too keen on the centralization of authority. Even though Semco has diversified and grown significantly, it has only three levels of hierarchy. Semler himself is one of six "counsellors" (top management), who take turns leading the company for six months at a time. Workers choose their own work hours, set their own salaries, and decide who will be their managers. Managers trust workers and treat them with dignity. As Semler notes, "Most of our programs are based on the notion of giving employees control over their own lives. In a word, we hire adults, and then we treat them like adults."

One final change worth noting is that Semler dismantled Semco's large departments, replacing them with smaller, more autonomous units of 150 or fewer members who each know that his or her participation truly matters. The heavy emphasis on participation is consistent with Semler's commitment to democracy, a watchword in Semco's culture.

Ricardo Semler revels in the fact that he is not a conventional manager, and he wants to keep it that way. Even though Semco has enjoyed an outstanding growth rate, Semler is very clear that growth and profits are not his primary goals: "I can honestly say that our growth, profit, and the number of people we employ are secondary concerns. Outsiders clamor to know these things because they want to quantify our business. These are the yardsticks they turn to first. That's one reason we're still privately held. I don't want Semco to be burdened with the ninety-day mind-set of most stock market analysts."

Semco demonstrates that organizations can thrive when they have cultures and structures that treat people with dignity, foster trust and participation, value experimentation and learning, and remain sensitive to the larger needs and opportunities around them. At Semco, these are the genuine fundamentals of organizing. Semler's approach seems to have attracted admiration among his peers, as an annual poll of 52,000 Brazilian executives has chosen him as "Business Leader of the Year" on several occasions.

Although humankind has a long history of organizing, modern-day organizations as we know them really became commonplace only during the last few hundred years. We live in a time when ideas such as division of labour are taken for granted, and we no longer marvel at the productivity and wealth they help to create. Nor do we give much thought to how formal organizational structures can affect our formal and informal interpersonal relationships.

When we take conventional ideas of organizing for granted, we forget how they influence us, just as we forget how we are influenced by the physical structures in which we live and work. For example, the floor plans of your home and your office influence which people you interact with, how you interact with them, and the informal culture that is fostered. Frank Lloyd Wright, the famous architect, reportedly said he could design a home that would cause newlyweds to get divorced within a few months. Along the same lines, Winston Churchill observed that "we shape our buildings, and thereafter our buildings shape us."[2]

Just as physical architecture shapes our buildings, conceptual architecture shapes our organizations. Conventional building blocks include ideas such as standardization, specialization, and centralization. And just as concerns about the natural environment and ergonomics are prompting the construction of increasingly energy-efficient and people-friendly physical buildings, similar concerns can prompt changes in organizational structures and cultures (see the opening case).

This chapter will focus on organizational culture and structure. **Organizational culture** is the set of shared assumptions, values, and experiences that influence the ways in which individuals, teams, and groups interact with one another and work toward company goals.[3] According to Edgar Schein, the specific culture of an organization is typically made up of ways of interacting that have worked well enough in the past to be passed on as the norms for how new members should think, feel, and act.[4] Put differently, an organization's culture is a shared understanding about accepted and valued behaviour that acts as a (usually unwritten) guide for organizational members.[5] We can describe cultures by their characteristics, as well as by how consistently members agree on cultural values and assumptions and use them as a guide for behaviour.[6]

The culture of an organization is important in that it can attract, motivate, and help to retain organizational members. An organization's culture can affect how satisfied members are with their jobs, how committed they are to the organization, how innovative they are, and the quality of the products and services they deliver.[7] It can even influence the way members manage the organization's expenses, satisfy its customers,[8] and contribute to a shared zeal that leads to higher sales.[9] Overall, organizational cultures with high levels of internal consistency—that is, cultures whose different elements fit together in a way that makes sense—tend to perform better.[10] And, as we'll see later, some evidence suggests that certain types of culture are related to financial measures of profitability and growth.[11]

Researchers have found it helpful to think of an organization's culture as having two basic categories of elements: (1) *informal* elements like basic assumptions and values, and (2) *formal* elements, including cultural artifacts and formal structures. The iceberg depicted in Figure 12.1 shows how the informal elements are usually less visible (beneath the waterline) compared to the formal elements (above the waterline).

Organizational structure is the formal arrangements and linkages among members and groups that specify work activities and subtasks and allow them to be completed. Although structure is not always included in the definition of organizational culture, there is general agreement that culture influences structure and vice versa.[12] For example, a change in values toward greater respect for the natural environment may result in the creation of a

Organizational culture is the set of shared assumptions, values, and experiences that influence the ways in which individuals, teams, and groups interact with one another and work toward company goals.

Organizational structure is the formal arrangements and linkages among members and groups that specify work activities and subtasks and allow them to be completed.

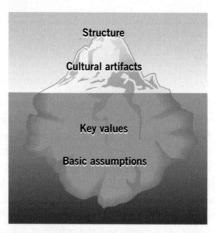

FIGURE 12.1 The Basic Elements and Levels of Organizational Culture and Structure

Department of Environmental Stewardship, and vice versa. In this chapter we will examine each of the main elements of culture and structure in some detail, and in the next chapter we will see how they fit together to form a coherent whole.

LEARNING OBJECTIVE 1
Identify the basic assumptions of organizational culture.

Basic Assumptions of Organizational Culture

ASSUMPTIONS VALUES ARTIFACTS STRUCTURE

There are many aspects of an organization's culture you won't find written down or described in detail in the company policy manual or annual report. You learn them when you become a member of the organization or by interacting with its members (see My OB: What Is the Culture of Your Class?). For example, anyone who takes a WestJet flight would get a sense that something is different about the company upon hearing the flight attendants telling jokes over the intercom or seeing them dramatically acting out the pre-flight safety instructions. Even so, only members acquire a complete picture of the organization's culture.

The basic assumptions at the core of an organization's culture are often held unconsciously or taken for granted, like the beliefs, feelings, and thoughts that inform members' values and actions.[13] Understanding organizational culture requires uncovering basic assumptions such as these. Developing such an understanding is important because it helps members fit into the organization, tells them what to pay attention to, helps them interpret what different behaviours mean, and helps them identify what actions are appropriate in various situations. Overall, basic assumptions provide the cognitive stability that permits groups to continue to function. However, basic assumptions can also distort how people interpret the actions of others, as illustrated by the following example provided by Edgar Schein:

> If we assume, on the basis of past experience or education, that other people will take advantage of us whenever they have an opportunity, [then] we expect to be taken advantage of, and then we interpret others in a way that coincides with those expectations. We observe people sitting in a seemingly idle posture at their desk and interpret their behaviour as "loafing" rather than "thinking out an important problem." We perceive absence from work as "shirking" rather than "doing work at home."[14]

In conventional organizations, common unspoken assumptions are that the primary focus should be the financial bottom line, that shareholder interests take precedence, and that everyone is out to pursue his or her self-interests. In sustainable organizations, common assumptions are likely to include focusing on the triple bottom line of financial, social, and

Buena Vista/Photofest

Each class has a unique feel to it. It starts the first day when you enter the classroom, with its particular layout and atmosphere, and is influenced by the personalities of the other students enrolled in the class and the style of the instructor. In the movie *Dead Poets Society*, Robin Williams makes a unique impression on his students through his unconventional behaviour and instructional methods.

QUESTIONS FOR REFLECTION

1. What was your first impression of this class?
2. If your course follows a traditional format, by the time you reach this chapter you are well into the course. What has been your experience so far?
3. What are the basic assumptions or core values influencing the behaviour of class members?
4. Do any specific events or experiences stand out in your mind?
5. Have you told any stories about this class to others?
6. How does the culture of the class contribute to your performance and/or learning?
7. Do you have any suggestions for how to improve the culture? Be specific. Your instructor may want to know.

ecological well-being, considering the interests of multiple stakeholders, and encouraging everyone to look out for others and not only for himself or herself.

Changing basic assumptions, even those that are dysfunctional, "is difficult, time-consuming, and highly anxiety-provoking."[15] Of course, this does not mean we should not try, but it does help to explain why such change is difficult even when our livelihood is at stake (for more on change, see chapter 15).

Key Values that Shape Organizational Culture

| ASSUMPTIONS | **VALUES** | ARTIFACTS | STRUCTURE |

LEARNING OBJECTIVE 2
Recognize the key values that shape organizational behaviour.

Many different kinds of values can influence an organization's culture. For example, family values influence how one family firm differs from others; regional or national values affect organizational practices (see chapter 2); and professional values influence, say, the organizational cultures of engineering firms versus marketing firms. Among all of these differences, researchers have found particular merit in looking at two sets of values for understanding organizational culture. Taken together, these values form the Competing Values Framework.

The Competing Values Framework

The **Competing Values Framework** (CVF) is a useful tool for helping to understand the shared values and assumptions that guide organizational behaviour.[16] The next chapter will show how the CVF has proven useful in identifying four basic forms of organizational culture, but in this chapter we simply look at two basic dimensions of culture found in the CVF.

The **Competing Values Framework** categorizes organizational cultures based on two dimensions: the relative emphasis members place on (1) predictability versus adaptability, and (2) having an external versus an internal focus.

Predictability versus Adaptability Some organizational cultures value stability and predictability. For example, members may take comfort in knowing that every Tuesday afternoon there is a staff meeting, every Friday lunch is catered by the company, and the format of budget statements is the same this year as it has been for the past 10 years. In these companies, norms and standards are welcome.

In contrast, other organizational cultures value flexibility and adaptability. Members seek and thrive on change—they would find it stifling and undesirable to have predictable meetings or any bias toward maintaining the status quo. Rather, they pride themselves on being able to "roll with the punches" and adapt to the latest technologies and wants of the marketplace. Indeed, these members will create change for the sake of change, just to keep things interesting. Of course, most organizational cultures lie on a continuum somewhere between these two extremes, and members usually know exactly where on the continuum theirs falls.

External versus Internal Focus   Some organizational cultures have an external focus whereby members are viewed as a means to meet organizational ends. In such cultures the organization's goals take primacy over the goals of members, and members are seen as servants to meet organizational goals.

In contrast, other organizational cultures have an internal focus, whereby the organization is a means to meet employees' ends. Members are encouraged to express themselves, and organizational goals are designed to be consistent with members' goals, strengths, and aspirations. For example, the Specialisterne organization described in this chapter's closing case was designed to meet the needs of a certain segment of the autistic population. Again, most organizations lie somewhere between the external and internal ends of the continuum; members know what their organization's culture is, and it affects their behaviour.

In addition to influencing the behaviour of members, the values emphasized within an organization also influence the implied psychological contract between the organization and its members (see chapter 8). For example, a culture that is flexible and participative contributes to employees believing the organization is concerned about them and their long-term well-being, whereas a more controlling and hierarchical culture contributes to employees believing the organization is primarily concerned with how they perform today, without much regard for their future.[17]

In most organizations, the culture is not as easily described by a formal set of values Moreover, sometimes the statement of values published on a company's website or espoused by its executives is quite different from the real feel of the organization. A classic irony occurs when an organization that touts people as important repeatedly lays employees off or cuts investments in training and development. This isn't the case at Toyota, which is rather an example of an organization that has attempted to live up to its values even in the tough economic times of a recession.[18] Employees at Toyota's plant in Princeton, Indiana, were not laid off when demand for the company's large Tundras and Sequoias plummeted and production was shut down for three months. Instead, the plant employees were put to work learning skills and processes that would make them more informed and efficient once production resumed. Toyota also invested in promoting and maintaining employee fitness by requiring and paying employees to exercise three times a week.

Differences between conventional and sustainable values can be illustrated in light of the two dimensions of the Competing Values Framework. For example, a conventional approach tends to favour a relatively narrow understanding of internal versus external factors, focusing especially on the instrumental needs of the external marketplace and of individual members within the organization. In contrast, a sustainable approach offers a more holistic understanding, highlighting social and ecological aspects of the external environment and group-based social aspects of its internal members. Similarly, a conventional approach would have a narrower range of things being considered along the dimension of predictability versus adaptability—again, focusing particularly on the instrumental needs of individuals—whereas a sustainable approach would have a more holistic orientation that would include multiple forms of well-being and multiple stakeholders. These differences will be discussed in greater detail in chapter 13.

Rocky Widner/NBAE via Getty Images

When Dwane Casey joined the Toronto Raptors as head coach for the 2011–2012 season, the team had just finished compiling a disappointing record of 22 wins and 60 losses—third worst in the NBA. Casey knew that changes needed to be made, and he identified the team's defence (an area that had been historically lacking) as one of the first areas to address.

Casey felt that part of the reason for the weak defence stemmed from a culture that did not demand consistency and tenacity from the players. He sought to change this by urging his team to "pound the rock." Rather than the phrase's traditional basketball meaning of (over)dribbling the ball, Casey's usage of it was inspired by a quote from Jacob Riis, a Danish American social reformer who lived from 1849 to 1914. As Casey explained it, the phrase comes "from a story about a stonecutter. Every time a stonecutter hits a rock it may not break, you may have to hit it 100 times but on that 101st time you hit it, now you crack the rock."

And so "Pound the Rock" became the team's motto. It was inscribed on the wall of the practice court and the doors of the Raptors's locker room, and players shouted the phrase as they left every huddle. Casey even had a three-foot-tall, 1,300 pound boulder, purchased from a quarry in Thornhill, Ontario, placed by the door of the locker room and had his players touch the boulder every time they entered and left as a literal reminder to "pound the rock."

The Raptors's defence has improved significantly through Casey's tenure, and their winning percentage has climbed steadily, going from .348 in the 2011–2012 season to .415 in the 2012–2013 season and culminating in a .585 winning percentage, a division title, and the first playoff appearance for the team in six years in the 2013–2014 season. Although Toronto traditionally had trouble wooing free agents, in 2014 the Raptors's star point guard, Kyle Lowry, chose to extend his contract with the club for four more years rather than test the free agent waters, claiming that "Toronto is just the right place for me."

QUESTIONS FOR DISCUSSION

1. Have you ever been part of an organization that was "the right place for you"? What was it about the culture that suited you?
2. What symbols or rituals does your school have? What messages do those things send about the school's culture?

Artifacts of Organizational Culture

| ASSUMPTIONS | VALUES | **ARTIFACTS** | STRUCTURE |

> **LEARNING OBJECTIVE 3**
> Discuss cultural artifacts and how they shape an organization's culture.

Whereas basic assumptions and values are often the less visible elements that shape an organization's culture, its **cultural artifacts**—which include physical features, shared stories, rituals, and formal structure and systems—are tangible evidence of the culture.[19] Consider how archeologists try to put together a picture of an ancient culture by hypothesizing about the purpose and significance of objects they dig up. These objects are clues to the past. Similarly, an organization has tangible clues that provide insight into its culture. Recall the boulder in the Raptors's locker room that was placed there as a constant reminder of their team commitment to hard work and consistency. Some physical features, like a wall of pictures of executives, may signal an emphasis on hierarchy, whereas others may express an emphasis on individual empowerment.

> **Cultural artifacts** provide tangible evidence of an organization's values and may include the organization's physical features, shared stories, rituals, and formal structure and systems.

Some artifacts showcase an emphasis on continuing tradition, while others serve to emphasize a spirit of innovation. Take, for example, the plaques on a company's wall: Are they devoted to past accomplishments or are they seen as symbols of future aspirations? Microsoft's Seattle headquarters has artifacts that recognize the past, and it also has several rooms that are devoted to showing what technology might look like in the home and office of the future. A building or facility can be another clue. Is an organization's headquarters located above an upscale coffee shop in a renovated brick building, or does it occupy the top level of a steel-and-glass skyscraper? Is the layout of an organization open and conducive to interactions, or are people divided into separate offices with closed doors?

Culture also is evident in the stories that members tell about experiences of the organization. **Shared stories** form the oral history of critical events that have shaped an organization. One story told at automotive parts supplier Dana Holding Corporation helps explain the company's move to a decentralized, empowered work environment by recounting how the acting CEO threw the firm's extensive policy manual into the trash during a headquarters meeting and pulled out a simple pamphlet with a vision statement and guiding values. The superior customer service provided by a Sport Chek sales associate, reported in chapter 1, if retold by Sport Chek leaders would serve to reinforce the culture of customer service more effectively than would almost any policy.

Rituals are behavioural practices that perpetuate, reinforce, and keep alive a particular value that defines an organization. Walmart's company chant is still practised today after being introduced by founder Sam Walton decades ago. This ritual reinforces a spirit of unity and helps employees feel that they are a part of the Walmart family. Similarly, the Raptors's ritual of ending team huddles by shouting "pound the rock" in unison or of touching the boulder that sits at the door to their locker room clarifies and reinforces the norms and standards that are expected from team members. Rituals may also be as simple as the way people address members in conversations; the use of formal titles communicates differences in status and importance, while the use of first names communicates a sense of equality.

The difference between conventional and sustainable artifacts of organizational culture may be subtle at times, but at other times they are very pronounced. A conventional culture may emphasize symbols of material and individual success like a corner office reserved for top executives, plaques that memorialize top-producing salespeople, and stories about financial achievements. Cultural artifacts in conventional organizations are also more likely to have been developed by top managers and introduced in a deliberate top-down fashion. A sustainable culture may emphasize symbols of community and other forms of success by means of collaborative office spaces, plaques indicating support provided to local non-profit organizations, and stories of exceptional service to customers or the community. Cultural artifacts in sustainable organizations are more likely to have been developed by organizational members from a variety of hierarchical levels and to have been introduced in an emergent bottom-up fashion. Other differences between conventional and sustainable approaches to organizational structure are evident in the fundamentals described in the next section.

Fundamentals of Organizational Structure

ASSUMPTIONS | VALUES | ARTIFACTS | **STRUCTURE**

An organization's structure is a particularly important artifact of organizational culture, and indeed it can shape the experiences and values of members.[20] According to Max Weber—one of the most influential thinkers in organization theory—the formal aspect of organizing includes managing four fundamental issues:

1. *Ensuring that work activities are completed in the best way.* This means breaking down the overall work of the organization into individual subtasks and identifying the best way to perform each.

2. *Ensuring that each member's subtasks contribute to the whole.* Each member should understand which specific organizational subtasks he or she is responsible for performing.

3. *Ensuring orderly deference among organizational members.* Members should know from whom to take their cues in the everyday operation of the organization.

4. *Ensuring that members work together harmoniously.* This can include placing members alongside people who have similar or complementary jobs to accomplish the overall work of the organization.[21]

Four Fundamentals of Organizing	Conventional OB	Sustainable OB
1. How to ensure that work activities are being completed in the best way	**Standardization:** The emphasis is on developing uniform practices for organizational members to follow in doing their jobs.	**Experimentation:** The emphasis is on an ongoing voluntary implementation of new ways of performing tasks on a trial basis.
2. How to ensure that members' subtasks contribute to the whole	**Specialization:** The emphasis is on grouping standardized organizational tasks into separate jobs.	**Sensitization:** The emphasis is on searching for and responding to needs and opportunities to improve the status quo.
3. How to ensure orderly deference	**Centralization:** The emphasis is on having decision-making authority rest with the top of an organization's hierarchy.	**Dignification:** The emphasis is on treating *everyone* in the organization with dignity and respect.
4. How to ensure members work together harmoniously	**Departmentalization:** The emphasis is on grouping members and resources together to achieve the work of the larger organization.	**Participation:** The emphasis is on mutuality and giving stakeholders a voice in how the organization is managed and how jobs are performed.

Knowing how an organization deals with these fundamental structural issues gives us insight into its culture. Conventional OB focuses more on the *content* of organizing, for instance, while sustainable OB tends to place greater emphasis on the *process*. In addition, conventional OB emphasizes *rational* competence, whereas sustainable OB emphasizes *relational* competence.[22] This is not to say that rationality and the content of formal structures are not important for sustainable OB. Indeed, as described in this chapter's opening case, Ricardo Semler understands that structures help determine behaviour and he intentionally chooses structures that promote experimentation, sensitization, dignification, and participation. These sustainable OB terms and their conventional counterparts are defined in Table 12.1.[23] We now turn to take an in-depth look at each of the four fundamentals of organizing.

Fundamental 1: Standardization versus Experimentation. **Standardization** is the conventional response to Weber's first fundamental of organization. It describes designing basic work activities so that members perform tasks in the best way to accomplish the overall work of the organization and avoid using suboptimal methods or doing unrelated tasks. By standardizing tasks, conventional organizations try to ensure that members perform the activities most appropriate for achieving overarching organizational goals. For example, to facilitate the overall goal of providing post-secondary education, most universities offer "standard" timetables that describe how long classes are and at what times of day they start and stop. This makes it easier for students to enroll in courses in more than one academic department. Also, if you complete an Organizational Behaviour course in one university, you can usually transfer the credit to another university because standardized curricula ensures that the same basic material will be covered in any location.

    The retail clothing sector is trying to increase standardization across organizations to address the fact that the same customer might be a size 8 in one store and, frustratingly, a size 12 in another.[24] When McDonald's opened its first restaurant in Moscow, it discovered that local farmers could not provide the high-quality potatoes needed to meet the company's standards. So McDonald's flew in experts, imported the appropriate seeds and harvesting machinery, and trained Russian farmers to grow and harvest the potatoes it needed.

Standardization is developing uniform practices for organizational members to follow in doing their jobs.

Additionally, Russians who were hired to manage the Moscow branches were trained in Canada and at "Hamburger University" in Chicago, Illinois.

The challenge from a conventional perspective is to develop standards that maximize productivity. As depicted in Figure 12.2, placing too little or too much emphasis on standards can cause undesired outcomes.[25] With an optimal level of standardization, members know which tasks need to be performed and how to perform them to reach organizational goals. Standards serve as guidelines for decision making, and they provide an overarching framework that gives members confidence and ensures coordinated decision making across departments and over time (see chapter 6). An optimal emphasis on performance standards can enhance the productivity of members (see the next OB in Action feature, which looks at Starbucks).

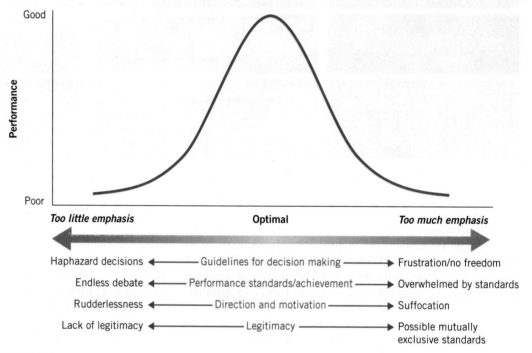

FIGURE 12.2 Characteristics of Optimal and Suboptimal Standardization

Too few standards may result in haphazard decision making, and their absence may lead to endless debate and uncertainty among members about precisely which goals should be pursued and how tasks should be performed. Inadequate standards may also undermine the perceived legitimacy of an organization and lead to inconsistent quality in its outputs. At the other extreme, placing too much emphasis on standardization and having too many standards may cause members to become frustrated because they have little opportunity to express their creativity. Members may also feel overwhelmed by the sheer number of standards they must meet, which can squelch initiative and organizational learning.[26]

From a sustainable perspective, the merits of standardization and the fears about too little standardization are both overrated. If there is a standard that sustainable OB emphasizes, it is the standard of **experimentation**. Rather than spending a lot of effort trying to ensure that organizational members conform to a host of specific standards, sustainable OB encourages members to try new ways of doing things and to make organizing a dynamic and experimental process focused on improvement rather than on static adherence to standards. Research indicates that this approach leads to higher levels of commitment and can improve organizational performance.[27]

With this approach some of the members' experiments may fail, in which case reverting to the old way is fine, but the organization has still gained new knowledge from the

Experimentation is the emphasis on an ongoing voluntary implementation of new ways of performing tasks on a trial basis.

Will a Spoonful of Efficiency Change the Culture of Starbucks?

Bloomberg/Getty Images

Chapter 5 described Starbucks as a motivational workplace. Highly trained baristas (those who brew and sell the coffee) have a strong sense of ownership in Starbucks's mission and contribute to its comfortable, friendly, and relaxed atmosphere. The focus on social responsibility and the promotion of new music also add a progressive and creative feel that is attractive to customers and baristas alike.

Tough economic times have led many companies to increase emphasis on cost savings and efficiency gains. For its part, Starbucks has standardized more of its baristas' behaviour in order to cut down on wasted effort and time. Corporate representatives went around to stores with a simple exercise to demonstrate the benefits of efficiency. The parts of a Mr. Potato Head toy were spread across several tables, and baristas were timed as they put him back together. Then they were asked how the time taken to do the task could be reduced. Simple suggestions like putting the pieces closer together and assembling them in a specific sequence turned out to be significant time savers that transferred over to making coffees, reloading the pastries, and other job tasks.

QUESTIONS FOR DISCUSSION

1. Do you think there is a downside to improved efficiency at Starbucks?
2. Will increasing standardization in baristas' movements and actions change the culture?
3. How might these changes affect a customer's experience at Starbucks?

experiment. When experiments are a rousing success, all members of the organization can benefit from and adapt to the lessons learned. Experimentation was evident when members of The Body Shop tried recycling and reusing different containers for their products, which subsequently became a model for other organizations.

Too little experimentation may result in organizational rigidity, making people feel stifled and complacent. Furthermore, a failure to take advantage of the most up-to-date knowledge of members can perpetuate systemic shortcomings and injustices. Of course, too much experimentation could lead to chaos, especially if the experimentation isn't coordinated and organizational members are not held accountable to others. This is especially true if experimentation is not linked to participation—it is participation of key stakeholders that lends coordination to experimentation. By inviting each member to experiment and improve the way that tasks are done, Semco fosters a culture of interpersonal trust, democracy, and information sharing that coordinates work while promoting meaningful work, motivation, work-life balance, and financial profitability.

Fundamental 2: Specialization versus Sensitization **Specialization** ensures that all organizational members know the specific subtasks they are required to perform. (If everyone performed identical tasks, organizations would provide little added value.) The positive aspects of specialization are reflected in the concept of division of labour, as famously illustrated by Adam Smith's pin factory, where productivity improved 1,000-fold when each worker performed specialized tasks rather than all of the tasks (see chapter 2). The challenge is to ensure that the activities each member performs are designed to enhance the productivity of the whole group.

Specialization refers to grouping standardized organizational tasks into separate jobs.

Job specialization takes standardized organizational tasks and allocates them to separate jobs. Job specialization can be narrow (which means that the tasks a member performs are fairly limited and focused) or broad (which means that each member performs a wide range of tasks). For example, Henry Ford revolutionized productivity in the automobile industry when he pioneered the assembly line, whereby each worker built a separate subcomponent of a car rather than assembling an entire car. Typically, the specialized knowledge, skills, abilities, and other characteristics required to perform each job are written out in job descriptions, which also may describe the formal qualifications required for jobholders. For example, an accounting firm might require a staff accountant to pass the CPA Exam before being promoted to senior accountant. Similarly, universities require qualifications to take courses, such as having a high school diploma and completing any prerequisites for a course.

The goal is to establish an optimal level of specialization (see Figure 12.3) and avoid the disadvantages of having too little or too much. From the conventional perspective, specialization is optimal when each member's specific tasks are clear and help to maximize productivity. Having specialization refers to grouping standardized organizational tasks into separate jobs. Having clear and well-defined job descriptions makes it easier to recruit, select, and train people for jobs. Specialization at its best provides members with a sense of purpose and understanding of how their work contributes to the overall organization, and it allows them to obtain a high degree of proficiency and expertise in their particular tasks. People who can thus take pride in their work will be motivated and will help maximize the productivity of the organization.

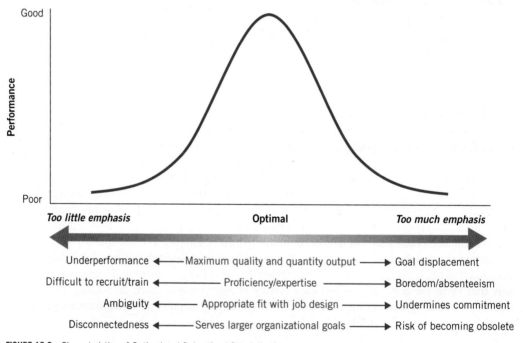

FIGURE 12.3 Characteristics of Optimal and Suboptimal Specialization

Too little specialization means tasks are not being performed as efficiently as possible, which results in underperformance. This extreme may also create difficulties in recruitment and training, because it is unclear which sorts of skills members need to perform. Finally, too little specialization may lead to ambiguity in decision making, because no one is quite sure who has the responsibility or the information needed to make different decisions, and people feel unsure about what is expected of them.

Conversely, too much specialization can result in jobs that are very repetitive and boring, like assembly line jobs in which workers perform the same task hundreds of times each hour or day. This may lead to high turnover and absenteeism, and it can contribute to people feeling insecure about being easily replaced or their job becoming obsolete due to advances in technology. Excessive specialization may also contribute to a form of **goal displacement**,[28] which occurs when people get so focused on specific goals that they lose sight of more important big-picture aims like providing innovative or high-quality services and products.

From a sustainable OB point of view, **sensitization** ensures that each member's subtasks contribute to the whole. Members should be sensitive to and continuously adapt and improve the way they do their jobs in harmony with others around them. If tasks are divided into separate jobs within sustainable organizations, this activity is often undertaken at a group level. Whereas the conventional emphasis on specialization tends to be at the level of the individual jobholder, the sustainable emphasis tends to focus on the specific tasks that need to be performed at a group, team, or departmental level of analysis. As a consequence, job descriptions and designs focus on the interrelationships among members rather than on the specific tasks of each member. The sustainable approach values the complementary skills of a team as a unit more than the individual skills of particular team members.

An optimal emphasis on sensitization enhances members' proficiency and expertise, not by spelling out beforehand exactly what they are to do, but rather by allowing and encouraging them to develop their existing skills and abilities. This phenomenon is illustrated by Semco's "Lost in Space" program, which gives new members and managers the opportunity to sensitively match their skills with jobs. By welcoming members and encouraging them to take initiative in areas where they think improvement is possible, the company gives them a greater feeling of purpose, meaningful work, and loyalty.[29] Interestingly, this type of arrangement does not hold up as well among employees from national cultures that defer to authority; it appears that these workers are less committed when given more opportunities to take initiative (see chapter 2).[30]

A sustainable approach emphasizes sensitization to opportunities and needs that go beyond the current specialized way of doing things. It also encourages sensitivity to other stakeholders' needs. For example, consider what happened at an historic urban church in the U.S. Southwest.[31] A series of unintended changes occurred when some young adult members began providing a hot breakfast to the neighbourhood's homeless people on Sunday mornings; their guests soon numbered more than 200. Six months later, a medical doctor brought along his stethoscope and a medical bag and began to examine people who wanted to discuss medical problems. Soon thereafter, full-scale medical, dental, and eye clinics emerged, and within a few years the church had opened a Day Center, was serving over 20,000 meals a year, and had hundreds of homeless people participating in worship services, singing in choirs, and serving as ushers. Because it allows for input and insight from a variety of organizational stakeholders, sensitization helps improve an organization's performance not only in terms of productivity but also in terms of social, ecological, and other measures of performance.

When there is too little sensitization in organizations, members are not encouraged and permitted to act on things to improve the organization or relationships with stakeholders. Too much sensitization, in contrast, can lead to inaction caused by being overwhelmed. For example, it can be overwhelming to know that there are millions of people in low-income countries whose lives could be made more bearable with available medicines, that hundreds of people in your local community have lost their jobs due to downsizings or company closures, or that members of your own organization may be suffering the stress of personal or family illness or financial stress. Managers and organizational members who are sensitized to multiple needs in their communities might start by focusing on those needs for which they have particularly appropriate resources and strengths to make a difference. For example, pharmaceutical companies such as Novartis are wellsuited to meeting needs for vaccines or medicines and are therefore able to devote some of their resources to treating diseases like malaria at little or no cost to those who are afflicted in poor countries.

Goal displacement occurs when people get so focused on specific subgoals that they lose sight of more important overarching goals.

Sensitization is the emphasis on searching for and being receptive to better ways of doing things in order to take advantage of existing opportunities or to address existing needs.

Fundamental 3: Centralization versus Dignification The third conventional fundamental of organizing from the conventional perspective is **centralization**. This addresses the need for members to know who has authority over whom and the extent to which that authority is centralized or decentralized in the organization. **Authority** refers to the formal power given to specific members—usually managers—to arrange resources, assign tasks, and direct the activities of other members so as to achieve organizational goals. Organizational members are expected to defer to those who have authority over them. An *organization chart* is a pictorial representation of the formal authority relationships within the organization's structure.

Delegation is the process of giving authority to a person or group to make decisions in a specified sphere of activity. When members have been delegated the authority to make decisions, they become both responsible and accountable for the decisions they make. The more authority managers delegate to others, the more decentralized an organization is said to be. In a highly centralized organization, the authority to make decisions rests with managers at the top of an organization's hierarchy. It is helpful to think of centralization as a continuum along which all organizational units find themselves.[32]

Structures with greater delegation and decentralization with wider spans of control have recently become popular. **Span of control** describes the number of members over whom a given manager has authority. Managers with wide spans have many subordinates reporting to them, whereas managers with narrow spans have few. Given a fixed number of members, a wide span of control reduces the number of hierarchical layers in an organization, such that the organization is said to have a "flat" or "short" structure.

As shown in Figure 12.4, an optimal level of centralization maximizes organizational performance.[33] When this occurs, there is timely and coordinated decision making, vertically balanced decision making at the various levels in the hierarchy, and a motivating environment for members. An optimal level of centralization frees up enough time for top management to develop overarching plans and strategies, and it allows lower-level managers and front-line workers to handle routine, everyday matters.

Centralization is having decision-making authority rest with managers at the top of an organization's hierarchy.

Authority refers to the formal power given to specific members—usually managers—to arrange resources, assign tasks, and direct the activities of other members so as to achieve organizational goals.

Span of control is the number of members a given manager has authority over.

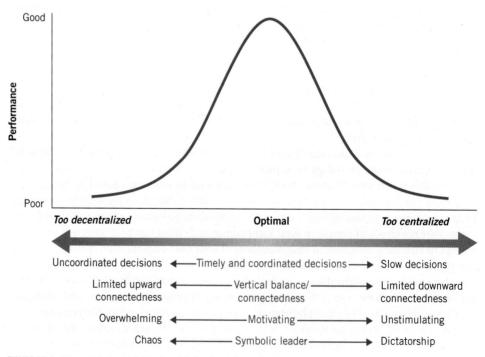

FIGURE 12.4 Characteristics of Optimal and Suboptimal Centralization

At one extreme—too much decentralization—each member of the organization has the right to make decisions on the spot, but members lack the larger perspective needed to ensure that their decisions are coordinated as a whole. For example, a salesperson unaware that supply is limited may promise a particular product unit to a customer while other salespeople are making the same promise. Too much decentralization also erodes a sense of belonging and connectedness with the larger organization. Members of organizations that are too decentralized may feel overwhelmed by responsibility and experience a sense of chaos from not having adequate centralized direction or support.

At the other extreme—too much centralization—the organization will be slow to take action because decisions have to work their way up and then back down the hierarchy. Similarly, insufficient responsibility and authority will erode members' sense of belonging, their connectedness with the larger organization, their commitment, and their creativity.[34] Finally, organizations that are too centralized may become dictatorships from which members will try to exit as quickly as they are able.

The sustainable perspective is less concerned about how much authority each member should have and more concerned about **dignification**—promoting the idea that everyone is better served if *all* stakeholders are treated with dignity. Instead of distributing *authority* throughout the organizational structure, sustainable organizations are more effective if they distribute *dignity*. Unlike authority, which is usually seen as a limited resource that must be parcelled out sparingly, dignity is an unlimited resource that can be distributed generously because everyone has inherent worth that should be recognized.

Dignification is the emphasis on treating everyone in the organization with dignity and respect.

Dignification entails treating people with respect as valued members of a community. This is the application of interactional justice, as described in chapter 8, to organizing. In the workplace, sustainable OB encourages organizational structures and cultures that contribute to treating people with respect and valuing their capabilities, and providing people with appropriate information to make decisions.[35] Dignifying others affects them personally by enhancing their self-esteem in the organization and decreases counterproductive behaviour such as complaining about work, acting rudely to co-workers, and taking unnecessary breaks that result from not feeling valued.[36]

Dignity may be present in an organization when members are given some discretion in setting their own work hours that permits them to accommodate family needs. An inflexible emphasis on regulations and monitoring by time clocks and electronic means can make members feel like a "number" rather than a person. The sustainable approach tends to favour decision making being pushed down to the front lines and even beyond the organization's boundaries where appropriate, such as to customers.[37] Consider how Ricardo Semler gives Semco employees the authority to set their own salaries. According to Semler, "Arguably, Semco's most controversial initiative is to let employees set their own salaries. Pundits are quick to bring up their dim view of human nature, on the assumption that people will obviously set their salaries much higher than feasible. It's the same argument we hear about people setting their own work schedules in a seven-day weekend mode. The first thing that leaps to mind is that people will come as late or little as possible—this has never been our experience."[38]

Treating people with dignity also means providing them with the information they require for responsible decision making. Semco employees are provided with market surveys that describe how much people earn who do similar work at competing organizations, information about what everyone else in the company earns, and profit forecasts for the company. Very seldom has the salary-setting system been abused, perhaps because employees know that if they request too large a salary, they run the risk of annoying their colleagues and suffering the personal stress that comes from making a decision that they know to be unjust and undignified.

An optimal emphasis on dignification will enhance decision making because, by its very nature, it allows decisions to be made at the appropriate level in the organization. If a member on the front lines of an organization has enough knowledge to make an informed and appropriate decision, then why push the decision up the hierarchy?[39] Dignification also encourages connectedness between and across organizational levels because lower-level members, rather than fearing managers with more authority, will be more trusting of higher-level managers and willing to share information with them that helps the overall organization.[40]

Research suggests that members treat one another with more dignity and respect when organizations lack centralized structures and systems to monitor behaviour.[41] For example, Semco does not set up structures and systems, like internal audits or inspections, to monitor whether workers are complying with regulations. Monitoring in a conventional way sends the message that workers cannot be trusted. At Semco there are no job descriptions, no dress codes, and no monitoring of expense accounts. Attendance at company meetings is voluntary and open to everyone, and meetings are chaired by the person most knowledgeable about the subject matter on the agenda.

Fundamental 4: Departmentalization versus Participation   As organizations grow in size, decisions must be made about where and with whom members will perform their tasks. From a conventional perspective, this effort is facilitated by **departmentalization**—the grouping of members and resources to achieve the work of the larger organization. Departmentalization has two key dimensions. The first dimension is *focus,* which is the relative emphasis on internal efficiency and external adaptiveness. The second dimension relates to the extent that departmental *membership* is permanent or short term.

The focus dimension describes the basis upon which an organization is divided into smaller, more manageable subgroups. At one end of this dimension are organizations with a **functional** structure. Here members are placed into the same department because they have similar technical skills and they use similar resources to perform similar tasks. For example, as illustrated in Figure 12.5(a), a computer manufacturing firm might have a Purchasing Department, a Production Department, and a Marketing Department, each of which might have subdepartments. The Production Department may have subdepartments for each factory (product departmentalization) or for each major region it serves (geographic departmentalization).

At the other end of the focus dimension are organizations with a **divisional** structure. Here each department provides specific products or services, serves specific customers, or works in a specific geographic region. Figure 12.5(b) shows a regionally based divisional structure with a Western Division, a Central Division, and an Eastern Division. A computer manufacturer might have a product-based structure with a Desktop Division, a Laptop Division, and a Handheld Division, or a customer-based structure with a Consumer Division, a Business Division, and an Educational Institutions Division.

As evident in Figure 12.5, a divisional structure will often have functional subdepartments, and a functional structure will often have divisional subdepartments. Thus, in the end, the same people might work in each organization, but the way they are grouped together depends on the departmentalization of the organization. This doesn't mean departmentalization is unimportant. Quite the contrary: We've seen that the structures we inhabit have a great deal of influence over how we see the world and the work we do. You have probably noticed the difference between taking a course comprising classmates from a wide variety of majors (akin to divisional departmentalization) versus taking one that comprises all business or all management majors (functional departmentalization). Of course, departmentalization can also have a profound effect on organizational culture—the culture of a department full of engineers (or marketers, or whatever) may be very different from that of a department whose members come from a variety of backgrounds.

Departmentalization is grouping members and resources together to achieve the work of the larger organization.

Functional departmentalization occurs when members are placed into the same department based on having similar technical skills and using similar resources to perform their tasks.

Divisional departmentalization occurs when members are placed together based on their working together as a subunit that provides specific products or services, serves specific customers, or works in a specific geographic region.

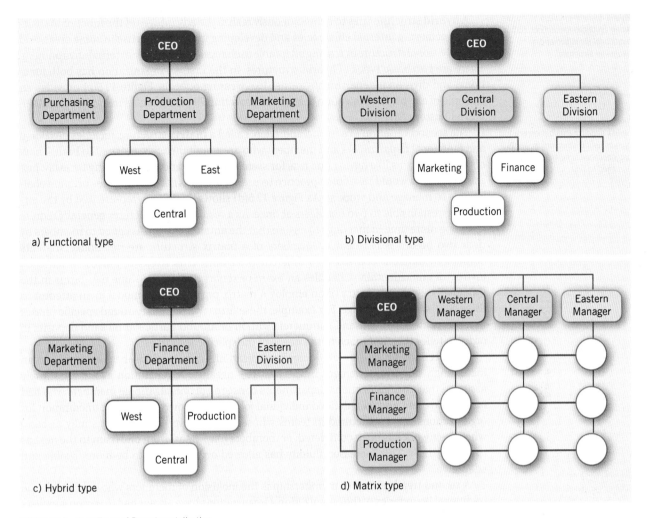

FIGURE 12.5 Four Types of Departmentalization

The relative strengths and weaknesses of divisional and functional approaches tend to mirror each other. On the one hand, consider the advantages an automobile manufacturer may enjoy by having functional departments rather than 10 separate divisions. First, the functional approach offers economies of scale. **Economies of scale** are evident when increases in volume are associated with lower organizational costs for providing a specific product or service. For example, the per-unit cost to produce 10,000 cars on a single assembly line is lower than it would be to produce 1,000 cars on each of 10 assembly lines scattered around the globe. Another advantage of the functional approach is that it offers opportunities for in-depth skill development in each area of specialization. For example, one legal department with 10 lawyers may have specialists in commercial, labour, patent, and international trade law, whereas having one lawyer in each of 10 divisions means the lawyers must necessarily be more generalists.

On the other hand, in a divisional approach, decision-making authority sits closer to the organization's customers. This allows the organization to readily adapt to changing preferences in their divisions' regions or customer groups. Also, accountability is promoted insofar as each division is responsible for making a profit as an independent unit.

> **Economies of scale** are evident when increases in volume are associated with lower organizational costs for providing a specific product or service.

Hybrid departmentalization occurs when an organization uses both a functional structure and a divisional structure.

A **hybrid** structure tries to simultaneously realize the advantages of the functional structure by achieving internal efficiencies and developing internal expertise in some areas, and of the divisional structure by staying adaptable to changes in a dynamic external environment. There are two basic types of hybrid structures. In the first, an organization has both functional and divisional departments, rather like wearing bifocals. Figure 12.5(c) provides an example of a hybrid organization that has a Marketing Department, a Finance Department, and an Eastern Division.

Matrix departmentalization is a type of hybrid structure in which members are simultaneously assigned to both functional and divisional departments.

The second variation of a hybrid approach, called a **matrix** structure, includes divisional and functional departments and members who are simultaneously assigned to both. Think of this structure as like having one lens for seeing close and another for seeing far away. Just as such glasses would take some practice to use, so too can matrix structures be quite challenging to manage and work in. As Figure 12.5(d) shows, members (represented by the circles) are responsible to two managers at once. As a result, these structures generally require spending more time in meetings to ensure that the amount of work assigned to members by their two bosses is reasonable. Members of a matrix structure are not unlike students enrolled in different courses with different professors. It is stressful, indeed, when each instructor coincidentally schedules an exam or report due on the same day. Firms in the Canadian oil sands industry often employ a matrix organizational model in an attempt to drive competitive advantage. For example, these firms will organize around specific phases of resource development and commercialization or around particular oil sand deposits in order to tailor their approach to the needs of the specific resource.[42]

The second dimension of departmentalization—membership—has emerged as an increasingly important element in the past few decades. A generation ago it was simply assumed that an organization's departments consisted of organizational members who had fairly permanent and well-defined individual jobs. Today, however, it is not uncommon for organizations to be structured in teams whose membership is fluid. Teams may disband when their work has been completed, or members may "float" from one team to the next as the need arises. This increased fluidity has allowed organizations to be more flexible and adaptable.

A second trend related to membership is the inclusion of members who are outside the traditional boundaries of the organization. Organizations have always had to rely on suppliers for their inputs, but recently the relationship with suppliers has changed due to the growing emphasis on outsourcing, network structures, and virtual organizations. **Outsourcing** is the practice of using contracts to transfer some of an organization's recurring internal activities and decision-making rights to outsiders better equipped to utilize the latest technologies and reduce costs through economies of scale.[43] Many U.S. companies outsource their payroll functions, for example. Even educators are taking up outsourcing; at an increasing number of American colleges, the grading for coursework is being outsourced to independent "evaluators" or even to software.[44]

Outsourcing is the practice of using contracts to transfer some of an organization's recurring internal activities and decision-making rights to outsiders better equipped to utilize the latest technologies and reduce costs through economies of scale.

Network structure occurs when an organization enters into fairly stable and complex relationships with a variety of other organizations that provide essential services, including manufacturing and distribution.

A **network structure** is evident when an organization enters into fairly stable and complex relationships with a variety of other organizations that provide essential services, including manufacturing and distribution. Warby Parker, an edgy producer of low-cost fashion eyewear, focuses its energy on designing its products, contracting with manufacturers of other boutique-quality eyewear to produce them. Unlike more expensive brands that also contract for the distribution of their eyewear in stores, Warby Parker sells to customers primarily through its website.[45] At the same time, it has entered a socially conscious partnership with non-profit VisionSpring to distribute eyewear through a network of over 9,000 sales agents in economically depressed areas, thereby providing jobs selling and servicing low-cost glasses in their community.[46]

A **virtual organization** is one in which members come and go on an as-needed basis and are networked together with an information technology architecture that enables them to synchronize their activities.

A **virtual organization** is one whose members come and go on an as-needed basis and are networked together through technology that enables them to synchronize their activities. For example, there is computer software that allows people in different parts of the world to work simultaneously on the same document. Virtual organizations can hire people from anywhere around the world for short or long periods. Members may never see one another, and they may not have any ongoing commitment to the organization. They are hired to do a specific job, and when the job is finished their membership may be over. Thanks to cyberspace, networked virtual organizations such as Nike are becoming increasingly commonplace, though they also have potential shortcomings (see My OB: What Brand of Shoes Are You Wearing?).

A sustainable approach recognizes the merits of departmentalization and of bundling tasks and assigning them to identifiable organizational units. Nevertheless, sustainable managers have a lighter hand, giving more freedom to members to collectively decide how specific tasks should be carried out. Sustainable OB emphasizes wide-ranging **participation.**

With regard to the *focus* of departments, the sustainable approach generally leans toward a divisional rather than a functional structure. Divisions operate as autonomous subunits, in which each member knows the overall goals of the unit and understands how his or her efforts contribute to meeting them. As is the case at Semco, the ideal size for a division is about 120 to 150 members. Once it grows much beyond this size, it should be subdivided into two divisions.[47]

With regard to *membership,* a sustainable approach is more likely to invite external stakeholders to participate in decision making. Inviting, listening to, and responding to a variety of stakeholders allows members to be sensitized to new opportunities. In addition, it enhances goodwill when the inevitable mistakes are made. For example, at Shell every business unit must create and implement a stakeholder engagement plan that identifies the specific external stakeholders with which the unit will work, including suppliers, environmental groups, labour organizations, local community, and non-profit energy organizations. The plan describes the precise role that each stakeholder should play in helping to monitor and improve Shell's programs and in enhancing its sustainability. These stakeholders are even offered uncensored space in Shell's annual sustainability report to comment on Shell's efforts.[48]

Participation is the emphasis on mutual discernment and giving stakeholders a voice in how the organization is managed and how jobs are performed.

M⊘B | WHAT BRAND OF SHOES ARE YOU WEARING?

© Crack Palinggi/Reuters/Corbis

Because it's a virtual organization, Nike can choose to have its shoes manufactured in places where the cost of labour is low. This provides jobs in less fortunate countries, but in the past Nike has been the target of criticism for its use of manufacturers in low-income regions that paid substandard wages, employed underage workers, or maintained poor working conditions. Moreover, critics claimed that in failing to disclose its supplier network, Nike was hiding its unethical conduct.

The company's perception changed in 2005 when Nike earned praise for becoming more transparent and revealing data about the nearly 750 factories around the globe that manufacture its shoes.

The company has also increased its charitable contributions to low-income countries, focusing on improving the lives of children and women. Facing pressure from student groups and universities, in 2010 Nike announced it would pay over $1.5 million to help 2,000 workers who had lost their jobs in Honduras when two subcontractors shut down their factories.

QUESTIONS FOR REFLECTION

1. What factors contributed to your decision to purchase the shoes you're wearing?
2. Were you concerned with who made the shoes and where they were made?
3. Are you among the increasing number of consumers who consider the social responsibility practices of companies in their purchasing decisions?

Mutual discernment is a process by which people deliberately learn from one another as they jointly address an issue.

Participation refers to the emphasis on **mutual discernment**, a process by which people deliberately learn from one another as they jointly address an issue—and the process of giving stakeholders a voice in the way the organization is managed and jobs are performed. This means members and other stakeholders join together in running the organization. Managers value stakeholders' input both in making decisions and in setting the agenda. Participation also describes how approachable managers are. Participative managers will facilitate the discussion of how to resolve an issue and then, as appropriate, invite people to participate in implementing the plan. Participation nurtures a collaborative atmosphere in which a variety of members assume joint responsibility for the organization's operations and share its goals.[49]

Ricardo Semler believes that participation is the key to having the kind of organization he wants. In his mind, creating an entirely new kind of organization means operating on "a deceptively simple principle—relinquishing control in order to institute true democracy at Semco."[50] Semler even trusts employees to choose their own managers. This is clearly a foreign concept to conventional management, as Semler attests:

At workshops outside Semco, participants tell me that they'd expect workers to choose leaders who are nice to them, even if those managers are ineffective. They also assume that employees favour bosses who are politically able but technically weak. But Semco's history proves that's not what happens. People will not follow someone they don't respect. Our employees know that their livelihood depends on the company doing well, and they won't support an ineffective leader.[51]

Of course, too much participation has drawbacks, including too many meetings. If input is sought for every little decision and if consensus is always required, activity can be stifled. Participation also may be dysfunctional if stakeholders have little desire to participate or if meetings are intended only as a show of activity or an excuse to delay action.

new ways of organizing for new needs[52]

Nicky Bonne/Redux

Autism rates have grown rapidly around the world. In Canada, about 1 in 94 children are diagnosed with autism, and in the United States the rate is around 1 in 64. However, according to experts, including Dr. Stuart Shanker of York University, the comparatively lower rate in Canada may be conservative and simply reflect a lack of autism services in the areas where data have been collected.

Although about half of all autistic people are considered high functioning (that is, they don't have an intellectual disability), currently only about 6 percent of adults diagnosed with autism spectrum disorder (ASD) find full-time work. Often the reason is that they don't do well in job interviews because they are easily distracted and small talk and eye contact are a challenge.

When Thorkil Sonne, a Danish software executive, discovered that his 2-year-old son Lars had autism, he realized that it would be very difficult for Lars to have a normal life in the traditional workforce. However, Sonne soon recognized that people like Lars have specific cognitive abilities that are both admirable and marketable. In particular, many are gifted at the challenging repetitive tasks that are necessary for testing software and that require enormous accuracy and an intense level of focus. During a TED Talk in 2010, Sonne spoke of how he'd met many people diagnosed with autism who are highly skilled but unable to secure work that tapped into their special skills.

This is what motivated Sonne to create a new business that hires and provides meaningful and dignified work for people with ASD, allowing them to participate in and contribute to society. He called the company Specialisterne (translation: The Specialists), and about 75 percent of its members have some degree of autism. Said Sonne of his company: "The genius of Specialisterne is that it was set up to take so-called 'odd' behaviour and make it the norm."

A typical employee, 30-year-old former teacher Torben Sorenson, says he likes working at Specialisterne because he can be himself, which includes obsessing with his work at times if he wants to: "In another company I might be expected to make small talk and be flexible. Here I can just concentrate on my work without being considered anti-social."

Sonne had to convince potential clients of the extraordinary skills that his consultants could contribute to their companies. The key strength of Specialisterne employees is that they can remain fully attentive doing repetitive tasks that cause other people's attention to wane. Specialisterne employees can earn market-comparable wages because, for example, their error rates are 0.5 percent on tasks where the standard rate is 5 percent—a 10-fold improvement.

Within five years Specialisterne's annual revenue was growing about 50 percent per year, and it had all the work that its 60 consultants could handle from global firms like Microsoft and LEGO. Specialisterne was soon ready to start responding to requests from 53 different countries to start Specialisterne branches beyond Denmark. "My company is a showcase, but my endgame is to get one million specialist people into meaningful work by providing a management model for large corporations to become attractive to people with special needs, so they know that they will be understood and supported."

In 2013 Specialisterne launched its Canadian branch, with offices in Toronto, Quebec City, and Vancouver. Today, Specialisterne is teaming up with the government, communities, and businesses with an aim to provide 10,000 Canadians on the autism spectrum with the opportunity to obtain meaningful and sustained employment. One such partnership is with SAP, who has partnered with Specialisterne Canada to provide employment opportunities in roles such as software testers, programmers, system administrators, and data quality assurance specialists in SAP's labs in Vancouver and Montreal.

QUESTIONS FOR DISCUSSION

1. How are each of the four fundamental issues in organizing evident at Specialisterne?
2. Describe the informal culture at Specialisterne, using but also going beyond the two basic dimensions of culture (predictability versus adaptability, and internal versus external focus).

Summary

Behaviour in an organization is influenced by the interrelated elements of its culture, which includes members' basic assumptions, key values, cultural artifacts, and the organization's structure.

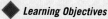 **Learning Objectives**

- Identify the basic assumptions of organizational culture.

- Recognize the key values that shape organizational behaviour.

- Discuss cultural artifacts and how they shape an organization's culture.

- Identify the four fundamentals of organizational structure.

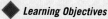 **From a conventional OB perspective:**

- **Basic assumptions** tend to take for granted a focus on the financial bottom line, the precedence of shareholder interests, and that everyone is out to pursue his or her self-interests.

- **Key values** include the relative emphasis placed on instrumental and individual-based flexibility versus predictability, and having an internal versus an external focus.

- **Key cultural artifacts** tend to be symbols of material and individual success, developed by top managers, and introduced in a deliberate top-down fashion.

- **Organizational structures** tend to emphasize:
  - *standardization* (i.e., developing uniform practices for organizational members to follow in doing their jobs) to ensure that work activities are completed in the best way
  - *specialization* (i.e., grouping standardized organizational tasks into separate jobs) to ensure that members know which subtasks to perform
  - *centralization* (i.e., having decision-making authority rest with managers at the top of an organization's hierarchy) to ensure orderly deference
  - *departmentalization* (i.e., grouping members and resources together to achieve the work of the larger organization) to ensure that members work together harmoniously

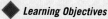 **From a sustainable OB perspective:**

- **Basic assumptions** tend to take for granted a focus on a triple bottom line that includes providing financial, social, and ecological well-being; considering the interests of multiple stakeholders; and ensuring that everyone is pursuing the common good.

- **Key values** include the relative emphasis placed on holistic flexibility versus predictability, and having an internal versus an external focus.

- **Key cultural artifacts** tend to be symbols of community and service, developed by organizational members from a variety of hierarchical levels, and introduced in an emergent bottom-up fashion.

- **Organizational structures** tend to emphasize:
  - *experimentation* (i.e., an ongoing voluntary implementation of new ways of performing tasks on a trial basis) to ensure that work activities are completed in the best way
  - *sensitization* (i.e., being aware of and responsive to needs and opportunities) to ensure that members know which subtasks to perform
  - *dignification* (i.e., treating everyone in the organization with dignity and respect) to ensure orderly deference
  - *participation* (i.e., mutual discernment and guidance) to ensure that members work together harmoniously

Key Terms

Authority (p. 272)
Centralization (p. 272)
Competing Values Framework (p. 263)
Cultural artifacts (p. 265)
Departmentalization (p. 274)
Dignification (p. 273)
Divisional (p. 274)
Economies of scale (p. 275)
Experimentation (p. 268)

Functional (p. 274)
Goal displacement (p. 271)
Hybrid (p. 276)
Matrix (p. 276)
Mutual discernment (p. 278)
Network structure (p. 276)
Organizational culture (p. 261)
Organizational structure (p. 261)
Outsourcing (p. 276)

Participation (p. 277)
Rituals (p. 266)
Sensitization (p. 271)
Shared stories (p. 266)
Span of control (p. 272)
Specialization (p. 269)
Standardization (p. 267)
Virtual organization (p. 276)

Questions for Reflection and Discussion

1. The less visible elements of organizational culture include its shared assumptions and values. Describe how members become aware of these. Do you think these invisible aspects are managed deliberately, or do they just "happen"? How can they be managed, and how can members contribute to developing these elements of culture?

2. Describe the four fundamentals of organizational structure. Which do you think is the most important, and which is the least important? Explain your answers.

3. Define, contrast, and compare standardization and experimentation. Is one merely the opposite of the other? What are the underlying assumptions for each?

4. If you treat others with dignity, will that change the amount of power you have? If so, how? Do you think that any change in power would depend, in part, on your position in the organizational hierarchy? What effect would it have on organizational culture? Explain.

5. Consider Semco, the company described in the opening case. Should employees be trusted to set their own salaries, choose their own hours, and choose their own managers? Identify the risks and benefits from the perspective of employees, managers, and owners. Would this degree of freedom be more appropriate in some organizations than in others? Explain.

ob activities

Where Are You along the Conventional–Sustainable Continuum?

Indicate the extent to which each of the two comparison statements fit you best. Rankings of 1 or 5 indicate strong agreement with the statement closest to the number, whereas a 3 indicates you are undecided or neutral.

Managers should develop standards to ensure that members complete their work activities in the best way.	① ② ③ ④ ⑤	Members should be encouraged to develop and experiment with new ways of performing tasks.
Managers should use specialized job descriptions to ensure that staff members do their specific jobs.	① ② ③ ④ ⑤	Members should be encouraged to be sensitive to and address the opportunities and needs around them.
A centralized hierarchy of authority is the best way to achieve orderly deference.	① ② ③ ④ ⑤	Everyone should be treated with dignity and respect.
Members should be grouped into departments to ensure that everyone works together harmoniously.	① ② ③ ④ ⑤	Members should be welcome to participate and practise mutual discernment and guidance.

Key: These questions measure your views about the four fundamentals of organizational structure. The 1s and 2s reflect conventional tendencies, and the 4s and 5s represent sustainable tendencies. Add up your scores. A sum of 12 means you do not tend to favour one approach over the other, a sum of 11 or lower suggests that you prefer a conventional approach, and a sum of 13 or higher suggests that you tend to favour a sustainable approach. Your score gives you a sense of the kind of manager you want to become and of the kind of organizational structure you would prefer to work in.

Because of pressure from his brokerage firm, a stockbroker recommended a type of bond that he did not consider to be a good investment.

Why might this scenario occur in organizations?

Use the following scale to indicate whether this behaviour is ethically acceptable:

NEVER ACCEPTABLE		SOMETIMES ACCEPTABLE		ALWAYS ACCEPTABLE	
①	②	③	④	⑤	⑥	⑦

Explain the ideas you considered in arriving at your answer.

DISCUSSION STARTER

Organizational Assessment

Option 1: Use the basic concepts in this chapter to analyze the structure of an organization you are familiar with. It could be your employer (past or present), the school you are attending, or a non-profit organization to which you belong. Analyze the organization and indicate which of the two components listed on each line below best describes the organization. Circle "Undecided" if it emphasizes both equally.

My organization can best be described by:		
Emphasis on predictability	Undecided	Emphasis on adaptability
Internal focus	Undecided	External focus
Standardization	Undecided	Experimentation
Specialization	Undecided	Sensitization
Centralization	Undecided	Dignification
Departmentalization	Undecided	Participation

Option 2: Use the concepts described in this chapter to analyze the structure of your Organizational Behaviour course. First, rate each factor based on the way the course is currently structured, and then repeat the exercise indicating how you think it would *ideally* be structured for maximizing students' learning about OB.

QUESTIONS FOR DISCUSSION

1. Based on your ratings, do you think the organizational structure makes sense?
2. Do the different structural elements fit together?
3. Should any of the components be changed? If so, why?

4. Compare your analysis with those of your classmates and identify any differences between large and small organizations and between for-profit and non-profit organizations. Why do you think these differences, if any, exist?

DISCUSSION STARTER

Chief Sustainability Officers[53]

An increasing number of companies are adding the position of Chief Sustainability Officer (CSO) to their organizational structure. A recent study found that organizations which indicate that sustainability contributes to their profitability are about three times more likely to have a CSO. The structures of these organizations are also twice as likely to have a separate function for sustainability and have separate sustainability reporting. Organizations with a CSO (or similar position) are three times more likely to be listed in the Dow Jones Sustainability Index (DJSI). Other organizations can achieve highly sustainable performance without a CSO if sustainability is embedded in their organizational culture and structure.

QUESTIONS FOR DISCUSSION

1. What are the pros and cons of organizations adding a CSO?

2. How would adding a CSO influence the specific cultural and structural elements described in this chapter? Explain.

This is the next in a series of journal entries that can be used for class discussion or be compiled and included in a self-reflection paper.

Think about a group or organization to which you belong that has a distinct culture (it could be your workplace, a particular class you are in, a sports team, a religious organization, etc.). Reflect on how the culture of this organization has changed you and on how you have helped to strengthen (or weaken) the culture. Have you been consciously aware of these changes as they were happening, or did you come to realize them upon further reflection? Do formal structures enhance, or do they squelch, the values and informal culture of group members?

Thirteen

Developing Organizational Culture and Structures

Now that we've introduced the ideas of organizational culture and the four fundamental elements of organizing, such as standardization/experimentation and specialization/sensitization (see chapter 12), we are ready to see how culture is created; how priorities shape the four basic forms of culture; how culture aligns with organizational artifacts like an organization's structure, technology, and strategy; and how these pieces all combine together to form one of four basic types of organizations. Understanding these four organizational types helps us understand much of what happens inside organizations.

Learning Objectives	Conventional OB	Sustainable OB
CREATING AN ORGANIZATIONAL CULTURE		
1. Discuss how an organizational culture is created.	Focus on leaders and strong culture	Focus on all members and weak culture
PRIORITIZING A FORM OF ORGANIZATIONAL CULTURE		
2. Describe the key assumptions and values associated with four basic organizational cultures.	Choose from Conventional Clan, Adhocracy, Hierarchy, or Market cultures	Choose from Sustainable Clan, Adhocracy, Hierarchy, or Market cultures
ALIGNING CULTURE WITH STRUCTURE, TECHNOLOGY, AND STRATEGY		
3. Explain how to align organizational culture with structure, technology, and strategy.	Attend to the fit between structure (mechanistic versus organic), technology (variety and analyzability), and strategy (cost leader versus differentiator)	Attend to the fit between structure (inward- versus outward-facing), technology (variety and analyzability), and strategy (minimizer versus transformer)
COMBINING THE PIECES TO MAKE FOUR ORGANIZATIONAL TYPES		
4. Identify the four basic organizational types and how they should fit together to form a coherent whole.	Develop a Conventional Simple type (an entrepreneurial start-up), a Conventional Defender (emphasizes internal efficiency), a Conventional Prospector (emphasizes external adaptability), or a Conventional Analyzer (balances internal efficiency and external adaptability)	Develop a Voluntary Simplicity type (an alternative to status quo), a Sustainable Defender (emphasizes internal well-being), a Sustainable Prospector (emphasizes external well-being), or a Sustainable Analyzer (balances internal well-being and external well-being)

managing a smile factory[1]

YOSHIKAZU TSUNO/
AFP/Getty Images

Managers at Disney theme parks have a big challenge: to design an organization that makes its parks "The Happiest Place on Earth." Which approach to organizing do they choose? How do they design a culture and shape the four fundamental elements of organizing to accomplish their goal? According to people who have worked there, Disney managers place a great deal of emphasis on standardization, specialization, centralization, and rigid departmentalization. With more than 18 million people visiting just one of its theme parks—Disney World in Orlando, Florida—every year, Disney managers need to run a tight ship. Disney needs to ensure not only that its millions of visitors get a consistent experience, but that families who may have saved up for a whole year for their Disney vacation feel that they had a great time and got their money's worth.

In terms of standardization, new hires at Disney attend "Disney University," a 40-hour program where they learn that customers are "guests," employees are "cast members," rides are "attractions," and accidents are "incidents." They learn standard answers to typical customer questions, such as why rain checks aren't offered. They receive elaborate checklists of behavioural standards, including the need to practise friendly smiles and use friendly and courteous phrases. "At Disney, we believe everything's important," says a former executive in charge of the Disney theme parks. "We don't want any paper on the ground. We're fanatical about it—you don't have to be happy to work at Disney, but you do have to act happy for eight hours." Some observers note that this sort of standardization can make employees' physical selves into "objects," with managers ensuring that each part of people's bodies and social lives are "polished, groomed, and controlled." Some new hires are so put off by the standardized rules they learn in orientation—such as the fact that if you are one minute late for

Company founder Walt Disney is said to have "ruled by fear."

your shift, you have to go home—that they quit before they start actually working.

As for specialization, once employees are assigned to a particular position based on specialized skills, there may be little room for change: "Once a sweeper, always a sweeper." The most skilled are the bilingual Ambassadors and Tour Guides, followed by those who operate tricky rides or rides that require live narration, then the operators of regular rides, the sweepers, and, finally, the food and concession workers.

Disney is centralized, with intense top-down management monitoring. Supervisors have been known to hide in observation posts to try to catch employees who break even minor rules. "Our managers are not bashful about enforcing policies, procedures, and operating guidelines," says the former theme park executive. A former Jungle Cruise operator describes how supervisors "are regarded by ride operators as sneaks and tricksters out to get them and representative of the dark side of park life. [Supervision] also draws operators together as cohesive little units who must look out for one another while they work (and shirk)." Company founder Walt Disney is said to have "ruled by fear."

As for departmentalization, employees' social status is greatly influenced by where they work in the park. Managers do not encourage movement across jobs, and when it does happen it is usually within the same area and job category. There is little overt fraternization across the different types of jobs.

In sum, it is quite an impressive feat of organizational design and socialization that Disney's front-line workers play their smiling roles so effectively, considering the work is fairly mindless, strictly supervised, and not particularly well-paid. Clear standards, specialized jobs, tight supervision, and rigid job groupings have worked for decades to help Disney develop its reputation as a leading vacation destination.

Have you ever noticed that one organization's members act very differently from another's, even if the two are in the same industry? Tim Hortons and Krispy Kreme are noticeably different. Walmart is different from Costco, and Air Canada from WestJet. There are organizations that feel like big bureaucracies in which employees simply go through the motions, and there are places where employees actually seem to be having fun at work. Some organizations are always on top of what their customers want; others have established a process for everything they do.

There are usually good reasons for such differences across organizations. This chapter will help you understand why there are different basic types of organizations, how they got to be that way, and how you can help to create, maintain, or change a certain type of organization. An organizational type is a specific, coherent way that an organization's culture and the four elements of its organizational structure[2] fit with each other and with the organization's technology and strategy. The chapter will proceed in four steps, as summarized in Figure 13.1. The numbering inside each box in the figure indicates the flow of the chapter, and the double-headed arrows show that the four parts of the figure all influence one another.

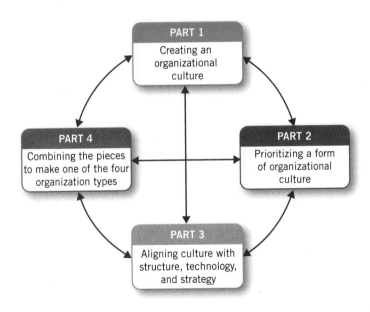

FIGURE 13.1 Overview of the Four Parts of the Chapter

Creating an Organizational Culture

`CREATING` `PRIORITIZING` `ALIGNING` `COMBINING`

LEARNING OBJECTIVE 1
Discuss how an organizational culture is created.

We saw in chapter 12 that *organizational culture* refers to the set of shared values, norms, standards, and expectations that influence the ways in which individuals, teams, and groups interact with one another and work toward organizational goals.[3] We also noted that basic assumptions and values form the core of culture. But we did not describe very fully how members develop and learn about their organization's culture. Where does organizational culture come from, and how is it created and maintained over time?

According to Edgar Schein, organizational culture is created by leaders. In fact, Schein contends that the most important thing leaders do, whether they know it or not, is create and manage an organization's culture.[4] Herb Kelleher, former CEO of Southwest Airlines, agrees.[5] Interestingly, if you think about it in reverse, whoever sets a group's culture can be seen as its leader, even if that person does not have a formal leadership role. For an example, consider teams in professional sports whose culture may be influenced more by their key players than by their formal captain or coach.[6] Sustainable OB emphasizes that it's not only an organization's formal leaders who bring their own values and assumptions about how the world works and what is important. Other members do the same.

To understand how leaders create organizational structure, consider a simple start-up organization. Whether leaders are consciously aware of them or not, they will have underlying assumptions about how the world works and what is important. This will influence their actions and the kinds of organizational structures and processes that they develop. If these actions and structures are positively reinforced in the marketplace—for example, if the organization is profitable and grows—then they will become the norms of behaviour in the organization, and, furthermore, other new and existing organizational members will learn to adopt these successful behaviours.[7] By following these patterns of behaviour, the members are (often unwittingly) adopting and reinforcing the assumptions and values on which they are based.[8]

For example, consider Walt Disney's assumptions about the need for top-down control, which was evident right from the beginning in the way he micromanaged the artists who made Disney films. As we saw in the opening case, these assumptions and their resulting organizational practices were also evident in the rigid top-down structures and systems at Disneyland. And thanks to Disney University, this hierarchical culture persisted long after Walt Disney's death.

Regardless of how it has been created, an organization is considered to have a strong culture when there are high levels of consistency among the assumptions and values held by organizational members. Research suggests that, in general, the greater the shared beliefs and values among members about their organization's culture, the stronger the culture; the greater the level of motivation, satisfaction, coordination, communication, and delegation; and the lower the levels of monitoring, influence activities, experimentation, and information collection.[9] A strong culture promotes consistent behaviour among organizational members, which in turn contributes to consistent organizational performance if the culture enjoys a good fit in a relatively stable environment.[10] Of course, if the organizational culture is not adaptable and does not fit with the organization's environment, or if the environment is changing, a strong culture can contribute to poor performance.[11] For example, a culture that emphasizes traditional methods and proven processes could prevent its members from adapting to changes in the industry that require innovation and flexibility. This helps explain why historic newspapers such as the *Chicago Tribune* and *Los Angeles Times* declared bankruptcy in recent years.

Organizational culture can be strengthened (or weakened) via selection, socialization, or reward recognition. First, selection is at work when organizations hire people from a similar socioeconomic class, the same university program of study, the same ethnic background, and so on. For example, in the past when a job applicant in Boston was said to "look like a banker," it was due to having certain physical attributes: male, Caucasian, short hair, and well dressed in a suit and tie. However, over time, some Boston banks deliberately began to hire people from a diverse variety of backgrounds, although the culture was such that it was initially difficult for these "outsiders" to get the same opportunities for promotion as did their peers who had the traditional look of bankers.[12] Theory from the "attraction-selection-attrition" framework sheds light on how organizational cultures can contribute to a sense of uniformity: (1) *attraction:* people are attracted to work in organizations with others who have similar values, interests, personalities, backgrounds, or other attributes; (2) *selection:* organizations recruit, hire, and promote people who are similar to others currently in the organization; (3) *attrition:* people who do not "fit" with other organizational members tend to exit the organization.[13]

Second, socialization occurs over time as people work in an organization. Recall from chapter 6 how quickly Dennis Gioia adopted the "scripts" at Ford Motor Company, which displaced the values and assumptions he had brought with him when hired. Similarly, consider how theories and practices taught in business schools, based on assumptions that people will act in their financial self-interests, tend to make students more materialistic and individualistic as they go through their programs of study.[14]

Third, when members are rewarded for specified actions, this recognition affects their assumptions and values. Recall how cognitive dissonance ensures that a person's beliefs and assumptions will tend over time to align with new actions that are rewarded (chapter 4). For example, if students learn that mastering their textbook material will reward them with

 **OB in Action** Reddit Revolt

© Carlos Osorio/Getty Images

To see the importance of a connection between the technology, culture, and values of an organization and its community, consider the recent case of Reddit. Founded in 2005 by college roommates Steve Huffman and Alexis Ohanian, Reddit is an entertainment, social networking, and news website where registered users ("redditors") submit content, in the form of web links or text, to different categories ("subreddits") that deal with specific topics. Redditors can discuss the posts and vote either for or against any of the content, with the highly rated submissions becoming more prominent.

The community-driven website relies on its members to create and moderate the various subreddits. Redditors see the website as a bastion of free speech. The topics covered by the subreddits are very diverse, and some of them are highly objectionable. From its inception, users were allowed to publish any sort of content, as long as it was legal. Management has described the various subreddits as ranging from "wonderful, creative, funny, smart, and silly," to "odious" and "reprehensible."

The Reddit community was up in arms shortly after the appointment of Ellen Pao as CEO in November 2014. Pao undertook a series of initiatives that were aimed at changing the culture of the organization and rumoured by the community to be aimed toward monetizing the more popular features of the site. These initiatives met with an immediate and severe backlash.

Pao first drew the wrath of redditors with the introduction of an anti-harassment policy and the subsequent use of the policy to ban five subreddits. While Pao said the policy would ban "behaviours, not ideas," many redditors considered the policy to be nebulous, inconsistently applied, and against the principle of freedom of expression, which is an essential part of the Reddit community. Pao was viciously attacked on the message boards for her role in instituting the new policies and the bannings.

Next, Reddit suddenly fired their Director of Talent, Victoria Taylor. Taylor oversaw one of the most popular features of the website, "Ask Me Anything," where both celebrities and average citizens would field questions from the community. Taylor was extremely popular with redditors. One of the few paid employees, she was seen as a crucial part of the community and responsive to the needs of the users.

The Reddit community saw Taylor's firing as more evidence that management's values were inconsistent with those of the users who were on the site daily. Subreddit moderators, most of whom were volunteers, protested by temporarily shutting down some of the most trafficked areas of the website. Other members began a Change.org petition calling for Pao's dismissal and the reinstatement of Taylor. The petition gathered over 210,000 signatures. An apology from Pao fell flat and she stepped down as CEO eight days after Taylor's firing.

In the wake of this incident, the board recruited Reddit co-founder and first CEO Steve Huffman to return to the role of CEO. In a statement to the community, board member Sam Altman said, "Product and community are the two legs of Reddit, and the board was very focused on finding a candidate who excels at both (truthfully, community is harder), which Steve does." It was the board's hope that Huffman, with "ten years of Reddit history in his head," would be able to use his understanding of the community to rebuild the trust between Reddit and its users.

QUESTIONS FOR DISCUSSION

1. Have you ever thought about the sorts of cultural "signals" your boss (or teacher) may be sending with his or her actions?
2. Do you think these signals are being sent without much thought, or with considerable deliberation and purpose (as in Pao's case)?
3. What additional challenges do organizations that rely on volunteers face when trying to change their culture or structure?
4. What assumptions and values are embedded in the structures and systems in your workplace (or school)?

higher grades, and if they begin to spend a lot of time reading their textbooks, then over time they will increasingly assume that textbooks are an important source of knowledge, that textbook authors know what they're talking about, and perhaps also that the sort of codified knowledge presented in textbooks is more valuable than tacit or experiential knowledge.

Of course, as might be emphasized by sustainable OB, these three mechanisms can also be used to deliberately create and maintain "weak cultures," which are characterized by diversity and multiculturalism. A key dysfunctional aspect of strong cultures is that they may lead to groupthink (see chapter 10) as members becoming increasingly focused on one way of doing things and less able to deal with changes in the environment.[15] The strength of weak cultures, in contrast, is that if the diversity inside the organization reflects the diversity outside of it, then members are more likely to maintain a better fit with their larger context. Research suggests that a flexible, balanced culture that supports a variety of values is more likely to respond to the diverse requirements of its customers and the demands of its changing industry.[16]

Finally, once a culture gets established in an organization's structures and systems, then no matter what kind of culture it is, it no longer needs the active support of leaders to create and maintain it. (This is evident in the substitutes-of-leadership literature discussed in chapter 9.) Indeed, as was evident at Apple in the years after Steve Jobs had passed away, an organization's established culture will persist even if the leader and founding members who helped create the organization's structures and systems leave the organization,[17] and often even when original leaders are replaced by a new leader who purposefully tries to change the values and assumptions of an organization's culture. However, as described in the OB in Action feature "Reddit Revolt," culture change is possible if a leader is able to successfully introduce systems and structures associated with a different culture, as members who act according to these new structures will, over time, begin to embrace their underlying values and assumptions.

Prioritizing a Form of Organizational Culture

CREATING **PRIORITIZING** ALIGNING COMBINING

Given the limitless ways people look at the world, you might expect to find a wide variety of organizational cultures, and it is probably true that every organization has a unique culture. Even so, past experience and research suggest it is helpful to think about a limited number of basic forms of organizational culture. Perhaps the best-known typology of organizational culture is the "Competing Values Framework."[18] This framework is shown in Figure 13.2, which identifies four basic forms of organizational culture that arise based on priorities along the two basic dimensions—the direction of the organization's focus and its degree of predictability—that were described in chapter 12.

With regard to the vertical dimension in Figure 13.2, recall from the preceding chapter that an organization's culture may value and prioritize predictability and control (in the form of rules, coordinated control systems, overall integration, direction, and role clarity), or it may value and prioritize flexibility and variety (in the form of innovation, adaptability, and differentiation). With regard to the horizontal dimension, an organization's culture may focus externally (responding to changes outside its boundaries) or internally (emphasizing human and technical systems inside the organization). We will briefly describe the resulting four forms of culture in turn, using our conventional and sustainable lenses for each.

Clan Organizational Culture

A conventional **clan culture** describes an organization that feels like a very personal place, much like an extended family. Teamwork, loyalty, commitment, and cohesion are the bonds that connect the organization's members. Its culture is participative and comfortable, with a high level of openness. It defines success in terms of teamwork, human

Clan cultures are like extended families that value developing human resources, loyalty, commitment, participation, and teamwork to meet organizational goals.

Clan Organizational Culture (Collaborate) Extended families that value developing human resources, loyalty, commitment, participation, and teamwork to meet organizational goals.	**Adhocracy Organizational Culture (Create)** Open systems that value innovating, risk-taking, bringing new products and services to market, and staying on the cutting edge of the market.
Hierarchy Organizational Culture (Control) Rule-based bureaucracies that value efficiency, low-cost production, predictability, low turnover, and formal procedures and processes.	**Market Organizational Culture (Compete)** Goal-focused and results-oriented culture that emphasizes productivity and the organization's position in the marketplace.

INTERNAL FOCUS — EXTERNAL FOCUS

PREDICTABILITY AND CONTROL

FIGURE 13.2 The Competing Values Framework: Key Assumptions and Values Associated with Four Basic Organizational Cultures
Source: Adapted from Cameron, K. S., & Quinn, R. E. (2011). *Diagnosing and changing organizational culture: Based on the Competing Values Framework* (3rd ed.). San Francisco, CA: Jossey-Bass.

resource development, and concern for people. Although it is characterized by teamwork and consensus, it does have a leader, often positioned as a parent figure or coordinator with skills in mentoring and facilitation.

A sustainable clan culture is similar, though it tends to place less emphasis on top-down organizational goals that originate from the leaders. Instead this type of culture promotes egalitarian and collaboratively chosen goals that everyone shares. And while a conventional approach might emphasize working together to reduce turnover costs or improving methods to increase profits for the clan, a sustainable clan is more likely to also emphasize treating one another with dignity and benefiting the community in ways that cannot be measured in financial terms.

Hierarchy Organizational Culture

The conventional **hierarchy culture** describes an organization held together by internal processes, formal procedures, policies, and rules. It defines success in terms of efficiency, low-cost production, dependable delivery, and smooth operations. Its leaders are often experts on efficiency and are characterized by predictability, longevity in the job, and skills in coordinating and monitoring.

Rather than centralized control, a sustainable hierarchy culture emphasizes collaboratively developed rules that minimize financial as well as other costs. For example, a sustainable approach seeks ecological and social justice efficiencies, even if they do not enhance the financial bottom line. Also, whereas a conventional approach would focus on monitoring employees, a sustainable approach might focus on 360-degree feedback (see chapter 14).

Hierarchy cultures are rule-based bureaucracies that value efficiency, low-cost production, predictability, low turnover, and formal procedures.

Adhocracy Organizational Culture

A conventional **adhocracy culture** is a dynamic and entrepreneurial organization whose members are willing to take risks and "stick their necks out." Innovation, development, and comfort with being on the cutting edge are the glue that holds this type of organization

Adhocracy cultures are entrepreneurial open systems that value innovation, risk-taking, bringing new products and services to market, and staying on the cutting edge of the market.

together. Members like to try new things and meet new challenges. The culture defines success as having the newest or most unique product or service, or as being a product leader and innovator. Its leadership style is characterized by innovation and initiative, and its leader is often considered an innovator, entrepreneur, or risk-taker with skills in brokering.

Whereas a conventional version of this culture tends to emphasize creating and offering innovative products and services that maximize profits, a sustainable version emphasizes innovations that are sustainable and that enhance ecological and community well-being. For example, a conventional adhocracy focuses on financially promising new opportunities (say, how to *maximize* profits by taking advantage of the growing demand for environmentally friendly products), whereas a sustainable adhocracy seeks new opportunities to enhance multiple forms of well-being for multiple stakeholders (say, how to provide environmentally friendly products in a financially *viable* way that also benefits other stakeholders). Innovative social entrepreneurship (discussed in chapter 16) would often be related to such an organizational culture.

Market Organizational Culture

Market cultures are goal-focused and results-oriented and emphasize productivity and the organization's position in the marketplace.

The conventional **market culture** is competitive, results-oriented, and constantly seeking the best way to get the job done. Achieving goals in both productivity and market aggressiveness are the hallmarks of organizations with this type of culture. Success is considered to consist of achieving both market penetration and market share, and the leadership style is hard-driving about both competitiveness and production.

A sustainable market culture places greater emphasis on goals like finding mutually beneficial ways to co-operate with other stakeholders and improve a community's overall productivity. For example, whereas a conventional market culture sees instrumental goals as rational and encourages actions that improve profits over the next quarter, a sustainable culture will value sustainable relationships and have a longer time horizon. From a sustainable perspective, productivity includes not only goods and services produced but also dimensions like productivity in terms of improved ecological standards and meaningful jobs. A sustainable approach values friendly competition but not winning at all costs: It considers markets more from a traditional perspective of a market in a community where everyone knows one another, rather than contemporary commodity markets where non-financial personal relationships are often downplayed.

Each form of culture has its advantages. For example, the external focus and predictability of conventional market cultures enable them to perform better on measures of financial

---

M⊘B | CULTURE AT YOUR WORKPLACE

VisitBritain/Pawel Libera/ Getty Images

Some cultural artifacts seem hard to understand. Ever wonder how those tall bearskin hats became a part of the Grenadier Guards's regimental uniform? Apparently it was done because it was thought to make the soldiers look larger and more impressive to enemies. Regardless of their particular history, cultural artifacts often provide evidence of the sorts of shared assumptions and values described in the Competing Values Framework, which can be combined to describe four forms of organizational cultures.

QUESTIONS FOR REFLECTION

1. Use the Competing Values Framework to describe the organizational culture at your current or past job. What key factors do you think influenced the culture?
2. Was it the personality or values of your boss, of your peers, or of the organization's founders?
3. Was it the size of the organization?
4. How much difference does it make if you are in a service job versus a manufacturing job, or if you interact directly with customers versus working behind the scenes?
5. Does the physical layout of the organization affect the culture? Compare your observations with those of your classmates.

success but somewhat less well than the internally focused and flexible clan culture on measures of employees' attitudes and commitment.[19] Each of these cultures is also created and maintained differently. For example, leaders in conventional market cultures place higher value on status than do leaders in clan cultures.[20] Some research has found that leaders of these four different cultural forms tend to differ on some of the "Big Five" personality traits (see chapter 3). For example, research suggests that leaders' agreeableness is associated with clan culture, conscientiousness is associated with hierarchical culture, openness to new ideas is associated with adhocracy culture, and assertiveness is associated with market culture.[21] Job satisfaction seems to vary across cultures depending on what sort of system is used to ensure fairness. In a clan culture, members are most satisfied with systems that ensure interpersonal fairness; in market cultures they prefer distributive fairness; in hierarchical cultures procedural fairness is felt to be most satisfying; as for adhocracy, satisfaction may be related to a lack of such systems.[22]

Finally, organizations can change from one culture to another over time. Steve Jobs initially founded Apple based on values like flexibility and adaptability. But when that culture no longer received adequate positive reinforcement in the marketplace, Jobs was replaced for a time by John Sculley from PepsiCo, who was a master at efficiency and who changed the culture. When that experiment failed, Jobs came back and changed Apple's culture once again to make it one of the leading companies in the world.[23] The challenges and dynamics of changing organizations, and their cultures, will be discussed further in chapter 15.

Aligning Organizational Culture with Structure, Technology, and Strategy

CREATING | PRIORITIZING | **ALIGNING** | COMBINING

LEARNING OBJECTIVE 3
Explain how to align organizational culture with structure, technology, and strategy.

An organization's assumptions and values tend to be consistent with its key organizational artifacts—in particular its structure, technology, and strategy. A simplified overview of these relationships is depicted in Figure 13.3, and we discuss each in turn.

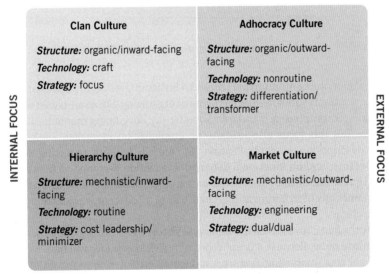

FLEXIBILITY AND VARIETY

INTERNAL FOCUS / **EXTERNAL FOCUS**

Clan Culture
Structure: organic/inward-facing
Technology: craft
Strategy: focus

Adhocracy Culture
Structure: organic/outward-facing
Technology: nonroutine
Strategy: differentiation/transformer

Hierarchy Culture
Structure: mechnistic/inward-facing
Technology: routine
Strategy: cost leadership/minimizer

Market Culture
Structure: mechanistic/outward-facing
Technology: engineering
Strategy: dual/dual

PREDICTABILITY AND CONTROL

FIGURE 13.3 Structure, Technology, and Strategy Aligned with Four Basic Organizational Cultures
Source: Adapted from Cameron, K. S., & Quinn, R. E. (2011). *Diagnosing and changing organizational culture: Based on the Competing Values Framework* (3rd ed.). San Francisco, CA: Jossey-Bass.

Organizational Structure

We begin by describing two continuums of structure and the way they relate to the Competing Values Framework. First, the conventional *mechanistic-organic structure* continuum is related to the vertical dimension depicted in Figure 13.3. Organizations in which predictability is valued tend to have a mechanistic structure, and organizations that value flexibility tend to have an organic structure. Second, the *outward- versus inward-facing structure* continuum, associated with a sustainable approach to structure, is related to the horizontal dimension of Figure 13.3. Organizations that primarily value external stakeholders tend to have an outward focus, and those that primarily value their own members tend to have an inward focus. We will look now at the components of each continuum in greater detail.

First, by far the best-known continuum in the study of organizational structure describes two basic kinds of conventional organizational structures: mechanistic and organic[24] (see Figure 13.4). Building on the discussion of the four fundamentals of structure in the previous chapter, we characterize a **mechanistic structure** as having relatively high levels of standardization, specialization, and centralization, and a functional departmentalization. The U.S. Postal Service is a good example of a mechanistic organizational structure. In contrast, an **organic structure** has relatively low levels of standardization, specialization, and centralization, and a divisional departmentalization. A neighbourhood Ultimate Frisbee league—where people show up on an as-available basis once a week and are divided into different teams—is an example of an organic structure.

A **mechanistic structure** is an organizational structure characterized by relatively high levels of standardization, specialization, and centralization, and by a functional departmentalization.

An **organic structure** is an organizational structure characterized by relatively low levels of standardization, specialization, and centralization, and by a divisional departmentalization.

MECHANISTIC	←——————→	ORGANIC
• Highly formalized	Standardization	• Low
• High/narrow	Specialization	• Low/broad
• Centralized	Centralization	• Decentralized
• Functional	Departmentalization	• Divisional

FIGURE 13.4 The Two Basic Kinds of Conventional Organization Structure and Their Characteristics

The logic behind the continuum in Figure 13.4 is that interrelationships exist among each of the four conventional fundamental elements of organizing. For example, in a mechanistic structure, managers emphasize standardization by, say, developing manuals filled with policies and rules. But this focus also leads to an emphasis on specialization in the form of detailed job descriptions, on centralization via carefully laid-out reporting and decision-making procedures, and on functional departmentalization designed to manage groups of people with similar rather than diverse functional skills. In sum, in a mechanistic structure, the four fundamentals of structure fit together to form a coherent whole that operates like a well-oiled machine.

To see how the four conventional fundamentals fit together in an organic structure, let's look at them in reverse order. Because it is unlikely that a division's leader will have full expertise in every functional area (marketing, finance, production, etc.), it is appropriate to decentralize decision making, giving authority to members who do have the relevant expertise. As they work together, members' specializations will broaden as they understand how the different functions fit together in the work of the division. Finally, because of this decentralization and collaborative specialization, it will be relatively difficult to have very detailed procedures and standards for the overall work that members do. Thus, in an organic structure, the four fundamentals also fit together to form a coherent whole, but the resulting organization operates in a less machine-like fashion and is more like a highly adaptive organism.[25]

It is rare to find an example of pure mechanistic or pure organic organizational structures. Instead, most organizations fall somewhere between these two extremes, or they divide their operations into a mechanistic and an organic component. For example, the LEGO Mindstorms team described in chapter 10 was designed to be more organic, while other parts of the LEGO company remained mechanistic.

Second, sustainable OB also emphasizes two basic, but different, kinds of organization structure: **inward-facing structure**, in which the four sustainable fundamental elements of organizing are emphasized for stakeholders *within* an organization, and **outward-facing structure**, in which the fundamentals are emphasized for stakeholders *outside* the organization. Figure 13.5 presents the inward–outward continuum.[26]

Inward-facing structure is an organizational structure that emphasizes experimentation, sensitization, dignification, and participation among an organization's internal stakeholders and operations.

Outward-facing structure is an organizational structure that emphasizes experimentation, sensitization, dignification, and participation among an organization's external stakeholders and operations.

INWARD–FACING (focus on stakeholders **within** organizational boundaries)		OUTWARD–FACING (focus on stakeholders **beyond** organizational boundaries)
Improve operations with and for stakeholders inside the organization	**Experimentation**	Improve relationships and links with stakeholders outside the organization
Focus on opportunities with and for stakeholders inside the organization	**Sensitization**	Focus on opportunities with and for stakeholders outside the organization
Respect co-workers	**Dignification**	Respect external stakeholders
Include all members	**Participation**	Include external stakeholders

FIGURE 13.5 A Continuum Showing the Two Basic Kinds of Sustainable Organizational Structure

Like the conventional mechanistic–organic continuum, the sustainable inward–outward continuum is based on the idea that the four fundamentals are interrelated, but related in their focus rather than their degree of predictability. Thus, in an inward-facing organizational structure, attention is directed inward to treating each other with respect (dignification), making mutual decisions (participation), improving task performance (sensitization), and improving internal operations (experimentation). In this way, the four fundamentals form a self-reinforcing system. This interplay is evident in the inward-facing organizational structure at Semco (see the opening case in chapter 12). Under the management of Ricardo Semler, members of this organization choose their own hours, experiment with different jobs, and call meetings to initiate change whenever they find worthwhile opportunities to do so.

Similarly, for an outward-facing organizational structure, when members focus on treating external stakeholders—especially those who are not well served by the status quo—with respect (dignification), then it follows that they will seek the advice of these stakeholders (participation), look for ways to raise overall well-being (experimentation), and try to improve the effect of the organization's activities on external stakeholders (sensitization). Muhammad Yunus and the Grameen Bank provide an example of an outward-facing organization structure in action (chapter 16 will provide more information about the formation of this bank). Poor people are treated with dignity and invited to participate in the bank, whose members are especially sensitive to the needs of marginalized women and children and are willing to experiment with new products, such as a program that provides loans to beggars.

ALIGNING ORGANIZATIONAL CULTURE WITH STRUCTURE, TECHNOLOGY, AND STRATEGY   **295**

OB in Action

Organizational Structure in the Global Marketplace

CHINATOPIX/AP Images

Sometimes organizational structures that are designed to minimize financial costs have the unintended result of creating very high human costs for employees. This may be especially true in a global environment where firms compete to minimize production costs. For example, Apple has faced criticism for tolerating poor working conditions in the Chinese factories where iPads are assembled. Among the cases reported were of workers being underage, working 60 hours a week, residing in crowded living conditions provided by their employers (sometimes 20 people sharing a three-bedroom apartment), and of workers with a college degree earning about $22 per day, often for a 12-hour shift.

Other times the flow of business practices and ideas from one country to another may help to improve structures and working conditions. For example, although it was not their original intention, when American Colin Flahive and three friends opened Salvador's Coffee House in Kunming, a city of 6 million that is the capital of China's Yunnan province, the business has had a positive effect on the working and living standards of its 24 employees (young female migrants from rural Yunnan). Contrary to the local business practices, the firm has a very flat organizational structure, provides housing for employees (with a maximum of one roommate), offers profit-sharing after three months, and has health care and vacation packages. In addition to this emphasis on an enhanced inward-facing structure, Flahive's experience has led him to create two new outward-facing initiatives: an organic grocery service called Green Kunming and a non-profit organization called Village Progress, in which international volunteers teach art and health classes in rural villages.

QUESTIONS FOR DISCUSSION

1. What sorts of factors influence the effect that the international flow of ideas and capital have on organizational structures overseas?
2. Do you ever consider the sort of working conditions associated with the products and services you purchase? Should you? Why or why not?

The inward–outward continuum does not describe perfectly what goes on in all sustainable organizations. Nevertheless, it does provide a helpful conceptual framework to think about organizational structure, about how changes in one of the fundamentals can affect the other three, and, in particular, about how to develop a sustainable organizational structure.

Technology

Technology refers to the combination of equipment (e.g., computers, machinery, tools) and skills (e.g., techniques, knowledge, processes) used to acquire, design, produce, and distribute goods and services. Different kinds of technology tend to be related to different kinds of organizational culture. Two dimensions—task analyzability and variety—have proven particularly helpful in thinking about and distinguishing different kinds of technology.[27] **Task analyzability** describes the ability to reduce work to mechanical steps and create objective, computational procedures for problem solving. **Task variety** is the frequency of unexpected, unfamiliar, or different activities involved in performing work.

A *routine technology* is characterized by work that has high analyzability and low variety. Work in such organizations can be broken down into separate steps, and there are few exceptions to standard ways of operating. Traditional assembly-line and data-entry work are highly routine. In her groundbreaking research on the influence of technology on structure, Joan Woodward found that when manufacturers relied on assembly-line technology, a mechanistic organizational structure was associated with increased financial performance.[28] In general, organizations that mass-produce items are more profitable when they emphasize standardization, specialization, centralization, and functional departmentalization. Routine technology is related to an inward orientation and a hierarchical culture.

Work in an *engineering technology* has high analyzability and high variety, meaning many unexpected or novel events. Examples include the work performed by lawyers, engineers, and

Technology refers to the combination of equipment (e.g., computers, machinery, tools) and skills (e.g., techniques, knowledge, processes) used to acquire, design, produce, and distribute goods and services.

Task analyzability refers to the ability to reduce tasks down to mechanical steps and to create objective, computational procedures for problem solving.

Task variety refers to the frequency of unexpected, unfamiliar, or different activities involved in performing work.

tax accountants. The best structure for this technology is moderately mechanistic, but not as mechanistic as routine technology. Here we find an outward orientation and a market culture.

A *non-routine technology* creates work with low analyzability and high variety. It cannot easily be broken down into separate steps, and many one-of-a-kind activities are necessary. Examples include the production of custom-built products and services and the work of university researchers and business strategists. Woodward found that when manufacturers relied on "small batch" technologies to do custom work, like producing unique short-run or one-of-a-kind products, then an organic organizational structure was associated with increased financial performance. In general, organizations that offer tailor-made products and services are more profitable when they adopt an organic structure. Non-routine technology is related to an outward orientation and an adhocracy culture.

Finally, work in a *craft technology* is low in both analyzability and variety. This means a lot of tacit knowledge must be applied but done so in fairly predictable settings, such as the performing arts or training-specific skills. Craft technology may also be evident in some "continuous process" organizations where much of the work is done by machines but people's tacit knowledge is required to oversee them and ensure that they are operating properly. For example, master brewers and taste-testers work as troubleshooters in areas where the nature of problems is often difficult to predict. Woodward found that continuous-process manufacturers achieved higher financial performance if they had a more organic organizational structure. Craft technology is related to an inward orientation and clan culture.

Strategy

Conventional theory and practice draws attention to four main possible strategies: (1) cost leadership, (2) differentiation, (3) focus, and (4) a combination of differentiation and cost leadership.[29]

First, a **cost leadership strategy** aims to keep an organization's financial costs lower than those of its competitors while still maintaining the price and quality of its goods and services at roughly the same level as their competitors. Cost leaders may use a portion of their cost savings by offering lower prices to buyers, thereby increasing their market share and realizing even greater cost savings from increased economies of scale. Choosing this strategy requires members to pay attention to efficiencies in production and distribution systems through tight controls. Walmart is a classic example of a company that uses a cost leadership strategy. Internally, the firm has a world-class supply chain and inventory management system that it uses to lower costs. Externally, volume provides it with massive buyer power that enables it to purchase products from suppliers at lower cost than its competitors can.[30] Although a cost leadership strategy could be supported by either an organic or a mechanistic structure, it is typically found in organizations with mechanistic structures designed to improve internal efficiency and reduce costs.

> **Cost leadership strategy** refers to increasing profit margins by keeping financial costs lower than those of competitors while still maintaining price and quality at roughly the same level as competitors.

Second, organizations following a **differentiation strategy** offer products or services for which buyers are willing to pay a higher price than competitors charge. Differentiators offer exceptionally high quality, extraordinary service, creative design, unique technical ability, and so on. Of course, their exceptional features must be sufficient for customers to pay a premium. The watches marketed by Patek Philippe—the only manufacturer that makes all its mechanical movements according to the strict specifications of the Geneva Seal—are a good example of differentiation. The firm's reputation for quality enables it to charge tens of thousands of dollars for its products.[31] A differentiation strategy can be associated with either an organic or a mechanistic structure, but it is often best supported by an organic structure designed to develop innovative products and services.

> **Differentiation strategy** refers to offering a unique product or service for which buyers are willing to pay a premium price.

Third, while differentiation and cost leadership focus on the overall market, managers might instead choose a **focus strategy**, targeting a small niche such as a specific geographic area or a small product segment. For example, a local pizza restaurant may decide to distribute flyers only in its local neighbourhood, to create an ambiance that appeals especially to

> **Focus strategy** refers to choosing a small niche in the overall market.

families, or to offer only pizza made from organic products. Indian company Tata Motors may decide to distribute its cars only in a particular region and sell only at the low end of the price range. It is possible to combine the focus strategy with either differentiation or cost leadership, and it can fit with either an organic or a mechanistic structure.

A fourth strategy combines cost leadership and differentiation, or perhaps more accurately, it pursues both in parallel. For example, a telephone company might use a cost leadership strategy for its land-line operations and a differentiation strategy for its cellular operations. Ivory soap may compete both as a cost leader and differentiate itself as being 99.44 percent pure.[32]

Sustainable OB theory and practice highlight four parallel strategies: (1) minimizer, (2) transformer, (3) focus, and (4) a combination of transformer and minimizer.

A **minimizer strategy** provides desired goods and services in a way that limits not just a firm's financial costs but rather a *variety* of costs, including financial, social, and ecological. An example is Mountain Equipment Co-op's approach to reducing its waste by recycling water and using environmentally friendly geothermal heating and cooling systems in its retail stores.[33] An inward-facing organizational structure and culture provide a good fit with a minimizer strategy, because both tend to focus on what happens inside an organization and the balance between multiple forms of intraorganizational well-being.

A **transformer strategy** provides desired goods and services by redeeming previously discarded or underappreciated resources. Organizations that recycle tires into floor mats, garden hoses, office supplies, and road surfacing are examples,[34] as are volunteer agencies, such as AARP Experience Corps, which encourages seniors to participate in after-school programs designed to help children with schoolwork.[35] An outward-facing organizational structure and culture provide a good fit with the transformer strategy because each has a focus outside of the organization and each seeks to transform underutilized external resources into valuable inputs and outputs.

Just as the two basic conventional strategies can vary according to their focus, so also can these two basic sustainable strategies operate in a broad or a narrow niche. Thus, a sustainable focus strategy can be associated with either an inward- or an outward-facing organizational structure.

Finally, some organizations may try to combine aspects of a minimizer strategy and a transformer strategy. For example, Staples minimizes its own ecological footprint by using

A **minimizer strategy** provides desired goods and services in a way that limits a variety of costs (e.g., financial, social, ecological).

A **transformer strategy** provides desired goods and services in a way that redeems what were previously discarded or underappreciated resources (e.g., waste, pollution).

OB in Action — Mission-Driven Organizations

© LivingImages/iStockphoto

Given that today's needs are different from those of yesterday, it is not surprising that new kinds of organizations are being created. For example, consider the rise of a new type of organization called the "B corporation," which is *designed* to deliver benefits beyond profits (B stands for beneficial). B Corporations are now operating in more than 20 countries and 60 industries. For example, Novo Nordisk, a Danish health care organization founded to defeat diabetes, has made its organizational priorities improving access to health care among the most vulnerable in developing countries and partnering with local communities to build long-term health care system capacity. Novo Nordisk is guided by a business philosophy of making decisions that consider "what is best for patients, our employees and our shareholders in the long run."

Other examples include ice cream producer Ben & Jerry's and Organic Valley, a producer-owned marketing co-operative whose mission is to save the family farm and which thus has no need for profits much over 2 percent ("We'd just pay taxes on it. We'd rather give it to the farmers").

QUESTIONS FOR DISCUSSION

1. B corporations are pushing the boundaries of organizational design and embracing new understandings of inward and outward-facing organizational structure. What sort of organizations do you want to work in?

2. What sort of culture will you help to create? Give examples.

and promoting recycled paper, and it helps customers transform waste by accepting computers and monitors for recycling (instead of sending them overseas where they would become an environmental problem).[36]

Combining the Pieces to Make Four Organizational Types

CREATING | PRIORITIZING | ALIGNING | **COMBINING**

LEARNING OBJECTIVE 4
Identify the four basic organizational types and how they should fit together to form a coherent whole.

Organizational researchers have long sought to discover the "one best way" to structure an organization. But by now the answer is quite obvious that there is no one best way! Rather, the best way to design an organization is to recognize that the different pieces of its culture and structure should fit together to form a coherent whole.[37]

We return to the question we raised at the beginning of the chapter: Why are there different **organizational types**? The answer is that people have different basic assumptions about how to organize, there are different ways to combine the fundamentals of organizational structures, and organizations use different technologies and strategies. All these different pieces of the puzzle fit together to form a coherent whole,[38] and there are surprisingly few basic types of organizations (though there is variation here too).

The best-known typology of organizations identifies Defender organizations, Prospector organizations, and a combination of the two called Analyzer organizations. A fourth type might be called a Simple organization. Figure 13.6 shows how these four types relate to the different components we have discussed so far in this chapter.[39] We will briefly describe each of the four types in turn, including both a conventional and a sustainable variation. Keep in mind here that there is considerable variation among organizations *within* each type.

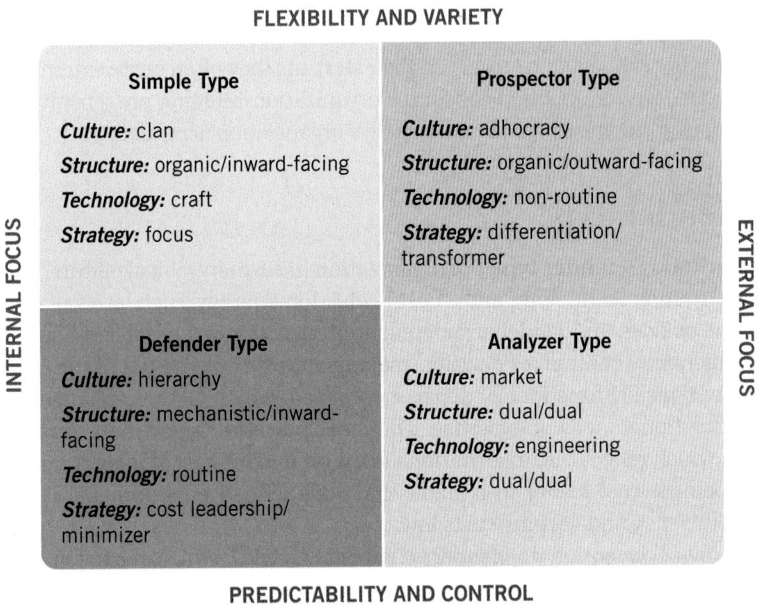

Organizational type is a specific, coherent way that an organization's culture and the four elements of its organizational structure fit with each other and with the organization's technology and strategy.

FLEXIBILITY AND VARIETY

INTERNAL FOCUS

Simple Type

Culture: clan

Structure: organic/inward-facing

Technology: craft

Strategy: focus

Prospector Type

Culture: adhocracy

Structure: organic/outward-facing

Technology: non-routine

Strategy: differentiation/transformer

Defender Type

Culture: hierarchy

Structure: mechanistic/inward-facing

Technology: routine

Strategy: cost leadership/minimizer

Analyzer Type

Culture: market

Structure: dual/dual

Technology: engineering

Strategy: dual/dual

EXTERNAL FOCUS

PREDICTABILITY AND CONTROL

FIGURE 13.6 Combining the Pieces: Four Basic Organizational Types
Source: Adapted from and building on Cameron, K. S., & Quinn, R. E. (2011). *Diagnosing and changing organizational culture: Based on the Competing Values Framework* (3rd ed.). San Francisco, CA: Jossey-Bass.

The Simple Type

Conventional Simple type organizations are small with a clan culture, an organic structure, a craft technology, and a focused strategy.

A typical **Conventional Simple type** is a small organization with a clan culture, an organic structure, a craft technology, and a focused strategy. Think of an entrepreneur who starts up a new organization in a garage or home office. For example, Winnipeg's Ken Reimer started Kendall's Automotive in a small shop in his backyard. Ken may be a mechanic, but his organizational structure was not mechanistic; it started off organic, relying on his own expertise and that of his suppliers to service customers' automobiles. The Simple organization starts with one person, so there is little need for developing written guidelines or job descriptions. The job description of the lone entrepreneur is to do everything and to work as a one-person profit centre. Entrepreneurs who manage Simple organizations are eager to demonstrate the viability of their new venture in order to make a profit and to attract investors. Their strategy is to focus on a particular segment of the market to which they tout their new offering or—because they have lower overhead and operating costs—their low price. Members, where there are more than one, have an opportunity to get to know everyone else in the firm, to know how their work fits with everyone else's, and to participate and share in decisions about the strategic direction of the organization. Small family firms are often of the Simple type, as are long-standing organizations that have remained small in size.

Voluntary Simplicity type organizations are small with a clan culture, an inward-facing structure, a craft technology, and a focused strategy.

The sustainable variation of this organizational type, called the **Voluntary Simplicity type**, is a small organization with a clan culture, an inward-facing structure, a craft technology, and a focused strategy. Often its members are people disillusioned with the conventional approach who are willing to take a pay cut in order to work where they are allowed to pursue multiple forms of well-being and are treated with dignity. For example, MBA graduates from elite business schools have recently begun to shun the high-paying but demanding investment banking industry, opting instead for entrepreneurial ventures where they can make an impact with a more reasonable work–life balance.[40] Some surveys have suggested that the number of Americans amenable to voluntary simplicity has grown from about 24 percent in 1995 to 35 percent in 2008,[41] and it is not unusual to hear sentiments such as "I quit my 40-hour-a-week slavery and got a 20-hour-a-week job that I love."[42] When people in this larger movement do not find working in conventional organizations satisfying, some start or join Voluntary Simplicity organizations such as organic grocery stores, restaurants, bakeries, used-clothing stores, bookstores, bicycle repair shops, child care centres, craft shops, alternative health care centres, alternative schools, and so on.[43] At their start-up, they often invite external stakeholders to help them develop a viable vision for the organization, and they are sensitive to different niches in the environment where their alternative organization is needed.

The Defender Type

Conventional Defender type organizations have a hierarchical culture, a mechanistic structure, a routine technology, and a cost leadership strategy.

The **Conventional Defender type**[44] of organization has a hierarchical culture, a mechanistic structure, routine technology, and a cost leadership strategy. High levels of standardization spell out policies and guidelines, detailed job descriptions emphasize specialization, and a clear hierarchy centralizes decision-making authority at the top of the organization. Defenders are typically functionally departmentalized, which further enhances specialization in the functional areas of expertise. The most powerful departments are production and finance, which reflect the organization's focus on maximizing efficiency and productivity and on being a cost leader in a stable and well-defined environment. The culture is focused on efficiency and keeping costs low.

A well-known Conventional Defender is Lincoln Electric,[45] which started in 1895 and has become one of the most successful manufacturing companies in the world, thanks to an organizational design that helps it achieve significantly lower production costs than its competitors. At the heart of the company's success are two policies built into its organizational structure. One guarantees employment for Lincoln Electric's workers even in down

Open-Source Philosophy at Tesla Motors Advances Industry

© Teddy Leung/Shutterstock

With issues such as climate change and energy security posing catastrophic threats to the planet, there is increased pressure on all sectors of society to improve energy efficiency and to embrace clean energy. Tesla Motors is a company committed to solving the carbon crisis and accelerating the creation and adoption of sustainable modes of transportation. In 2014, Tesla made all of its patented technology available to the public. Elon Musk, CEO and Product Architect at Tesla, believes that intellectual property barriers work against the company's goal of creating compelling electric vehicles and that the "open sourcing" of Tesla's technology will encourage that goal.

As a Sustainable Prospector, Tesla is concerned with pursuing new markets and technologies for the betterment of society.

According to Musk, "Tesla, other companies making electric cars, and the world would all benefit from a common, rapidly-evolving technology platform." Less than a year later, Toyota followed Tesla's initiative and announced that the company will share thousands of fuel cell patents with competitors. From Musk's perspective, technological leadership is not defined by patents but rather by the ability of a company to attract and motivate talent, and he believes that applying an open-source philosophy to its patents will strengthen Tesla's position.

QUESTIONS FOR DISCUSSION

1. Do you know of other organizations who willingly shared secrets of their success with their competitors?
2. Under what conditions might it be in the long-term interests of a firm to share its secrets, and when might it be inadvisable? Consider the views of various stakeholders, including employees and shareholders.

---

times, and the other guarantees that the standard rates for piecework will not be changed simply because employee earnings are deemed to be too high. The resulting structure provides workers with the incentive to increase efficiency and no disincentives. Average wages are about twice the going rate for similar work in other firms.

The **Sustainable Defender type** has a hierarchy culture, an inward-facing structure, a routine technology, and a minimizer strategy. It might appear on "Best Green Companies" or "Best Employers of the Year" lists because of its highly satisfying jobs and corporate social responsibility record. Examples, such as Wegmans Food Markets and REI,[46] are known for experimenting with new ways to treat employees with dignity and sensitivity. They often have a specific niche in the marketplace, and they strive to continuously make their internal operations more socially just and environmentally friendly. The culture is one in which everyone shares a goal to reduce the waste they produce, whether it be financial (in the form of inefficient practices), social (workplace stress), or ecological (pollution). Another excellent example is Semco, described in the opening case of chapter 12.

> **Sustainable Defender type** organizations have a hierarchy culture, an inward-facing structure, a routine technology, and a minimizer strategy.

The Prospector Type

The **Conventional Prospector type** focuses on a differentiation strategy and constant innovation; its members are always searching for new market opportunities and trying to remain flexible and entrepreneurial. Prospectors tend to have an adhocracy culture, non-routine technology, and an organic structure that is characterized by many different divisions acting as relatively independent profit centres. Decision-making authority is decentralized down to the level of the profit centre or lower, standardization is low to permit flexibility, and specialization is also low to permit people to adapt to change and do what is needed. Both Apple and 3M are companies that have a Prospector strategy, and each is known for being an innovation leader in its industry.[47]

Sustainable Prospectors—like The Body Shop, Experience Corps, and manufacturers of composting boxes made from recycled materials—promote environmentally friendly

> **Conventional Prospector type** organizations have an adhocracy culture, an organic structure, a non-routine technology, and a differentiation strategy.

> **Sustainable Prospector type** organizations have an adhocracy culture, an outward-facing structure, a non-routine technology, and a transformer strategy.

products and technology. They tend to have an adhocracy culture, an outward-facing structure, a non-routine technology, and a transformer strategy. Members work closely with suppliers and customers—often because of their high interdependence—and educate them about the benefits of their products and services. The culture fosters relationships and mutual learning with the larger community.

Sustainable Prospector organizations are aware that for Western society to become truly sustainable, everyone ultimately needs to consume less. They therefore encourage customers to purchase *fewer* products, and they promote alternative products that are healthier or produced locally. For example, whereas other grocers have vacated the inner city to maximize their profits, Canadian grocer Neechi Foods Co-op Ltd. has deliberately opened new stores in downtown Winnipeg neighbourhoods to serve the people living there. While other grocery stores promote sweets and processed foods to children, Neechi places fruit at the front of its stores to sell to children at prices subsidized by Neechi staff. To promote community health, the co-op refuses to sell cigarettes. Neechi Foods also purchases as much of its produce as possible from local producers rather than seeking volume discounts from distant distributors.[48]

The Analyzer Type

Conventional Analyzers often have two spheres of operations and develop hybrid structures to accommodate them. Thus, they may support both functional departments (with high levels of standardization, specialization, and centralization) and divisional profit centres (with relatively low levels of standardization, specialization, and centralization). Analyzer organizations use a cost leadership strategy and predictable technologies in stable sectors of the environment, and use a differentiation strategy and evolving technology in sectors that are changing. The culture focuses on refining production methods and on learning from and keeping up with the competition in bringing new products and services to market.

One conventional analyzer is Tech Data Corporation, a *Fortune* 100 company that distributes computer software, hardware, and networking products throughout the world. Its main customers are "resellers," organizations that purchase computer components, package them, and then resell the bundled components to end-user companies that lack a network infrastructure. The key to Tech Data's success has been its ability to operate like a Defender in distribution and like a Prospector in offering new products and entering new markets. The structure on the Defender side is highly mechanistic for distribution, with functionally organized distribution centres that have high levels of standardization and routines designed to maximize efficiency. The structure on the Prospector side relies on monitoring and adapting to changes in the environment; it uses face-to-face technology, such as quarterly customer "summit meetings" to aid in identifying viable new products.[49]

Finally, the **Sustainable Analyzer type** has a market culture, a dual inward- and outward-facing structure, an engineering culture, and a dual minimizer and transformer strategy. Managers strive to achieve the best of both worlds, providing excellent workplaces and helping external stakeholders to achieve structures and practices that meet multiple forms of well-being. As is described in this chapter's closing case, this type is evident in the twofold vision of the carpeting firm Interface, which is (1) to be a world-leading sustainable organization in its internal operations (Sustainable Defender), and (2) to become a restorative organization that helps suppliers and customers put back more than they take from the earth (Sustainable Prospector). Interface's vision statement recognizes that all components of its organizational design must work together to achieve this twofold goal. The dematerialization of internal operations and the collaboration and capacity-sharing that characterize its relationships with external stakeholders requires having a sustainable structure that treats both internal and external stakeholders with dignity.

about face at interface[50]

© Brooks Kraft/Corbis

With more than USD $1 billion in annual sales, Interface is the largest supplier of modular carpeting in the world. A Sustainable Analyzer, Interface pursues the dual goals of minimizing overall costs related to production in its internal operations and of collaborating with suppliers and customers to help them put back more than they take from the earth.

When Interface was started in 1969 by its founder, the late Ray C. Anderson, it was more of a Conventional Prospector with what had been a novel product: 18-inch squares of carpet that could be installed without glue and easily changed and rearranged. This product was ideal for the growing market in offices, which required easy access to underfloor wiring for computers and flexibility to accommodate open floor plans. Thanks to its differentiated product for this new and growing market—and thanks to a "Compete, compete, compete!" approach—by the end of the millennium Interface had become a global giant with 29 factories in six countries, selling about 40 percent of the world's carpet tiles and enjoying the largest market share in almost all of the 110 countries in which it competed.

Around 1990, Anderson was embarrassed to discover that, in the preceding year, Interface had used 1.2 trillion pounds of the earth's stored natural capital and that more than 5 billion pounds of carpet in landfills had "Interface" on the label. "I was running a company that was plundering the earth . . . someday people like me will be put in jail!" Thus began Interface's transformation to become a Sustainable Analyzer, which is evident in three general areas of the company.

First are Interface's achievements in reducing its inputs and waste, which minimize its overall cost of using natural resources, not merely the financial costs. In the first year of this initiative, Interface was able to keep its resource inputs stable despite a 20 percent increase in sales. Part of its success has come from designing new products that maintain quality but use less material. Within three years, a program known as QUEST (Quality Utilizing Employee Suggestions and Teamwork) helped the company reduce its total global waste by 40 percent, which in turn led to financial savings ($67 million) that could be invested in other changes. Interface's goal is to halve its waste every three years, and to eliminate toxic waste altogether by 2020.

Second, the restorative side of Interface's operations includes enabling its suppliers and customers to become more ecologically sustainable. For example, its Cool Blue initiative helps Interface become "waste positive" by reclaiming the waste of other organizations and people, thereby reducing the total amount of waste in society. Interface also offers education and provides other services and products that help its stakeholders become increasingly sustainable. This has included helping companies like Walmart develop their own sustainability vision. Interface has a particular focus on minimizing its customers' waste, which it achieves in part by recycling used carpets—rather than having them be thrown into landfills—which also further reduces Interface's input costs. With its innovative Evergreen Lease, customers do not purchase carpets but instead perpetually lease the service of carpeting (which Interface cleans and replaces as required).

Third, Interface recognizes the importance of promoting social equity within its organization and beyond. For example, it builds and operates overseas factories in lower-income countries according to the same high standards that are applied in North America, Europe, and Australia. Interface has been successful in providing jobs in poor urban communities in the United States, and it encourages its members to become involved in such initiatives.

Four years after introducing its new structure and strategy, Interface was recognized by *Fortune* magazine as one of the "Best 100 Companies to Work For," and it had doubled its employment and tripled its profits. By 2007 Interface's use of fossil fuels was down 45 percent, its net production of greenhouse gas production was down 60 percent, its contribution to landfill sites was down 80 percent, and its use of water to manufacture carpeting was a third of what it had been.

1. Use the Competing Values Framework to describe the culture at Interface. What do you think have been key challenges in creating and maintaining this culture?

2. Describe how the culture at Interface fits with its structure, technology, and strategy. What do you think will be key challenges for Interface in the future?

3. Interface is a global leader in its initiative to minimize its impact on the natural environment, seeking to reclaim more resources than it uses (Anderson called this "climbing higher than Mount Everest"). Why don't more organizations follow Interface's lead?

Summary

Organization culture theory suggests that there will be coherent relationships among the following factors: (1) how an organizational culture is created and maintained; (2) the values and assumptions that guide behaviour in organizations, which may be represented by one of four basic forms of culture; (3) the organization's structure, technology, and strategy; and (4) the organization's design type.

◆ *Learning Objectives*

- Discuss how an organizational culture is created.

- Describe the key assumptions and values associated with four basic organizational cultures.

- Explain how to align organizational culture with structure, technology, and strategy.

- Identify the four basic organizational types and how they should fit together to form a coherent whole.

◆ *From a conventional OB perspective:*

- Organizational leaders seek to create and maintain a strong culture.

- It is helpful to think about organizational culture in terms of prioritizing one of four different forms of culture (conventional clan, adhocracy, hierarchy, or market), depending on whether the basic values and assumptions have an emphasis on predictability versus variety, and whether they have an emphasis on an internal versus an external focus.

- The organizational culture tends to align with key organizational artifacts, including its structure (mechanistic versus organic), its technology (based on its variety and analyzability), and its strategy (cost leadership, differentiation, focus, or a combination of cost leadership and differentiation).

- Taken together, all these factors combine to form four coherent types of organizations:
  - A **Conventional Simple type** has a clan culture, an organic structure, a craft technology, and a focus strategy.
  - A **Conventional Defender type** has a hierarchy culture, a mechanistic structure, routine technology, and a cost leadership strategy.
  - A **Conventional Prospector type** has an adhocracy culture, an organic structure, non-routine technology, and a differentiation strategy.
  - A **Conventional Analyzer type** has a market culture, a dual mechanistic–organic structure, an engineering technology, and a dual cost leadership and differentiation strategy.

◆ *From a sustainable OB perspective:*

- Organizational members typically prefer to create and maintain a weak culture.

- It is helpful to think about organizational culture in terms of prioritizing one of four different forms of culture (sustainable clan, adhocracy, hierarchy, or market), depending on whether the basic values and assumptions have an emphasis on predictability versus variety, and whether they have an emphasis on an internal versus an external focus.

- The organizational culture tends to align with key organizational artifacts, including its structure (inward- versus outward-facing), its technology (based on its variety and analyzability), and its strategy (minimizer, transformation, focus, or a combination of minimizer and transformation).

- Taken together, all these factors combine to form one of four coherent types of organizations:
  - A **Voluntary Simplicity type** has a clan culture, an inward-facing structure, a craft technology, and a focus strategy.
  - A **Sustainable Defender type** has a hierarchy culture, an inward-facing structure, routine technology, and a minimizer strategy.
  - A **Sustainable Prospector type** has an adhocracy culture, an outward-facing structure, non-routine technology, and a transformer strategy.
  - A **Sustainable Analyzer type** has a market culture, a dual inward- and outward-facing structure, an engineering culture, and a dual minimizer and transformer strategy.

Key Terms

Adhocracy culture (p. 291)
Clan culture (p. 290)
Conventional Analyzer type (p. 302)
Conventional Defender type (p. 300)
Conventional Prospector type (p. 301)
Conventional Simple type (p. 300)
Cost leadership strategy (p. 297)
Differentiation strategy (p. 297)
Focus strategy (p. 297)

Hierarchy culture (p. 291)
Inward-facing structure (p. 295)
Market culture (p. 292)
Mechanistic structure (p. 294)
Minimizer strategy (p. 298)
Organic structure (p. 294)
Organizational type (p. 299)
Outward-facing structure (p. 295)

Sustainable Analyzer type (p. 302)
Sustainable Defender type (p. 301)
Sustainable Prospector type (p. 301)
Task analyzability (p. 296)
Task variety (p. 296)
Technology (p. 296)
Transformer strategy (p. 298)
Voluntary Simplicity type (p. 300)

Questions for Reflection and Discussion

1. What generic elements in organizational design are important from both a conventional and a sustainable approach?

2. How are the four fundamental aspects of organizational structure related to one another? Why might it be difficult to change one fundamental without also changing the others?

3. Which do you think is easier to change, an organization's structure or its underlying values? Explain your reasoning.

4. What sort of organizational type best describes the management of Disney theme parks as profiled in the opening case?

Do you think there is a better way to manage a "smile factory"? Explain.

5. The basic typologies presented in this chapter have proven helpful to both scholars and practitioners, and yet they are also acknowledged to be an over-simplification of reality. Can you think of organizations that don't fit into one of the four organizational types described in this chapter? Why are these typologies deemed to be valuable, even if there are important exceptions to them?

ob activities

Where Are You along the Conventional–Sustainable Continuum?

Indicate the extent to which the following list of two comparison statements fit you best. Rankings of 1 or 5 indicate strong agreement with the statement closest to the number, whereas a 3 indicates you are undecided or neutral.

The following are more likely to be effective:

Small organizations that have a clan culture, an organic structure, a craft technology, and a focused cost leadership or transformer strategy.	① ② ③ ④ ⑤	Small organizations that have a clan culture, an inward-facing structure, a craft technology, and a focused minimizer or transformer strategy.
Organizations that have a hierarchy culture, a mechanistic structure, a routine technology, and a cost leadership strategy.	① ② ③ ④ ⑤	Organizations that have a hierarchy culture, an inward-facing structure, a routine technology, and a minimizer strategy.
Organizations that have an adhocracy culture, an organic structure, non-routine technology, and a differentiation strategy.	① ② ③ ④ ⑤	Organizations that have an adhocracy culture, an outward-facing structure, non-routine technology, and a transformer strategy.

Organizations that essentially have two spheres of operations, with some parts of the organization operating like a Conventional Defender and other parts operating like a Conventional Prospector.

Organizations that essentially have two spheres of operations, with some parts of the organization operating like a Sustainable Defender and other parts operating like a Sustainable Prospector.

Key: These questions measure your views about the four basic organizational types. The 1s and 2s reflect conventional organizational types, and the 4s and 5s represent sustainable types. Add up your scores. A sum of 11 or lower suggests that you prefer conventional organizational types, a sum of 13 or higher suggests that you tend to favour sustainable types, and a sum of 12 means that you do not tend to favour one over the other. Your score gives you a sense of the kind of organization you might prefer to work in and the kind of manager you might become.

ETHICS SCENARIO

An engineer discovered what she perceived to be a design flaw that constituted a safety hazard. Her company declined to correct the flaw. The engineer decided to keep quiet rather than take her complaint outside the company.

Use the following scale to indicate whether this behaviour is ethically acceptable:

NEVER ACCEPTABLE		SOMETIMES ACCEPTABLE			ALWAYS ACCEPTABLE	
1	2	3	4	5	6	7

Explain the ideas you considered in arriving at your answer.

DISCUSSION STARTER

Introducing Sustainable Culture and Structures in the Classroom

When it comes to designing courses and assigning grades, many students have grown accustomed to and developed a preference for a mechanistic structure. For example, students want to know ahead of time what percentage they need to earn on exams and assignments to earn a particular letter grade, how much weight is given to each test and assignment, and which parts of the textbook they are responsible for knowing. They also typically prefer objective multiple-choice questions to subjective essay questions. Imagine that one of your instructors has asked you to redesign the course you are currently enrolled in to make it more closely resemble a sustainable organization type.

QUESTIONS FOR DISCUSSION

1. Considering each of the factors in the organizational design process, what would you suggest changing?

2. Which changes might be relatively easy to make, and which might be difficult to make?

3. Which changes would students prefer, and which might your instructors prefer? Why?

DISCUSSION STARTER

Design for a Soup Kitchen

Your friend Nancy, who has volunteered in a soup kitchen, tells you about three basic types of this sort of service organization. The first model she calls the "carrot and stick" soup kitchen, which requires clients to enter through a church or chapel and hear a sermon before getting a meal. The second model has a large staff and is able to raise hundreds of thousands of dollars, but only a small percentage of the money actually goes to purchase food for hungry people. Staff in these "self-serving" organizations, as Nancy describes them, see feeding the hungry as a means to raise funds for their own livelihood. The third type Nancy calls the "charity" model. She worked for an organization of this type for five years. Here, well-meaning people donate money and volunteer to feed people who are less fortunate than themselves and who need only walk through the door to eat.

At first, Nancy said, she thought the charity model was the best way to organize. She worked hard and successfully in that setting and after a few years became the paid manager of one such soup kitchen. The organization also had two part-time staff members and an abundance of volunteers who would come in to serve the 200 or so simple hot lunches prepared each day in a church basement. Most of the food served was donated through a local food bank. The organization was governed by a board of individuals who wanted to help people less fortunate than themselves. After a while, however, Nancy began to have doubts about how the charity model worked. Her misgivings were triggered by the things she heard people say who came there to eat: "I never thought I'd drop so low as to become a charity case." "It is humiliating for me to be here." "I feel that I have no more dignity." Nancy described how this affected her:

I started to think about those comments, and I talked about them with my friends and associates. Were we robbing people of their dignity? Was our organization designed in such a way that we could not help but rob people of dignity? It bothered me to see how the attitude of our "regulars" seemed to change. At first, they felt bad because they felt that they did not have anything to contribute back.

Then, after a while, they started to think that they should not contribute anything.

She listened some more and asked herself probing questions: "Would I like to be treated as a charity case? What would it do to me, to my sense of self-worth, to depend on handouts?" She decided to try to change her organization into a "dignity model," but because her board has resisted her efforts, she is thinking of starting a new soup kitchen.

Nancy asks whether you would be willing to give her some advice on designing a "dignity" model organization. She has already made some progress in identifying sources where she thinks she can get food donations to start up such a soup kitchen, and she has some friends and acquaintances who could provide start-up money. She also says she has a site she could use. Nancy just needs help in envisioning this new organization.

QUESTIONS FOR DISCUSSION

1. Draw on concepts from this and earlier chapters to describe the culture Nancy is envisioning. How will this culture be established and maintained?

2. What would you suggest as an organizational design for Nancy's dignity-model soup kitchen?

3. Describe each of the four fundamentals of organizing as well as how your design fits with strategy and technology.

APPLICATION JOURNAL

This is the next in a series of journal entries that can be used for class discussion or be compiled and included in a self-reflection paper.

Think of an organization you are very familiar with based on your personal experience. How was its culture created, and how is it maintained? What organizational type described in this chapter does it most closely correspond to? How do your personal values align with the values and culture of this organization? Can you think of other organizations that fit better with your personal values? What does this analysis tell you about yourself or the kind of organization(s) you would like to work for?

Fourteen

Motivating with Systems

In your journey through this chapter, you will read about motivational systems within organizations. The systems may also serve other functions, such as ensuring legal compliance, but our main interest is the effect that each system has on individual and group behaviour. We will begin by exploring the motivating potential of the way jobs are designed and end by discussing the motivating potential of organizational goals and mission statements. In between, we will review the ongoing rewards and development systems within organizations that reinforce and improve job performance in pursuit of organizational goals.

Learning Objectives	Conventional OB	Sustainable OB
JOB DESIGN		
1. Explain how jobs are designed.	Focus on the individual job Use input primarily from jobholders Emphasize efficiency	Focus on team or system Use input from multiple stakeholders Emphasize meaning
PERFORMANCE MANAGEMENT		
2. Discuss the two components of performance management and how the outcomes influence organizational members' behaviour, motivation, and learning.	Use appraisals to reward members Reinforce independent performance through individual rewards Focus on financial rewards	Use appraisals to develop members Reinforce interdependent performance through group-based rewards Balance financial and non-financial rewards
TRAINING AND DEVELOPMENT		
3. Discuss how training and career development improves job performance and prepares employees for future positions.	Provide training in exchange for short-term production Favour organizational needs over personal development	Provide training as a long-term investment in people Favour personal development over organizational needs
MISSION AND VISION		
4. Explain how mission and vision work together to contribute to organizational performance.	Emphasize the organization's purpose and aspirations	Emphasize the shared purpose and aspirations of the organization

high-tech loyalty at SAS Institute[1]

CP Images/Karen Tam

"I'm never gonna leave SAS; just bury me here. I'm just gonna stay here forever," said one employee of SAS Institute, a software pioneer that has an impressive record of more than 30 years of consecutive increases in revenue growth and profitability. It is the largest privately held software company, with 400 offices across the world and more than 13,000 employees. At the heart of its success is a simple employee-focused philosophy: "Satisfied employees create satisfied customers." In an industry characterized by hyper-competition, where employees tend to act like free agents signing with the highest bidder, SAS has maintained a high level of loyalty and a low level of turnover (historically, less than 5 percent).

Guiding principles at SAS are to treat people fairly and to treat them with dignity.

When they established SAS, Jim Goodnight, John Sall, Anthony Barr, and Jane Helwig set out to create a workplace that was as much fun for employees to work in as it was for top managers. The co-founders recognized that their most important assets, their people, leave each night and it is management's job to give them compelling reasons to return the next day. The grounds of SAS's Cary, North Carolina, headquarters are designed to be aesthetically pleasing, with picnic areas and hiking trails winding through the property. On-site are an expansive fitness facility with basketball courts and a pool, a subsidized Montessori daycare centre, and a 7,500-square-foot medical facility offering free care to employees. Inside, all employees have access to a subsidized cafeteria and enough free M&M'S candy to compel use of the fitness facilities. The attractive setting might be perceived as an attempt to lure people to spend all their waking hours at SAS, but the opposite is actually true: Company policy encourages employees and managers to maintain a healthy work–life balance and keep reasonable hours. This is echoed in an often repeated company proverb: "After eight hours, you're probably just adding bugs."

Two guiding principles at SAS are to treat people fairly and to treat them with dignity. In a business that depends on its intellectual capital for success, SAS's co-founders believe that these guiding principles will attract and motivate their employees. Flexible work schedules allow employees to make their own decisions about when to show up and when to leave early, which enables them to work around personal commitments. Jobs are designed to be interesting and challenging to emphasize intrinsic motivation over extrinsic incentives. Employees are given opportunities to use the latest technology tools, encouraged to experiment in developing new software, and provided opportunities to work on projects with talented colleagues.

SAS follows a simple formula for performance management: provide people with the necessary resources for the job, empower them to do their work, and hold them accountable. Managers set high expectations, formal appraisals of job performance are conducted to provide employees with regular feedback, and managers are available to support employees. If an employee is not meeting expectations, a corrective action plan is developed and the person either improves or is asked to leave. Pay practices at SAS also are different from those of other companies in the same industry. Instead of using stock options to entice employees to work harder, the company pays a competitive market wage, regularly makes contributions to employees' profit-sharing retirement plans, and gives small annual bonuses based on company performance (typically ranging from 5 to 8 percent of the employee's base salary). SAS de-emphasizes individual pay for performance, believing that it is not an effective motivator compared to meaningful work and a long-term loyal employment relationship.

SAS managers hope that their company's culture of loyalty will encourage employees to spend a majority of their working lives with SAS. Although employees may have several careers, SAS makes room for those careers within its organization. If an employee has the skill set to contribute to the organization in another role, the firm's structure makes it easy to move laterally across the organization. Training for new positions as well as orientation for new hires is handled almost entirely by long-term employees who enjoy training others—keeping it within the family, so to speak. SAS supports its employees in the process of discovering what they like to do and what they are good at doing, then allows them a great deal of freedom to do what they like to do and do it well.

The people-friendly focus of SAS's organizational systems is an intentional approach to achieving the company's primary mission of delivering superior software and continually enhancing customer relationships. A track record of consistent revenue growth and profitability offers compelling evidence that everyone benefits from a motivating work environment, which is a main reason why so many people want to work there and so few want to leave. The strategy has certainly worked: One estimate from a Stanford University professor is that SAS saves more than $85 million per year thanks to its high morale and low turnover.

In organizations, motivational systems are developed and maintained to influence members' motivation and behaviour. These motivational systems include several human resource management (HRM) practices that organize, reward, and improve the work of organizational members and that emphasize the organization's mission and vision. These systems have been proven to enhance motivation and organizational performance[2] and are gaining prominence as potential sources of competitive advantage. In this age of hyper-competition, products and services—and even many technologies—are easily copied. As a consequence, they quickly become obsolete as sources of competitive advantage. In contrast, the motivational systems that affect how an organization's members are organized, rewarded, developed, and inspired are more difficult to copy. Stanford University professor Jeffrey Pfeffer is among a growing group of researchers who have shown that people-focused motivational systems can have enormous economic benefits as well as enhance social well-being.[3]

Figure 14.1 illustrates how these motivational systems influence motivation that, in turn, contributes to lower turnover and higher individual and organizational performance.[4]

We will discuss four motivational systems in this chapter: job design, performance management, training and development, and the organization's mission and goals. Although these systems are most often implemented by managers or HRM professionals within the organization, the specific practices can also be applied by other members seeking to enhance motivation throughout the organization.

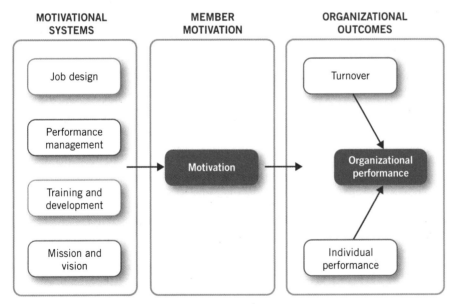

FIGURE 14.1 Motivational Systems and Outcomes

Job Design

JOB DESIGN | PERFORMANCE MANAGEMENT | TRAINING & DEVELOPMENT | MISSION & VISION

Job design answers the question of what work should be done in specific jobs. At a basic level, it identifies the knowledge, skills, abilities, and other characteristics—known as **KSAOs**—necessary for a given job. The design of a job also describes the job's characteristics and how it relates to other jobs and people in other positions.

Job analysis, the beginning point for designing a job, is an investigative process of gathering and interpreting information about a job and its required KSAOs. There are several methods of collecting this information. For example, a job analyst or manager might observe a job being performed by another employee or might even perform the actual job. More often, job analysts interview or survey **subject matter experts (SMEs)**, who either hold the job or observe the job regularly, to generate a list of job tasks or KSAOs.

Although the job analysis process can sometimes be very detailed and formal, when Darin Hartley was an HRM professional for Dell, he used a process he called Job Analysis at the Speed of Reality (JASR), whereby he would bring together a group of jobholders for a few hours to negotiate job expectations and tasks.[5] Like commitment to goals, the jobholder's motivation is likely to be increased by participation in the analysis process. Whereas the conventional approach to gathering information for a job analysis is dominated by getting input from subject matter experts like jobholders, a sustainable approach is likely to include more extensive participation in the process; more stakeholders, such as customers; and a greater emphasis on the role of a job in the larger system or workflow of the department or business unit.

The information from a job analysis feeds into the drafting of a job description that summarizes the characteristics of a particular position. The job description specifies the duties associated with the position as well as the knowledge, skills, education and training, credentials, prior experience, physical abilities, and other characteristics required to fulfill those duties. Generally, a job description can be motivating because it clarifies tasks and roles. Clarity in a job can improve employee satisfaction and performance, whereas ambiguity and conflicting expectations can be demotivating and immobilizing.[6]

The characteristics of a job also contribute to how motivating the job is to the jobholder. The **job characteristics model**, illustrated in Figure 14.2, specifies how to increase the motivational potential of a job by improving the meaningfulness, autonomy, and feedback associated with the job.[7] The *meaningfulness* of a job comes from the variety of skills required

KSAOs are the knowledge, skills, abilities, and other characteristics associated with specific positions.

Job analysis is an investigative process of gathering and interpreting information about a job and its required KSAOs.

Subject matter experts (SMEs) are experts in a specific occupation or specific task.

The **job characteristics model** specifies how to increase the motivational potential of a job by improving the meaningfulness, autonomy, and feedback associated with the job.

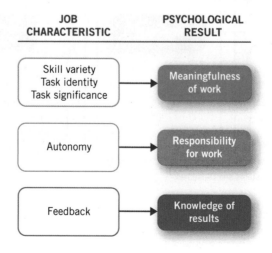

FIGURE 14.2 Components of the Job Characteristics Model

to complete the work (skill variety), the extent to which the job tasks allow for completing more or all of a project or product (task identity), and the degree to which the work is understood to affect the lives of other people (task significance). *Autonomy* is the extent to which the job provides the freedom and responsibility to decide how the work is done. *Feedback* describes the knowledge of results the jobholder receives from the job itself, co-workers, or supervisors regarding the quality or quantity of the work. When jobholders experience their work as meaningful, feel responsible for their work, and receive feedback on their results, the experience is motivating for those who value opportunities to grow and who have the basic knowledge and skills to perform their jobs.[8] For those who don't value growth or who lack basic skills or abilities, holding an important job with high levels of responsibility and feedback may be discouraging.

Redesigning one or all of the job characteristics in the model is a way to increase motivation. We can increase *meaningfulness*, for example, by expanding the variety of skills employed in the job, perhaps through cross-training in jobs of similar complexity. We can also move away from an assembly-line type of organization in which a person does one part of a larger project and instead consider having one person or one team of people complete a whole job or project. For example, at American-Lincoln their industrial sweepers and cleaning machines are completed almost entirely by a team rather than by individuals on an assembly line. This increased task identity gives members a sense of pride and ownership that is less likely when each person does only one part and does not see how he or she is contributing to the final product. Another strategy is to elevate the work's importance by highlighting its effect on others. In episodes of the television show *Cake Boss*, Buddy Valastro is often heard telling his staff to do excellent work on a cake for the sake of the person receiving it. Increasing the job's connection to its impact on customers can have a similar effect for a variety of jobs.

We can increase job *autonomy* by allowing employees more freedom and responsibility in the way they accomplish tasks. At Mouvement des caisses Desjardins, a financial institution based in Lévis, Quebec, employees are encouraged to strike a balance between work and personal commitments, and they are given the flexibility to adjust their schedules so that work-related stress becomes manageable. As a socially responsible and environmentally conscious organization, this company tailors its benefits package to meet the specific needs of its employees and their families.[9] Increased autonomy is a key feature of self-managed teams. Management may work with the team to agree on goals, but the team members decide how they will pursue them, making decisions about scheduling and roles, suppliers, machines, or tools and communicating directly with customers.

We can increase *feedback* by providing the jobholder with information about the quality or quantity of the work. Sometimes this feedback comes in the form of more frequent interaction with supervisors, but it can also consist of reports or performance dashboards that provide up-to-the-minute information about work processes and outputs. More information allows jobholders to receive reinforcement or to get early warning of adjustments they need to make in order to improve outcomes.

The conventional approach to job analysis and design tends to be mechanistic, strongly rooted in scientific management, and oriented toward maximizing efficiency through individual task specialization and task simplification. The main objective is to create defensible, verifiable specifications and descriptions that are independent of any particular person. This approach to job design may ensure that the required work gets done, but it isn't likely to spur innovation.[10] Also, if job design focuses on individual jobs that don't change much, this approach does not fit well with jobs that require working interdependently or that change frequently.[11]

A sustainable approach builds on research findings from job characteristics theory to encourage putting more control of decisions in the hands of the jobholder in order to spur creativity and innovation.[12] This approach is also likely to emphasize the dignifying and motivating aspects of social characteristics of jobs that were not included in the original job

Luciano Mortula/Shutterstock

Fast food restaurants and other service franchises are masters of a mechanistic approach to job design: Their jobs are highly specified, and people are plugged in as needed to efficiently run the system to produce a uniform output. Under this approach, a job at a McDonald's in Manhattan, New York, should essentially be the same as a job at a McDonald's restaurant in Toronto or even in Yellowknife, Northwest Territories. That's something you might appreciate if you hunger for a Big Mac while travelling and hope to receive "two all-beef patties, special sauce, lettuce, cheese, pickles, and onions on a sesame seed bun." Without clear procedures in place for employees to follow, your order could be a big mistake.

QUESTIONS FOR REFLECTION

1. Have you ever worked at a fast food restaurant?
2. How were the jobs designed?
3. Did they allow much room for you to make decisions or innovate?
4. How would you describe your motivation level?
5. On the other hand, as a customer at a fast food restaurant, do you *want* innovative employees making your food?

---

characteristics model. Working interdependently, receiving feedback from people rather than the job itself, being helped or supported by others, and interacting with people outside the organization increase motivation over and above the original job characteristics and decrease stress and intentions to leave the organization.[13]

A sustainable alternative to focusing on individual jobs may be to analyze and design team jobs where appropriate. That is, the tasks and KSAOs of the team, rather than the individual, are designated in the job description and specifications, along with a description of whom the team interacts with and influences through its work. Researchers have already identified KSAOs that can be applied to teams, such as managing conflict, coordinating work responsibilities, and communicating effectively.[14] Focusing on the team may make the characteristics of individual jobs less clear, but it can be motivational for different reasons. Some people simply enjoy working in teams, and others are motivated by the accountability that comes from working alongside others.[15] Self-managed teams also can increase autonomy by allowing the team, rather than managers, to make many operational decisions, and they can increase job significance by focusing the work on larger challenges. Merck & Co., an American-based pharmaceutical company, experienced an increase in employee motivation and innovation when it moved its scientists from a job-focused approach of completing individual responsibilities to a team-focused approach of working together to provide solutions for the challenges associated with cancer and diabetes.[16]

LEARNING OBJECTIVE 2
Discuss the two components of performance management and how the outcomes influence organizational members' behaviour, motivation, and learning.

Performance Management

| JOB DESIGN | **PERFORMANCE MANAGEMENT** | TRAINING & DEVELOPMENT | MISSION & VISION |

Performance management is the process of ensuring that each employee's activities and outputs are aligned with the organization's goals.

Reinforcement is a response or consequence linked to a behaviour.

Performance management refers to HRM and management processes that ensure that employees' activities and outputs are aligned with the organization's goals.[17] Performance management has two components: performance appraisal and compensation. Conventionally, each of these tools relies on reinforcement theories that draw attention to the ways people with power can use outcomes or consequences to influence organizational members' behaviour, motivation, and learning. A **reinforcement** is a response or consequence linked to a behaviour. Reinforcement theories help explain how new behaviours are learned and how behaviour can be changed.

Psychologist B. F. Skinner described the process of motivating behaviour by manipulating its consequences as *operant conditioning*. Another name for this process is *behaviour modification*—that is, the use of reinforcement techniques to modify human motivation and behaviour. In organizations, reinforcement techniques are utilized to help employees learn new behaviours for their jobs or to change their on-the-job behaviour. Reinforcements also can encourage individuals to act co-operatively in organizations.[18] Four basic techniques are associated with reinforcement theory:

- Positive reinforcement
- Punishment
- Negative reinforcement (or avoidance)
- Extinction

Positive reinforcement is the administration of a pleasant and rewarding consequence following a desired behaviour. When a person observes someone doing an especially good job and offers praise, that praise serves as a positive way to reinforce the behaviour of good work. In organizations, positive reinforcers include pay raises, promotions, and almost anything that people regard as a desirable consequence. Of course, a reinforcer is positive only if it is something that is valued by the person who receives the reinforcement. For example, tickets to an NHL hockey game might be a positive outcome for some people but not for others.

Punishment seeks to decrease the frequency of or eliminate an undesirable behaviour by following the behaviour with an unpleasant consequence. For example, a supervisor might assign extra work to an employee who is observed wasting time on the job, or a professor might deduct points for a late assignment. Both hope that punishment will reduce the likelihood that the unwanted behaviour will recur. Punishment has been proven to reduce certain types of behaviour, and it can send a signal to others that people are held accountable for their behaviour.[19] However, punishment should be used for the right reasons—not to satisfy the need for attention or to demonstrate power—and sparingly, because it can have some undesirable side effects, including resentment, loss of self-respect, and desire for retaliation.

Negative reinforcement, sometimes called *avoidance learning*, is the removal of an unpleasant consequence following a desired behaviour. People learn to do certain things to avoid unpleasant consequences. For example, many of us have learned that if we fasten our seatbelt shortly after we get in our car, we can avoid the annoying warning bell. Employees learn to complete work before a deadline to avoid the stress of working up to the last minute or having to explain a missed deadline to the boss. Note the key difference between negative reinforcement and punishment: Whereas punishment causes unwanted behaviour to occur less frequently, negative reinforcement causes *desired* behaviour to be repeated.

Extinction is the absence of any reinforcement—either positive or negative—following the occurrence of a behaviour. The idea is that a behaviour that is not positively reinforced will be less likely to occur in the future. For example, if you stop smiling and laughing in response to a co-worker who often stops by to get attention from crude jokes, your lack of response removes the expected positive reinforcement and makes the employee more likely to stop the disruptive behaviour.

In organizations, positive reinforcement is a common and effective method for managers to motivate or shape the behaviour of employees. Not only is it a powerful motivator, but its influence depends to some extent on when it occurs. *Schedules of reinforcement* describe the frequency and regularity of recurring reinforcement:

- *Fixed-interval schedules* reward employees at fixed intervals of time, such as with regular paycheques or annual appraisals.
- *Fixed-ratio schedules* reward employees after a specific number of desired responses or behaviours have occurred. For example, in many sales situations, salespeople receive a bonus or prize after selling a specific quantity of products, such as medical devices, computers, or cars.

Positive reinforcement is the administration of a pleasant and rewarding consequence following a desired behaviour.

Punishment seeks to decrease the frequency of or eliminate an undesirable behaviour by following the behaviour with an unpleasant consequence.

Negative reinforcement, sometimes called *avoidance learning*, is the removal of an unpleasant consequence following a desired behaviour.

Extinction is the absence of any reinforcement—either positive or negative—following the occurrence of a behaviour.

OB in Action — Where Is the Motivation?

The classic film comedy *Office Space* makes light of several examples of reinforcement techniques. In an interview with consultants, for instance, a disgruntled programmer named Peter, played by Ron Livingston, asks, "Where is the motivation?" He says he doesn't see a dime if his company makes more money (no positive reinforcement), but he does get berated if he makes a mistake or turns work in late (punishment). In fact, Peter has eight bosses, so he hides out in his office and keeps a low profile in order to avoid interacting with them and being assigned more work (negative reinforcement). The response of Peter and many others to misused motivational tools is that they "just don't care."

QUESTIONS FOR DISCUSSION

1. Have you ever worked in an organization where members just don't care?
2. Can you point to the absence or presence in that organization of any of the reinforcement principles identified in this chapter?
3. What would you suggest be changed to improve motivation?

- *Variable-interval schedules* provide reinforcement at varying intervals of time, such as occasional visits by the supervisor.
- *Variable-ratio schedules* provide reinforcement at variable amounts of output, such as sales bonuses tied to a certain number of sales calls one month and a different number another month.

Fixed-interval schedules and ratios have the motivational benefit of providing a clear message about when reinforcement will occur so that recipients can look forward to it, but they also can contribute to a drop in motivation if there is a long time lag before the next possible reinforcement, or if a scheduled reinforcement is not provided (say, no annual bonus one year). Variable schedules tend to result in more consistent and enduring motivation, partly because people don't quite know when their behaviour might lead to reinforcement, so they work at a higher level more of the time. The downside is that employees may feel it is unfair when they don't know when reinforcement is coming.

Findings from research on reinforcement theory influence how performance management systems are designed and used. This is evident in the following sections describing performance appraisal and compensation practices in organizations.

Performance Appraisal

Performance appraisal is the process of specifying what performance is expected of a member of the organization and then providing feedback on the member's performance.

The foundation of an effective performance management system is the **performance appraisal** process, which specifies the level of performance expected for an employee, typically in the form of goals or behavioural standards, and then provides feedback on the employee's performance. Although performance appraisals have the potential to be motivating, they also can be uncomfortable. The appraiser can feel uneasy delivering feedback that isn't positive, and being on the receiving end of such an appraisal may not feel much better; feedback that was meant to be constructive can be perceived as inaccurate or biased. Fortunately, performance appraisals do not need to be a motivational drain for everyone involved. If performed well, they can be valuable in conveying important information and increasing motivation. The key is to follow these steps, which we look at in detail further below:

1. Design the appraisal system with a clear purpose, specified performance criteria, and defined roles.
2. Deliver the appraisal by measuring performance and providing feedback.
3. Reinforce and review the appraisal process.[20]

Design a System   The first step in designing an appraisal system is to decide on its specific purpose. There are at least two types that serve different purposes: **administrative appraisals** are used to justify pay and promotion decisions, and **developmental appraisals** provide feedback on progress toward expectations and identify areas for improvement. Administrative appraisals tend to focus on the average performance of the person being rated, whereas developmental appraisals tend to focus on identifiable strengths and weaknesses and trends in performance.[21] When the appraisal is linked to an administrative decision, such as a raise or promotion, the value of that feedback in encouraging growth or stimulating learning is often lost, or at least diminished, as the recipient focuses on what he or she has to do in order to get the "carrots." It also is less valuable because administrative ratings are less accurate.[22] In practice, most organizations use annual or semi-annual administrative appraisals; some also include a developmental appraisal at a separate time. In any case, both the rater and the person being appraised should understand the basic purpose of the appraisal system.

Next, the system must state the performance criteria that will be assessed. These are the goals or behaviours that an employee should work to achieve or demonstrate. For example, a branch manager for Umpqua Bank, a regional bank based out of Oregon in the United States, will have sales goals for various financial products as well as behaviour goals, such as showing initiative in contributing to the company's vision of being known as the "World's Greatest Bank."[23] Some performance criteria are more objective, such as the sales example, and some are more subjective, such as showing initiative. In either case, these performance criteria must be discussed and agreed upon prior to attempts to perform.

Managers should also specify who will be appraising whom and at what times. Clarifying these roles is important to ensure perceptions of fairness; no one wants to be surprised about who is providing input into decisions about their performance. An increasingly popular appraisal method, called *360-degree feedback*, relies on self-report ratings and input from supervisors, co-workers, subordinates, and, possibly, customers. The advantage of this approach is that it increases the quantity and variety of information while reducing the bias that might come from using a single rating source. Dangers include subordinates who use an anonymous program to get revenge on a boss, and managers who coerce their subordinates to give them good evaluations.

Deliver the Appraisal   Delivering an appraisal first requires measuring performance. A rating form is a tool to measure performance. Typically, a rating form has one or more of the following elements: (1) a place to rate specific characteristics or KSAOs, (2) assessments of progress toward goals, and (3) a summary judgement or rating. Graphic rating scales are one of the oldest and most popular methods to appraise KSAOs. These often offer a 5-point scale along which raters assess the degree to which they believe a person exhibits a characteristic. For example, in class evaluations students may be asked to rate the degree to which a professor was organized, used time wisely, demonstrated concern for students' learning, or explained assignments clearly. The more specific the scale's descriptions of work behaviour, the more valid and reliable it tends to be.

Some rating forms go one step further by asking for a numerical rating and specific examples of performance to justify it. Rating forms also may contain—or in some cases exclusively focus on—goals and progress toward goals, especially in organizations that systematically use a management-by-objectives (MBO) approach for planning and goal

Administrative appraisals are performance appraisals that are used to justify pay and promotion decisions.

Developmental appraisals are performance appraisals that are used to provide feedback on progress toward expectations and to identify areas for improvement.

setting. In such cases, the focus is on outcomes, such as volume of sales, and less on the means by which the outcomes were achieved. Regardless of the types of ratings, an appraisal typically ends with a summary rating. This can be subjective, consisting of the rater's overall judgement of the employee's performance, or it can simply be a summation of the individual item ratings, combined mathematically to yield an overall score.

A major challenge is delivering feedback in such a way that is constructive for the employee's development and improvement. Eliciting a positive reaction is a critical determination of whether the feedback will be used to change behaviour and improve performance.[24] Complicating the appraisal process is the reality that many managers, peers, and subordinates give lenient ratings or exclude negative feedback to avoid the negative reactions of those who receive the ratings.[25] The potential for leniency increases in collectivistic and high power distance cultures, particularly when lower-level employees provide ratings for others.[26] To improve positive reactions, the appraisal process must use a fair process in which employees understand expectations and provide their input; it must deliver unbiased and accurate ratings; and raters must be familiar with the employee's jobs and be trained to focus on agreed-upon performance criteria.[27]

Reactions also are more positive when the feedback focuses on task performance rather than on how the recipient's performance compares to others.[28] Although participation in the appraisal process and the favourability of the ratings can influence reactions to an appraisal, the quality of the relationship (level of trust, support, and satisfaction) between the supervisor providing the rating and the employee is more important in determining employee reactions to an appraisal.[29]

Reinforce and Review the Process   The third step in a performance appraisal system is reinforcing the importance of the appraisal process. To begin, top leaders must model a thoughtful, thorough, and timely approach to appraising their own subordinates. This behaviour sends the message "Do what I do" rather than "Do what I say." Some organizations also hold leaders accountable for the quality and timeliness of their appraisals. Another clear way to communicate the importance of the appraisal process is to subject the whole process to regular review.

An important consideration in designing or reviewing an appraisal system to maximize motivation to improve performance is the cultural context. Practices in one culture may not be appropriate or acceptable in another. Hofstede's dimensions of culture, discussed in chapter 2, can help illustrate this point. For example, participation in the appraisal process (providing input or having a conversation about future goals) is not appreciated in collectivist cultures where preserving harmony is important or in high power distance cultures where avoiding conflicts is desirable.[30] Additionally, in low power distance cultures, like Finland and Sweden, appraisals are more likely to include peer and subordinates as appraisers, but not so in Hong Kong or Singapore.[31] A misfit between the performance appraisal process and the culture can lead to increased absenteeism and higher levels of turnover.[32]

Although we've outlined the general appraisal system, organizations may adjust a step in the process to fit the culture in which they operate or the organization's internal culture. For example, at global consumer products company WD-40, the appraisal process includes clear goals, but the delivery of feedback takes the form of frequent coaching throughout the year instead of only during an annual review. Garry Ridge, CEO of WD-40, attributes his employees' high levels of motivation to this "no surprises" approach to appraising performance with an emphasis on coaching.[33]

A sustainable appraisal system is likely to recognize and assess a broader range of goals and behaviours. Island Savings Credit Union in Duncan, British Columbia, has provided more than $1 million to family-focused initiatives since 2010 through its community investment program. Each of its branches can provide volunteer support to local groups and organizations that implement and execute these initiatives.[34] A sustainable approach values

© Brooks Kraft/Corbis

Some organizations use performance appraisal information to comparatively rate or rank employees every year and then fire the bottom 10 percent. Under former CEO Jack Welch, General Electric (GE) utilized this "rank and yank" process. Although GE later abandoned the system, other companies such as LendingTree have embraced it. Defenders of rank-and-yank argue that it is motivational because few people want to be rated in the lower 10 percent category and have their jobs be put in jeopardy. Understandably, it can make the performance appraisal process more stressful for both the manager and the person receiving the rating.

QUESTIONS FOR REFLECTION

1. How would you like to be ranked based on your performance in this class and know that the bottom 10 percent will be periodically dropped from the class?
2. Would that have any effect on class dynamics?
3. Would this make you concerned about how your performance was appraised?
4. How would you feel if you found out your class was filled with mostly honours students?

---

actions that are not easy to quantify, such as organizational citizenship behaviours like helping co-workers with their tasks or volunteering to represent the organization at community functions. It reinforces a sense of community within the organization by emphasizing contributions to the group over individual performance. If performance criteria emphasize individual outcomes, those who are being rated will focus on individual performance; in the same way, performance criteria focused on contributions made to the group will contribute to group performance.[35]

A sustainable approach may also invite people from all levels in the organization to participate in appraising others. When it is not only people in positions of power who can provide feedback, the wider participation dignifies and empowers more members. The sustainable approach also is more likely to emphasize transparency along with inviting participation. When he was CEO at India's HCL Technologies, Vineet Nayar was rated in his developmental appraisal as needing to improve his project management and time management skills. Not only was he aware that this was his lowest rating, but everyone else knew too because the appraisals of the top managers get posted on the company's intranet for all members to see.[36]

Compensation

Monetary payments such as wages, salaries, and bonuses as well as other goods or commodities used to reward organizational members are collectively referred to as **compensation**. *Benefits*, a subset of compensation, are typically not directly contingent on performance. They may include retirement plans; health, disability, and life insurance; and perks such as access to workout facilities, on-site daycare services, subsidized cafeteria food, education reimbursement, and laundry services. Some benefits are mandated by laws, such as those set forth in the Canada Labour Code. For example, Canadian employers are required to provide at least 37 weeks of parental leave to employees (which includes mothers, fathers, and adoptive parents).[37]

At Dell and a variety of other organizations, employees receive an annual statement of total compensation that details the value of their direct monetary compensation as well as the estimated value of their indirect compensation, such as benefits. To enhance employees' appreciation of benefits, some organizations offer cafeteria-style plans that allow members to pick and choose their benefits within a certain dollar amount. Recall from chapter 5 that Herzberg considers most benefits to be hygiene factors. In addition to

Compensation is monetary payments such as wages, salaries, and bonuses as well as other goods or commodities that are used to reward organizational members.

reducing dissatisfaction, benefits may attract people to an organization or affect their decision to remain despite offers of better-paying jobs. Despite these potential advantages of benefits, organizations conventionally rely more heavily on pay or incentive compensation to motivate performance.

The most basic employee compensation system is job-based pay, which pays employees based on the jobs that they hold. Generally, the higher the pay level, the greater the satisfaction with pay, but pay level is only moderately related to *job* satisfaction.[38] Although there may be some variability across employees in the same job (owing to individual differences in experience or job tenure), job-based pay is usually "banded"; that is, it is bounded by a pre-determined minimum and maximum. Increases can be either uniform—such as cost-of-living raises given to everyone in the organization—or merit-based. In merit-based pay systems, employees essentially earn an increase in compensation based on past performance as reflected in the performance appraisal. Even the Canadian government uses some degree of merit-based pay in its compensation structure for public servants. The Treasury Board of Canada Secretariat (which oversees the management of government agencies) uses the concept of "at-risk pay," whereby a portion of an employee's base pay must be re-earned each year based on the level of achievement against corporate and individual commitments.[39]

Despite being intended as an incentive to increase performance, merit-based pay has a weak effect because the long time lag between behaviour and reward makes it difficult for employees to link the two. It also may not be received well by employees due to concerns about distributive justice and perceptions that favouritism and politics influenced the pay decision.[40] Because of these weaknesses and the permanent nature of merit raises, many organizations are moving away from relying primarily on merit pay. To encourage members to advance their competencies, some organizations such as Quaker Oats, Sherwin-Williams, and Au Bon Pain have adopted a skill-based pay system. Members are paid a base hourly wage rate for doing their jobs and then get additional increments for acquiring other skills valuable to the organization, such as knowing how to use a software program or being certified to operate a piece of machinery.

Pay-for-performance (PFP) is a compensation scheme in which each member's pay is linked directly to individual, group, or organizational performance. The direct relationship is expected to raise productivity.

An increasing number of organizations today rely on **pay-for-performance (PFP)** to raise productivity. With PFP (sometimes called *incentive pay*), a member's pay is linked directly to individual, group, or organizational performance. Most companies now offer some form of incentive pay, including piece-rate systems for individuals, such as those made famous by Lincoln Electric, that pay employees a fixed amount for every unit of output. Another example of PFP is evident when salespeople work on an individual commission basis, whereby their compensation is tied to their sales and they may earn additional rewards for meeting specified goals. PFP also can include gain-sharing plans (in which employees within a group are rewarded for reaching agreed-upon productivity improvements), goal-sharing plans (in which employees within a group receive bonuses for reaching strategically important goals), profit-sharing plans (in which a portion of an organization's profits is paid to employees), and stock options plans (in which employees earn the right to purchase shares of their organization's stock at a potentially reduced cost). These types of PFP plans are particularly helpful in aligning employee goals with organizational performance goals.

Not surprisingly, research on employee attitudes suggests that financial compensation can be an important motivator for many people.[41] Whereas some sustainable leaders attempt to de-emphasize money (see this chapter's opening case), others use money to communicate their values by paying above-market wages to front-line employees and limiting the pay of executives. The Men's Wearhouse, for example, competes in a market environment that typically employs low-skilled labour at low wages. Bucking industry norms, The Men's Wearhouse pays its salespeople (who are called "wardrobe consultants") above-market wages as well as commissions.[42] Furthermore, almost 100 percent of the firm's employees and managers own stock in the company. Although they benefit from shared or group incentives, the top managers at The Men's Wearhouse are paid less than executives are paid at similar-performing organizations.[43] This practice is consistent with sustainable organizational leaders' concerns about justice and fairness, which make them less likely to accept compensation that is perceived to be excessive. For example, at Reell Precision Manufacturing, executive pay is limited to roughly 7 to 10 times that of the lowest-paid employee.[44]

Sustainable performance management tends to emphasize group- or team-based reward systems. These systems encourage collaboration and promote sharing of information. The use of individual incentives may stimulate individual productivity, but when work requires collaboration, the use of group incentives promotes more attention to doing the task correctly and helping others.[45] When all team members share in the success of the team, its members are more likely to widely share tactical or technical information and to help find solutions that benefit the whole team. Furthermore, team-oriented reward and feedback systems are often a practical necessity, as it is usually impossible to separate out the contributions of individuals when the work is completed interdependently.

Members of sustainable organizations are more likely to be motivated by rewards that go beyond financial benefits. For example, they may choose to work in organizations known for empowering workers (such as Semco, chapter 12) or known for being ecologically friendly (such as Interface, chapter 13). If money is made the primary reward and motivator in the workplace, then members will tend to focus on working for money instead of for the enjoyment of their work or the benefit their work offers to others. Thus, sustainable motivating systems draw attention to non-financial rewards.[46] Just as people's behaviour can be reinforced with money, so can it be reinforced by simple recognition like a "thank you" or a creative reward. Bob Nelson, in his book *1001 Ways to Reward Employees*,[47] provides numerous examples of how people can use their imagination to devise non-financial forms of compensation that deliver creative rewards to others. For example, after a team reaches a goal or stays late to meet a deadline, a manager might bake a treat to serve to employees the next morning. Of course, not every manager has baking skills, but almost every manager can send employees home early on a Friday or acknowledge the team's work in the company newsletter. It sends a powerful message to employees when leaders demonstrate creativity, self-sacrifice, and thoughtfulness in their rewards.

Finally, an important form of compensation associated with sustainable motivation systems is the intrinsic satisfaction of working for an organization that does not place *primary* emphasis on financial matters. Putting the focus on money has a tendency to turn jobs into commodities and turn relationships with other people into opportunities to maximize profits. In sustainable organizations, members are able to treat co-workers, customers, and suppliers with dignity and to act on their concerns about how organizational practices are affecting the environment, impacting the local neighbourhood and community, or contributing to the quality of working conditions in developing countries. These forms of non-financial compensation motivate members.[48]

Training and Development

JOB DESIGN | PERFORMANCE MANAGEMENT | **TRAINING & DEVELOPMENT** | MISSION & VISION

Most motivational theories recognize the value of providing opportunities for organizational members to learn and grow personally and professionally. Many organizations have training and career development systems to address these innate or developed needs. The terms *training* and *development* are sometimes used interchangeably. For the purposes of our discussion, however, **training** refers to learning activities that improve skills or performance in a specific area or current position, whereas **development** describes learning activities that result in broader growth, usually beyond the scope of the current job, and that prepare a person for future positions. Development activity is often referred to as *career development*. Let's look at these two functions separately.

Training refers to learning activities that improve an individual's skills or performance in a specific area or current position.

Development refers to learning activities that result in broad growth for a person, including growth in terms of a larger career or beyond the scope of the person's current job.

Training

The most common method of training is **on-the-job training (OJT)**, in which a more experienced member shows a newer member how to complete the job tasks. OJT has a long history, going back centuries to the days when apprentices worked with master craftspeople to become, first, journeymen and then masters themselves. When it works, OJT is considered the fastest and most effective form of training. Some organizations engage in cross-training or job rotation, by which they provide members with OJT in a variety of positions so that employees can better understand how their jobs fit into the overall picture and the organization has flexibility if another employee is unable to come to work for an extended period of time. Tedd Hoff, the Vice-President of Human Resources at IBM, says employees acquire as much as 80 percent of their skills from OJT.[49]

OJT is not appropriate for every training need. When it causes too much disruption in normal operations, such as it would for judges in a court of law, for example, it is not effective. Likewise, when tasks are too complex to learn by OJT, organizations instead use *off*-the-job training methods, such as formal education, classroom lectures, podcasts and videos, and simulation exercises. IBM combines OJT experiences with on-site classes, role-playing experiences, podcasts, coaching, and other forms of training to ensure its employees' skills are up-to-date. IBM has one of the largest internal training and development programs, spending approximately USD $575 million annually to provide 28.6 million hours of training.[50]

In off-the-job training environments, the successful transfer of the training to the work environment depends on several factors:[51]

- Training should be offered to those who have an interest in and aptitude for it. In other words, trainees must be able and motivated to be trained.

- The training content itself must be relevant and the instruction designed so that trainees are given multiple opportunities to practise using each component of the target skill or knowledge domain.

- There must be support for applying the training in the work environment. Many employees have returned from training eager to apply what they have learned, only to find no opportunities to use their new knowledge on the job.

From a conventional perspective, training must be instrumental or linked to immediate returns in task performance. In contrast, from a sustainable perspective, education and training are worth doing whether or not the organization will directly reap the benefits of that investment. For example, Baylor Health Care System in Dallas, Texas, offers a range of training programs, some that have direct application to work, and others—such as negotiations training—that develop skills for both professional and personal use. Research affirms that training that is focused on learning broad principles instead of prescribed behaviours is more likely to transfer back to the workplace.[52] A sustainable approach to training also encourages members to explore a range of interests and to learn from others. For example, IBM has a well-developed on-demand, organization-wide e-learning system in which employees can try a simulation, read about best practices, or even chat with a colleague about a specific work challenge or learning need.[53]

Some sustainable businesses are very deliberate in providing training and apprenticeship opportunities that benefit their larger community, even if these do not lead to productivity improvements for the firms themselves. This holistic perspective can motivate members who want their work to be about more than just maximizing financial profits and be something that reminds them they belong to a larger human family. For example, one director of a sustainable business in Brazil describes an apprenticeship program his company has for young people with drug addiction problems:

This year we have taken on two young people ages 15–17 . . . Of course the productivity of the business is important and our employees have to work, but we have to be sensitive, above all, with one boy who has problems even if he doesn't contribute in terms of productivity . . . For us, however, he is a brother.[54]

Career Development

Not many people nowadays stay in one job for most of their lives. In fact, most people will have several different jobs throughout their work career. The conventional perspective on careers focuses on immediate and narrow exchanges between the employee and the organization. This approach is sometimes called the "new employment contract" in which— instead of offering the old model of a secure career and consistent raises—employers offer challenging jobs, pay-for-performance compensation packages, and opportunities to learn skills that will increase employee marketability.[55] In this economic-exchange relationship, the employer asks for immediate and well-defined contributions from employees and, in return, delivers short-term financial benefits to them.

From this conventional approach, just as training is appropriate to the extent that it yields skills contributing to improving short-term productivity, career development is also appropriate if it improves competencies needed for a future position in the organization. A common development activity is to have a member complete difficult or challenging tasks that extend the scope and complexity of the member's job, such as leading a cross-functional problem-solving team or researching process improvements. If an employee is interested in a different sort of development opportunity, this is viewed as his or her own responsibility. A few suggestions that most managers indicate are important development opportunities are:[56]

- Receiving opportunities to be mentored by senior managers
- Volunteering for challenging/difficult job assignments
- Visiting other departments/organizations
- Engaging in formal career planning

 **B in Action** Whataburger, Whatacompany

Getty Images/James McKinley

Harmon Dobson had an idea to make a burger so big and so good that after one bite customers would proclaim, "What a burger!" Dobson turned his idea into reality seven decades ago by opening his first burger stand in Corpus Christi, Texas. The founder's original vision and appetite for impressing customers still inspires everything employees do today at Whataburger.

The family-owned and -operated business has expanded to over 700 stores, but it has kept its recipe simple: They hire people they believe in, train them for success, and help them build careers at the company. Nora Garcia was hired during high school into a Whataburger training program, and she never left. Now as a store manager, she loves to train her employees to be successful, and she also helps train employees from other stores.

Whataburger values all of its employees and engages them in training with a twist. Employees can compete as team members in the WhataGames, a skills competition designed to promote a sense of family and pride in the job. It seems to have worked, because employees talk of working at the stores not as being a job but as being part of a family.

QUESTIONS FOR DISCUSSION

1. How does training enhance motivation for employees at Whataburger?
2. How might training contribute to employee retention or turnover?
3. Have you worked at a fast food restaurant? If so, what was motivating or not motivating about your work environment?

Although managers and other organizational members are interested in receiving formal career development–planning assistance, few organizations offer this service. Anyone can engage in career planning, however, by doing an annual personal career SWOT (Strength, Weakness, Opportunity, Threat) analysis. In addition to identifying personal and professional strengths and weaknesses, the analysis considers how your strengths and weaknesses match opportunities and threats in your industry, in your profession, or in the broader job market (see the OB Activities section "Personal Career SWOT Analysis" at the end of this chapter).

A sustainable approach to career development is consistent with several of the assumptions in the "old" employment contract, in which the employer asks for both immediate and long-term contributions from the employee—including loyalty—and offers more security and benefits as well as broad development opportunities to the employee. Research comparing this long-term mutual investment relationship to the new short-term economic-exchange relationship (which is more typical of the conventional approach) indicates that the old approach allows members to be more committed to the organization as well as to perform better, help other employees more, and be absent less often.[57] Moreover, some evidence suggests that the whole organization performs better under the "old" approach.[58]

The sustainable version of the old employment contract is not paternalistic. Rather, it is particularly sensitive to how members are labelled and treated in organizations. For example, instead of considering employees to be subordinates, resources, commodities, or expenses (which is where employment costs show up on the income statement), a sustainable approach to career development emphasizes dignity and broad development for all members. Practically, this may mean offering career interest assessments and counselling to align organizational members with their interests. This alignment can improve job performance and reduce turnover.[59]

A sustainable approach is more likely to invest in and support long-term development, even if the payoff to the organization is undefined. In one year, the American consulting firm Booz Allen Hamilton paid out more than $10 million in tuition reimbursements for 21 percent of its employees.[60] The company may benefit directly from its investment in education, or it may not if employees leave to pursue other opportunities. Nonetheless, the firm's culture emphasizes development even when it is not clear how those development activities might address immediate needs within the organization. A sustainable approach also is more likely to support development activities that involve other stakeholders, such as taking time away from the organization to work on a community-education project or to help clean up the local environment. Interacting with people in other organizations can stimulate creativity and enhance awareness of the needs, challenges, and concerns of others. For example, footwear manufacturer Timberland introduced a program that pays its employees for up to 40 hours of service to the community. Timberland's motto, "Doing well and doing good," has been lived out in projects such as improving the drinking water in the Dominican Republic, reducing soil erosion in New York City's Bronx River by planting native plants on the shore, or, as described in chapter 1, planting a million trees in a Chinese desert.[61]

Taken as a whole, the sustainable approach to training and development is rooted in promoting human development and multiple forms of well-being. Sport Chek and its people-centred customer service philosophy, profiled in the opening case of chapter 1, suggests that a career model is emerging in which establishing good relationships—not amassing large sums of money—is the indicator of success. Instead of focusing on tangible career outcomes like money and position titles, this approach balances material needs and intangibles such as enriching the lives of others. In other words, success is making a living and making a meaningful difference.[62]

Mission and Vision

JOB DESIGN | PERFORMANCE MANAGEMENT | TRAINING & DEVELOPMENT | **MISSION & VISION**

LEARNING OBJECTIVE 4
Explain how mission and vision work together to contribute to organizational performance.

Perhaps the broadest system of motivation consists of the organization's mission and vision. These formal statements can work together to contribute to organizational performance by shaping and maintaining a consensus about the organization's purpose and direction.[63]

A **mission statement** identifies the fundamental purpose of the organization, often by describing what the organization does, whom it serves, and how it differs from similar organizations. In this way mission statements can provide motivation and a sense of identity for members. Those that are most effective in contributing to organizational performance describe the distinctiveness of the organization and the way the organization relates to its key stakeholders, doing so briefly and without referring to financial goals.[64] One study suggests that as many as 90 percent of companies have mission statements.[65]

Here are two examples of mission statements, the first from a non-profit international service organization and the second from a for-profit association of co-operative banks:

> **International Committee of the Red Cross (ICRC):** "[The ICRC is] an impartial, neutral and independent organization whose exclusively humanitarian mission is to protect the lives and dignity of victims of war and internal violence and to provide them with assistance."[66]
>
> **Mouvement des caisses Desjardins:** "To contribute to improving the economic and social well-being of people and communities within the compatible limits of its field of activity by continually developing an integrated cooperative network of secure and profitable financial services, owned and administered by the members, as well as a network of complementary financial organizations with competitive returns, controlled by the members; and by educating people, particularly members, officers and employees, about democracy, economics, solidarity, and individual and collective responsibility."[67]

An ideal mission statement contains a small set of key instrumental or terminal values that have significant motivating potential. The Red Cross's values consist of protecting the lives and dignity of victims of war, while Mouvement des caisses Desjardins's values consist of improving the economic and social well-being of people and communities. These values may not be equally motivating to all people, but for members of each organization the values can provide a sense of purpose for their efforts.

Many mission statements sound very similar. One reason is that organizations are influenced by the mission statements of other organizations in their industry. For example, one study found that more than 60 percent of banking organizations mention employees in their mission statement (e.g., "We value our employees"), but fewer than 25 percent of computer hardware firms do. Similarly, about half of all banks mention the philosophy of the firm (e.g., "We believe in quality"), but fewer than 25 percent of computer software or hardware firms do.[68] Some firms deliberately try to set themselves apart from other members of their industry. Southwest Airlines was the first air carrier to see itself primarily as a service provider; in fact, its mission statement doesn't even mention air travel:

> The mission of Southwest Airlines is dedication to the highest quality of customer service delivered with a sense of warmth, friendliness, individual pride, and company spirit. To our employees: We are committed to provide a stable work environment with equal opportunity for learning and personal growth. Creativity and innovation are encouraged for improving the effectiveness of Southwest Airlines. Above all, employees will be provided the same concern, respect, and caring attitude within the organization that they are expected to share externally with every Southwest customer.[69]

Mission statements identify the fundamental purpose of the organization, often by describing what the organization does, whom it serves, and how it differs from similar organizations.

Despite the great motivational potential of a mission statement, some organizational members can be cynical about it, particularly if it espouses values that are not practised in the organization. The overuse of buzz words can also make the mission statement seem meaningless to employees.[70]

When it is meaningful and motivational, a mission statement can contribute to the financial success of the organization. Walmart provides a notable example of how commitment to a simple mission can yield financial success. The essence of the company's mission is to save customers money: "We save people money so they can live better." In 1962, when Sam Walton opened the first Walmart, he "somehow knew in his gut" the power of this phrase. Walmart's brilliant, obsessive focus on this core mission—delivering low prices—has created what some call "the largest and most powerful company in history."[71] Walmart generates more than USD $444 billion in annual sales and is the largest employer in the world with over 2.2 million employees.[72] Almost all of the actions of Walmart managers and employees are focused on fulfilling the company's mission statement.

Mission statements may change over time as the organization grows, adopts new strategies, or experiences significant change. At one point in its history, Internet and media giant AOL had a mission to "build a global medium as central to people's lives as the telephone or television . . . and even more valuable."[73] Later, in an attempt to update a mission that had been largely accomplished, AOL made its mission "to serve the world's most engaged community."[74] More recently, AOL's mission was stated as "to inform, entertain and connect the world."[75]

A mission statement is often accompanied by a change-oriented **vision statement**, which describes what the organization is striving to achieve and, in this way, provides guidance to organizational members. Typically, the vision statement describes goals that the organization hopes to achieve five or more years into the future. For example, the *mission* of a university may be to teach students, engage in research, and provide service to the community; its *vision* may be to become a world leader in medical research, to maximize diversity in the classroom, or to foster a sense of global citizenship. A tourist destination may have the *mission* to provide local employment and be friendly to tourists and the *vision* of becoming the honeymoon capital of the world.

From a conventional view, vision statements focus on factors that will contribute to the organization's future competitiveness and financial success. Research suggests that managers should develop vision statements that have a future orientation and are inspiring, challenging, brief, clear, and stable.[76] As with mission statements, the content of a vision statement may be influenced by the industry to which an organization belongs. For example, one study showed that the growth of entrepreneurial firms is associated with vision statements expressing a need for power (e.g., "We will be number one in our industry"), whereas in government service agencies, high performance is related to vision statements that recognize the need for members to have strong interpersonal relationships (e.g., "We will provide excellent working conditions and service").[77]

Although we have described the conceptual difference between a mission statement and a vision statement, they are not always so distinct in practice. A vision statement can include elements of the organization's mission, such as its guiding philosophy, purpose, and core beliefs. Some organizations do not have a formal mission or vision statement but instead have similar statements that function in the same way.

Two organizations may have similar mission and vision statements but implement them differently because their underlying values and priorities differ or because they lean toward either a conventional or a sustainable approach. Consider the similarity between Walmart's mission statement and that of Costco, whose $50 billion in annual sales make it the number one warehouse club retailer in the United States. Costco's mission is "to continually provide our members with quality goods and services at the lowest possible prices." This is not unlike Walmart's mission; however, Costco has a markedly different management philosophy. For managers at Costco, keeping prices low and rewarding shareholders do not come

OB in Action — Kasasa against the World

The word "mission" can evoke military images for some people, but at Kasasa (formerly BancVue) the association is intentional. Kasasa's mission is to "Enable a powerful network of community financial institutions to re-establish themselves as the go-to-place for banking products and services and win the war." The organization's mission, spirit, and values are inspired by the Battle of Thermopylae of 480 BC, in which 300 Spartan soldiers played a critical role in repelling the assault of a much larger enemy consisting of 300,000 soldiers. Despite the great odds against them, the Spartans' courageous stand prevented the demise of Western civilization.

In a similar vein, Kasasa is at war to save from the threat of megabanks the approximately 14,000 small rural banks that make up the community banking system. Kasasa believes that the community bank system is central to supporting millions of farmers and entrepreneurs in rural cities. Founded in 2004, as BancVue,

Kasasa has already made a substantial impact by creating software and other solutions for community banks, thereby helping them compete with megabanks. The innovative company is led by its CEO, Gabe Krajicek.

Krajicek admits that early in his entrepreneurial experience he realized he couldn't succeed alone: "To survive, I had no choice but to ask the few employees we had to help me lead. Since then, I've been a believer in bottom-up leadership and the impact a strong culture can have not only on your employees' job satisfaction but also on your bottom line."

Krajicek knew that a company's mission, culture, and its values are essential to success. Kasasa's value system combines interdependence, 5-star leadership, love, and "badassitude," which are symbolized by "The Patch," shown here. The idea behind The Patch is to inspire emotion and a sense of connection and understanding of the value system, rather than a cold set of standards no one cares much about. Kasasa even incorporates The Patch into everyday items like T-shirts and tattoos, to keep the values from appearing stuffy.

QUESTIONS FOR DISCUSSION

1. What is your reaction to Kasasa's mission?
2. What are the benefits and drawbacks of using a military metaphor as part of the mission?
3. Which of Kasasa's values are motivating? Explain why.
4. Why might you want to work at Kasasa?

---

before taking care of the firm's customers, employees, and suppliers.[78] Perhaps most notable is Costco's commitment to pay its front-line workers $3 to $4 more per hour than employees in comparable positions at Walmart's warehouse club subsidiary, Sam's Club.[79]

Another difference is that a sustainable approach to drafting mission and vision statements is more participative. If possible, a variety of stakeholders, including owners, managers, employees, suppliers, customers, and members of the community, are engaged in the development of a sustainable organization's mission and vision statements. The benefits of such an approach are twofold:

- It permits the development of more broadly motivating mission and vision statements.
- It increases outside support for the work of the organization.

At Eliza Jennings Group, a long-term health care provider with five residential facilities in the American state of Ohio, a consultant once interviewed top executives in order to develop a mission statement. Under the leadership of CEO Deborah Hiller, however, the mission statement was revised with the input from a cross-section of stakeholders—employees at multiple levels, managers, and patients and their children. The revised mission statement, though similar in many ways to the old version, was enthusiastically embraced as a result of the participative process.[80]

When a variety of key stakeholders become aware of an organization's mission and vision, everyone has a greater appreciation of the organization's work. It is also valuable for all organizational members to understand how their daily work fits with that of others in their organization *and beyond*. Front-line workers should see how they contribute to their organization's mission and vision, just as top managers should understand how their work contributes to the experience of front-line members.[81] Furthermore, when organizational plans are sensitive to the needs of the larger socioeconomic and ecological environment, members may experience their work as more meaningful and motivating. Research points out the merits of developing long-term trusting relationships with key suppliers (and customers) to gain the advantage of their expertise and knowledge in making organizational decisions.[82] This is one of the points illustrated in the values and behaviours of Mountain Equipment Co-op, described in chapter 2. Altogether, the benefits of stakeholder participation in drafting the mission and vision statements can translate into improved organizational performance, even if this is not the primary focus of the statements.[83]

Finally, a sustainable approach is also more likely to encourage members to reflect on what drives them personally and how that motivation overlaps with the mission of their organization. Yoling Sevilla (introduced in chapter 9), CEO of The Leather Collection in Manila, Philippines, calls this being "aware of what is driving you," and she believes that it includes contemplating the way your actions affect other organizational stakeholders. "For me," Sevilla says, "that would be the most important. To observe, to analyze, to be both self-aware and aware of the environment."[84]

people, the planet, and profits at herman miller[85]

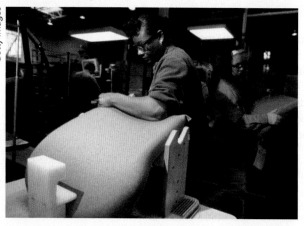

to emphasize a profound respect for people, and he instilled a commitment to being a good steward of the environment.

DePree had an epiphany about the potential of people when he visited the family of a deceased millwright from his company, Herman Rummelt. In conversations with his widow about Rummelt's passion for poetry, DePree was struck by the realization that everyone is exceptional in unique ways and that he was viewing his employees too narrowly, based only on their job descriptions. The person he had known as a mechanic was in fact a wonderful poet. In DePree's words,

> I think at that point it really changed the tone and the way the company operated. [We became more] inclusive not only in ownership and results, but inclusive in solving problems and letting the people be involved in the creation of ideas and their implementation.

Drawing on this insight, DePree launched initiatives that welcomed the ideas and creativity of employees. Many of these ideas benefited everyone in the firm, and when they also improved Herman Miller's financial performance, the company became one of the first to share its success with members by paying them bonuses. It was also an industry leader in adopting annual profit-sharing plans and allowing employees to share in the equity of the company through stock ownership.

Herman Miller is an innovative furniture design and manufacturing company located in the fields of Zeeland, Michigan. It has 5,000 employees worldwide and operates manufacturing facilities in the United States, the United Kingdom, China, and Italy; its products are sold in more than 100 countries. Herman Miller's current systems and policies, and its success, can be attributed to the influence and leadership of D. J. DePree, who was the company's president from 1923 to 1962. Early in DePree's tenure he began

Eventually DePree's sons Hugh and Max took over as leaders of the company, with a deep and ongoing commitment to its culture and history. As Max DePree put it, "Around here, the employees act as if they own the place," which in a real sense they do. Hugh DePree adds, "It was a change from 'piece work' and every man for himself to each person being not only responsible for himself but for every other person in the organization."

Under the leadership of Hugh and Max, a statement of the firm's values was developed with employees from across the organization. The statement notes that a "key value, and the one that is at the heart of Herman Miller values, is participation," defined as "the opportunity and the responsibility each employee-owner has to be included in the decision-making process to the level of one's competence and job responsibility."

Herman Miller also values its employees by offering an attractive menu of benefits, including a variety of family-friendly subsidies for child care expenses, reimbursement of adoption costs, and resources for elder care, as well as flex-time, compressed workweeks, and telecommuting and job sharing. The company also has on-site fitness facilities that offer exercise classes.

Another prominent value espoused by D. J. DePree that continues to guide employees is the commitment to being good stewards of the earth and its resources. For example, the company decided to accept an annual $2.5 million increase in costs in order to avoid using the toxic substance polyvinyl chloride (PVC) in its furniture. And when wasps began to infest its environmentally friendly manufacturing facility in Holland, Michigan, rather than use ecologically destructive pesticides, the company introduced honey bees onto the grounds. The bees soon rid the facility of wasps, and the honey they produce is given to visitors to the facility.

As a result of the global recession, in 2009 Herman Miller experienced a sharp decline in net income, from $152 million to $68 million, suggesting that massive layoffs would be necessary. To limit the number of layoffs, senior executives decided to reduce their own financial compensation, and employees' hours were temporarily cut back. Employees were promised that if the company could return to profitability, hours would be restored and a portion of the lost income would be returned. Generous severance packages for those who were laid off included three paid weeks for every year of employment.

Throughout its history, Herman Miller has been known for its unique focus on people, the planet, and profits. *Fortune* magazine has identified it as one of the most admired companies, research firm KLD has consistently cited it as one of its "best corporate citizens," and, not surprisingly, the firm is considered one of the "100 Best U.S. Companies to Work For" By *Fortune* magazine. Its attention to diversity, evident in its work with the Women's Business Enterprise Council and the National Minority Supplier Development Council, has also won praise. Little wonder that Herman Miller has a motivated workforce.

QUESTION FOR DISCUSSION

1. Which practices at Herman Miller do you think are the most motivating for employees?
2. What, if anything, would attract you to work at Herman Miller?
3. How might Herman Miller's approach to being a good steward of the environment be motivational?

Summary

People work and interact in organizational contexts with systems that influence their motivation. There are at least four motivational systems that can be considered and implemented from a conventional or sustainable perspective.

 **Learning Objectives**

- Explain how jobs are designed.

- Discuss the two components of performance management and how the outcomes influence organizational members' behaviour, motivation, and learning.
- Discuss how training and career development improves job performance and prepares employees for future positions.
- Explain how mission and vision work together to contribute to organizational performance.

A conventional OB approach to motivational systems includes:

- *Job design:* Identify what people need to do by focusing on individual jobs, using input primarily from jobholders, and emphasizing efficiency.
- *Performance management:* Provide sufficient feedback and rewards for people through using appraisals to reinforce and reward individual performance, aligning compensation with individual performance, and focusing on financial rewards.
- *Training and development:* Prepare and develop people by providing training to improve short-term production and targeting employee development toward the future needs of the organization.
- *Mission and vision:* Identify a mission and vision for the organization that motivates members to maximize the financial return for the organization's owners.

A sustainable OB approach to motivational systems includes:

- *Job design:* Identify what people need to do by focusing on the team or system, using input from multiple stakeholders, and emphasizing meaning.
- *Performance management:* Provide sufficient feedback and rewards for people through using appraisals to reinforce and reward interdependence, aligning compensation with team performance, and balancing financial and non-financial rewards.
- *Training and development:* Prepare and develop people by providing training to improve short-term and long-term production and recognizing employee development as an end in itself.
- *Mission and vision:* Together, develop a mission and vision for the organization that motivates stakeholders to enhance multiple forms of well-being (including financial viability).

Key Terms

Administrative appraisals (p. 317)

Compensation (p. 319)

Development (p. 321)

Developmental appraisals (p. 317)

Extinction (p. 315)

Job analysis (p. 312)

Job characteristics model (p. 312)

KSAOs (p. 312)

Mission statements (p. 325)

Negative reinforcement (p. 315)

On-the-job training (OJT) (p. 322)

Pay-for-performance (PFP) (p. 320)

Performance appraisal (p. 316)

Performance management (p. 314)

Positive reinforcement (p. 315)

Punishment (p. 315)

Reinforcement (p. 314)

Subject matter experts (SMEs) (p. 312)

Training (p. 321)

Vision statements (p. 326)

Questions for Reflection and Discussion

1. What would you like about working at SAS (the company featured in the opening case of this chapter)? What would cause you to concern? If you did work there, what would it take for you to leave? Do you think it is reasonable for other organizations to adopt SAS's approach? Why or why not?

2. Keeping job designs up-to-date can be a time-consuming and laborious task. If someone you are managing asked you to explain why the job design process is necessary, what would you say?

3. Would you accept a lower salary if the organization that was offering it emphasized environmental sensitivity in its products and services? If so, how much lower, and why?

4. Which type of employment contract is more motivating to you: the "new" (conventional) contract, which is based on short-term exchanges, or the "old" (sustainable) contract, which encouraged long-term commitments?

5. What aspects of a mission would be motivating to you?

ob activities

SELF-ASSESSMENT EXERCISE

Diagnosing Your Job

This questionnaire challenges you to examine the motivating potential in your job. If you are not currently working, complete the questionnaire for a job you have held or for which you want to examine the motivating potential. For each of the following five questions, circle the number that corresponds (in terms of its proximity) to the most accurate description of the job. Be as objective as you can in describing the job by answering these questions.

1. How much *autonomy* is there in the job? In other words, to what extent does the job permit a person to decide *on his or her own* how to go about doing the work?

Very little; the job gives a person almost no personal say about how and when the work is done.

Moderate autonomy; many things are standardized and not under the control of the person, but he or she can make some decisions about the work.

Very much; the job gives a person almost complete responsibility for deciding how and when the work is done.

2. To what extent does the job involve doing a *whole* and *identifiable piece of work*? For example, is the job a complete piece of work that has an obvious beginning and end, or is it a small *part* of the overall piece of work that is finished by other people or by automatic machines?

①　　　**②**　　　**③**　　　**④**　　　**⑤**　　　**⑥**　　　**⑦**

The job is only a tiny part in the overall piece of work; the results of the person's activities cannot be seen in the final product or service.

The job is a moderate-sized "chunk" of the overall piece of work; the person's own contribution can be seen in the final outcome.

The job involves doing the whole piece of work, from start to finish; the results of the person's activities are easily seen in the final product or service.

3. How much *variety* is there in the job? To what extent does the job require a person to do many different things at work, using a variety of his or her skills and talents?

①　　　**②**　　　**③**　　　**④**　　　**⑤**　　　**⑥**　　　**⑦**

Very little; the job requires the person to do the same routine things over and over again.

Moderate variety.

Very much; the job requires the person to do many different things, using a number of different skills and talents.

4. In general, how *significant or important* is the job? For example, are the results of a person's work likely to significantly affect the lives or well-being of other people?

①　　　**②**　　　**③**　　　**④**　　　**⑤**　　　**⑥**　　　**⑦**

Not at all significant; the outcome of the work is not likely to affect anyone in any important way.

Moderately significant.

Highly significant; the outcome of the work can affect other people in very important ways.

5. To what extent does the job provide a person with *feedback or information* about his or her work performance? Does the actual *work itself* provide clues about how well the person is doing—aside from any feedback that co-workers or supervisors may provide?

①　　　**②**　　　**③**　　　**④**　　　**⑤**　　　**⑥**　　　**⑦**

Very little; the job itself is set up so that a person could work forever without finding out how well he or she was doing.

Moderately; sometimes doing the job provides feedback to the person; sometimes it does not.

Very much; the job is set up so that, as he or she works, a person gets almost constant feedback about how well he or she is doing.

To score your questionnaire, place your responses to questions 3, 2, 4, 1, and 5, respectively, in the following equation:

$$\frac{\overset{Q\#3}{[\quad]} + \overset{Q\#2}{[\quad]} + \overset{Q\#4}{[\quad]}}{3} \times \overset{Q\#1}{[\quad]} \times = \frac{\overset{Q\#5}{[\quad]}}{\text{Score (MPS)}}$$

Motivating

Key: If the MPS for the job you rated is between 0 and 119, it is low in motivating potential; if between 200 and 343, it is high in motivating potential; if between 120 and 199, it is moderate in motivating potential.

Source: Adapted from J. R. Hackman and G. R. Oldham (1974). *The Job Diagnostic Survey: An Instrument for the Diagnosis of Job and the Evaluation of Job Redesign Projects* (Technical Report No. 4), Yale University.

Personal Career SWOT Analysis

The objective of this exercise is to think reflectively and proactively about your career.

The first step is to look at yourself. Take a piece of paper and write down two headings: "Strengths" and "Weaknesses." Under Strengths, write down areas in which you have excelled and in which others say you do well (you might even ask a friend, co-worker, or boss). Under Weaknesses, list areas of struggle or failure, bad habits, and areas that others say are "not your strength."

The second step is to look outside yourself. Flip the paper over and write the heading "Opportunities" on one side of it. List promising opportunities in the job market, or trends for certain careers or jobs and their availability. Below these list a few development activities you could pursue to make yourself more attractive in these fields, such as internships or leadership roles in student organizations. Label the other side of the paper "Threats," and list some factors such as competition or changes in technology that might prevent you from getting the jobs or pursuing the careers that interest you. You might also consider other factors such as personal or professional relationships that could either offer you opportunities for growth and encouragement or threaten your career aspirations.

The final step is to take an honest look at your strengths, weaknesses, opportunities, and threats and make specific action plans to enhance your strengths, develop your weaknesses, increase your opportunities, and minimize your threats. On a separate sheet of paper, make specific plans for each of these four activities and assign yourself clear deadlines.

A corporation increased the annual compensation of its CEO from $5 million to $9 million over a four-year period during which profits declined and the dividend was cut.

Why might this scenario occur in organizations?

Use the following scale to indicate whether this behaviour is ethically acceptable:

NEVER ACCEPTABLE		SOMETIMES ACCEPTABLE			ALWAYS ACCEPTABLE	
1	**2**	**3**	**4**	**5**	**6**	**7**

Explain the ideas you considered in arriving at your answer.

Interview a Business Owner or Manager

Visit an organization and observe how it operates. Interview a manager to determine how the company operates and what motivational systems are in place. Ask questions about job design, performance management, training and development, and mission and vision statements.

QUESTIONS FOR DISCUSSION

1. How would you rate the motivational influence of each system you observed?

2. Are the systems primarily conventional or sustainable?

3. Would you want to work at this organization? Why?

Advertising a Mission (Group activity)

Have each group member individually consider a favourite television commercial that promotes an organization's motto or mission. Before discussing your examples with the group, write down the motto/mission and describe what about it might be motivational for you as an employee. As a group, share your examples and your explanations of the motivating potential of the organization's motto or mission.

QUESTIONS FOR DISCUSSION

1. Rate the attractiveness of each mission statement or motto as low, moderate, or high. Share your ratings with group members and discuss differences in the ratings.

2. What made the top-rated mission statements motivational?

APPLICATION JOURNAL

This is the next in a series of journal entries that can be used for class discussion or be compiled and included in a self-reflection paper.

In your experience in organizations, which of the motivational systems discussed in this chapter influenced your motivation? What was it about the system that was motivating? Were others also motivated? What can you take from your experience and apply to other workplaces?

Fifteen

Leading Organizational Change

Like the view that a traveller sees when looking back on the journey, this chapter will illustrate how many of the concepts (such as motivation and leadership) we visited in earlier chapters can help us understand the basic four-step change process. It is in times of change that we see most clearly the differences between the approaches to OB. The conventional view is characterized by a top-down approach to organizational change, whereby change and its implementation are controlled by top managers. In contrast, the sustainable view takes a bottom-up approach, in which change and its implementation involve more stakeholders.

Learning Objectives | Conventional OB | Sustainable OB

ORGANIZATIONAL CHANGE

Learning Objectives	Conventional OB	Sustainable OB
1. Discuss organizational change and the ways to differentiate the type of change.	Change is managed by a top-down process, whereby leaders work to ensure that their changes are implemented in the organization.	The change process is much more bottom-up, so that everyone participates in developing and implementing the change

STEP 1: RECOGNIZE NEED

Learning Objectives	Conventional OB	Sustainable OB
2. Discuss recognizing the need for change, the first step in leading organizational change.	Base on managerial insight and sense of urgency	Base on organization-wide sensitization and openness

STEP 2: UNFREEZE

Learning Objectives	Conventional OB	Sustainable OB
3. Discuss unfreezing, or understanding the need for change, the second step in leading organizational change.	Overcome members' resistance and sell new vision of change	Include multiple stakeholders and treat one another with consideration and dignity

STEP 3: CHANGE

Learning Objectives	Conventional OB	Sustainable OB
4. Describe how change takes the form of interventions in the third step of leading organizational change.	Provide direction and use persuasion to gain commitment	Use broad participation to gain commitment

STEP 4: REFREEZE

Learning Objectives	Conventional OB	Sustainable OB
5. Explain the refreezing stage, the fourth step of leading organizational change, in which leaders make adjustments to the design of the organization.	Choose structures and systems that reinforce and reward members who implement change	Choose structures and systems that facilitate continuous learning and celebrate improvement

learning from the journey[1]

© Lars Hagberg/CP Images

For over two decades, the Canadian National Railway Company (CN) has been on a journey that has transformed a laggard Crown corporation into North America's leading publicly held railway company. In 1992, when Paul Tellier was appointed CEO and President of the corporation, it was bloated with bureaucracy and suffering from a culture of entitlement. Tellier wanted to streamline operations and engage employees, and he knew that in order to do so extensive changes would need to be made. He began by creating urgency and a focus on improving bottom-line performance and customer relationships. He launched changes to CN's strategic vision, culture, and structure, as well as to its operations and technologies. These changes were designed to prepare the organization for privatization and to capitalize on the eventual enactment of the North American Free Trade Agreement.

The spectre of privatization was a powerful tool that helped align employees toward Tellier's vision of making CN the best railroad company in North America. Employees understood that customer satisfaction would be paramount, and attitudes toward performance began to change.

By the time CN was privatized in 1995, a more bottom line–oriented culture had been created, consisting of people who wanted to see improved performance and higher share prices, and the change to CN's corporate culture had begun in earnest.

When he became CEO, Tellier had until then had little involvement in the railroad industry. Early on, he put together a team of experienced executives and relied on their knowledge and experience to help drive change. Through the acquisition of the Illinois Central Railroad (IC) in 1998, Tellier found the right person to help guide CN's transition to a performance-oriented culture. He appointed Hunter Harrison, formerly IC's President, as the COO of CN. An experienced railroader, Harrison understood the industry and how to transform CN's new-found enthusiasm into improved performance. He introduced the Five Guiding Principles (Service, Cost Control, Asset Utilization, Safety, and People) that became the core pillars of CN, and he created the "precision railroading" philosophy, a game-changing way to operate a railroad company that created new value for customers. To make this new

The spectre of privatization was a powerful tool that helped to align employees toward Tellier's vision of making CN the best railroad company in North America.

philosophy work, Harrison needed employees throughout the organization to reconceptualize their roles and responsibilities. Each employee was encouraged to share knowledge with company leaders and take initiative by spotting issues and fixing them.

Tellier resigned from CN in 2002, and Harrison was appointed CEO on the first day of 2003. Although changes to the culture had yielded improvements, there were still those who had not bought in. Adding to this was the fact that CN had made multiple acquisitions and mergers. Harrison faced the challenge of integrating a broad company culture across multiple regions. Harrison and his team set out a seven-step plan to create a company-wide culture of discretionary performance—one in which employees want to go above and beyond the formal requirements of their jobs—and year-over-year improvements.

1. *Clarify the vision. We needed to ensure that everyone across the company understood the vision, the Five Guiding Principles, and how we planned to get there by creating a new culture.*

2. *Choose the right switchpoints. With the vision set and a clear understanding of our culture, we needed to determine how to change that culture into one of an engaged, committed workforce.*

3. *Select the tools for change. You need the right tools to ensure change. At CN, we found those tools in Behavioural Science.*

4. *Align the switches. With a clear vision of our desired culture, and the tools to do it right, we were ready to begin by aligning the switches in the right direction. This required finding sponsorship, testing the business case for the tools, and setting a plan to broaden our efforts.*

5. *Assess switchpoints' impact. Once we had expanded the cultural change across the organization, we needed to track progress to determine if we were on the right route.*

6. *Spike the switches. For each decision and change, we needed to spike the switch to ensure that the culture would continue forward and not fall back into old habits. To spike the switches, we put in place changes in organizational and management processes to support the new direction.*

7. *Learn from the journey. This would be an ongoing effort to keep the company moving in the right direction. We took time to take stock of the learnings, so we could replicate the successes and avoid repeating the failures in the future.*

Despite struggling with issues such as union strikes during his tenure, Harrison felt that CN made substantial progress and created changes that would set the tone for the future. Rather than a process that would have a specific beginning and ending, he viewed change as "an ongoing, multi-year effort to keep the company moving in the right direction." In 2015, CN continues to develop its culture of engagement under the direction of its president and CEO Claude Mongeau. Mongeau also views ongoing change ("you can't go from A to D in one fell swoop") as an important part of maintaining organizational excellence. "Once you are the leader in the industry," says Mongeau, "you have to set a course for the next level of performance."

Organizational Change

ORGANIZATIONAL CHANGE | RECOGNIZE NEED | UNFREEZE | CHANGE | REFREEZE

LEARNING OBJECTIVE 1
Discuss organizational change and the ways to differentiate the type of change.

Most organizations operate in rapidly changing environments that require change and continuous improvement in order to survive and thrive.[2] Unprecedented advances in technology, opportunities and threats from globalization, dramatic fluctuations in the economy, stakeholder activism, heightened sensitivity to environmental concerns, new laws and regulations, and changes in customer preferences all exert pressure on organizations to change. **Organizational change** is any substantive modification to some aspect of an organization. It may consist of a change in the workforce, technologies, structure, work processes, culture, values, or strategic vision. Yet change is difficult. One half to two-thirds of organizational changes fail to achieve their expected results.[3] "In a rapidly changing environment, the knowledge that is most useful to organizations is knowledge that helps them change and adapt to perform effectively."[4] Leaders must understand *when* change is needed and *how* to guide their organization through it.

Organizational change is any substantive modification to some aspect of an organization.

The way a change unfolds depends, of course, on the type of change. As Figure 15.1 shows, there are at least three ways to differentiate between types of change: the change's scope, intentionality, and source.

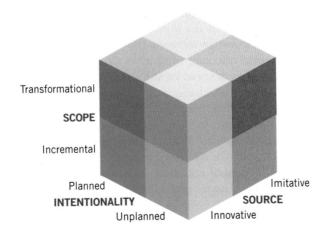

FIGURE 15.1 Types of Change

First, the scope of a change can be either transformational or incremental.[5] **Transformational change** occurs when an organization changes its strategic direction or re-engineers its culture or operations in response to dramatic changes, such as a technological breakthrough or a merger.[6] **Incremental change** occurs when an organization takes relatively smaller steps toward its goal, perhaps by restructuring to be more efficient or by expanding its line of products or services to promote more growth.

Transformational changes are often a reaction to a major problem or challenge in the competitive environment. For example, organizations in the music sales industry underwent a transformational change in response to losing revenue to iTunes and other Internet software that made it more accessible to download songs. These types of changes require leaders and members to embrace learning and innovation in order to succeed.[7] Other organizations change incrementally, experiencing long periods of "equilibrium" during which the focus is on fine-tuning existing practices. For example, the airline industry has historically experienced long periods of stability; however, equilibrium is occasionally interrupted or punctuated by bursts of transformational change, as was experienced by the airline industry when it was deregulated and following the September 11 terrorist attacks.[8]

Second, the intentionality of the organization's actions can vary.[9] A common problem that organizations face is members' failure to anticipate or respond to changing competitive conditions; instead of planned change, they then must resort to reactive or unplanned change. **Planned change** designs and implements changes in an orderly and timely fashion. It is generally a direct response to the recognition of a performance gap—that is, a discrepancy between the desired and the actual state of affairs. For instance, the employees of Rakuten, Japan's online shopping equivalent of Amazon, were asked to communicate in English—a planned change designed to allow them to improve their ability to participate in the global community. **Unplanned change** involves ad hoc or piecemeal responses to unanticipated opportunities and threats as they occur. Unexpected strategic moves by competitors are a common reason for unplanned change. These reactive changes usually need to be implemented quickly to minimize negative consequences and maximize possible benefits.

Third, we can differentiate types of changes by discerning whether they arise from innovation or from imitation. **Innovation** is the development and implementation of *new* ideas and practices. For example, organizational innovation has taken place when an automotive manufacturer develops and implements a sophisticated virtual design process that will save time and money.[10] **Imitation**, in contrast, is the application of *existing* ideas, which may come from other units within the organization or from outside the organization. For example, organizational imitation takes place when an automotive manufacturer changes its design process to follow another firm's process. Innovation is considered to be more difficult to manage than imitation.

In the remainder of this chapter, we will describe the change process as having four steps, as illustrated in Figure 15.2, based on the work of Kurt Lewin.[11] The conventional and sustainable perspectives on the four steps represent the ends of a continuum of approaches to managing the change process. Although approaches differ in their descriptions of how to perform each step, they agree on the need for all four steps.

From a conventional perspective, change and learning in each step are essentially managed with a top-down process, whereby leaders work to ensure that their changes are implemented in the organization. The expertise and ideas come largely from executives or consultants who provide their expertise related to the opportunities or threats in the organization's environment that need to be addressed through changes. A vision or description of what needs to change is formulated, and those at the top persuade others of the need to change, direct and oversee the changes, and implement structural and cultural changes to reinforce the new vision.

In a sustainable approach to change, the process is much more bottom-up, so that everyone participates in developing and implementing the change. This is consistent with a

Transformational change occurs when an organization changes its strategic direction.

Incremental change occurs when an organization makes improvements in moving in its current strategic direction.

Planned change is designed and implemented in an orderly and timely fashion; it is generally a direct response to the recognition of a performance gap—that is, a discrepancy between the desired and the actual state of affairs.

Unplanned change involves making ad hoc or piecemeal responses to unanticipated events or crises as they occur.

Innovation involves the development and implementation of new ideas and practices.

Imitation involves the replication of existing ideas, which may come from other units within the organization or from outside the organization,

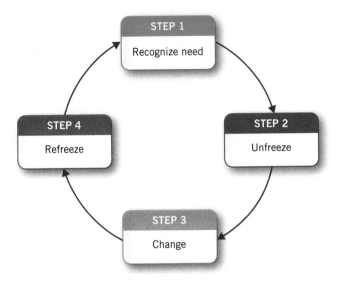

FIGURE 15.2 Four Steps in the Change Process

servant leadership orientation and reflects many of the core values of the **organizational development (OD)** approach to change management. OD is a process of planned change that draws on behavioural science to systematically improve and renew the personal, social, and structural components of organizations.[12] Both OD and servant leadership affirm that

Organizational development (OD) is a process of planned change that draws on behavioural science to systematically improve and renew the personal, social, and structural components of organizations.

OB in Action Delivering Change

© Roberto Machado Noa/ Getty Images

Canada Post is in the midst of a planned transformational change that will reshape the venerable Crown corporation. Although it had been profitable for 16 straight years until labour disruptions in 2011, Canada Post formulated a strategic action plan to confront emerging challenges that threaten future operations.

With the increasing ease and prevalence of electronic communication, Canada Post is no longer handling the volume of mail that it requires in order to maintain profitability. In 2014, Canada Post delivered 1.4 billion fewer pieces of mail than it did in 2006. Although demand for parcel delivery is growing (thanks to e-commerce), projections suggest that the number of physical pieces of mail sent via postal service will continue to decline as more people and businesses stop sending letters and start using various forms of electronic communication instead.

As a result, Canada Post proposed a number of changes to realign operations so that it would remain profitable in the future. These changes included a five-point action plan:

- moving from door-to-door delivery to community mailboxes
- raising prices for sending letter mail

- replacing post offices with postal franchises located in local businesses
- streamlining operations
- addressing the high cost of labour

The proposed changes have met with considerable resistance from postal workers' unions and the general public. Workers have already made a number of concessions on wages and benefits and fear that many of the restructuring measures will result in further layoffs and cuts to their pensions, while the public bemoans the higher costs and reductions in service. One particular sticking point for the voting public is the elimination of door-to-door delivery. After the Liberal's federal election victory in late 2015, the party stopped Canada Post's rollout of the new community mailboxes.

QUESTIONS FOR DISCUSSION

1. If you were a postal employee, how would you respond to these changes?
2. How might the fact that Canada Post is a (public) Crown corporation help or hinder this change? Which is more important, profitability or providing service?
3. What if your school decided that, in order to cut costs, classes would only be held online? How would this change affect the quality of instruction and your educational experience?

(1) organizational members are inherently valuable and should be engaged in shaping changes; (2) changes should help enhance meaningful interpersonal relationships in organizations; and (3) organizational structures and systems should be set up to encourage personal development and to support teams and collaboration. Research comparing top-down with participative approaches to leading change points to the benefits of participation and open dialogue among members in gaining commitment to change.[13] Participative approaches are particularly important to engaging minority or marginalized members in contributing to positive organizational change.[14]

Step 1: Recognize Need

LEARNING OBJECTIVE 2
Discuss recognizing the need for change, the first step in leading organizational change.

Everything and anything can be changed in an organization, including its name, its human resources policies, the way it processes its payroll, its dress code, its location, its structure, its products, and so on. A conventional approach concentrates on looking for and recognizing the need for changes that will help to maximize an organization's profits, efficiency, productivity, and competitiveness. These conventional criteria determine which change opportunities are urgent and which can be overlooked (at least for the moment). To identify opportunities for change, leaders rely on a variety of sources, ranging from formal information systems to the intuition that comes from having a deep understanding of existing operations. Recognition of the need for change can be triggered by internal or external factors.

With regard to internal factors, an organization may implement changes to decentralize structures or processes in response to recognizing that some functions impede the performance of others. For example, General Motors recently decentralized the control network of its powertrain assembly plant to prevent a single malfunction from shutting down the entire assembly line.

Organizational leaders also may recognize the need for change based on external factors, such as a shift in consumer buying habits. For example, in the home improvement sector, members of the unhandy baby boomer generation replaced their do-it-yourself parents as the dominant consumer group. As a result, home improvement stores are more successful if they offer homeowners simple training seminars and easy-to-install decor elements like stylish plumbing fixtures, in addition to selling tradespeople necessary products such as nuts and bolts.[15] Change also may be triggered externally by leaders' recognition that natural raw materials the company relies upon as inputs (such as coal and oil for energy companies) have been depleted or that workers with specific skills (such as nurses) are growing scarce. An organization may also need to respond to new government regulations like affirmative action programs or pollution regulations, or to new directives from shareholders, such as requests for greater transparency about senior managers' compensation packages. Finally, organizations may need to respond to technological innovations introduced by competitors or suppliers.

Recognizing the need for change is not always easy. Managers who keep their proverbial nose to the grindstone and push out products and profits can miss or dismiss internal or external triggers that suggest the need for change. (Recall the decision-making pitfalls, such as selective perception and escalation of commitment, described in chapter 6.) In particular, success has a way of blinding managers to the wisdom of change. Consider IBM managers, who, given the success of the company's large mainframe computers, for many years dismissed the potential market for personal computers.

Like conventional leaders, leaders in sustainable organizations lack the time or interest to change everything or to change just for the sake of change. However, in contrast to conventional leaders who focus primarily on identifying change opportunities that will improve an organization's immediate productivity or enhance its competitive position, sustainable leaders are more likely to take a long-term perspective that values opportunities that develop people and enhance capabilities that will contribute to sustainable performance.[16] Such leaders also watch for opportunities to improve members' on-the-job experience, to foster positive relationships with the community, and to reduce harmful impacts on the natural environment. Leaders of sustainable organizations are also predisposed to be attuned to the needs of the least privileged in society, whether at home or abroad (recall from chapter 12 how Thorkil Sonne recognized the unique needs and talents of those with autism).

Like conventional leaders, leaders of sustainable organizations draw on their experience and unique vantage point to identify areas that can be changed. But unlike conventional organizations, where change is a top-down process, sustainable organizations engage a variety of members at all levels in a *joint diagnosis* process that exposes both leaders and members to information and ideas that might suggest change is necessary. Thus, sustainable organizations are characterized by an openness that invites all members to become sensitized to the broader issues that concern the company and its stakeholders.

The sustainable approach is often enhanced when all organizational members have learned to read financial statements and link their own actions to the organization's financial health and well-being. This policy is sometimes referred to as **open-book management**; its core principle is that significant change occurs when people at the bottom are meaningfully engaged and allowed to have a voice. We saw a sustainable variation at Semco in chapter 12. Jack Stack was another pioneer in sharing information with employees: "It's amazing what you can come up with when you have no money, zero outside resources, and 119 people all depending on you for their jobs, their homes, even their prospects for dinner in the foreseeable future."[17] Stack and a handful of managers purchased their small manufacturing company from International Harvester when given the choice of either ownership or a shutdown. By requiring employees to understand the business, Stack and his managers were able to take advantage of the combined wisdom of the whole company and thus succeeded in changing it for the better. Margaret Meggy, a co-founder of Canadian packaging company Great Little Box, agrees that an open approach is motivating and can sensitize her company's 219 employees to the way money is spent. One suggested change to a packaging process from a maintenance worker saved the company several thousand dollars a month.[18]

Differences between conventional and sustainable approaches to recognizing needs and the next step (unfreezing) are both reflected in OB in Action: Diverging Thoughts at Harvard.

Open-book management is an approach to management whereby leaders share detailed information concerning the financial and operational condition of the organization.

Step 2: Unfreeze

| ORGANIZATIONAL CHANGE | RECOGNIZE NEED | **UNFREEZE** | CHANGE | REFREEZE |

Generally, when members perceive changes as positive opportunities, they increase their support for change and decrease their support for the status quo (the current way of doing work). However, when members perceive changes as threats, they may increase their commitment to the status quo, something researchers call the "threat-rigidity" response.[19] This response can be described as members being "frozen" to the current way of doing their work. Although it may be easier to persuade others to make incremental changes, that is often not the case for transformational change. This requires that leaders plan to *unfreeze* members. The primary objectives for leaders in the unfreezing step are to ensure that organizational members understand the need for change to reduce possible resistance to change and to create a sense of openness and willingness to change.

In the unfreezing step, organizational leaders must convince employees there is a need for change that requires them to behave differently. If the change is perceived by organizational members to be bad or harmful, as may have been the case at pharmaceutical company Pfizer Inc., this task can be particularly challenging. Pfizer struggled with a string of mergers and acquisitions that were undertaken to spur revenues and replace drugs that had

declining revenues or expiring patents (e.g., Lipitor, Viagra, Plavix). In response, the company moved to reduce costs, which it did primarily by cutting benefits to retirees and by laying off approximately 55,000 employees.[20] These major changes were part of broader transformational changes that began under CEO Jeffrey Kindler and continued under his successor, CEO Ian Read. Although the initial changes did not require broad acceptance by employees, ongoing changes are likely to be difficult without a critical mass of support among remaining members.

The unfreeze step requires that leaders help members understand the need for change and provide them with information that reduces uncertainty. Commonly recommended influence tactics to unfreeze organizational members typically draw attention to either the *threat* that demands change or the *opportunity* that a change offers. The first approach can create an almost painful sense of discomfort or dissonance among members because it identifies alarming information or potential negative consequences by using rational persuasion or pressure (recall the influence tactics descriptions from chapter 8). In John Kotter's words, identifying a threat creates a **burning platform**—a metaphor based on the real-life experiences of oil platform workers, such as those in the Gulf of Mexico.[21] Oil rigs situated in deep water are built to a height that ensures the machinery and its operators remain above the swells of the ocean. Of course, this design also means that in case of a fire, which is not uncommon in this environment, workers are stranded on a burning platform they can escape only by diving into the water below, despite the

Burning platform is an approach to unfreezing organizational members that may be painful; it may involve using rational persuasion or pressure to expose members to alarming information or potential negative consequences.

uncertainty of surviving the fall or the possibility of encountering sharks. A burning platform in organizations is a clear recognition that the organization needs to change and that members may even need to jump into the uncertainty of something new to avoid potential dangers, such as a loss of market share or organizational extinction.

The second approach, much less harrowing and more pleasant, is to show organizational members that they will be better off if they change. This approach draws attention to a compelling picture of the future that offers personal benefits, doing so through the use of inspirational appeal or exchange tactics. For example, the change can be described to employees as providing greater opportunities for growth or advancement, improving how they perform their jobs, or offering the potential for financial rewards. Another way to describe the differences in approaches is to say that threat-based approaches use the potential for pain to *push* people to change, whereas opportunity-based approaches use the potential for pleasure to *pull* people to change.

Although both approaches to unfreezing are based on creating a sense of dissonance or discomfort about not changing, the threat-based approach may only result in just enough change to avoid a looming painful outcome; it may not result in employees fully embracing the change and new ways of behaving once the threat subsides. Also, threats might backfire if employees perceive the change itself to be a threat that endangers their job, work relationships, compensation, or continued employment. In response, they are likely to quit or become disengaged.[22]

Helping members understand the need for change can be helpful in thawing members who are frozen in the status quo, but there are other perceptions of change illustrated in Figure 15.3 that also explain why members might still resist change.

First, people may resist change because they perceive it to break a formal or informal agreement or promise.[23] For example, employees may suspect that a change will require them to work harder, receive less resources, or be denied developmental opportunities that were expected. A broken promise creates a sense of inequity or the perception that a psychological contract with the firm has been violated. As described in chapter 8, a psychological contract is an unwritten expectation about what a person will receive from the organization in exchange for the person's contributions. That is, an employee might feel that when more hours of work are expected, something should be offered in return, or if they have faithfully worked for years, they should be safe from downsizing. When a person's psychological contract is violated, resistance to change is one response, but other responses can include increased cynicism and absenteeism and lower levels of performance, job satisfaction, and organizational commitment.[24]

Second, members may resist change because their personal identity is closely tied to their job and to the organization's identity. For example, one of the first questions we ask when meeting new people is, "What do you do?" or "Where do you work?" Many of us rely on our job for a large part of our self-concept. Our self-understanding is also shaped by our position within a social structure and the power we hold in the system, whether it is an educational institution like the school we attend or a company, government agency, or non-profit organization where we work. Organizational change may be perceived to threaten or diminish an employee's work identity.[25]

Third, change brings with it uncertainty and ambiguity, which make many employees anxious and nervous. Because many people prefer a stable but mediocre status quo to a potentially promising but ambiguous change, a major cause of employee resistance to change is lack of information about the vision for change. Uncertainty is especially threatening for employees who have a low tolerance for change and who fear the new and unusual. In the absence of a compelling justification for change and clear plans for how it will be implemented, employees will resist change.[26]

REASONS FOR RESISTANCE

Broken promises

Threat to identity

Uncertain plans

Cultural differences

FIGURE 15.3 Reasons for Resistance

Fourth, change is received differently in each cultural context.[27] When Switzerland-based Puma Energy acquires companies in countries such as Vietnam, one of its challenges is to overcome resistance due to cultural differences.[28] The Swiss culture is characterized by low power distance and high individualism, whereas the Vietnamese culture is characterized by high power distance and high collectivism.[29] Thus, changes such as an empowerment initiative or an individual pay-for-performance process that challenges cultural norms may meet resistance. This potential resistance is not insurmountable. Vietnam represents a growing list of developing countries with transitioning economies influenced by their cultural heritage but whose employees also may be receptive to new management practices under the right conditions.[30]

Regardless of the culture or context, leaders can reduce resistance by showing respect for employees and concern for their long-term well-being.[31] Leaders must communicate a commitment to act fairly and supportively during the change process; if these OB practices are absent, resistance will likely grow and, eventually, employees will leave the organization.[32]

In contrast to the conventional approach, whereby leaders use their power of influence to get other members to accept their vision and the need for change, the sustainable

OB in Action

Managing the Morning after the Merger

Universal Studios/ Photofest

A big merger or acquisition is a transformational change of dramatic proportions. In the movie *In Good Company*, seasoned advertisement sales executive Dan Foreman (played by Dennis Quaid) experiences a corporate takeover that has him now reporting to Carter Duryea (Topher Grace), who is half his age. Like many Hollywood movies, it has a happily-ever-after ending, but that is not always the case in real corporate life.

Mergers and acquisitions are common in corporate America. For example, United Airlines and Continental Airlines merged to form the world's single largest airline, and Bank of America acquired Merrill Lynch to expand its client base. These bold mergers and acquisitions are undertaken with the hope of achieving efficiency gains and/or enhanced growth; unfortunately, however, many fail to realize their potential. Somewhat like marriages based on the partners' superficial or idealistic view of each other, corporate mergers often run into difficulties caused by a lack of full disclosure and insufficient effort given to work through the details of becoming one entity.

The failures of such mergers and acquisitions are not necessarily due to financial or structural irreconcilable differences. Instead, failure is often attributed to a weak understanding of or a lack of attention to important human and cultural factors. Culture clashes are a common source of misunderstandings and problems. In the wake of poorly implemented partnerships, traumatized employees often exhibit attitudinal and performance problems that ultimately may result in a "breakup," with the employees leaving the organization.

One way to address the human side of change is for leaders to provide clear and consistent communication about what direction the merged company will take, and how and when changes will occur. Even more pressing is the need to align systems across the two organizations. Often in mergers, employees from each organization are paid different salaries for doing similar jobs; news of these discrepancies spread quickly through the grapevine.

QUESTIONS FOR DISCUSSION

1. When it comes to businesses, mergers are not made in heaven—they are achieved through hard work. If you were working in an organization that is acquired, what would you want from your leaders?
2. What would unfreeze you from the way you've always done things?
3. Does the metaphor of a marriage give you any ideas for how to achieve a successful union of two companies? Explain.

approach overcomes resistance by using participative methods. The bottom-up involvement of members sensitizes them to the need for the change and contributes to a *shared vision* to change. A participative approach creates a readiness to change and a powerful sense of ownership.[33] As management guru Tom Peters says, when you allow people to share in the process of gathering information, it becomes theirs.[34]

Sustainable organizations assume that most organizational members want to grow and develop and to make a meaningful difference. Tapping into this desire encourages them to embrace change. Put differently, the sustainable view treats members not as mere pieces of a puzzle or parts of a solution, but rather as human beings who desire to help their organization become a better place. Thus, when a crisis or an opportunity is recognized, members have a standing invitation to help develop mutually beneficial solutions. In return, they have less reason to fear that management will take advantage of them. By being informed and involved in the process, they are more likely even to accept changes that are not in their own material self-interests.

Becton, Dickinson and Company (BD), a medical technology and supplies company, used a participative process of co-creation to reduce infections associated with unsafe injection and syringe-disposal processes.[35] BD leaders invited an initial set of employees to begin interacting with the goal of creating sustainable solutions and encouraged them to expand their community to include others in the organization who might have insights into the problem and benefit from finding solutions. Eventually, hospital administrators, doctors, and nurses from outside BD were invited to join these co-creation conversations. This empowered a participative, process-built commitment to change and contributed to innovative solutions. BD leaders also believe the co-creation process deepened relationships with the participating hospital and even attracted new partner hospitals.[36]

Step 3: Change

ORGANIZATIONAL CHANGE | RECOGNIZE NEED | UNFREEZE | **CHANGE** | REFREEZE

LEARNING OBJECTIVE 4
Describe how change takes the form of interventions in the third step of leading organizational change.

In the third stage, the change ideas are put into practice and the change becomes a tangible reality. Change takes the form of **interventions**, planned activities that target specific outcomes such as improving individual, group, or organizational performance or well-being.[37] We can think about organizational change interventions as occurring in four different areas of the organization that, as illustrated in Figure 15.4, are often interrelated.[38]

Interventions to change technology affect the conversion process by which organizational members transform inputs into outputs and generally focus on workflows, production methods, equipment, and information systems. They are designed to make products or services more efficient or to increase organizational capabilities. For example, companies such as Cenovus Energy use information technology systems to more efficiently obtain greenhouse gas offset credits, which improves operational efficiency and reduces greenhouse emissions. Because of the rapid rate at which technological advancements are emerging, these changes occur frequently.

Interventions to change an organization's structures are directed at its levels of centralization, standardization, specialization, and departmentalization (recall chapter 12). For instance, when computer manufacturing giant Dell Inc. acquired Perot Systems, a service-based information technology company, the change to integrate customized service solutions required

Interventions are planned activities that target specific outcomes such as improving individual, group, or organizational performance or well-being.

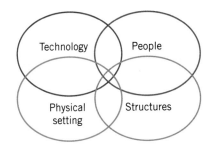

FIGURE 15.4 Target Areas for Organizational Change Interventions

adjustments to Dell's organizational structure. Structures also include the formal systems of the organization, such as how people are hired and compensated.

Interventions to change an organization's physical setting target the space where people work. The type of buildings, the surrounding grounds, the way offices or cubicles are configured, and the overall aesthetic appeal of an organization's physical characteristics are part of its work setting. The characteristics of the physical setting can affect communication, collaboration, creativity, productivity, and stress levels. For example, Nike created a physical space within the company called the Innovation Kitchen. It is an open-space "creative playpen, with every type of tool, material, machine, toy, instrument, software, game, and inspirational image at the ready."[39]

Often changes in technology, structures, or physical setting can also have a profound effect on people, but some changes are directed primarily at the attitudes, behaviours, and performance of people in the organization. The focus of these changes can be individuals, teams, or the overall culture of the organization. Coaching, conflict resolution, training, leadership development, team building, and participation and empowerment programs are a few of the many interventions designed to change people. For example, encouraging dialogue using *appreciative inquiry (AI)* is known to create positive energy for organizational change.[40] AI uses positive questions and reflections about peak performances to draw out the ideas and evoke the energy of organizational members and other stakeholders.[41] A typical AI format includes explaining the process, asking questions, imagining a possible future, and planning to take action.[42] For example, the Canadian Broadcasting Corporation (CBC) brought together an 1,100-person global news unit for a three-day summit to invent new ways to collect, edit, produce, and evaluate the news. Overall, interventions directed toward people have the greatest influence on changes in individual behaviour and the work environment.[43]

HOW DOES CHANGE MAKE YOU FEEL?

EMMANUEL DUNAND /AFP/Getty Images

Marissa Mayer assumed the reins at Yahoo! Inc. in 2012 with the charge to turn around the struggling Internet search engine giant. As CEO, she has enthusiastically embraced the challenges of transforming the company's image and setting a new strategic direction toward profitability. Certainly, shareholders will be pleased if she accomplishes the turnaround, but the exit of several key leaders during the initial stages of the change suggests that it wasn't good news for everyone.

Change is inevitable, but is it necessarily good? Change evokes a range of emotions from those who are facing or experiencing it. In the workplace, unsuccessful or difficult changes often leave employees stressed, disengaged, and cynical. The very nature of planned organizational change, whether successful or not, can expose employees to increased uncertainty, disrupt informal networks of support, and entrench the power of management. Employees under such conditions experience a loss of control and become dependent on managers to provide them with direction, stability, and, possibly, self-assurance. Even if the change seems to be in the best interests of all organizational stakeholders, there is little doubt it exerts a heavy toll on members.

QUESTIONS FOR REFLECTION

1. Consider a change you have experienced (at work, in school, or within an organization in which you participate). How did you feel when you first heard about the change and then later as you began adjusting to it?

2. Were you angry or enthused; frustrated or encouraged; numb or invigorated; sad or happy?

3. What would have made you feel better or worse? What can you do to help other organizational members minimize the negative emotions associated with change and promote positive emotions?

Most organizational changes are a combination of changes to technology, structures, physical settings, and people. When multiple changes are aligned with and support each other, they have the greatest positive effect and are more likely to result in lasting change.[44] It is during change that the leader's role moves from words to actions. Leaders must become change agents to ensure that the proposed change results in changes in the work setting. A **change agent** is someone who acts as a catalyst and takes leadership and responsibility for managing part of the change process. Change agents make things happen. They are most often leaders, middle-level managers, human resources specialists, or influential members of the organization, although they may also be outside consultants.

Change agents sometimes work in conjunction with **idea champions**, people who actively and enthusiastically support new ideas. Together, change agents and idea champions promote productive change within the organization by building support, overcoming resistance, and ensuring that innovations are implemented. For example, as a middle manager in a multinational auto parts supplier, Mike McDaniel took it upon himself to promote his organization's continuous-improvement initiatives by being one of the first leaders to implement participative methods of problem solving in his department.[45] His early adoption served as an example for others to follow.

A leader's goal in this stage is to ensure that organizational members are committed to the change. Commitment is important because it influences individual behaviour and the performance of tasks that are critical to implementing the change.[46] Commitment to change is influenced by the following factors:

- Members' confidence in the competence of the leaders promoting the change
- Members' confidence in their own ability to put the change into practice
- Members' attitude toward the change

Next we look at each factor separately and from both a conventional and a sustainable perspective. Figure 15.5 presents a model that summarizes how conventional leaders contribute to members' commitment to an organizational change.

Members' Confidence in Organizational Leaders

Members will be more committed to change if they have confidence in the competence of their leaders.[47] Research suggests that this confidence can develop in at least four ways:

- If members are convinced that leaders have the skill set required to manage a change and to provide the necessary support that members will need
- If leaders themselves model the desired behaviour and don't fall back into the previous pattern of behaviour
- If leaders have integrity and are consistent in their actions to gain members' commitment to change
- If leaders have good planning skills and take care not to create crises by exhibiting reactionary behaviour

Leaders who are capable and demonstrate integrity earn the trust of others. Trust in management is one of the strongest and most consistent predictors of positive responses from employees.[48] From a sustainable perspective, members will have confidence in leaders they feel they can trust and who dignify the contributions and skills of others through participation and teamwork. Sustainable leaders nurture empowered or team-based work environments in which members have a greater voice and more autonomy in decision making. When organizational leaders are humble and share power, members are more likely to commit to change because they have greater confidence that the manager is doing what is best for the organization.[49]

A **change agent** is someone who acts as a catalyst and takes leadership and responsibility for managing part of the change process.

An **idea champion** is a person who actively and enthusiastically supports new ideas.

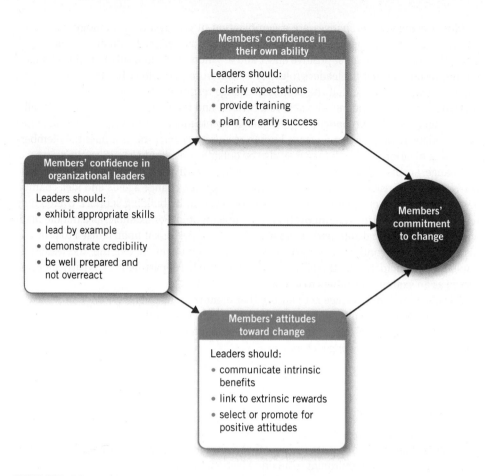

FIGURE 15.5 A Conventional Approach to Increasing Members' Commitment to Change

At Eliza Jennings Group, a long-term health care provider that was mentioned in the previous chapter, leaders worked in partnership with a broad cross-section of organizational stakeholders to revise the company's mission and vision statement. Following the development of a draft statement, Eliza Jennings's leaders met in small forums with all employees to hear their responses to the proposed changes. These meetings not only served to increase commitment to the changes, they also brought to light a few additional changes to the statement before it was adopted throughout the facilities. From the sustainable perspective, commitment to change is not a specific goal as much as it is a natural result of treating others with dignity and consideration.

Members' Confidence in Their Own Ability

Members will be more committed to a change if they have confidence in their own ability to put the change into practice.[50] Research suggests that leaders can strengthen this confidence in at least four ways:

- By providing frequent information so that members have clear expectations about how to perform in the new work environment
- By providing training to enhance the skills and behaviours needed for change

- By planning for early successes or small wins to build confidence and celebrate them
- By providing the appropriate resources and time to help members adapt to their new responsibilities

A sustainable perspective values the benefits of clear expectations, training, recognition, and resources in building members' own confidence. Yet sustainable organizations are likely to also create spaces or opportunities for informal or peer learning to enhance the skills of employees and to provide relevant information. Instead of tightly controlling and delivering training and information, sustainable organizations nurture an environment where people learn from one another.

Sustainable leaders may also include other stakeholders in the learning process. Their inclusion has two key benefits. First, it builds participants' confidence by enhancing their understanding of stakeholder relationships and the complexity of the system. Second, broad participation brings more resources and perspectives to bear on meeting the challenge of implementing changes, which in turn inspires confidence that the changes will succeed. For example, in the BC Ferries change process described at the end of this chapter, management interacted with union officials and the public before creating action plans on how to best implement changes.

Members' Attitudes toward the Change

Members will be more committed to a change if they can see the personal benefits they will gain from it.[51] Research suggests that leaders can facilitate this motivation in at least three ways:

- By persuading members that the change is good for them; beyond pure facts, people respond best to emotional appeals that target the heart. If they fail to see the benefits of the change, particularly how benefits relate to their own jobs, their motivation will decrease and they will direct their efforts elsewhere
- By providing extrinsic incentives such as bonuses, pay raises, or potential promotions
- By promoting those members who have a disposition that facilitates coping with change and who have a positive attitude toward it

The importance of communication in shaping positive attitudes cannot be overemphasized. In a study comparing two plants operated by a company that was involved in a merger, one plant experienced an increase in employee stress and turnover and a decrease in employee satisfaction and commitment in the months following the announcement. In contrast, communication at the other plant—which included a hotline, a merger newsletter, and frequent updates in departmental meetings—dramatically minimized these negative effects.[52]

Like conventional leaders, sustainable leaders can affect members' attitudes by communicating the benefits of a change, but the process is likely to be more of a dialogue.[53] At Yahoo!, Mayer (mentioned earlier) introduced a program known as PB&J (Process, Bureaucracy, and Jams) and encouraged members from throughout the organization to share their ideas and discuss the benefits and challenges of any changes through this forum. Other means to facilitate information sharing might include intra-organizational chat rooms, testimonials in newsletters, and members lent to other departments as internal trainers. Through means such as these, positive attitudes about the change are spread and gain momentum throughout the organization, not by top managers who are separated from employees by hierarchy, but rather by members throughout the organization who understand and accept the change or have come up with new means to implement it.[54]

A sustainable perspective is more likely than a conventional one to focus on intrinsic motivations such as opportunities for growth, the significance of employees' work, and the

Top 10 Causes	Percent Citing the Cause	Consequences
Ineffective communication skills/practices	80%	Leaves employees uncertain and stressed, making it difficult to make informed business decisions
Poor work relationships and interpersonal skills	79%	Isolates managers from the informal network of knowledge that is necessary to cope with change
Person-job mismatch/skills gap	69%	Puts managers in positions in which they are ill-equipped to deliver results
Failing to set clear direction/clarify performance expectations	61%	Hinders planning, saps motivation, and, ultimately, immobilizes staff
Delegation and empowerment breakdowns	56%	Contributes to confusion and frustration
Failing to break old habits and adapt	54%	Perpetuates behaviours and actions that no longer add value in the new work environment
Inability to develop co-operation/teamwork	51%	Destroys collective performance
Lack of personal integrity and trustworthiness	49%	Destroys a leader's credibility with the people who are essential to getting results
Inability to lead/motivate others	45%	Leads to minimal performance at a time when change requires extra effort
Poor planning practices/reactionary behaviour	44%	Creates disruptive crises that damage performance and morale

Source: Longenecker, C., Neubert, M. J., & Fink. L. (2007). Causes and consequences of managerial failure in rapidly changing organizations. *Business Horizons, 50*(2), 145–155.

needs of others being positively affected by the change (this is evident in OB in Action: TOMS Walks the Talk). Instead of focusing primarily on offering short-term inducements to encourage commitment, sustainable leaders also make long-term investments to the employee's development, encourage open communication and information sharing, and provide meaningful opportunities to participate in shaping the implementation.[55]

The growing pressure on leaders to successfully implement change has been documented in a number of research studies. In two studies, one of more than 2,000 U.S. managers and another of more than 5,000, "getting results" was cited as the single most important factor for keeping a job and career on track. Recent research, in which more than 1,000 front-line managers participated in 160 focus groups, helps explain the causes and consequences of failing to get results in the midst of organizational change. The results are described in Table 15.1, starting with the most frequently mentioned cause, ineffective communication skills or practices (noted by 80 percent of respondents).

Step 4: Refreeze

ORGANIZATIONAL CHANGE | RECOGNIZE NEED | UNFREEZE | CHANGE | **REFREEZE**

LEARNING OBJECTIVE 5
Explain the refreezing stage, the fourth step of leading organizational change, in which leaders make adjustments to the design of the organization.

Once changes have been implemented, they need to be reinforced and become institutionalized. As a result of this process of refreezing, the change will become second nature to members, embedded in their everyday actions and thoughts. Achieving this goal requires creating structures and systems that reinforce the change and dismantling those that undermine it.

OB in Action — TOMS Walks the Talk

Blake Mycoskie (pictured here in the background), founder and Chief Shoe Giver of TOMS Shoes, embodies a spirit of hope that pervades the organization. In Mycoskie's One for One model, the company gives one pair of shoes free to a poor child for every pair purchased. The plan has been a phenomenal success, and well over a million pairs of shoes have been given away. The rapid growth of TOMS and the success of its business model, which integrates profitability and social concern, earned the company the U.S. Secretary of State's Award for Corporate Excellence in 2009.

Since its founding in 2006, change at TOMS has continued. The company has expanded operations to more than 24 countries and begun a program called Sight Giving, through which the purchase of a pair of glasses helps give sight to someone in need elsewhere in the world. Outside TOMS, Mycoskie is active in public speaking and influencing others with the goal of inspiring a new generation of leaders to incorporate giving into their business practices. He also frequently visits his on-the-ground distribution partners, soliciting their input about what is going well and what needs improving. Mycoskie builds trust by openly sharing his thoughts with his staff regarding what is troubling him, what is inspiring him, and where he thinks TOMS should go in the future.

QUESTIONS FOR DISCUSSION

1. If you were working for TOMS, what would motivate you to work through the inevitable growing pains of this expanding organization?
2. How does Blake Mycoskie inspire commitment to change?

In the refreezing stage, leaders make adjustments to the design of the organization and its systems (see chapters 12, 13, and 14). This may include making structural changes in the way work is organized (more or less standardization, specialization, centralization) and changing who reports to whom (departmentalization). It also requires revising job descriptions, aligning the performance appraisal and reward systems with the new expectations, and adapting recruitment and promotion practices to reinforce the new culture. Ideally, by this stage everyone affected by the change will have acquired new attitudes and competencies, so the final step of refreezing is merely reinforcing these changes structurally and systematically to ensure that the new ways of doing things are repeated and rewarded.

Like the conventional approach, a sustainable approach seeks to ensure that positive changes are implemented throughout the organization. The two approaches differ in that the sustainable approach seeks to "re-slush"—rather than refreeze—the organization, in order to facilitate ongoing experimentation and additional changes. That is, sustainable leaders do make changes to their structures and systems (such as adjusting misaligned reward systems), but they place greater emphasis on changes that facilitate learning and flexibility. They view change as an ongoing process, not an event that happens once every few years. Thus, sustainable leadership encourages flexible structures that can support continuous change.

The building of flexible structures requires agreeing on the organization's ends but also allowing latitude on the means used to achieve them. For example, Mike McDaniel, the manager from the automotive supplier who was mentioned earlier as a change agent, realized that job roles were outdated after his division was restructured. A conventional approach would have been to instruct the firm's human resources staff to make a formal assessment and revision of all jobs in this new department. Although this step would have improved the role clarity that McDaniel was seeking, instead department members were invited to revise the job descriptions themselves during an afternoon session. As employees arrived, they noticed the existing job descriptions blown up and taped to the walls. Over the course of the next few hours, they used Post-it notes and markers to add or subtract responsibilities and negotiate new agreed-upon job descriptions. This approach helped to provide ownership and role clarity for a fraction of the time and money that a formal process typically requires, and it set an example of working and learning collaboratively.

"Slushing" assumes that a change may not work uniformly well throughout the organization. It acknowledges that making wholesale changes to systems can cause unintended consequences when the changes do not fit perfectly within particular contexts. A sustainable approach thus encourages experimentation and celebrates the learning associated with both successful *and* unsuccessful attempts to implement change. Members of sustainable organizations are diligent in keeping one another informed about what is working and what is not, and they are encouraged to make adjustments that best suit their work environment. The outcomes of experimental changes are monitored, and members are provided opportunities to share these success stories with others to promote further learning. When it's clear that new changes are having the desired effects, other members are given an opportunity to implement them. Positive change is celebrated and disseminated, not as a mandate but instead as a possible example for others to follow. Ultimately, changes that begin and grow informally may be institutionalized, but the process is bottom-up (not top-down, where management decides what is best).

In practice, it will be up to you to decide whether a conventional or sustainable approach might work better in leading change, or whether one approach fits your values better than the other. Regardless of your choice, the success of organizational change will depend on working through the four general steps of change: (1) Recognize the Need, (2) Unfreeze, (3) Change, and (4) Refreeze.

calming the waters[56]

© Bayne Stanley/CP Images

British Columbia Ferry Services Inc. (BC Ferries) has grown to be the largest ferry operating service in North America and the second largest in the world. The company operates a fleet of 35 vessels that provide vehicle and passenger service on 24 routes to 47 terminals in western Canada off the coast of British Columbia. In 2003, BC Ferries was transformed from a Crown corporation to an independent and privately held company with the provincial Crown as its sole shareholder.

On March 22, 2006, one of BC Ferries's ships, the Queen of the North, ran aground on a routine voyage between Prince Rupert and Port Hardy. The ship sank in 425 metre–deep water and lost two passengers who are presumed to have drowned. This tragic day was the critical incident that spurred the corporation to create a company-wide culture emphasizing safety.

The accident had a tremendous impact on President and CEO of BC Ferries, Mike Corrigan. Corrigan became COO days after the incident. From that point on, he made organizational safety the company's top focus and single most important goal. While third-party experts had given BC Ferries good marks for safety and it was considered "as good as any other ferry outfit out there," Corrigan decided this was not good enough and started his journey to making BC Ferries the safest ferry service in the world. He quickly realized that to achieve this goal he would need overwhelming support from BC Ferries's 10,000-plus employees.

Corrigan immediately set out by sharing his safety vision with the unions. After several conversations, he spearheaded the launch of SailSafe, a company-wide program that targets incident and injury prevention as well as employee wellness. The program includes a process called ALERT (All Learning Events Reported Today), which empowers every employee to report any safety issue to a supervisor and log it into a computer system where reports are reviewed in order to identify and prevent hazards.

To help implement SailSafe, BC Ferries brought in FORCE Technology and WrightWay Training, both of which have a great deal of international experience in maritime safety, human factors, and culture change. As FORCE Technology describes the endeavour on its website:

The task included a significant change in core aspects of the company such as the training approach, the way the different levels of the company communicate, leadership styles and operational practices. This change in culture meant moving from a "wagging finger" model towards a Just Culture model in which individuals are not punished for mistakes, flaws or wrong decisions, and instead such undesired events are capitalized as learning opportunities for the entire workforce.

Since its implementation, the SailSafe program has been viewed, internally and externally, as a success. Employee and passenger injuries have both decreased by nearly 60 percent, on-time service has increased by 78 percent, and insurance premiums have dropped by nearly $1.1 million annually, making the initial $8 million investment into the program a positive financial return. Above all, SailSafe has been successful in changing "the company culture with a new view on safety" and embarking BC Ferries on "the process of continuous improvement."

Corrigan believes that it is the partnership BC Ferries has with the unions and their employees, and their commitment to safety that have been the fundamental building blocks of the company's new safety culture.

Questions for Discussion

1. Describe and evaluate the changes that were made in response to the Queen of the North incident. Was the approach deployed by Corrigan sufficient in gaining a long-term commitment to safety from BC Ferries's employees?
2. What suggestions would you offer Mike Corrigan in helping him transform BC Ferries into the safest ferry service in the world?

Summary

Organizational change is complex and varies in its scope (transformational versus incremental change), intentionality (planned versus unplanned change), and source (innovative versus imitative change).

◆ **Learning Objectives**	◗ **The conventional OB approach to the four-step change model is typically a top-down, content-driven approach:**	◗ **The sustainable OB approach to the four-step change model is typically an inclusive, bottom-up, process-driven approach:**
• Discuss organizational change and the ways to differentiate the type of change.	• Change process is top-down	• Change process is bottom-up.
• Discuss recognizing the need for change, the first step in leading organizational change.	• Leaders conceive of the need for change.	• Leaders and members are sensitized to a wider scope of areas where change may be appropriate (not just changes that enhance materialism and individualism).
• Discuss unfreezing, or understanding the need for change, the second step in leading organizational change.	• Leaders use influence tactics to overcome resistance and get others to buy into the change.	• Members consider how to define the need for change.
• Describe how change takes the form of interventions in the third step of leading organizational change.	• Leaders provide direction to implement the change and use persuasion to gain commitment.	• Participative practices are used to implement change and gain commitment.
• Explain the refreezing stage, the fourth step of leading organizational change, in which leaders make adjustments to the design of the organization.	• Leaders set up structures and systems to ensure the change remains entrenched.	• Members are encouraged to learn from one another and through experimentation

Key Terms

Burning platform (p. 342)

Change agent (p. 347)

Idea champion (p. 347)

Imitation (p. 338)

Incremental change (p. 338)

Innovation (p. 338)

Interventions (p. 345)

Open-book management (p. 341)

Organizational change (p. 337)

Organizational development (OD) (p. 339)

Planned change (p. 338)

Transformational change (p. 338)

Unplanned change (p. 338)

Questions for Reflection and Discussion

1. Identify the four steps in the process of change. What do you believe are the main differences between the conventional and the sustainable approaches of each step?

2. Which approach to change—conventional or sustainable—do you think would be the most effective in the organizations where you have worked? Why?

3. How do you generally react to change? Why do you think people resist change? What can be done to minimize resistance and increase commitment?

4. What are the benefits and drawbacks to including more stakeholders in shaping and implementing the change process?

5. Consider for a moment how you might respond to changes within your class. How would you respond to a professor who started out very directive and demanding but later loosened up?

6. How would you respond to a professor who was initially very inclusive and encouraging but later became more demanding?.

7. Many organizations talk about the need to be collaborative and work as a team. What changes would be necessary in an organization's human resources systems to reinforce teamwork?

ob activities

How Do You Cope with Change?

Using the scale of 1 – Strongly Disagree (SD), 2 – Disagree (D), 3 – Neutral (N), 4 – Agree (A), and 5 – Strongly Agree (SA), indicate your level of agreement with each statement on the 5-point scale.

Typically . . .	SD	D	N	A	SA
1. When dramatic changes happen, I feel that I handle them with ease.	1	2	3	4	5
2. I have been a leader of major changes within an organization.	1	2	3	4	5
3. When changes happen, I react by trying to manage the change rather than complain about it.	1	2	3	4	5
4. When changes occur in organizations of which I am a member, the situation causes me stress.	1	2	3	4	5
5. I see changes that occur as opening up new opportunities for me.	1	2	3	4	5
6. When changes are announced, I try to react in a problem-solving mode rather than in an emotional mode.	1	2	3	4	5
7. I often find myself leading change efforts in organizations.	1	2	3	4	5
8. I think I cope with change better than most of those with whom I work.	1	2	3	4	5

Key: This is an assessment of your behaviour and attitudes related to coping with change. Add up your scores. A score of 33–40 indicates strong and proactive change-coping skills; a score of 25–32 indicates some hesitation and concerns about change; and a score of 24 or less indicates resistance to change or a passive approach to coping with change.

Source: Adapted from Judge, T. A., Thoresen, C. J., Pucik, V., & Welbourne, T. M., (1999). Managerial coping with organizational change: A dispositional perspective. *Journal of Applied Psychology, 84*(1), 107–122.

Where Are You along the Change Continuum?

Indicate the extent to which the two comparison statements fit you best. Rankings of 1 or 5 indicate strong agreement with the statement closest to the number, whereas a 3 indicates that you are undecided or neutral.

Change should be based on research, expertise, and insights of top management.	1	2	3	4	5	Change should be based on organization-wide sensitization, openness, and discernment.
Communication about the vision should be used to increase members' willingness to change.	1	2	3	4	5	Involvement in formulating the vision should be used to increase members' willingness to change.

Leaders should employ their power and influence to overcome resistance and gain commitment for a change.	① ② ③ ④ ⑤			Leaders should employ participative approaches to overcome resistance and gain commitment for a change.
Leaders should set up structures and systems that reward members who implement the change consistently.	① ② ③ ④ ⑤			Leaders should set up structures and systems that facilitate continuous improvement and celebrate improvement.

Key: These questions measure your views about the four main steps of the change process. The 1s and 2s reflect conventional tendencies, and the 4s and 5s represent sustainable tendencies. Add together the scores for all items. Higher scores (16–20) on this assessment indicate favouring a sustainable approach to change, while lower scores (1–8) indicate favouring a conventional approach to change.

ETHICS SCENARIO

A corporate director learned that his company intended to announce a stock split and increase its dividend. On the basis of this information, he bought additional shares and sold them at a gain following the announcement.

Use the following scale to indicate whether this behaviour is ethically acceptable:

NEVER ACCEPTABLE		SOMETIMES ACCEPTABLE		ALWAYS ACCEPTABLE	
① ②	③	④	⑤	⑥	⑦

Explain the ideas you considered in arriving at your answer.

DISCUSSION STARTER

Balls of Fun

This exercise will require a dozen or more tennis balls, a stopwatch, and a space large enough for the whole class to participate. The participants should be organized in a circle, given two balls, and instructed to remain stationary while making sure everyone in the circle touches the balls once without dropping them. The leader, who is not part of the circle, puts the balls into a participant's hand, says "start," and records the time it takes for the balls to complete the circuit. (If the group is large, two or more groups can participate as long as there is a leader for each.)

Have the group perform the task several times, without making changes to the instructions or welcoming any suggestions.

Participants are simply to do what they are told. After the group begins performing well, introduce some of the following changes:

- Add more balls.
- Alter the system by moving a participant, or several, into (or out of) the circle.
- Alter process requirements by instructing participants to bounce the balls to each other or to hand them off while standing back to back.
- Adjust the leadership style by asking for input or allowing the group(s) to self-manage.
- Add or swap members if there are two groups.

QUESTIONS FOR DISCUSSION

1. How did you feel when things changed?
2. What was most frustrating in this exercise?
3. What was most satisfying?

4. Are there any lessons that can apply to leading or surviving change?

Engineering Change in Bangladesh[57]

For many years, the people in Bangladesh and their crops suffered due to difficulties accessing water. Most villagers drank water from hand-dug wells or ponds that were shared with bathing cows and water buffaloes. Cholera and diarrhea flourished, and each year hundreds of thousands of deaths resulted from drinking contaminated water. The insufficient access to water also hampered the use of irrigation in farming, which was the occupation of most villagers.

This distressing situation prompted various organizations to import and subsidize diesel-powered and cast-iron pumps that, based on members' experience in other contexts, they believed would solve the problem. Unfortunately, these imported technologies cost too much money to purchase, required expensive fuel to operate, and could not be easily repaired locally when they broke down. Little wonder that farmers resisted these imposed attempts at change.

Enter George Klassen, a North American engineer employed by Mennonite Central Committee (MCC), who had been working alongside Bangladeshi farmers in the fields for several years, contributing to community building and earning the farmers' trust. Despite his emphasis on building relationships and mutual understanding, Klassen at first had few concrete results to show for his efforts. However, he did have the insight to realize that these rural farmers required a pump that could be operated by one person, could be

manufactured locally, and was an affordable low-tech option that could be serviced locally. With that understanding, he was able to develop a "rower pump" (so named because operating it requires a motion that looks like the operator is rowing a boat).

Klassen's good working relationship with the farmers had two additional positive benefits. First, because the farmers had learned to trust him they were motivated and willing to work alongside him in refining the rower pump. Second, Klassen benefited greatly from the knowledge the farmers shared with him as they developed and tested many different prototypes. They experimented with different designs, talked about how to deliver the product, learned from one another, and worked together to achieve what none could have done alone.

After the prototype had been developed, other staff at MCC developed relationships with local businesses to build, sell, and service the pumps. This effort led to the development of a local infrastructure of expertise in installation, repair, and inventory of parts. MCC workers also did field tests and trained people to use the pump. In the early years, MCC provided subsidies for the pump but with clear plans to phase out the organization's involvement to ensure that the pump would be self-supporting.

Today the use of the rower pump has become second nature to Bangladeshi farmers, enabling access to water for irrigation and providing safe drinking water for the whole village.

QUESTIONS FOR DISCUSSION

1. Identify each of the four steps in the change process that introduced the rower pump to Bangladeshi agriculture. Why did attempts to introduce cast-iron pumps and diesel-powered pumps fail?

2. Which steps do you think were the most challenging to manage?

This is the next in a series of personal journal entries that can be used for class discussion or be compiled and included as input in a self-reflection paper.

What are a few of the changes you will face in the next year? Why are they necessary? What do you hope will be the results of these changes? What might help (or hinder) your commitment to change? List a set of actions and plans that are likely to contribute to your success.

Sixteen

Creating Organizations

When changing an organization is warranted but unlikely, or when an attractive opportunity pulls people away from the current organization, starting a new venture is a possible solution. People who embark on the adventure of starting a new organization usually follow a path that includes four steps: (1) they identify an opportunity, (2) they take initiative, (3) they develop plans for the new venture, and (4) they mobilize resources.

Learning Objectives	Conventional OB	Sustainable OB
IDENTIFY OPPORTUNITY		
1. Discuss how entrepreneurs focus on identifying needs that can provide financial payoffs and/or enhance well-being.	Offer a product or service that meets a need that people are willing to pay for	Offer a product or service that meets or eliminates a need people have
TAKE INITIATIVE		
2. Identify the factors that influence taking the initiative to act on an opportunity.	Move from ideas to action as influenced by personality traits and potential benefits for the entrepreneur	Move from ideas to action as influenced by personality traits and potential benefits for others
DEVELOP PLANS		
3. Discuss how entrepreneurs develop a plan for their new venture.	Focus on having firm plans in place prior to start-up Highlight financial costs and benefits	Focus on flexible, ongoing learning Highlight financial, social, and ecological costs and benefits
MOBILIZE RESOURCES		
4. Identify how entrepreneurs acquire and mobilize the necessary resources for their new venture.	Attract financial resources and get started	Establish community support and get started

One Person's Trash Is Another Person's Treasure[1]

© Tony Kurdzuk/Star Ledger/Getty Images

Tom Szaky immigrated with his leaned family at an early age from Budapest, Hungary, to Toronto, Ontario. His parents were doctors, but Szaky leaned toward being an entrepreneur and started his own business, a webdesign firm, at the age of 14. Despite earninga five-figure income from the venture, he decided to move to the United States to attend Princeton University.

Szaky had known people who were exploring the use of "worm poop" as a fertilizer. Intrigued by the idea, he and his friends at Princeton began to experiment with feeding their leftover cafeteria food to worms. The results produced an excellent fertilizer—one that could be gathered and bottled in recycled pop bottles, no less. This got Szaky thinking differently about waste. He realized that he had found an interesting opportunity to produce something useful from things that were being thrown out. He devoted his spare time to refining the idea, particularly as it related to worm feces. Szaky's hope was to turn waste into marketable products, a simple idea that became the basis for a business plan he submitted to a student competition. Although he did not win that competition, he continued to work on the concept.

To expand his fledgling experiment in organic fertilizer production, Szaky begged and borrowed and came up with $20,000 to construct a "worm gin" to house worms and handle cafeteria waste. Potential investors were difficult to find and many laughed in his face when he described his plans, but Szaky persevered and eventually founded TerraCycle, based in New Jersey.

Later, as TerraCycle grew, Szaky struggled to find distribution channels for his bottled fertilizer. With no retail experience and a product that was unknown to many, he faced a difficult challenge. After initial rejections from many retail outlets, he finally convinced Home Depot, Walmart, Target, Petco, and Whole Foods to carry his

His hope was to turn waste into marketable products.

initial product, and later to also carry many other organic items and a range of recycled goods.

Every month, TerraCycle collects about a billion pieces of waste that otherwise would end up in a landfill. A major source of these inputs comes through its partnerships with major consumer products companies, such as Kraft, Nestlé, Johnson & Johnson, and Colgate-Palmolive, on whose behalf TerraCycle oversees waste collection programs. These partners pay for consumers and groups, such as schools, to collect non-recyclable packaging, like Capri Sun drink pouches, for upcycling to new products, such as purses that are of higher value than the waste they are manufactured from. TerraCycle is continually looking for new types of waste to recycle. It now recycles millions of cigarette butts in Canada and other countries and candy wrappers in countries such as New Zealand.

Maybe the most impressive recycling project is the fact that TerraCycle takes most of its profits and puts them back into the business. Szaky limits the profit margin to just 1% so TerraCycle can do more good for the environment. "We're in this to show that you can be a very successful social enterprise with the key goal of eliminating as much waste from being burned or buried as possible, while being profitable," Szaky says. He's quick to point out that his motivation is not entirely altruistic. "I want to make a lot of money by doing good. People are also motivated by personal return. If I sell this company I'll make millions, and that's a human motivator." In 2014, TerraCycle had roughly $20 million in revenues.

From an original sustainable entrepreneurial idea, TerraCycle has grown to produce more than 1,500 different products made from waste collected in more than 20 countries. The company has even spawned a Facebook video game called Trash Tycoon. It seems that transforming trash can also result in treasure.

This chapter will look at the initial creation of organizations, also called entrepreneurship. **Entrepreneurship** is the process of conceiving an opportunity to offer new or improved goods or services, taking the initiative to pursue that opportunity, making plans, and mobilizing the resources necessary to convert that opportunity into reality. It often leads to the creation of a new organizational start-up, and almost every organization we know today (including Liz Claiborne, Microsoft, FedEx, and the pizza place down the street) had an entrepreneurial beginning. **Entrepreneurs** are people who engage in entrepreneurial action to pursue an opportunity, often without control over the necessary resources or without certainty about the results.[2]

Sometimes entrepreneurship occurs within *existing* organizations, a phenomenon often referred to as **intrapreneurship**.[3] An intrapreneur is a person who, within a larger organization, behaves like an entrepreneur. Intrapreneurs see an opportunity that has potential to benefit the organization, and they take action to pursue it. Intrapreneurship is evident, for example, in organizations like 3M and Google, where managers expect employees to allocate as much as 20 percent of their time to dreaming up innovations that will eventually become the organization's future products and services.

The term "entrepreneurship" is sometimes used interchangeably with the terms "small business management" and "family business management." This is understandable, because these ideas often overlap. For example, many entrepreneurs manage small businesses, and many small business managers are entrepreneurs. Nevertheless, some entrepreneurs manage large businesses (e.g., Microsoft and Grameen Bank are quite large), and some small business managers are not entrepreneurs (e.g., someone who manages a local hardware store in much the same way as his or her entrepreneurial parent did is not an entrepreneur). Similarly, some family firms are small businesses run by entrepreneurs, but many *Fortune* 500 companies are also family owned or family controlled (e.g., the Mars family owns the world's largest chocolate company).

Note also that entrepreneurship can occur in non-profit organizations whenever someone recognizes an opportunity, demonstrates initiative, formulates plans, and gathers resources. For example, entrepreneurs started the non-profit Digger Foundation in 1998 to develop an affordable technology for the removal of land mines. The resulting machine increased the amount of land one worker can de-mine in a day from approximately 50 square metres to 250.[4] The opportunity, as exploited through entrepreneurial initiative, addressed an important need in countries recovering from war. Thus, entrepreneurship, generally defined, is simply the pursuit of new or innovative opportunities, regardless of organization type or size.

From a sustainable OB perspective, entrepreneurship includes both for-profit and non-profit entrepreneurial activity, but it focuses on a broader set of stakeholder needs with a long-term perspective. It is in many ways synonymous with a widely used definition of **social entrepreneurship:** "a process involving the innovative use and combination of resources to pursue opportunities to catalyze social change and/or address social needs."[5] This general definition is broad enough to include the sorts of non-profit organizations common in Europe (like a community child care co-operative) and those that combine social and profit motives and are more prominent in North America (such as TerraCycle).[6] And so we can define sustainable entrepreneurship as identifying an opportunity to provide benefits for multiple stakeholders, relentlessly pursuing that opportunity, developing and continuously adapting plans, and mobilizing the present and future resources necessary to sustainably convert the opportunity into reality.[7]

Entrepreneurship is the process of conceiving an opportunity to offer new or improved goods or services, taking the initiative to pursue that opportunity, making plans, and mobilizing the resources necessary to convert that opportunity into reality.

Entrepreneurs are people who engage in entrepreneurial action to pursue an opportunity.

Intrapreneurship is entrepreneurship that occurs within *existing* organizations.

Social entrepreneurship involves the innovative use and combination of resources to pursue opportunities to catalyze social change and/or address social needs.

Whereas the goal of conventional entrepreneurship is to maximize the *financial* wealth of the entrepreneurs and other investors, the goal of sustainable entrepreneurship is to maximize *multiple* forms of well-being for the entrepreneur, other investors, as well as other stakeholders. This goal takes form in the triple-bottom-line approach, introduced in chapter 1, through which sustainable entrepreneurs try to enhance financial, social, *and* ecological well-being simultaneously. The triple bottom line is depicted in Figure 16.1, which shows three overlapping circles: one representing financial interests, one ecological issues, and one social issues. The centre, where all three circles overlap, is the "sweet spot" that triple-bottom-line sustainable entrepreneurs aim for. Of course, sustainable entrepreneurs may also look at quadruple- or quintuple-bottom-line opportunities and pursue opportunities related to a variety of forms of well-being.

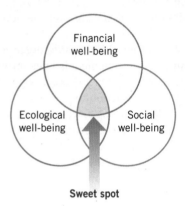

FIGURE 16.1   The Sustainable Sweet Spot in the Triple-Bottom-Line Approach

Like conventional entrepreneurship, sustainable entrepreneurship can occur in a wide variety of organizations, including for-profit and non-profit, small and large, and family-run or publicly traded organizations. Sustainable OB among entrepreneurs has been evident for years in well-known companies such as Ben & Jerry's, Patagonia, AES Corporation, ServiceMaster, Timberland, and many others. Sir Edmund Hillary is remembered more for climbing Mount Everest than for his four decades of entrepreneurial activity that helped establish more than 30 schools, 12 medical clinics, and two hospitals for impoverished Nepalese people. But he claimed, "My most worthwhile things have been the building of schools and medical clinics. That has given me more satisfaction than a footprint on a mountain."[8]

The basic four-step entrepreneurial process (see Figure 16.2) is the same for most entrepreneurs, but its focus may vary according to the founders' values and goals. We will describe each of the steps from a conventional OB perspective and then supplement each with a look at how the step unfolds from a sustainable OB perspective.

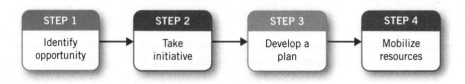

FIGURE 16.2   The Four Steps of the Entrepreneurial Process

Identify Opportunity

IDENTIFY OPPORTUNITY | TAKE INITIATIVE | DEVELOP PLANS | MOBILIZE RESOURCES

LEARNING OBJECTIVE 1
Discuss how entrepreneurs focus on identifying needs that can provide financial payoffs and/or enhance well-being.

Harvard psychologist Ellen Langer visits classrooms and shows students a picture of a person in a wheelchair. In one class she'll ask, "Can this person drive a car?" Students usually answer "no" and give plenty of reasons why not. In another class Langer will ask, "How can this person drive a car?" and students often come up with many creative ideas. The orientation evident in the second classroom is more consistent with the way entrepreneurs, by their very nature, look at the world.[9]

In short, entrepreneurs are more likely than others to see unmet needs in the internal or external environment and think about how something can be done rather than see reasons why it "can't" be done. Conventional entrepreneurs are constantly looking for better and more financially rewarding ways to meet needs. They are looking for places where they can outperform existing competitors, either by lowering costs or by providing unique added value. They look for opportunities to invest resources that will yield a higher financial return than they currently get. As the French economist Jean-Baptiste Say put it at the turn of the 19th century: "The entrepreneur shifts resources out of an area of lower and into an area of higher productivity and greater yield."[10] Because of their capacity to see opportunities where others see problems, entrepreneurs make very important contributions to society. Most notably, entrepreneurship plays an important role in keeping the economy going in areas such as job creation and innovation.[11] For example, in Canada, small businesses (defined as firms with fewer than 100 employees) make up 98.2 percent of the firms that employ others, and they create nearly half of all private-sector jobs.[12]

Sometimes the best entrepreneurial ideas come from people who have little or no experience in an industry, so they are able to bring a fresh perspective to it. For example, as featured in the opening case, Tom Szaky knew little about the fertilizer industry when he recognized the benefits of worm feces. More often, however, the best entrepreneurial ideas occur when people build on experience and expertise that they developed by working in a particular industry or sector. This is illustrated by the entrepreneurs who started PayPal and the dozens of people who left the company after eBay purchased it for $1.5 billion in 2002. Since then, PayPal alumni have participated in starting up YouTube, Room 9 Entertainment, Slide, and LinkedIn. The experience of working together at PayPal seems to have increased the likelihood and the success of future start-ups created by the former employees.[13]

Sometimes a new invention enjoys greater success if its creator does not seek to control it. For example, Tim Berners-Lee invented the World Wide Web, the importance of which cannot be overstated in terms of its effect on the world's economy, and he launched the world's first website in August 1991. The invention could have made Berners-Lee very wealthy, but he explains why he decided to leave the Web in the public domain rather than patenting it: "It was simply that, had the technology been proprietary, and in my total control, it would probably not have taken off."[14]

Both conventional and sustainable entrepreneurs think about how new products or services can meet people's needs; however, sustainable entrepreneurs differ from their conventional counterparts in two ways. First, whereas conventional entrepreneurs focus on identifying needs that can provide financial payoffs, sustainable entrepreneurs look at needs that, once met, can enhance a variety of forms of well-being—financial, social, and ecological. For example, sustainable entrepreneurs may seek to reduce environmental degradation in a financially sustainable way.[15] They also may seek to invent new ways of taking care of the environment or explore ways to improve employment opportunities for the marginalized members of society. In short, the sustainable approach represents a different way of seeing entrepreneurial opportunities. Muhammad Yunus spearheaded Grameen

Bank because he saw this venture as a way to help poor entrepreneurs in Bangladesh—not because he wanted to maximize financial returns for himself and other investors. In his own words:

> I met a woman who was making bamboo stools. After a long discussion I found out that she made only two pennies U.S. each day, and I couldn't believe anybody could work so hard and make such beautiful bamboo stools and make such a tiny amount of profit. So I tried to understand. She explained to me that she didn't have the money to buy the bamboo to make the stools, so she had to borrow from the trader—and the trader imposed the condition that she had to sell the product to him alone, at a price that he decided . . . she was virtually in bonded labor to this person. And how much did the bamboo cost? She said, "Oh, about 20 cents."[16]

Yunus recognized an opportunity that conventional managers had not been able to see: providing loans to the poor to help reduce a barrier that prevented them from becoming successful entrepreneurs. Now, many years later and thanks to the success of organizations such as Grameen Bank, big banks have begun participating in the microcredit business because their managers are increasingly recognizing its merits. As one-time McKinsey & Company consultant Vikram Akula notes, the "magic" of microfinancing is that it can work even if banks are "driven only by greed."[17]

A second difference between sustainable and conventional entrepreneurs is that, whereas conventional entrepreneurs often seek to *create* needs or a demand for their products or services, success for sustainable entrepreneurs sometimes comes when they *eliminate* needs or the demand for their products or services. In short, sustainable organizations often try to work themselves out of a job. For example, the entrepreneurs who founded the Digger Foundation and its volunteers who design machinery to remove landmines would be thrilled if all landmines were eliminated and there was no longer a need for their equipment. Similarly, Muhammad Yunus is looking forward to eliminating poverty, thereby eliminating the need to provide loans to impoverished people. Others may be seeking to eliminate social injustice, illness, pollution, or other societal problems.

Take Initiative

| IDENTIFY OPPORTUNITY | **TAKE INITIATIVE** | DEVELOP PLANS | MOBILIZE RESOURCES |

LEARNING OBJECTIVE 2
Identify the factors that influence taking the initiative to act on an opportunity.

Of course, simply identifying an opportunity does not automatically make someone an entrepreneur. The word *entrepreneur* originates from a French word meaning "to undertake." Many people love the idea of having a great cup of coffee in a nice coffee shop, but Howard Schultz actually did something about it when he started Starbucks.[18] Research suggests that almost half of Canadian students plan on starting a small business upon graduation and that almost 130,000 small businesses are created annually.[19]

We know that personal characteristics and life circumstances (situations that people face at a particular point in their lives) have an effect on whether people take entrepreneurial initiative (see Figure 16.3). The personality characteristics most often associated with entrepreneurs from the Big Five are conscientiousness, openness to experience, extraversion, and emotional stability.[20] These traits predict both the intention to start a business and the performance of the business. Risk propensity also plays a role, but it predicts only intention to start a business, not success.[21]

A high achievement motivation[22] and a high level of self-confidence[23] also are associated with entrepreneurs. Entrepreneurship is not for the timid. Entrepreneurs must be driven to succeed and trust their own abilities to fulfill the unmet needs they have identified. Their self-confidence must run deep, as many will fail several times before they finally attain success. The Hershey Company's founder, Milton S. Hershey, was the son of a man who tried

17 different new ventures, none of which earned him a living. Listening to the advice of his father also contributed to Milton's first venture going bankrupt.[24]

Research indicates that different levels of entrepreneurial activity can be explained by personal characteristics such as gender, ethnicity, or educational level, but these differences can also be explained by other factors.[25] For example, in Canada, men are almost twice as likely as are women to be actively engaged in starting a new firm, and immigrants account for 17.7 percent of the self-employed. Educational level also makes a difference, with more than half of the self-employed having completed a post-secondary certificate or diploma.[26]

Life circumstances also affect the likelihood that someone will start a new organization. People are more likely to act on their entrepreneurial urges if they are

- in the midst of a transition in life,
- being pushed away from the status quo, or
- being pulled into an entrepreneurial venture.

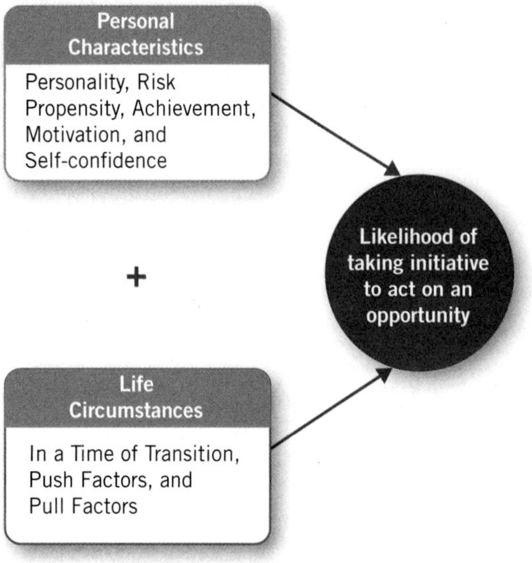

FIGURE 16.3 Factors that Influence Taking the Initiative to Act on an Opportunity

First, people are more likely to start a new organization if they have just gone through a big transition in their lives, be it planned or unplanned. Such an event might be completing an education or training program, finishing a major project, having a mid-life crisis, moving, or having recently been divorced or fired. For example, the people who left PayPal when it was purchased by eBay were in a period of transition, looking for the next project to work on.

Second, people are more likely to start a new organization if their current job is dissatisfying or if they have little hope of finding satisfying employment. This group includes intrapreneurs who believe that their good ideas are being stifled or who face dead-end jobs in their current workplace. Silicon Valley is filled with engineers and executives who left a company to start a new one. For example, Fairchild Semiconductor was started by eight engineers who left Shockley Semiconductor Laboratory; subsequently, two of those engineers (Robert Noyce and Gordon Moore) left Fairchild to start Intel Corporation,[27] and two others (William Hewlett and David Packard) left Fairchild to form Hewlett-Packard. Entrepreneurship can be especially important for those who have been marginalized in the larger society, such as minorities and women who face glass ceilings.[28]

Third, people are more likely to become entrepreneurs if they have positive pull influences, such as availability of financial resources and active encouragement from mentors, family, and friends. One pull factor is membership in a group of people who want you to join them in a new venture. Indeed, countering the myth of the "lone entrepreneur" is the fact that a start-up is more likely to find success if it is led by a group of entrepreneurs,[29] as were YouTube and Intel. Approximately one-fifth of existing organizations in a variety of industries started when a group of people left a common parent organization.

Many new ventures have been started by frustrated intrapreneurs who left an existing organization. As it turns out, they are often following a predictable path similar to the four-step entrepreneurial process.[30]

Step 1: A subgroup of members in an existing organization *identify an opportunity* for a new good or service. Members seldom act on this new idea until doing so has been legitimized by, for example, a senior manager saying the organization encourages members to develop initiatives based on new ideas.

M⦶B | WHEN A HOBBY BECOMES A NEW VENTURE

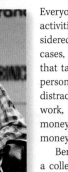

Jordon Naylor/WireImage/Getty Images

Everyone has interests or activities that might be considered a hobby. In most cases, a hobby is something that takes place outside of a person's work, is a refreshing distraction from the stress of work, and usually requires money instead of producing money.

Ben Silbermann has been a collector all his life. If you talk with him long enough about where he got the idea for Pinterest, he will mention his hobby of collecting bugs. His boyhood hobby was finding these bugs and then pinning them to a board. "I really liked insects," he says, "M1 kinds: flies, grasshoppers, weevils." He also might mention that later in life he developed an interest in infographics—the visual or graphical display of data.

Before Pinterest, Silbermann had worked at Google and with a college friend in a failed start-up that was focused on creating a shopping app. In exploring the use of that app with an initial group of customers, Silbermann noticed that the primary use people made of it was to take pictures of products to look at later. The combination of his life and work experience thus became the basis of Pinterest, a virtual information-sharing and networking pinboard.

Silbermann was particularly choosy about who could join the site at first, knowing that early users would be role models who would set the norms for the new community. He himself learned a great deal from them: "It's exciting to see people using the product in ways that we never really expected." Who knew that Pinterest could help spouses who live in the same house understand each other better by visiting each other's virtual pinboard?

Silbermann is not done learning from Pinterest users or even from his friends. "It's important to have people in your life who can talk to you about other stuff: life, sports. It's going to take a long time to build a big product that'll change the world," he says. Not only do friends balance out your life, they may help you recognize your next opportunity.

QUESTIONS FOR REFLECTION

1. What are the activities or interests that take up most of your time?
2. Have you invented better ways to do what you love doing?
3. Are there any ideas or practices you can take from your hobbies that might be the seed of entrepreneurial opportunity?

Step 2: Once their goals have been sanctioned, the intrapreneurs actively begin to *initiate changes*. These changes are tolerated at first, but after a while other members begin to resist.

Step 3: The intrapreneurs recognize that their *plans* for change are being opposed, and after a short struggle, they are told their new initiatives are not welcome.

Step 4: Members of the intrapreneurial group exit their parent organization and *mobilize resources* to create a new start-up.

The personalities of conventional and sustainable entrepreneurs may be similar and both types may be highly motivated, but for conventional entrepreneurs the focus is on achieving tangible and quantifiable financial goals, whereas sustainable entrepreneurs are more likely to want to accomplish something that may defy measurement but is significant and timeless. Conventional entrepreneurs may ground their confidence in themselves, whereas sustainable entrepreneurs find it in a community; they recognize that they cannot make a venture happen on their own—the support and co-operation of other stakeholders are required. For example, Muhammad Yunus worked with clients, university students, and other bankers as he developed Grameen Bank. Because sustainable entrepreneurs are more likely to seek other stakeholders' advice and involve them in developing a new venture, they can be confident of their support.

We also see contrasts in the conventional and the sustainable entrepreneur's responses to transition, push, and pull. For sustainable entrepreneurs, *transitions* often result from realizing they want to escape the pursuits and pressures of the status quo. Many well-paid professionals have chosen to become "downwardly mobile" in an effort to escape jobs and lifestyles associated with excessive materialism.[31] For example, Tom Chappell left the corporate world in 1968 to "move back to the land" and eat and live healthier. When he and his wife, Kate, were unable to find natural personal-care products, they co-founded Tom's of Maine in 1970 with a $5,000 loan from a friend. The company grew, but when Chappell saw that its founding values were being challenged by MBA-trained managers, he became the first sitting CEO to enrol in the Harvard Divinity School. His goal was to rediscover the mission for both himself and his company—that is, to simultaneously be financially successful and socially and environmentally responsible. By 2006, the company had become the leading natural-care brand in the United States, and the Chappells decided they could best meet the growing demand for their products by partnering with a larger company. They were very careful to choose a partner they felt would honour their firm's values and ended up selecting the Colgate-Palmolive Company.[32]

People may experience *positive pulls* to become sustainable entrepreneurs from friends or others who are encouraging and offer support for a new venture or from one's own desire to make a difference. Tom Williams started his own computer game company when he was 13 and became famous at 14 for being one of the youngest people ever hired to work for Apple Inc. Although he earned "an absurd amount of money" and achieved great success there as a pioneer in online music, by the time he was in his mid-20s Williams realized that meaning was missing from his life.[33] Eventually he left Apple to start GiveMeaning.com, a website that enables people to post project-specific appeals for capital and provides donors with a hassle-free and tax-efficient way to make contributions.[34] In short, Tom Williams is an entrepreneur who makes it easier for people to take initiative when they see opportunities to help others.

Empathy for a disadvantaged segment of the population can be another pull factor. Katie Davis, just a few years out of high school, started a non-profit organization for orphans in Uganda after she had lived there and encountered their needs first-hand.[35] Others are *pushed* to become entrepreneurs, such as whistleblowers who are not welcome back in their industry or frustrated intrapreneurs whose ideas are not accepted by their former organizations or industries.[36] At times, pull and push factors can work together, like they did for Muhammad Yunus. He recognized the great needs of the poor, and the banking industry would not accept his ideas for addressing the problem.

Even so, seeing needs first-hand is not enough; entrepreneurs still need to act. For example, many people have ideas about how to help poor people but do nothing to execute those ideas. Yunus did. According to him,

> I debated whether I should give her [the bamboo-stool-making entrepreneur] 20 cents, but then I came up with another idea—let me make a list of people who needed that kind of money. I took a student of mine and we went around the village for several days and came up with a list of 42 such people. When I added up the total amount they needed, I got the biggest shock of my life: it added up to 27 dollars! . . . . I took the money out of my pocket and gave it to my student. I said: "You take this money and give it to those 42 people that we met and tell them this is a loan that they can pay me back whenever they are able to. In the meantime, they can sell their product wherever they can get a good price."[37]

The story of social entrepreneur George Willdridge provides an example in which all three life circumstances—transition, push, and pull—are evident. Willdridge had become the very successful managing director of an import/export firm when, as part of his job to entertain wealthy Asian customers who enjoyed high-stakes gambling, he became addicted to gambling himself. Soon he had no job (transition), no money, and huge debts, and he contemplated suicide every day for six weeks. Willdridge knew his behaviour needed to change (push). He became a social entrepreneur when The Salvation Army asked him to set up the Oasis Centre for Problem Gamblers in Auckland, New Zealand (pull). For Willdridge, the depths of despair resulting from his gambling addiction led to a life-changing moment when he came to realize that "quality of life does not stem from wealth. Once you have enough, it makes no difference."[38]

OB in Action   From Failure to Fame

© Nomi Ellenson/FilmMagic/ Getty Images

J. K. Rowling, author of the Harry Potter series, went through an extraordinary and stressful transition period before penning the wildly successful books. Seven years after finishing university, her life had undergone a radical change: She had left her marriage, her job, and the country in which she worked. Returning to Britain a single mother living in poverty, Rowling saw herself as a failure. However, these failures spurred her to focus on her passion for writing and launch what would become a billion-dollar empire. Rowling's writing and the industry it spurred would land her on *Forbes's* billionaire list by 2011, although she subsequently fell off the list after donating a substantial portion of her fortune to charity.

In her 2008 commencement address at Harvard University, Rowling suggested that failure can have "fringe benefits" and that those who experience failure can emerge wiser and stronger. As she stated, "It is impossible to live without failing at something, unless you live so cautiously that you might as well not have lived at all—in which case, you fail by default." Failure is not an uncommon occurrence for entrepreneurs. In fact, research suggests that nearly three-quarters of venture-backed firms fail to pay back their investors. However, entrepreneurs can build upon and learn from their previous failures so that they can launch endeavours that are ultimately a success.

QUESTIONS FOR DISCUSSION

1. Do you know of other people who experienced failure but moved on to greater success?
2. What can you learn from the failures you have experienced?
3. What personal characteristics are important in making the best of difficult circumstances?

Develop Plans

| IDENTIFY OPPORTUNITY | TAKE INITIATIVE | **DEVELOP PLANS** | MOBILIZE RESOURCES |

Even though entrepreneurs tend to be action oriented, before they start a new venture they need to do some research to find out whether their idea is feasible. In particular, they must develop a plan for the new venture. This plan, usually referred to as a business plan, provides a clear direction by laying out the strategy necessary to reach the objectives. Perhaps not surprisingly, teaching students how to prepare such plans has been identified as the most important feature of entrepreneurship education; though, as we shall see, sometimes detailed plans may not be as helpful in practice.[39]

Preparing a plan for a new venture prior to start-up provides several benefits. Following are the principal benefits:

- It forces entrepreneurs to set standards or milestones against which to measure performance. For example, an entrepreneur may decide that a new organization should have at least $100,000 in revenue within the first year or a positive cash flow within three years. If these milestones are not met, then the entrepreneur (and investors) can walk away from the venture before investing any more resources in it.

- It helps the venture win the support of other stakeholders, whether they are financiers, employees, suppliers, or customers. Having a plan improves both the likelihood of success and the potential for securing outside funding.

- It ensures that entrepreneurs, before they start their venture, think through the different aspects of planning mentioned below. Once a new venture is under way, the ongoing pressures of running it often leave little time for reflection.

There are different ways to structure a business plan, but most include an executive summary, the concept of the venture, a description of the team, a discussion of operational resources, and the short-term and long-term goals for the venture.

The first part of the start-up plan is the *executive summary*. Although it typically appears at the beginning of a plan, the summary isn't written until after the other parts have been written because it includes the highlights of the other parts of the plan as well as the mission of the new venture. The executive summary should capture the reader's attention and be no longer than three pages. For a new venture utilizing a sustainable approach, the summary would not only describe how the new venture can enhance financial well-being but also how it may enhance other forms of well-being.

The second part of the plan is the *concept of the venture*. This part describes customers and other organizations in the new venture's external environment and describes the new venture's product or service. Once you have identified the attributes of key customers and other relevant organizations, you should evaluate the strengths and weaknesses of your new venture relative to the opportunities and threats you have identified. This analysis, in turn, will allow you to develop and describe an appropriate strategy that your new venture will pursue. A sustainable approach takes this general approach but does so in light of a wide range of social and ecological concerns. For example, a new daycare centre may be promoted as operating in a community that has many single parents who cannot afford existing daycares. Similarly, the description of the product or service itself will draw attention to its multiple benefits, perhaps including a reduced ecological footprint compared to that of competitors.

Sometimes the basic concept can develop very quickly. For example, at a restaurant during the 29th birthday party for Max Levchin, one of PayPal's co-founders, a conversation began about how difficult it can be to find a good dentist. Two former PayPal engineers who were at the party, Jeremy Stoppelman and Russel Simmons, started talking about creating a website on which people could review the professional services available in their neighbourhoods. The conversation continued on the walk back to their offices after lunch, at which time they pulled Levchin aside and pitched the basic concept of the new venture. Levchin liked the idea. The next day he agreed to back it with $1 million—and thus Yelp was born.[40]

The start-up plan also must communicate that you have an appropriately skilled *team* of organizational members and partners to carry out the work of the new venture. Studies suggest that venture capitalists place great emphasis on the characteristics of the entrepreneurs who are leading a new start-up, especially their ability to work as a cohesive team.[41] A **venture capitalist** is a company or individual that invests money in an organization in exchange for a share of its ownership and profits. In addition, the business plan should provide information on your basic management philosophy and how members will relate to one another and in what roles. For example, Jawed Karim, one of the three entrepreneurs who co-founded YouTube, never took a salary, benefits, or even a formal title in the company. He simply assumed the role of an informal advisor to the other two co-founders, Chad Hurley and Steve Chen. All three had left PayPal after selling it to eBay for $1.5 billion. Karim initially pitched the basic idea of video sharing but ultimately decided to go back to university; Hurley and Chen subsequently turned the idea into what became YouTube.[42]

A sustainable plan is likely to include key external stakeholders in the design and ongoing operation of the organization. For example, for every pair of Eco eyeglass frames (made entirely of recycled materials) that Modo Eyewear sells,[43] the company plants a tree through its partnership with Trees for the Future. The eyewear packaging is also environmentally friendly, and it includes a return envelope so customers can donate unwanted glasses to OneSight, an organization that helps some of the millions of people worldwide whose poor eyesight hinders learning and employment.[44]

The start-up plan also should include a section describing the *resources* required to operate your new venture. A key resource is suppliers. For example, if you are starting a new daycare centre, then your plan may describe how a key supplier of your human resources will be a local community college that trains credentialed daycare professionals. Other key resources for most organizations are physical buildings and location. For example, what are

A **venture capitalist** is a company or individual that invests money in an organization in exchange for a share of ownership and profits.

potential sites for the daycare centre, and what are the zoning regulations, property taxes, and insurance costs? What sorts of equipment and supplies do you need—crayons, floor mats, indoor/outdoor climbing structures, and so on? A final component is to identify the new venture's sources of financing (e.g., bank loans, venture capitalists' investments, entrepreneurs' personal savings) and specify when specific amounts of money will be needed.

Perhaps the most distinct features of a sustainable approach to discussing resources is the inclusion of environmental and social implications for the new venture. A sustainable start-up plan is much more likely to cover issues such as the energy efficiency of the physical plant and equipment, a description of how waste will be minimized and recycled, and so on. Bioplaneta is a sustainable network started by Héctor Marcelli to promote fair trade, organic agriculture, and sustainable development in Mexico. Bioplaneta helps Mexican entrepreneurs develop plans for new ventures that protect natural resources and minimize ecological impact (sometimes called ecopreneurship).[45] A sustainable plan is also more likely to describe how suppliers are chosen based on their perceived corporate social responsibility and to look at how hiring practices affect social justice.

The final section of the start-up plan describes to what ends or *goals* resources will be mobilized; forecasts expected financial performance over time; and, possibly, discusses contingency plans that will be put in place in case events do not unfold as planned. Central features of this last section are the goals and financial projections for the first five years, including analysis of expected expenses and revenues. The plan should include budgets and financial statements that describe the specific times and amounts of financing that will be required over a period of several years. Often plans identify specific "milestones" that are designed to help the entrepreneurs and investors know whether they should pull out. For example, if a new daycare centre needs 40 children to be viable and it has only 20 children after two years of operation, then it may be prudent to close the business. A start-up plan also may include contingency plans to follow if goals or milestones are not met or circumstances change.

A sustainable plan is more likely to supplement financial concerns and measures with social and ecological measures of performance. For example, success measures at Windigo Catering (see OB in Action: Gourmet Just Got Better) may include satisfied customers, financial viability, job opportunities for First Nations peoples, and a small ecological footprint. Sustainable plans will seek to enhance overall well-being in the long term, which may in turn influence things like decisions about overseas expansion. Contingency plans will include social and ecological contingencies.

Another significant difference between conventional and sustainable entrepreneurship is that, whereas conventional entrepreneurs *use the plan to convince stakeholders* to support the organization, sustainable entrepreneurs *use stakeholders to write a convincing plan*. This difference in perspective is what makes writing a sustainable plan a process of continual revision. Consider what happened when managers of Kowalski's Markets, a Minnesota grocery chain, purchased four store locations, one of which was an existing grocery store in a lower- to middle-class neighbourhood that did not fit the grocer's typical upscale demographic. Rather than sell this property, managers decided they had an obligation to provide the neighbourhood with a viable grocery store (which the former tenant had failed to do). Founders Mary Anne and Jim Kowalski shared their vision for their newly acquired store at a community meeting in the neighbourhood. They promised to provide a clean, safe store and vowed not to sell lottery tickets or cigarettes. They then invited residents of the neighbourhood to name the store and to spend all of its profits in ways that served the interests of the surrounding community.

The residents shocked the Kowalskis by saying they believed that keeping the Kowalski name would attract more businesses to the community and that they would rather have profits put back into improving the store. As expected, the store has made a valuable contribution to the neighbourhood nonetheless, including an increased sense of community spirit

OB in Action Gourmet Just Got Better

© Ilya Shapovalov/iStock photo

Windigo Catering Limited Partnership is owned by five member communities of the Windigo First Nations Council in northwestern Ontario. Based in Sioux Lookout, the company operates a business-to-business model, providing gourmet catering services as well as housekeeping services. Although the company serves a wide range of short-term and long-term clients, its largest client by far is Goldcorp's Musselwhite Mine fly-in camp on Opapimiskan Lake (located 800 kilometres north of Thunder Bay), with which the company has been partnered since 1998. Through co-operation and a formal partnership with Goldcorp, Windigo provides employment, skills training, and economic development opportunities to its communities and people. The company currently generates approximately CAD $6 million in revenue annually and shares its profits among the five First Nations communities that own it: Bearskin Lake, Cat Lake, North Caribou Lake, Sachigo Lake, and New Slate Falls.

While many relationships between First Nations communities and mining companies are characterized by hostility, Frank McKay, President of Windigo Ventures General Partner Ltd., states that Windigo's relationship with Goldcorp "embodies cooperation, understanding and mutual respect [. . .] and is based on shared values and continues to strengthen."

From its founding in the early 1990s, Windigo has taken pride in contributing to the socio-economic development of First Nations communities by creating employment opportunities. Debbie Korobanik, General Manager of Windigo, says the company not only offers employment opportunities that never existed before, it also pays its employees higher-than-industry-average wages and provides benefit packages.

Committed to building a long-term sustainable business, Windigo continues to improve its ability to better cater to its clients while benefiting nearby First Nations communities. Unlike many catering services that operate at mines, Windigo offers gourmet and freshly prepared meals to Goldcorp. The company has even started to recruit and train certified bakers, so the cafeteria smells like fresh bread and other baked goods when workers arrive. Korobanik notes that this focus on quality yields two major benefits: (1) it helps with retention in what is usually a high-turnover industry, and (2) it creates more jobs and employment opportunities. As the company states on its website: "With our roots in Northwestern Ontario, we are determined to expand throughout the region and beyond, hiring local labour to work alongside our qualified chefs, managers and well-trained staff."

Recognized by the Prospectors and Developers Association of Canada for its excellence in service and contribution to the mining industry, Windigo continues to excel and contribute to the greater development of neighbouring First Nations communities and their people.

QUESTIONS FOR DISCUSSION

1. What is your reaction to the fact that Windigo is providing services to a company that is potentially contributing to environmental degradation?
2. What concerns do you have about a recipe for sustainable business that includes a mix of social justice and profits?
3. How would you expect investors to respond to it?

---

and increased property values. Thus, even though the store did not turn a profit in its first few years, the Kowalskis viewed it as a success. As Mary Anne Kowalski notes, this entrepreneurial endeavour shows the importance of neighbourliness and citizenship: Business can't do it on its own.[46]

Probably the most striking sign of a sustainable new-venture plan is its consistent reference to multiple forms of well-being, the triple-bottom-line approach. For example, any plan that Muhammad Yunus wrote about Grameen Bank mentioned how the organization would help poor people escape poverty, would provide women with greater opportunities to meet their needs and those of their children, and would develop a sense of community. Despite having a positive experience loaning his own money, Yunus found few interested partners when he tried to get traditional banks to pick up on the opportunity. He had to formulate his own plan to find money to lend to the poor. In his words,

Finally, after several days of running around I offered myself as a guarantor. I'll guarantee the loan, I'll sign whatever they wanted me to sign, but they can give the money, and I'll give it to the people that I want to. So that was the beginning. They warned me repeatedly that the poor people who receive the money will never pay back. I said, "I'll take a chance." And the surprising thing was, they repaid me every penny—there was not a single penny missing.[47]

The bankers still questioned the viability of his business model and continued to question whether the idea of microlending would work on a large scale. Yunus spent a great deal of time trying to convince bankers to join him, but they had been trained to believe the poor were too risky. As he described,

> Luckily, I was not trained that way so I could believe whatever I am seeing, as it revealed itself. But their minds, their eyes were blinded by the knowledge they had. Finally I had the thought: Why am I trying to convince them? I am totally convinced that poor people can take money and pay back. Why don't we set up a separate bank? That excited me, and I wrote down the proposal and went to the government to get the permission to set up the bank. It took me two years to convince the government.[48]

Aspiring entrepreneurs should take heart from this example; it can be difficult to convince others of the merit of plans, even if they have the potential to become Nobel Prize–winning entrepreneurial ventures.

Planning has value, but on the other hand, the value of developing a detailed plan for a new venture may be somewhat overrated.[49] For example, one study found that only 28 percent of a sample of *Inc.* 500 firms had completed a prototypical business plan, and other research has shown no relationship between having a new-venture plan and future profitability.[50] Critics of developing detailed plans for new ventures argue that planning may be irrelevant and constraining, limiting the likelihood of ongoing experimentation as the organization grows.

Managers at the World Bank, for example, encourage flexible planning to foster intrapreneurship. In one case, a team had been given the goal of increasing milk production for rural farmers in Africa. When team members visited the field, however, they found that the real problem was *spoilage* of milk as it travelled from producer to consumers. The flexibility they were given allowed them to change their focus. As the team leader put it, "I now realize how much of the overall success of the effort depends on people discovering for themselves what goals to set and what to do to achieve them."[51] While an emphasis on planning reinforces convergent thinking, by which managers seek to find a single precise answer, a sustainable approach encourages divergent thinking, by which managers discover multiple alternative solutions based on the same information (see chapter 7).[52]

Mobilize Resources

IDENTIFY OPPORTUNITY | TAKE INITIATIVE | DEVELOP PLANS | **MOBILIZE RESOURCES**

With a detailed plan for the new venture in place, the entrepreneur is now prepared to acquire and mobilize the necessary resources. This phase includes arranging the required financing, establishing relationships with suppliers and other stakeholders, and creating and implementing the organizational structure and systems.

For most new ventures, adequate financing is the key resource that needs to be mobilized. Unless the entrepreneurs are self-financed, they will need either debt or equity financing. **Debt financing** consists of funds that entrepreneurs borrow money from family members, friends, a bank, or another financial institution that must be paid back at some future date. *Collateral*—such as personal assets or business assets—is often required to guarantee such a loan. **Equity financing** occurs when investors in a new venture receive shares in return for their infusion of cash and become part owners of the organization; this type of financing usually comes from venture capitalists. Venture capitalists often become quite heavily involved in the operations of a business, sometimes providing advice or even requiring that they approve any major decisions regarding the organization.

Debt financing occurs when entrepreneurs borrow money from family members, friends, a bank, or another financial institution that must be paid back at some future date.

Equity financing occurs when investors in a new venture receive shares of stock and become part owners of the organization.

OB in Action

Can Entrepreneurs Take the Heat?

CBC Licensing

Dragons' Den is a reality television show on which aspiring Canadian entrepreneurs pitch their businesses to a panel of potential investors, who are known as the Dragons. The show's name is appropriate because the investors will instigate an aggressive attack when they sense that an entrepreneur is unprepared or that there is an opportunity for a profitable return on investment. Among those who have invested millions in promising start-ups on the show are successful entrepreneurs, senior executives of multinational corporations, real estate moguls, and venture capitalists. The pitch—a short explanation of the product or service, business plan, and estimated financial needs—is pivotal in securing money from the Dragons or from other investors who are tamer.

A few examples from the show highlight the importance of a well-prepared pitch. The founder of CrowdFanatic, an online engagement platform for debates, left the Dragons confused and unimpressed when he failed to explain his revenue model and justify his company's valuation. In contrast, the founders of Steeped Tea, a loose-leaf tea company, provided a succinct and compelling explanation of what they were offering, what problem they were solving, and what made them the best people to solve that problem. In the end, CrowdFanatic failed to yield a single offer from any of the five investors on the panel, whereas Steeped Tea yielded four. However, the founders of Steeped Tea decided to accept only two of the four offers because two of the Dragons were asking for too much ownership and control. In 2015, Steeped Tea was ranked 27th on the *PROFIT* 500 list of Canada's fastest-growing companies, and its co-founder and president, Tonia Jahshan, was named by Ernst & Young as one of the six Entrepreneurial Women to Watch in *Forbes* magazine.

It helps your pitch to know your product and numbers; to be persuasive, personable, and yet humble; and to have a good story. Lori Greiner, a successful entrepreneur who holds more than 100 patents and has launched 400 new products, has a few specific suggestions for women when making their pitch: Know your stuff and view yourself as equal to men, don't back down. "Do not let any man put you down or be chauvinistic to you," she says. Instead forge ahead with confidence, and command respect by being prepared and knowledgeable.

QUESTIONS FOR DISCUSSION

1. Entrepreneurs make sales pitches to investors, but everyone has to make a pitch at some point to persuade others to co-operate. When do you need to pitch to others to get their investment of resources, such as money or time?
2. What can you learn from *Dragons' Den* about pitching ideas to make improvements in your organization or intrapreneurship?
3. How is an employment interview like a pitch?

Sometimes governments provide resources specifically geared to support entrepreneurial activity. This support may include supporting educational programs for potential entrepreneurs, including partnerships with local community colleges and universities. Government "incubators" designed to help particular types of entrepreneurs get started may provide subsidized office space, support services, and management advice. Governments may also provide subsidies or incentives to help people start particular types of organizations. For example, wind farms that generate electricity by harnessing the power of the wind were initially subsidized but are now self-sustaining.

Sustainable entrepreneurs also need to mobilize financial resources to get their organizations started. As the history of Grameen Bank illustrates, conventional financial institutions may prefer providing financing to conventional entrepreneurs, and as a result sustainable entrepreneurs need to become more creative in gaining access to financial resources.

In any case, sustainable entrepreneurs are more likely to recognize the importance of non-financial resources and, especially, the fact that good relationships with stakeholders can reduce the need for financial resources. Sustainable entrepreneurs develop social networks to develop their credibility. While doing so, they invite stakeholders to give shape to, identify with, and create opportunities to support the values and basic concept of the new venture. For example, ever since its earliest days, Celestial Seasonings, the leading herbal tea company in the United States, has done extensive product testing with consumers.[53] This same emphasis on developing relationships with stakeholders is also evident in the examples set by entrepreneurs like Muhammad Yunus and the Kowalskis.

Sustainable entrepreneurs are also more mindful of the way they mobilize the physical resources required for their new venture. They would consider, for example, what is the effect of operations on the ecological footprint? Again, concerns like this are addressed by working with stakeholders who are concerned about the ecological environment. For instance, every year thousands of "bioneers" gather for a three-day conference in San Rafael, California, with another 10,000 participating by satellite. Attendees include entrepreneurs like Jay Harman, who demonstrated an energy-saving technology for pumps and fans, and John Maus, a contractor looking for the latest information about green building.[54]

Because sustainable entrepreneurs are more sensitive to responsibly using the variety of resources they require, and because they are more likely to welcome input from key stakeholders, their venture should be more sustainable over the long term and should enjoy wider support in the larger community. This support can also come from financial institutions. For example, there is increasing interest in socially responsible investing—such portfolios now account for approximately $2 trillion in investments.[55] Specialist networks can help sustainable organizations find venture capital; examples include Cleantech Venture Network, Investor's Circle, and World Resources Institute's New Ventures.[56] Organizations like Ashoka look for social entrepreneurs to invest in when no one else will.[57] In short, because of their attention to non-financial resources and benefits, sustainable ventures will be more attractive to certain investors; particularly to those who look for more than simply maximizing their financial return.

In Muhammad Yunus's own words,

> A bank which started its journey with 27 dollars, giving loans to 42 people, coming all the way to a billion dollars in loans, is a cause for celebration, we thought. And we felt good. Nobody had believed in us, everybody said, Well, you can give tiny amounts to tiny people—so what? You cannot expand, you cannot reach out to the poor people. So coming all the way to a billion dollars in loans to so many borrowers was quite an excitement.*

When Yunus received the Nobel Peace Prize in 2006, Grameen Bank had 6.6 million borrowers, more than 95 percent of whom were women,[58] and 18,795 employees in 2,225 branches[59] working in 71,371 villages. Since its inception, the bank has disbursed more than $5.7 billion to help people escape poverty by starting businesses. Its loan recovery rate is 98.85 percent, and it has made a profit almost every year of its operations. The compellingly simple idea of providing credit to the world's poorest micro-entrepreneurs has proven to be enormously effective. Yunus is known for saying that our grandchildren will need to go to a museum to see poverty. The creation of this bank was a great opportunity that has delivered a wealth of benefits to society.

---

* Yunus , M. (1996 , November/December). Fighting poverty from the bottom up: An address by Muhammad Yunus. Retrieved from \www.grameen-info.org.

googling google[60]

Robert Cardin/Redux

By almost any measure, Google Inc. represents an amazing entrepreneurial success story. Within the span of eight years (1996–2004), it went from being a student research project in a university dorm room to a company valued at almost USD $30 billion. Its initial public offering (IPO) raised $1.6 billion, which was a new record for a technology IPO. The company is known for its motto "Do no evil," for bringing unbiased information in many languages to people around the world, for giving small businesses affordable access to advertising, for creating a stimulating work environment, and even for being a leader in ecological responsibility. Following is a brief summary of Google's formative years.

Larry Page and Sergey Brin, Google's co-founders, met in 1995 when they were graduate students at Stanford University. At the time, Brin was 23 years old and had been assigned to show the 24-year-old Page around campus. The pair argued with each other about almost everything, but their divergent points of view came together in January 1996 when they began working on one of the biggest challenges in computing—namely, retrieving relevant information from a huge data set. Their unique approach was based on developing the ability to analyze the "back links" that pointed to a given website. Google's mission continues to be "to organize the world's information and make it universally accessible and useful." For Page and Brin, a better search engine was everything—profit was peripheral.

After a couple of years' work, Page and Brin had developed their ideas and built a beta version of their better mousetrap. They never intended to start a new venture; instead they wanted to license their search technology to an existing organization. However, when managers at potential partner organizations failed to see the value of their technology, the pair took a break from their university studies to start their firm. In an early attempt at finding an investor, they demonstrated a prototype to Andy Bechtolsheim, a co-founder of Sun Microsystems and a legend in Silicon Valley for his ability as an engineer and his nose for talent. Brin recalls, "We gave him a quick demo. He had to run off somewhere, so he said, 'Instead of us discussing all the details, why don't I just write you a check?' It was made out to Google Inc. and was for $100,000." Google became the official name of their firm.

By September 1998, the pair had accumulated an initial investment of almost $1 million from family, friends, and acquaintances, and Google opened its first off-campus office in a friend's garage in Menlo Park, California. At the time it had a staff of three, and the beta version of Google.com was answering nearly 10,000 search queries per day. By February 1999 the beta version was answering 500,000 queries per day and Google's staff, now numbering eight, had relocated to an office in Palo Alto.

Page and Brin were aware that their $1 million wouldn't last long, so they went looking for support from leading venture capitalists in Silicon Valley. Specifically, they sought the support of John Doerr of Kleiner Perkins Caufield & Byers, arguably the most influential venture capitalist in the Valley, and Michael Moritz of Sequoia Capital, who had backed Yahoo! Inc. Both Doerr and Moritz were as impressed as Bechtolsheim had been—they were not concerned by the lack of a detailed business plan—but both wanted to do the deal alone. Page and Brin insisted that they wanted both Doerr and Moritz as backers, something that had never been done before. Doerr and Moritz agreed to invest jointly only after Page and Brin threatened to look for investment capital elsewhere. On June 7, 1999, Google secured $25 million from Doerr and Moritz, who both joined the company's board of directors (which met around a ping-pong table). Soon, daily traffic on Google surpassed 3 million searches, and on September 21, 1999, the "beta" label came off the website. By the end of 2000, Google was handling more than 100 million search queries every day.

In 2001 Google barely turned a profit with $87 million in revenues; by 2003, however, its revenues were $1.5 billion and its profits totalled $340 million. Meanwhile, Google's unique organizational culture flourished as the company kept growing. The desks of its 60 or so employees each consisted of a door laid across a pair of sawhorses, and office chairs were often large rubber exercise balls. Google hired a company chef who prepared health-conscious recipes. Twice a week, employees used the parking lot to play roller hockey. The informal culture fostered collegiality and facilitated the exchange of ideas.

Not surprisingly, given these unconventional management practices, Doerr and Moritz insisted that Page and Brin hire a professional manager to become CEO of the firm. At first Page and Brin resisted, but they saw the merits of having a professional manager after Doerr arranged meetings with a variety of leading industry executives in Silicon Valley. Eric Schmidt, former CEO of Novell, became Google's CEO in 2001. Schmidt said upon joining the team, "We're not just three random guys. We're all computer scientists with the same interests and backgrounds. The first time we met, we argued for an hour and a half over pretty much everything—and it was a really good argument." Schmidt noted that the three had found a new way of doing business, breaking all the rules—a triumvirate of equals with no hierarchy.

Page and Brin were not eager to offer shares in Google for public sale. After all, the main reason any firm goes public is to raise cash, but Google already had enough. They also knew that previous IPOs had created "forces of greed and envy that wreaked havoc on promising start-ups." But Doerr and Moritz were eager to cash in on their investment, and the employees who had been working hard for years were also eager for the payday that would come with an IPO. Page and Brin relented, but they insisted that the IPO be set up in such a way that made it clear that managers at Google would not feel compelled to play the short-term financial games typically required by Wall Street. And so, before Google's IPO in 2004, they penned "An Owner's Manual" for Google's shareholders that expressed this desire.

QUESTIONS FOR DISCUSSION

1. Can you identify the four steps of the entrepreneurship process in the formation of Google? Which step was the most important for this firm? Which was least important?
2. What are the secrets to the entrepreneurial success of Page and Brin? Which aspects of their approach can be applied to other entrepreneurial ventures?
3. Where would you place them along the conventional–sustainable continuum? Why?

Summary

Both conventional and sustainable entrepreneurs follow a similar four-step entrepreneurial process, but there are differences in how the process unfolds.

◆ Learning Objectives	◇ In the conventional OB approach, entrepreneurs:	◇ In the sustainable OB approach, entrepreneurs:
• Discuss how entrepreneurs focus on identifying needs that can provide financial payoffs and/or enhance well-being. • Identify the factors that influence taking the initiative to act on an opportunity.	• Identify opportunities to offer a product or service that meets a need that people are willing to pay for. • Take initiative resulting from a combination of the entrepreneur's personality characteristics (predisposed to see financial opportunities) and his or her life circumstances (transition, push, pull).	• Identify opportunities to offer a product or service that meets or eliminates needs that people have. • Take initiative resulting from a combination of the entrepreneur's personality characteristics (predisposed to see opportunities that enhance multiple forms of well-being, a need to help, and confidence in the community) and their life circumstances (transition, push, pull).
• Discuss how entrepreneurs develop a plan for their new venture. • Identify how entrepreneurs acquire and mobilize the necessary resources for their new venture.	• Develop a plan for the new venture with an emphasis on financial costs and benefits. • Mobilize resources, especially attracting the required start-up financing.	• Develop a plan for the new venture with an emphasis on financial, social, and ecological costs and benefits. • Mobilize resources, especially attracting the support of other stakeholders.

Key Terms

Debt financing (p. 372) Equity financing (p. 372) Venture capitalist (p. 369)
Entrepreneurs (p. 361) Intrapreneurship (p. 361)
Entrepreneurship (p. 361) Social entrepreneurship (p. 361)

Questions for Reflection and Discussion

1. Identify and describe the four steps of the entrepreneurial process. What are the differences between the conventional and sustainable approaches in each step?

2. How often do you talk with your friends or family about ideas for starting a new venture? Where do your ideas come from?

3. How are you different from the entrepreneurs in this chapter who also had good ideas and put them into practice? How are you similar? Which do you think is more important for entrepreneurial initiative: personality traits or life circumstances? Explain your answer.

4. Identify and describe the five parts of a new venture's plan. What are some differences based on the type of venture—conventional or sustainable?

5. What are the pros and cons of developing a detailed plan for a new venture prior to start-up?

6. What are the benefits of entrepreneurship for society?

ob activities

What Kind of Entrepreneur Might You Be?

Indicate the extent to which the two comparison statements fit you best. Rankings of 1 or 5 indicate strong agreement with the statement closest to the number, whereas a 3 indicates that you are undecided or neutral.

I have a high need to achieve defined goals.	① ② ③ ④ ⑤	I have a high need to help others.
I have confidence in myself.	① ② ③ ④ ⑤	I have confidence in the community to which I belong.
I tend to focus on the financial costs and benefits of a business opportunity.	① ② ③ ④ ⑤	I tend to focus on the social and ecological costs and benefits of a business opportunity.
Financial resources are key to a successful organizational start-up.	① ② ③ ④ ⑤	Community support is key to a successful organizational start-up.

Key: These questions measure your views about engaging in entrepreneurship. The 1s and 2s reflect conventional tendencies, and the 4s and 5s represent sustainable tendencies. Add up your scores. A sum of 12 means you do not tend to favour one approach over the other, a sum of 11 or lower suggests you prefer a conventional approach, and a sum of 13 or higher suggests you tend to favour a sustainable approach. Your score gives you a sense of the kind of communicator you want to become and also of the kind of organization you would prefer to work in.

A company president found out that a competitor had made an important scientific discovery that would sharply reduce the profits of his own company. The president then hired a key employee who'd been working at the competing company in an attempt to learn the details of the discovery.

Why might this scenario occur in organizations?

Use the following scale to indicate whether this behaviour is ethically acceptable:

NEVER ACCEPTABLE		SOMETIMES ACCEPTABLE			ALWAYS ACCEPTABLE	
1	2	3	4	5	6	7

Explain the ideas you considered in arriving at your answer.

DISCUSSION STARTER

Intrapreneurship in Academia

As a student reading this book, you have experience as part of a college or university. When you consider your experiences, what opportunities emerge for improving the services or the educational product you are receiving? With a small group of students, make a list of possible opportunities and solutions (products or services or changes) that would improve students' educational experiences. Pick one opportunity and rough out a plan on four notecards, using the content guide in the next column, and present your plan to the class.

Content of four notecards:

1. Concept: Specify the unmet need or opportunity and describe how your idea addresses the opportunity.
2. Team: List the people who would need to be involved to make the idea a reality.
3. Resources: Describe the key resources necessary for making the change or for offering the new product or service.
4. Goals: Specify SMART goals (refer to chapter 5) you hope to accomplish with this intrapreneurship.

QUESTIONS FOR DISCUSSION

1. Which part of the process was most challenging to complete?
2. What are the strengths and weaknesses of your plan?
3. In listening to others' plans, which ideas seemed most compelling? Why?

DISCUSSION STARTER

U2 Can Be a Social Entrepreneur[61]

A U2 concert is a grand musical extravaganza with social reflection woven in. The production is the culmination of a band turned enterprise, with a unique form of entrepreneurship.

The members of U2 and their manager, Paul McGuinness, took a long-term perspective on their enterprise. They ensured their autonomy to live out their values and social concerns by gaining control of their copyrights, maintaining control of their image and their schedule, and ensuring that they are directly connected with their fans. The band is also known for being on the cutting edge of technology, releasing one of the first music videos and, decades later, creating a unique partnership with iTunes.

In addition to swaying to the soaring guitar solos and taking in the band's hit music, concert goers are encouraged to reflect on the significant needs of the world and how they might take action. Harvard Business School historian Nancy Koehn says U2's songs resonate with many who seek a higher purpose in life. "U2's appeal has always been about our common humanity and the yearning we all experience to follow a higher path," Koehn says. "People are looking for the light, and U2's music has spoken to that search since the band started recording more than two decades ago."

One of the things U2 hopes to inspire is sustainable entrepreneurship. Band leader Bono and his wife, Ali Hewson, founded EDUN, a fashion brand whose mission is to bring about positive change through trading relationships with the poor of Africa. EDUN produces close to 40 percent of its clothing in Africa and aims to increase trade in the future.

QUESTIONS FOR DISCUSSION

1. U2 uses its platform as a successful band to promote social causes that fit its members' particular values. Do you think it works? Explain.
2. What are some potential benefits and drawbacks in connecting values with entrepreneurship?

This is the next in a series of journal entries that can be used for class discussion or be compiled and included as input in a self-reflection paper.

Consider your sources of expertise that might allow you to recognize opportunities and novel solutions. Do you have skills, training, knowledge, or unique experiences in a particular area, or do you have extensive experiences as a user of a product or service? Does this reflection bring to mind any opportunities for improving something, addressing a need, or providing a new product or service? Try to come up with one or two ideas. State the idea (opportunity) and a possible solution. If you are willing to take initiative, share it with someone you trust.

glossary

A

ABC framework of attitudes consists of affect, behavioural intentions, and cognitions.

Abilities are innate capabilities to perform a specific task.

Adhocracy cultures are entrepreneurial open systems that value innovation, risk-taking, bringing new products and services to market, and staying on the cutting edge of the market.

Administrative appraisals are performance appraisals that are used to justify pay and promotion decisions.

Administrative inertia describes what happens when existing organizational structures and systems persist simply because they are already in place.

Administrative method of decision making is evident when decision makers have *some* knowledge and at least *partial* goal consensus.

Agreeableness is a personality trait associated with being good-natured, cooperative, trustful, and not jealous.

Aspiration point is what you hope for in a given situation; it is your preferred result.

Attitudes are summary evaluations of a particular object or person.

Attributions are people's explanations of the causes of behaviours or performance.

Authenticity is the state of being true to oneself; it is a way of living in which your outward actions match up with your inner self because you know who you are and what you want to be.

Authentic leadership is authenticity in organizational leadership roles.

Authority refers to the formal power given to specific members—usually managers—to arrange resources, assign tasks, and direct the activities of other members so as to achieve organizational goals.

B

Behaviours are the ways or manner in which people act.

Beliefs are ideas or opinions we hold to be true.

Best alternative to a negotiated agreement (BATNA) is the most attractive option available to you outside of the current negotiations.

Brainstorming is an unstructured process of sharing ideas.

Burning platform is an approach to unfreezing organizational members that may be painful; it may involve using rational persuasion or pressure to expose members to alarming information or potential negative consequences.

C

Calling is an experienced passion and sense of meaning toward work or a career.

Centralization is having decision-making authority rest with managers at the top of an organization's hierarchy.

Change agent is someone who acts as a catalyst and takes leadership and responsibility for managing part of the change process.

Channel is the pathway along which a message travels through a medium.

Charisma is a special ability or "gift" to attract and inspire others.

Clan cultures are like extended families that value developing human resources, loyalty, commitment, participation, and teamwork to meet organizational goals.

Coaching is a high-direction, high-support leadership style.

Code of ethics is a formal written statement of an organization's primary values and the ethical rules it expects its members to follow.

Cognitive dissonance is the uncomfortable mental state we experience if a current perception, belief, or behaviour conflicts with a past perception, deeply held belief or previous behaviour.

Collective decoding occurs when a message is interpreted by a group of two or more people with the result that each member learns more than any one member could alone (and typically more than the sender could have put into the original message).

Commitments are attachments or bonds to people, actions, or organizations.

Communication is the process of transferring information by using meaningful symbols so that a message is understood by others.

Compensation is monetary payments such as wages, salaries, and bonuses as well as other goods or commodities that are used to reward organizational members.

Competing Values Framework categorizes organizational cultures based on two dimensions: the relative emphasis members place on (1) predictability versus adaptability, and on (2) having an external versus an internal focus.

Conceptual skills refer to the capability to understand complex issues and underlying causes and to solve problems with broad implications.

Conflict style is the way people handle conflict.

Conscientiousness is a personality trait associated with being achievement-oriented, responsible, persevering, and dependable.

Consequentialist theory considers the consequences of an action when determining what is ethical.

Conservation of resources theory proposes that people strive to gain and maintain resources that help them achieve goals.

Consideration is a category of visible leadership behaviours that are supportive, relationship-oriented and/or employee-centred.

Consistent contributor is someone who contributes regardless of how little his or her teammates contribute.

Constructive criticism is a serious examination or judgement delivered in a way that is intended to help the receiver to improve.

Contingency theories assert that the *situation* determines which leadership style is most effective at maximizing productivity.

Conventional Analyzer type organizations have a market culture, a dual mechanistic and organic structure, an engineering technology, and a dual cost leadership and differentiation strategy.

Conventional Defender type organizations have a hierarchical culture, a mechanistic structure, a routine technology, and a cost leadership strategy.

Conventional OB tends to emphasize material or financial well-being and the interests of a narrow range of stakeholders in the immediate future.

Conventional Prospector type organizations have an adhocracy culture, an organic structure, a non-routine technology, and a differentiation strategy.

Conventional Simple type organizations are small and have a clan culture, an organic structure, a craft technology, and a focused strategy.

Convergent thinking means looking at a problem from a traditional perspective and then trying to find the best solution by thinking logically.

Core self-evaluation is a broad trait that integrates an individual's sense of self-esteem, generalized self-efficacy, level of emotional stability, and locus of control.

Corporate social responsibility (CSR) is the responsibility of organizations to act in ways that protect and improve the welfare of multiple stakeholders.

Cost leadership strategy refers to increasing profit margins by keeping financial costs lower than those of competitors while still maintaining price and quality at roughly the same level as competitors.

Courage is the willingness to take action to do what is good regardless of personal consequences.

Creativity is the process of coming up with novel and useful ideas for solving a problem or developing an opportunity.

Critical thinking involves actively questioning and evaluating assumptions and information.

Cultural artifacts provide tangible evidence of an organization's values and may include the organization's physical features, shared stories, rituals, and formal structure and systems.

D

Debt financing occurs when entrepreneurs borrow money from family members, friends, a bank, or another financial institution that must be paid back at some future date.

Decision is a choice that is made among a number of available alternatives.

Decoding is the process by which the receiver attributes meaning to a message.

Delegating is a low-direction, low-support leadership style.

Delegation is the process through which a person trusts another person with the authority to accomplish a task or make decisions.

Deliberative dialogue refers to structured multidirectional communication that enables multiple stakeholders to learn from one another what is best for the overall community.

Delphi technique is a technique in which questions are posed to team members remotely and responses are returned to the leader.

Departmentalization is grouping members and resources together to achieve the work of the larger organization.

Development refers to learning activities that result in broad growth for a person, including growth in terms of a larger career or beyond the scope of the person's current job.

Developmental appraisals are performance appraisals that are used to provide feedback on progress toward expectations and to identify areas for improvement.

Differentiation strategy refers to offering a unique product or service for which buyers are willing to pay a premium price.

Dignification is the emphasis on treating everyone in the organization with dignity and respect.

Directing is a high-direction, low-support leadership style.

Distributive bargaining is a negotiation behaviour that assumes there is a limited amount of money, resources, or opportunities that must be divided because people have competing interests.

Distributive justice compares the individual's inputs and outcomes to other members' inputs and outcomes.

Divergent thinking means looking at a problem in a unique way.

Diversity is a state of having or being composed of differing attributes.

Divisional departmentalization occurs when members are placed together based on their working together as a subunit that provides specific products or services, serves specific customers, or works in a specific geographic region.

E

Economies of scale are evident when increases in volume are associated with lower organizational costs for providing a specific product or service.

Egalicentrism is the assumption that people from different cultures working together in a manner characterized by two-way, give-and-take communication fosters deeper mutual understanding, community, and new insights.

Egoism is a moral philosophy based on what benefits "me" the most.

Emotional intelligence (EI) is the innate or developed capability to recognize, manage, and exercise emotions in relationships.

Emotional labour is a term given to the display and management of appropriate emotion as part of fulfilling job responsibilities.

Emotional stability is a personality trait associated with being calm, placid, poised, and not neurotic.

Emotions are affective states that arise in response to information or messages a person receives from specific sensory inputs.

Empowering is freeing people to be responsible for their work.

Enabling is sharing or explaining information related to a job and its context.

Encoding is putting a message in understandable terms by using symbols and media.

Engaging is encouraging community and enhancing intrinsic motivators.

Entrepreneurs are people who engage in entrepreneurial action to pursue an opportunity.

Entrepreneurship is the process of conceiving an opportunity to offer new or improved goods or services, taking the initiative to pursue that opportunity, making plans, and mobilizing the resources necessary to convert that opportunity into reality.

Equipping is creating an environment for continuous and collaborative learning.

Equity financing occurs when investors in a new venture receive shares of stock and become part owners of the organization.

Equity theory is based on the logic of social comparisons, and it assumes that people are motivated to seek and preserve social equity in the rewards they expect for performance.

ERG theory describes three universal categories of needs: existence, relatedness, and growth.

Escalation of commitment occurs when a decision maker perseveres with the implementation of a poor decision despite evidence that it is not working.

Ethical climate describes the informal shared perceptions of what are appropriate practices and procedures.

Ethical culture consists of the formal and informal systems aimed at influencing the ethical behaviour of organizational members.

Ethics are a set of principles or standards that differentiate right from wrong.

Ethnocentrism is the assumption that members of one's own home country offer the best way to manage an organization in a host country.

Expectancy is the probability perceived by an individual that exerting a given amount of effort will lead to a certain level of performance.

Expectancy theory states that motivation depends on an individual's learned expectations about his or her ability to perform certain tasks and receive desired rewards.

Experimentation is the emphasis on an ongoing voluntary implementation of new ways of performing tasks on a trial basis.

Explicit knowledge is information that can be articulated or codified.

Extinction is the absence of any reinforcement—either positive or negative—following the occurrence of a behaviour.

Extraversion is a personality trait associated with being sociable, talkative, assertive, and adventurous.

Extrinsic motivation is a source of motivation that comes from factors outside the task itself.

F

Fairness is a judgement about whether treatment has been just, equitable, and impartial.

Feedback lets the sender know whether the message has been received as intended.

Feedback-seeking behaviour is asking for feedback or collecting information from the work environment to better understand how you are performing.

Feedforward communication is the combination of relationships and prior communication that influences subsequent messages.

Fiedler's contingency theory of leadership is based on matching a person's leadership style with the appropriate situation.

Filtering occurs when information is withheld or not communicated to others.

Focus strategy refers to choosing a small niche in the overall market.

Framing refers to presenting ideas and alternatives in a way that has an influence on the choices that people make.

Free riding is doing less than your best or contributing less than your fair share to reach the team's goal.

Frustration-regression principle suggests that people who are unable to satisfy higher-order needs will compensate by focusing on over-satisfying lower-order needs.

Functional departmentalization occurs when members are placed into the same department based on having similar technical skills and using similar resources to perform their tasks.

G

Generalized self-efficacy is a person's belief or confidence in his or her capability to cope with and perform in a variety of situations.

Globalization refers to the increased interdependence and integration among people and organizations around the world.

Goal consensus is the level of agreement among members about which goals the organization should pursue.

Goal displacement occurs when important overarching goals are displaced by other specific goals.

Goal-setting theory states that goals direct and motivate behaviour.

Grapevine is the informal information network in an organization.

Group is a collection of two or more people who share a common interest or association.

Group efficacy is the collective belief about the group's performance capability.

Groupthink is a term describing the tendency of group members to strive for and maintain consensus on a decision rather than disrupt the group.

H

Hawthorne effect is an improvement in work productivity resulting from people receiving attention from observers.

Hierarchy cultures are rule-based bureaucracies that value efficiency, low-cost production, predictability, low turnover, and formal procedures.

Hubris is a "grandiose sense of self" evident in excessive confidence and narcissism.

Human relations focuses on how the social environment of work influences attitudes and behaviour.

Hybrid departmentalization occurs when an organization uses both a functional structure and a divisional structure.

Hygiene factors refer to the presence or absence of sources of job dissatisfaction.

I

Idea champion is a person who actively and enthusiastically supports new ideas.

Ideal types are fundamental models or theoretical extremes.

Image theory describes decisions as being made not "by the numbers," but rather in comparison with ideal states or ideal images of self or outcomes.

Imitation involves the replication of existing ideas, which may come from other units within the organization or from outside the organization.

Impression management is an actor's active attempt to limit or influence the information the perceiver receives.

Incremental change occurs when an organization makes improvements in moving in its current strategic direction.

Incremental trial-and-error method of decision making is evident when decision makers have a high agreement on goals but a low level of technical knowledge.

Influence tactics are specific behaviours exercised to achieve an outcome, particularly getting personal interests satisfied.

Information distortion refers to the tendency to overlook or downplay feedback that makes a decision look bad and focus instead on feedback that makes it look good.

Infrastructural behaviour is a category of leadership behaviours, which may or may not be visible to followers, that are directive, task-oriented, and production-centred and that promote information exchange and learning.

Initiating structure is a category of visible leadership behaviours that are directive, task-oriented, and production-centred.

Innovation takes a creative idea and puts it into practice; often involves the development and implementation of new ideas and practices.

Institutionalization has occurred when organizational practices or rules are accepted and perpetuated without regard to instrumental rationality.

Instrumental values are desirable means to achieve end states.

Instrumentality refers to the perceived probability that successfully performing at a certain level will result in attaining a desired outcome.

Integrative models are combinations of various leadership theories, research findings, and leaders' experiences with a focus on practical application.

Integrative negotiation is an alternative to distributive bargaining that seeks to achieve a win-win result for both parties.

Interactional justice is the interpersonal form of justice concerned with the behaviour of leaders in their relationship to followers or direct reports.

Interpersonal trust consists of the expectations, assumptions, or beliefs about the likelihood that another's future actions will be beneficial, favourable, or at least not detrimental to one's interests.

Interventions are planned activities that target specific outcomes such as improving individual, group, or organizational performance or well-being.

Intrapreneurship is entrepreneurship that occurs within *existing* organizations.

Intrinsic motivation is a source of motivation that comes from doing the activity or work itself.

Intuition refers to making decisions based on tacit knowledge, which can be based on experience, insight, hunches, or "gut" feelings.

Inward-facing structure is an organizational structure that emphasizes experimentation, sensitization, dignification, and participation among an organization's internal stakeholders and operations.

J

Job analysis is an investigative process of gathering and interpreting information about a job and its required KSAOs.

Job characteristics model specifies how to increase the motivational potential of a job by improving the meaningfulness, autonomy, and feedback associated with the job.

Job involvement is the extent to which a person thinks about, is immersed in, and is concerned about his or her job.

Job satisfaction is a person's general attitude toward his or her job or job experiences.

Justice is a sense of "fairness" that ensures that everyone connected with an organization gets his or her due.

K

KSAOs are the knowledge, skills, abilities, and other characteristics associated with specific positions.

L

Leader-Member Exchange (LMX) is a measure of the quality of exchanges between a leader and a follower.

Leadership is the purposeful and relational process of influencing others.

Leadership Grid identifies different leadership styles based on combinations of concern for production and concern for people.

Locus of control is a person's consistent belief about the sources of success and failure.

M

Management is the process of planning, organizing, leading, and controlling human and other organizational resources toward the achievement of organizational goals.

Market cultures are goal-focused and results-oriented and emphasize productivity and the organization's position in the marketplace.

Maslow's hierarchy of needs is the theory that people are motivated to satisfy five need levels: physiological, safety, social, esteem, and self-actualization.

Matrix departmentalization is a type of hybrid structure in which members are simultaneously assigned to both functional and divisional departments.

McClelland's acquired needs theory states that certain types of needs or desires are acquired during an individual's lifetime.

Mechanistic structure is an organizational structure characterized by relatively high levels of standardization, specialization, and centralization, and by a functional departmentalization.

Media richness refers to a communication medium's ability to resolve ambiguity.

Medium is the vehicle that is used to carry a message from the sender to the receiver.

Message is a specific idea or general information that a sender wants to convey to receivers.

Minimizer strategy provides desired goods and services in a way that limits a variety of costs (e.g., financial, social, ecological).

Mission statements identify the fundamental purpose of the organization, often by describing what the organization does, whom it serves, and how it differs from similar organizations.

Moral development is the state or level of a person's moral reasoning.

Moral point of view is a framework of values we use to develop our internally consistent and logically justified principles and standards of right and wrong.

Motivation is a psychological force that helps to explain what arouses, directs, and maintains human behaviour.

Motivator factors refer to the presence or absence of sources of job satisfaction.

Multinational company (MNC) is an organization that receives more than 25 percent of its total sales revenue from outside its home country.

Mutual discernment is a process by which people deliberately learn from one another as they jointly address an issue.

Myers–Briggs Type Indicator (MBTI) is a personality inventory based on Carl Jung's work on psychological types.

N

National culture includes the shared values, beliefs, knowledge, and general patterns of behaviour that characterize a country's citizens.

Natural environment is composed of all living and non-living things that have not been created by human technology or human activity.

Negative affect describes a person who is generally angry, anxious, and pessimistic.

Negative reinforcement, sometimes called *avoidance learning*, is the removal of an unpleasant consequence following a desired behaviour.

Negotiation is a social interaction between two (or more) parties who attempt to persuade or influence each other regarding some end.

Network structure occurs when an organization enters into fairly stable and complex relationships with a variety of other organizations that provide essential services, including manufacturing and distribution.

Noise refers to potential barriers that may impede communication at all four steps of the communication process.

Nominal group technique is an information-sharing technique in which the leader asks participants to silently and individually write down all of their ideas related to a specific question.

Nonprogrammed decisions involve developing and choosing among new alternatives in situations where programmed alternatives are not available or not appropriate.

Norms are shared beliefs about social and task behaviours in a group.

O

On-the-job training (OJT) is a type of training in which a more experienced member of the organization teaches a specific job or task to a newer member.

Open-book management is an approach to management whereby leaders share detailed information concerning the financial and operational condition of the organization.

Openness to experience is a personality trait associated with being intellectual, original, imaginative, and cultured.

Organic structure is an organizational structure characterized by relatively low levels of standardization, specialization, and centralization, and by a divisional departmentalization.

Organizational behaviour (OB) refers to explaining human behaviour in organizations, which includes examining the behaviour of individuals, groups, or all the members of an organization as a whole.

Organizational change is any substantive modification to some aspect of an organization.

Organizational citizenship behaviour (OCB) is work behaviour that goes above and beyond normal role or job expectations to help others or benefit the organization.

Organizational commitment is an attachment or bond to a particular organization.

Organizational culture is the set of shared assumptions, values, and experiences that influence the ways in which individuals, teams, and groups interact with one another and work toward company goals.

Organizational development (OD) is a process of planned change that draws on behavioural science to systematically improve and renew the personal, social, and structural components of organizations.

Organizational politics refers to the activities that individuals in organizations pursue to reach their own desired outcomes.

Organizational structure is the formal arrangements and linkages among members and groups that specify work activities and subtasks and allow them to be completed.

Organizational type is a specific, coherent way that an organization's culture and the four elements of its organizational structure fit with each other and with the organization's technology and strategy.

Organizations are "social structures created by individuals to support the collaborative pursuit of specific goals."

Organization-specific responsibility (OSR) is the responsibility of organizations to focus on the organization's owners and their financial interests.

Outsourcing is the practice of using contracts to transfer some of an organization's recurring internal activities and decision-making rights to outsiders better equipped to utilize the latest technologies and reduce costs through economies of scale.

Outward-facing structure is an organizational structure that emphasizes experimentation, sensitization, dignification, and participation among an organization's external stakeholders and operations.

P

Participation is the emphasis on mutual discernment and giving stakeholders a voice in how the organization is managed and how jobs are performed.

Path-goal theory focuses on what leaders can do to motivate and align their followers' behaviour to achieve organizational goals.

Pay-for-performance (PFP) is a compensation scheme in which each member's pay is linked directly to individual, group, or organizational performance. The direct relationship is expected to raise productivity.

Perceptions are the subjective interpretations we give to information and messages we receive from sensory inputs.

Performance appraisal is the process of specifying what performance is expected of a member of the organization and then providing feedback on the member's performance.

Performance management is the process of ensuring that each employee's activities and outputs are aligned with the organization's goals.

Personality is the unique and relatively stable pattern of behaviours, thoughts, and emotions shown by individuals.

Planned change is designed and implemented in an orderly and timely fashion; it is generally a direct response to the recognition of a performance gap—that is, a discrepancy between the desired and the actual state of affairs.

Political method of decision making is evident when there is much debate about which goal to pursue, even though a lot of knowledge is available.

Polycentrism is the assumption that members in a host country know the best way to manage an organization in their country.

Positive affect describes a person who is generally happy, enthused, and optimistic.

Positive reinforcement is the administration of a pleasant and rewarding consequence following a desired behaviour.

Practical wisdom (prudence) is exercising foresight, reason, and discretion to achieve what is good for the community.

Procedural justice is the extent to which policies and rules are jointly developed, transparent, and fairly administered without bias or favouritism.

Programmed decisions involve choosing a standard alternative in response to recurring organizational problems or opportunities.

Psychological contract is an unwritten expectation about the exchanges that will take place between an employee and the organization.

Punishment seeks to decrease the frequency of or eliminate an undesirable behaviour by following the behaviour with an unpleasant consequence.

R

Rational choice as a method of decision making is evident when goal consensus is high and there is adequate time to collect all of the required information.

Reinforcement is a response or consequence linked to a behaviour.

Relational skills are talents for getting along with and motivating people.

Reservation point is the bottom-line offer you would accept.

Rituals are behavioural practices that perpetuate, reinforce, and keep alive a particular value that defines an organization.

S

Satisficing is evident when managers choose an *adequate* response to a problem or opportunity, rather than make the effort to develop an *optimal* response.

Scientific management focuses on analyzing and improving the efficiency of work processes.

Scripts are learned frameworks that provide direction for people by helping them to interpret and respond to what is happening around them.

Self-control relates to a person's emotional regulation and ability to overcome impulsive actions and greed.

Self-efficacy is a person's belief that he or she will be able to complete a task successfully.

Self-esteem is an individual's self-evaluation of worth.

Self-fulfilling prophecy effect is the idea that people often live up (or down) to the expectations of others.

Self-leadership practices are self-regulatory actions that help us manage and motivate ourselves.

Semantic problems arise when words have different meanings for people who are from different demographic groups or who have had different experiences.

Sensitization is the emphasis on searching for and being receptive to better ways of doing things in order to take advantage of existing opportunities or to address existing needs.

Servant leadership is an active approach to leadership that promotes the interests of others.

Shared stories are well-known narrative accounts that form the oral history of critical events that have shaped an organization.

Situational Leadership II describes four leadership situations and the appropriate leadership styles based on the development level of followers.

Social categorization theory proposes that we use characteristics to categorize others into groups, and this shapes our attitudes and behaviour toward them.

Social cohesion is the attachment and attraction of team members to one another.

Social construction of reality is the idea that what we perceive to be real is influenced by the social environment.

Social entrepreneurship involves the innovative use and combination of resources to pursue opportunities to catalyze social change and/or address social needs.

Social networks are patterns of repeated interactions that influence the flow of resources, information, and support among organizational members.

Socioemotional behaviour is a category of leadership behaviours, which may or may not be visible to followers, that are supportive, relationship-oriented, and employee-centred and that promote personal and collective well-being.

Span of control is the number of members a given manager has authority over.

Specialization refers to grouping standardized organizational tasks into separate jobs.

Stakeholder is any group within or outside an organization that is directly affected by the organization and has a stake in its performance.

Standardization is developing uniform practices for organizational members to follow in doing their jobs.

States are dynamic conditions of a person evident in what he or she thinks, feels, or acts.

Stereotypes are general perceptions about a group of people with similar characteristics.

Stress is the body's state of heightened readiness for action in response to challenges or pressures in the environment.

Stressors can be situations, events, people, or perceptions that contribute to experiencing stress.

Stretch goal is one so difficult that people do not immediately know how to reach it.

Subject matter expert (SME) is an expert in a specific occupation or specific task.

Subjective method of decision making is evident when there is little or no agreement on goals and there is limited information.

Substitutes-for-leadership theory argues that characteristics of the task and work environment may substitute for, neutralize, or enhance leadership behaviour.

Superordinate goal is a higher-level goal recognized as important by team members.

Supporting is a low-direction, high-support leadership style.

Sustainable Analyzer type organizations have a market culture, a dual inward- and outward-facing structure, an engineering culture, and a dual minimizer and transformer strategy.

Sustainable Defender type organizations have a hierarchy culture, an inward-facing structure, a routine technology, and a minimizer strategy.

Sustainable development is development that meets the needs of the present without compromising the ability of future generations to meet their own needs.

Sustainable OB tends to emphasize multiple forms of well-being (e.g., financial, social, ecological, spiritual) and the interests of a broad range of stakeholders in the immediate as well as the distant future.

Sustainable Prospector type organizations have an adhocracy culture, an outward-facing structure, a non-routine technology, and a transformer strategy.

Sustaincentrism is a perspective promoting balance between the human and ecological concerns in organizational endeavours.

Systems theory highlights the complex interdependencies between individuals, features of organizations, and the broader organizational context.

T

Tacit knowledge is information people possess that is difficult to articulate or codify.

Task analyzability refers to the ability to reduce tasks down to mechanical steps and to create objective, computational procedures for problem solving.

Task cohesion is the shared commitment among members to achieving a goal.

Task variety refers to the frequency of unexpected, unfamiliar, or different activities involved in performing work.

Team is a task-oriented collection of people who work interdependently as a unit to achieve common goals and are accountable to one another to achieve those goals.

Team conflict is a real or perceived difference in interests between two or more team members.

Team diversity is the extent to which member characteristics differ within the team.

Team identity is the collective sense of identification and loyalty that team members feel toward the team.

Team task interdependence refers to the extent to which team members require resources or support from other team members to complete their tasks.

Technical skills refer to expertise in a particular task or field.

Technology refers to the combination of equipment (e.g., computers, machinery, tools) and skills (e.g., techniques, knowledge, processes) used to acquire, design, produce, and distribute goods and services.

Teleopathy is an addiction to the unbalanced pursuit of a single purpose or goal.

Terminal values are related to desirable ends (what a person values achieving in life).

Theory X states that managers assume people are inherently lazy, dislike work, will avoid working hard unless forced to do so, and prefer to be directed rather than accept responsibility.

Theory Y states that managers assume people are inherently motivated to work and will feel unfulfilled if they do not have the opportunity to work and make a contribution to society.

Training refers to learning activities that improve an individual's skills or performance in a specific area or current position.

Traits are personal characteristics that are relatively stable.

Transactional leaders focus on having fair exchanges with organizational members to motivate them to achieve established goals.

Transformational change occurs when an organization changes its strategic direction.

Transformational leaders focus on inspiring change in members and the organization.

Transformer strategy provides desired goods and services in a way that redeems what were previously discarded or underappreciated resources (e.g., waste, pollution).

U

Uncertainty is evident when decision makers do not know what outcomes to expect as a result of choosing a particular alternative.

Unplanned change involves making ad hoc or piecemeal responses to unanticipated events or crises as they occur.

Utilitarianism is a moral philosophy that holds that ethical managers strive to produce "the greatest good for the greatest number."

V

Valence is the value an individual attaches to an outcome.

Values are a set of personal tenets that guide a person's actions in evaluating and adapting to his or her world.

Venture capitalist is a company or individual that invests money in an organization in exchange for a share of ownership and profits.

Virtual organization is one in which members come and go on an as-needed basis and are networked together with an information technology architecture that enables them to synchronize their activities.

Virtue theory focuses on character and the ways in which people practise and facilitate the practice of virtues in community, thereby facilitating happiness.

Virtues are good ways of acting that are noble or have value *regardless* of the end result or consequences.

Vision statements describe what the organization is striving to achieve and, in this way, provide guidance to organizational members.

Voluntary Simplicity type organizations are small and have a clan culture, an inward-facing structure, a craft technology, and a focused strategy.

W

Work–family conflict is role conflict that results from the incompatibilities and pressures of work and family roles.

Work–life conflict exists when work role demands interfere with life role demands.

Z

Zone of possible agreements (ZOPA) is a range of possible offers you and the other party are willing to accept.

Endnotes

Preface

[1]Pfeffer, J. (2010). Building sustainable organizations: The human factor. *Academy of Management Perspectives, 24*(1), 34–45.

[2]See for example the "Best AMR Paper of 2005" winner Ferraro, F., Pfeffer, J., & Sutton, R. I. (2005). Economic language and assumptions: How theories can become self-fulfilling. *Academy of Management Review, 30*(1), 8–24; Ghoshal, S. (2005). Bad management theories are destroying good management practices. *Academy of Management Learning and Education, 4*(1), 75–91.

[3]See Dyck, B., Walker, K., Starke, F. A., & Uggerslev, K. (2012). Enhancing critical thinking by teaching two distinct approaches to management. *Journal of Education for Business, 87*(6), 343–357.

[4]Safian, R. (2012, January 9). This is Generation Flux: Meet the pioneers of the new (and chaotic) frontier of business. *Fast Company,* http://www.fastcompany.com/magazine/162/generation-flux-future-of-business

[5]Barton, D. (2011). Capitalism for the long term. *Harvard Business Review*, 85–91.

[6]According to the literature reviewed in Giacalone (2004), the ratio between those holding primarily materialist values versus those holding these emerging nonmaterialist values changed from 4:1 in 1970 to 4:3 by 1990. Giacalone, R. A. (2004). A transcendent business education for the 21st century. *Academy of Management Learning and Education, 3*(4), 415–420.

[7]See fn 1, Pfeffer (2010); Mintzberg, H. (2009). Rebuilding companies as communities. *Harvard Business Review, 87*(7/8), 140–143; Spreitzer, G. (2007). Giving peace a chance: Organizational leadership, empowerment, and peace. *Journal of Organizational Behavior, 28*(8), 1077–1095; Hamel, G. (2009). Moon shots for management. *Harvard Business Review, 87*(2), 91–98; Kanter, R. (2010). How to do well and do good. *MIT Sloan Management Review, 52*(1), 12–15.

[8]It is very important to note that the concepts and theory that underpin this book have the scholarly integrity that they deserve, as evident in having been published in leading scholarly journals (e.g., *Journal of Management Studies, Academy of Management Review, Administrative Science Quarterly, Journal of Applied Psychology*).

[9]Based on two recent studies—"The Spiritual Life of College Students: A National Study of College Students' Search for Meaning and Purpose" and "Spirituality and the Professoriate: A National Study of Faculty Beliefs, Attitudes, and Behaviors"—both done by the Higher Education Research Institute, University Graduate School of Education & Information Studies, University of California, Los Angeles.

Chapter 1

[1]Friedman, M. (1970, September 13). A Friedman doctrine: The social responsibility of business is to increase its profits. *The New York Times Magazine*, p. SM17; The Canadian Press. (2008, December 16). Forzani dropping 'hard-sell' approach. *The Globe and Mail*. Retrieved June 26, 2015, from http://www.theglobeandmail.com/report-on-business/forzani-dropping-hard-sell-approach/article1210339/; Canadian Tire. (2012). *Annual Report 2012: Canadian Tire Corporation: A Family of Companies*. Toronto, Canada: Canadian Tire, p. 12; FGL Sports. FGL Sports profile: corporate mission: FGL Sports leadership brand. Retrieved June 26, 2015, from https://www.fglsports.com/fglprofile.aspx?selected=mission; Canadian Tire. (2011). *Annual Report 2011: Canadian Tire Corporation: Life in Canada for 90 Years*. Toronto, Canada: Canadian Tire, p. 19; FGL Sports. FGL Sports profile: Corporate mission. Retrieved June 26, 2015, from https://www.fglsports.com/fglprofile.aspx?selected=mission; McKenna, H. (2012, May 30). Canadian Tire plans aggressive overhaul for sports unit. *The Globe and Mail*. Retrieved June 26, 2015 from http://www.theglobeandmail.com/globe-investor/canadian-tires-fgl-to-add-100-new-stores-close-others/article4217499/; McKenna, H. (2012, May 30). Canadian Tire plans aggressive overhaul on sports units. *The Toronto Star*. Retrieved June 26, 2015, from http://www.thestar.com/business/2012/05/30/canadian_tire_plans_aggressive_overhaul_of_sports_unit.html

[2]Parsons, T. (1960). *Structure and process in modern societies.* Glencoe, IL: Free Press.

[3]Scott, W. R. (1998). *Organizations: Rational, natural, and open systems.* (4th Ed.). Upper Saddle River, NJ: Prentice Hall.

[4]Rousseau, D. M., & McCarthy, S. (2007). Educating managers from an evidence-based perspective. *Academy of Management Learning & Education, 6*(1), 84–101.

[5]Pages 12–13 in Drucker, P. F. (2001) *The essential Drucker.* New York, NY: Harper Collins.

[6]Bonini S., and Mendonca, L. (2011). Doing good by doing well: Shaping a sustainable future. McKinsey & Company. http://mckinseyonsociety.com/downloads/articles/Social-Innovation/MOS_030311_Doing_Good_V8.pdf

[7]Weber (1958, original 1904, pp. 181 and 182). *The protestant ethic and the spirit of capitalism.* (transl. T Parsons). New York: Scribner's.

[8]Smith, Adam (1982) [1759]. *The theory of moral sentiments.* In D. D. Raphael and A. L. Macfie (Eds). Glasgow Edition. Indianapolis, IN: Liberty Press.

[9]Smith (1982, p. 237). "The man who acts according to the rules of perfect prudence, of strict justice, and of proper benevolence may be said to be perfectly virtuous. But the most perfect knowledge of those rules will not alone enable him to act in this

manner: his own passions are very apt to mislead him; sometimes to drive him and sometimes to seduce him to violate all the rules which he himself, in all his sober and cool hours, approves of. The most perfect knowledge, if it is not supported by the most perfect self-command, will not always enable him to do his duty." McCloskey, D. (2008). Adam Smith, the last of the former virtue ethicists. *History of Political Economy, 40*(1), 43–71.

[10]For example, perspectives like corporate social responsibility and stakeholder theory offer a counterpoint to conventional's focus maximizing the self-interests of shareholders.

[11]E. F. Schumacher, in his cleverly subtitled book *Small Is Beautiful: A Study of Economics as if People Mattered,* argues that there are many classic moral points of view that could be used to underpin an alternative to the conventional approach. In particular, he suggests that "there is perhaps no body of teaching which is more relevant and appropriate to the modern predicament than the marvelously subtle and realistic doctrines of the Four Cardinal Virtues—*prudential* [practical wisdom], *justitia* [justice], *fortitudo* [courage], and *temperentia* [self-control]" (pp. 248–249 in Schumacher, E. F. (1973). *Small is beautiful: A study of economics as if people mattered.* London, England: Blond & Briggs Ltd). This section draws from Dyck, B., & Kleysen, R. (2001). Aristotle's virtues and management thought: An empirical exploration of an integrative pedagogy. *Business Ethics Quarterly, 11*(4), 561–574. Of course, the challenge that others have raised (e.g., Hartman, Edwin M. (1998). The role of character in business ethics. *Business Ethics Quarterly, 8,* 547–59; MacIntyre, A. (1981). *After virtue: A study in moral theory.* Notre Dame, IN: University of Notre Dame Press; Neubert M. (2011). Introduction: The value of virtue to management and organizational theory and practice. *Canadian Journal of Administrative Sciences, 28*(3), 227–230.), and which informs this textbook, is to make virtues observable in management practice and a relevant guiding framework for management theory.

[12]Aristotle. (1962). *Nichomachean ethics* (trans. M. Oswald). New York: MacMillan Publishing.

[13]Dyck, B., Walker, K., Starke, F., & Uggerslev, K. (2011). Addressing concerns raised by critics of business schools by teaching multiple approaches to management. *Business and Society Review, 116,* 1–27.

[14]Bonini, S., & Mendonca, L. (2011); Lubin, D. A., & Esty, D. C. (2010). The sustainability imperative. *Harvard Business Review, 88*(5), 42–50; Pfeffer, J. (2010). Building sustainable organizations: The human factor. *Academy of Management Perspectives, 24*(1), 34–45; Mintzberg, H. (2009). Rebuilding companies as communities. *Harvard Business Review, 87*(7/8), 140–143; Hamel, G. (2009). Moon shots for management. *Harvard Business Review, 87*(2), 91–98; Kanter, R. (2010). How to do well and do good. *MIT Sloan Management Review, 52*(1), 12–15.

[15]Martin, R. (2007). How successful managers think. *Harvard Business Review, 85*(6), 60–67.

[16]Dyck, B., Walker, K., Starke, F., & Uggerslev, K. (2012). Enhancing critical thinking by teaching two distinct approaches to management. *Journal of Education for Business, 87*(6), 343–357.

[17]Henri Fayol's original mention of the functions was in Fayol, H. (1916). Administration industrielle et générale, *Bulletin de la Société de l'Industrie Minérale, 10,* 5–164.

Réédité 13 fois chez Dunod. He identified the five functions of management as planning, organizing, commanding, coordinating, and controlling. A translation in 1949 by C. Storrs led to its wider dissemination. Coordinating was later dropped by most management scholars in recognition of its being instrumental to the other functions. Commanding also was revised to be leading.

[18]Practical wisdom is the opposite of an attitude to life that is small and calculating and "which refuses to see and value anything that fails to promise an immediate utilitarian advantage" (Schumacher, 1973, 249).

[19]Solomon, R.C. (1992). *Ethics and excellence: Cooperation and integrity in business.* Oxford, UK: Oxford University Press.

[20]Neisser, D. (2010, July 28). A 7-point guide to doing well by doing good. *Fast Company.* Retrieved from http://www.fastcompany.com/1674513/7-point-guide-doing-well-doing-good; Lipton, J. (2010, May 19). Religious CEOs: Timberland's Jeffrey Swartz. Retrieved from http://www.minyanville.com/special-features/articles/jeff-swartz-timberland-religious-ceos-wolverine/5/19/2010/id/28272; Cody, T., & MacFadyen, K. (2011). CSR: An asset or albatross? *Mergers & Acquisitions: The Dealermakers Journal, 46*(8), 14–48.

[21]Spreitzer, G. M., McCall, M. W., & Mahoney, J. D. (1997). Early identification of international executive potential. *Journal of Applied Psychology, 82*(1), 6–29; Bamber, D., & Castka, P. (2006). Personality, organizational orientations and self-reported learning outcomes. *Journal of Workplace Learning, 18*(2), 73–92.

[22]Longenecker, J., Moore, C., Palich, L., Petty, W., & McKinney, J. (2006). Ethical attitudes in small businesses and large corporations: Theory and empirical findings from a tracking study spanning three decades. *Journal of Small Business Management, 44,* 167–183; Emerson, T. L., McKinney, J. A., & Neubert, M. J. (2010). The effects of ethical codes on ethical perceptions of actions toward stakeholders. *Journal of Business Ethics, 97,* 505–516.

[23]Zimbardo, P. (1982). Pathology of imprisonment. In D. Krebs (Ed.), *Readings in social psychology: Contemporary perspectives* (2nd ed., p. 249). New York: Harper & Row. Cited in Brady, F. N., & Logsdon, J. M. (1988). Zimbardo's "Stanford Prison Experiment" and the relevance of social psychology for teaching business ethics. *Journal of Business Ethics, 7*(9), 703–710.

[24]"The individual comes to the job in a state of what we have previously defined as role-readiness, a state that includes the acceptance of legitimate authority and compliance with its requests, a compliance that for many people extends to acts that they do not understand and that may violate many of their own values" [Katz, D., & Kahn, R. (1978). *The social psychology of organizations* (2nd ed., p. 194). New York: John Wiley & Sons. Cited in Brady & Logsdon, 1988].

Feature Notes

My OB: Does Money Buy Happiness? Don't indulge. Be happy. *The New York Times.* Retrieved from http://www.nytimes.com/2012/07/08/opinion/sunday/dont-indulge-be-happy.html?_r=1&pagewanted=all; Aknin,

L. B., Dunn, E. W., & Norton, M. I. (2012). Happiness runs in a circular motion: Evidence for a positive feedback loop between prosocial spending and happiness. *Journal of Happiness Studies, 13*(2), 347–355; Hsieh, C. (2011). Money and happiness: Does age make a difference? *Ageing & Society, 31*(8), 1289–1306; Kasser, T. (2003) *The High Price of Materialism.* Cambridge, MA: Bradford Book, MIT Press; Burroughs, J. E., & Rindfleisch, A. (2002). Materialism and well-being: A conflicting values perspective, *Journal of Consumer Research, 29*, 348–370.

My OB: The Bottom Line(s) about Effectiveness
Pfeffer, J. (2010). Building sustainable organizations: The human factor. *Academy of Management Perspectives, 24*(1), 34–45; Gimenez, C., Sierra, V, & Rodon, J. (2012). Sustainable operations: Their impact on the triple bottom line. *International Journal of Production Economics, 140*(1), 149–159; Deckop, J. R., Jurkiewicz C. L., & Giacalone R. A. (2010). Effects of materialism on work-related personal well-being. *Human Relations, 63*(7), 1007–1030.

OB in Action: The Importance of Critical Thinking
Dyck, B., Walker, K., Starke, F., & Uggerslev, K. (2012). Enhancing critical thinking by teaching two distinct approaches to management. *Journal of Education for Business, 87*(6), 343–357; Dyck, B., Walker, K., Starke, F., & Uggerslev, K. (2011). Addressing concerns raised by critics of business schools by teaching multiple approaches to management. *Business and Society Review, 116*, 1–27; Ferraro, F., Pfeffer, J., & Sutton, R. I. (2005). Economic language and assumptions: How theories can become self-fulfilling. *Academy of Management Review, 30*(1), 8–24; Ghoshal, S. (2005). Bad management theories are destroying good management practices. *Academy of Management Learning and Education, 4*(1), 75–91; Pfeffer, J. (2010). Building sustainable organizations: The human factor. *Academy of Management Perspectives, 24*(1), 34–45; Mintzberg, H. (2009). Rebuilding companies as communities. *Harvard Business Review, 87*(7/8), 140–143; Spreitzer, G. (2007). Giving peace a chance: Organizational leadership, empowerment, and peace. *Journal of Organizational Behavior, 28*(8), 1077–1095; Kanter, R. (2010). How to do well and do good. *MIT Sloan Management Review, 52*(1), 12–15; Barton, D. (2011). Capitalism for the long term. *Harvard Business Review,* 85–91.

OB in Action: Moonshots for Management 2.0
Hamel, G. (2011). First, let's fire all the managers. *Harvard Business Review, 89*(12), 48–60; Hamel, G. (2009). Moon Shots for Management. *Harvard Business Review, 87*(2), 91–98; Hamel, G. (2007, p. 98). *The future of management.* Boston, MA: Harvard Business School Press.

Chapter 2

[1]Mountain Equipment Co-op. (2014). *MEC 2014 annual report.* Retrieved from http://www.mec.ca/media/Images/pdf/annualreport/MEC_2014_Annual_Report_v2_m5657756 9836365900.pdf; Perkins, T. (2014, June 6). Top company profile: Mountain Equipment Co-op. *Corporate Knights.* Retrieved from http://www.corporateknights.com/magazines/health-in-the-age-of-climate-change/top-company-profile-mountain-equipment-co-op-14020616/; Mediacorp Canada Inc. (2015). Canada's top 100 employers: Previous winners: 2007, 2014. Retrieved from http://www.canadastop100.com/national/; Beedie Newsroom. (2013, October 9). MEC CEO talks importance of corporate-social responsibility: CEO series. Beedie School of Business. Simon Fraser University. Story posted to http://beedie.sfu.ca/newsroom/2013/10/mec-ceo-talks-about-the-importance-of-corporate-social-responsibility-ceo-series/; O'Kane, J. (2015, March 30). Office Space: Inside Mountain Equipment Co-op's modern, woodsy HQ. *The Globe and Mail.* Retrieved from http://www.theglobeandmail.com/report-on-business/industry-news/property-report/inside-mecs-modern-woodsy-hq/article23686912/; Mountain Equipment Co-op. (2015). About MEC: Working here. Retrieved from http://www.mec.ca/AST/ContentPrimary/AboutMEC/Jobs/Inside.jsp; Mountain Equipment Co-op. (2015). About MEC: Sustainability. Retrieved from http://www.mec.ca/AST/ContentPrimary/AboutMEC/Sustainability.jsp; Mountain Equipment Co-op. (2015). About MEC: Our co-op: MEC's roots. Retrieved from http://www.mec.ca/AST/ContentPrimary/AboutMEC/AboutOurCoOp.jsp

[2]A guild is an organization, typically of merchants or craftworkers, that influences local markets by controlling the quality of goods or services and their price, production, and distribution. Guilds also sometimes provide welfare services for their members. See Van Leeuwen, M. (2012). Guilds and middle-class welfare, 1550–1800: Provisions for burial, sickness, old age, and widowhood. *Economic History Review, 65*(1), 61–90.

[3]Community was also fostered by the fact that people often were more vulnerable to the whims of weather and disease, and so there was a greater dependence on other people.

[4]Hawken, P. (1993). *The ecology of commerce: A declaration of sustainability.* New York: Harper Business.

[5]Cited from p. 42 in Daft, R. L. (2003). *Management.* Mason, Ohio: Southwestern. Taylor's concern for maximizing materialism is evident in Taylor, F. W. (1911). *Principles of scientific management.* New York: Harper; Taylor states that "the principal object of management should be to secure maximum prosperity for the employer, coupled with maximum prosperity for the employee" (cited on p. 93 in Schermerhorn, J. R. (2002). *Management* (7th ed.). New York: John Wiley & Sons). See also Taylor, F. W. (1903). *Shop management.* New York: Harper; Wrege, C.,& Stoka, A. M. (1978). Cooke creates a classic: The story behind F. W. Taylor's *Principles of Scientific Management. Academy of Management Review,* October, 736–749; Kanigel, R. (1997). *The one best way: Frederick Winslow Taylor and the enigma of efficiency.* New York: Viking.

[6]Gilbreth, F. B. (1911). *Motion study.* New York: Van Nostrand Reinhold; Gilbreth, F. B. (1912). *Primer of scientific management.* New York: Van Nostrand Reinhold; Gilbreth, F. B. & Gilbreth, L. M. (1916). *Fatigue study.* New York: Sturgis & Walton.

[7]Gilbreth, F. B. Jr., & Carey, E. G. (1948/1963). *Cheaper by the dozen.* New York: Thomas Y. Crowell.

[8]Pages 39 and 40 in Jones, G. R., & George, J. M. (2003). *Contemporary management* (3rd edition). New York, NY: McGraw-Hill

Irwin. See the interestingly titled: Ford, H. (1926). Sustainable manufacture. *Encyclopedia Britannica* (13th ed.). New York: Encyclopedia Co.

[9]Gilbreth, F. B. (1911). *Motion study*. New York: Van Nostrand; Gilbreth, F. B., & Gilbreth, L. M. (1916). *Fatigue study*. New York: Sturgis & Walton; Graham, L. D. (1998). *Managing on her own: Dr. Lillian Gilbreth and women's work in the interwar era*. Norcross, GA: Engineering & Management Press.

[10]Cited on p. 45 in Daft (2003). See also Follett, M. P. (1918). *The new state: Group organization: The solution of popular government*. London: Longmans, Green; Parker, L. D. (1984). Control in organizational life: The contribution of Mary Parker Follett. *Academy of Management Review*, 9, 736–745; Graham, P. (1995). *M. P. Follett—Prophet of management: A celebration of writings from the 1920s*. Boston: Harvard Business School Press. We also draw on descriptions of Follett's contributions found in Jones and George (2003, p. 55). and Schermerhorn (2002, p. 95).

[11]Roethlisberger, F. J., Dickson, W. J., & Wright, H. A. (1939). *Management and the worker*. Cambridge, MA: Harvard University Press; Mayo, E. (1933). *The human problems of an industrial civilization*. New York: MacMillan; Mayo, E. (1945). *The social problems of an industrial civilization*. Boston: Harvard Business School; Adair, J. G. (1984). The Hawthorne effect: A reconsideration of a methodological artifact. *Journal of Applied Psychology* 69(2), 334–345; Diaper, G. (1990). The Hawthorne effect: A fresh examination. *Education Studies*, 16(3), 261–268; Jones, S. R. (1992, November). Was there a Hawthorne effect? *American Sociological Review*, 451–468; O'Connor, E. S. (1999). The politics of management thought: A case study of the Harvard Business School and the human relations school. *Academy of Management Review*, 24, 117–131.

[12]Actually, the term "Hawthorne effect" was not coined by the original researchers, but rather by French. French, J. R. P. (1953). Experiments in field settings. In Festinger, L., & Katz, D. (Eds). *Research methods in the behavioral sciences* (pp. 98–135). New York: Holt, Rinehart and Winston. French used it to describe "marked increases in production which were related only to the special position and social treatment they [workers] received" (cited on p. 452 of Jones (1992). Was there a Hawthorne effect? *American Journal of Sociology*, 98(3), 451–468). The idea that the Hawthorne effect shows that it is giving "attention to employees, not working conditions per se, that has the dominant impact on productivity." *In Search of Excellence*. New York: HarperCollins. Peters, T. J. & Waterman Jr., R. H. (1982); this idea cited on p. 454 in Jones (1992) has been perpetuated in the popular management literature. However, scholars today use the term to refer to "the problem in field experiments that subjects' knowledge that they are in an experiment modifies their behavior." Adair, J. G. (1984). The Hawthorne effect: A reconsideration of the methodological artifact. *Journal of Applied Psychology*, 69(2), 334–345. Indeed, they question whether the original data even demonstrate a Hawthorne effect (e.g., Adair, 1984; Jones, 1992).

[13]Thompson, J. D. (1967) *Organizations in action*. New York: McGraw-Hill; Katz, D., & Kahn, R. L. (1966). *The social psychology of organizations*. New York: Wiley.

[14]Gartner, W. B., & Naughton, M. J. (2000). Out of crisis. In Pierce, J. L., & Newstrom, J. W. (Eds.). *The manager's bookshelf* (pp. 53–58). Upper Saddle River, NJ: Prentice Hall.

[15]Schein, E. H. (1985). *Organizational culture and leadership*. San Francisco: Jossey-Bass Publishers.

[16]Selznick, P. (1949). *TVA and the grassroots*. Berkely, CA: University of California Press; Selznick, P. (1957) *Leadership and administration*. New York: Harper & Row.

[17]Selznick (1949) defines *institutionalization* as occurring when something is "infused with value beyond the technical requirements of the task at hand."

[18]See p. 52 in Berger, P. L., & Luckmann, T. (1966). *The social construction of reality: A treatise in the sociology of knowledge*. Garden City, NY: Anchor Books.

[19]Garfinkel, H. (1964). Studies of the routine grounds of everyday activities. *Social Problems*, 11(3), 225–250.

[20]See fn 18, Berger & Luckman (1966).

[21]"Universities and professional training institutions are important centers for the development of organizational norms among professional managers and their staff." Page 152 in DiMaggio, P. F., & W. W Powell (1983). The iron cage revisited: Institutional isomorphism and collective rationality in organizational fields. *American Sociological Review*, 48(April), 147–160.

[22]Pfeffer, J. (1977). The ambiguity of leadership. *Academy of Management Review*, 2(1), 104–112.

[23]Page 87 in Ghoshal, S. (2005). Bad management theories are destroying good management practices. *Academy of Management Learning and Education*, 4(1), 75–91.

[24]Mintzberg, H. (2005). How inspiring. How sad. Comment on Sumantra Ghoshal's paper. *Academy of Management Learning & Education*, 4, 108; Donaldson, L. (2005). For positive management theories while retaining science: Reply to Ghoshal. *Academy of Management Learning & Education*, 4(1), 109–113; Pfeffer, J. (2010). Building sustainable organizations: The human factor. *Academy of Management Perspectives*, 24(1), 34–45; Kanter, R. M. (2010). How to do well and do good. *MIT Sloan Management Review*, 52(1), 12–15.

[25]World Business Coucil for Sustainable Development. (2013). Low Carbon Technology Partnerships intitiave. Retrieved from http://www.wbcsd.org/home.aspx

[26]Albino, V., Balice, A., Dangelico, R. M., & Iacobone, F. A. (2012). The effect of the adoption of environmental strategies on green product development: A study of companies on world sustainability indices. *International Journal of Management*, 29(2), 525–538.

[27]Barton, D. (2011). Capitalism for the long term. *Harvard Business Review*, 85–91.

[28]For a summary, see Kasser, T. (2003) *The high price of materialism*. Cambridge, MA: A Bradford Book, MIT Press.

[29]For example, some people oppose Walmart because of its aesthetics (Dicker, J. [2005, November 6]). All the rage: Walmart as the great divider. *The Boston Globe*. Retrieved from http://www.boston.com/business/articles/2005/11/06/all_the_rage?mode=PF). See also Dobson, J. (2007). Aesthetics as a foundation for business activity. *Journal of Business Ethics*, 72(1), 41–46.

[30]Tracey, P. (2012). Religion and organization: A critical review of current trends and future directions. *The Academy of Management Annals*, 6, 87–134.

[31]According to the literature reviewed in Giacalone (2004), the ratio between those holding primarily materialist values versus those holding these emerging nonmaterialist values changed from 4:1 in 1970 to 4:3 by 1990. Giacalone, R. A. (2004). A transcendent business education for the 21st century. *Academy of Management Learning and Education*, 3(4), 415–420.

[32]Mastny, L. (2011, January 11). New American dream survey report: September 2004. Retrieved from http://www.new-dream.org/blog/2011-01-new-american-dream-survey-report-september-2004

[33]Judge, T. A., Piccolo, R. F., Podsakoff, N. P., Shaw, J. C., & Rich, B. L. (2010). The relationship between pay and job satisfaction: A meta-analysis of the literature. *Journal of Vocational Behavior*, 77(2), 157–167.

[34]Johnson, P., & Cassell, C. (2001). Epistemology and work psychology: New agendas. *Journal of Occupational & Organizational Psychology*, 74(2), 125–143.

[35]Neubert M. (2011). Introduction: The value of virtue to management and organizational theory and practice. *Canadian Journal of Administrative Sciences*, 28(3), 227–230; Gimenez, C. Sierra, V., & Rodon, J. (2012). Sustainable operations: Their impact on the triple bottom line. *International Journal of Production Economics*, 140(1), 149–159.

[36]Suddaby, R., Hardy, C., & Huy, Q. (2011). Where are the new theories of organization? *Academy of Management Review*, 36(2), 236–246.

[37]Starbuck, W. H. (2009). The constant causes of never-ending faddishness in the behavioral and social sciences. *Scandinavian Journal of Management*, 25(1), 108–116.

[38]Charlier, S. D., Brown, K. G., & Rynes, S. L. (2011). Teaching evidence-based management in MBA programs: What evidence is there? *Academy of Management Learning & Education*, 10(2), 222–236.

[39]Scherer, A., & Palazzo, G. (2011). The new political role of business in a globalized world: A review of a new perspective on CSR and its implications for the firm, governance, and democracy. *Journal of Management Studies*, 48(4), 899–931.

[40]Hakanen, T., & Jaakkola, E. (2012). Co-creating customer-focused solutions within business networks: A service perspective. *Journal of Service Management*, 23(4), 593–611.

[41]For a discussion of benefits and drawbacks, see Chang, S., Chung, J., & Moon, J. (2013). When do wholly owned subsidiaries perform better than joint ventures? *Strategic Management Journal*, 34(3), 317–337.

[42]Glen, B. (2006, February 13). His work is a precious place. *Western Catholic Reporter*. Retrieved from http://www.wcr.ab.ca/news/2006/0213/business021306.shtml

[43]Deutsch, C. H. (2007, May 12). Incredible shrinking packages. *New York Times*. Retrieved from http://www.nytimes.com/2007/05/12/business/12package.html?scp=1&sq=&st=nyt&_r=0; Mitchell, D. (2006, October 14). Going, going, trying to go green. *New York Times*. Retrieved from http://www.nytimes.com/2006/10/14/business/14online.html?scp=1&sq=&st=nyt

[44]This is what is alleged to have happened in the Ivory Coast with the Probo Koala, a Greek-owned tanker that flew a Panamanian flag and was leased by the London branch of a Swiss trading corporation that had its fiscal headquarters in the Netherlands.

See Polgreen, L., & Simons, M. (2006, October 2). Global sludge ends in tragedy for Ivory Coast. *New York Times*. Retrieved from http://www.nytimes.com/2006/10/02/world/africa/02ivory.html?scp=1&sq=&st=nyt

[45]U.S. Environmental Protection Agency. (2005). *Willamette Industries wood products settlement*. Washington, DC. Retrieved from http://www.epa.gov/compliance/resources/cases/civil/caa/willamette.html

[46]Clifford, S., & Martin, A. (2011, April 11). As consumers cut spending, "green" products lose allure. *New York Times*. Retrieved from http://www.nytimes.com/2011/04/22/busi-ness/energy-environment/22green.html?pagewanted=all

[47]Larson, C. (2013). Ma Jun: Director of Institute of Public and Environmental Affairs, how to clean up China's environment. *Fast Company*. Retrieved from http://www.fastcompany.com/most-creative-people/2012/ma-jun

[48]TerraCycle. (2013). About us: TerraCycle is a proud triple bottom line company. Retrieved from http://www.terracycle.net/en-US/about-us.html

[49]Underwood, A. (2007, August: 20–27). The green campus: How to teach respect for the environment? The three R's: Reduce your carbon footprint, reuse and recycle. *Newsweek*. Retrieved from http://www.thedailybeast.com/newsweek/2007/08/15/the-green-campus.html

[50]Based on the definition developed in 1987 by the World Commission on Environment and Development (the Brundtland Commission).

[51]Cox, P. L., Friedman, B. A., & Tribunella, T. (2011). Relationships among cultural dimensions, national gross domestic product, and environmental sustainability. *Journal of Applied Business and Economics*, 12(6), 46–56.

[52]For a helpful discussion of the implications of globalization, see Wiersema, M. F., & Bowen, H. P. (2008). Corporate diversification: The impact of foreign competition, industry globalization, and product diversification. *Strategic Management Journal*, 29(2), 115–132; and Noriko, Y., & Kleinberg, J. (2011). Boundary work: An interpretive ethnographic perspective on negotiating and leveraging cross-cultural identity. *Journal of International Business Studies*, 42(5), 629–653.

[53]This quote has been attributed to U.S. president John F. Kennedy, who used it in a speech in Frankfurt, Germany, in June 1963. On July 18, 1984, the Reverend Jesse Jackson spoke to the Democratic National Convention and said, "Rising tides don't lift all boats, particularly those stuck at the bottom." Cited in http://www.phrases.org.uk/bulletin_board/42/messages/1052.html. Research lends support to both views. For example, some research suggests that globalization leads to greater income inequality, whereas other studies contend that it may help the poorest people. Atkinson, A. B. (2003). Income inequality in OECD countries: Data and explanations. *CESifo Economic Studies*, 49(4), 479–513; Milanovic, B. (2005). Can we discern the effect of globalization on income distribution? Evidence from household surveys. *World Bank Economic Review*, 19(1), 21–44.

[54]Clarke, T., Dopp, S., et al. (2005). *Challenging McWorld*. (2nd ed.). Ottawa, ON: Canadian Centre for Policy Alternatives.

[55]This discussion draws from and builds upon ideas found in Roesen, R. (2004). How to overcome ethnocentrism: Approaches

to a culture of recognition by history in the twenty-first century. *History and Theory*, *43*(4), 118–129; and Michailova, S., & Nielsen, B. B. (2006). MNCs and knowledge management: A typology and key features. *Journal of Knowledge Management*, *10*(1), 44–54.

[56]This discussion of ethnocentrism, polycentrism, and egalicentrism draws from and builds upon ideas found in Roesen (2004) and Michailova and Nielsen (2006).

[57]See http://www.worldvaluessurvey.org/and for GLOBE, see House, R. J., Hanges, P. J., Javidan, M., Dorfman, P., & Gupta, V. (Eds). (2004). *Culture, leadership, and organizations: The GLOBE study of 62 societies*. Newbury Park, CA: Sage; Javidan, M., Dorfman, P. W., de Luque, M. S., & House, R. J. (2006). In the eyes of the beholder: Cross cultural lessons in leadership from Project GLOBE. *Academy of Management Perspectives*, *20*(1), 67–90.

[58]Minkov, M., & Hofstede, G. (2011). The evolution of Hofstede's doctrine. *Cross Cultural Management*, *18*(1), 10–20.

[59]Minkov, M., & Hofstede, G. (2012). Hofstede's fifth dimension: New evidence from the World Values Survey. *Journal of Cross-Cultural Psychology*, *43*(1), 3–14.

[60]For example, see Rinne, T., Steel, G., & Fairweather, J. (2012). Hofstede and Shane revisited: The role of power distance and individualism in national-level innovation success. *Cross-Cultural Research: The Journal of Comparative Social Science*, *46*(2), 91–108; Fischer, R., & Mansell, A. (2009). Commitment across cultures: A meta-analytical approach. *Journal of International Business Studies*, *40*(8), 1339–1358.

[61]Masculinity is also a term used to describe this dimension of a culture. Although we follow others in emphasizing materialism over masculinity; see Deresky, H. (1997). *International management: Managing across borders and cultures* (p. 75). Reading, MA: Addison Wesley Longman; Brice, W (2012). The effects of ethnic culture on managerial attitudes and practices: A survey in Hong Kong, Taiwan and China. *International Journal of Management*, *29*(1), 267–278. Hofstede's Values Survey continues to use the terms masculinity and femininity (available online at http://www.geert-hofstede.com/).

[62]See fn 61, Deresky (1997).

[63]This may be the most ambiguous of Hofstede's five dimensions to interpret, because it equates avoiding uncertainty with resisting change. However, when managers present a very careful plan of the future that reduces the uncertainty of the status quo, then people who want to avoid uncertainty may, in fact, welcome change.

[64]For categorizing individualism scores, "low" means that Hofstede's score was from 6 through 26 (number of countries, N = 18); "medium" scores were from 27 through 60 (N = 18); and "high" scores were from 63 through 91 (N = 17). For categorizing materialism scores, "low" means that Hofstede's score was from 5 through 43 (N = 17); "medium" scores were from 44 through 58 (N = 18); and "high" scores were from 61 through 95 (N = 18).

[65]Costa Rica ranked low in both individualism (15) and materialism (21). Moreover, Costa Rica is an appropriate comparison country for the United States because, like the United States but unlike some other countries with low materialism and individualism scores, Costa Rica has enjoyed a relatively stable political situation, democratic institutions, and a free press.

[66]See Venetoulis, J., & Talberth, J. (2005). *Ecological footprint of nations*. Oakland, CA: Redefining Progress. www.Redefining-Progress.org. As readers familiar with this literature will recognize, these are Ecological Footprint 2.0 data, which try to address some of the concerns raised by others on the original ecological footprint research (Rees, W., & Wackernagel, M. [1996]. *Our ecological footprint*. Gabriola Island, BC: New Society Publishers; van den Bergh, J. C. M., & Verbruggen, H. (1999). Spatial sustainability, trade and indicators: An evaluation of the ecological footprint. *Ecological Economics*, *29*(1), 61–72). For example, unlike the original index, Ecological Footprint 2.0 attempts to measure use of cropland, built space, and marine and inland fisheries.

[67]See Marks, N., Abdallah, S., Simms, A., & Thompson, S. (2006). *The unhappy planet: An index of human well-being and environmental impact*. London, UK: New Economics Foundation (Economics as if People and the Planet Mattered). www.happyplanetindex.org. This publication draws on a variety of sources, but most heavily on Veenhoven, R. (2005). Average happiness in 91 nations 1995–2005. World Database of Happiness (see Veenhoven, R. States of Nations, World Database of Happiness, Erasmus University, Rotterdam, Netherlands. www.worlddatabaseofhappiness.eur.nl/statnat).

[68]Content for this case was drawn from Cadbury's corporate website (www.cadbury.com), which was taken offline after its acquisition by Kraft in 2010 and the split of Kraft's confectionery business into Mondelēz International (http://www.mondelezinternational.com/SiteCollectionDocuments/pdf/about/corporate_timeline_Cadbury.pdf). The word "chocolate" comes from the Mayan word *xocolatl*, which means "bitter water"; the Mexican Indian word for chocolate comes from the terms *choco* (foam) and *atl* (water). For most of its history, chocolate was consumed as a beverage. The bitter beverage was made from roasted cocoa beans, water, and spices. Joseph Fry, a Quaker, made the first chocolate bar in Great Britain in 1847. Quakers, also known as the Society of Friends, were a nonconformist and pacifist group that emerged in the 17th century in protest against the formalism of the established Church of England. Their strong beliefs and ideals motivated Quakers to pursue projects that fostered justice, equality, and social reform and that alleviated poverty and deprivation. George, O., Owoyemi, O., & Onakala, U. (2012). Hofstede's "software of the mind" revisited and rested: The case of Cadbury Worldwide and Cadbury (Nigeria) Plc—A qualitative study. *International Business Research*, *5*(9), 148–157. The definition of fair trade used here was adapted from the TransFair USA and TransFair Canada websites. Retrieved from http://www.transfairusa.org/content/about/overview.php and http://www.transfair.ca/en/fairtrade/, respectively. http://www.fairtrade.net/cocoa.html. Accessed October 7, 2015; http://www.divinechocolate.com/about/story.aspx. Accessed February 8, 2013; https://www.bvt. org.uk/. Accessed February 8, 2013.

[69]This short version of the NEP scale is taken from the following source: Stern, P. C., Dietz, T., Abel, T., Guagnano, A., & Kalof, L. (1999). A value-belief-norm theory of support for social movements: The case of environmentalism. *Research in Human Ecology 6*(2), 81–97.

[70]Byrka, K., Hartig, T., & Kaiser, F. G. (2010). Environmental attitudes as a mediator of the relationship between psychological restoration in nature and self-reported ecological behavior. *Psychological Reports*, *107*(3), 847–859.

[71]This example is taken from Hawken, P. (1993). *The ecology of commerce: A declaration of sustainability*, New York: Harper Business; Hawkins, P. (2010). *The ecology of commerce: A declaration of sustainability* (rev. ed.). New York: HarperCollins.

Feature Notes

OB in Action: Hungry for Evidence de Ridder, D. D., Lensvelt-Mulders, G., Finkenauer, C., Stok, F., & Baumeister, R. F. (2012). Taking stock of self-control: A meta-analysis of how trait self-control relates to a wide range of behaviors. *Personality and Social Psychology Review, 16*(1), 76–99; Mischel, W., Ayduk, O., Berman, M. G., Casey, B. J., Gotlib, I. H., Jonides, J., Kross, E., Teslovich, T., Wilson, N. L., Zayas, V., & Shoda, Y. (2011). "Willpower" over the life span: Decomposing self-regulation. *Social, Cognitive, and Affective Neuroscience, 6*(2), 252–256; Lehrer, J. (2009, May 18). Don't: The secret of self-control. *The New Yorker.* Retrieved from http://www.newyorker.com/reporting/2009/05/18/090518fa_fact_lehrer

OB in Action: Growing with Your Suppliers and Stakeholders 49th Parallel Coffee Roasters. (2015). *Transparency Update: 2015.* Retrieved from https://cdn.shopify.com/s/files/1/0803/6099/files/Transparency_Update_2015.pdf?1196856430600340079; 49th Parallel Coffee Roasters. (2015). Sourcing. Retrieved from http://49thcoffee.com/pages/sourcing; Goldberg, E. (2015, January 10). 11 of the world's best cities for coffee lovers. Matador Network. Retrieved from http://matadornetwork.com/life/11-worlds-best-cities-coffee-lovers/; Perry, L. (2015, June 22). Learn: How we work with people. 49th Parallel Coffee Roasters. Retrieved from http://49thcoffee.com/blogs/learn/35337409-how-we-work-with-people; Potts, M. (2015, July 3). Blog: Small lots series. 49th Parallel Coffee Roasters. Retrieved from http://49thcoffee.com/blogs/blog/36376129-small-lots-series; Scout Magazine. (2012). 49th Parallel Coffee Roasters: About 49th Parallel.

Chapter 3

[1]Black Entrepreneurs and Executives Profile. (2015). *Angela Samuels.* Retrieved from http://www.blackentrepreneurprofile.com/profile-full/article/angela-samuels/; Campbell, R. (2012, November 27). Angela Samuels' fashion line, Voluptuous, celebrates full-figured women. *Madame Noire.* Retrieved from http://madamenoire.com/196687/angela-samuels-fashion-line-voluptuous-celebrates-full-figured-women/; TorontoVerve Street Style. (2014, November 20). *Voluptuous: Angela Samuels' inspiring journey.* Retrieved from http://www.torontoverve.org/2014/11/voluptuous-angela-samuels-inspiring.html; Voluptuous Clothing. (2014). *Angela Samuels - Voluptuous Clothing founder and CEO.* Retrieved from http://www.voluptuousclothing.com/about-voluptuousclothing-and-ceo-angela-samuels/#.VVqRZvlVhBc

[2]Fassinger, R. E. (2008). Workplace diversity and public policy: Challenges and opportunities for psychology. *American Psychologist, 63*(4), 252–268.

[3]Scott, K. A., Heathcote, J. M., & Gruman, J. A. (2011). The diverse organization: Finding gold at the end of the rainbow. *Human Resource Management, 50*(6), 735–755.

[4]Hogg, M. A., & Terry, D. J. (2000). Social identity and self-categorization processes in organizational contexts. *Academy of Management Review, 25,* 121–140; Tsui, A. S., Egan, T. D., & O'Reilly, C. A. (1992). Being different: Relational demography and organizational attachment. *Administrative Science Quarterly, 37,* 549–579; Van Knippenberg, D., De Dreu, C. K. W., & Homan, A. C. (2004). Work group diversity and group performance: An integrative model and research agenda. *Journal of Applied Psychology, 89*(6), 1008–1022.

[5]Van Knippenberg, De Dreu, & Homan. (2004).

[6]Webber, S.S., & Donahue, L. M. (2001). Impact of highly and less job-related diversity on work group cohesion and performance: A meta-analysis. *Journal of Management, 27,* 141–162.

[7]The Toronto-Dominion Bank. (2015). *TD 2014 corporate responsibility report.* Retrieved from http://www.td.com/document/PDF/corporateresponsibility/2014-Final-CRR_EN.pdf; Canada's Best Diversity Employers, The *Globe and Mail* & Mediacorp Canada Inc. (2015). *2015 Canada's best diversity employers.* Retrieved from http://issuu.com/ct100./docs/diversity-2015?e=14200235/11978967

[8]Milian, M. (2012, May 8). Zuckerberg's hoodie a "mark of immaturity," analyst says. *Bloomberg.* Retrieved from http://go.bloomberg.com/tech-deals/2012-05-08-zuckerbergs-hoodie-a-mark-of-immaturity-analyst-says-2/; The Canadian Press. (2014, December 11). Fashion comes at a cost, Don Cherry's suits occupy almost every closet. *NHL - News.* Retrieved from www.nhl.com/ice/news.htm?id=743427

[9]Harrison, D. A., Price, K. H., Gavin, J. H., & Florey, A. T. (2002). Time, teams, and task performance: Changing effects of surface- and deep-level diversity on group functioning. *Academy of Management Journal, 45,* 1029–1045.

[10]Ely, R. J., Padavic, I., & Thomas, D. A. (2012). Racial diversity, racial asymmetries, and team learning environment: Effects on performance. *Organization Studies (01708406), 33*(3), 341–362.

[11]Van Knippenberg, D., Haslam, S. A., & Platow, M. J. (2007). Unity through diversity: Value-in-diversity beliefs, work group diversity, and group identification. *Group Dynamics: Theory, Research, and Practice, 11*(3), 207–222.

[12]Yamashita, M. (2011, May 19–25). Great waffles and the hugs are free. *Alibi.com* Retrieved from http://alibi.com/food/37211/Great-Waffles-and-the-Hugs-Are-Free.html

[13]http://timsplaceabq.com/about-tim. Accessed February 2, 2013.

[14]La Rose, L. (2014, October 7). As more workers get inked, some companies easing rules on visible tattoos. *CTV News.* Retrieved from http://www.ctvnews.ca/lifestyle/as-more-workers-get-inked-some-companies-easing-rules-on-visible-tattoos-1.2042732

[15]Cheng, H., & Furnham, A. (2012). Childhood cognitive ability, education, and personality traits predict attainment in adult occupational prestige over 17 years. *Journal of Vocational Behavior, 81*(2), 218–226.

[16]McGrew, K. S. (2009). CHC theory and the human cognitive abilities project: Standing on the shoulders of the giants of psychometric intelligence research. *Intelligence, 37*(1), 1–10.

[17]Kuncel, N. R., Ones, D. S., & Sackett, P. R. (2010). Individual differences as predictors of work, educational, and broad life outcomes. *Personality and Individual Differences, 49*(4), 331–336.

[18]Ackerman, P. L. (1992). Predicting individual differences in complex skill acquisition: Dynamics of ability determinants. *Journal of Applied Psychology, 77,* 598–614; LePine, J. A., Colquitt, J. A., & Erez, A. (2000). Adaptability of changing task contexts: Effects of general cognitive ability, conscientiousness, and openness to experience. *Personnel Psychology, 53,* 563–593.

[19]Dilchert, S., Ones, D. S., Davis, R. D., & Rostow, C. D. (2007). Cognitive ability predicts objectively measured counterproductive work behaviors. *Journal of Applied Psychology, 92*(3), 616–627.

[20]Menkes, J. (2005). Hiring for smarts. *Harvard Business Review, 83*(11), 100–109.

[21]See Barrick, M. R., Stewart, G. L., & Piotrowski, M. (2002). Personality and job performance: Test of the mediating effects of motivation among sales representatives. *Journal of Applied Psychology, 87,* 1–9; Judge, T. A., & Ilies, R. (2002). Relationship of personality to performance motivation: A meta-analytic review. *Journal of Applied Psychology, 87,* 797–807.

[22]Alarcon, G., Eschleman, K. J., & Bowling, N. A. (2009). Relationships between personality variables and burnout: A meta-analysis. *Work & Stress, 23*(3), 244–263.

[23]Britton, A. R., Sliter, M. T., & Jex, S. M. (2012). Is the glass really half-full? The reverse-buffering effect of optimism on undermining behavior. *Personality and Individual Differences, 52*(6), 712–717.

[24]O'Boyle, E. R., Forsyth, D. R., Banks, G. C., & McDaniel, M. A. (2012). A meta-analysis of the Dark Triad and work behavior: A social exchange perspective. *Journal of Applied Psychology, 97*(3), 557–579.

[25]Digman, J. M. (1990). Personality structure: Emergence of the five-factor model. In M. R. Rosenzweig & L. W. Porter (Eds.), *Annual review of psychology* (Vol. 41, pp. 417–440). Palo Alto, CA: Annual Reviews.

[26]Chiaburu, D. S., Oh, I., Berry, C. M., Li, N., & Gardner, R. G. (2011). The five-factor model of personality traits and organizational citizenship behaviors: A meta-analysis. *Journal of Applied Psychology, 96*(6), 1140–1166; Barrick, M. R., & Mount, M. K. (1991). The Big Five personality dimensions and job performance: A meta-analysis. *Personnel Psychology, 44,* 1–26; Tett, R. P., Jackson, D. N., & Rothstein, M. (1991). Personality measures as predictors of job performance: A meta-analytic review. *Personnel Psychology, 44,* 703–742.

[27]See fn 26, Chiaburu et al. (2011).

[28]Barrick, M. R., Mount, M. K., & Strauss, J. P. (1993). Conscientiousness and performance of sales representatives: Test of the mediating effects of motivation among sales representatives. *Journal of Applied Psychology, 78,* 715–722.

[29]Alarcon, G., Eschleman, K. J., & Bowling, N. A. (2009). Relationships between personality variables and burnout: A meta-analysis. *Work & Stress, 23*(3), 244–263.

[30]Thoresen, C. J., Kaplan, S. A., Barsky, C. R., Warren, C. R., & de Chermont, K. (2003). The affective underpinnings of job perceptions and attitudes: A meta-analytic review and integration. *Psychological Bulletin, 129,* 914–945.

[31]Nai-Wen, C., Grandey, A. A., Diamond, J. A., & Krimmel, K. (2011). Want a tip? Service performance as a function of emotion regulation and extraversion. *Journal of Applied Psychology, 96*(6), 1337–1346.

[32]Judge, T. A., Bono, J. E., Ilies, R., Gerhardt, M. W. (2002). Personality and leadership: A qualitative and quantitative review. *Journal of Applied Psychology, 87*(4), 765–780.

[33]Hunter, E. M., Neubert, M. J., Perry, S. J., Witt, L. A., Penney, L. M., & Weinberger, E. L. (2013). Servant leaders inspire servant followers: Outcomes for employees and the organization. *The Leadership Quarterly, 24,* 316–331.

[34]George, J. M., & Zhou, J. (2001). When openness to experience and conscientiousness are related to creative behavior: An interactional approach. *Journal of Applied Psychology, 86*(3), 513–524.

[35]Ekehammar, B., & Akrami, N. (2003). The relation between personality and prejudice: A variable- and person-centered approach. *European Journal of Personality, 17,* 449–464.

[36]Homan, A. C., Hollenbeck, J. R., Humphrey, S. E., Van Knippenberg, D., Ilgen, D. R., & Van Kleef, G. A. (2008). Facing differences with an open mind: Openness to experience, salience of intragroup differences, and performance of diverse work groups. *Academy of Management Journal, 51*(6), 1204–1222.

[37]Barrick, M. R., Stewart, G. L., Neubert, M. J., & Mount, M. K. (1998). Relating member ability and personality to work-team processes and team effectiveness. *Journal of Applied Psychology, 83,* 377–391.

[38]Chiaburu, Oh, Berry, Li, & Gardner. (2011).

[39]See fn 32, Judge et al. (2002).

[40]See Chiaburu, Oh, Berry, Li, & Gardner. (2011); Organ, D. W. (1994). Personality and organizational citizenship behavior. *Journal of Management, 20*(2), 465–478.

[41]Neubert, M. J., Taggar, S., & Cady, S. H. (2006). The role of conscientiousness and extraversion in affecting the relationship between perceptions of group potency and volunteer group member selling behavior: An interactionist perspective. *Human Relations, 59*(9), 1235–1260.

[42]See fn 21, Barrick et al. (1998).

[43]Kuipers, B. S., Higgs, M. J., Tolkacheva, N. V., & de Witte, M. C. (2009). The influence of Myers-Briggs Type Indicator profiles on team development processes: An empirical study in the manufacturing industry. *Small Group Research, 40*(4), 436–464; Gentry, W. A., Mondore, S. P., & Cox, B. D. (2007). A study of managerial derailment characteristics and personality preferences. *Journal of Management Development, 26*(9), 857–873.

[44]Furnham, A. (1996). The Big Five versus the Big Four: The relationship between the Myers-Briggs Type Indicator (MBTI) and NEO-PI five factor model of personality. *Personality and Individual Differences, 21*(2), 303–307.

[45]Judge, T. A., Erez, A., Bono, J. E., & Thoresen, C. J. (2003). The Core Self-Evaluations Scale (CSES): Development of a measure. *Personnel Psychology, 56,* 303–331.

[46]Ng, T. W. H., Sorenson, K. L., & Eby, L. T. (2006). Locus of control at work: A meta-analysis. *Journal of Organizational Behavior, 27,* 1057–1087.

[47]Tong, J., & Wang, L. (2012). Work locus of control and its relationship to stress perception, related affections, attitudes and behaviours from a domain-specific perspective. *Stress and*

Health: Journal of the International Society for the Investigation of Stress, 28(3), 202–210.

[48]Judge, T. A., Bono, J. E., Erez, A., & Locke, E. A. (2005). Core self-evaluations and job and life satisfaction: The role of self-concordance and goal attainment. *Journal of Applied Psychology, 90,* 257–268.

[49]Trzesniewski, K. H., Donnellan, M. B., & Robins, R. W. (2003). Stability of self-esteem across the life span. *Journal of Personality and Social Psychology, 84,* 205–220.

[50]Graves, L. M., Ruderman, M. N., Ohlott, P. J., & Weber, T. J. (2012). Driven to work and enjoyment of work: Effects on managers' outcomes. *Journal of Management, 38*(5), 1655–1680.

[51]Bandura, A. (1986). *Social foundations of thought and action: A social cognitive theory.* Englewood Cliffs, NJ: Prentice-Hall; Cady S. H., Grey-Boyd, D., & Neubert, M. J. (2001). Multilevel performance probability: A meta-analytic integration of expectancy and self-efficacy. *Psychological Reports, 88,* 1077–1090.

[52]Judge, T. A., Jackson, C. L., Shaw, J. C., Scott, B. A., & Rich, B. L. (2007). Self-efficacy and work-related performance: The integral role of individual differences. *Journal of Applied Psychology, 92*(1), 107–127.

[53]Eden, D., Ganzach, Y., Flumin-Granat, R., & Zigman, T. (2010). Augmenting means efficacy to boost performance: Two field experiments. *Journal of Management, 36*(3), 687–713.

[54]Chen, G., Gully, S. M., & Eden, D. (2001). Validation of a new generalized self-efficacy scale. *Organizational Research Methods, 4,* 62–83.

[55]Chang, C., Ferris, D., Johnson, R. E., Rosen, C. C., & Tan, J. A. (2012). Core self-evaluations: A review and evaluation of the literature. *Journal of Management, 38*(1), 81–128.

[56]Chen, G., Gully, S. M., & Eden, D. (2004). General self-efficacy and self-esteem: Toward theoretical and empirical distinction between correlated self-evaluations. *Journal of Organizational Behavior, 25*(3), 375–395.

[57]Anderson, C., Brion, S., Moore, D. A., & Kennedy, J. A. (2012). A status-enhancement account of overconfidence. *Journal of Personality and Social Psychology, 103*(4), 718–735.

[58]Chang et al. (2012); Judge, T. A. (2009). Core self-evaluations and work success. *Current Directions in Psychological Science, 18*(1), 58–62.

[59]Joo, B., Yoon, H., & Jeung, C. (2012). The effects of core self-evaluations and transformational leadership on organizational commitment. *Leadership & Organization Development Journal, 33*(6), 564–582; Stumpp, T., Muck, P. M., Hülsheger, U. R., Judge, T. A., & Maier, G. W. (2010). Core self-evaluations in Germany: Validation of a German measure and its relationships with career success. *Applied Psychology: An International Review, 59*(4), 674–700.

[60]Grant, A. M., & Wrzesniewski, A. (2010). I won't let you down . . . or will I? Core self-evaluations, other-orientation, anticipated guilt and gratitude, and job performance. *Journal of Applied Psychology, 95*(1), 108–121.

[61]De Cremer, D., van Knippenberg, D., Dijke, M., & Bos, A. E. R. (2006). Self-sacrificing leadership and follower self-esteem: When collective identification matters. *Group Dynamics: Theory, Research, and Practice, 10*(3), 233–245.

[62]Zhang, A., Tsui, A. S., & Wang, D. (2011). Leadership behaviors and group creativity in Chinese organizations: The role of group processes. *The Leadership Quarterly, 22*(5), 851–862.

[63] Canadian Business Staff. (2014, October 24). How Hootsuite built a cool office (that makes people work harder). *Canadian Business.* Retrieved from http://www.canadianbusiness.com/innovation/how-to/hootsuite-cool-office-that-makes-people-work-harder/?gallery_page=1

[64]Heslin, P. A., & Vandewalle, D. (2008). Managers implicit assumptions about personnel. *Current Directions in Psychological Science, 17*(3), 219–223.

[65]McGregor, D. (1960). *The human side of enterprise.* New York: McGraw-Hill.

[66]McGregor. (1960). See also Heil, G., Bennis, W., & Stephens, D. (2000). *Douglas McGregor revisited: Managing the human side of the enterprise.* New York: John Wiley & Sons.

[67]Ouchi, W. G. (1981). *Theory Z.* Reading, MA: Addison-Wesley.

[68]Vo, A., & Hannif, Z. (2012). The transfer of training and development practices in Japanese subsidiaries in Vietnam. *Asia Pacific Journal of Human Resources, 50*(1), 75–91.

[69]Nicholson, N. (2000). *Executive instinct: Managing the human animal in the Information Age.* New York: Crown; Pierce, B. D., & White, R. (1999). The evolution of social structure: Why biology matters. *Academy of Management Review, 24*(4), 843–853.

[70]Batson, C. (2011). *Altruism in humans.* New York: Oxford University Press. See also Oliner, S. P. M., & Oliner, P. M. (1988). *The altruistic personality: Rescuers of Jews in Nazi Europe.* New York: Free Press.

[71]Heslin, P. A., Vandewalle, D., & Latham, G. P. (2006). Keen to help? Managers' implicit person theories and their subsequent employee coaching. *Personnel Psychology, 59*(4), 871–902.

[72]Kahle, L. R., & Goff, T. G. (1983). A theory and method for studying values. In L. R. Kahle (Ed.), *Social values and social change: Adaptation to life in America* (pp. 43–69). New York: Praeger.

[73]Rokeach, M. (1973). *The nature of human values.* New York: Free Press.

[74]Walker, K. R. (2006). *Examining ethics from a moral point of view framework: A longitudinal analysis.* Master of Science thesis, Faculty of Management, University of Manitoba.

[75]http://about.puma.com/category/company/glance/. Accessed February 2, 2013.

[76]http://www.guardian.co.uk/sustainable-business/best-practice-exchange/puma-impact-environment-counting-cost. Accessed February 2, 2013.

[77]Schwartz, S. H., & Boehnke, K. (2004). Evaluating the structure of human values with confirmatory factor analysis. *Journal of Research in Personality, 38*(3), 230–255; Schwartz, S. H., Melech, G., Lehmann, A., Burgess, S., Harris, M., & Owens, V. (2001). Extending the cross-cultural validity of the theory of basic human values with a different method of measurement. *Journal of Cross-Cultural Psychology, 32*(5), 519–542.

[78]van Vianen, A. E. M., De Pater, I. E., & Van Dijk, F. (2007). Work value fit and turnover intention: Same-source or different-source fit. *Journal of Managerial Psychology, 22*(2), 188–202.

[79]Kristof-Brown, A. L. (2000). Perceived applicant fit: Distinguishing between recruiters' perceptions of person-job and person-organization fit. *Personnel Psychology, 53*(3), 643–671.

[80]Klein, P. (2014, December 15). Here's the right way for companies to donate to charity. *Canadian Business* Retrieved from http://www.canadianbusiness.com/blogs-and-comment/the-right-way-to-donate-to-charity/

[81]Vance, A. (2012, September 13). Elon Musk, the 21st century industrialist. *Bloomberg Businessweek.* Retrieved from http://www.businessweek.com/articles/2012-09-13/elon-musk-the-21st-century-industrialist; http://www.biography.com/people/elon-musk-20837159. Accessed February 2, 2013; Kluger, J. (2012, June 18). Rocket man. *Time Magazine.* Retrieved from http://www.time.com/time/magazine/article/0,9171,2116714,00.html

[82]See fn 77, Schwartz et al. (2001).

Feature Notes

My OB: Do Generational Differences Make a Difference? Lyons, S. T., Ng, E. S. & Schweitzer, L. (2012). Generational career shift: Millennials and the changing nature of careers in Canada. *Managing the New Workforce: International Perspectives on the Millennial Generation,* 64–85.; Avery, D. R., McKay, P. F., & Wilson, D.C. (2007). Engaging the aging workforce: The relationship between perceived age similarity, satisfaction with coworkers, and employee engagement. *Journal of Applied Psychology, 92*(6), 1542–1556.

OB in Action: Employee Candidacy Tests Wilkinson, K. (2013, July 11). Companies turn to psych tests to screen out workplace weirdos. *Canadian Business.* Retrieved from http://www.canadianbusiness.com/business-strategy/psychological-testing-job-search/; [Company website landing page]. (n.d.). Retrieved from http://www.aplin.com/

My OB: Humility or Hard Work? Hempel, J. (2012, September 20). IBM's Ginni Rometty looks ahead. CNN Money. Retrieved from http://management.fortune.cnn.com/2012/09/20/powerful-women-rometty-ibm/; Hymowitz, C., & Frier, S. (2012, October 26). IBM's Rometty breaks ground as 100-year-old company's first female leader. *Bloomberg.* Retrieved from http://www.bloomberg.com/news/print/2011-10-25/ibm-names-rometty-to-succeed-palmisano-as-its-first-female-chief-executive.html; Tong, J., & Wang, L. (2012). Work locus of control and its relationship to stress perception, related affections, attitudes and behaviours from a domain-specific perspective. *Stress and Health: Journal of the International Society for the Investigation of Stress, 28*(3), 202–210; Ng, T. W. H., Sorenson, K. L., & Eby, L. T. (2006). Locus of control at work: A meta-analysis. *Journal of Organizational Behavior, 27,* 1057–1087.

OB in Action: Political Values and Geographical Differences Political Culture. *The Canadian Encyclopedia.* Retrieved from http://www.thecanadianencyclopedia.ca/en/article/political-culture/; J.J.'s Complete Guide to Canada. (2015). *Political Parties of Canada.* Retrieved from http://www.thecanadaguide.com/political-parties

Chapter 4

[1]Strauss K. (July 25, 2012). The new billionaire behind Twitter and Square: Jack Dorsey. *Forbes.* Retrieved from http://www.forbes.com/sites/karstenstrauss/2012/07/25/the-new-billionaire-behind-twitter-and-square-jack-orsey/; Kirkpatrick, D. (April, 2011). Twitter was act one. *Vanity Fair.* Retrieved from http://www.vanityfair.com/business/features/2011/04/jack-dorsey-201104; Segall, L. (October 9, 2012). Square CEO Jack Dorsey scales back at Twitter. CNN. Retrieved from http://money.cnn.com/2012/10/09/technology/social/jack-dorsey-square/index.html

[2]Canadian Foundation for Advancement of Investor Rights. (2011). *A report on a decade of financial scandals.* Retrieved from http://faircanada.ca/wp-content/uploads/2011/01/Financial-scandals-paper-SW-711-pm_Final-0222.pdf

[3]Lahey, L. (2012, January 6). Top 5 business scandals of 2011. *Yahoo Finance Canada.* Retrieved from https://ca.finance.yahoo.com/blogs/insight/top-5-business-scandals-2011-174754706.html

[4]Adams, P., & Yauch, B. (2013, November 4). How Canada encourages corrupt companies. *Financial Post.* Retrieved from http://business.financialpost.com/fp-comment/how-canada-encourages-corrupt-companies

[5]See fn 2, Canadian Foundation for Advancement of Investor Rights (2011).

[6]McKenna, B. (2015, February 16). Largest Ponzi scheme in Canadian history exploited boom time Alberta. *The Globe and Mail.* Retrieved from http://www.theglobeandmail.com/report-on-business/largest-ponzi-scheme-in-canadian-history-exploited-boom-time-alberta/article23010870/

[7]McCall, M. W., & Lombardo, M. M. (1983). Off the track: Why and how successful executives get derailed. (Technical Report No. 21). Greensboro, NC: Center for Creative Leadership.

[8]As this relates to abusive supervision, see Carlson, D. S., Ferguson, M., Perrewé, P. L., & Whitten, D. (2011). The fallout from abusive supervision: An examination of subordinates and their partners. *Personnel Psychology, 64*(4), 937–961; and Carlson, D., Ferguson, M., Hunter, E., & Whitten, D. (2012). Abusive supervision and work-family conflict: The path through emotional labor and burnout. *The Leadership Quarterly, 23*(5), 849–859.

[9]Kish-Gephart, J. J., Harrison, D. A., & Treviño, L. (2010). Bad apples, bad cases, and bad barrels: Meta-analytic evidence about sources of unethical decisions at work. *Journal of Applied Psychology, 95*(1), 1–31; Ashkanasy, N. M., Windsor, C. A., & Treviño, L. K. (2006). Bad apples in bad barrels revisited: Cognitive moral development, just world beliefs, rewards, and ethical decision making. *Business Ethics Quarterly, 16*(4), 449–473; Henle, C. A. (2006). Bad apples or bad barrels? A former CEO discusses the interplay of person and situation with implications for business education. *Academy of Management Learning & Education, 5*(3), 346–355; O'Boyle, E. H., Forsyth, D. R., & O'Boyle, A. S. (2011). Bad apples or bad barrels: An examination of group- and organizational-level effects in the study of counterproductive work behavior. *Group & Organization Management, 36*(1), 39–69.

[10]McCabe, D. L., Butterfield, K. D., & Treviño, L. (2006). Academic dishonesty in graduate business programs: Prevalence, causes,

and proposed action. *Academy of Management Learning & Education, 5*(3), 294–305; Li-Ping Tang, T., Yuh-Jia, C., & Sutarso, T. (2008). Bad apples in bad (business) barrels: The love of money, Machiavellianism, risk tolerance, and unethical behavior. *Management Decision, 46*(2), 243–253.

[11]See fn 9, Kish-Gephart et al. & Treviño, L. (2010); and Ashkanasy et al. (2006).

[12]Farnsworth, J. R., & Kleiner, B. H. (2003). Trends in ethics education at U.S. colleges and universities. *Management Review Research News, 26*(2–4), 130–140.

[13]Kohlberg, L. (1969). Stage and sequence: The cognitive development approach to socialization. In D. A. Goslin (Ed.), *Handbook of socialization theory and research* (pp. 347–380). Chicago: Rand McNally.

[14]Pojman, L. (1995). *Ethics: Discovering right and wrong.* Belmont, CA: Wadsworth.

[15]Deckop, J. R., Cirka, C. C., & Andersson, L. M. (2003). Doing unto others: The reciprocity of helping behavior in organizations. *Journal of Business Ethics. 47*(2), 101–113.

[16]See fn 9, Kish-Gephart et al. (2010).

[17]See fn 9, Ashkanasy et al. (2006).

[18]See fn 9, Kish-Gephart et al. (2010).

[19]MacIntyre, A. (1981). *After virtue: A study in moral theory.* Notre Dame, IN: University of Notre Dame Press.

[20]For differing opinions on the extent to which rights should govern decisions see Werhane, P. H., & Gorman, M. (2005). Intellectual property rights, moral imagination, and access to life-enhancing drugs. *Business Ethics Quarterly, 15*(4), 595–613; and Portillo, J., & Block, W. (2012). Anti-discrimination laws: Undermining our rights. *Journal of Business Ethics, 109*(2), 209–217.

[21]For more on this issue, see Frey, D. E. (1998). Individualist economic values and self-interest: The problem in the Puritan ethic. *Journal of Business Ethics, 17*, 1573–1580; and Bragues, G. (2009). Adam Smith's vision of the ethical manager. *Journal of Business Ethics, 90*, 447–460.

[22]Aristotle. (1962). *Nichomachean ethics* (trans. M. Oswald). New York. MacMillan.

[23]Neubert, M. J. (2011). Introduction: The value of virtue to management and organizational theory and practice. *Canadian Journal of Administrative Science, 28*(3), 227–230; Weaver, G. R. (2006). Virtue in organizations: Moral identity as a foundation for moral agency. *Organizational Studies, 27*(3), 341–368.

[24]These questions are found on p. 832 of Mintz, S. M. (1996). Aristotelian virtue and business ethics education. *Journal of Business Ethics, 15*, 827–838; who is citing Pincoffs, E. L. (1986). *Quandaries and virtues.* Lawrence, KS: University Press of Kansas.

[25]Audi, R. (2012). Virtue ethics as a resource in business. *Business Ethics Quarterly, 22*(2), 273–291; Neubert (2011).

[26]Hunter, E. M., Neubert, M. J., Perry, S. J., Witt, L. A., Penney, L. M., & Weinberger, E. L. (2013). Servant leaders inspire servant followers: Outcomes for employees and the organization. *The Leadership Quarterly*; van Dierendonck, D. (2011). Servant leadership: A review and synthesis. *Journal of Management, 37*(4), 1228–1261.

[27]See fn 9, Kish-Gephart et al. (2010).

[28]Valente, M. (2012). Theorizing firm adoption of sustaincentrism. *Organization Studies, 33*(4), 563–591.

[29]Valente (2012); Johnson, P. (1996). Development of an ecological conscience: Is ecocentrism a prerequisite? *Academy of Management Review, 21*(3), 607–611.

[30]Ferraro, F., Pfeffer, J., & Sutton, R. I. (2005). Economic language and assumptions: How theories can become self-fulfilling. *Academy of Management Review, 30*, 8–24; and Krishnan, V R. (2003). Do business schools change students' values along desirable lines? A longitudinal study. In A. F. Libertella & S. M. Natale (Eds.), *Business education and training: A value-laden process* (Vol. 8, pp. 26–39). Lanham, MD: University Press of America. However, students often do not recognize that their ethics are changing, or that becoming more materialist-individualist is a moral concern: By propagating ideologically inspired amoral theories, business schools have actively freed their students from any sense of moral responsibility (Ghoshal, 2005, p. 76). Bad management theories are destroying good management practices. *Academy of Management Learning and Education, 4*(1), 75–91.

[31]Weeks, B., Longenecker, J., McKinney, J., & Moore, C. (2005). The role of mere exposure effect on ethical tolerance: A two-study approach. *Journal of Business Ethics, 58*(4), 281–294.

[32]Grojean, M. W., Resick, C. J., Dickson, M. W., & Smith, B. (2004). Leaders, values, and organizational climate: Examining leadership strategies for establishing an organizational climate regarding ethics. *Journal of Business Ethics, 55*, 223–241.

[33] See fn 9, Kish-Gephart et al. (2010); Appelbaum, S. H., Deguire, K. J., & Lay, M. (2005). The relationship of ethical climate to deviant workplace behaviour. *Corporate Governance, 5*(4), 43–55.

[34]Schaubroeck, J. M., Hannah, S. T., Avolio, B. J., Kozlowski, S. J., Lord, R. G., Treviño, L. K., & Peng, A. C. (2012). Embedding ethical leadership within and across organizational levels. *Academy of Management Journal, 55*(5), 1053–1078; Trevino, L. K., Butterfield, K. D. & McCabe, D. L. (1998). The ethical context in organizations: Influences on employee attitudes and behavior. *Business Ethics Quarterly, 8*, 447–477.

[35]Emerson, T. L., McKinney, J. A., & Neubert, M. J. (2010). The effects of ethical codes on ethical perceptions of actions toward stakeholders. *Journal of Business Ethics, 97*, 505–516; and Kish-Gephart et al. (2010).

[36]Schwartz, M. (2001). The nature of the relationship between corporate codes of ethics and behavior. *Journal of Business Ethics, 32*(3), 247–262.

[37]Tenbrunsel, A. E., Smith-Crowe, K., & Umphress, E. (2003). Building houses on rocks: The role of ethical infrastructure in organizations, *Social Justice Research 16*(3), 285–307.

[38]http://www.loreal.com/_en/_ww/html/our-company/interview-of-the-director-of-ethics.aspx? Accessed February 2, 2013.

[39] Falcione, A. (2012, February 29). Canadian Centre for Ethics & Corporate Policy: Compliance & Ethics Program Best Practices [Presentation slides]. Retrieved from http://www.ethicscentre.ca/EN/files/speeches/2012%20Canadian%20Centre%20for%20Ethics.pdf

[40]Badaracco, J. L. Jr., & Webb, A. (1995). Business ethics: A view from the trenches. *California Management Review, 37*(2), 8–28.

[41]Salter, M. S. (2004). *Innovation corrupted: The rise and fall of Enron.* Boston: Harvard Business School Publishing.

[42]Neubert, M. J., Carlson, D. S., Kacmar, K. M., Roberts, J. A., & Chonko, L. B. (2009). The virtuous influence of ethical leadership

behavior: Evidence from the field. *Journal of Business Ethics, 90,* 157–170; Keith, N. K., Pettijohn, C. E., & Burnett, M. S. (2003). An empirical evaluation of the effect of peer and managerial ethical behaviors and the ethical predispositions of prospective advertising employees. *Journal of Business Ethics, 48*(3), 251–265.

[43]Brown, M. E., Trevino, L. K., & Harrison, D. A. (2005). Ethical leadership: A social learning perspective for construct development and testing. *Organizational Behavior and Human Decision Processes, 97,* 117–134.

[44]Mayer, D. M., Kuenzi, M., Greenbaum, R., Bardes, M., & Salvador, R. (2009). How low does ethical leadership flow? Test of a trickle-down model. *Organizational Behavior and Human Decision Processes, 108,* 1–13.

[45]MacDonald, C. (2013, March 15). Can SNC's reputation recover? *Canadian Business.* Retrieved from http://www.canadianbusiness.com/companies-and-industries/can-sncs-reputation-recover/

[46]Gibbs, J. P. (1975). *Crime, punishment, and deterrence.* Amsterdam: Elsevier.

[47]Stansbury, J., & Barry, B. (2007). Ethics programs and the paradox of control. *Business Ethics Quarterly, 17*(2), 239–261; Tenbrunsel, A. E., & Messick, D. M. (1999). Sanctioning systems, decision frames, and cooperation. *Administrative Science Quarterly, 44*(4), 684–707.

[48]See fn 47, Stansbury & Barry (2007).

[49]Gardner, W. L., & Schermerhorn, J. R. Jr. (2004). Unleashing individual potential performance gains through positive organizational behavior and authentic leadership. *Organizational Dynamics, 33*(3), 270–281.

[50]See p. 145 in Gold, L. (2010). *New financial horizons: The emergence of an economy of communion.* Hyde Park, NY: New City Press.

[51]Goodpaster, K. (2007). *Conscience and culture.* Malden, MA: Blackwell.

[52]Spreier, S., Fontaine, M., & Malloy, R. (2006, June). Leadership run amok: The destructive potential of overachievers. *Harvard Business Review,* 72–82.

[53]http://www.adidas-group.com/en/sustainability/Suppliers/Our_Workplace_standards/default.aspx. Accessed February 8, 2013.

[54]Ajzen, I. 2001. Nature and operation of attitudes. *Annual Review of Psychology, 52,* 27–58.

[55]Brief, A. (1998). *Attitudes in and around organizations.* Thousand Oaks, CA: Sage.

[56]Harrison, D. A., Newman, D. A., & Roth, P. L. (2006). How important are job attitudes? Meta-analytic comparisons of integrative behavioral outcomes and time sequences. *Academy of Management Journal, 49*(2), 305–325.

[57]For examples of how individual differences influence job attitudes, see Ng, T. H., & Feldman, D. C. (2010). The relationships of age with job attitudes: A meta-analysis. *Personnel Psychology, 63*(3), 677–718; Avey, J. B., Reichard, R. J., Luthans, F., & Mhatre, K. H. (2011). Meta-analysis of the impact of positive psychological capital on employee attitudes, behaviors, and performance. *Human Resource Development Quarterly, 22*(2), 127–152.

[58]Newman, P. C. (2008, December 11). Ted Rogers: A visionary leader. *Maclean's.* Retrieved from http://www.macleans.ca/economy/business/a-visionary-leader/

[59]Sorenson, C. (2013, November 7). Really bad bosses. *Maclean's.* Retrieved from http://www.macleans.ca/economy/business/really-bad-bosses/

[60]See fn 56, Harrison et al. (2006); Judge, T. A., Thoresen, C. J., Bono, J. E., & Patton, G. K. (2001). The job satisfaction-job performance relationship: A qualitative and quantitative review. *Psychological Bulletin, 127,* 376–407.

[61]Chuang, A., Judge, T. A., & Liaw, Y. (2012). Transformational leadership and customer service: A moderated mediation model of negative affectivity and emotion regulation. *European Journal of Work and Organizational Psychology, 21*(1), 28–56

[62]Diefendorff, J. M., Brown, D. J., Kamin, A. M., & Lord, R. G. (2002). Examining the roles of job involvement and work centrality in predicting organizational citizenship behaviors and job performance. *Journal of Organizational Behavior, 23*(1), 93–108.

[63]Erdogan, B., Bauer, T. N., Truxillo, D. M., & Mansfield, L. R. (2012). Whistle while you work: A review of the life satisfaction literature. *Journal of Management, 38*(4), 1038–1083.

[64]Caza, A., Barker, B. A., & Cameron, K. S. (2004). Ethics and ethos: The buffering and amplifying effects of ethical behavior and virtuousness. *Journal of Business Ethics, 52,* 169–178.

[65]Kooij, D. M., Jansen, P. W., Dikkers, J. E., & De Lange, A. H. (2010). The influence of age on the associations between HR practices and both affective commitment and job satisfaction: A meta-analysis. *Journal of Organizational Behavior, 31*(8), 1111–1136.

[66]Saari, L. M., & Judge, T. A. (2004). Employee attitudes and job satisfaction. *Human Resource Management, 43*(4), 395–407.

[67]See fn 65, Kooij et al. (2010).

[68]Duffy, R. D., Bott, E. M., Allan, B. A., Torrey, C. L., & Dik, B. J. (2012). Perceiving a calling, living a calling, and job satisfaction: Testing a moderated, multiple mediator model. *Journal of Counseling Psychology, 59*(1), 50–59; Valentine, S., & Fleischman, G. (2008). Ethics programs, perceived corporate social responsibility and job satisfaction. *Journal of Business Ethics, 77*(2), 159–172.

[69]Neubert, M. J., Carlson, D. S., Kacmar, K. M., Roberts, J. A., & Chonko, L. B. (2009). The virtuous influence of ethical leadership behavior: Evidence from the field. *Journal of Business Ethics, 90,* 157–170.

[70]Avey, J. B., Reichard, R. J., Luthans, F., & Mhatre, K. H. (2011). Meta-analysis of the impact of positive psychological capital on employee attitudes, behaviors, and performance. *Human Resource Development Quarterly, 22*(2), 127–152.

[71]Culpepper, R. A. (2011). Three-component commitment and turnover: An examination of temporal aspects. *Journal of Vocational Behavior, 79*(2), 517–527.

[72]Klein, H., Molloy, J., & Brinsfield, C. T. (2009). Understanding commitment in the workplace: Differentiating commitment strength, rationales and targets. In Klein, H. J., Becker, T. E., & Meyer, J. P. (Eds.), *Commitment in organizations: Accumulated wisdom and new directions.* Mahwah, NJ: Lawrence Erlbaum Associates.

[73]Meyer, J. P., & Herscovitch, L. (2001). Commitment in the workplace: Toward a general model. *Human Resource Management Review, 11,* 299–326.

[74]See fn 72, Klein et al. (2009).

[75] See fn 56, Harrison et al. (2006).

[76] Cohen, A. (2003). *Multiple commitments in the workplace: An integrative approach.* Mahwah, NJ: Lawrence Erlbaum Associates.

[77] See fn 65, Kooij et al. (2010).

[78] See fn 71, Culpepper (2011).

[79] See fn 76, Cohen (2003).

[80] See fn 65, Kooij et al. (2010).

[81] http://www.accenture.com/us-en/company/overview/awards/Pages/recognition-best-companies.aspx. Accessed February 8, 2013.

[82] Simpson, B., Markovsky, B., & Steketee, M. (2011). Power and the perception of social networks. *Social Networks, 33*(2), 166–171.

[83] Kenny, D. A. (2004). PERSON: A general model of interpersonal perception. *Personality and Social Psychology Review, 8*(3), 265–280.

[84] Weiner, B. (1986). *An attributional theory of motivation and emotion.* New York: Springer-Verlag; LePine, J. A., & Van Dyne, L. (2001). Peer responses to low performers: An attributional model of helping in the context of groups. *Academy of Management Review, 26,* 67–84.

[85] Taggar, S., & Neubert, M. J. (2004). The impact of poor performers on team outcomes: An empirical examination of attribution theory. *Personnel Psychology, 57,* 935–968.

[86] Kacmar, K., & Carlson, D. S. (1999). Effectiveness of impression management tactics across human resource situations. *Journal of Applied Social Psychology, 29*(6), 1293–1315; Carlson, J., Carlson, D., & Ferguson, M. (2011). Deceptive impression management: Does deception pay in established workplace relationships? *Journal of Business Ethics, 100*(3), 497–514.

[87] Zaidman, N. N., & Drory, A. A. (2001). Upward impression-management in the work place cross-cultural analysis. *International Journal of Intercultural Relations, 25*(6), 671–690.

[88] Mealy, M., Stephan, W., & Urrutia, I. (2007). The acceptability of lies: A comparison of Ecuadorians and Euro-Americans. *International Journal of Intercultural Relations, 31*(6), 689–702.

[89] LeDoux, J. A., Gorman, C. A., & Woehr, D. J. (2012). The impact of interpersonal perceptions on team processes: A social relations analysis. *Small Group Research, 43*(3), 356–382.

[90] Kahneman, D., & Tversky, A. (1973). On the psychology of prediction. *Psychological Review, 80,* 237–251.

[91] Festinger, L. (1957). *A theory of cognitive dissonance.* Stanford, CA: Stanford University Press; Matz, D. C., & Wood, W. (2005). Cognitive dissonance in groups: The consequences of disagreement. *Journal of Personality and Social Psychology, 88*(1), 22–37.

[92] Ross, L., & Nisbett, R. E. (1991). *The person and the situation: Perspectives of social psychology.* New York, NY: McGraw-Hill.

[93] Pronin, E., Gilovich, T., & Ross, L. (2004). Objectivity in the eye of the beholder: Divergent perceptions of bias in self versus others. *Psychological Review, 111,* 781–799.

[94] Choi, I., Dalai, R., Kim-Prieto, C., & Park, H. (2003). Culture and judgement of causal relevance. *Journal of Personality and Social Psychology, 84*(1), 46–59.

[95] Hoever, I. J., van Knippenberg, D., van Ginkel, W. P., & Barkema, H. G. (2012). Fostering team creativity: Perspective taking as key to unlocking diversity's potential. *Journal of Applied Psychology, 97*(5), 982–996.

[96] Fehr F., & Gachter, S. (2002). Altruistic punishment in humans. *Nature, 415,* 137–140; Taggar & Neubert (2004).

[97] See fn 85, Taggar & Neubert (2004).

[98] Rothbard, N. P., & Wilk, S. L. (2011). Waking up on the right or wrong side of the bed: Start-of-the-day mood, work events, employee affect, and performance. *Academy of Management Journal, 54*(5), 959–980.

[99] Gray, E. K., & Watson, D. (2007). Assessing positive and negative affect via self-report; In J. A. Coan & J. J. B. Allen (EDs.), *Handbook of emotion elicitation and assessment.* (pp. 171–183). New York, NY: Oxford University Press.

[100] Hatfield, E., Cacioppo, J. T., &Rapson, R. T. (1994). *Emotional contagion.* New York: Cambridge University Press.

[101] George, J. M. (1995). Leader positive mood and group performance: The case of customer service. *Journal of Applied Social Psychology, 25*(9), 778–794.

[102] Brescoll, V L., & Uhlmann, E. L. (2008). Can an angry woman get ahead? Status conferral, gender, and expression of emotion in the workplace. *Psychological Science, 19*(3), 268–275.

[103] Kiefer, T., & Barclay, L. J. (2012). Understanding the mediating role of toxic emotional experiences in the relationship between negative emotions and adverse outcomes. *Journal of Occupational & Organizational Psychology, 85*(4), 600–625.

[104] Frost, P. J. (2004). Handling toxic emotions: New challenges for leaders and their organization. *Organizational Dynamics, 33*(2), 111–127.

[105] Hochschild, A. R. (1983). *The managed heart.* Berkeley, CA: University of California Press; Brotheridge, C. M., & Lee, R. T. (2008). The emotions of managing: An introduction to the special issue. *Journal of Managerial Psychology, 23*(2) 108–117.

[106] Tsai, W. C. (2001). Determinants and consequences of employee displayed positive emotions. *Journal of Management, 27,* 497–512.

[107] Zapf, D., & Holz, M. (2006). On the positive and negative effects of emotion work in organizations. *European Journal of Work and Organizational Psychology, 15*(1), 1–28.

[108] Bar-On, R. (2000). Emotional and social intelligence: Insights from the Emotional Quotient Inventory. In Bar-On, R., & Parker, J. D. A. (Eds.), *The handbook of emotional intelligence* (pp. 363–388). San Francisco: Jossey-Bass; Salovey, P., & Mayer, J. D. (1990). Emotional intelligence. *Imagination, Cognition, and Personality, 9.* 185–211.

[109] Joseph, D. L., & Newman, D. A. (2010). Emotional intelligence: An integrative meta-analysis and cascading model. *Journal of Applied Psychology, 95*(1), 54–78.

[110] Wong, C. S., & Law, K. S. (2002). The effects of leader and follower emotional intelligence on performance attitude: An exploratory study. *The Leadership Quarterly, 13,* 243–274.

[111] Pugh, S., Groth, M., & Hennig-Thurau, T. (2011). Willing and able to fake emotions: A closer examination of the link between emotional dissonance and employee well-being. *Journal of Applied Psychology, 96*(2), 377–390.

[112] Case sources: Alaga, E. (2011). Pray the devil back to hell: Women's ingenuity in the peace process in Liberia. Background

brief, PeaceBuild: The Canadian Peacebuilding Network, 1–21; Disney, A., & Gbowee, L. (2012). Gender and sustainable peace. In Coleman, P. T., & Deutsch, M. (Eds.), *Psychological components of sustainable peace*, 197–203 (ch. 10). Peace psychology book series; Gbowee, L. (with Mithers, C.). (2011). *Mighty be our powers*. New York: Beast Books; Hanna, H., & Alfaro, A. L. (2012). The future development in Liberia: Keeping women on the agenda. *Women's Policy Journal of Harvard, 9* (spring), 77–79; Hunt, A. S., & Laresen, Z. (2012). Why they won the Nobel Peace prize. *Women's Policy Journal of Harvard, 9* (spring), 3–4.

[113]See fn 112, Alaga (2011).

[114]See fn 112, Gbowee (with Mithers) (2011).

[115]See fn 112, Disney & Gbowee (2012).

[116]See fn 112, Alaga (2011).

[117]Naughton, M, J., & Bausch, T. A. (1994). The integrity of a Catholic management education. *California Management Review, 38*(4), 119–140; and Weber, M. (1958). *The Protestant ethic and the spirit of capitalism*. New York: Scribner.

[118]Sackett, P. R., & Schmitt, N. (2012). On reconciling conflicting meta-analytic findings regarding integrity test validity. *Journal of Applied Psychology, 97*(3), 550–556.

[119]Quotes from Wagner, P. (1991, September-October). Pagsunog-Kilay. *Women's Concerns Report, 89*, 4–6.

Feature Notes

OB in Action: Business Ethics and Personal Standards of Honesty   Tracey, P. (2012). Religion and organization: A critical review of current trends and future directions. *The Academy of Management Annals*, 1–46; Boswell, R. (2012, April 7). Religion not important to most Canadians, although majority believe in God: poll. *National Post*. Retrieved from http://news.nationalpost.com/news/religion/religion-not-important-to-most-canadians-although-majority-believe-in-god-poll; Chan-Serafin, S., Brief, A. P., & George, J. M. (in press). How does religion matter and why? Religion and the organizational sciences. *Organization Science*. Advance online publication doi: 10.1287/orsc.1120.0797; Ariely, D. (2008, January 29). How honest people cheat. Retrieved at http://blogs.hbr.org/cs/2008/01/how_honest_people_cheat.html#

My OB: What Makes A Job Satisfying?   Rowe, M. (2008). Seven dirty habits of highly effluent people. *Fast Company, 122,* 69; Wegge, J., Schmidt, K., Parkes, C., & van Dick, R. (2007). "Taking a sickie": Job satisfaction and job involvement as interactive predictors of absenteeism in a public organization. *Journal of Occupational and Organizational Psychology, 80*(1), 77–89; Hadi, R., & Adil, A. (2010). Job characteristics as predictors of work motivation and job satisfaction of bank employees. *Journal of the Indian Academy of Applied Psychology, 36*(2), 294–299; Hackman, J. R., & Oldham, G. R. (1976). Motivation through the design of work: Test of a theory. *Organizational Behavior & Human Performance, 16*(2), 250–279.

OB in Action: Deceptive First Impressions   Sisario, B. (2010, April 30). Susan Boyle tops global sales chart.

New York Times. Retrieved from http://artsbeat.blogs.nytimes.com/2010/04/30/susan-boyle-tops-global-sales-chart/; http://www.ifpi.org/content/section_news/20100428.html. Accessed February 2, 2013; Sisario, B. (2009, December 2). Susan Boyle, top seller, shakes up CD trends. *New York Times*. Retrieved from http://www.nytimes.com/2009/12/03/arts/music/03sales.html

My OB: When Managing Emotions Matters   Kiefer, T., & Barclay, L. J. (2012). Understanding the mediating role of toxic emotional experiences in the relationship between negative emotions and adverse outcomes. *Journal of Occupational & Organizational Psychology, 85*(4), 600–625; Brescoll, V. L., & Uhlmann, E. L. (2008). Can an angry woman get ahead? Status conferral, gender, and expression of emotion in the workplace. *Psychological Science, 19*(3), 268–275; Frost, P. J. (2004). Handling toxic emotions: New challenges for leaders and their organization. *Organizational Dynamics, 33*(2), 111–127.

Chapter 5

[1]Certner, J. (2012). Starbucks: For infusing a steady stream of new ideas to revive its business. *Fast Company, 163,* 112–149; Ignatius, A. (2010). We had to own the mistakes. *Harvard Business Review, 88*(7/8), 108–115; Starbucks Corporation. (2015). *Starbucks global responsibility report: Exploring the role of a public company*. https://news.starbucks.com/news/starbucks-2014-global-responsibility-report. Accessed July 5, 2015; Weiss, N. (1998). How Starbucks impassions workers to drive growth. *Workforce, 77*(8), 60–64; Great Place to Work Award for credibility. (2003). http://www.greatplacetowork.com; http://money.cnn.com/magazines/fortune/bestcompanies/2011/snapshots/98.html; Starbucks Corporation. (2015). *Working at Starbucks*. Retrieved from http://www.starbucks.ca/careers/working-at-starbucks; Starbucks Coffee Company. (2013). *Starbucks Coffee Canada: Your special blend brimming with benefits!.* Retrieved from http://globalassets.starbucks.com/assets/d7ea56b34e27429e8171d7c4e8d65fc7.pdf

[2]Deci, E. L., & Ryan, R. M. (2000). The "what" and "why" of goal pursuits: Human needs and the self-determination of behavior. *Psychological Inquiry, 11*(4), 227–268.

[3]Meyer, J. P., Becker, T. E., & Vandeberghe, C. (2004). Employee commitment and motivation: A conceptual analysis and integrative model. *Journal of Applied Psychology, 89*(6), 991–1007.

[4]Mitchell, T. R., & Daniels, D. (2003). Motivation. In W. C. Borman, D. R. Ilgen, & R. J. Klimoski (Eds.), *Handbook of psychology: Industrial and organizational psychology* (Vol. *12*, pp. 225–254). Hoboken, NJ: John Wiley & Sons.

[5]Kooij, D. M., de Lange, A. H., Jansen, P. W., Kanfer, R., & Dikkers, J. E. (2011). Age and work-related motives: Results of a meta-analysis. *Journal of Organizational Behavior, 32*(2), 197–225.

[6]Mitchell, T. R., & Daniels, D. (2003). Observations and commentary on recent research in work motivation. In L. Porter, G. Bigley, & R. Steers (Eds.), *Motivation and work behavior* (7th ed.). New York: McGraw Hill.

[7]Alderfer, C. P. (1969). An empirical test of a new theory of human needs. *Organizational Behavior and Human Performance, 4,* 142–175.

[8]Bassett-Jones, N., & Lloyd, G. C. (2005). Does Herzberg's motivation theory have staying power? *Journal of Management Development*, *24*(10), 929–943.

[9]McCullough, M. (2015, March 12). Former Lululemon CEO Christine Day wants to reinvent the frozen dinner. *Canadian Business*. Retrieved from http://www.canadianbusiness.com/innovation/christine-day-life-after-lululemon-starbucks-luvo/

[10]Lindenberg, S., & Foss, N. J. (2011). Managing joint production motivation: The role of goal framing and governance mechanisms. *Academy of Management Review*, *36*(3), 500–525.

[11]Luthans, F., & Youssef, C. M. (2007). Emerging positive organizational behavior. *Journal of Management*, *33*(3), 321–349.

[12]Bluestein, A. (2007). Cafeteria 2.0. *Fast Company*, *119*, 60–62.

[13]See fn 6, Mitchell & Daniels (2003), p. 33.

[14]Locke, E. A., & Latham, G. P. (1990). *A theory of goal setting and task performance*. Englewood Cliffs, NJ: Prentice Hall.

[15]Neubert, M. J. (1998). The value of feedback and goal setting over goal setting alone and potential moderators of this effect: A meta-analysis. *Human Performance*, *11*, 321–335.

[16]Neubert, M. J., & Wu, C. (2009). Action commitments. In H. J. Klein, T. E. Becker, & J. P. Meyer (Eds.), *Commitment in organizations: Accumulated wisdom and new directions*. Mahwah, NJ: Lawrence Erlbaum Associates.

[17]Shaw, K. N. (2004). Changing the goal-setting process at Microsoft. *Academy of Management Executive*, *18*(4), 139–142.

[18]Latham, G. P. (2004). The motivational benefits of goal-setting. *Academy of Management Executive*, *18*(4), 126–129.

[19]See fn 17, Shaw (2004).

[20]Hemmadi, M. (2014, November 21). Clearpath Robotics is changing the world with its life-saving robots. *Canadian Business*. Retrieved from http://www.canadianbusiness.com/innovation/clearpath-robotics-passion-capitalists-2014/

[21]Kerr, S., & Landauer, S. (2004). Using stretch goals to promote organizational effectiveness: General Electric and Goldman Sachs. *Academy of Management Executive*, *18*(4), 134–138.

[22]Locke, E. A. (2004). Linking goals to monetary incentives. *Academy of Management Executive*, *18*(4), 130–133.

[23]Schweitzer, M., Ordonez, L., & Douma, B. (2004). Goal setting as a motivator of unethical behavior. *Academy of Management Journal*, *47*, 422–432.

[24]Wright, P. M., George, J. M., Farnsworth, S. R., & McMahan, G. C. (1993). Productivity and extra-role behavior: The effects of goals and incentives on spontaneous helping. *Journal of Applied Psychology*, *78*(3), 374–381.

[25]http://www.gatesfoundation.org/about/Pages/bill-melinda-gates-letter.aspx

[26]Grant, A. M., & Berry, J. W. (2011). The necessity of others is the mother of invention: Intrinsic and prosocial motivations, perspective taking, and creativity. *Academy of Management Journal*, *54*(1), 73–96.

[27]See fn 21, Kerr & Landauer (2004).

[28]http://money.cnn.com/magazines/fortune/bestcompanies/2007/snapshots/12.html. Accessed February 8, 2013; http://www.davidweekleyhomes.com/Site/SubPage.aspx?UID=3bc2e249-2b54-42af-ab52-3c36e41c3bba. Accessed February 8, 2013.

[29]See fn 18, Latham (2004), p. 129. Of course, this rule of thumb—to permit participation when there are multiple goals—applies all the time to sustainable management, because sustainable management has as its premise the existence of multiple goals and multiple forms of well-being.

[30]MEC. (2012). *MEC stakeholder panel report*. Retrieved from http://www.mec.ca/media/Images/pdf/accountability-2012-stakeholderpanel_v2_m56577569831501419.pdf; Almack, K. (2013, Nov 27). Increasing the impact of CSR through multi-stakeholder collaboration. *Canadian Business for Social Responsibility*. Retrieved from http://www.cbsr.ca/blog/increasing-impact-csr-through-multi-stakeholder-collaboration

[31]Holloway, A. (2009, March 12). Lorenzo Donadeo, CEO and president, Vermilion Energy Trust. *Canadian Business*. Retrieved from http://www.canadianbusiness.com/business strategy/now-hear-this-lorenzo-donadeo-ceo-and-president-vermilion-energy-trust/

[32]Coates, J., Gray, M., & Hetherington, T. (2006). An "ecospiritual" perspective: Finally, a place of indigenous approaches. *British Journal of Social Work*, *36*, 381–399.

[33]Eden, D. (2003). Self-fulfilling prophecies in organizations. In J. Greenberg (Ed.), *Organizational behavior: The state of the science* (2nd ed., pp. 91–122). Mahwah, NJ: Lawrence Erlbaum Associates.

[34]Campion, M. A., Medsker, G. J., & Higgs, A. C. (1993). Relations between work group characteristics and effectiveness: Implications for designing effective work groups. *Personnel Psychology*, *46*, 823–850; Jung, D. I., Sosik, J. J., & Baik, K. B. (2002). Investigating work group characteristics and performance over time: A replication and cross-cultural extension. *Group Dynamics: Theory, Research, & Practice*, *6*, 153–171.

[35]Tyran, K., & Gibson, C. B. (2008). Is what you see, what you get? The relationship among surface- and deep-level heterogeneity characteristics, group efficacy, and team reputation. *Group & Organization Management*, *33*(1), 46–76.

[36]Wright, P. M., George, J. M., Farnsworth, S. R., & McMahan, G. C. (1993). Productivity and extra-role behavior: The effects of goals and incentives on spontaneous helping. *Journal of Applied Psychology*, *78*(3), 374–381.

[37]Paine, J. B., & Organ, D. W. (2000). The cultural matrix of organizational citizenship behavior: Some preliminary conceptual and empirical observations. *Human Resource Management Review*, *10*(1), 45–59.

[38]Carlson, D. S., & Kacmar, K. M. (2000). Work-family conflict in the organization: Do life role values make a difference? *Journal of Management*, *26*(5), 1031–1054.

[39]Service Canada. (2014). *Firefighters*. Retrieved from http://www.servicecanada.gc.ca/eng/qc/job_futures/statistics/6262.shtml

[40]Adams, J. S. (1965). Inequity in social exchange. In L. Berkowitz (Ed.), *Advances in experimental social psychology* (Vol. *2*, pp. 267–299). New York: Academic Press.

[41]See fn 6, Mitchell & Daniels (2003). See also Greenberg, J. (1988). Equity and workplace status: A field experiment. *Journal of Applied Psychology*, *73*, 606–613.

[42]This example is based on one of the author's personal experiences with the employees of Dana Corporation.

[43]See Cooper, C., Dyck, B., & Frohlich, N. (1992). Improving the effectiveness of gainsharing: The role of participation and fairness. *Administrative Science Quarterly, 37*, 471–490.

[44]Gildan Activewear Inc. (2015). *Raw material.* Retrieved from http://www.genuinegildan.com/en/product/raw-material/

[45]Cropanzano, R., Bowen, D. E., & Gilliland, S. W. (2007). The management of organizational justice. *Academy of Management Perspectives, 21*(4), 34–48.

[46]Cohen, A. (2003). *Multiple commitments in the workplace: An integrative approach.* Mahwah, NJ: Lawrence Erlbaum Associates.

[47]Canadian Business Staff. (2014 November 10). Canada's best employers 2015: The top 50 large companies. *Canadian Business.* Retrieved from http://www.canadianbusiness.com/lists-and-rankings/best-jobs/2015-best-employers-top-50/; WestJet Airlines Ltd. (2015). *What's in it for you?* Retrieved from http://www.westjet.com/pdf/greatWestJetJobs.pdf

[48]Yukl, G. (2013). *Leadership in organizations* (8th ed.) Upper Saddle River, NJ: Pearson Education Inc.

[49]Becker, T. E. (2009). Interpersonal commitments. In H. J. Klein, T. E. Becker, & J. P. Meyer (Eds.), *Commitment in organizations: Accumulated wisdom and new directions.* Mahwah, NJ: Lawrence Erlbaum Associates.

[50]Choi, J., & Sy, T. (2010). Group-level organizational citizenship behavior: Effects of demographic faultlines and conflict in small work groups. *Journal of Organizational Behavior, 31*(7), 1032–1054.

[51]For a discussion of different types of commitments, motivational bases, and levels of identification, See Johnson, R. E., Chang, C., & Yang, L. (2010). Commitment and motivation at work: The relevance of employee identity and regulatory focus. *Academy of Management Review, 35*(2), 226–245

[52]Dierdorff, E. C., Bell, S. T., & Belohlav, J. A. (2011). The power of "we": Effects of psychological collectivism on team performance over time. *Journal of Applied Psychology, 96*(2), 247–262.

[53]Lululemon Athletica Inc. (2015). *Our sustainability vision.* Retrieved from http://sustainability.lululemon.com/our-sustainability-vision/; Lululemon Athletica Inc. (2015). *People-powered projects.* Retrieved from http://sustainability.lululemon.com/people-power-projects/

[54]Lululemon Athletica Inc. (2015). *Responsible supply chain.* Retrieved from http://sustainability.lululemon.com/responsible-supply-chain/

[55]Lululemon Athletica Inc. (2015). *The metta movement.* Retrieved from http://sustainability.lululemon.com/giving-communities/

[56]Beckett, J. (1998). *Loving Monday: Succeeding in business without selling your soul.* Downers Grove, IL: Intervarsity Press.

[57]French, J. R. P., & Raven, B. (1959). The bases of social power. In D. Cartwright & A. Zander (Eds.), *Studies in social power* (pp. 150–167). Ann Arbor, MI: University of Michigan, Institute for Social Research.

[58]Wagner, J., Leana, C. R., Locke, E. A., & Schweiger, D. M. (1997). Cognitive and motivational frameworks in U.S. research on participation: A meta-analysis of primary effects. *Journal of Organizational Behavior, 18*(1), 49–65.

[59]Subramony, M. (2009). A meta-analytic investigation of the relationship between HRM bundles and firm performance. *Human Resource Management, 48*(5), 745–768.

[60]Spreitzer, G. M., & Quinn, R. E. (2001). *A company of leaders: Five disciplines for unleashing power in your workforce.* University of Michigan Business School Management Series. San Francisco, CA: Jossey-Bass.

[61]See fn 60, Spreitzer & Quinn (2001).

[62]Nguyen, M. (2014, November 10). Canada's best employers 2015: How the Keg keeps its sizzle. *Canadian Business.* Retrieved from http://www.canadianbusiness.com/lists-and-rankings/best-jobs/2015-best-employers-keg-restaurants/

[63]Canadian Business Staff. (2010, September 28). Heather Reisman [Video]. *Canadian Business.* Retrieved from http://www.canadianbusiness.com/business-news/heather-reisman/; Mohamed, F. (2013, Aug 30). She-lanthropy: Heather Reisman and her commitment to improving children's literacy one school at a time. *The Huffington Post.* Retrieved from http://www.huffingtonpost.com/farah-mohamed/shelanthropy-heather-reis_b_3831908.html; Mompreneur Staff. (2010, November). Businesses that speaks volumes . . . and values. *Mompreneur.* Retrieved from http://www.themompreneur.com/documents/MPN_11_12_2010.pdf; Shaw, H. (2013, October 29). American Girl debuts in Canada with boutiques in two Indigo stores. *Financial Post.* Retrieved from http://business.financialpost.com/news/retail-marketing/american-girl-debuts-in-canada-with-boutiques-in-two-indigo-stores; Indigo Inc. (2015). *Our company: Indigo timeline.* Retrieved from http://www.chapters.indigo.ca/en-ca/our-company/timeline/

Feature Notes

My OB: Understanding Motivation Inside-Out   Shea, C. (2015, January 2). Trainer to the stars Harley Pasternak on keeping people motivated. *Canadian Business.* Retrieved from http://www.canadianbusiness.com/leadership/harley-pasternak-interview/

OB in Action: Olympic-Sized Aspirations   Heil, J. (2014, February 24). Jennifer Heil salutes the gold-medal parents who instill much more than a love of sport. *The Globe and Mail.* Retrieved from http://www.theglobeandmail.com/life/health-and-fitness/health-advisor/jennifer-heil-salutes-the-gold-medal-parents-who-instill-much-more-than-a-love-of-sport/article17064240/

OB in Action: Changing Vice to Virtuous Goals   Gandhi, A. (2003). Foreword: My grandfather's footsteps. In C. Ingram, *In the footsteps of Gandhi: Conversations with spiritual social activists* (rev. ed., pp. 9–12). Berkeley, CA: Parallax Press; Gandhi, M. (1999). *The collected works of Mahatma Gandhi.* New Delhi: Publications Division, Ministry of Information and Broadcasting.

My OB: Is Your Motivation Intrinsic or Extrinsic?   Killed by carrots: The pay for performance myth. (2011, April 13). WordPress.com. Retrieved from http://theexecutiveroundtable.wordpress.com/2011/04/13/killed-by-carrots-the-pay-for-performance-myth/; Deci, E. L., Koestner, R., & Ryan, R. M. (1999). *A meta-analytic review of experiments examining the effects of extrinsic rewards on intrinsic motivation, Psychological Bulletin, 125(6),* 627–668; Deci, E. L., & Ryan, R. M. (1985). *Intrinsic motivation and self-determination in human behavior.* New York: Plenum.

[1]The quotes in this case are taken from pages 382 and 384 in Gioia, D. A. (1992). Pinto fires and personal ethics: A script analysis of missed opportunities. *Journal of Business Ethics, 11,* 379–389. Dennis Gioia served as Ford's Recall Coordinator from 1973 to 1975. When he started in 1973, he inherited the oversight of approximately 100 active recall campaigns and had additional files of incoming safety problems, one of which included reports of Pintos "lighting up." The decision described in the opening paragraphs, to pay damages instead of issuing a recall, was made after Gioia had left the position. Important stories in the public media on Pinto problems were published in 1976 and 1977. After three teenage girls died in a Pinto fire, a grand jury took the unprecedented step of indicting Ford on charges of reckless homicide. See also Nutt, P. C. (2002). *Why decisions fail: Avoiding blunders and traps that lead to debacles.* San Francisco: Berret-Kohler; Birsch, D., & Fielder, J. H. (Eds.). (1994). *The Ford Pinto case: A study in applied ethics, business, and technology.* New York: State University of New York Press. Hora, M., Bapuji, H., & Roth, A. V. (2011). Safety hazard and time to recall: The role of recall strategy, product defect type, and supply chain player in the U.S. toy industry. *Journal of Operations Management, 29,* 766–777.

[2]Dyck, B. (1991). Prescription, description and inscription: A script theoretic leadership model. Presented to the Organization and Management Theory Interest Group, Administrative Sciences Association of Canada, Niagara Falls, Ontario.

[3]Dawes, R. (1988). *Rational choice in an uncertain world.* Orlando, FL: Harcourt Brace Jovanovich.

[4]Li, L., Ambani, S., & Ni, J. (2009). Plant-level maintenance decision support system for throughput improvement. *International Journal of Production Research, 47*(24), 7047–7061.

[5]Timm, J. (2011, April 25). Canadian Tire: Fixing a flat. *Canadian Business.* Retrieved from http://www.canadianbusiness.com/business-strategy/canadian-tire-fixing-a-flat/

[6]Dyck, B., & Weber, J. M. (2006). Conventional and radical moral agents: An exploratory look at Weber's moral-points-of-view and virtues. *Organization Studies, 27*(3), 429–450.

[7]Biggart, N. W., & Delbridge, R. (2004). Systems of exchange. *Academy of Management Review, 29*(1), 28–49.

[8]Barney, J. B. (2004). An interview with William Ouchi. *Academy of Management Executive, 18*(4), 108–116.

[9]Alvesson, M., & Spicer, A. (212). A stupidity-based theory of organizations. *Journal of Management Studies, 49*(7), 1194–1120.

[10]Castaldo, J. (2012, January 19). How management has failed at RIM. *Canadian Business.* Retrieved from http://www.canadianbusiness.com/technology-news/how-management-has-failed-at-rim/

[11]Research suggests that having a short-term versus long-term time horizon tends to make decision makers favour shorter-term instrumental rewards possibly at cost to long-term organizational reputations. Martin, J., & Davis, K. (2010). Late in the game: How does a short time horizon impact CEO decision making? *Academy of Management Perspectives, 24*(3), 105–106.

[12]No author. (2012, October 30). The Toyota Prius C received the best overall expected reliability score for 2013 model-year cars from *Consumer Reports.* Japanese vehicles rate most reliable. *Winnipeg Free Press,* p. B8.

[13]Alexiev, A., Jansen, J., Van den Bosch, F., & Volberda, H. (2010). Top management team advice seeking and exploratory innovation: The moderating role of TMT heterogeneity. *Journal of Management Studies, 47*(7), 1343–1364.

[14]Thompson, G., & Driver, C. (2005). Stakeholder champions: How to internationalize the corporate social responsibility agenda. *Business Ethics: A European Review, 14*(1), 56–66. doi: 10.1111/j.1467-8608.2005.00386.x

[15]For the classic, though debated, discussion of uncertainty and risk, see Knight, F. H. (1921). *Risk, uncertainty, and profit.* Boston, MA: Hart, Schaffner & Marx; Houghton Mifflin Company, 1921.

[16]Bazerman, M. (1998). *Judgment in managerial decision making* (4th ed.). New York: John Wiley & Sons; Miller, C. C., & Ireland, R. D. (2005). Intuition in strategic decision making: Friend or foe in the fast-paced 21st century? *Academy of Management Executive, 19*(1), 19–30.

[17]Burke, L. A., & Miller, M. K. (1999). Taking the mystery out of intuitive decision-making. *Academy of Management Executive, 13*(4), 91–99. See also Sadler-Smith, E., & Shefy, E. (2004). The intuitive executive: Understanding and applying "gut feel" in decision-making. *Academy of Management Executive, 18*(4), 76–91.

[18]Salas, E., Rosen, M.A., & Diaz Granados, D. (2010). Expertise-based intuition and decision making in organizations. *Journal of Management, 36*(4), 941–973.

[19]See fn 16, Miller & Ireland (2005).

[20]Gladwell, M. (2005). *Blink.* New York: Little, Brown.

[21]Simon, H. A. (1947). *Administrative behavior.* New York: Mac-Millan; Simon, H. A. (1957). *Models of man.* New York: Wiley; March, J. G., & Simon, H. A. (1958). *Organizations.* New York: Wiley; Simon, H. A. (1960). *The new science of management decision.* New York: Harper & Row; Simon, H. A. (1987, February). Making management decisions: The role of intuition and emotion. *Academy of Management Executive, 1*(1), 57–63.

[22]The work of Daniel Kahneman and Amos Tversky suggests that how the facts are presented, or framed, has an effect on the kinds of decisions people make. For example, see Kahneman, D., & Tversky, A. (1979). Prospect theory: An analysis of decision under risk. *Econometrica, 47,* 263–291.

[23]This example is adapted from and builds on the discussion described in Bazerman (1998) (see fn 16).

[24]Seo, M., Goldfarb, B., & Barrett, L. (2010). Affect and the framing effect within individuals over time: Risk taking in a dynamic investment simulation. *Academy of Management Journal, 53*(2), 411

[25]For a more detailed explanation of these decision-making biases, see Dawes, R. M. (1988). *Rational choice in an uncertain world.* Orlando, FL: Harcourt Brace Jovanovich, Inc.

[26]Barton, D. (2013, June 25). The rise of the social CEO: Dominic Barton. *Canadian Business.* Retrieved from http://www.canadianbusiness.com/blogs-and-comment/the-rise-of-the-social-ceo/

[27]Wong, E., Ormiston, M., & Tetlock, P. (2011). The effects of top management team integrative complexity and decentralized decision making on corporate social performance. *Academy of Management Journal, 54*(6), 1207–1228.

[28]deLuque, M., Washburn, N., Waldman, D., & House, R. (2008). Unrequited profit: How stakeholder and economic values

relate to subordinates' perceptions of leadership and firm performance. *Administrative Science Quarterly, 53*(4), 626–654.

[29]For more information, please see the *Principles of Responsible Management Education* website at http://www.unprme.org/. Accessed February 22, 2013. See also the special issue in *Journal of Management Education,* including Clasco, M. (2012). Aligning the hidden curriculum of management education with PRME: An inquiry-based framework. *Journal of Management Education, 36*(3), 364–388.

[30]Zhong, C. (2011). The ethical dangers of deliberative decision making. *Administrative Science Quarterly, 56*(1), 1–25.

[31]Beach, L. (1990). *Image theory: Decision making in personal and organizational contexts.* New York: Wiley.

[32]Giacalone, R. A. (2004). A transcendent business education for the 21st century. *Academy of Management Learning and Education, 3*(4), 415–420.

[33]See fn 31, Beach (1990).

[34]Cowan, J. (2012, April 16). Can Air Canada be saved? *Canadian Business.* Retrieved from http://www.canadianbusiness.com/business-strategy/can-air-canada-be-saved/

[35]See Vroom, V. H. (2000). Leadership and the decision-making process. *Organizational Dynamics, 28*(4), 82–94; see also Vroom, V H., & Yetton, P. W. (1973). *Leadership and decision-making.* Pittsburgh, PA: University of Pittsburgh Press.

[36]This is adapted from principles in Vroom, V. H. (2003). Educating managers for decision making and leadership. *Management Decision, 41*(10), 968–978.

[37]Moreover, almost all failures are due to actions of the decision maker, not problems that are inherent in the situation itself. Nutt, P. C. (2004). Expanding the search for alternatives during strategic decision-making. *Academy of Management Executive, 18*(4), 13–28.

[38]*Canadian Business* Staff. (2014, October 1). Fail Forward's Ashley Good on how to screw up in the best possible way. *Canadian Business.* Retrieved from http://www.canadianbusiness.com/innovation/how-to/fail-forwards-ashley-good-on-how-to-screw-up-in-the-best-possible-way/

[39]Guarnaccia, S. (1998). The truth is, the truth hurts. *Fast Company, 14,* 93. Retrieved from http://www.fastcompany.com/33876/truth-truth-hurts. Accessed February 24, 2013.

[40]Castaldo, J. (2013, January 25). Why BlackBerry 10 will be a stunning success—and an inevitable failure. *Canadian Business.* Retrieved from http://www.canadianbusiness.com/technology-news/rims-last-stand-bb10-will-be-a-stunning-success-and-an-inevitable-failure/

[41] Shimizu, K., & Hitt, M. A. (2004). Strategic flexibility: Organizational preparedness to reverse ineffective strategic decisions. *Academy of Management Executive, 18*(4), 44–59.

[42]Gina, F., & Pisano, G. P. (2011, April). Why leaders don't learn from success. *Harvard Business Review, 89*(4), 68–74.

[43]See fn 41, Shimizu & Hitt (2004).

[44]The proportion of African-American managers at AT&T increased from about 0.5 percent to 4.5 percent. This voluntary improvement—achieved in a time when there were no orders from top management to increase the number of African-American employees being promoted, no timetables, no quotas, no performance reviews tied to promoting African-American managers, and so on—was especially impressive in contrast to the subsequent increase achieved at AT&T with much acrimony and struggle via the legislated Civil Rights Act (Nielsen, 1998).

[45]McFarland, J. (2014, November 19). Women gain on corporate boards but visible minority representation dips. *The Globe and Mail.* Retrieved from http://www.theglobeandmail.com/report-on-business/corporate-boards-now-have-more-women-fewer-minorities/article21641463/

[46]Quote taken from Dyck, B. (2002). A grounded, faith-based moral point of view of management. In Teresa Rose (Ed.), *Proceedings of Organizational Theory Division, 23,* 12–23, Administrative Sciences Association of Canada, Winnipeg, MB.

[47]Samuel, H., & Allen, N. (2008). Jérôme Kerviel: Bank knew what I was doing. *Telegraph.* Retrieved from http://www.telegraph.co.uk/finance/newsbysector/banksandfinance/2783483/Jerome-Kerviel-Bank-knew-what-I-was-doing.html. Accessed February 22, 2013; Clark, N. (2008, February 6). French trader says he won't be made a scapegoat. *New York Times.* Retrieved from http://www.nytimes.com/2008/02/06/business/worldbusiness/06bank.html?pagewanted=all&_r=0. Accessed February 22, 2013; Anderson, J. (2008, February 7). Craving the high that risky trading can bring. *New York Times.* Retrieved from http://www.nytimes.com/2008/02/07/business/worldbusiness/07trader.html. Accessed February 22, 2013; Schwartz, N. D., & Bennhold, K. (2008, February 5). A trader's secrets, a bank's missteps. *New York Times.* Retrieved from http://www.nytimes.com/2008/02/05/business/worldbusiness/05bank.html?pagewanted=all. Accessed February 22, 2013. In 2013 he sued Société Générale for 4.9 billion euros, the same amount he is said to have lost, insisting that his managers had known what he had been doing and had turned a blind eye as long as he was making a profit; see article dated February 12, 2013: Rogue trader Jerome Kerviel sues Société Générale for €4.9bn. *The Telegraph.* Retrieved from http://www.telegraph.co.uk/finance/financial-crime/9866292/Rogue-trader-Jerome-Kerviel-sues-Societe-Generale-for-4.9bn.html. Accessed February 24, 2013.

[48]Hannah, S. T., Avolio, B. J., & Walumbwa, F. O. (2011). Relationships between authentic leadership, moral courage, and ethical and pro-social behaviors. *Business Ethics Quarterly, 21*(4), 555–578.

[49]Backhaus, K., & Liff, J. P. (2007). Cognitive styles and approaches to studying in management education. *Journal of Management Education, 31*(4), 445–466. See also Vance et al. (2007).

[50]Gill, D.W. (2011, June 25). Was Aaron Feuerstein wrong? *Ethix, 75.* Retrieved from http://ethix.org/2011/06/25/was-aaron-feuerstein-wrong; Page 133 in Batstone, D. (2003). *Saving the corporate soul and (who knows?) maybe your own.* San Francisco: Jossey-Bass; The mensch of Malden Mills. (2003, July 3). CBSNews.com, *60 Minutes*; Browning, L. (2001, November 28). Management: Fire could not stop a mill, but debts may. *New York Times.* Retrieved from http://www.nytimes.com/2001/11/28/business/management-fire-could-not-stop-a-mill-but-debts-may.html?pagewanted=all; Kerber, R. (2007, January 11). Malden Mills files for second chapter 11. *Boston Globe.* Retrieved from http://www.tmcnet.com/usubmit/2007/01/11/2239997.htm

[51]Kahneman, D., Lovallo, D., & Sibony, O. (2011) The big idea: Before you make that big decision. *Harvard Business Review,*

89(6), 50–60. See also description in Zhang, H. (n.d.). How to avoid cognitive biases in decision-making. Retrieved from http://www.zhangzhiyong.cn/decision_making/avoiding_biase.htm. Accessed February 22, 2013.

Feature Notes

My OB: Neuroscience and Decision Making Rilling, J. K., & Sanfey, A. G. (2011). The neuroscience of social decision-making. *Annual Review of Psychology, 62,* 23–48; Turner, J. (2011). Your brain on food: A nutrient-rich diet can promote cognitive health. *Journal of the American Society on Aging, 35*(2), 99–106; Wehrenberg, M. (2010). *The 10 best-ever depression management techniques: Understanding how your brain makes you depressed & what you can do to change it.* New York: W. W. Norton & Company, Inc.; Schwarz, A. (2012, June 9). Risky rise of the good-grade pill. *New York Times.* Retrieved from http://www.nytimes.com/2012/06/10/education/seeking-academic-edge-teenagers-abuse-stimulants.html?pagewanted=all&_r=0. Accessed February 22, 2013.

My OB: Networks That Promote Sustainable OB Decision Making The MBA Oath was retrieved from http://www.mbaoath.com/. Accessed February 22, 2013; Vermaelen, T., & Gren, C. H. (2010, January 21). The debate room: MBA Oath is nothing to swear by. *Bloomberg Businessweek.* Retrieved from http://www.businessweek.com/debateroom/archives/2010/01/mba_oath_is_not.html. Accessed February 22, 2013; Clayton, W. (2012, March 26). Why we should have an MBA Oath and why I will take it. *The Harbus Online.* Retrieved from http://www.harbus.org/2012/mba-oath/. Accessed February 22, 2013; Barry, C. (2012, March 26). I'm not taking any MBA Oaths, and you shouldn't either. *The Harbus Online.* Retrieved from http://www.harbus.org/2012/mba-oath/. Accessed February 22, 2013.

OB in Action: How Do Managers Actually Make Ethical Decisions? Badaracco, J. L. Jr., & Webb, A. (1995). Business ethics: A view from the trenches. *California Management Review, 37*(2), 8–28; Jackall, R. (1988). *Moral mazes: The world of corporate managers.* New York: Oxford University Press; Van Yperen, N. W., Hamstra, M. R. W., & van der Klauw, M. (2011). To win, or not to lose, at any cost: The impact of achievement goals on cheating. *British Journal of Management, 22,* S5–S15.

OB in Action: Culture and the Decision-Making Process Cowan, J. (2013, February 19). Why Tim Hortons can't rrroll into the United States. *Canadian Business.* Retrieved from http://www.canadianbusiness.com/blogs-and-comment/tim-hortons-american-expansion-failure/; McMahon, T. (2012, July 20). Doing business with Americans? HSBC has some (hilarious) cultural advice. *Maclean's.* Retrieved from http://www.macleans.ca/economy/business/doing-business-across-the-border-hsbc-has-some-hilarious-cultural-advice/; Alvesson, M., & Spicer, A. (2012). A stupidity-based theory of organizations. *Journal of Management Studies, 49*(7), 1194–1120; Barney, J. B. (2004). An interview with William Ouchi. *Academy of Management Executive, 18*(4), 108–116;

Deresky, H. (2007). *International management: Managing across borders and cultures* (6th ed.). Upper Saddle River, NJ: Prentice-Hall; Glisby, M., & Holden, N. (2003). Contextual constraints in knowledge management theory: The cultural embeddedness of Nonaka's knowledge-creating company. *Knowledge and Process Management, 10*(1), 29–36; Ryan, R. M., & Deci, E. R., (2001). Self-determination theory and the facilitation of intrinsic motivation, social development, and well-being. *American Psychologist, 52,* 141–166.

Chapter 7

[1]Ripley, A. (2008, February 4). Q&A: Whistle-blower Cynthia Cooper. *Time.* Retrieved from http://www.time.com/time/arts/article/0,8599,1709695,00.html; Watkin, S. (2011, March 29). Cooper details WorldCom fraud experience at Xavier speech. *Cincinnati Business Courier.* Retrieved from http://www.bizjournals.com/cincinnati/blog/2011/03/coo-per-details-worldcom-fraud.html?page=all; Katz, D. M., & Homer, J. (2008, February 1). WorldCom Whistle-blower Cynthia Cooper: What she was feeling and thinking as she took the steps that, as it turned out, would change Corporate America. *CFO Magazine.* Retrieved from http://www.cfo.com/article.cfm/10590507; Meyer, P. J. (2002). *Unlocking your legacy: 25 keys for success.* Chicago, IL: Moody Publishers; Personal Interview (May 26, 2008); What it takes to be a winner: The Paul J. Meyer story. *Success* (June/July 2008), pp. 84–89. Carozza, D. (March/April 2008). Extraordinary circumstances: An interview with Cynthia Cooper. *Fraud Magazine.* Pulliam, S., and D. Solomon. (October 30, 2002). How three unlikely sleuths exposed fraud at WorldCom. *The Wall Street Journal.*

[2]Gardner, W. L., Cogliser, C. C., Davis, K. M., & Dickens, M. P. (2011). Authentic leadership: A review of the literature and research agenda. *Leadership Quarterly, 22*(6), 1120–1145.

[3]Kernis, M. H., & Goldman, B. M. (2006). A multicomponent conceptualization of authenticity: Theory and research. In M. P. Zanna (Ed.), *Advances in Experimental Social Psychology, 38,* pp. 283–357, San Diego: Academic Press; Toor, S., & Ofori, G. (2009). Authenticity and its influence on psychological well-being and contingent self-esteem of leaders in Singapore construction sector. *Construction Management and Economics, 27,* 299–313.

[4]Macik-Frey, M., Quick, J., & Cooper, C. L. (2009). Authentic leadership as a pathway to positive health. *Journal of Organizational Behavior, 30*(3), 453–458.

[5]Calvasina, G. E., Calvasina, R. V., & Calvasina, E. J. (2012). The Dodd-Frank Act: Whistleblower protection piled higher and deeper. *Business Studies Journal, 4*(1), 51–60.

[6]Walumbwa, F. O., Avolio, B. J., Gardner, W. L., Wernsing, T. S., & Peterson, S. J. (2008). Authentic leadership: Development and validation of a theory-based measure. *Journal of Management, 34,* 89–126.

[7]Avolio, B. J., Walumbwa, F. O., & Weber, T. J. (2009). Leadership: Current theories, research, and future directions. *Annual Review of Psychology, 60,* 421–449.

[8]Leroy, H., Palanski, M., & Simons, T. (2012). Authentic leadership and behavioral integrity as drivers of follower commitment and performance. *Journal of Business Ethics, 107*(3), 255–264; Peus, C., Wesche, J., Streicher, B., Braun, S., & Frey, D. (2012). Authentic

leadership: An empirical test of its antecedents, consequences, and mediating mechanisms. *Journal of Business Ethics, 107*(3), 331–348; Peterson, S. J., Walumbwa, F. O., Avolio, B. J., & Hannah, S. T. (2012). The relationship between authentic leadership and follower job performance: The mediating role of follower positivity in extreme contexts. *The Leadership Quarterly, 23*(3), 502–516.

[9]Luthans, F., Avolio, B. J., Avey, J. B., & Norman, S. M. (2007). Positive psychological capital: Measurement and relationship with performance and satisfaction. *Personnel Psychology, 60,* 541–572.

[10]Findings reported in Gardner et al. (2011) meta-analysis (see fn 2) and in Moorman, R. H., Darnold, T. C., & Priesemuth, M. (2013). Perceived leader integrity: Supporting the construct validity and utility of a multi-dimensional measure in two samples. *The Leadership Quarterly,* doi:10.1016/j.leaqua.2013.02.003.

[11]Drawn from his website, http://www.davidwhill.com/portfolio.htm, and a personal conversation with lead author.

[12]Rego, A., Sousa, F., Marques, C., & Cunha, M. (2012). Authentic leadership promoting employees' psychological capital and creativity. *Journal of Business Research, 65*(3), 429–437.

[13]Hsiung, H. (2012). Authentic leadership and employee voice behavior: A multi-level psychological process. *Journal of Business Ethics, 107*(3), 349–361.

[14]Hmieleski, K. M., Cole, M. S., & Baron, R. A. (2012). Shared authentic leadership and new venture performance. *Journal of Management, 38*(5), 1476–1499.

[15]Clapp-Smith, R., Vogelgesang, G. R., & Avey, J. B. (2009). Authentic leadership and positive psychological capital: The mediating role of trust at the group level of analysis. *Journal of Leadership and Organizational Studies, 15,* 227–240.

[16]Wong, C. A., Spence Laschinger, H. K., & Cummings, G. G. (2010). Authentic leadership and nurses' voice behavior and perceptions of care quality. *Journal of Nursing Management, 18*(8), 889–900.

[17]Spitzmuller, M., & Ilies, R. (2010). Do they [all] see my true self? Leader's relational authenticity and followers' assessments of transformational leadership. *European Journal of Work and Organizational Psychology, 19*(3), 304–332.

[18]Campbell, J. D., Trapnell, P. D., Heine, S. J., Katz, I. M., Lavallee, L. F., & Lehman, D. R. (1996). Self-concept clarity: Measurement, personality correlates, and cultural boundaries. *Journal of Personality and Social Psychology, 70*(1), 141–156.

[19]Eriksen, M. (2009). Authentic leadership: Practical reflexivity, self-awareness, and self-authorship. *Journal of Management Education, 33*(6), 747–771; and fn 8, Peus et al., (2012).

[20]Dyck, B., Starke, F. A., & Weimer, J. (2012). Toward understanding management in first century Palestine. *Journal of Management History, 18*(2), 137–165.

[21]Although this general tendency exists to a degree, other factors can offset this relationship. See Ferris, D., Lian, H., Brown, D. J., Pang, F. J., & Keeping, L. M. (2010). Self-esteem and job performance: The moderating role of self-esteem contingencies. *Personnel Psychology, 63*(3), 561–593.

[22]Petit, V., & Bollaert, H. (2012). Flying too close to the sun? Hubris among CEOs and how to prevent it. *Journal of Business Ethics, 108*(3), 265–283.

[23]Li, J., & Tang, Y. (2010). CEO hubris and firm risk taking in China: The moderating role of managerial discretion. *Academy of Management Journal, 53*(1), 45–68; Hayward, M. L. A., &

Hambrick, D. C. (1997). Explaining the premiums paid for large acquisitions: Evidence of CEO hubris. *Administrative Science Quarterly, 42,* 103–127.

[24]Fisher, M. (2015, March *23).* Brazilian aircraft maker Embraer's decision to target regional jet market pays off. *National Post.* Retrieved from http://news.nationalpost.com/news/world/brazillian-aircraft-maker-embraers-decision-to-target-regional-jet-market-pays-off.

[25]Kirby, J. (2015, February 18). Bombardier is just the latest warning about government support. *Maclean's.* Retrieved from http://www.macleans.ca/economy/business/bombardier-is-just-the-latest-warning-about-government-oversight/.

[26]Quan, K. (2015, February 12). Bombardier's shakeup was a long time coming. Is it enough? *Canadian Business.* Retrieved from http://www.canadianbusiness.com/companies-and-industries/bombardier-management-shakeup/.

[27]Diddams & Chang. (2012). Only human: Exploring the nature of weakness in authentic leadership. *Leadership Quarterly, 23*(3), 593–603. See also Weick, K. E. (2003). Positive organizing and organizational tragedy. In Cameron, K. S., Dutton, J. E., & Quinn, R. E. (Eds.), *Positive organizational scholarship: Foundations of a new discipline* (pp. 66–80). San Francisco, CA: Berrett-Koehler.

[28]Owens, B. P., & Hekman, D. R. (2012). Modeling how to grow: An inductive examination of humble leader behaviors, contingencies, and outcomes. *Academy of Management Journal, 55*(4), 787–818; Nielsen, R., Marrone, J., & Slay, H. (2010). A new look at humility: Exploring the humility concept and its role in socialized charismatic leadership. *Journal of Leadership and Organizational Studies, 17,* 33–43.

[29]Page 1331 in Morris, J. A., Brotheridge, C. M., and Urbanski, J. C. (2005). Bringing humility to leadership: Antecedents and consequences of leader humility. *Human Relations, 58*(10): 1323–1350.

[30]Lawrence, P. (2008). Neohumility/Humility and business leadership: Do they belong together? *Journal of Business and Leadership, 2*(1): 116–126.

[31]See fn 29, Morris et al. (2012).

[32]Johnson, M. K., Rowatt, W. C., & Petrini, L. (2011). A new trait on the market: Honesty-humility as a unique predictor of job performance ratings. *Personality and Individual Differences, 50*(6), 857–862.

[33]Pages 718–119 in Dyck, B. & Schroeder, D. (2005). Management, theology and moral points of view: Towards an alternative to the conventional materialist-individualist ideal-type of management. *Journal of Management Studies, 42* (4), 705–735; see also pages 13–14 in Greenleaf, R. K. (1977). *Servant leadership: A journey in the nature of legitimate power and greatness.* New York: Paulist Press.

[34]LaBouff, J., Rowatt, W. C., Johnson, M. K., Tsang, J., & Willerton, G. (2012). Humble persons are more helpful than less humble persons: Evidence from three studies. *The Journal of Positive Psychology, 7*(1), 16–29.

[35]See fn 27, Diddams & Chang (2012).

[36]Dunning, D., Heath, C., & Suls, J. (2004). Flawed self-assessment: Implications for health, education and the workplace. *Psychological Science in the Public Interest, 5*(3), 69–106.

[37]Coates, B. (2010). Cracking into the panes of corporate denial. *Business Renaissance Quarterly, 5*(3), 23–46.

[38]The Johari Window is attributed to Joseph Luft and Harry Ingham in use at Western Training Laboratory in Group

Development in 1955. Luft, J. (1984). *Group processes—An introduction to group dynamics*. Palo Alto: Mayfield.

[39]Ashford, S. J. (1986). Feedback-seeking in individual adaptation: A resources perspective. *Academy of Management Journal, 29*(3), 465–487.

[40]De Stobbeleir, M. K. E., Ashford, S. J., & Buyens, D. (2011). Self-regulation of creativity at work: The role of feedback seeking behavior in creative performance. *Academy of Management Journal, 54*(4), 811–831.

[41]Lord, R. G., & Hall, R. J. (2005). Identity, deep structure, and the development of leadership skill. *The Leadership Quarterly, 16*(4), 591–615; Branson, C. (2007). Effects of structured self-reflection on the development of authentic leadership practices among Queenstand primary school principals. *Educational Management Administration & Leadership, 35*(2), 225–246.

[42]Shamir, B., & Eilam, G. (2005). "What's your story?" A life stories approach to authentic leadership development. *The Leadership Quarterly, 16*(3), 395–417.

[43]Shepherd, M. (2006). Using a learning journal to improve professional practice: A journey of personal and professional self-discovery. *Reflective Practice, 7*(3), 333–348.

[44]Manz, C.C. (1986). Self-leadership: Toward an expanded theory of self-influence processes in organizations. *Academy of Management Review, 11*, 585–600; Neck, C., & Houghton, J. (2006). Two decades of self-leadership theory and research: Past developments, present trends, and future possibilities. *Journal of Managerial Psychology, 21*, 270–295.

[45]See fn 41, Branson (2007); fn 42, Shamir & Eilam (2005).

[46]Stewart, G. L., Courtright, S. H., & Manz, C. C. (2011). Self-Leadership: A multilevel review. *Journal of Management, 37*(1), 185–222; Neck, C. P., & Manz, C. C. (2010). *Mastering self-leadership: Empowering yourself for personal excellence* (5th ed.). Upper Saddle River, NJ: Prentice Hall.

[47]See fn 46, Stewart et al. (2011).

[48]Raabe, B., Frese, M., & Beehr, T. A. (2007). Action regulation theory and career self-management. *Journal of Vocational Behavior, 70*, 297–311.

[49]Unsworth, K. L., & Mason, C. M. (2012). Help yourself: The mechanisms through which a self-leadership intervention influences strain. *Journal of Occupational Health Psychology, 17*, 235–245.

[50]Birdi, K., Clegg, C., Patterson, M., Robinson, A., Stride, C. B., Wall, T. D., & Wood, S. J. (2008). The impact of human resources and operational management practices on company productivity: A longitudinal study. *Personnel Psychology, 61*, 467–501.

[51]Neubert, M. J., & Wu, C. (2006). An investigation of the generalizability of the Houghton and Neck revised self-leadership questionnaire to a Chinese context. *Journal of Managerial Psychology, 21*(4), 360–373.

[52]Stewart, G. L., Carson, K. P., & Cardy, R. L. (1996). The joint effects of conscientiousness and self-leadership training on employee self-directed behavior in a service context, *Personnel Psychology, 49*, 143–164.

[53]See fn 46, Stewart et al. (2011).

[54]See fn 46, Stewart et al. (2011).

[55]Tucker, S., Turner, N., Barling, J., Reid, E., & Elving, C. (2006). Apologies and transformational leadership. *Journal of Business Ethics, 63*(2), 195–207.

[56]A clip of this SNL skit can be seen at http://www.youtube.com/watch?v=-DIETlxquzY. Accessed October 1, 2012.

[57]See fn 46, Stewart et al. (2011); Houghton, J. D., & Jinkerson, D. L. (2007). Constructive thought strategies and job satisfaction: A preliminary examination. *Journal of Business and Psychology, 22*(1), 45–53.

[58]O'Boyle, T. F. (1998). *At any cost: Jack Welch, General Electric, and the pursuit of profit*. New York: Alfred A. Knopf.

[59]See fn 57, Houghton & Jinkerson (2007).

[60]Dyck, B., Walker, K., Starke, F. A., & Uggerslev, K. (2012). Enhancing critical thinking by teaching two distinct approaches to management. *Journal of Education for Business, 87*(6), 343–357.

[61]Robinson, J. (2011). The years of living dangerously. *Entrepreneur, 39*(9), 75–78.

[62]See fn 61, Robinson (2011).

[63]Weber, M. (1958; original 1904). *The protestant ethic and the spirit of capitalism*. (trans. T Parsons). New York: Scribner's.

[64]Hirschi, A. (2011). Callings in career: A typological approach to essential and optional components. *Journal of Vocational Behavior, 79*, 60–73; Bunderson, J. S., & Thompson, J. A (2009). The call of the wild: Zookeepers, callings, and the double-edged sword of deeply meaningful work. *Administrative Science Quarterly, 54*, 32–57.

[65]Dobrow, S. R., & Tosti-Kharas, J. (2011). Calling: The development of a scale measure. *Personnel Psychology, 64*, 1001–1049.

[66]Duffy, R. D., Dik, B. J., & Steger, M. S. (2011). Calling and work related outcomes: Career commitment as a mediator. *Journal of Vocational Behavior, 78*, 210–218; Peterson, C., Park, N., Hall, N., & Seligman, M. E. P. (2009). Zest and work. *Journal of Organizational Behavior, 30*, 161–172.

[67]Duffy, R. D., Bott, E. M., Allan, B. A., Torrey, C. L., & Dik, B. J. (2012). Perceiving a calling, living a calling, and job satisfaction: Testing a moderated, multiple mediator model. *Journal of Counseling Psychology, 59*, 50–59.

[68]Le Fevre, M., Matheny, J., & Kolt, S.K. (2003). Eustress, distress, and interpretation in occupational stress. *Journal of Managerial Psychology, 18*(7), 726–744.

[69]Nixon, A. E., Mazzola, J. J., Bauer, J., Krueger, J. R., & Spector, P. E. (2011). Can work make you sick? A meta-analysis of the relationships between job stressors and physical symptoms. *Work & Stress, 25*(1), 1–22.

[70]Ciccone, A. (2012, August 9). Bad bosses cause employee stress, poor health. *The Huffington Post*. Retrieved from http://www.huffingtonpost.com/2012/08/06/bad-bosses-employee-stress_n_1747565.html.

[71]Livingston, G. (2013, Mary 14). Work a source of anxiety for many Canadians. *The Globe and Mail*. Retrieved from http://www.theglobeandmail.com/report-on-business/careers/career-advice/life-at-work/work-a-source-of-anxiety-for-many-canadians/article11918348/

[72]Maslach, C., Schaufeli, W. B., & Leiter, M. P. (2001). Job burnout. *Annual Review of Psychology, 52*, 397–422.

[73]Semmer, N. K., McGrath, J. E., & Beehr, T. A. (2005). Conceptual issues in research on stress and health. In C. L. Hooper (Ed.), *Handbook of stress medicine and health* (pp. 1–43). 2nd ed. London: CRC Press.

[74]Purvanova, R. K., & Muros, J. P. (2010). Gender differences in burnout: A meta-analysis. *Journal of Vocational Behavior, 77*(2), 168–185.

[75]See fn 69, Nixon et al. (2011).

[76]Crompton, S. (2014, April 23). What's stressing the stressed? Main sources of stress among workers. Statistics Canada. Retrieved from http://www.statcan.gc.ca/pub/11-008-x/2011002/article/11562-eng.htm

[77]Hecht, T. D., & McCarthy, J. M. (2010). Coping with employee, family, and student roles: Evidence of dispositional conflict and facilitation tendencies. *Journal of Applied Psychology, 95*(4), 631–647.

[78]Michel, J. S., Kotrba, L. M., Mitchelson, J. K., Clark, M. A., & Baltes, B. B. (2011). Antecedents of work-family conflict: A meta-analytic review. *Journal of Organizational Behavior, 32*(5), 689–725; Kahn, R. L., Wolfe, D. M., Quinn, R. P., Snoek, J. D., & Rosenthal, R. A. (1964). *Organizational stress: Studies in role conflict and ambiguity.* New York: Wiley.

[79]McMillan, H. S., Morris, M., & Atchley, E. (2011). Constructs of the work/life interface: A synthesis of the literature and introduction of the concept of work/life harmony. *Human Resource Development Review, 10*(1), 6–25.

[80]Grawitch, M. J., Maloney, P. W., Barber, L. K., & Mooshegian, S. E. (2013). Examining the nomological network of satisfaction with work-life balance. *Journal of Occupational Health Psychology,* doi:10.1037/a0032754.

[81]Carlson, D. S., Kacmar, K. M., & Williams, L. J. (2000). Construction and initial validation of a multidimensional measure of work-family conflict. *Journal of Vocational Behavior, 56,* 249–276.

[82]See fn 79, McMillan et al. (2011).

[83]Greenhaus, J. H., & Beutell, N. J. (1985). Sources of conflict between work and family roles. *Academy of Management Review, 10,* 76–88.

[84]Seiger, C. P., & Wiese, B. S. (2009). Social support from work and family domains as an antecedent or moderator of work-family conflicts? *Journal of Vocational Behavior, 75,* (2009), 26–37.

[85]See fn 78, Michel et al. (2011); Allen, T. D., Johnson, R. C., Saboe, K. N., Cho, E., Dumani, S., & Evans, S. (2012). Dispositional variables and work-family conflict: A meta-analysis. *Journal of Vocational Behavior, 80*(1), 17–26.

[86]Hoobler, J. M., Hu, J., & Wilson, M. (2010). Do workers who experience conflict between the work and family domains hit a 'glass ceiling'?: A meta-analytic examination. *Journal of Vocational Behavior, 77*(3), 481–494.

[87]Carlson, D. S., Grzywacz, J. G., Ferguson, M., Hunter, E., Clinch, C. R., & Acury, T. (2011). Health and turnover of working mothers after childbirth via the work-family interface: An analysis across time. *Journal of Applied Psychology, 96,* 1045–1054.

[88]Watkin, S. (2011, March 29). Cooper details WorldCom fraud experience at Xavier speech. *Cincinnati Business Courier.* Retrieved from http://www.biz-journals.com/cincinnati/blog/2011/03/cooper-details-world-com-fraud.html?page=all.

[89]Health Canada. (2008, January). *Mental health - Coping with stress.* Retrieved from http://www.hc-sc.gc.ca/hl-vs/iyh-vsv/life-vie/stress-eng.php

[90]Shea, C. (2014, December 19). Conrad Black on creative problem-solving (and how to write 3,000 words a day). *Canadian Business.* Retrieved from http://www.canadianbusiness.com/leadership/conrad-black-rise-to-greatness/.

[91]Hobfoll, S. E. (1989). Conservation of resources: A new attempt at conceptualizing stress. *American Psychologist, 44,* 513–524; Hobfoll, S. (2002). Social and psychological resources and adaptations. *Review of General Psychology, 6,* 302–324.

[92]See fn 77, Hecht & McCarthy (2010); fn 86, Hoobler et al. (2010).

[93]Gilbreath, B. (2012). Educating managers to create healthy workplaces. *Journal of Management Education, 36*(2), 166–190.

[94]Jex, S. M., Bliese, P. D., Buzzell, S., & Primeau, J. (2001). The impact of self-efficacy on stressor-strain relations: Coping style as an explanatory mechanism. *Journal of Applied Psychology, 86*(3), 401–409.

[95]de Jonge, J., Spoor, E., Sonnentag, S., Dormann, C., & van den Tooren, M. (2012). 'Take a break?' Off-job recovery, job demands, and job resources as predictors of health, active learning, and creativity. *European Journal of Work and Organizational Psychology, 21*(3), 321–348; Fritz, C., Sonnentag, S., Spector, P. E., & McInroe, J. A. (2010). The weekend matters: Relationships between stress recovery and affective experiences. *Journal of Organizational Behavior, 31*(8), 1137–1162; Kühnel, J., & Sonnentag, S. (2011). How long do you benefit from vacation? A closer look at the fade-out of vacation effects. *Journal of Organizational Behavior, 32*(1), 125–143.

[96]See fn 78, Michel et al. (2011).

[97]Byron, K., Khazanchi, S., & Nazarian, D. (2010). The relationship between stressors and creativity: A meta-analysis examining competing theoretical models. *Journal of Applied Psychology, 95,* 201–212.

[98]McNall, L. A., Nicklin, J. M., & Masuda, A. D. (2010). A meta-analytic review of the consequences associated with work-family enrichment. *Journal of Business and Psychology, 25*(3), 381–396.

[99]Nickerson, R. S. (1999). Enhancing creativity. In R. J. Sternberg (Ed.), *Handbook of Creativity* (pp. 392–430). New York: Cambridge University Press, 1999 (pp. 392–430); Kabanoff, B., & Rossiter, J. R. (1994). Recent developments in applied creativity. *International Review of Industrial and Organizational Psychology, 9,* 283–324; Oxenfeldt, A., Miller, D., & Dickinson, R. (1978). *A basic approach to executive decision making.* New York: Amacon.

[100]Appelo, T. (2011, October 14). How a calligraphy pen rewrote Steve Jobs' life. *The Hollywood Reporter.* Retrieved from http://www.hollywoodreporter.com/news/steve-jobs-death-apple-calligraphy-248900.

[101]Amabile, T. M. (2000). Stimulate creativity by fueling passion. In E. A. Locke (Ed.), *The Blackwell Handbook of Principles of Organizational Behavior* (pp. 331–341). Oxford, England: Blackwell; Weisberg, R. W. (1999). Creativity and knowledge: A challenge to theories. In R. J. Sternberg (Ed.), *Handbook of Creativity* (pp. 226–250). New York: Cambridge University Press; Amabile, T. M. (1988). A model of creativity and innovation in organizations. *Research in Organizational Behavior, 10,* 123–167; Woodman, R., Sawyer, J. E., & Griffin, R. W. (1993). Toward a theory of organizational creativity. *Academy of Management Review, 18,* 293–321.

[102]Simonton, D. K. (2000). Creativity: Cognitive, personal, developmental, and social aspects. *American Psychologist, 55,* 151–158; Barron, F. B., & Harrington, D. M. (1981). Creativity, intelligence, and personality. *Annual Review of Psychology, 32,* 439–476; MacKinnon, D. W. (1965). The nature and nurture of creative talent. In H. J. Leavitt (Ed.), *Readings in Managerial Psychology.* Chicago: University of Chicago Press; Vessels, G. (1982). The creative process: An open systems conceptualization. *Journal of Creative Behavior, 16,* 185–196.

[103]Mumford, M. D. (2000). Managing creative people: Strategies and tactics for innovation. *Human Resource Management Review, 10*, 313–351; Amabile, T. M. (1998, September-October). How to kill creativity. *Harvard Business Review,* 76–87; Steiner, G. A. (1965). *The creative organization.* Chicago: University of Chicago Press; Zaltman, G., Duncan, R., & Holbek, J. (1973). *Innovations and organizations.* New York: Wiley; Femina, J. D., & Sopkin, C. (1970). *From those wonderful folks who brought you Pearl Harbor.* New York: Simon and Schuster; Baker, N. R., Winofsky, E., Langmeyer, L., & Sweeney, D. J. (1976). *Idea generation.* Cincinnati: University of Cincinnati.

[104]Bell, S. T., Villado, A. J., Lukasik, M. A., Belau, L., & Briggs, A. L. (2011). Getting specific about demographic diversity variable and team performance relationships: A meta-analysis. *Journal of Management, 37*(3), 709–743.

[105]See fn 104, Bell et al. (2011).

[106]PwC Canada. (2015). Transaction services: Helping compete deals with less disruption. Retrieved from http://www.pwc.com/ca/en/transaction-service/index.jhtml.

[107]Glass, D. (1996, June 10). Hallmark nurtures worker creativity. *The Globe and Mail,* p. B9.

[108]Shea, C. (2015, February 20). Elaine "Lainey Gossip" Lui on turning a passion into a job. *Canadian Business.* Retrieved from http://www.canadianbusiness.com/leadership/interview-elaine-lui-lainey-gossip/; Rinehart, D. (2014, April 4). Lainey Gossip blogger Elaine Lui reveals all in her new book. *Toronto Star.* Retrieved from http://www.thestar.com/life/2014/04/04/laineygossip_blogger_elaine_lui_reveals_all_in_her_new_book.html; Landau, E. (2014, April 2). In lurv with Lainey: Elaine Lui's rise to the top of the gossip pantheon. *Toronto Life.* Retrieved from http://www.torontolife.com/informer/features/2014/04/02/in-lurv-with-lainey/?page=all#tlb_multipage_anchor_3; Kingston, A. (2013, February 19). Lainey Lui: Canada's gossip magnate. *Maclean's.* Retrieved from http://www.macleans.ca/economy/business/canadas-gossip-magnate-2/; TEDx. (2013, February 6). The sociology of gossip: Elaine Lui at TEDxVancouver [video]. Retrieved from http://tedxtalks.ted.com/video/The-Sociology-of-Gossip-Elaine; CTV. (2015). About The Social - Lainey Lui. Retrieved from http://www.thesocial.ca/About/Lainey; Allen, J. (2014, January 15). Five questions with Elaine Lui. CTV. Retrieved from http://www.thesocial.ca/thejessfiles/five-questions-with-elaine-lui.

[109]Ning, D., Lew, M., & Schmidt, H.G. (2011). Writing to learn: Can reflection journals be used to promote self-reflection and learning? *Higher Education Research & Development, 30*(4), 519–532.

Feature Notes

My OB: How Real Is Reality TV?   Writers Guild of America, West. (2015). How reality TV works. Retrieved from http://www.wga.org/organizesub.aspx?id=1091;   Feloni, R. (2015, February 4). 'Shark Tank' investor Kevin O'Leary explains why 'business is war'. *Business Insider.* Retrieved from http://www.businessinsider.com/shark-tank-investor-kevin-oleary-2015-2; MacRae, D. (2014, October 24). From cameraman to Mr. Wonderful: Kevin O'Leary on where he started and what's coming up on 'Shark Tank.' CTV. Retrieved from http://www.ctv.ca/SharkTank/Articles/News/Kevin_OLeary_Shark_Tank.aspx.

OB in Action: Conrad Black in the Red   Shea, C. (2014, December 19). Conrad Black on creative problem-solving (and how to write 3,000 words a day). *Canadian Business.* Retrieved from http://www.canadianbusiness.com/leadership/conrad-black-rise-to-greatness/; Hustak, A. & Marshall, T. (2015, June 23). Conrad Moffat Black. *The Canadian Encyclopedia.* Retrieved from http://www.thecanadianencyclopedia.ca/en/article/conrad-moffat-black/; Harper, T. (2014, January 31). Conrad Black joins exclusive club of shame. *Toronto Star.* Retrieved from http://www.thestar.com/news/canada/2014/01/31/conrad_black_joins_exclusive_club_of_shame_tim_harper.html; The Canadian Press. (2014, January 31). Conrad Black stripped of the Order of Canada. *The Globe and Mail.* Retrieved from http://www.theglobeandmail.com/news/national/conrad-black-stripped-of-the-order-of-canada/article16644365/

OB in Action: Is First Really the Worst?   Pachner, J. (2010, March 15). How to recognize work burnout. *Canadian Business.* Retrieved from http://www.canadianbusiness.com/business-strategy/how-to-recognize-work-burnout/.

OB Action: Give Me a Break   FullContact. (2011–2013). About us. Retrieved from http://www.fullcontact.com/about/; Sandell, C. (2012, July 14). Boss gives employees $7,500 for vacations. Retrieved from http://news.yahoo.com/blogs/abc-blogs/boss-gives-employees-7-500-vacations-143431561-abc-news-topstories.html.

Chapter 8

[1]Acharya-Tom Yew, M. (2015, February 27). OSC slaps permanent ban on Conrad Black. *The Toronto Star.* Retrieved from http://www.thestar.com/business/2015/02/27/osc-slaps-permanent-ban-on-conrad-black.html; CBC News. (2010, July 5). Timeline: Conrad Black through the years. Retrieved from http://www.cbc.ca/news/canada/conrad-black-through-the-years-1.868133; Globe Debate. (2007, July 14). The fall of Conrad Black. *The Globe and Mail.* Retrieved from http://www.theglobeandmail.com/globe-debate/the-fall-of-conrad-black/article1078338/; KPMG. (2013). *KPMG Forensic: Integrity survey 2013.* Retrieved from https://www.kpmg.com/CN/en/IssuesAndInsights/ArticlesPublications/Documents/Integrity-Survey-2013-O-201307.pdf; KPMG. (2011). *KPMG Analysis of global patterns of fraud: Who is the typical fraudster?* Retrieved from https://www.kpmg.com/CEE/en/IssuesAndInsights/ArticlesPublications/Documents/who-is-the-typical-fraudster.pdf; KPMG. (2013). *Global profile of the fraudster: White-collar crime—present and future.* Retrieved from http://advisory.kpmg.us/content/dam/kpmg-advisory/PDFs/RiskConsulting/global-profiles-fraudster.pdf; Pitts, D. (2012, May 3). Analysis: Claiming Conrad Black as our own. *CBC News.* Retrieved from http://www.cbc.ca/news/business/claiming-conrad-black-as-our-own-1.1197701; Tedesco, T. (2012, May 24). Conrad Black moves to end Hollinger CCAA. *Financial Post.* Retrieved from http://business.financialpost.com/news/fp-street/conrad-black-moves-to-end-hollinger-ccaa. "Biography of Conrad Black," *National Post.* Retrieved from http://www.financialpost.com/story.html?id=ff18a624-c20b-481c-ab6b-822b4111258c. The Canadian Press, "Ontario regulator allows Conrad Black to testify on activities at Hollinger," CP24.

(2014, October 8). Retrieved from http://www.cp24.com/news/ontario-regulator-allows-conrad-black-to-testify-on-activities-at-hollinger-1.2044875. "Conrad Black stripped of Order of Canada," BBC News. (2014, February 1). Retrieved from http://HYPERLINK "http://www.bbc.com/news/world-us-canada-25996644" www.bbc.com/news/world-us-canada-25996644. "SEC files fraud charges against Conrad Black, F. David Radler and Hollinger Inc." U.S. Securities and Exchange Commission news release. (2004, November 15).

[2]Starke, F., & Sexty, R. (1998), *Contemporary management.* (p. 380). Scarborough, ON: Prentice-Hall Canada, Inc.

[3]Kacmar, K. M., Andrews, M., Harris, K., & Tepper, B. (2013). Ethical leadership and subordinate outcomes: The mediating role of organizational politics and the moderating role of political skill. *Journal of Business Ethics, 115*(1), 33–44; Ferris, G. R., Treadway, D. C., Perrewe, P. L., Brouer, R. L., Douglas, C., & Lux, S. (2007). Political skill in organizations. *Journal of Management, 33,* 290–320.

[4]See fn 3, Kacmar et al. (2013).

[5]Chang, C., Rosen, C. C., & Levy, P. E. (2009). The relationship between perceptions of organizational politics and employee attitudes, strain, and behavior: A meta-analytics examination. *Academy of Management Journal, 52*(4), 779–801; Kacmar, K. M., Bozeman, D. P., Carlson, D. S., & Anthony, W. P. (1999). An examination of the perceptions of organizational politics model: Replication and extension. *Human Relations, 52*(3), 383–416.

[6]Kiewitz, C., Restubog, S. D., Zagenczyk, T., & Hochwarter, W. (2009). The interactive effects of psychological contract breach and organizational politics on perceived organizational support: Evidence from two longitudinal studies. *Journal of Management Studies, 46*(5), 806–834.

[7]See fn 5, Kacmar et al. (1999).

[8]Gandz, J. V., & Murray, V. V. (1980). The experience of workplace politics. *Academy of Management Journal, 23,* 237–251.

[9]Goldner F. H. (1970). Success vs. failure: Prior managerial perspective. *Industrial Relations,* 457–474.

[10]Atinc, G., Darrat, M., Fuller, B., & Parker, B. W. (2010). Perceptions of organizational politics: A meta-analysis of theoretical antecedents. *Journal of Managerial Issues, 22*(4), 494–513.

[11]See fn 3, Kacmar et al. (2013).

[12]See fn 10, Atinc et al. (2010).

[13]Kacmar, K., Bachrach, D. G., Harris, K. J., & Zivnuska, S. (2011). Fostering good citizenship through ethical leadership: Exploring the moderating role of gender and organizational politics. *Journal of Applied Psychology, 96*(3), 633–642.

[14]Dickler, J. (2010, January 21). I work for one of the 10 best companies. *CNN Money.* Retrieved from http://money.cnn.com/galleries/2010/fortune/1001/gallery.Bestcom-panies_employees.fortune/2.html

[15]Uzzi, B. (1997). Social structure and competition in interfirm networks. *Administrative Science Quarterly, 42*(1), 35–68.

[16]Robinson, S. L. (1996). Trust and breach of the psychological contract. *Administrative Science Quarterly, 41,* 574–599.

[17]Rousseau, D. M. (1995). *Psychological contracts in organizations: Understanding written and unwritten agreement.* Thousand Oaks, CA: Sage.

[18]Zagenczyk, T. J., Gibney, R., Few, W. T., & Scott, K. L. (2011). Psychological contracts and organizational identification: The mediating effect of perceived organizational support. *Journal of Labor Research, 32*(3), 254–281.

[19]Johnson, J. L., & O'Leary-Kelly, A. M. (2003). The effects of psychological contract breach and organizational cynicism: Not all social exchange violations are created equal. *Journal of Organizational Behavior, 24,* 627–647.

[20]Chua, R., Ingram, P., & Morris, M. W. (2008). From the head and the heart: Locating cognition- and affect-based trust in managers professional networks. *Academy of Management Journal, 51*(3), 436–452; Ibarra, H., & Andrews, S. B. (1993). Power, social influence, and sense making: Effects of network centrality and proximity on employee perceptions. *Administrative Science Quarterly, 38*(2) 277–303.

[21]Colquitt, J. A., & Rodell, J. B. (2011). Justice, trust, and trustworthiness: A longitudinal analysis integrating three perspectives. *Academy of Management Journal, 54*(6), 1183–1206; Mayer, R. C., Davis, J. H., & Schoorman, F. D. (1995). An integrative model of organizational trust. *Academy of Management Review, 20,* 709–734.

[22]Chua, R. J., Morris, M. W., & Mor, S. (2012). Collaborating across cultures: Cultural metacognition and affect-based trust in creative collaboration. *Organizational Behavior & Human Decision Processes, 118*(2), 116–131.

[23]Ibid.

[24]Peus, C., Wesche, J., Streicher, B., Braun, S., & Frey, D. (2012). Authentic leadership: An empirical rest of its antecedents, consequences, and mediating mechanisms. *Journal of Business Ethics, 107*(3), 331–348; Avolio, B. J., Gardner, W. L., Walumbwa, F. O., Luthans, F., & May, D. R. (2004). Unlocking the mask: A look at the process by which authentic leaders impact follower attitudes and behaviors. *The Leadership Quarterly, 15,* 801–823.

[25]Leroy, H., Palanski, M., & Simons, T. (2012). Authentic leadership and behavioral integrity as drivers of follower commitment and performance. *Journal of Business Ethics, 107*(3), 255–264.

[26]Niven, K., Holman, D., & Totterdell, P. (2012). How to win friendship and trust by influencing people's feelings: An investigation of interpersonal affect regulation and the quality of relationships. *Human Relations, 65*(6), 777–805.

[27]Colquitt, J. A., Scott, B. A., & LePine, J. A. (2007). Trust, trustworthiness, and trust propensity: Meta-analytic test of their unique relationships with risk taking and job performance. *Journal of Applied Psychology, 92,* 909–927; Mayer, R. C., & Gavin, M. B. (2005). Trust in management and performance: Who minds the shop while the employees watch the boss? *Academy of Management Journal, 48,* 874–888; Khazanchi, S., & Master-son, S. S. (2011). Who and what is fair matters: A multi-foci social exchange model of creativity. *Journal of Organizational Behavior, 32*(1), 86–106.

[28]Dirks, K. T., & Ferrin, D. L. (2002). Trust in leadership: Meta-analytic findings and implications for research and practice. *Journal of Applied Psychology, 87,* 611–628.

[29]Guenzi, P., & Georges, L. (2010). Interpersonal trust in commercial relationships: Antecedents and consequences of customer trust in the salesperson. *European Journal of Marketing, 44*(1–2), 114–138.

[30]Malloch, T. (2010). Doing virtual business. (Transcript). Retrieved from http://www.w.fyi.org/doingvirtuousbusiness/DVBtranscript.pdf.

[31]Ibid.

[32]Adapted from Clifton Williams, *Effective Leadership.* LTrek Corporation Inc.

[33]Leana, C. R. (1986). Predictors and consequences of delegation. *Academy of Management Journal, 29*(4), 754–774; Yukl, G., & Fu, P. (1999). Determinants of delegation and consultation by managers. *Journal of Organizational Behavior, 20*(2), 219–232.

[34]See fn 33, Yukl & Fu (1999).

[35]See fn 33, Leana (1986); Yukl & Fu (1999).

[36]Locke, E. A., & Latham, G. P. (1990). *A theory of goal setting and task performance.* Englewood Cliffs, NJ: Prentice Hall.

[37]Klein, K. J., Ziegert, J. C., Knight, A. P., & Xiao, Y. (2006). Dynamic delegation: Shared, hierarchical, and deindividualized leadership in extreme action teams. *Administrative Science Quarterly, 51*(4), 590–621.

[38]Colquitt, J. A., Conlon, D. E., Wesson, M. J., Porter, C. O., & Ng, K. Y. (2001). Justice at the millennium: A meta-analytic review of 25 years of organizational justice research. *Journal of Applied Psychology, 86,* 425–445.

[39]Jones, D. A., & Martens, M. L. (2009). The mediating role of overall fairness and the moderating role of trust certainty in justice-criteria relationships: The formation and use of fairness heuristics in the workplace. *Journal of Organizational Behavior, 30*(8), 1025–1051.

[40]Maxham III, J. G., & Netemeyer, R. G. (2003). Firms reap what they sow: The effects of shared values and perceived organizational justice on customers' evaluations of complaint handling. *Journal of Marketing, 67*(1), 46–62.

[41]Cropanzano, R., Bowen, D. E., & Gilliland, S. W. (2007). The management of organizational justice. *Academy of Management Perspectives, 21*(4), 34–48.

[42]Colquitt, J. A. (2001). On the dimensionality of organizational justice: A construct validation of a measure. *Journal of Applied Psychology, 86*(3), 386–400.

[43]Viswesvaran, C., & Ones, D. S. (2002). *Journal of Business Ethics, 38*(3), 193–203.

[44]Colquitt, J. A., Noe, R. A., & Jackson, C. L. (2002). Justice in teams: Antecedents and consequences of procedural justice climate. *Personnel Psychology, 55*(1), 83–109.

[45]Wu, J. C., Neubert, M. J., & Yi, X. (2007). Transformational leadership, cohesion perceptions, and employee cynicism about organizational change: The mediating role of justice perceptions. *Journal of Applied Behavioral Science, 43*(3), 327–351.

[46]Colquitt, J. A., Piccolo, R. F., LePine, J. A., Zapata, C. P., & Rich, B. L. (2012). Explaining the justice-performance relationship: Trust as exchange deepener or trust as uncertainty reducer? *Journal of Applied Psychology, 97*(1), 1–15.

[47]Hooker, J. (2009, November 2). A cross cultural view of corruption. Ethisphere. Retrieved from http://ethisphere.com/a-cross-cultural-view-of-corruption/.

[48]Maaravi, Y., Ganzach, Y., & Pazy, A. (2011). Negotiation as a form of persuasion: Arguments in first offers. *Journal of Personality and Social Psychology.* Advance online publication. doi: 10.1037/a0023331.

[49]Lewicki, R. J., Saunders, D. M., & Barry, B. (2011). *Essentials of negotiation.* (5th ed.) New York, NY: McGraw-Hill.

[50]Sebenius, J. K. (2001). Six habits of merely effective negotiators. *Harvard Business Review, 79*(4), 87–95.

[51]Kipnis, D., Schmidt, S. M., & Wilkinson, I. (1980). Intraorganizational influence tactics: Explorations in getting one's way. *Journal of Applied Psychology, 65,* 440–452.

[52]Higgins, C. A., Judge, T. A., & Ferris, G. R. (2003). Influence tactics and work outcomes: A meta-analysis. *Journal of Organizational Behavior, 24*(1), 89–106.

[53]Yukl, G. (2002). *Leadership in organizations.* Upper Saddle River, NJ: Prentice Hall.

[54]Ibid.

[55]Gunia, B. C., Brett, J. M., Kamdar, D., & Nandkeolyar, A. (2011). Paying a price: Culture, trust, and negotiation consequences. *Journal of Applied Psychology, 96*(4), 774–789.

[56]Galinsky, A., & Mussweiler, T. (2001). First offers as anchors: The role of perspective-taking and negotiator focus. *Journal of Personality and Social Psychology, 81*(4), 657–669.

[57]Hilty & Carnevale. (1993). Black hat/white hat strategy in bilateral negotiation. *Organizational Behavior and Human Decision Processes, 55*(3), 444–469.

[58]Fisher, R., & Ury, W. (1981). *Getting to yes: Negotiating agreement without giving in.* Boston, MA: Houghton Mifflin.

[59]Pinkley, R. L., Neale, M. A., & Bennett, R. J. (1994). The impact of alternatives to settlement in dyadic negotiation. *Organizational Behavior and Human Decision Processes, 57,* 97–116.

[60]Pinkley, R. L., Griffith, T. L., & Northcraft, G. B. (1995). "Fixed-pie" à la mode: Information availability, information processing, and the negotiation of suboptimal agreements. *Organizational Behavior and Human Decision Processes, 62,* 101–112.

[61]Adapted from Patton, B. (2004). Building relationships and the bottom line: The circle of value approach to negotiation. *Negotiation 7*(4), 4–7.

[62]Trötschel, R., Hüffmeier, J., Loschelder, D. D., Schwartz, K., & Gollwitzer, P. M. (2011). Perspective taking as a means to overcome motivational barriers in negotiations: When putting oneself into the opponent's shoes helps to walk toward agreements. *Journal of Personality and Social Psychology, 101*(4), 771–790.

[63]Han, I., Kwon, S., Bae, J., & Park, K. (2012). When are integrative tactics more effective? The moderating effects of moral identity and the use of distributive tactics. *International Journal of Conflict Management, 23*(2), 133–150.

[64]Cai, D. A., & Fink, E. L. (2002). Conflict style differences between individualists and collectivists. *Communication Monographs, 69*(1), 67–87; Volkema, R. J., & Bergmann, T. J. (1995). Conflict styles as indicators of behavioral patterns in interpersonal conflicts. *Journal of Social Psychology, 135*(1), 5–15; Rahim, M. A. (1983). A measure of styles of handling interpersonal conflict. *Academy of Management Journal, 26*(2), 368–376; Antonioni, D. (1999). Relationship between the big five personality factors and conflict management styles. *Journal of Conflict Management, 9*(4), 336–355.

[65]Gundlach, M., Zivnuska, S., & Stoner, J. (2006). Understanding the relationship between individualism–collectivism and team performance through an integration of social identity theory and the social relations model. *Human Relations, 59*(12), 1603–1632.

[66]Ma, Z. (2007). Conflict management styles as indicators of behavioral pattern in business negotiation: The impact of contextualism in two countries. *International Journal of Conflict Management, 18*(3–4), 260–279.

[67]Yale School of Management. (2010). *The Tata Group: Can Indian-style capitalism survive global capital markets?* Retrieved from http://nexus.som.yale.edu/tata/?q=node/114.

[68]Connon, H. (2008). Tea, cars, steel, IT . . . Tata, the headiest brew in the world. *The Observer.* Retrieved from http://

www.guardian.co.uk/business/2008/may/04/mergersand acquisitions.india.

[69]Graham, A. (2010, February 23). Too good to fail. *strategy+business, 58.* Retrieved from http://www.strategy-business.com/article/10106?gko= 74e5d.

[70]Seetharaman, G. (2012, March 4). Caregiver: TCS tops best companies to work for list. *Business Today.* Retrieved from http://businesstoday.intoday.in/story/tata-consultancy-services-tcs-best-companies-to-work-indi/1/22285.html.

[71]Ibid.

[72]Mukherjee, D., Lahiri, S., Mukherjee, D., & Billing, T. K. (2012). Leading virtual teams: How do social, cognitive, and behavioral capabilities matter? *Management Decision, 50*(2), 273–290.

[73]Yukl, G. (1998). *Leadership in organizations.* (4th ed.). Upper Saddle River, NJ: Prentice Hall.

Feature Notes

My OB: Machiavellianism in the Workplace Christie, R., & Geis, F. L. (1970). *Studies in machiavellianism.* New York, NY: Academic Press.

OB in Action: Keeping a Lid on Layoffs CB Staff. (2014, November 10). Canada's best employers 2015: The top 50 large companies. *Canadian Business.* Retrieved from http://www.canadianbusiness.com/lists-and-rankings/best-jobs/2015-best-employers-top-50/; Grant, T. (2009, January 30). Where layoffs are not an option. *The Globe and Mail.* Retrieved from http://www.theglobeandmail.com/report-on-business/where-layoffs-are-not-an-option/article1152844/; Haddi, G. (2014, January 8). Empowering teamwork through trust (interview). *Trend Reports.* Retrieved from http://www.trendreports.com/article/delta-hotels; Zatzick, C., & Iverson, R. D. (2007). High-involvement management practices and work-force reduction: Competitive advantage or disadvantage? *Academy of Management Journal, 49*(5), 999–1015.

My OB: Fair or Foul Selvarajan, T. T., & Cloninger, P. A. (2012). Can performance appraisals motivate employees to improve performance? A Mexican study. *The International Journal of Human Resource Management, 23*(15), 3063–3084; Salimäki, A., & Jarnsen, S. (2010). Perceptions of politics and fairness in merit pay. *Journal of Managerial Psychology, 25*(3), 229–251; Cannon, M. D., & Witherspoon, R. (2005). Actionable feedback: Unlocking the power of learning and development. *Academy of Management Executive, 19,* 120–134.

My OB: How Skilled Are You at Understanding Others? Covey, S. R. (1989). *The 7 habits of highly effective people.* New York, NY: Simon & Schuster, Inc.; Bradberry, T., & Greaves, J. (2009). *Emotional intelligence 2.0.* San Diego, CA: TalentSmart; Trötschel, R., Hüffmeier, J., Loschelder, D. D., Schwartz, K., & Gollwitzer, P. M. (2011). Perspective taking as a means to overcome motivational barriers in negotiations: When putting oneself into the opponent's shoes helps to walk toward agreements. *Journal of Personality and Social Psychology, 101*(4), 771–790.

Chapter 9

[1]G Adventures. (2015). About us. Retrieved from https://www.gadventures.com/about-us/; G Adventures. (2015). Careers. Retrieved from https://www.gadventures.com/careers/?l=fnav; Lapelosová, K. (2014, April 11). Creating a company built on happiness: Bruce Poon Tip on Looptail and transformative travel with G Adventures. Matador Network. Retrieved from http://matadornetwork.com/bnt/creating-company-built-happiness-bruce-poon-tip-looptail-transformative-travel-gadventures/; Maimona, M. (2013, June 17). A travel guru's guide to good leadership. *Financial Post.* Retrieved from http://business.financialpost.com/entrepreneur/a-travel-gurus-guide-to-good-leadership; NSB. (2015). Bruce Poon Tip: Founder of G Adventures & NY Times bestselling author. National Speakers Bureau. Retrieved from http://nsb.com/speakers/bruce-poon-tip/; Poon Tip, B. (2013). *Looptail: How one company changed the world by reinventing business.* Toronto: HarperCollins; Smith, C. (2013, November 20). Dalai Lama helps G Adventures founder Bruce Poon Tip discover Looptail to happiness. *The Georgia Straight.* Retrieved from http://www.straight.com/life/534131/dalai-lama-helps-g-adventures-founder-bruce-poon-tip-discover-looptail-happiness; Poon Tip, B. (2010, October 8). Beyond the triple bottom line. TEDxToronto. Retrieved from https://www.youtube.com/watch?v=xbeUftMoFUQ

[2]This definition is drawn from the list of definitions on p. 3 of Yukl, G. (2013). *Leadership in organizations* (8th ed.). Upper Saddle River, NJ: Prentice Hall.

[3]Bass, B. M. (1985). *Leadership and performance beyond expectations.* New York: Free Press; Burns, J. M. (1978). *Leadership.* New York: Harper & Row.

[4]Judge, T. A., & Piccolo, R. F. (2004). Transformational and transactional leadership: A meta-analytic test of their relative validity. *Journal of Applied Psychology, 89*(5), 755–768; Pawar, B. S., & Eastman, K. K. (1997). The nature and implications of contextual influences on transformational leadership: A conceptual examination. *Academy of Management Review, 22*(1), 80–109.

[5]Farrell, G. (2005, April 25). A CEO and a gentleman. *USA Today,* B.1.

[6]Covin, G. (2008, Jan 8). AmEx gets CEO pay right. *Fortune.* http://money.cnn.com/magazines/fortune/fortune_archive/2008/01/21/102659595/indexhtm. Accessed January 6, 2009.

[7]American Express's Kenneth I. Chenault on Leadership. *FastCompany.* http://www.fastcompany.com/1276671/american-express%E2%80%99s-kenneth-i-chenault-leadership. Accessed May 14, 2013.

[8]DeCelles, K., & Pfarrer, M. (2004). Heroes or villains? Corruption and the charismatic leader. *Journal of Leadership and Organizational Studies, 11*(1), 67–77.

[9]See fn 2, Yukl (2013); Kirkpatrick, S. A., & Locke, E. A. (1991). Leadership: Do traits matter? *Academy of Management Executive, 5*(2), 48–60.

[10]Judge, T., Ilies, R., Bono, J., & Gerhardt, M. (2002). Personality and leadership: A qualitative and quantitative review. *Journal of Applied Psychology, 87*(4), 765–780.

[11]Waldman, D. A., & Javidan, M. (2009). Alternative forms of charismatic leadership in the integration of mergers and acquisitions. *The Leadership Quarterly, 20*(2), 130–142; McCall, M., & Lombardo, M. (1983). *Off the track: Why and how successful executives get derailed* (Technical Report No. 21). Greensboro, NC: Center for Creative Leadership.

[12]Spreier, S., Fontaine, M., & Malloy, R. (June 2006). Leadership run amok: The destructive potential of overachievers. *Harvard Business Review, 84*(6), 72–82.

[13]Collins, J. (2001). *Good to great: Why some companies make the leap . . . and others don't.* New York: HarperCollins.

[14]MFI International. Our company. http://www.mfiintl.com/our_company.asp. Accessed May 16, 2013.

[15]Renteria, R. (2011, September 4). A force for change: Maquiladora owner works to transform Juarez in campaign. *El Paso Times.* Retrieved from http://www.elpasotimes.com/business/ci_18821677

[16]The AES Corporation. (2013). About us. Retrieved from http://www.aes.com/about-us/about-us-overview/default.aspx; Bakke, D. (2005). *Joy at work: A revolutionary approach to fun on the job.* Seattle: PVG; Wetluafer, S. (1999). Organizing for empowerment: An interview with Roger Sant and Dennis Bakke. *Harvard Business Review, 77*(1), 110–123.

[17]Charan, R. (2007). *Know how: The 8 skills that separate people who perform from those who don't.* New York: Crown.

[18]Goleman, D. (2001). Emotional intelligence: Issues in paradigm building. In C. Cherniss & D. Goleman (Eds.), *The emotionally intelligent workplace* (pp. 13–26). San Francisco: Jossey-Bass; Goleman, D. (January 1998). What makes a leader. *Harvard Business Review, 82*(1), 93–102.

[19]Goleman, D., Boyatzis, D., & McKee, A. (2002). *Primal leadership: Realizing the power of emotional intelligence.* Cambridge, MA: HBR Press; *see fn 18,* Goleman (1998).

[20]Cherniss, C., Extein, M., Goleman, D., & Weissberg, R. P. (2006). Emotional intelligence: What does the research really indicate? *Educational Psychologist, 41*(4), 239–245.

[21]Fox, S., & Amichai-Hamburger, Y. (2001). The power of emotional appeals in promoting organizational change. *Academy of Management Executive, 15,* 84–94.

[22]See fn 20, Cherniss et al. (2006).

[23]Druskat, V., & Wolff, S. (2001). Building the emotional intelligence of groups. *Harvard Business Review, 79,* 80–91.

[24]Alon, I., & Higgins, J. (2005). Global leadership success through emotional intelligence and cultural intelligence. *Business Horizons, 48,* 501–512.

[25]See fn 19, Goleman et al. (2002); fn 18, Goleman (1998).

[26]See fn 20, Cherniss et al. (2006).

[27]Stogdill, R. M. (1950). Leadership, membership and organization. *Psychological Bulletin, 47,* 1–14.

[28]Judge, T. A., Piccolo, R. F., & Ilies, R. (2004). The forgotten ones? The validity of consideration and initiating structure in leadership research. *Journal of Applied Psychology, 89*(1), 36–51.

[29]Based on personal conversations with the lead author and information retrieved from http://www.dwyergroup.com/management-team.asp. Accessed on July 5, 2013.

[30]Dina Dwyer-Owens's leadership concern for her employees was evident an *Undercover Boss* episode that is highlighted at http://www.dwyergroup.com/undercoverboss/. Accessed on July 5, 2013.

[31]Blake, R. R., & Mouton, J. S. (1968). *The managerial grid: Key orientations for achieving production through people.* Houston, TX: Gulf Publishing Company; Blake, R. R., & Mouton, J. (1982). A Comparative Analysis of Situationalism and 9, 9 Management by Principle. *Organizational Dynamics, 10*(4), 20–43; Blake, R.R.,

& McCanse, A.A. (1991). *Leadership dilemmas: Grid solutions.* Houston, TX: Gulf Publishing Company.

[32]See fn 31, Blake & Mouton (1982).

[33]For a list of socioemotional behaviours in the context of teams, see Barry, B., & Stewart, G. L. (1997). Composition, process, and performance in self-managed groups: The role of personality. *Journal of Applied Psychology, 82*(1), 62–78.

[34]van Dierendonck, D. (2011). Servant leadership: A review and synthesis. *Journal of Management, 37*(4), 1228–1261. Servant leadership shares characteristics with other types of leadership, but also differs in meaningful ways. It can be distinguished from transformational leadership in emphasizing growth and engagement for the sake of the person and not primarily for the organization. It can be differentiated from the authentic leadership in chapter 7, in that servant leadership moves beyond a focus on self to a focus on all stakeholders. It differs from ethical leadership discussed in chapter 4 by encouraging experimentation and autonomy over ensuring conformity and compliance.

[35]See fn 34, van Dierendonck (2011).

[36]Greenleaf, R. (1977/2002). *Servant leadership.* New York: Paulist Press.

[37]Neubert, M. J., Kacmar, K. M., Carlson, D. S., Chonko, L. B., & Roberts, J. A. (2008). Regulatory focus as a mediator of the influence of initiating structure and servant leadership on employee behavior. *Journal of Applied Psychology, 93*(6), 1220–1233.

[38]Ehrhart, M. G. (2004). Leadership and procedural justice climate as antecedents of unit-level organizational citizenship behavior. *Personnel Psychology, 57,* 61–94; Hunter, E. M., Neubert, M. J., Perry, S. J., Witt, L. A., Penney, L. M., & Weinberger, E. L. (2013). Servant leaders inspire servant followers: Antecedents and outcomes for employees and the organization. *The Leadership Quarterly, 24*(2), 316–331.

[39]Pollard, W. (2003). Leading in turbulent times. *Baylor Business Review, 20*(1), 22.

[40]Buckingham, M., & Coffman, C. (1999). *First break all the rules: What the world's greatest managers do differently.* New York: Simon and Schuster.

[41]House, R. J. (1971). A path-goal theory of leadership effectiveness. *Administrative Science Quarterly, 16,* 321–339.

[42]Vroom, V. H., & Jago, A. G. (2007). The role of the situation in leadership. *American Psychologist, 62*(1), 17–24.

[43]See fn 2, Yukl (2013); Nahrgang, J. D., Morgeson, F. P., & Ilies, R. (2009). The development of leader-member exchanges: Exploring how personality and performance influence leader and member relationships over time. *Organizational Behavior and Human Decision Processes, 108*(2), 256–266.

[44]Dansereau, F., Jr., Graen, G., & Haga, W. J. (1975). A vertical dyad linkage approach to leadership within formal organizations: A longitudinal investigation of the role making process. *Organizational Behavior and Human Performance, 13,* 46–78.

[45]See fn 2, Yukl (2013).

[46]Hu, J., & Liden, R. C. (2013). Relative leader-member exchange within team contexts: How and when social comparison impacts individual effectiveness. *Personnel Psychology, 66*(1), 127–172.

[47]Graen, G. B., & Uhl-Bien, M. (1995). Relationship-based approach to leadership: Development of leader-member exchange (LMX) theory of leadership over 25 years: Applying a

multi-level multi-domain perspective. *The Leadership Quarterly*, *25*, 219–247.

[48]See fn 2, Yukl (2013).

[49]Carewest. (2015). Innovative health care: The Carewest difference. Retrieved from https://carewestwebsite.wordpress.com/the-carewest-difference/

[50]Forbes, D. (2014, April 30). Staff experience survey. *Carewest* [company newsletter]. Retrieved from https://carewestwebsite.files.wordpress.com/2014/10/april-2014-carewrite.pdf

[51]Buckingham, M. (2005). What great managers do. *Harvard Business Review*, *83*(3), 70–79.

[52]Blanchard, K., Zigarmi, P., & Zigarmi, D. (1985). *Leadership and the one-minute manager: Increasing effectiveness through situational leadership*. New York: William Morrow.

[53]Norrise, W. R., & Vecchio, R. P. (1992). Situational leadership theory: A replication. *Group and Organization Management*, *17*(3), 331–342.

[54]Thompson, G., & Vecchio, R. P. (2009). Situational leadership theory: A test of three versions. *The Leadership Quarterly*, *20*(5), 837–848.

[55]Principles of situational leadership inform this model, particularly the idea of leadership styles changing based on the needs of the follower. Even so, the integrated model relaxes the boundaries of situational leadership to allow for more than four combinations of leader behaviours.

[56]Kerr, S., & Jermier, J. M. (1978). Substitutes for leadership: Their meaning and measurement. *Organizational Behavior & Human Performance*, *22*(3), 375–403.

[57]Podsakoff, P. M., & MacKenzie, S. B. (1997). Kerr and Jermier's substitutes for leadership model: Background, empirical assessment, and suggestions for future research. *The Leadership Quarterly*, *8*(2), 117–132.

[58]Wu, C., Neubert, M. J., & Yi, X. (2007). Transformational leadership, cohesion perceptions, and employee cynicism about organizational change: The mediating role of justice perceptions. *Journal of Applied Behavioral Science*, *43*(3), 327–351.

[59]Bligh, M. C., & Kohles, J. C. (2012). From radical to mainstream? How follower-centric approaches inform leadership. *Zeitschrift Für Psychologie/Journal of Psychology*, *220*(4), 205–209; Fairhurst, G. T., & Uhl-Bien, M. (2012). Organizational discourse analysis: Examining leadership as a relational process. *The Leadership Quarterly*, *23*(6), 1043–1062; Cunliffe, A. L., & Eriksen, M. (2011). Relational leadership. *Human Relations*, *64*(11), 1425–1449.

[60]Wu, C., McMullen, J., Neubert, M. J., & Yi, X. (2008). The influence of leader regulatory focus on employee creativity. *Journal of Business Venturing*, *23*, 587–602; Kark, R., & Van Dijk, D. (2007). Motivation to lead, motivation to follow: The role of the self-regulatory focus in leadership processes. *Academy of Management Review*, *32*(2), 500–528.

[61]See fn 37, Neubert et al. (2008).

[62]See fn 54, Thompson & Vecchio (2009).

[63]Luchman, J. N., & González-Morales, M. (2013). Demands, control, and support: A meta-analytic review of work characteristics interrelationships. *Journal of Occupational Health Psychology*, *18*(1), 37–52.

[64]Vandewalle, D. (2001). Why wanting to look successful doesn't always lead to success. *Organizational Dynamics*, *30*(2), 162–171;

Yperen, N. W. V. (2003). The perceived profile of goal orientation within firms: Differences between employees working for successful and unsuccessful firms employing either performance-based pay or job-based pay. *European Journal of Work & Organizational Psychology*, *12*(3), 229–244.

[65]Kozlowski, S. W. J., Gully, S. M., Brown, K. G., Salas, E., Smith, E. M., & Nason, E. H. (2001). Effects of training goals and goal orientation traits on multidimensional training outcomes and performance adaptability. *Organizational Behavior & Human Decision Processes*, *85*(1), 1–31.

[66]Vansteenkiste, M., Simons, J., Lens, W., Soenens, B., Matos, L., & Lacante, M. (2004). Less is sometimes more: Goal content matters. *Journal of Educational Psychology*, *96*(4), 755–764.

[67]Sellers, P. (2013, March 25). What men can learn from Sheryl Sandberg's lean in. *Fortune*. http://money.cnn.com/2013/03/21/news/sandberg-chenault-lean-in.pr.fortune/index.html

[68]American Express Commits $25 Million to Leadership Development. http://www.bloomberg.com/apps/news?pid=conewsstory&tkr=AXP:US&sid=aP13eiS_mdBE

[69]Hamel, G. (2010, July 6). HCL: Extreme management makeover. *Wall Street Journal*. Retrieved from http://blogs.wsj.com/management/2010/07/06/hcl-extreme-management-makeover/

[70]Spreitzer, G. M., & Quinn, R. E. (2001). *A company of leaders: Five disciplines for unleashing the power in your workforce*. San Francisco: Jossey-Bass.

[71]Comments taken from speech at Baylor University. September 28, 2005.

[72]Home page of The Leather Collection Inc. http://www.leather collection.ph/Home.html. Accessed May 17, 2013; *The secrets of successful business leaders—Ms Yolanda Sevilla*. Video prepared by the Business Management Society of De La Salle University, Manila, Philippines. http://www.youtube.com/watch?v=5I1ie7N4Hbg&feature=player_embedded. Accessed May 17, 2013; "Yoling Sevilla—Leather Collection." Philippine Venture Capital Investment Group, Meeting 3254, April 29, 2010. Video- grapher Vivien Mangalindan. http://www.youtube.com/watch?v=YbFahM-n9Jk. Accessed May 17, 2013.

[73]See fn 38, Hunter et al. (2013).

[74]See fn 37, Neubert et al. (2008); fn 38, Hunter et al. (2013).

Feature Notes

OB Action: Rock Star Businessman http://www.virg-ingalactic.com/. Accessed February 22, 2013; Branson, R. (2010, September 9). Richard Branson: Five secrets to business success. *Entrepreneur*. Retrieved from http://www.entrepreneur.com/article/217284; Greenburg, Z. (2011, September 19). Billionaire Richard Branson on being a rock star businessman. *Forbes*. Retrieved from http://www.forbes.com/sites/zackomalleygreenburg/2011/09/19/billionaire-richard-branson-on-being-a-rock-star-businessman/

My OB: All for One or One for All? http://www.dramatica.com/story/analyses/analyses/braveheart.html. Accessed December 14, 2012; Waldman, D. A., & Javidan, M. (2009). Alternative forms of charismatic leadership in the integration of mergers and acquisitions. *The Leadership Quarterly*, *20*(2), 130–142; McCall, M., & Lombardo, M. (1983). *Off the track: Why and how successful executives get derailed* (Technical Report No. 21). Greensboro, NC: Center for Creative Leadership.

My OB: Gender and Leadership—Does One Size Fit All? Koenig, A. M., Eagly, A. H., Mitchell, A. A., & Ristikari, T. (2011). Are leader stereotypes masculine? A meta-analysis of three research paradigms. *Psychological Bulletin, 137*(4), 616–642; van Emmerik, H., Wendt, H., & Euwema, M. C. (2010). Gender ratio, societal culture, and male and female leadership. *Journal of Occupational and Organizational Psychology, 83*(4), 895–914; Neubert, M. J., & Taggar, S. (2004). Pathways to informal leadership: The moderating role of gender on the relationship of individual differences and team member network centrality to informal leadership emergence. *Leadership Quarterly, 15,* 175–194; Tannen, D. (1995). The power of talk: Who gets heard and why. *Harvard Business Review, 73*(5), 138–148; Lyness, K. S., & Heilman, M. E. (2006). When fit is fundamental: Performance evaluations and promotions of upper-level female and male managers. *Journal of Applied Psychology, 91*(4), 777–785.

OB in Action: "Krafting" a New Culture of Empowerment and Entrepreneurial Spirit Rosenfeld, I. (2010, November 6). *Financial Times.* Retrieved from http://www.ft.com/cms/s/0/c78aa1ea-ed93-11df-9085-00144feab49a.html#ixzz2TDRo2yjQ; Rosenfeld, I. (2011, August 24). *Forbes.* Retrieved from http://www.forbes.com/sites/jennagoudreau/2011/08/24/power-women-forbes-anna-wintour-ann-curry-irene-rosenfeld/; Irene Rosenfeld hopes Mondēlez International can create delicious moments of joy. (2013, May 1). Retrieved from http://www.sbnonline.com/2013/05/irene-rosenfeld-hopes-mondelez-international-can-create-delicious-moments-of-joy/; Irene Rosenfeld discusses belief in concept of servant leadership. http://eclips.cornell.edu/clip.do?isCUWA=null&type=null&id=10855&tab=TabClip Page. Accessed May 15, 2013.

Chapter 10

[1]Barmak, S. WestJet: Friendly skies and then some. *Canadian Business.* Retrieved from http://www.canadianbusiness.com/lists-and-rankings/westjet-friendly-skies-and-then-some/; Jang,B. (2009, March 13). Why WestJet's culture guru chooses to fly under the radar. *The Globe and Mail.* Retrieved from http://www.theglobeandmail.com/report-on-business/why-westjets-culture-guru-chooses-to-fly-under-the-radar/article960441/; Lu, V. (2012, May 28). WestJet's CEO may be big boss, but emphasizes team attitude. *Toronto Star.* Retrieved from http://www.thestar.com/business/2012/05/28/westjets_ceo_may_be_big_boss_but_emphasizes_team_attitude.html; McCullough, M. (2014, August 7). Interview: WestJet CEO Gregg Saretsky on the power of culture. *Canadian Business.* Retrieved from http://www.canadianbusiness.com/leadership/gregg-saretsky-westjet-interview/; WestJet. (n.d.). About WestJet. [Corporate website]. Retrieved from https://www.westjet.com/guest/en/about/; WestJet. (n.d.). [Corporate website]. Retrieved from http://www.westjet.com/pdf/investorMedia/westjetBackgrounder.pdf; WestJet. (2012). *Expanding our reach: WestJet annual report 2011.* Retrieved from http://www.westjet.com/guest/en/media-investors/2011-annual-report/meet-our-team/executive-team.shtml

[2]Hunter, L. W., MacDuffie, J. P., & Doucet, L. (2002). What makes teams take? Employee reactions to work reforms. *Industrial and Labor Relations Review, 55*(3), 448–472.

[3]Glassop, L. I. (2002). The organizational benefits of teams. *Human Relations, 55*(2), 225–249.

[4]Bezrukova, K., Jehn, K. A., Zanutto, E. L., & Thatcher, S. B. (2009). Do workgroup faultlines help or hurt? A moderated model of faultlines, team identification, and group performance. *Organization Science, 20*(1), 35–50; Cohen, S. G., & Bailey, D. E. (1997). What makes teams work: Group effectiveness research from the shop floor to the executive suite. *Journal of Management, 23,* 239–290.

[5]Somech, A., Desivilya, H., & Lidogoster, H. (2009). Team conflict management and team effectiveness: The effects of task interdependence and team identification. *Journal of Organizational Behavior, 30*(3), 359–378.

[6]Gardner, H. K. (2012). Performance pressure as a double-edged sword: Enhancing team motivation but undermining the use of team knowledge. *Administrative Science Quarterly, 57*(1), 1–46

[7]Millikin, J. P., Hom, P. W., & Manz, C. C. (2010). Self-management competencies in self-managing teams: Their impact on multiteam system productivity. *The Leadership Quarterly, 21*(5), 687–702; Yang, S., & Guy, M. E. (2011). The effectiveness of self-managed work teams in government organizations. *Journal of Business and Psychology, 26*(4), 531–541.

[8]Cohen, S., Ledford, G., & Spreitzer, G. (1996). A predictive model of self-managing work team effectiveness. *Human Relations, 49*(5), 643–676.

[9]Batt, R. (2004). Who benefits from teams? Comparing workers, supervisors, and managers. *Industrial Relations, 43*(1), 183–212.

[10]Maynard, M., Mathieu, J. E., Rapp, T. L., & Gilson, L. L. (2012). Something(s) old and something(s) new: Modeling drivers of global virtual team effectiveness. *Journal of Organizational Behavior, 33*(3), 342–365.

[11]Colquitt, J., Noe, R. A., & Jackson, C. L. (2002). Justice in teams: Antecedents and consequences of procedural justice climate. *Personnel Psychology, 55*(1), 83–109.

[12]For more on this topic, see Burnette, J. L., Pollack, J. M., & Forsyth, D. R. (2011). Leadership in extreme contexts: A groupthink analysis of the May 1996 Mount Everest disaster. *Journal of Leadership Studies, 4*(4), 29–40; Kayes, D. C. (2004). The 1996 Mount Everest climbing disaster: The breakdown of learning in teams. *Human Relations, 57*(10), 1263–1284.

[13]Tuckman, B. W. (1965). Developmental sequence for small groups. *Psychological Bulletin, 63,* 384–399.

[14]Gersick, C. J. G. (1988). Time and transition in work teams: Toward a new model of group development. *Academy of Management Journal, 31*(1), 9–41.

[15]Subramony, M., Beehr, T. A., & Johnson, C. M. (2004). Employee and customer perceptions of service quality in an Indian firm. *Applied Psychology: An International Review, 53*(2), 311–327.

[16]Mathieu, J., Maynard, M., Rapp, T., & Gilson, L. (2008). Team effectiveness 1997–2007: A review of recent advancements and a glimpse into the future. *Journal of Management, 34*(3), 410–476.

[17]Bell, S. T., Villado, A. J., Lukasik, M. A., Belau, L., & Briggs, A. L. (2011). Getting specific about demographic diversity variable

and team performance relationships: A meta-analysis. *Journal of Management, 37*(3), 709–743.

[18]Knippenberg, D., De Dreu, C. K. W., & Homan, A. C. (2004). Work group diversity and group performance: An integrative model and research agenda. *Journal of Applied Psychology, 89*(6), 1008–1022; Milliken, F. J., & Martins, L. L. (1996). Searching for common threads: Understanding the multiple effects of diversity in organizational groups. *Academy of Management Review, 21*(2), 402–433; Barrick, M. R., Stewart, G. L., Neubert, M. J., & Mount, M. K. (1998). Relating member ability and personality to work-team processes and team effectiveness. *Journal of Applied Psychology, 83*(3), 377–391.

[19]Mohammed, S., & Nadkarni, S. (2011). Temporal diversity and team performance: The moderating role of team temporal leadership. *Academy of Management Journal, 54*(3), 489–508.

[20]Michailova, W., & Minbaeva, D. A. (2012). Organizational values and knowledge sharing in multinational corporations: The Danisco case. *International Business Review, 21*(1), 59–70.

[21]Cheng, C., Chua, R. J., Morris, M. W, & Lee, L. (2012). Finding the right mix: How the composition of self-managing multicultural teams' cultural value orientation influences performance over time. *Journal of Organizational Behavior, 33*(3), 389–411; Staples, D., & Zhao, L. (2007). The effects of cultural diversity in virtual teams versus face-to-face teams. *Group Decision & Negotiation, 15*(4), 389–406.

[22]Hopkins, W. E., Hopkins, S. A., & Gross, M. A. (2005). Cultural diversity recomposition and effectiveness in monoculture work groups. *Journal of Organizational Behavior, 26*(8), 949–964.

[23]McDowell, W. C., Herdman, A. O., & Aaron, J. (2011). Charting the course: The effects of team charters on emergent behavioral norms. *Organization Development Journal, 29*(1), 79–88.

[24]Salas, E., Rozell, D., Mullen, B., & Driskell, J. E. (1999). The effect of team building on performance and integration. *Small Group Research, 30*(3), 309–329.

[25]CB Staff. Canada's best employers 2015: The top 50 large companies. (2014, November 10). *Canadian Business*. Retrieved from http://www.canadianbusiness.com/lists-and-rankings/best-jobs/2015-best-employers-top-50/.

[26]http://www.campbellfamilyinstitute.com/. Accessed December 15, 2012.

[27]Mullen, B., & Copper, C. (1994). The relation between group cohesiveness and performance: An integration. *Psychological Bulletin, 115*(2), 210–227; Jordan, M. H., Feild, H. S., & Armenakis, A. A. (2002). The relationship of group process variables and team performance: A team-level analysis in a field setting. *Small Group Research, 33*(1), 121–150.

[28]Bhattacharyya, R. & Basu, S. D. Self-forming teams improve productivity and help organisations save costs. *The Economic Times*. Retrieved from http://articles.economictimes.india times.com/2013-06-25/news/40186861_1_edelweiss-financial-services-marico-employees-group.

[29]DeChurch, L. A., Mesmer-Magnus, J. R., & Doty, D. (2013). Moving beyond relationship and task conflict: Toward a process-state perspective. *Journal of Applied Psychology, 98*(4), 559–578.

[30]Ibid.

[31]Hoch, J. E., & Kozlowski, S. J. (2012). Leading virtual teams: Hierarchical leadership, structural supports, and shared team leadership. *Journal of Applied Psychology*. Advance online publication. doi: 10.1037/a0030264.

[32]Cameron, K. S., Dutton, J. E., & Quinn, R. E. (2003). *Positive organizational scholarship: Foundations of a new discipline* (pp. 48–65). San Francisco, CA: Berrett-Koehler.

[33]See fn 31. Hoch & Kozlowski (2012).

[34]Dyck, B., Bruning, S., & Driedger, L. (1996). Potential conflict, conflict stimulus, and organizational performance: An empirical test. *International Journal of Conflict Management, 7,* 295–313.

[35]See fn 29, DeChurch et al. (2013).

[36]See fn 29, DeChurch et al. (2013).

[37]See fn 5, Somech et al. (2009).

[38]LePine, J. A., Buckman, B. R., Crawford, E. R., & Methot, J. R. (2011). A review of research on personality in teams: Accounting for pathways spanning levels of theory and analysis. *Human Resource Management Review, 21*(4), 311–330.

[39]Taggar, S., & Neubert, M. (2004). The impact of poor performers on team outcomes: An empirical examination of attribution theory. *Personnel Psychology, 57,* 935–968.

[40]Faraj, S., & Yan, A. (2009). Boundary work in knowledge teams. *Journal of Applied Psychology, 94*(3), 604–617.

[41]See fn 5, Somech et al. (2009).

[42]Bradley, B. H., Klotz, A. C., Postlethwaite, B. E., & Brown, K. G. (2013). Ready to rumble: How team personality composition and task conflict interact to improve performance. *Journal of Applied Psychology, 98*(2), 385–392.

[43]Goncalo, J. A., Polman, E., & Maslach, C. (2010). Can confidence come too soon? Collective efficacy, conflict and group performance over time. *Organizational Behavior and Human Decision Processes, 113*(1), 13–24.

[44]Bradley, B. H., Postlethwaite, B. E., Klotz, A. C., Hamdani, M. R., & Brown, K. G. (2012). Reaping the benefits of task conflict in teams: The critical role of team psychological safety climate. *Journal of Applied Psychology, 97*(1), 151–158.

[45]Gaynier, L. P. (2005). Transformative mediation: In search of a theory of practice. *Conflict Resolution Quarterly, 22*(3), 397–408; Putnam, L. L (2004). Transformations and critical moments in negotiations. *Negotiation Journal, 20*(2), 275–295.

[46]De Dreu, C. K. W., & West, M. (2001). Minority dissent and team innovation: The importance of participation in decision making. *Journal of Applied Psychology, 86*(6), 1191–1202.

[47]See fn 45, Putnam (2004).

[48]Janis, I. L. (1972). *Victims of groupthink*. Boston, MA: Houghton Mifflin.

[49]Taggar, S., & Ellis, R. (2007). The role of leaders in shaping formal team norms. *Leadership Quarterly, 18,* 105–120.

[50]Lim, B., & Klein, K. J. (2006). Team mental models and team performance: A field study of the effects of team mental model similarity and accuracy. *Journal of Organizational Behavior, 27*(4), 403–418; Edwards, B. D., Day, E. A., Arthur, W., & Bell, S. T. (2006). Relationships among team ability composition, team mental models, and team performance. *Journal of Applied Psychology, 91*(3), 727–736.

[51]Cialdini, R. B., & Goldstein, N. J. (2004). Social influence: Compliance and conformity. *Annual Review of Psychology, 55,*

591–621; Feldman, D. C. (1984). The development and enforcement of group norms. *Academy of Management Review, 9,* 47–53.

[52]Kim, P. H. (2003). When private beliefs shape collective reality: The effects of beliefs about coworkers on group discussion and performance. *Management Science, 49*(6), 801–815.

[53]Biron, M., & Bamberger, P. (2012). Aversive workplace conditions and absenteeism: Taking referent group norms and supervisor support into account. *Journal of Applied Psychology, 97*(4), 901–912.

[54]See fn 49, Taggar & Ellis (2007).

[55]Porter, C. H., Gogus, C., & Yu, R. (2010). When does teamwork translate into improved team performance? A resource allocation perspective. *Small Group Research, 41*(2), 221–248.

[56]Barnes, C. M., Hollenbeck, J. R., Wagner, D. T., DeRue, D., Nahrgang, J. D., & Schwind, K. M. (2008). Harmful help: The costs of backing-up behavior in teams. *Journal of Applied Psychology, 93*(3), 529–539.

[57]Kameda, T., Tsukasaki, T., Hastie, R., & Berg, N. (2011). Democracy under uncertainty: The wisdom of crowds and the free-rider problem in group decision making. *Psychological Review, 118*(1), 76–96; Kidwell, R. E., & Bennett, N. (1993). Employee propensity to withhold effort: A conceptual model to intersect three avenues of research. *Academy of Management Review, 18,* 429–456; Olson, M. (1965). *The logic of collective action: Public goods and the theory of groups.* Cambridge, MA: Harvard University Press.

[58]Neubert, M. J., Taggar, S., & Cady, S. H. (2006). The role of conscientiousness and extraversion in affecting the relationship between perceptions of group potency and volunteer group member selling behavior: An interactionist perspective. *Human Relations, 59*(9), 1235–1260.

[59]Taggar, S., & Neubert, M. J. (2008). A cognitive (attributions)-emotion model of observer reactions to free-riding poor performers. *Journal of Business and Psychology, 22*(3), 167–177.

[60]Kerr, N. L. (1983). Motivation losses in small groups: A social dilemma analysis. *Journal of Personality and Social Psychology, 45,* 819–828.

[61]Mesmer-Magnus, J. R., & DeChurch, L. A. (2009). Information sharing and team performance: A meta-analysis. *Journal of Applied Psychology, 94*(2), 535–546.

[62]Mesmer-Magnus, J. R., DeChurch, L. A., Jimenez-Rodriguez, M., Wildman, J., & Shuffler, M. (2011). A meta-analytic investigation of virtuality and information sharing in teams. *Organizational Behavior and Human Decision Processes, 115*(2), 214–225.

[63]March, J. G., & Simon, H. A. (1958). *Organizations.* New York: Wiley.

[64]Alquist, J. L., Ainsworth, S. E., & Baumeister, R. F. (2013). Determined to conform: Disbelief in free will increases conformity. *Journal of Experimental Social Psychology, 49*(1), 80–86.

[65]This section draws heavily from Weber, J. M. (2004). *Catalysts for cooperation: Consistent contributors in public good dilemmas.* Doctoral dissertation, *Management and Organizations,* Northwestern University, Evanston, IL.

[66]Barrick, M., Stewart, G., Neubert, M. J., & Mount, M. (1998). Relating member ability and personality to work-team processes and team effectiveness. *Journal of Applied Psychology, 83,* 377–319.

[67]See fn 61, Mesmer-Magnus & DeChurch (2009).

[68]See fn 49, Taggar & Ellis (2007).

[69]Quan, K. (2015, February 18). How Google's Canadian office design encourages collaboration. *Canadian Business.* Retrieved from http://www.canadianbusiness.com/leadership/office-space/sam-sebastian-google-canada-managing-director/; Globe Careers. Take a tour of Google's new Toronto office. (2012, November 16). *The Globe and Mail.* Retrieved from http://www.theglobeandmail.com/report-on-business/careers/take-a-tour-of-googles-new-toronto-office/article5220954/.

[70]Chen, G., Kirkman, B. L., Kanfer, R., Allen, D., & Rosen, B. (2007). A multilevel study of leadership, empowerment, and performance in teams. *Journal of Applied Psychology, 92*(2), 331–346.

[71]Kleingeld, A., van Mierlo, H., & Arends, L. (2011). The effect of goal setting on group performance: A meta-analysis. *Journal of Applied Psychology, 96*(6), 1289–1304.

[72]Guzzo, R. A., & Shea, G. P. (1992). Group performance and intergroup relations in organizations. In M. D. Dunnette & L. M. Hough (Eds.), *Handbook of industrial and organizational psychology* (2nd ed., Vol. 1, pp. 269–313). Palo Alto, CA: Consulting Psychologists Press.

[73]Campion, M. A., Medsker, G. J., & Higgs, A. C. (1993). Relations between work group characteristics and effectiveness: Implications for designing effective work groups. *Personnel Psychology, 46,* 823–847; Pritchard, R. D., Jones, S. D., Roth, P. L., Stuebing, K. K., & Ekeberg, S. E. (1988). Effects of group feedback, goal setting, and incentives on organizational productivity. *Journal of Applied Psychology, 73,* 337–358.

[74]See fn 70, Kleingeld et al. (2011).

[75]Beer, J. (2012, April 11). How to build a better call centre. *Canadian Business.* Retrieved from http://www.canadianbusiness.com/business-strategy/how-to-build-a-better-call-centre/.

[76]Neubert, M. J., & Scullen, S. (2004). The potential and volitional accuracy of supervisors and team members as ratings sources of individual team members. Working paper.

[77]Weinreb, M. (2003). Power to the people. *Sales and Marketing Management, 155*(4), 30–36.

[78]Schippers, M. C., Homan, A. C., & Van Knippenberg, D. (2013). To reflect or not to reflect: Prior team performance as a boundary condition of the effects of reflexivity on learning and final team performance. *Journal of Organizational Behavior, 34*(1), 6–23.

[79]Tjosvold, D., Yu, Z., & Hui, C. (2004). Team learning from mistakes: The contribution of cooperative goals and problem-solving. *Journal of Management Studies, 41*(7), 1223–1245.

[80]Carroll, J. S., Hatakenaka, S., & Rudolph, J. W. (2006). Naturalistic decision making and organizational learning in nuclear power plants: Negotiating meaning between managers and problem investigation teams. *Organization Studies, 27*(7), 1037–1057.

[81]Kesler, K. (2006). Robots are child's play. *Portable Design, 12*(12), 7–8; Oliver, D., & Roos, J. (2003). Dealing with the unexpected: Critical incidents in the LEGO Mindstorms team. *Human Relations, 56*(9), 1057–1082; Koerner, B. (2006, February) Geeks in Toyland, *Wired, 14*(2), Retrieved from http://www.wired.com/wired/archive/14.02/lego_pr.html; http://nxtrobots.org/nxt-robots-3-0-release/. Accessed December 17, 2012; http://firstlegoleague.org/mission/support. Accessed February 28, 2013.

Feature Notes

OB in Action: Groupthink Goncalo, J. A., Polman, E., & Maslach, C. (2010). Can confidence come too soon? Collective efficacy, conflict and group performance over time. *Organizational Behavior and Human Decision Processes, 113*(1), 13–24; Forsyth, D. (1990). *Group dynamics.* Pacific Grove, CA: Brooks/Cole; Janis, I. L. (1972). *Victims of groupthink.* Boston, MA: Houghton Mifflin; Katzenstein, G. (1996). The debate on structured debate: Toward a unified theory. *Organizational Behavior and Human Decision Processes, 66*(3), 316–332.

My OB: Stimulating Information Sharing Garrett, A. G. (2006, October). Crash course . . . in brainstorming. *Management Today, 16*; Delbecq, A. L., Van de Ven, A. H., & Gustafson, D. H. (1975). *Group techniques for program planning: A guide to nominal group technique and Delphi processes.* Glenview, IL: Scott-Foresman; Lago, P. P., Beruvides, M. G., Jian, J., Canto, A., Sandoval, A., & Taraban, R. (2007). Structuring group decision making in a web-based environment by using the nominal group technique. *Computers & Industrial Engineering, 52*(2), 277–295; Rowe, G., & Wright, G. (1999). The Delphi technique as a forecasting tool: Issues and analysis. *International Journal of Forecasting, 15*(4), 353–375.

OB in Action: Front-Line Management Teams Longenecker, C., & Neubert, M. J. (2000). Barriers and gateways to management cooperation and teamwork. *Business Horizons, 43,* 37–44; Janssen, O., & Huang, X. (2008). Us and me: Team identification and individual differentiation as complementary drivers of team members' citizenship and creative behaviors. *Journal of Management, 34*(1), 69–88.

Chapter 11

[1]Kopun, F. (2015, June 15). Hudson's Bay buys Germany's Kaufhof chain in $3.3B deal. *Toronto Star.* Retrieved from http://www.thestar.com/business/2015/06/15/hudsons-bay-buys-germanys-kaufhof-chain.html; Shaw, H. (2015, June 20). How Richard Baker engineered Hudson's Bay Co.'s stunning turnaround with a 'leap of faith' in real estate. *Financial Post.* Retrieved from http://business.financialpost.com/executive/management-hr/how-richard-baker-engineered-hudsons-bay-co-s-stunning-turnaround-with-a-leap-of-faith-in-real-estate; Strauss, M. (2013, June 18). Five years in, the turnaround 'is real' at Hudson's Bay. *The Globe and Mail.* Retrieved from http://www.theglobeandmail.com/report-on-business/hudsons-bay-narrows-loss-canadian-sales-climb/article12489101/; Toller, C. (2015, July 13). Interview: Hudson's Bay president Liz Rodbell on taking retail upscale. *Canadian Business.* Retrieved from http://www.canadianbusiness.com/leadership/liz-rodbell-hudsons-bay/; Wahba, P. (2015, February 25). Saks, Lord & Taylor owner HBC looks to cash in on its valuable real estate. *Fortune.* Retrieved from http://fortune.com/2015/02/25/saks-lord-and-taylor/

[2]This is based on the classic study by Mintzberg, H. (1973). *The nature of managerial work.* New York: Harper and Row. These figures have been pretty stable over time, though there is some variation based on the kind of manager. For example, managers who are starting a new organization spend a lower percent of their time (64 percent) communicating than managers in the growth stage of entrepreneurship (82 percent; of this, 56 percent is with organization members and 22 percent with outsiders; 53 percent was face-to-face, 14 percent telephone, and 11 percent email). (Mueller, S., Volery, T., and von Siemens, B. (2012). What do entrepreneurs actually do? An observational study of entrepreneurs' everyday behavior in the startup and growth stages. *Entrepreneurship Theory and Practice, 36,* 995–1017.) Another study found that managers of growth-oriented small and medium-sized organizations spend 78 percent of their time communicating with others (O'Gorman, C., Bourke, S., & Murray, J. A. (2005). The nature of managerial work in small growth-orientated businesses. *Small Business Economics, 25*(1), 1–16.

[3]For an early variation of this four-step model adapted here, see Shannon, C. E., & Weaver, W. (1949). *The mathematical theory of communication.* Urbana-Champaign: University of Illinois Press.

[4]Lawrence, T. B., & Maitlis, S. (2012). Care and possibility: Enacting an ethic of care through narrative practice. *Academy of Management Review, 37*(4), 641–663; Putnam, L. L., Phillips, N., & Chapman, P. (1996). Metaphors of communication and organization. In S. R. Clegg, C. Hardy, & W. R. Nord (Eds.), *Managing organizations: Current issues* (pp. 125–158). London: Sage.

[5]Boyes-Watson, C. (2006). Community is not a place but a relationship: Lessons for organizational development. *Public Organization Review: A Global Journal, 5,* 359–374.

[6]Page 74 in Autry, J. A. (1991). *Love and profit: The art of caring leadership.* New York: William Morrow.

[7]Clampitt, P. G., DeKoch, R. J., & Cashman, T. (2000). A strategy for communicating about uncertainty. *Academy of Management Executive, 14*(4), 41–57.

[8]Ibid.

[9]Fenton C., & Langley A. (2011). Strategy as practice and the narrative turn. *Organization Studies, 32*(9), 1171–1196.

[10]See fn 7, Clampitt et al. (2000).

[11]Ibid.

[12] See fn 4, Putnam et al. (1996); Despain, J. M., & Brulle, R. J. (2003). Media's social construction of environmental issues: Focus on global warming—a comparative study. *International Journal of Sociology and Social Policy, 23*(10), 74–105.

[13]See pp. 223–229 in Narayan, D. (with R. Patel, K. Schafft, A. Rademacher, & S. Koch-Schulter). (1999). *Can anyone hear us? Voices from 47 countries.* Poverty Group, World Bank.

[14]Haigh, N., & Griffiths, A. (2009). The natural environment as a primary stakeholder: The case of climate change. *Business Strategy and the Environment, 18*(6), 347–359.

[15]Vandenbosch, B., Saatcioglu, A., & Fay, S. (2006). Idea management: A systemic view. *Journal of Management Studies, 43*(3), 259–288.

[16]Portilla, J. (2004). Interview with John Paul Lederach. Retrieved from http://www.beyondintractability.org/audiodisplay/lederach-j; Accessed February 22, 2013; see also Huebner, C. K. (2006). *A precarious peace.* Waterloo, ON: Herald Press.

[17]Lederach, J. P. (1995). *Preparing for peace: Conflict transformation across cultures.* Syracuse, NY: Syracuse University Press.

[18]Farndale, E., Van Ruiten, J., Kelliher, C., & Hope-Hailey, V. (2011). The influence of perceived employee voice on organizational commitment: An exchange perspective. *Human Resource Management, 50*, 113–129.

[19]CB Staff. (2015, January 5). What Founders and CEOs learned in 2014, part two. *Canadian Business.* Retrieved from http://www.canadianbusiness.com/leadership/what-founders-and-ceos-learned-in-2014-part-2/; Quan, K. How Tangerine Bank CEO Peter Aceto gets his whole company to pitch in. *Canadian Business.* Retrieved from http://www.canadianbusiness.com/innovation/change-agent/peter-aceto-president-ceo-tangerine-bank/

[20]Knowles, M. (2012, August 24). Anchor accidentally propositions co-worker on live TV. *Trending Now.* Retrieved from http://news.yahoo.com/blogs/trending-now/anchor-accidentally-propositions-co-worker-live-tv-165257175.html

[21]Cross, R., & Sproull, L. (2004). More than an answer: Information relationships for actionable knowledge. *Organization Science, 15*(4), 446–462.

[22]See fn 7, Clampitt et al. (2000).

[23]This may be based on a comment made by Blaise Pascal, who wrote to a friend: "I have made this letter longer than usual because I lack the time to make it shorter." Quote comes from Charles Loewen at a time when he was CEO of Loewen Windows, cited in Kroeker, W. (2007, August 20). Dear editor. *Canadian Mennonite, 11*(16), p. 11.

[24]See literature review in Cuddy, A. J. C., Glick, P., & Beninger, A. (2011). The dynamics of warmth and competence judgments, and their outcomes in organizations. *Research in Organizational Behavior, 31*, 73–98.

[25]Côté, S., & Hideg, I. (2011). The ability to influence others via emotion displays: A new dimension of emotional intelligence. *Organizational Psychology Review, 1*(1), 53–71.

[26]Semnani-Azad, Z., & Adair, W. L. (2011, July). Nonverbal cues associated with negotiation 'styles' across cultures. In 24th Annual International Association of Conflict Management Conference (Istanbul, Turkey).

[27]Daft, R. L., & Lengel, R. H. (1986). Organizational information requirements, media richness and structural design. *Management Science, 32*(5), 554–571; Daft, R. L., Lengel, R. H., & Trevino, L. K. (1987). Message equivocality, media selection, and manager performance: Implications for information systems. *MIS Quarterly, 11*, 335–366; Neufeld, D. J., Brotheridge, C. M., & Dyck, B. (2001). Electronic mail as a rich communication medium in global virtual organizations. *HICSS 34*, Minitrack Information Systems in Global Business, Hawaii, January 3–6, 2001. Neves, P., & Eisenberger, R. (2012). Management communication and employee performance: The contribution of perceived organizational support. *Human Performance, 25*(5), 452–464. Richness also includes the ability to express language variety.

[28]Lengel, R. H., & Daft, R. J. (1988). The selection of communication media as an executive skill. *The Academy of Management Executive, 11*(3), 225–232.

[29]Some research suggests the non-verbal and para-verbal messages account for 93 percent of the inferred meaning in expressions of emotion or liking: Gifford, R. (2011). The role of nonverbal communication in interpersonal relations. In L. M. Horowitz, & S. N. Strack (Eds.), *Handbook of interpersonal psychology,* pp. 171–190. New York: Wiley; Martin, S. (1995). The role of nonverbal communications in quality improvement. *National Productivity Review, 15*(1), 27–40; Fatt, J. P. T. (1998). Nonverbal communication and business success. *Management Research News, 21*(4/5), 1–10.

[30]Mackenzie, M. L. (2010). Manager communication and workplace trust: Understanding manager and employee perceptions in the e-world. *International Journal of Information Management, 30*(6), 529–541.

[31]This discussion builds on Peters, L. D. (2006). Conceptualising computer-mediated communication technology and its use in organizations. *International Journal of Information Management, 26*, 142–152.

[32]Hart, R. K. B. (2002). *The conversation of relationships: The communication content and quality of strong and weak relationships in geographically dispersed teams.* PhD dissertation, Department of Organizational Behavior, Case Western Reserve University, Cleveland, OH; Muethel, M., Siebdrat, F., & Hoegl, M. (2012). When do we really need interpersonal trust in globally dispersed new product development teams? *R&D Management, 42*(1), 31–46.

[33]Rafter, M. V. (2012, January 4). 10 workplace trends to watch in 2012. *Second Act.* Retrieved from http://www.secondact.com/2012/01/top-workplace-trends-in-2012/. Accessed February 22, 2013.

[34]See fn 31, Peters (2006, p. 145).

[35]Wajcman, J., & Rose, E. (2011). Constant connectivity: Rethinking interruptions at work. *Organization Studies, 32*(7), 941–961.

[36]Allen, J., Jimmieson, N. L., Bordia, P., & Irmer, B. E. (2007). Uncertainty during organizational change: Managing perceptions through communication. *Journal of Change Management, 7(2),* 187–210.

[37]DiFonzo, N. (2010). Ferreting facts or fashioning fallacies? Factors in rumor accuracy. *Social and Personality Psychology Compass, 4*, 1124–1137.

[38]This was practised by Charles Loewen when he was the CEO of Loewen Windows (Dyck, B. & Neubert, M. (2010). *Management: Current practices and new directions.* Boston MA: Cengage/Houghton Mifflin).

[39]Kron, D., Kruschwitz, N., Haanaes, K., & von Streng Velken, I. (2011). Sustainability nears a tipping point. *MIT Sloan Management Review, 53*(2), 69–74.

[40]Buchanen, A., & O'Neill, M. (2001). *Inclusion and diversity: Finding common ground for organizational action: A deliberative dialogue guide.* Ottawa: Canadian Council for International Cooperation; Fleming, P. (2013). Down with big brother: The end of corporate culturalism. *Journal of Management Studies, 50*, 447–473.

[41]Hermans, C., Howarth, R. B., Noordewier, T., & Erickson, J. D. (2008). Constructing preferences in structured group deliberative processes. In C. Zografos & R. B. Howarth (Eds.), *Deliberative Ecological Economics* (pp. 50–79). Delhi, India: Oxford University Press.

[42]Barley, S. R. (1986). Technology as an occasion for structuring: Evidence from observations of CT scanners and the social order of radiology departments. *Administrative Science Quarterly, 31,* 78–108; Brotheridge, C. (2003). *Structuring deference and solidarity in a manager-expatriate employee dyad in the context of changing communications media within the Mennonite*

Central Committee. Ph.D. dissertation, University of Manitoba; Sjöberg, A. (2013). Making sense of technology—A study of how professionals use, understand and create a sense of Facebook, LinkedIn and Twitter and what factor's that might influence these processes. *Master Thesis in Strategic HRM and Labour Relations*. University of Gothenburg: Gothenburg, Sweden. Retrieved from http://hdl.handle.net/2077/31935.

[43]See fn 31, Peters (2006).

[44]Mesch, G., & Talmud, I. (2006). The quality of online and offline relationships: The role of multiplexity and duration of social relationships. *Information Society, 22,* 137–148. Another study—which examined members of geographically dispersed teams and looked at whether the choice of media and the content of messages sent were influenced by the strength of interpersonal relationships—found that when interpersonal relationships were weak, the preferred medium was group meetings (see fn 32, Hart, 2002).

[45]Reich, S. M., Subrahmanyam, K., & Espinoza, G. (2012). Friending, Ming, and hanging out face-to-face: Overlap in adolescents' online and offline social networks. *Developmental psychology, 48*(2), 356–368.

[46]Szulanski, G. (1996). Exploring internal stickiness: Impediments to the transfer of best practice within the firm. *Strategic Management Journal, 17,* 27–43.

[47]See review by Klimoski, R. (2011). Deception: From ancient empires to internet dating (B. Harringotn, Ed.), *Administrative Science Quarterly, 55,* 328–331.

[48]See fn 29, Fatt (1998).

[49]Weingarten, G. (2007, April 8). Pearls before breakfast: Can one of the nation's great musicians cut through the fog of a D.C. rush hour? Let's find out. *The Washington Post,* p. W10.

[50]Ucok, O. (2006). Transparency, communication and mindfulness. *Journal of Management Development, 25*(10), 1024–1028.

[51]In one sense, everyone receives and decodes messages from others in terms of their own context, agenda, fear, and filters (Ucok, 2006). Sustainable managers try to be aware of their own voice and their own agenda, and they try to hear the voices of others without judging or criticizing.

[52]See fn 39, Kron et al. (2011).

[53]This discussion builds on Jacobs, C., & Coghlan, D. (2005). Sound from silence: On listening in organizational learning. *Human Relationships, 58*(1), 115–138. See also Nonaka, I. (1994). A dynamic theory of organizational knowledge creation. *Organization Science, 5*(1), 14–37.

[54]This description about Westward Industries builds on case material found in Dyck, B., Starke, F. A., & Mauws, M. K. (2008). Teaching versus learning: An exploratory longitudinal case study. *Journal of Small Business and Entrepreneurship, 21*(1), 37–58.

[55]See fn 53, Jacobs & Coghlan (2005).

[56]Lawrence, T., Dyck, B., Maitlis, S., & Mauws, M. (2006). The underlying structure of continuous change. *MIT Sloan Management Review, 47*(4), 59–66.

[57]Crossan, M., Lane, H., & White, R. (1999). An organizational learning framework: From intuition to institution. *Academy of Management Review, 24,* 522–537. See also fn 53, Nonaka (1994).

[58]This definition builds on the definition of criticism as "a serious examination and judgment of something" and "constructive criticism is always appreciated." Retrieved from http://wordnetweb. princeton.edu/perl/webwn. Accessed February 22, 2013.

[59]Tourish, D., & Robson, P. (2006). Sensemaking and the distortion of critical upward communication in organizations. *Journal of Management Studies, 43*(4), 711–730. They also show that receptivity to upward feedback was identified as a strength for only 16 percent of managers, and was rated as the lowest of 49 measures of managerial effectiveness. This finding is problematic given the fact that decision making improves when upward feedback systems are functioning well.

[60]Folkman, J. R. (2006). *The power of feedback.* Hoboken, NJ: John Wiley & Sons.

[61]Knudsen, M. (2011). Forms of inattentiveness: The production of blindness in the development of a technology for the observation of quality in health services. *Organization Studies, 32*(7), 963–989.

[62]Page 70 in Baker, D., Greenberg, C., & Hemingway, C. (2006). *What happy companies know.* Upper Saddle River, NJ: Pearson Prentice-Hall.

[63]See fn 60, Folkman (2006).

[64]Put in more scholarly terms, feedforward communication prepares the ground for intersubjective meaning generation (see fn 53, Jacobs & Coghlan, 2005).

[65]See fn 53, Jacobs & Coghlan (2005, p. 127).

[66]Despain, J., & Converse, J. B. (2003). *And dignity for all: Unlocking greatness through values-based leadership.* Upper Saddle River, NJ: Prentice Hall, pp. 142–143.

[67]Ibid., p. 169.

[68]Ideas and quotes in this case are drawn from research done by Fang Chen, Hari Bapuji, Bruno Dyck, and Xiaoyun Wang. The first quote comes from p. 114 in Chen, F., Wang, X., Bapuji, H., & Dyck, B. (2007). I learned more than I taught: Exploring the feedback loop of knowledge transfer. *Proceedings of OLKC,* pp. 105–117. The remaining three quotes come from pp. 14–16 in Chen, F. Bapuji, H., Dyck, B., & Wang, X. (2009). I learned more than I taught: The hidden dimension of learning in knowledge transfer. Academy of Management Annual Conference, Chicago, United States. The second quote can also be found on p. 115 in Chen, F., Bapuji, H., Dyck, B., & Wang, X (2012). I learned more than I taught: The hidden dimension of learning in knowledge transfer. *The Learning Organization, 19*(2), 109–120. There are currently more students studying English in China than in the United States.

[69]Inspired by comments made at the International Symposium on Catholic Social Thought and Management, Dayton, Ohio, June 2012 conference (with thanks to the person who described the basic idea of "Grace" and the "empty seat," and apologies for forgetting that person's name).

Feature Notes

OB in Action: Your Seat at the Table Sends a Message
Wickhorst, V., & Geroy, G. (2006). Physical communication and organization development. *Organization Development Journal, 24*(3), 54–63; Loyle, D. (2009). Where to sit in a business meeting . . . and why it mat-

ters. *BizME*. Retrieved from http://www.bizme.biz/biz-class/meeting-seating-the-fundamentals/; Brown, G. (2011). Setting (and choosing) the table: The influence of the physical environment in negotiation. In M. Benoliel (Ed.), *Negotiation excellence: Successful deal making* (pp. 39–56). Singapore: World Scientific Publishing.

My OB: Communicating across Cultures Lauring, J. (2011). Intercultural organizational communication: The social organizing of interaction in international encounters. *Journal of Business Communication, 48*(3), 231–255; van den Born, F., & Peltokorpi, V. (2010). Language policies and communication in multinational companies. *Journal of Business Communication, 47*(2), 97–118; Chen, F., Bapuji, H., Dyck, B., & Wang, X. (2012). I learned more than I taught: The hidden dimension of learning in knowledge transfer. *The Learning Organization, 19*(2), 109–120.

My OB: Impersonally Delivering What Is Personal Derks, D., & Bakker, A. (2010). The impact of e-mail communication on organizational life. *Cyber-psychology: Journal of Psychosocial Research on Cyberspace, 4*(1). Retrieved from http://www.cyber-psychology.eu/view.php?cisloclanku=2010052401&arti cle1; Baliet, D. (2010). Communication and cooperation in social dilemmas: A meta-analytic review. *Journal of Conflict Resolution, 54*(1), 39–57; Sheer, V. C. (2012). Does e-mail facilitate negative performance feedback giving? Supervisor and subordinate responses compared via the concept of social accountability. *Communication Studies, 63*(2), 220–242; Bies, R. J. (2012). The delivery of bad news in organizations: A framework for analysis. *Journal of Management, 39*(1), 136–162.

My OB: Trouble for Organizations When Members Text and Tweet? Gossit, L. M. (2013). Fired over Facebook: Issues of employee monitoring and personal privacy on social media websites. In S. May (Ed.) *Case studies in organizational communication: Ethical perspectives and practices* (2nd ed.) (pp. 207–218). Los Angeles, CA: Sage Publications; Melanson, T. (2013, April 18). 3 big Twitter no-noes for athletes. *Canadian Business*. Retrieved from http://www.canadianbusiness.com/technology-news/3-big-twitter-no-noes-for-athletes/; Calcaterra, C. (2012, March 14). Major League Baseball releases its social media policy—and it's pretty good. Retrieved from http://hardballtalk.nbcsports.com/2012/03/14/major-league-baseball-releases-its-social-media-policy-and-its-pretty-good/; Silverman, R. E. (2012, May 14). Facebook and Twitter postings cost CFO his job. *The Wall Street Journal*. Retrieved from http://online.wsj.com/article/SB10001424052702303505504577404542168061590.html

Chapter 12

[1]This case is developed based on information found in the following: John, E., & Fisher, A. (2011, February 6). Ethical pioneers changing the way we live: Ricardo Semler: Classroom revolutionary. *The Guardian*. Retrieved from http://www.guardian.co.uk/environment/2011/feb/06/ethical-living-martha-lane-fox; Semler, R. (1989, September/October). Managing without managers. *Harvard Business Review*, 76–84; Semler, R. (2004). *The seven-day weekend*. New York: Portfolio/Penguin Group. Note that the quote in the second paragraph ("I'd come from . . .") is drawn from John & Fisher (2011). The quote in the fifth paragraph ("Most of our programs . . .") is drawn from Semler (1989, p. 77). The quote in the seventh paragraph ("I can honestly say . . .") is drawn from Semler (2004, p.12).

[2]This quote and the reference to Frank Lloyd Wright are taken from Orr, D. (2006). Design: Part I. *Geez, 3*, 8.

[3]Alvesson M. (2011). Organizational culture: Meaning, discourse, and identity. In N. Ashkanasy, C. Wilderom, & M. Peterson (Eds.), *The handbook of organizational culture and climate* (2nd ed.) (pp. 11–28). Thousand Oaks, CA: Sage; Schein, E.H. (2010). *Organizational culture and leadership* (4th ed.). San Francisco, CA: Wiley; O'Reilly, C. A., & Chatman, J. A. (1996). Culture as social control: Corporations, culture, and commitment. In B. M. Staw & Cummings. L. L. (Eds.), *Research in organizational behavior* (pp. 157–200). Greenwich, CT: JAI Press.

[4]Schein, E. (1999). *The corporate culture survival guide*. San Francisco: John Wiley & Sons, Inc. and cited in Nazari, J. A., Herremans, I. M., Isaac, R. G., Manassian, A., & Kline, T. (2011). Organizational culture, climate and IC: An interaction analysis, *Journal of Intellectual Capital, 12*(2), 224–248.

[5]O'Reilly, C. A. (2001, Summer). Corporations, culture, and commitment: Motivation and social control in organizations. *California Management Review*, 9–25.

[6]Kotrba, L. M., Gillespie, M. A., Schmidt, A. M., Smerek, R. E., Ritchie, S. A., & Denison, D. R. (2012). Do consistent corporate cultures have better business performance? Exploring the interaction effects. *Human Relations, 65*(2), 241–262; Flynn F. J., & Chatman, J. A. (2001). Innovation and social control: Oxymoron or opportunity? In C. Cooper, S. Cartwright & P. C. Earley (Eds.) *Handbook of organizational culture* (pp. 263–287). Chichester: John Wiley & Sons.

[7]Hartnell, C. A., Ou, A., & Kinicki, A. (2011). Organizational culture and organizational effectiveness: A meta-analytic investigation of the competing values framework's theoretical suppositions. *Journal of Applied Psychology, 96*(4), 677–694.

[8]Gregory, B. T., Harris, S. G., Armenakis, A. A., & Shook, C. L. (2009). Organizational culture and effectiveness: A study of values, attitudes, and organizational outcomes. *Journal of Business Research, 62*, 673–679.

[9]Reported in Mindlin, A. (2009, November 22). The influence of zealous employees. *The New York Times*.

[10]Bezrukova, K., Thatcher, S. B., Jehn, K. A., & Spell, C. S. (2012). The effects of alignments: Examining group faultlines, organizational cultures, and performance. *Journal of Applied Psychology, 97*(1), 77–92; see fn 6, Kotrba et al. (2012).

[11]See fn 7, Hartnell et al. (2011).

[12]For example, Edgar Schein has "defined and described culture as a *structural* concept"; see p. 69 in Schein, E. H. (2010). *Organizational culture and leadership* (4th ed.). San Francisco, CA: Wiley. For more on the idea that the elements of culture and structure are related to and influence one another, see Shepherd, D. A., Patzelt, H., & Haynie, J. M. (2010). Entrepreneurial spirals: Deviation-amplifying loops of an entrepreneurial mindset and organizational culture. *Entrepreneurship Theory and Practice, 34*, 59–82.

[13]See fn 12, Schein (2010).

[14]See fn 12, Schein (2010, p. 29).

[15]See fn 12, Schein (2010, p. 33).

[16]For more on the Competing Values Framework, see Cameron, K. S., and Quinn, R. E. (2011). *Diagnosing and changing organizational culture: Based on the competing values framework* (3rd ed.). San Francisco, CA: Jossey-Bass. See also fn 8, Gregory et al. (2009); Giberson, T. R., Resick, C. J., Dickson, M. W., Mitchelson, J. K., Randall, K. R., & Clark, M.A. (2009). Leadership and organizational culture: Linking CEO characteristics to cultural values. *Journal of Business Psychology, 24,* 123–137; Hartnell, C.A., Ou, A.Y., & Kimicki, A. (2011). Organizational culture and organizational effectiveness: A meta-analytic investigation of the competing values framework's theoretical suppositions. *Journal of Applied Psychology, 96*(4), 677–694; Quinn, R. E., Spreitzer, G. M. (1991). The psychometrics of the competing values culture instrument and an analysis of the impact of organizational culture on the quality of life. In R. W. Woodman & W. A. Pasmore (Eds.), *Research in organizational change and development* (pp. 115–158). Greenwich, CT: JAI Press.

[17]Richard, O.C., McMillan-Capehart, A., Bhuian, S. N., & Taylor, E. C. (2009). Antecedents and consequences of psychological contracts: Does organizational culture really matter? *Journal of Business Research, 62,* 818–825.

[18]See Shaw, D. (2008, November 1) Toyota: Making the most of downtime. *Evansville Courier & Press*. Retrieved from http://www.courierpress.com/news/2008/nov/01/making-the-most-of-down-time-toyota-uses-for/

[19]Schneider, B., Ehrhart, M. G., & Macey, W H. (2013). Organizational climate and culture. *Annual Review of Psychology, 64*(1), 361–388.

[20]One study found a link between religious organizations' structures and its values, as expressed in their statements of faith. Dyck, B., Starke, F., Harder, H., & Hecht, T. (2005). Do the structures of religious organizations reflect their statements-of-faith? An exploratory study. *Review of Religious Research, 47*(1), 51–69.

[21]This is an adapted and somewhat simplified interpretation of Weber's ideas. A more detailed description of these four fundamentals, as well as theoretical and empirical support for the conventional versus sustainable approaches to the four fundamentals, can be found in Dyck, B., & Schroeder, D. (2005). Management, theology and moral points of view: Towards an alternative to the conventional materialist-individualist ideal type of management. *Journal of Management Studies, 42*(4), 705–735; and Dyck, B., & Weber, J. M. (2006). Conventional and radical moral agents: An exploratory look at Weber's moral-points-of-view and virtues. *Organization Studies, 27*(3), 429–450. See also Weber, M. (1958). *The Protestant ethic and the spirit of capitalism* (trans. T. Parsons). New York: Scribner's.

[22]This sustainable emphasis on process and relational competence is consistent with Mintzberg and Waters's (1985) notion of "strategic learning." Mintzberg, H., & Waters, J. 1985. Of strategies, deliberate and emergent. *Strategic Management Journal, 6,* 257–272. The sustainable approach does not see a lack of conventional formal structure as a weakness to be overcome, but rather embraces it as a hallmark of an appropriate way to manage the organizing function process.

[23]Dyck and Weber (2006; see fn 20) explicitly examined the relative emphasis that managers place on materialism and individualism. They found that managers who placed more emphasis on materialism and individualism placed more emphasis on standardization, specialization, centralization, and formalization, and less emphasis on experimentation, sensitization, dignification, and participation. In addition, they found that managers who placed less emphasis on materialism and individualism placed less emphasis on standardization, specialization, centralization, and formalization, and more emphasis on experimentation, sensitization, dignification, and participation.

[24]Clifford, S. (2011, April 24). One size fits nobody: Seeking a steady 4 or a 10. *The New York Times*. Retrieved from http://www.nytimes.com/2011/04/25/business/25sizing.html

[25]Note that the curvilinear relationships between structure and performance depicted in Figures 12.2, 12.3, and 12.4 are generally accepted in the literature, but have proven difficult to study empirically, with some important exceptions: Davis, J. P., Eisenhardt, K. M., & Bingham, C. G. (2009). Optimal structure, market dynamism, and the strategy of simple rules. *Administrative Science Quarterly, 54,* 413–452; Bradach, J. L. (1997). Using the plural form in the management of restaurant chains. *Administrative Science Quarterly, 42,* 276–304; Gibson, C., & Birkinshaw, J. (2004). The antecedents, consequences and mediating role of organizational ambidexterity. *Academy of Management Journal, 47,* 209–226; Mintzberg, H., & McHugh, A. (1985). Strategy formation in an adhocracy. *Administrative Science Quarterly, 30,* 160–197. Rothaermel, F. T., Hitt, M., & Jobe, L. (2006). Balancing vertical integration and strategic outsourcing: Effects on product portfolios, new product success, and firm performance. *Strategic Management Journal, 27,* 1033–1056.

[26]Hirst, G., van Knippenberg, D., Chen, C. H., & Sacramento, C.A. (2011). How does bureaucracy impact individual creativity? A cross-level investigation of team contextual influences on goal orientation-creativity relationships. *Academy of Management Journal, 54*(3), 624–641.

[27]Ussahawanitchakit, P. (2008). Organizational learning capability, organizational commitment, and organizational effectiveness: An empirical study of accounting firms. *Journal of International Business Strategy, 8*(3), 1–12.

[28]We recognize that Selznick's idea of goal displacement goes beyond our definition. For example, see Raab, J. (2004). Selznick revisited: Goal displacement as an unavoidable consequence of cooptation? Working paper, Department of Organization Studies, Tilburg University, Netherlands.

[29]Badaracco, J. L. Jr., & Webb, A. (1995). Business ethics: A view from the trenches. *California Management Review, 37*(2), 8–28.

[30]Newman, A., & Sheikh, A. Z. (2012). Organizational rewards and employee commitment: A Chinese study. *Journal of Managerial Psychology, 27*(1), 71–89.

[31]Some of the details in this study have been disguised. Plowman, D. A., Baker, L. T, Beck, T. E., Kulkarni, M., Solansky, S. T., & Travis, D. V. (2007). Radical change accidentally: The emergence and amplification of small change. *Academy of Management Journal, 50*(3), 515–543.

[32]Note that an overall organization may be very centralized (i.e., authority for most decisions is retained in the CEO's office), while a particular subunit within that organization may be relatively

decentralized (i.e., what little decision-making authority resides in the marketing department is dispersed widely throughout that department). The reverse is also true: A relatively decentralized organization may have centralized departments if the department head insists on making all the major and minor decisions for the department. Finally, the organization and its subunits can both be centralized, or both can be decentralized.

[33]Zheng, W., Yang, B., and McLean, G.N. (2010). Linking organizational cultural, structure, strategy, and organizational effectiveness: Mediating role of knowledge management. *Journal of Business Research, 63,* 763–771.

[34]See fn 26, Hirst et al. (2011).

[35]Colquitt, J. A. (2001). On the dimensionality of organizational justice: A construct validation of a measure. *Journal of Applied Psychology, 86*(3), 386–400.

[36]Ferris, D., Spence, J. R., Brown, D. J., & Heller, D. (2012). Interpersonal injustice and workplace deviance: The role of esteem threat. *Journal of Management, 38*(6), 1788–1811.

[37]Coviello, N. E., & Joseph, R. M. (2012). Creating major innovations with customers: Insights from small and young technology firms. *Journal of Marketing, 76*(6), 87–104.

[38]See fn 1, Semler (2004, p. 179). Semler talks about trusting employees to choose their own hours, and how when people from CNN were at Semco to do a special program, they found no one in the building on the first day of filming (which happened to be the day after Carnival): "But later, after interviewing, they calculated that our employees worked more hours than their counterparts at other companies. Which goes to say that when people are given freedom, they'll do whatever it takes to get the job done" [quoted on p. 34 of Vogl, A. J. (2004, May/June). The anti-CEO. *Across the Board,* 30–36].

[39]This sustainable OB approach is consistent with Baake's principle of allowing everyone in the organization to make important decisions, to "shoot the game-winning basket." See chapter 15 in Baake, D. (2005). *Joy at work: A revolutionary approach to fun on the job.* Seattle, WA: PVG.

[40]Colquitt, J. A., & Rodell, J. B. (2011). Justice, trust, and trustworthiness: A longitudinal analysis integrating three theoretical perspectives. *Academy of Management Journal, 54*(6), 1183–1206.

[41]Even weak monitoring systems undermine interpersonal respect. Note also that introducing sanctions tends to make members see decisions more in terms of business rather than ethical terms. Tenbrunsel, A. E., & Messick, D. M. (1999). Sanctioning systems, decision frames, and cooperation. *Administrative Science Quarterly, 44*(4), 684–707.

[42]DeGeer, R., McCollum, J., & Peterson, R. (2012, December 5). Organizing for growth: Scaling up in Canadian oil sands. *Oil + Gas Monitor.* Retrieved from http://www.oilgasmonitor.com/organizing-growth-scaling-canadian-oil-sands/3412/

[43]Mol, M. J., & Kotabe, M. (2011). Overcoming inertia: Drivers of the outsourcing process, *Long Range Planning, 44*(3), 160–178.

[44]Young, J. R. (2011, August 7). Professors cede grading power to outsiders—even computers. *The Chronicle of Higher Education.* Retrieved from http://chronicle.com/article/Professors-Cede-Grading-Power/128528/

[45]See "How can we offer such high-quality prescription glasses for $95? We cut out the middlemen." Retrieved from http://www.warbyparker.com/how-we-do-it. Accessed February 20, 2013.

[46]Bansal, S. (2012, May 9). Shopping for a better world. *The New York Times.* Retrieved from http://opinionator.blogs.nytimes.com/2012/05/09/shopping-for-a-better-world/

[47]The advantages of relatively small organizational subunits and organizations are also described in Dyck & Schroeder (2005); see fn 21.

[48]Savitz, A. W., & Weber, K. (2006). *The triple bottom line: How today's best-run companies are achieving economic, social, and environmental success—and how you can too.* San Francisco: Jossey-Bass.

[49]Amason, A. C., & Sapienza, H. J. (1997). The effects of top management size and interaction norms on cognitive and affective conflict. *Journal of Management, 23*(4), 495–516; Van Der Westhuizen, D. W., Pacheco, G., & Webber, D. J. (2012). Culture, participative decision making and job satisfaction. *The International Journal of Human Resource Management, 23*(13), 2661–2679.

[50]See fn 1, Semler (2004, pp. 10–11).

[51]See fn 1, Semler (2004, p. 185).

[52] George, L. (2009, June 8). Channeling autism: A Danish tech firm harnesses the power of the autistic brain. *Maclean's,* pp. 40–42; Booth, M. (2009, May 31). Better, faster . . . and no office politics: The company with the autistic specialists. *The Independent.* Retrieved from http://www.independent.co.uk/life-style/gadgets-and-tech/features/bet-ter-faster-and-no-office-politics-the-company-with-the-autistic-specialists-1693057.html; Carey B. (2012, January 19). New definition of autism will exclude many, study suggests. *The New York Times.* Retrieved from http://www.nytimes.com/2012/01/20/health/research/new-autism-definition-would-exclude-many-study-suggests.html?pagewanted=all; Cook, G. (2012). The autism advantage. *New York Times.* Retrieved from http://www.nytimes.com/2012/12/02/magazine/the-autism-advantage.html?pagewanted=all; Autism Rates Rocket—1 in 38 British Boys—Cambridge Study. Retrieved from http://childhealthsafety.wordpress.com/2009/03/21/autism-rates-rocket/; O'Grady, K.. (2015, July 31). Three things you need to know about autism in Canada. *Huffington Post.* Retrieved from http://www.huffingtonpost.ca/kathleen-oagrady/asd-canada_b_7905686.html; Ozretic, A. (2013, October 28). Creating great employees (who happen to be autistic). *Forbes.* Retrieved from http://www.forbes.com/sites/techonomy/2013/10/28/creating-great-employees-who-happen-to-be-autistic/; Specialisterne Canada. (2013). SAP and Specialisterne: Working together to employ people with autism. Retrieved from http://ca.specialisterne.com/about-specialisterne/sap-partnership/; Winter, S. (2013). Specialisterne launches in Canada. Retrieved from http://ca.specialisterne.com/2013/11/04/specialisterne-launches-in-canada/

[53]We thank one of our reviewers for the idea for this Discussion Starter. Research cited comes from Kiron, D., Kruschwitz, N., Haanaes, K., & Velken, I. V S. (2012). Sustainability nears a tipping point. *MIT Sloan Management Review, 53*(2), 69–74; Strand, R. (2013). The chief officer of corporate social responsibility: A study of its presence in top management teams. *Journal of Business Ethics,* 1–14; see also Mink, K. E. (2012). The effects of organizational structure on sustainability report compliance. College of Technology Masters Theses. Paper 62. http://docs.lib.purdue.edu/techmasters/62

Feature Notes

OB in Action: Pounding the Rock Associated Press (2011, December 25). Raptors and new coach will keep chipping away. *The New York Times*. Retrieved from http://www.nytimes.com/2011/12/26/sports/basketball/raptors-coach-dwane-casey-plans-to-chip-away.html; Koreen E., (2011, December 12). Casey urges Raptors to persevere. *National Post*. Retrieved from http://news.nationalpost.com/sports/nba/eric-koreen-casey-urges-raptors-to-pound-the-rock; Sandler, A. (2011, December 27). Here's why the Toronto Raptors have a 1,300-pound boulder sitting in their locker room. Business Insider. Retrieved from http://www.businessinsider.com/toronto-raptors-boulder-2011-12; Smith, D. (2014, October 24). Two decades of turmoil. *The Toronto Star*. Retrieved from http://www.thestar.com/sports/raptors/2014/10/24/toronto_raptors_20th_season_two_decades_of_turmoil.html

OB in Action: Will a Spoonful of Efficiency Change the Culture of Starbucks? Jargon, J. (2010, October 13). At Starbucks, Baristas told no more than two drinks. *The Wall Street Journal*. Retrieved from http://www.wsj.com/articles/SB10001424052748704164004575548403514060736; Jargon, J. (2009, August 4). Latest Starbucks buzzword: 'Lean' Japanese techniques. *The Wall Street Journal*. Retrieved from http://www.wsj.com/articles/SB124933474023402611; [Starbucks employee reviews.] Retrieved from http://www.jobitorial.com/starbucks-job-reviews-C941?PageNum=3. Accessed February 20, 2013.

My OB: What Brand of Shoes Are You Wearing? Doorey, D. J. (2011). The transparent supply chain: From resistance to implementation at Nike and Levi-Strauss. *Journal of Business Ethics*, 103(4), 587–603; Greenhouse, S. (2010, July 26). Pressured, Nike to help workers in the Honduras. The New York Times. Retrieved from http://www.nytimes.com/2010/07/27/business/global/27nike.html. See also video posted by Sweatshop Free. (2011, October 29). "Behind the Swoosh." Retrieved from http://sweatfreeshop.com/sweatshop-videos/behind-the-swoosh/

Chapter 13

[1]Of course, some of the practices described here may have changed since the research was conducted upon which this case is based. Unless otherwise noted, the quotes in this case were drawn from Van Maanen, J. (1991). The smile factory: Work at Disneyland. In P. J. Frost, L. Moore, M. Louis, C. Lundberg, & J. Martin (Eds.), *Reframing organizational culture* (pp. 58–76). Newbury Park, CA: Sage. Information was also drawn from Boje, D. M. (1995). Stories of the storytelling organization: A postmodern analysis of Disney as "*Tamara*-land." *Academy of Management Journal*, 38(4), 997–1035; MacDonald, C. (2005). The quest for perfect customer service never stops. *Amusement Business*, 17(5), 18–19; and Brannan, M. Y. (2004). When Mickey loses face: Recontextualization, semantic fit, and the semiotics of foreignness. *Academy of Management Review*, 29(4), 593–616. The first quote in the second paragraph ("At Disney, we believe . . .") was drawn from A. Meek (January 26, 2015). Former executive shares the secrets to

how Disney runs its empire. *Fast Company*. The quotes in the last sentence of the second paragraph ("polished, groomed . . .") were drawn from p. 305 of Fjellman, S. M. (1992). *Vinyl leaves: Walt Disney World and America*. Boulder, CO: Westview Press; cited in Boje (1995). See also Brannan (2004). In the fourth paragraph, the quote "Our managers. . ." was drawn from Meek (2015), the quote "are regarded by . . ." was drawn from Van Maanen (1991), and the quote "rule by fear" was drawn from Boje (1995, p. 1027).

[2]As described in chapter 12, organizational structure can be seen as the combination of the four fundamental elements of organizing that describe how (1) work activities are being completed in the best way; (2) members know which subtasks they should perform; (3) there is orderly deference among members; and (4) members work together harmoniously.

[3]Alvesson M. (2011). Organizational culture: Meaning, discourse, and identity. In N. Ashkanasy, C. Wilderom, & M. Peterson (Eds.). *The handbook of organizational culture and climate* (2nd ed.) (pp. 11–28). Thousand Oaks, CA: Sage; Schein, E. (1985). *Organizational culture and leadership*. San Francisco, CA: Jossey-Bass; O'Reilly, C. A., & Chatman, J. A. (1996). Culture as social control: Corporations, culture, and commitment. In B. M., Staw & L. L. Cummings (Eds.), *Research in organizational behavior* (pp. 157–200). Greenwich, CT: JAI Press.

[4]A unique function of leadership is the "creation and management of culture," p. 171 in Schein, E. H. (1991) *Organizational culture and leadership*. San Francisco: Jossey-Bass.

[5]See "Podcast: Culture eats strategy for breakfast" from Knowledge@ W. P. Carey. Retrieved from http://knowledge.wpcarey.asu.edu/article.cfm?articleid=1506. Accessed February 21, 2013.

[6]Brett Ledbetter interviews Maya Moore (WNBA player), who "explains how one player can make the difference in creating a culture of success around a basketball program." See "How to create a winning culture." Retrieved from http://www.ihoops.com/training-room/player-psychology/How-to-Create-a-Winning-Culture.htm. Accessed February 21, 2013.

[7]The research in Van den Steen, E. (2010). The origin of shared beliefs (and corporate culture). *The RAND Journal of Economics*, 4(4), 617–648 shows that strong performance creates a strong culture, rather than the other way around (a view held by other scholars).

[8]Building on analysis in Fry, L.W., & Cohen, M. P. (2009). Spiritual leadership as a paradigm for organizational transformation and recovery from extended work hours cultures. *Journal of Business Ethics*, 84, 265–278.

[9]See fn 7, Van den Steen (2010), and Van den Steen, E. (2009). Culture clash: The costs and benefits of homogeneity. *Management Science*, 56(10), 1718–1738.

[10]Sorensen, J. B. (2002). The strength of corporate culture and the reliability of firm performance. *Administrative Science Quarterly*, 47(1), 70–82.

[11]Kotrba, L. M., Gillespie, M. A., Schmidt, A. M., Smerek, R. E., Ritchie, S. A., & Denison, D. R. (2012). Do consistent corporate cultures have better business performance? Exploring the interaction effects. *Human Relations*, 65(2), 241–262.

[12]Sommers, D. B., & Dyck, B. (2011). A process model of social intrapreneurship within a for-profit company: First Community Bank. In G.T. Lumpkin & J. A. Kats (Eds.), *Advances in entrepreneurship, Firm Emergence and Growth*. Volume 13, pp. 141–177. Bingley, UK: Emerald Group Publishing.

[13]Schneider, B., Goldstein, H. W., & Smith, D. B. (1995). The ASA framework: An update. *Personnel Psychology, 48,* 747–779; De Cooman, R. (2013). Attraction-selection-attrition model. *Encyclopedia of management theory*. KU Leuven.

[14]Dyck, B., Walker, K., Starke, F., & Uggerslev, K. (2011). Addressing concerns raised by critics of business schools by teaching multiple approaches to management. *Business and Society Review, 116*(1), 1–27.

[15]Kabanoff, B., & Brown, S. (2008). Knowledge structures of prospectors, analyzers, and defenders: Content, structure, stability, and performance. *Strategic Management Journal, 29,* 149–171; Miller D. (1993). The architecture of simplicity. *Academy of Management Review, 18,* 116–138.

[16]See fn 10, Sorensen (2002).

[17]Stewart, J. B. (2012, October 5). The shadow of Steve Jobs in Apple's Maps push. *The New York Times*. Retrieved from http://www.nytimes.com/2012/10/06/business/apples-map-app-could-raise-antitrust-concerns.html?_r=1&. Accessed February 21, 2013.

[18]For more on using the Competing Values Framework, see Cameron, K. S., & Quinn, R. E. (2011). *Diagnosing and changing organizational culture: Based on the Competing Values Framework* (3rd ed.). San Francisco, CA: Jossey-Bass. Using the Competing Values Framework's four organizational culture types to describe four conventional types and four parallel sustainable types is not inconsistent with the original framework and theory, which were designed to be applied to all sorts of different organizations. This four-part culture typology has been identified as "one of the 40 most important management theoretical models: Ten Have, S., Ten Have, W., Stevens, F., & van der Elst, M. (2003). *Key management models: What they are and when you use them*. Upper Saddle River, NJ: FT Press (cited in Giberson, T. R., Resick, C. J., Dickson, M. W., Mitchelson, J. K., Randall, K. R., & Clark, M. A. (2009). Leadership and organizational culture: Linking CEO characteristics to cultural values. *Journal of Business Psychology, 24,* 123–137. The Competing Values Framework has also been described as an organizational culture taxonomy widely used in the literature: Hartnell, C. A., Ou, A. Y., & Kimicki, A. (2011). Organizational culture and organizational effectiveness: A meta-analytic investigation of the Competing Values Framework's theoretical suppositions. *Journal of Applied Psychology, 96*(4), 677–694; citing Ostroff, C., Kinicki, A. J., & Tamkins, M. M. (2003). Organizational culture and climate. In W. C. Borman, D. R. Ilgen, R. J. Klimoski, & I. Weiner (Eds.), *Handbook of psychology* (Vol. 12, pp. 565–593). Hoboken, NJ: Wiley.

[19]See fn 18, Hartnell, Ou, & Kimicki (2011).

[20]See fn 18, Giberson et al. (2009).

[21]Belasen, A., & Frank, N. (2008). Competing values leadership: Quadrant roles and personality traits. *Leadership & Organization Development Journal, 29*(2), 127–143.

[22]Long, C., Bendersky, C., and Long, C. (2011). Fairness monitoring: Linking managerial controls and fairness judgments in organizations. *Academy of Management Journal, 54*(5), 1045–1068.

[23]See pages 6 and 67 in Cameron & Quinn (2011); see fn 18.

[24]Our discussion of conventional organizational structure builds on the work of Burns, T., & Stalker, G. M. (1966). *The management of innovation* (2nd ed.). London: Tavistock.

[25]Note there are at least two caveats of this continuum. First, in actual practice there are exceptions to the tendency for the four fundamentals to appear precisely as shown on the continuum. New ventures, for example, may have high centralization (e.g., the entrepreneur makes all of the decisions) and low standardization and specialization (e.g., the entrepreneur does things "on the fly" and creates policies only on an as-needed basis). Also, some start-up organizations may require high standardization because they are operating in highly regulated industries or because of key customer demands. Other exceptions to the continuum may occur in light of departmentalization, such as when large mechanistic organizations have divisional departmentalization, and when smaller organic organizations adopt functional departments. Second, while thinking about the mechanistic–organic structure along a continuum has proven to be both useful and elegant, it has been noted that some of its dimensions may be oversimplified. In particular, rather than place centralization and decentralization on opposite ends of a *single* continuum, it may be more useful to have two separate scales, where the organization could conceivably be seen to be becoming simultaneously more centralized and more decentralized. This could occur, for example, if decision-making authority was removed from middle management, with some of that authority going to top managers (centralization) and some going to lower-level managers (decentralization). For more discussion on this issue, see Cullen, J. B., & Perrewe, P. L. (1981). Decision making configurations: An alternative to the centralization/decentralization conceptualization. *Journal of Management, 7*(2), 89–103; Boumgarden, P., Nickerson, J., & Zenger, T. R. (2012). Sailing into the wind: Exploring the relationships among ambidexterity, vacillation, and organizational performance. *Strategic Management Journal, 33,* 587–610.

[26]The sustainable continuum is similar to, but also different than, the conventional mechanistic–organic continuum, where the organic structure tends to focus on external concerns and the mechanistic structure deals with internal issues. Also, parallel caveats apply here as to the mechanistic–organic continuum. First, there will be exceptions to the tendency for organizations to place their emphasis across each of the four sustainable fundamentals of organizing either internally or externally. For example, an organization may be very sensitive to *external* stakeholders, but emphasize *internal* experimentation, dignification, and experimentation. Second, rather than use a continuum, it may be more helpful to offer two separate scales for each of the four dimensions so that, for example, dignification could be high (or low) *both* internally and externally. That said, as with the mechanistic–organic continuum, the elegance and parsimony of the inward–outward distinction are useful for understanding sustainable organizational types and organizational design.

[27]Perrow, C. (1967). A framework for the comparative analysis of organizations. *American Sociological Review, 32,* 194–208; Daft, R., & Macintosh, N. (1978). A new approach to design and use of management information. *California Management Review, 21,* 82–92.

[28]Woodward, J. (1965). *Industrial organizations: Theory and practice*. London: Oxford University Press; and Woodward, J. (1958). *Management and technology*. London: Her Majesty's Stationery Service. Note that Woodward herself does not classify her work using the terms from the four quadrants we use here, but rather her work was foundational in developing subsequent thinking

in the relationship between technology and organizational structure. Perrow, C. (2010). From medieval history to smashing the medieval account of organizations. *Research in the Sociology of Organizations, 29,* 25–28.

[29]Porter, M. E. (1980). *Competitive strategy: Techniques for analyzing industries and competitors.* New York: Free Press; and Porter, M. E. (1985). *Competitive advantage: Creating and sustaining superior performance.* New York: Free Press. Note that, with regard to the fourth strategy described here, Porter himself argues against combining cost leadership and differentiation strategies. Despite this, the two can be seen to have been combined in a very highly regarded framework developed by Miles and Snow; see Miles, R. E., & Snow, C. C. (1978). *Organizational strategy, structure, and process.* New York: McGraw-Hill.

[30]Stankevit, E., Grunda, R., & Bartkus, E. V. (2012). Pursuing a cost leader strategy and business sustainability objectives: Walmart case study. *Economics and Management, 17*(3), 1200–1206.

[31]Mathur, S., & Kenyon, A. (2012). *Creating valuable business strategies.* New York: Routledge.

[32]Again, note that Michael Porter argues against simultaneously pursuing both low-cost and differentiation strategies because it is a recipe for getting stuck in the middle, though others have argued that an integrated low-cost/differentiation strategy may well work (e.g., Murray, A. I. [1988]. A contingency view of Porter's "generic strategies." *Academy of Management Review, 13*(3), 390–400). Indeed, Porter himself uses the example of Ivory soap as a low-cost exemplar, which can clearly be argued to have a differentiation strategy (99.44 percent pure).

[33]See MEC Accountability Report. Retrieved from http://www.mec.ca/AST/ContentPrimary/Sustainability/Accountability-Report.jsp. Accessed February 21, 2013.

[34]For a list of such organizations, see http://www.ciwmb.ca.gov/Tires/Products/. Accessed February 21, 2013.

[35]Hynes, M. E., & Weiss, S. (2004). Experience after school: Engaging older adults in after school programs: Experience Corps. Retrieved from http://www.experiencecorps.org/images/pdf/toolkit.pdf. Accessed February 21, 2013.

[36]Zeng, A. Z. (2013). Coordination mechanisms for a three-stage reverse supply chain to increase profitable returns. *Naval Research Logistics (NRL), 60*(1), 31–45; Jewell, M. (2007). Staples starts computer recycle program. Associated Press. http://www.physorg.com/news98937884.html. Accessed February 21, 2013.

[37]Conventional management theory adopts a contingency theory approach to organization design. For a classic article on this, see Child, J. (1972). Organizational structure, environment, and performance: The role of strategic choice. *Sociology, 6,* 1–22. For a more recent discussion on this, see Du Gay, P., & Vikkels, S. (2013). Exploitation, exploration and exaltation: Notes on a metaphysical (re)turn to 'one best way of organizing.' *Research in the Sociology of Organizations, 37,* 249–279.

[38]Of course, there are other factors and artifacts related to culture that are not discussed in this chapter. An obvious one is organizational size, where larger generally means more emphasis on predictability, standardization, formalization, and specialization. This makes intuitive sense: It may be possible to manage 5 or even 50 people with minimal formal rules and standards and a clan culture, but to manage 5,000 or 50,000 people requires a more mechanistic structure and hierarchical structure. It is exactly for this reason that Semco (opening case, chapter 12) limits the size of its departments to 150 members—Semco does not want a hierarchical culture! Another important factor is the larger business environment. The more stable the environment, the more opportunity there is for a hierarchical or market culture. Of course, the national culture where an organization is operating is also important (see chapter 3). For example, one study found that clan cultures are dominant in Finland and Estonia, market cultures more prevalent in countries like Germany, Japan, China, and Russia, and hierarchical cultures are especially likely to be found in Czech and Slovakia; see Übius, Ü., & Alas, R. (2009). Organizational culture types as predictors of corporate social responsibility. *Engineering Economics, 61*(1), 90–99.

[39]For more information on the Defender, Prospector, and Analyzer types, see Miles & Snow (1978); see fn 29. The four-part typology described in this chapter draws from and elaborates on their work, as well as others who link culture, strategy, and organizational design. For example, research in Bindu Gupta (2011). A comparative study of organizational strategy and culture across industry. *Benchmarking: An International Journal, 18*(4), 510–528 points to a relationship between a Prospector strategy and an adhocracy culture, and between a Defender strategy and a hierarchy culture (but also with an Analyzer strategy and adhocracy or clan cultures). A study by Slater. S. F., Olson, E. M., & Finnega, C. (2011). Business strategy, marketing organization culture, and performance. *Marketing Letters, 22,* 227–242 also shows a link between Prospectors and adhocracy cultures, and links the Analyzer to market (and to hierarchy) cultures. An article by Miles, R. E., Snow, C. C., & Sharfman, M. P. (1993). Industry synergy, variety, and performance. *Strategic Management Journal, 14,* 163–177 illustrates overlaps between a Prospector/differentiation strategy (e.g., Hewlett-Packard), whose culture fostered risk-taking, innovation, and individuality, and between a Defender/low-cost strategy (e.g., Emerson Electric), whose culture emphasized frugality, discipline, and attention to detail. This is not to downplay the difficulties in linking all these pieces (Ketchen [2003, 100]). Ketchen, D. J. (2003) An interview with Raymond E. Miles and Charles C. Snow. *Academy of Management Executive, 17*(4), 97–104. For others doing work in this area, see Sallee, A., & Flaherty, K. (2003). Enhancing salesperson trust: An examination of managerial values, empowerment, and the moderating influence of SBU strategy. *Journal of Personal Selling & Sales Management, 23*(4), 299–310; Cabrera, E. F., & Bonache. J. (1999). An expert HR system for aligning organizational culture and strategy. *Human Resource Planning, 22*(1), 51–60; O'Reilly, C., Chatman, J., & Caldwell, D. (1991). People and organizational culture: A profile comparison approach to assessing person-organization fit. *Academy of Management Journal, 34,* 487–516.

[40]Economist. (2014, October 11). Banks? No, thanks! *The Economist.* Retrieved from http://www.economist.com/news/business/21623673-graduates-worlds-leading-business-schools-investment-banking-out-and-consulting

[41]Giacalone, R. A., Jurkiewicz, C. L., & Knouse, S. B. (2012). The ethical aftermath of a values revolution: Theoretical bases of change, recalibration, and principalization. *Journal of Business Ethics, 110*(3), 1–11; Etzioni, A. (2001). *The monochrome society.* Princeton, NJ: Princeton University Press.

[42]There is also strong interest in sustainable organizations among retired people. A survey among Americans aged 50 to 70 years indicated that the majority wanted to dedicate their time to community or national service after their primary career had ended. This finding prompted the Harvard Business School to develop a new multidisciplinary leadership studies program to help such people design multidimensional solutions to pressing external problems (described in Dearlove, D., & Crainer, S. [2006]. Recent research: AARP University. *Strategy + Business, 43*, 1–4).

[43]Elgin, D. (1993). *Voluntary simplicity: Toward a way of life that is outwardly simple, inwardly rich* (rev. ed.). New York: Quill; Vannini, P., & Taggart, J. (2013). Voluntary simplicity, involuntary complexities, and the pull of remove: The radical ruralities of off-grid lifestyles. *Environment and Planning A, 45*(2), 295–311.

[44]For more information on the Defender, Prospector, and Analyzer types, see Miles & Snow (1978), fn 29.

[45]Charles Snow is confident that Lincoln Electric is an example of a Defender type (Ketchen [2003]; see fn 39). See also Roberts, J., & Saloner, G. E., & Milgrom, P. (2013). Strategy and organizations. In R. Gibbons & J. Robers (Eds.), *The Handbook of Organizational Economics*, (pp. 799–852). Princeton, New Jersey: Princeton University Press.

[46]Best companies to work for. (2006). *Fortune*. Retrieved from. http://money.cnn.com/magazines/fortune/best-companies/2012/snapshots/4.html. Accessed February 21, 2013.

[47]Menguc, B., Auh, S., & Shih, E. (2007). Transformational leadership and market orientation: Implications for the implementation of competitive strategies and business unit performance. *Journal of Business Research, 60*, 314–321.

[48]For more information, visit Neechi Foods's home page at http://neechi.ca/. Accessed February 21, 2013.

[49]Brunk, S. E. (2003). From theory to practice: Applying Miles and Snow's ideas to understand and improve firm performance. *Academy of Management Executive, 17*(4), 105–108.

[50]Haque, U. (2011). *The new capitalist manifesto: Building a disruptively better business*. Boston: Harvard Business School Press; Interface website, http://www.interfaceglobal.com/Company/Culture.aspx. Accessed February 21, 2013; Anderson, R. C. (1998). *Mid-course correction: Toward a sustainable enterprise: The Interface model*. Atlanta, GA: Peregrinzilla Press. Quote in third paragraph taken from Dean, C. (2007, May 22). Executive on a mission: Saving the planet. *The New York Times*. Retrieved from http://www.nytimes.com/2007/05/22/science/earth/22ander.html?_r=1&scp=1&sq=&st=nyt&oref=slogin. Accessed February 21, 2013; Nature and the industrial enterprise: Mid-course correction: An interview with Ray C. Anderson. (2004) *Engineering Enterprise* (Spring), 6–12. Retrieved from http://www.lionhrtpub.com/ee/spring04/nature.html. Accessed February 21, 2013; Company website: http://www.interfaceinc.com. Accessed February 21, 2013; Hawken, P., Lovins A., & Lovins, L. H. (1999). *Natural capitalism: Creating the next Industrial Revolution*. Boston: Little, Brown; Bryant, A. (2013, February 17). So why aren't you at your desk on Sunday? *The New York Times*. Retrieved from http://www.nytimes.com/2013/02/17/business/daniel-hendrix-of-interface-inc-on-work-life-balance.html?_r=0. Accessed February 21, 2013.

Feature Notes

OB in Action: Reddit Revolt Debigare, A., & Weinberger, D. (2015, July 14). How Reddit the business lost touch with Reddit the culture. *Harvard Business Review*. Retrieved from https://hbr.org/2015/07/how-reddit-the-business-lost-touch-with-reddit-the-culture+&cd=7&hl=en&ct=clnk&gl=ca; Kulwin, N. (2015, July 14). New CEO: Some people on Reddit 'shouldn't be here at all'. Retrieved from http://recode.net/2015/07/14/new-ceo-some-people-on-reddit-shouldnt-be-here-at-all/; Lynch, B., & Swearingen, C. (2015, July 8). Why we shut down Reddit's "ask me anything" forum. *The New York Times*. Retrieved from http://www.nytimes.com/2015/07/08/opinion/why-we-shut-down-reddits-ask-me-anything-forum.html?_r=1; McArdle, M. (2015, July 13). Reddit's Ellen Pao can only blame herself. *Bloomberg View*. Retrieved from http://www.bloombergview.com/articles/2015-07-13/reddit-s-ellen-pao-can-only-blame-herself; Pengelly, M., & Rawlinson, K. (2015, July 11). Reddit chief Ellen Pao resigns after receiving 'sickening' abuse from users. *The Guardian*. Retrieved from http://www.theguardian.com/technology/2015/jul/10/ellen-pao-reddit-interim-ceo-resigns; Tracy, A. (2015, July 13). A timeline of the Reddit drama and Ellen Pao's fall from power. *Forbes*. Retrieved from http://www.forbes.com/sites/abigailtracy/2015/07/13/a-timeline-of-the-reddit-drama-and-ellen-paos-fall-from-power/; Vela, M. (2015, July 10). Reddit CEO Ellen Pao is stepping down. *Time*. Retrieved from http://time.com/3953655/reddit-ellen-pao/

My OB: Culture at Your Workplace Irish Guards. Retrieved from http://en.wikipedia.org/wiki/Irish_Guards. Accessed October 9, 2013.

OB in Action: Organizational Structure in the Global Marketplace Duhigg C., & Barboza, D. (2012, January 25). In China, human costs are built into an iPad. *The New York Times*. Retrieved from http://www.nytimes.com/2012/01/26/business/ieconomy-apples-ipad-and-the-human-costs-for-workers-in-china.html? pagewanted=all; Duhigg, C., & Greehouse, S. (2012, March 29). Electronic giant vowing reforms in China plants. *The New York Times*. Retrieved from http://www.nytimes.com/2012/03/30/business/apple-supplier-in-china-pledges-changes-in-working-conditions.html?ref=charlesduhigg; Barboza, D., & Duhigg, C. (2012, September 12). China contractor again faces labour issue on iPhones. *The New York Times*. Retrieved from http://www.nytimes.com/2012/09/11/technology/foxconn-said-to-use-forced-student-labor-to-make-iphones.html?pagewanted=all; Ives, M. (2013, July 11). Colin Flahive opened a restaurant in China that's a beacon of enlightened management. *The Christian Science Monitor*. Retrieved from http://www.csmonitor.com/World/Making-a-difference/2013/0711/Colin-Flahive-opened-a-restaurant-in-China-that-s-a-beacon-of-enlightened-management

OB in Action: Mission-Driven Organizations Kelly, M. (2012). *Owning our future: The emerging ownership revolution: Journeys to a generative economy*. San Francisco, CA: Berrett-Koehler. Quote about Organic Valley is taken from Kelly, M. (Spring 2009). Not just for profit: Emerging alternatives to the shareholder-centric model could help companies avoid ethical mishaps and contribute more to the world at large. *Strategy + Business,* 54. Retrieved from http://www.strategy-business.com/article/09105?pg=all. Accessed February 21, 2013; http://www.bcorporation.net/. Accessed February 21, 2013. Information about Novo Nordisk retrieved from http://www.novonordisk.com/about_us/default.asp and http://www.novonor-disk.com/about_us/novo_nordisk_way/nnway_default.asp. Accessed February 21, 2013. For more on Ben & Jerry's as a B corporation, see http://www.bcorporation.net/community/ben-jerrys. Accessed July 5, 2013.

OB in Action: Open-Source Philosophy at Tesla Motors Advances Industry Associated Press. (2015, January 6). Toyota opens fuel-cell patents to competitors in bid to spur development of hydrogen-powered vehicles. *Financial Post.* Retrieved from http://business.financialpost.com/news/transportation/toyota-opens-fuel-cell-patents-to-competitors-in-bid-to-spur-development-of-hydrogen-powered-vehicles; Musk, E. (2014, June 12). All our patents belong to you. Tesla Motors. Retrieved from http://www.teslamotors.com/en_CA/blog/all-our-patent-are-belong-you

Chapter 14

[1]Florida, R., & Goodnight, J. (2005). Managing for creativity. *Harvard Business Review, 83*(7/8), 124–131; http://www.cbsnews.com/stories/2001/02/08/eveningnews/main270458.shtml; O'Reilly, C. III, & Pfeffer, J. (2000). *Hidden value: How great companies achieve extraordinary results with ordinary people.* Boston, MA: Harvard Business School Press; http://www.sas.com/corporate/overview/index.html; London, S. (2003, September 26). Profit machines that put the people first. *Financial Times.* Retrieved from http://search.ft.com/ftArticle?queryText=SAS+Institute+talent+&y=7&aje=false&x=14&id=030926000481&ct=0; Hardy, Q. (2011, June 9). SAS—We spurned IBM, now to win. *Forbes.* Retrieved from http://www.forbes.com/sites/quentinhardy/2011/06/09/sas-ibms-bad-culture-how-well-win/.

[2]Jiang, K., Lepak, D. P., Hu, H., & Baer, J. C. (2012). How does human resource management influence organizational outcomes? A meta-analytic investigation of mediating mechanisms. *Academy of Management Journal, 55*(6), 1264–1294; Bart, C. K., Bontis, N., & Taggar, S. (2001). A model of the impact of mission statements on firm performance. *Management Decision, 39*(1), 19–35; Messersmith, J. G., Patel, P. C., Lepak, D. P., & Gould-Williams, J. S. (2011). Unlocking the black box: Exploring the link between high-performance work systems and performance. *Journal of Applied Psychology, 96*(6), 1105–1118.

[3]Pfeffer, J., & Veiga, J. (1999). Putting people first for organizational success. *Academy of Management Executive, 13*(2), 37–48; and Pfeffer, J. (2005). Producing sustainable competitive advantage through the effective management of people. *Academy of Management Review, 19*(4), 95–106.

[4]This model is a compilation of findings from Jiang et al. (2012), Messersmith et al. (2011), and Bart et al. (2001). HRM systems also positively influence human capital development, but the contribution of skills to organizational outcomes is secondary to motivation. Further, HRM practices can contribute to relational coordination that contributes to organizational performance; see Gittell, J., Seidner, R., & Wimbush, J. (2010). A relational model of how high-performance work systems work. *Organization Science, 21*(2), 490–506.

[5]Hartley, D. (2004, September). Job analysis at the speed of reality. *Training and Development,* 20–24.

[6]Neubert, M., & Longenecker, C. (2003). Creating job clarity: HR's role in improving organizational focus and performance. *HR Advisor, 9*(4), 17–21.

[7]Oldham, G. R., & Hackman, J. (2010). Not what it was and not what it will be: The future of job design research. *Journal of Organizational Behavior, 31*(2–3), 463–479; Humphrey, S. E., Nahrgang, J. D., & Morgeson, F. P. (2007). Integrating motivational, social, and contextual work design features: A meta-analytic summary and theoretical extension of the work design literature. *Journal of Applied Psychology, 92*(5), 1332–1356; Hackman, R., & Oldham, G. (1980). *Work redesign.* Boston: Addison-Wesley.

[8]See fn 7, Oldham & Hackman (2010).

[9]Desjardins Group. See what Desjardins has to offer [Company website]. Retrieved from https://www.desjardins.com/ca/about-us/careers/why-work-at-desjardins/what-desjardins-offers/index.

[10]Holman, D., Totterdell, P., Axtell, C., Stride, C., Port, R., Svensson, R., & Zibarras, L. (2012). Job design and the employee innovation process: The mediating role of learning strategies. *Journal of Business and Psychology, 27*(2), 177–191.

[11]See fn 7, Oldham & Hackman (2010).

[12]See fn 10, Holman et al. (2012).

[13]See fn 7, Humphrey et al. (2007).

[14]Leach, D. J., Wall, T. D., Rogelberg, S. G., & Jackson, P. R. (2005). Team autonomy, performance, and member job strain: Uncovering the teamwork KSA link. *Applied Psychology: An International Review, 54*(1), 1–24; Stevens, M. J., & Campion, M. A. (1994). The knowledge skill and ability requirements for teamwork: Implications for human resource management. *Journal of Management, 20,* 503–530.

[15]Zajonc, R. B. (1980). Compresence. In P. B. Paulus (Ed.), *Psychology of group influence* (pp. 35–60). Hillsdale, NJ: Lawrence Erlbaum.

[16]Weintraub, A. (2007, July 30). Is Merck's medicine working? *BusinessWeek,* 67–70.

[17]Noe, R., Hollenbeck, J., Gerhart, B., & Wright, P. (2006). *Human resource management: Gaining a competitive advantage.* New York: McGraw-Hill.

[18]Balliet, D., Mulder, L. B., & Van Lange, P. A. M. (2011). Reward, punishment, and cooperation: A meta-analysis. *Psychological Bulletin, 137,* 594–615.

[19]Butterfield, K. D., Trevino, L. K., & Ball, G. A. (1996). Punishment from the manager's perspective: A grounded investigation and inductive model. *Academy of Management Journal, 39*(6), 1479–1512.

[20]Longenecker, C., & Fink, L. (1999). Creating effective performance appraisals. *Industrial Management, 41*(5), 18–23; Kondrasuk, J. N. (2011). So what would an ideal performance appraisal look like? *Journal of Applied Business and Economics, 12*(1), 57–71.

[21]Reb, J., & Greguras, G. J. (2010). Understanding performance ratings: Dynamic performance, attributions, and rating purpose. *Journal of Applied Psychology, 95*(1), 213–220.

[22]Ibid.

[23]Umpqua Bank. (2015). Careers at the world's greatest bank. [Company website]. Retrieved from http://umpquabank.com/1.0/pages/Careers.aspx?prodCAT=qCareers.

[24]Anseel, F., Van Yperen, N. W., Janssen, O., & Duyck, W. (2011). Feedback type as a moderator of the relationship between achievement goals and feedback reactions. *Journal of Occupational and Organizational Psychology, 84*(4), 703–722; Jawahar, I. M. (2010). The mediating role of appraisal feedback reactions on the relationship between rater feedback-related behaviors and ratee performance. *Group & Organization Management, 35*(4), 494–526.

[25]Kok-Yee, N., Koh, C., Ang, S., Kennedy, J. C., & Kim-Yin, C. (2011). Rating leniency and halo in multisource feedback ratings: Testing cultural assumptions of power distance and individualism-collectivism. *Journal of Applied Psychology, 96*(5), 1033–1044; Murphy, K. R., & Cleveland, J. N. (1995). *Understanding performance appraisal: Social, organizational, and goal-based perspectives.* Thousand Oaks, CA: Sage.

[26]See fn 25, Kok-Yee et al. (2011).

[27]See fn 24, Jawahar (2010).

[28]See fn 24, Anseel et al. (2011).

[29]Pichler, S. (2012). The social context of performance appraisal and appraisal reactions: A meta-analysis. *Human Resource Management, 51*(5), 709–732.

[30]Chiang, F. T., & Birtch, T. A. (2010). Appraising performance across borders: An empirical examination of the purposes and practices of performance appraisal in a multi-country context. *Journal of Management Studies, 47*(7), 1365–1393.

[31]ibid.

[32]Peretz, H., & Fried, Y. (2012). National cultures, performance appraisal practices, and organizational absenteeism and turnover: A study across 21 countries. *Journal of Applied Psychology, 97*(2), 448–459.

[33]Witt, D. (2010, November 8). Helping people win at work—3 keys to stop evaluating and start coaching instead. Retrieved at http://leaderchat.org/2010/11/08/helping-people-win-at-work-3-keys-to-stop-evaluating-and-start-coaching-instead/.

[34]CB Staff. (2014, November 10). Canada's best employers 2015: The top 50 large companies. *Canadian Business.* Retrieved from http://www.canadianbusiness.com/lists-and-rankings/best-jobs/2015-best-employers-top-50/

[35]Kleingeld, A., van Mierlo, H., & Arends, L. (2011). The effect of goal setting on group performance: A meta-analysis. *Journal of Applied Psychology, 96*(6), 1289–1304.

[36]McGregor, J. (2007, November 19). The employee is always right. *BusinessWeek,* 80–82.

[37]Canada Labour Code, R.S.C., 1985, c. L-2, c 7, s 206.1.

[38]Judge, T. A., Piccolo, R. F., Podsakoff, N. P., Shaw, J. C., & Rich, B. L. (2010). The relationship between pay and job satisfaction: A meta-analysis of the literature. *Journal of Vocational Behavior, 77*(2), 157–167.

[39]Treasury Board of Canada Secretariat. (2014, August 13). Frequently asked questions on the performance management program results for executives: What is performance pay? Retrieved from http://www.tbs-sct.gc.ca/prg/faq-eng.asp#a6.

[40]Salimäki, A., & Järnsén, S. (2010). Perceptions of politics and fairness in merit pay. *Journal of Managerial Psychology, 25*(3), 229–251.

[41]Rynes, S. L., Colbert, A. E., & Brown, K. G. (2002). HR professionals' beliefs about effective human resource practices: Correspondence between research and practice. *Human Resource Management, 41*(2), 149–174.

[42]Men's Wearhouse. (2015). Advantages: Compensation and benefits [Company website]. Retrieved from http://employment.menswearhouse.com/ats/advantage Selector.action?type=compensation.

[43]See fn 1, O'Reilly & Pfeffer (2000).

[44]Benefiel, M. (2005). *Soul at work (p. 21).* New York: Seabury Books.

[45]Barnes, C. M., Hollenbeck, J. R., Jundt, D. K., DeRue, D., & Harmon, S. J. (2011). Mixing individual incentives and group incentives: Best of both worlds or social dilemma? *Journal of Management, 37*(6), 1611–1635.

[46]Dyck, B., Starke, F., & Dueck, C. (2009). Management, prophets and self-fulfilling prophecies. *Journal of Management Inquiry, 18*(3), 184–196.

[47]Nelson, B. (2005). *1001 ways to reward employees* (2nd ed.). New York, NY: Workman.

[48]For examples of such organizations, see Gold, L. (2010). *New financial horizons: The emergence of an economy of communion.* Hyde Park, NY: New City Press.

[49]Weinstein, M. (2006). Suite success: On demand delivers for IBM. *Training, 43*(3), 18–20.

[50]IBM. (2011). A commitment to employee education. IBM at 100. Retrieved from http://www-03.ibm.com/ibm/history/ibm100/us/en/icons/employeeedu/.

[51]Blume, B. D., Ford, J. K., Baldwin, T. T., & Huang, J. L. (2010). Transfer of training: A meta-analytic review. *Journal of Management, 36,* 1065–1105; Baldwin, T. T., & Ford, J. K. (1988). Transfer of training: A review and directions for future research. *Personnel Psychology, 41,* 63–105; Colquitt, J. A., LePine, J. A., & Noe, R. A. (2000). Toward an integrative theory of training motivation: A meta-analytic path analysis of 20 years of research. *Journal of Applied Psychology, 85*(5), 678–707.

[52]See fn 51, Blume et al. (2010).

[53]See fn 49, Weinstein (2006).

[54]See fn 48, Gold (2010, pp. 137–138).

[55]Tsui, A., & Wu, J. (2005). The new employment relationship versus the mutual investment approach: Implications for human resource management. *Human Resource Management, 44*(2), 115–121.

[56]Longenecker, C., & Neubert, M. J. (2003). The management development needs of front-line managers: Voices from the field. *Career Development International, 8*(4), 210–218.

[57]Tsui, A., Pearce, J., Porter, L., & Tripoli, A. (1997). Alternative approaches to the employee-organization relationship: Does investment in employees pay off? *Academy of Management Journal, 40,* 1089–1121.

[58]Wang, D., Tsui, A., Zhang, Y., & Ma, L. (2003). Employment relationships and firm performance: Evidence from an emerging economy. *Journal of Organizational Behavior, 24,* 511–535.

[59]Van Iddekinge, C. H., Roth, P. L., Putka, D. J., & Lanivich, S. E. (2011). Are you interested? A meta-analysis of relations between vocational interests and employee performance and turnover. *Journal of Applied Psychology, 96*(6), 1167–1194.

[60]Kronick, J. (2006). Booz Allen Hamilton puts people first: One firm, one goal. *Training, 43*(3), 11–16.

[61]Timberland. (2015). Timberland responsibility. [Company website]. Retrieved from http://community.timberland.com/.

[62]Sanders, D. (2008). *Built to serve: How to drive the bottom line with people-first practices.* New York, NY: McGraw-Hill.

[63]Kellermanns, F. W., Walter, J., Floyd, S. W., Lechner, C., & Shaw, J. C. (2011). To agree or not to agree? A meta-analytical review of strategic consensus and organizational performance. *Journal of Business Research, 64*(2), 126–133.

[64]Desmidt, S., Prinzie, A., & Decramer, A. (2011). Looking for the value of mission statements: A meta-analysis of 20 years of research. *Management Decision, 49*(3), 468–483.

[65]Cited in Peyrefitte, J., & David, F. R. (2006). A content analysis of the mission statements of United States firms in four industries. *International Journal of Management, 23*(2), 296–310.

[66]Internationl Committee of the Red Cross. (2008, June 19). The ICRC's mission statement. [Company website]. Retrieved from http://www.icrc.org/eng/resources/documents/misc/icrc-mission-190608.htm.

[67]Desjardins Group. (2015). Vision, mission and values. [Company website]. Retrieved from https://www.desjardins.com/ca/about-us/desjardins/who-we-are/mission/index.jsp?navigMW=mm&.

[68]See fn 65, Peyrefitte & David (2006).

[69]Southwest. (2015). About Southwest: The mission of Southwest Airlines. [Company website]. Retrieved from http://www.southwest.com/about_swa/mission.html.

[70]If motivational potential and meaning in a mission statement are not of much interest to top managers, the Internet offers a quick way to create a mission statement—see the Mission Statement generator at http://www.netinsight.co.uk/portfolio/mission/missgen.asp. Accessed March 8, 2013.

[71]P. 7 in Fishman, C. (2006). The Walmart effect and a decent society: Who knew shopping was so important? *Academy of Management Perspective, 20*(3), 6–25.

[72]Walmart. (2015). Our story. [Company website]. Retrieved from http://corporate.walmart.com/our-story/.

[73]Case, D. (2008, p. 115). Dead man walking. *Fast Company, 124,* 112–119.

[74]Ibid., 115.

[75]AOL. (2015). Our values: Our mission. [Company website]. Retrieved from http://corp.aol.com/our-values/our-mission.

[76]Baum, J. R., Locke, E. A., & Kirkpatrick, S. A. (1998). A longitudinal study of the relation of vision and vision communication to venture growth in entrepreneurial firms. *Journal of Applied Psychology, 83,* 43–54. Cited in Kirkpatrick, S. A., Wofford, J. C., & Baum, J. R. (2002). Measuring motive imagery contained in the vision statement. *Leadership Quarterly, 13,* 139–150.

[77]See fn 76, Kirkpatrick et al. (2002).

[78]Costco. (2015). About us: Costco Code of Ethics. [Company website]. Retrieved from http://www.costco.ca/about-us.html#code.

[79]Holmes S., & Zellner, W. (2004). Good jobs and good wages. *BusinessWeek* online cover story, May 31.

[80]Wong-Ming Ji, D. J., & Neubert, M. J. (2001). *Voices in visioning: Multiple stakeholder participation in strategic visioning.* Washington, DC: Academy of Management Meetings.

[81]For example, as we will see in chapter 9, this understanding facilitates the emphasis on emergent strategic learning, which further differentiates the sustainable approach from the conventional approach.

[82]Pirson, M., & Malhotra, D. (2011). Foundations of organizational trust: What matters to different stakeholders? *Organization Science, 22*(4), 1087–1104.

[83]See fn 64, Desmidt et al. (2011).

[84]See *The Secrets of Successful Business Leaders—Ms. Yolanda Sevilla* (The Leather Collection, Inc.), produced by the Business Management Society, De La Salle University, Manila, Philippines. The fascinating interview with this sustainable business executive can be found at http://www.youtube.com/watch?v=5 I1ie7 N4Hbg&feature=channel&list=UL (published July 3, 2012). Viewed March 8, 2013.

[85]Herman Miller case study, The Yale Center for Faith and Culture. http://nexus.som.yale.edu/hermanmiller/?q=node/100. Accessed March 14, 2013; Manz, C. C., Manz, K. P., Adams, S. B., & Shipper, F. (2011). Sustainable performance with values-based shared leadership: A case study of a virtuous organization. *Canadian Journal of Administrative Sciences, 28*(3), 284–296; DePree, H. (1986). *Business as unusual: The people and principles at Herman Miller.* Zeeland, MI: Herman Miller, Inc.; DePree, M. (1989, p. 6). *Leadership is an art.* New York: Doubleday.

Feature Notes

My OB: Is Rank-and-Yank an Effective Motivational Method? Kwoh, L. (January 31, 2012). Rank and yank retains vocal fans. WSJ Online. Retrieved from http://online.wsj.com/article/SB10001424052970203636350457 7186970064375222.html; Mattioli, D. (February 2, 2011). Reinventing LendingTree. WSJ Online. Retrieved from http://online.wsj.com/article/SB10001424052748703960 80457620313730379694.html.

OB in Action: Whataburger, Whatacompany Breal, J. (2007). Secret sauce. *Fast Company*, 115, 61–63; http://www.whataburger.com/Company. Accessed March 8, 2013; Ruggless, R. (2004, January). WHATABURGER: Nora Garcia. *Nation's Restaurant News*, 38(4), 196–197.

OB in Action: BancVue against the World Dahl, D. (2010, September 1). How I beat the Fed. *Inc.* Retrieved from http://www.inc.com/magazine/20100901/how-i-beat-the-fed.html; Krajicek, G. (2011, March 4). Find creative ways to convey corporate values, build culture. *Austin Business Journal*. Retrieved from http://www.bizjournals.com/austin/print-edition/2011/03/04/find-creative-ways-to-convey-corporate.html; Morrison, C. (2012, August 16). Local bank leaders host gas giveaway to bring attention to brand alliance. Retrieved from http://www.nooga.com/156794/local-bank-leaders-host-gas-giveaway-to-bring-attention-to-brand-alliance/; http://www.bancvue.com/about/bancvue.html.

Chapter 15

[1]Dakens, L., Edwards, P., Johnson, J., & and Morse, N. (2008). *SwitchPoints: Culture change on the fast track to business success.* Somerset, NJ: John Wiley & Sons; Financial Post. (2013, February 4). Accountability and courage are values that define CN's corporate culture. Retrieved from http://business.financialpost.com/uncategorized/accountability-and-courage-are-values-that-define-cns-corporate-culture; Financial Post. (2013, February 4).

CN's remarkable story of transformation in Canadian business. Retrieved from http://business.financialpost.com/uncategorized/cns-remarkable-story-of-transformation-in-canadian-business; Mclean, D., & Finn, P. (2014). *A road taken: My journey from a CN station house to the CN boardroom*. Vancouver, BC: Greystone Seven steps are taken from Dakens et al., pp. 18–20.

[2]Mohrman, S. A., & Lawler, III, E. E. (2012). Generating knowledge that drives change. *Academy of Management Perspectives, 26*(1), 41–51.

[3]Shin, J., Taylor, M., & Seo, M. (2012). Resources for change: The relationships of organizational inducements and psychological resilience to employees' attitudes and behaviors toward organizational change. *Academy of Management Journal, 55*(3), 727–748.

[4]See fn 2, Mohrman & Lawler (2012, p. 41).

[5]Van de Ven, A. H., & Poole, M. S. (1995). Explaining development and change in organizations. *Academy of Management Review, 20*(3), 510–540.

[6]Kavanagh, M. H., & Ashkanasy, N. M. (2006). The impact of leadership and change management strategy on organizational culture and individual acceptance of change during a merger. *British Journal of Management, 17,* 81–103.

[7]García-Morales, V., Jiménez-Barrionuevo, M., & Gutiérrez-Gutiérrez, L. (2012). Transformational leadership influence on organizational performance through organizational learning and innovation. *Journal of Business Research, 65*(7), 1040–1050.

[8]Goll, I., & Rasheed, A. A. (2011). The effects of 9/11/2001 on business strategy variability in the US air carrier industry. *Management Decision, 49*(6), 948–961; Greiner, L. E. (1998). Evolution and revolution as organizations grow. *Harvard Business Review, 76*(3), 55–68; Haveman, H. A., Russo, M. V., & Meyer, A. D. (2001). Organizational environments in flux: The impact of regulatory punctuations on organizational domains, CEO succession, and performance. *Organization Science, 12*(3), 253–273.

[9]Nadler, D., & Tushman, M. (1990). Beyond the charismatic leader and organizational change. *California Management Review, 32*(2), 77.

[10]Vaccaro, A., Brusoni, S., & Veloso, F. M. (2011). Virtual design, problem framing, and innovation: An empirical study in the automotive industry. *Journal of Management Studies, 48*(1), 99–122.

[11]Although the four-step description provided here is based on Kurt Lewin's (1951) basic change model, it draws from and builds on a variety of studies, including the four-phase learning model in Crossan, M., Lane, H. W., & White, R. E (1999). An organizational learning framework: From intuition to institution. *Academy of Management Review, 24*(3), 522–537.

[12]Worley, C. G., & Feyerherm, A. E. (2003). Reflections on the future of organization development. *Journal of Applied Behavioral Science, 39*(1), 97–115.

[13]Michael, B., Neubert, M. J., Michael, R. (2012). Three alternatives to organizational value change and formation: Top down, spontaneous decentralized, and interactive dialogical. *Journal of Applied Behavioral Science, 48*(3), 380–409.

[14]Yang, Y., & Konrad, A. M. (2011). Diversity and organizational innovation: The role of employee involvement. *Journal of Organizational Behavior, 32*(8), 1062–1083.

[15]Gaudes, A. J. (2005). A longitudinal study of incumbent retailers and the arrival of large-format competitors in the home improvement industry: A look at the effectiveness of incumbent product specialization, customer specialization, and adaptation on firm performance. PhD. Thesis, University of Manitoba.

[16]Eisenstat, R. A., Beer, M., Foote, N., Fredberg, T., & Norrgren, F. (2008). The uncompromising leader. *Harvard Business Review, 86*(7/8), 50–57.

[17]Stack, J., & Burlingham, B. (1992). *The great game of business*. New York: Doubleday.

[18]Heymann, J. (2010, September 27). Bootstrapping profits by opening the books. *Bloomberg Businessweek*, (4197), 62.

[19]Muurlink, O., Wilkinson, A., Peetz, D., & Townsend, K. (2012). Managerial autism: Threat-rigidity and rigidity's threat. *British Journal of Management, 23*(Suppl 1), S74–S87; Dyck, B. (1996). The role of crises and opportunities in organizational change. *Non-profit and Voluntary Sector Quarterly, 25,* 321–346.

[20]Edwards, J. (2011, August 15). Pfizer plans 16,300 layoffs amid health benefit cuts for retirees. *Money Watch*. Retrieved from http://www.cbsnews.com/8301-505123_162-42849477/pfizer-plans-16300-layoffs-amid-health-benefit-cuts-for-retirees/

[21]Kotter, J. (1996). *Leading change*. Boston, MA: Harvard University Press.

[22]Fugate, M., Prussia, G. E., & Kinicki, A. J. (2012). Managing employee withdrawal during organizational change: The role of threat appraisal. *Journal of Management, 38*(3), 890–914.

[23]Ford, J. D., Ford, L. W., & D'Amelio, A. (2008). Resistance to change: The rest of the story. *Academy of Management Review, 33*(2), 362–377.

[24]Johnson, J. L., & O'Leary-Kelly, A. M. (2003). The effects of psychological contract breach and organizational cynicism: Not all social exchange violations are created equal. *Journal of Organizational Behavior, 24,* 627–647.

[25]Kira, M., Balkin, D. B., & San, E. (2012). Authentic work and organizational change: Longitudinal evidence from a merger. *Journal of Change Management, 12*(1), 31–51.

[26]See fn 23, Ford et al. (2008).

[27]Danişman, A. (2010). Good intentions and failed implementations: Understanding culture-based resistance to organizational change. *European Journal of Work and Organizational Psychology, 19*(2), 200–220.

[28]Ngoc, B. (2012, November 3). Puma Energy completes acquisition in Vietnam. *Vietnam Investment Review*. Retrieved at http://www.vir.com.vn/news/business/puma-energy-completes-acquisition-in-vietnam.html.

[29]Nguyen, L. D., Mujtaba, B. G., & Boehmer, T. (2012). Stress, task, and relationship orientations across German and Vietnamese cultures. *International Business & Management, 5*(1), 10–20.

[30]Vo, A., & Stanton, P. (2011). The transfer of HRM policies and practices to a transitional business system: The case of performance management practices in the US and Japanese MNEs operating in Vietnam. *International Journal of Human Resource Management, 22*(17), 3513–3527.

[31]Shin, J., Taylor, M., & Seo, M. (2012). Resources for change: The relationships of organizational inducements and psychological

resilience to employees' attitudes and behaviors toward organizational change. *Academy of Management Journal, 55*(3), 727–748.

[32]See fn 22, Fugate et al. (2012).

[33]Armenakis, A. A., & Harris, S. G. (2009). Reflections: Our journey in organizational change research and practice. *Journal of Change Management, 9*(2), 127–142.

[34]Peters, T., & Waterman, R. H. (2004). *In search of excellence.* New York: HarperCollins.

[35]Gouillart, F., & Billings, D. (2013). Community-powered problem solving. *Harvard Business Review, 91*(4), 70–77.

[36]Ibid.

[37]Tetrick, L. E., Quick, J., & Gilmore, P. L. (2012). Research in organizational interventions to improve well-being: Perspectives on organizational change and development. In C. Biron, M. Karanika-Murray, C. Cooper (Eds.), *Improving organizational interventions for stress and well-being: Addressing process and context* (pp. 59–76). New York, NY: Routledge/Taylor & Francis Group.

[38]Robertson, P. J., Roberts, D. R., & Porras, J. I. (1993). Dynamics of planned organizational change: Assessing empirical support for a theoretical model. *Academy of Management Journal, 36*(3), 619–634.

[39]McGirt, E. (2010, September). Artist. Athlete. CEO. *Fast Company, 114*, 66–74. Retrieved from http://www.fastcompany.com/1676902/how-nikes-ceo-shook-shoe-industry

[40]Bushe, G. R., & Kassam, A. F. (2005). When is appreciative inquiry transformational: A meta-case analysis. *The Journal of Applied Behavioral Science, 41(2)* 161–181.

[41]Cooperrider, D.L. (2005). *Appreciative inquiry: A positive revolution in change.* San Francisco, CA: Berrett-Koehler.

[42]Mishra, P., & Bhatnagar, J. (2012). Appreciative inquiry: Models & applications. *Indian Journal of Industrial Relations, 47*(3), 543–558.

[43]Ledema, J. D., Whitney, D., Mohr, B. J., & Griffin, T. J. (2003). *The appreciative inquiry summit: A practitioner's guide for leading large-group change.* San Francisco, CA: Berrett-Koehler.

[44]Boss, R., Dunford, B. B., Boss, A. D., & McConkie, M. L. (2010). Sustainable change in the public sector: The longitudinal benefits of organization development. *Journal of Applied Behavioral Science, 46*(4), 436–472.

[45]Mike McDaniel shared this example with one of the authors.

[46]See fn 31, Shin et al. (2012); Neubert, M. J., & Cady, S. H. (2001). Program commitment: A multi-study longitudinal field investigation of its impact and antecedents. *Personnel Psychology, 54*, 421–448; Herscovitch, L., & Meyer, J. P. (2002). Commitment to organizational change: Extension of a three-component model. *Journal of Applied Psychology, 87*(3), 474–487.

[47]Neves, P. (2011). Building commitment to change: The role of perceived supervisor support and competence. *European Journal of Work & Organizational Psychology, 20*(4), 437–450; Reichers, A. E., Wanous, J. P., & Austin, J. T. (1997). Understanding and managing cynicism about organizational change. *Academy of Management Executive, 11*(1), 48–59; see fn 21,Kotter (1996).

[48]Oreg S., Vakola, M., & Armenakis, A. (2011). Change recipients' reactions to organizational change: A 60-year review of quantitative studies. *Journal of Applied Behavioral Science, 47*(4), 461–524.

[49]Hurley, R. F. (2006). The decision to trust. *Harvard Business Review, 84*(9), 55–62.

[50]See fn 46, Neubert & Cady (2001); fn 48, Oreg et al. (2011); Herold, D. M., Fedor, D. B., & Caldwell, S. D. (2007). Beyond change management: A multilevel investigation of contextual and personal influences on employees' commitment to change. *Journal of Applied Psychology, 92*, 942–951.

[51]Peccei, R., Giangreco, A., & Sebastiano, A. (2011). The role of organisational commitment in the analysis of resistance to change. *Personnel Review, 40*(2), 185–204; Fox, S., & Amichai-Hamburger, Y. (2001). The power of emotional appeals in promoting organizational change. *Academy of Management Executive, 15*, 84–94; fn 31, Shin et al. (2012).

[52]Schweiger, D. M., & DeNisi, A. S. (1991). Communication with employees following a merger: A longitudinal field experiment. *Academy of Management Journal, 34*(1), 110–135.

[53]See fn 13, Michael et al. (2012).

[54]Hill, N., Seo, M., Kang, J., & Taylor, M. (2012). Building employee commitment to change across organizational levels: The influence of hierarchical distance and direct managers' transformational leadership. *Organization Science, 23*(3), 758–777.

[55]See fn 31, Shin et al. (2012); Holt, D. T., Armenakis, A A., Feild, H. S., & Harris, S. G. (2007). Readiness for organizational change: The systematic development of a scale. *Journal of Applied Behavioral Science, 43*, 232–255.

[56]BC Ferries. (2015). Our company: Corporate profile. Retrieved July 3, 2015, from http://www.bcferries.com/about/More_Information.html; BC Ferries. (2006). *B.C. Ferry Authority: Annual Report 2005/06.* Victoria, BC: British Columbia Ferry Services Inc. & B.C. Ferry Authority. Retrieved from http://www.bcferries.com/files/AboutBCF/AR/BCF_Annual_Report_2005-2006.pdf; *CBC News.* (2012, January 19). BC Ferries safety record gets thumbs-up. **CBC News:** British Columbia. Retrieved from http://www.cbc.ca/news/canada/british-columbia/bc-ferries-safety-record-gets-thumbs-up-1.1157078; Gary, G. (2013). Safety culture boosts safety, performance and profits. *Maritime News 2013: Fuel Efficiency*; Force Technology. (2015). Retrieved July 4, 2015, from http://www.forcewindengineering.dk/forcewindengineeringdk_docs/showdoc.asp?id=140331153719&type=doc&pdf=true; Norbury, K. (2013, January 17). Smooth sailing: The challenge. *Up front.* Retrieved from http://upfront.pwc.com/trust/334-smooth-sailing; Watts, R. (2015, May 24). B.C. Ferries aims to be safest in the world. *Times Colonist.* Retrieved from http://www.timescolonist.com/life/islander/b-c-ferries-aims-to-be-safest-in-the-world-1.1945311

[57]This case is based information found in Dyck, B., Buckland, J., Harder, H., & Wiens, D. (2000). Community development as organizational learning: The importance of agent-participant reciprocity. *Canadian Journal of Development Studies, 21*, 605–620; Personal correspondence with Harold Harder (most recently March 13, 2008).

Feature Notes

OB in Action: Delivering Change Canada Post. (2015). Canada Post's five-point action plan: Our progress to date. Retrieved from https://www.canada-post.ca/cpo/mc/assets/pdf/aboutus/5_en.pdf; Staff (2015, March 11). Union Says Canada Post's franchises will mean job losses for postal workers. *Cape Breton Post*. Retrieved from http://www.capebretonpost.com/News/Local/2015-03-11/article-4073930/Union-says-Canada-Posts-franchises-will-mean-job-losses-for-postal-workers/1; *CBC News*. (2015, July 30). Letters disappearing, more radical changes needed at Canada Post, prof says. *CBC News:* Saskatchewan. Retrieved from http://www.cbc.ca/news/canada/saskatchewan/letters-disappearing-more-radical-changes-needed-at-canada-post-prof-says-1.3174395; Lee, I. (2015). Is the cheque still in the mail?: The Internet, e-commerce, and the future of Canada Post Corporation. Macdonald-Laurier Institute. Retrieved from http://www.macdonaldlaurier.ca/files/pdf/MLI_PostOffice_F_web.pdf; McKenna, B. (2013, April 17). Canada Post swings to profit but red ink looms. *The Globe and Mail: Report on Business*. Retrieved from http://www.theglobeandmail.com/report-on-business/canada-post-swings-to-profit-but-red-ink-looms/article11327974/; Sturgeon, J. (2013, December 11). 7 things to know about Canada Post's plan to axe home delivery. *Global News*. Retrieved from http://globalnews.ca/news/1023396/seven-things-to-know-about-canada-posts-plan-to-axe-mail-service/.

OB in Action: Diverging Thoughts at Harvard Kotter, J. (2005). *The heart of change*. Boston, MA: Harvard University Press; Kotter, J. (1995). Leading change: Why transformation efforts fail. *Harvard Business Review, 73*(2), 59–67; Beer, M., Eisenstat, R., & Spector, B. (1990). Why change programs don't produce change. *Harvard Business Review, 68*(6), 158–166; Beer, M., & Nohria, N. (2000). Cracking the code of change. *Harvard Business Review, 78*(3), 133–141.

OB in Action: Managing the Morning after the Merger Snyder, B. (2010, June 16). Continental and United: This "merger of equals" isn't a great plan. *CBS News: Moneywatch*. http://www.cbsnews.com/8301-505123_162-43641867/continental-and-united-this-merger-of-equals-isnt-a-great-plan/. Accessed February 8, 2013; King, D. R., Dalton, D. R., Daily, C. M., & Covin, J. G. (2004). Meta-analyses of post-acquisition performance: Indicators of unidentified moderators. *Strategic Management Journal, 25*(2), 187–200; Mirvis, P. H. (1995). Negotiations after the sale: The roots and ramifications of conflict in an acquisition. *Journal of Occupational Behavior, 6,* 65–84; Covin, T. J., Sightler, K. W., Kolenko, T. A., & Tudor, R. K. (1996). An investigation of postacquisition satisfaction with the merger. *Journal of Applied Behavioral Science, 32*(2), 125–142; Martin, H. (2012, March 5). Merged United and Continental operations off to a bumpy start. *Los Angeles Times*. Retrieved from http://articles.latimes.com/2012/mar/05/business/la-fi-mo-united-glitches-20120305

My OB: How Does Change Make You Feel? Pepitone, J. (2012, September 26). Marissa Mayer's Yahoo turnaround starts to take shape. *CNN MoneyTech*. Retrieved from http://money.cnn.com/2012/09/26/technology/yahoo-strategy/index.html; Oreg, S., Vakola, M., & Armenakis, A. (2011). Change recipients' reactions to organizational change: A 60-year review of quantitative studies. *Journal of Applied Behavioral Science, 47*(4), 461–524; McKendall, M. (1993). The tyranny of change: Organizational development revisited. *Journal of Business Ethics, 12,* 93–104.

OB in Action: TOMS Walks the Talk Cole, P. (2010, September 15). Toms free shoe plan, boosted by Clinton, reaches million mark. *Bloomberg*. Retrieved from http://www.bloomberg.com/news/2010-09-16/toms-shoe-giveaway-for-kids-boosted-by-bill-clinton-reaches-million-mark.html; http://www.toms.com/blakes-bio; http://www.toms.com/eyewear/blog; Accessed March 8, 2013; Schweitzer, T. (2012, May 7). The way I work: Blake Mycoskie of Toms Shoes. *Inc.com*. Retrieved from http://www.inc.com/magazine/20100601/the-way-i-work-blake-mycoskie-of-toms-shoes.html

Chapter 16

[1]Bradford, H. (July 30, 2013). TerraCycle recycles the "non-recyclable"—cigarette butts, candy wrappers and its own profits. The Huffington Post. Retrieved from http://www.huffingtonpost.com/2013/07/30/terracycle_n_3678691.html. Young, E. (February 2, 2015). Waste not, want not—making money from rubbish. BBC News. Retrieved from http://www.bbc.com/news/business-31036601.

[2]Schurenberg, E. (2012, January 9). What's an entrepreneur? The best answer ever. *Inc*. Retrieved from http://www.inc.com/eric-schurenberg/the-best-definition-of-entrepreneurship.html

[3]For a description of intrapreneurs and how they differ from entrepreneurs, see Martiarena, A. (2013). What's so entrepreneurial about intrapreneurs? *Small Business Economics, 40*(1), 27–39.

[4]Koop, P. J. (2006). Engineering answers to landmine problem. *Peace Projections, 22*(1), 1–2. http://www.digger.ch/foundation/history/?lang=

[5]Mair, J., & Marti, I. (2006). Social entrepreneurship research: A source of explanation, prediction, and delight. *Journal of World Business, 41*(1), 36–44.

[6]Desa, G. (2012). Resource mobilization in international social entrepreneurship: Bricolage as a mechanism of institutional transformation. *Entrepreneurship: Theory & Practice, 36*(4), 727–751.

[7]This definition builds on and incorporates the ideas from the following sources: McMullen, J. S. (2011). Delineating the domain of development entrepreneurship: A market-based approach to facilitating inclusive economic growth. *Entrepreneurship: Theory & Practice, 35*(1), 185–193; definition found on website of The Schwab Foundation for Social Entrepreneurship. Accessed October 10, 2007, at http://www.schwabfound.org/definition.htm; Chell, E. (2007). Social enterprise and entrepreneurship: Towards a convergent theory of entrepreneurial process. *International Small Business Journal, 25*(1), 5–26.

[8]Cited on p. 48 in Roberts, D., & Woods, C. (2005, Autumn). Changing the world on a shoestring: The concept of social entrepreneurship. *Business Review* (University of Auckland), 45–51.

[9]This example is taken from pp. 3 and 4 in Dees, J. G., Emerson, J., & Economy, P. (2001). *Enterprising nonprofits: A tool kit for social entrepreneurs*. New York: John Wiley & Sons.

[10]See fn 9, Dees et al. (2001, p. 3).

[11]Reynolds, P. D., Carter, N. M., Gartner, W. B., & Greene, P. G. (2004). The prevalence of nascent entrepreneurs in the United States: Evidence from the panel study of entrepreneurial dynamics. *Small Business Economics, 23*, 263–284.

[12]Industry Canada. (2013, October 9). Key small business statistics—July 2012. Retrieved from https://www.ic.gc.ca/eic/site/061.nsf/vwapj/KSBS-PSRPE_July-Juillet2012_eng.pdf/$FILE/KSBS-PSRPE_July-Juillet2012_eng.pdf

[13]Helft, M. (2006, October 17). It pays to have pals in Silicon Valley. *The New York Times*. Retrieved from http://www.nytimes.com/2006/10/17/technology/17paypal.html?scp=1&sq=&st=nyt.

[14]Avery, S. (2004, June 15). Idea finally spins gold for web's inventor: Tim Berners-Lee will receive $1.7 million for concept that changed the world. *The Globe and Mail*, p. B9.

[15]Thomas, D. J., & McMullen, J. (2007). Toward a theory of sustainable entrepreneurship: Reducing environmental degradation through entrepreneurial action. *Journal of Business Venturing, 22*(1), 50–76.

[16]Yunus, M. (1996, November/December). Fighting poverty from the bottom up: An address by Muhammad Yunus. *TIMELINE*. Retrieved from http://www.grameen-info.org/mcredit/time-line.html

[17]Quotes taken from Bellman, E. (2006, May 15). Entrepreneur gets big banks to back very small loans. *The Wall Street Journal*, pp. A1, A12.

[18]Allen, K. R. (2006). *Launching new ventures: An entrepreneurial approach* (4th ed.). Boston: Houghton Mifflin.

[19]McKenna, H. (2013, September 6). Nearly half of students plan to start own business: survey. *The Globe and Mail*. Retrieved from http://www.theglobeandmail.com/report-on-business/small-business/starting-out/nearly-half-of-students-plan-to-start-own-business-survey/article14163719/

[20]Brandstätter, H. (2011). Personality aspects of entrepreneurship: A look at five meta-analyses. *Personality and Individual Differences, 51*, 222–230.

[21]Zhao, H., Seibert, S. E., & Lumpkin, G. T. (2010). The relationship of personality to entrepreneurial intentions and performance: A meta-analytic review. *Journal of Management, 36*, 381–404.

[22]Collins, C. J., Hanges, P. J., & Locke, E. A (2004). The relationship of achievement motivation to entrepreneurial behavior: A meta-analysis. *Human Performance, 17*(1), 95–117.

[23]Although management textbooks often talk about entrepreneurs' self-confidence, the scholarly research typically focuses on self-esteem or self-efficacy. For example, see Laguna, M. (2013). Self-efficacy, self-esteem, and entrepreneurship among the unemployed. *Journal of Applied Social Psychology*. doi: 10.1111/j.1559-1816.2012.00994.x

[24]Brenner, J. G. (1999). *The emperors of chocolate: Inside the secret world of Hershey and Mars*. New York: Broadway Books.

[25]Kim, P. H., Aldrich, H. E., & Keister, L. A. (2006). Access (not) denied: The impact of financial, human, and cultural capital on entrepreneurial entry in the United States. *Small Business Economics, 27*, 5–22.

[26]Delage, B. (2002). Results from the survey of self-employment in Canada. Human Resources Development Canada: Applied Research Branch. Retrieved from http://publications.gc.ca/collections/Collection/RH64-12-2001E.pdf

[27]See fn 13, Helft (2006).

[28]For example, see Jalbert, S. E. (2000). Women entrepreneurs in the global economy. Centre for International Private Enterprise. Retrieved from http://www.cipe.org/pdf/programs/women/jalbertpdf; Das, Debabrata. (2012, February 17). A social entrepreneur-ship model & policy framework for social inclusion in India. In S. Mathews, N. Raina, N. Sapkal, J. Jacob, & S. Ray (Eds.) *Inclusive Growth in India: Varied Dimensions and Challenges* (pp. 1–6). SCAC.

[29]Dyck, B., & Starke, F. A. (1999). The formation of breakaway organizations: Observations and a process model. *Administrative Science Quarterly, 44*, 792–822; Berman, N., Mellon, E. (2012, March). Contextualising the self and social change making: An evaluation of the Young Social Pioneers program. *Cosmopolitan Civil Societies: An Interdisciplinary Journal*, North America, *4*. Available at http://epress.lib.uts.edu.au/journals/index.php/mcs/article/view/2275. Accessed February 2, 2013.

[30]See fn 29, Dyck & Starke (1999).

[31]The voluntary simplicity movement is characterized by people who start up organizations such as used-book stores, bicycle repair shops, organic coffee shops, and other ventures that are inherently slower paced and more environmentally friendly: Elgin, D. (1993). *Voluntary simplicity: Toward a way of life that is outwardly simple, inwardly rich* (rev. ed.). New York: Quill; Alexander, S., & Ussher, S. (2012) The voluntary simplicity movement: A multi-national survey analysis in theoretical context. *Journal of Consumer Culture, 12*(1), 66–86.

[32]Taken from the Tom's of Maine company website: http://www.tomsofmaine.com/. For more on Chappell's story, see Chappell, T. (1993). *The soul of a business: Managing for profit and the common good*. New York: Bantam Press.

[33]Spaner, D. (2007, March 11). Family ties bring meaning to his life. *The Province* (Vancouver, BC), p. B.10. Retrieved from http://www.canada.com/story_print.html?id=0967eb92-c0c2-4702-b5b8-12510335f0e4&sponsor=

[34]Williams, T. (2007, August 30). The $5 philanthropist: Thoughts on social networks, philanthropy, markets. www.givemeaning.com.

[35]Smietana, B. (2011, October 11). At 22, a Tennessee woman is mom to 13 Uganda orphans. *USA Today*. Retrieved from http://usatoday30.usatoday.com/news/religion/story/2011-10-10/katie-davis-uganda/50723100/1

[36]These individuals are identified as "frustrated corporate social entrepreneurs" in the following article: Hemingway, C. A. (2005). Personal values as a catalyst for corporate social entrepreneurship. *Journal of Business Ethics, 60*, 233–249.

[37]See fn 16, Yunus (1996).

[38]Willdridge is irritated by being called an *entrepreneur*, because for him this label implies that the Oasis Centre was created by one person, which it clearly was not. Example and quote taken from Roberts & Woods (2005); see fn 8.

[39]Honig, B. (2004). Entrepreneurship education: Toward a model of contingency-based business planning. *Academy of Management Learning and Education, 3*(3), 258–273.

[40]Helft, M. (2006b, October 12). With YouTube, grad student hits jackpot again. *The New York Times*. Retrieved from http://www.nytimes.com/2006/10/12/technology/12tube.html?scp=1&sq=&st=nyt

[41]Franke, N., Gruber, M., Harhoff, D., & Henkel, J. (2008). Venture capitalists' evaluations of start-up teams: Trade-offs, knock-out criteria, and the impact of VC experience. *Entrepreneurship: Theory & Practice, 32*(3), 459–483.

[42]See fn 40, Helft (2006b).

[43]http://www.modo.com/press.php?release=Modo and EcoBonus 2011. Accessed October 12, 2012.

[44]http://www.onesight.org/na/about_us/. Accessed October 12, 2012.

[45]Kruks-Wisner, G. (2005). Promoting sustainability, building networks: A green entrepreneur in Mexico. In M. Schaper (Ed.), *Making ecopreneurship: Developing sustainable entrepreneurship* (pp. 225–238). Aldershot, Hampshire, UK: Ashgate.

[46]Taken from Pennington, A. Y. (2004, October). A world of difference. *Entrepreneur Magazine*. Retrieved from http://www.entrepreneur.com/article/printthis/72618.html

[47]See fn 33, Spaner (2007).

[48]Ibid.

[49]See fn 39, Honig (2004). See also Gumpert, D. E. (2002). *Burn your businessplan: What investors really want from entrepreneurs*. Need-ham, MA: Lauson.

[50]See fn 39, Honig (2004, p. 259).

[51]See fn 39, Honig (2004, p. 268). Also see p. 112 in Matta, N., & Ashkenas, R. (2003). Why good projects fail anyway. *Harvard Business Review, 8*, 109–113.

[52]See fn 39, Honig (2004).

[53]The importance of developing strong relationships with stakeholders is underscored in Dees et al. (2001); see fn 9.

[54]Taken from Brown, P. L. (2006, October 26). At this gathering, the only alternative is to be alternative. *The New York Times*. Accessed February 19, 2008, at http://www.nytimes.com/2006/10/24/science/24conference.html?scp=1&sq=&st=nyt

[55]Savitz, A. W., & Weber, K. (2006). *The triple bottom line: How today's best-run companies are achieving economic, social, and environmental success—and how you can too*. San Francisco: Jossey-Bass.

[56]O'Rourke, A. F. (2005). Venture capital as a tool for sustainable entrepreneurship. In M. Schaper (Ed.), *Making ecopreneurship: Developing sustainable entrepreneurship* (pp. 122–128). Aldershot, Hampshire, UK: Ashgate.

[57]See fn 8, Roberts & Woods (2005). Ashoka works in more than 40 countries with more than 1,400 social entrepreneurs and has provided the equivalent of about $40 million in financing.

[58]According to Yunus: "When we started, we looked at all the other banks in Bangladesh and found that only 1 percent of their membership were women. We aimed for 50/50 in the beginning. The main challenge for a poor woman was overcoming the fear in her which was holding her up. We found that compared to men who spent money more freely, women benefited their families much more. Women wanted to save and invest and create assets, unlike men who wanted to enjoy right away. Women are more self-sacrificing, they want to see their children better fed, better dressed, and, as a result, the conditions of the entire community improved." [Tharoor, I. (2006, October 13). Paving the way out of poverty: Bangladeshi economist Muhammad Yunus was awarded the 2006 Nobel Peace Prize not for giving to the poor, but for helping them to help themselves. *Time*. Accessed November 8, 2006, at http://www.time.com/time/world/article/0,8599,1546100,00.html].

[59]According to Yunus: "Each branch is self-contained, its own Grameen Bank, made up of a community of borrowers and local staff who all know each other. We have a total staff of 20,000, and lend $800 million a year to 6.6 million members nationwide. The Bank is very close to its community; there is a relationship of trust and the system as a whole [that] encourages repayment. There is no attempt on anyone's part to outsmart anyone. After all, everyone wants to keep the door open to opportunity and we present that opportunity." (Tharoor, 2006, see fn 58).

[60]Google website: http://www.google.com/about/company/. Accessed March 18, 2013; Heilmann, J. (2005, March). Journey to the (revolutionary, evil-hating, cash-crazy, and possibly self-destructive) center of Google. *GQ*. Retrieved from http://www.gq.com/news-politics/newsmakers/200502/google-larry-sergey; Richterl, M. (2006, October 17). Search power takes a stand for sun power. *The New York Times*. Retrieved from http://www.nytimes.com/2006/10/17/technology/17solar.html?_r=0; Sloan, A. (2004, August 24). IPO's success doesn't justify Google's price. *The Washington Post*, p. E03; Williams, A. (2006, October 15). Planet Google wants you. *The New York Times*. Retrieved from http://www.nytimes.com/2006/10/15/fashion/15google.html?pagewanted=all

[61]Neetal. (2011, June 9). Behind U2's ONE campaign, "I Am One." Innov8social. Retrieved from http://www.innov8social.com/2011/06/behind-u2s-one-campaign-i-am-one.html; Girard, K. (2011, June 11). Fame, faith, and social activism: Business lessons from Bono. *Harvard Business School*. Retrieved from http://d/hbswk.hbs.edu/item/6700.html; http://www.edun.com/about-edun. Accessed March 22, 2013.

Feature Notes

My OB: When a Hobby Becomes a New Venture Chafkin, M. (2012, October 12). Can Ben Silbermann turn Pinterest into the world's greatest shopfront? *Fast Company*. Retrieved from http://www.fastcodesign.com/1670681/ben-silbermann-pinterest; Rosman, K. (2011, September 25). Technology: The glue to my marriage. *Inc.* Retrieved from http://www.inc.com/30under30/christine-lagorio/ben-silbermann-evan-sharp-founders-pinterest.html; Rosman, K. (2011, September, 25). Technology: My marriage's secret glue. *The Wall Street Journal*. http://www.wsj.com/articles/SB10001424053111903703604576591272533051998

OB in Action: From Failure to Fame Gage, D. (2012, September 20). The venture capital secret: 3 out of 4 start-ups fail. *The Wall Street Journal*. Retrieved from http://www.wsj.com/articles/SB1000087239639044372

0204578004980476429190; Rowling, J. K. (2008, June 5). Text of J. K. Rowling's speech. *Harvard Gazette*. Retrieved from http://news.harvard.edu/gazette/story/2008/06/text-of-j-k-rowling-speech/; Rowling, J. K. (2012). Biography. [Author's website]. Retrieved from http://www.jkrowling.com/en_US/#/about-jk-rowling; Smith, S. (2003*). J. K. Rowling: A biography*. London: Michael O'Mara Books; Herald Online Staff. (2012, March 12). JK Rowling: Billionaire to millionaire. *The New Zealand Herald*. Retrieved from http://www.nzherald.co.nz/books/news/article.cfm?c_id=134&objectid=10791515

OB in Action: Gourmet Just Got Better Goldcorp. (2013). Above ground: Our world of community responsibility. Goldcorp Inc. Retrieved from http://www.goldcorp.com/files/12383_GC_AboveGround_Web144dpi.pdf; OMA. (2013, March 11). Award is icing on the cake for Aboriginal mine service company. Ontario Mining Association. Retrieved from http://www.oma.on.ca/en/news/index.aspx?newsId=78ad40e0-a945-43e9-8eb0-a678b121fa5c; Strong, G. (2013 , May 24). Award-winning First Nation caterer diversifies. *Sudbury Mining Solutions Journal*. Retrieved from http://www.sudburyminingsolutions.com/award-winning-first-nation-caterer-diversifies.html; Windigo Catering. (2015). About: Who we are. [Company website]. Retrieved from http://windigocatering.ca/about/who-we-are/

OB in Action: Can Entrepreneurs Take the Heat? Johne, M. (2012, December 7). How couple's perfect pitch yielded four offers on *Dragons' Den*. *The Globe and Mail*. Retrieved from http://www.theglobeandmail.com/report-on-business/small-business/starting-out/how-couples-perfect-pitch-yielded-four-offers-on-dragons-den/article6007914/; Steeped Tea. (2015). About us. [Company website]. Retrieved from http://www.steepedtea.com/our-story/

name index

Note: Page numbers with "*f*" indicate figures; those with "*t*" indicate tables

A

Aceto, Peter, 242
Adams, John Stacey, 104
Aisenstat, David, 107
Akula, Vikram, 364
Alderfer, Clayton, 94–96
Altman, Sam, 289
Anderson, Gillian, 10
Anderson, Ray C., 303
Aniston, Jennifer, 83
Ariely, D., 174*n*
Aristotle, 8, 72, 96
Arouet, François-Marie, 31
Atkinson, Thomas, 229
Austen, Jane, 79
Autry, James, 240
Avrea, Darren, 202

B

Baker, Richard, 238
Baker, Winifred Mitchell, 188
Bakke, Dennis, 190
Balsillie, Jim, 118, 127
Barnard, Chester, 25
Barr, Anthony, 310
Barton, Dominic, 10
Beach, Lee Roy, 123
Bechtolsheim, Andy, 375
Beckett, John, 106
Beddoe, Clive, 212
Beeman, Darcy, 165
Beer, Michael, 342
Bell, Donald, 212
Bell, Joshua, 249
Bentham, Jeremy, 71
Berners-Lee, Tim, 363
Black, Conrad, 144, 150, 162–163
Blake, Robert R., 192–193, 193*n*
Blanchard, Ken, 198
Bono, 378
Boyle, Susan, 81

Branson, Richard, 189
Briggs, Katherine, 52
Brin, Sergey, 375–376
Brinkley, David, 111
Brooks, Bonnie, 238
Buckingham, Marcus, 196, 198
Buffett, Warren, 100
Burgess, S., 58*n*

C

Cadbury, George, 38–39
Cadbury, John, 38
Cameron, K. S., 291*n*, 293*n*, 299*n*
Casey, Dwane, 265
Cashman, T., 241*n*
Chambers, Ray, 68
Chappell, Tom, 367
Charan, Ram, 190
Chen, Steve, 369
Chenault, Ken, 187–188, 203
Cherry, Don, 48
Christie, Richard, 164
Churchill, Winston, 261
Clampitt, P. G., 241*n*
Clooney, George, 246
Coffman, Curt, 196
Collins, Jim, 189
Confucius, 195
Cooper, Bradley, 116
Cooper, Cynthia, 138, 149
Corrigan, Mike, 353
Covey, Stephen, 176

D

Daft, R. L., 245*n*
Davis, Katie, 367
Day, Christine, 95
DeKoch, R. J., 241*n*
Deming, W. Edwards, 26
DePree, D. J., 328–329
DePree, Hugh, 329

DePree, Max, 329
Despain, James, 252
Disney, Walt, 286, 288
Dobson, Harmon, 323
Doerr, John, 375–376
Dorsey, Jack, 68
Drucker, Peter, 6
Duchovny, David, 10
Duke, Mike, 6
Dwyer-Owens, Dina, 192

E

Ebbers, Bernie, 138, 188
Ehrhart, M., 208n

F

Favreau, Jon, 60
Fayol, Henri, 11, 187
Fenton, Peter, 68
Fernandez, Martir, 33
Feuerstein, Aaron, 133
Fiedler, Fred, 195–197
Fields, W. C., 126
Fink, L., 351n
Flahive, Colin, 296
Follett, Mary Parker, 25
Ford, Henry, 25, 269–270
Foster, Dave, 202
Fox, Megan, 93
Franken, Al, 146
French, John R. P. Jr., 107
Friedman, Milton, 4, 72

G

Gandhi, Arun, 101
Gandhi, Mahatma, 101, 195
Gandhi, Mohandas
    Karamchand, 101
Garcia, Nora, 323
Gariepy, Ryan, 98–99
Gates, Bill, 60, 100, 251
Gates, Melinda, 100
Gbowee, Leymah, 84–85
Geis, Florence, 164
Ghoshal, Sumantra, 27
Gibson, Mel, 190
Gilbreth, Frank B., 24–25
Gilbreth, Lillian, 24–25
Gioia, Dennis, 114, 118, 289

Goleman, Daniel, 191
Good, Ashley, 126
Goodnight, Jim, 310
Goodpaster, Kenneth, 75
Grace, Topher, 344
Greenleaf, Robert, 128, 194–195
Greiner, Lori, 373
Groves, K. S., 133n

H

Hackman, J. R., 331n
Hamel, Gary, 11–12
Hanks, Tom, 170
Hansen, Ken, 195
Hardman, Stephanie, 49
Harman, Jay, 374
Harris, M., 58n
Harris, Tim, 48–49
Harrison, Hunter, 336–337
Hartley, Darin, 312
Heger, Milan, 146
Heil, Jennifer, 98
Heins, Thorsten, 127
Helwig, Jane, 310
Hersey, Paul, 198
Hershey, Milton S., 364–365
Herzberg, Frederick, 95, 319
Hesse, Hermann, 195, 201
Hewlett, William, 365
Hewson, Ali, 378
Hewson, Paul David, 378
Hill, David W., 140
Hill, Mark, 212
Hillary, Edmund, 362
Hiller, Deborah, 327
Hitler, Adolf, 188
Hoff, Tedd, 322
Hofstede, Geert, 35, 36f, 37,
    38f, 42, 318
Houghton, J. D., 157n
House, Chuck, 126
House, Robert, 196–197
Huffman, Steve, 289
Hughes, Howard, 60
Hurley, Chad, 369

J

Jack, Robbie, 151
Jahshan, Tonia, 373
Jefferson, Thomas, 71

Jesus Christ, 195
Jobs, Steve, 60, 152, 290, 293
Johansson, Scarlett, 244
John Paul II, Pope, 189
Johnson-Sirleaf, Ellen, 84–85
Judge, T. A., 355n
Jun, Ma, 32
Jung, Carl, 52
Jurvetson, Steve, 60

K

Kant, Immanuel, 71
Karim, Jawed, 369
Karman, Twawkkul, 85
Kastner, Danny, 50
Kelleher, Herb, 288
Keller, Gary, 204
Kendrick, Anna, 246
Kerviel, Jérôme, 130
Kindler, H., 133n
Kindler, Jeffrey, 342
Klassen, George, 357
Koehn, Nancy, 378
Kohlberg, Lawrence, 70–71
Korobanik, Debbie, 371
Kotter, John, 342–343
Kowalski, Jim, 370–371, 374
Kowalski, Mary Anne, 370–371, 374
Krajicek, Gabe, 327
Kroc, Ray, 121

L

Labistour, David, 22–23
Langer, Ellen, 363
Latham, Gary, 97
Lazaridis, Mike, 118, 127
Leiter, Michael, 149
Lencioni, Patrick M., 234, 234n
Lengel, R. H., 245n
Levchin, Max, 369
Lewin, Kurt, 338
Livingston, Ron, 316
Locke, John, 71
Longenecker, C., 234n, 351n
Lorang, Bart, 151
Lowewenstein, G., 174n
Lowry, Kyle, 265
Lui, Elaine "Lainey," 154–155
Luke, the Evangelist, 31
Lulin, Emmanuel, 73

M

Machiavelli, Niccolò, 164
Madoff, Bernie, 69
Marcelli, Héctor, 370
Mars family, 361
Martinson, Patrick, 98–99
Maslow, Abraham, 94–96, 94f
Maus, John, 374
Mauws, Larry, 250
Mayer, Marissa, 346, 349
Mayo, Elton, 25
McClelland, David, 96–97
McDaniel, Mike, 347, 351
McGregor, Douglas, 56
McGuinness, Paul, 378
McKay, Frank, 371
Medline, Michael, 5, 10
Meggy, Margaret, 341
Melech, G., 58n
Mill, John Stuart, 71
Mintzberg, Henry, 10
Mischel, Walter, 29
Mongeau, Claude, 337
Moore, Gordon, 365
Morgan, Tim, 212
Moritz, Michael, 375–376
Moss Kanter, Rosabeth, 10
Mouton, Jane, 192–193, 193n
Murray, Bill, 244
Musk, Elon, 60–61, 301
Musk, Kimbal, 60
Mycoskie, Blake, 350
Myers, Isabel Briggs, 52

N

Nayar, Vineet, 122, 203, 319
Neck, C. P., 157n
Neider, L. L., 158n
Nelson, Bob, 321
Neubert, M. J., 351n
Newton, Isaac, 23
Noyce, Robert, 365

O

O'Leary, Kevin, 143
Ochoa Levine, Cecilia,
    189–190
Ohanian, Alexis, 289
Oldham, G. R., 331n

Ouchi, William, 56
Owens, V., 58n

P

Packard, David, 126, 365
Page, Larry, 375–376
Paik, Y., 133n
Palmisano, Sam, 55
Pao, Ellen, 289
Pasternak, Harley, 93
Patton, B., 175n
Perry, Katy, 93
Perry, Laura, 33
Peters, Tom, 345
Pfeffer, Jeffrey, 10, 311
Phelan, Paul James (P.J.), 7
Phillippe, Ryan, 49
Piccolo, Vince, 33
Pohlmann, Andreas, 74
Pollard, William, 195
Poon Tip, Bruce, 186–187, 189
Prelec, D., 174n
Pucik, V., 355n

Q

Quaid, Dennis, 344
Quinn, R. E., 291n, 293n, 299n

R

Rahim, M. A., 182n
Rajaratnam, Raj, 69
Raven, Bertram, 107
Read, Ian, 342
Reimer, Ken, 300
Reisman, Heather, 108
Rendall, Matthew, 98–99
Riboud, Franck, 168
Ridge, Garry, 318
Rihanna, 93
Riis, Jacob, 265
Robbins, Tim, 49
Roberts, Amy, 100
Rockefeller, John D., 60
Rodbell, Liz, 238
Roethlisberger, Fritz, 25
Rogers, Ted, 76
Rokeach, Milton, 57
Rometty, Virginia "Ginni," 55
Roosevelt, Eleanor, 111

Rosenfeld, Irene, 204
Rowe, Mike, 77
Rowling, J. K., 368
Rummelt, Herman, 328

S

Sall, John, 310
Samuels, Angela, 46, 50, 52
Saretsky, Gregg, 212
Say, Jean-Baptiste, 363
Schein, Edgar, 261–262, 288
Schmidt, Eric, 376
Schriesheim, C. A., 158n
Schultz, Howard, 92, 364
Schwartz, S. H., 58n
Sculley, John, 293
Sebenius, James, 172
Selznick, Philip, 27
Semler, Ricardo, 260, 267, 273, 278, 295
Sevilla, Federico, 205
Sevilla, Yoling, 205–206, 328
Shanker, Stuart, 279
Shannon, C. E., 239n
Sheung, Lee Kum, 171
Silbermann, Ben, 366
Simmons, Russel, 369
Simon, Herbert, 121
Skilling, Jeffrey, 188
Skinner, B. F., 315
Skorton, David, 34
Smith, Adam, 7–8, 24, 72, 269
Smith, Ben, 229
Smith, Janice, 167
Socrates, 11
Sonne, Thorkil, 279, 341
Sorenson, Gary, 69
Sorenson, Torben, 279
Spreitzer, Gretchen, 10
Stack, Jack, 341
Stoppelman, Jeremy, 369
Sullivan, Scott, 138
Swartz, Jeffrey, 15
Szaky, Tom, 34, 360, 363

T

Tannen, Deborah, 194
Tat, Lee Man, 171
Tata, Ratan, 179
Taylor, Charles, 84
Taylor, Frederick W., 24–25

Taylor, Victoria, 289
Tellier, Paul, 336
Temple, David, 199–200
Temple, John, 199–200
Thiel, Peter, 60
Thoresen, C. J., 355n
Trevino, L. K., 245n

V

Valastro, Buddy, 313
van Houten, C. J., 38
Vance, C. M., 133n
Voltaire, 31
Vroom, Victor H., 101, 125n, 197

W

Walton, Sam, 266, 326
Weaver, W., 239n
Webb, Bryan, 98–99
Weber, Max, 7, 25, 266–267
Weisinger, H., 87n

Welbourne, T. M., 355n
Welch, Jack, 146, 319
Wetmore, Stephen, 117
Wiens, Dan, 177
Wiens, Wilma, 177
Willdridge, George, 367
Williams, C., 168n
Williams, Robin, 263
Williams, Tom, 367
Woodward, Joan, 296
Wright, Frank Lloyd, 261

Y

Yukl, G., 172n
Yunus, Muhammad, 295, 363–364,
    366–367, 371–372, 374, 374n

Z

Zahn, Steve, 83
Zuckerberg, Mark, 48

organization index

Note: Page numbers with "*f*" indicate figures; those with "*t*" indicate tables

A

AARP Experience Corps., 298, 301–302
Academy of Management, 28
Academy of Management Journal, 182*n*
Academy of Management Learning and Education,
 133*n*
Acadia University, 149
Accenture, 78
Adidas-Salomon, 75
Aecon Group, 217
AES Corporation, 190, 362
AIG, 69
Air Canada, 124, 287
Amazon, 338
American Express, 187, 203
American Girl, 108
American-Lincoln, 313
Aon Hewitt, 167
Apple Inc., 118, 151, 290, 293, 296, 301, 367
Ashoka, 374
Asnæs Power Plant, 42
Athletes World, 4
AT&T, 25, 128, 195
Au Bon Pain, 320
Avon, 69
AvreaFoster, 202

B

BancVue, 327
Bank of America, 344
Baylor Health Care Systems, 322
Becton, Dickinson and Company (BD), 345
Ben & Jerry's, 298, 362
Bethlehem Steel, 24
Bioplaneta, 370
BlackBerry, 118, 126–127
Blastar, 60
The Body Shop, 269, 301–302
Bombardier Inc., 142
Booz Allen Hamilton, 324
Botanical PaperWorks, 34

Bournville Village Trust, 38–39
British Airlines, 191
British Columbia Ferry Services Inc. (BC Ferries), 349,
 353
British Petroleum, 69
Brixx, 247
Business Horizons, 351*n*

C

C&A, 117
Cadbury Limited, 38–39
Campbell Family Institute for Breast Cancer
 Research, 217
Canada Post, 339
Canadian Board Diversity Council, 128
Canadian Broadcasting Corporation (CBC), 346
Canadian Centre for Ethics and Corporate Policy, 73
Canadian National Railway Company (CN), 336–337
Canadian Press, 49
Canadian Space Agency, 99
Canadian Tire, 4, 117
Capri Sun, 360
Cara Operations Ltd., 7
Carewest, 197–198
Caterpillar Inc., 252
CBC (Canadian Broadcasting Corporation), 346
Celestial Seasonings, 374
Cenovus Energy, 345
Centennial College, 46
Centre for Organizational Research and
 Development, 149
Change.org, 289
Chapters Inc., 108
Chicago Sun Times, 162
Chicago Tribute, 288
Chrysalis Capital Partners, 133
Cleantech Venture Network, 374
Clearpath Robotics, 98–99
Clorox, 32
Colgate-Palmolive Company, 360, 367
Compaq Computer Corporation, 60
Continental Airlines, 344

Cornell University, 34
Corporate Knights, 22
Costco, 287, 326–327
Covenant House, 154
CrowdFanatic, 373
CTVnews.ca, 49

D

Daily Telegraph, 162
Dalhousie University, 122
Dana Holding Corporation, 266
Danisco, 216
The Dannon Company, 167–168
David Aplin Group, 51
Day Chocolate Company, 39
Dell Inc., 213, 312, 319, 345–346
Delta Hotels and Resorts, 167
Digger Foundation, 361, 364
Discovery Channel, 77
Disney, 82, 286
Disneyland, 288
Disney University, 286, 288
Divine Chocolate, 39
DuPont, 216
The Dwyer Group, 192

E

East Side Mario's, 7
eBay, 96, 365, 369
EDUN, 378
Edward Jones, 165
Eliza Jennings Group, 327, 348
Enron, 69, 73, 188
Environmental Protection Agency
    (EPA), 190
Ernst & Young, 373
etalk, 154–155
Eurex, 130
Euro Disney, 35

F

Facebook, 48, 246, 247, 360
Fail Forward, 126
Fairchild Semiconductor, 365
Fairtrade Canada, 39
Fairtrade International, 23, 39
FedEx, 361
FGL Sports Ltd., 4–5, 10
Finance Canada, 123

Forbes, 368, 373
FORCE Technology, 353
Ford Motor Company, 114–116, 118, 289
Fortune, 55, 240, 302, 303, 329, 361
49th Parallel Coffee Roasters, 33
Francesca's Holdings Corp., 247
FullContact Inc., 151

G

G Adventures, 186–187, 189
Galeria Kaufhof, 238
Gallup Organization, 196
GAP Adventures, 186
General Electric (GE), 25–26, 32, 34, 146, 319
General Motors (GM), 340
George Brown College, 46
Gildan Activewear Inc., 105
GiveMeaning.com, 367
Glass Doctor, 192
GLOBE, 35
Goldcorp, 371
Google Canada, 225–226
Google Inc., 118, 361, 366, 375–376
Grameen Bank, 295, 361, 363–364, 366,
    371, 373–374
Great Little Box Company (GLBC), 341
Green Kumming, 296
Green Works, 32
Grenadier Guards, 292
Groupe Danone, Inc., 168
Gyproc A/S, 42

H

Hallmark Cards, Inc., 154
Hamburger University, 268
Harvard Business Review, 194, 198
Harvard Business School, 12, 123, 124, 342, 378
Harvard Divinity School, 367
Harvard University, 363, 368
Harvey's, 7
HCL Technologies, 122, 203, 319
Health Canada, 149–150
Herman Miller, 328–329
Hershey Company, 364–365
Hewlett-Packard (HP), 126, 365
Hollinger International, 144, 162–163
Holt Renfrew, 238
Home Depot, 360
Home Outfitters, 238
Honda, 119

Hootsuite, 55
Hudson's Bay Company (HBC), 46, 238

I

IBM, 35, 55, 322, 340
Illinois Central Railroad (IC), 336
Inc., 372
Indigo Books & Music, 108
ING Direct, 242
Intel Corporation, 365
Interface, 302–303, 321
International Committee of the
　　Red Cross (ICRC), 325
International Harvester, 341
Investor's Circle, 374
Island Savings Credit Union, 318
Ivory, 298

J

Jerusalem Post, 162
Journal of Cross-Cultural Psychology, 58n
Journal of Managerial Psychology, 157n

K

Keg Restaurants Ltd., 107
Keller Williams Realty, Inc., 204
Kemira, 42
Kendall's Automotive, 300
Kleiner Perkins Caufield & Byers, 375
Kleinfeld Bridal, 238
Kmart, 46
Kobo Inc., 108
Kowalski's Markets, 370
KPMG, 162–163
Kraft Foods, 204, 360
Krispy Kreme, 287
Kythe Foundation, 58

L

LaineyGossip.com, 154–155
The Leather Collection Inc., 205, 328
Lee Kum Kee Ltd. (LKK), 171
The LEGO Group, 229–230, 279, 295
Lehman Brothers, 69
Lincoln Electric, 300–301, 320
LinkedIn, 363
Liz Claiborne, 361
London School of Business, 123

Lord & Taylor, 238
L'Oréal, 73
Los Angeles Times, 288
Love of Reading Foundation, 108
LTrek, Inc., 232n
Lucent Technologies, 191
Lululemon Athletica Inc., 95, 106
Luvo Inc., 95

M

Major League Baseball (MLB), 247
Malden Mills Industries, 133
Management, 83
Management Decision, 125n
Mars Inc., 39, 361
Massachusetts Institute of Technology (MIT), 99
Matador Network, 33
Mattamy Homes, 100
Mattel, 114
McDonald's, 121, 267, 314
McGill-HEC School of Management, 123
McKinsey & Company, 10, 364
Mennonite Central Committee (MCC), 357
Men's Wearhouse, 320–321
Merck & Co., 314
Merrill Lynch, 344
Microsoft, 97–99, 251, 265, 279, 361
Milestones, 7
Modo Eyewear, 369
Mondelēz International, 39, 204
Mountain Equipment Co-op (MEC), 22–23,
　　100, 298, 328
Mouvement des caisses Desjardins, 313, 325
Mozilla Corporation, 188
Mr. Rooter, 192

N

NASA (National Aeronautics Space
　　Administration), 222
National Minority Supplier Development
　　Council, 329
National Post, 162
NBA (National Basketball Association), 247, 265
Neechi Foods Co-op Ltd., 302
Negotiation, 175n
Nestlé, 39, 360
Netscape, 188
New Jersey Bell Telephone Company, 25
NFL (National Football League), 247
NHL (National Hockey League), 247, 315

Nike, 277, 346
Nissan, 119
Nordstrom, 238
Nortel, 69
North York Sheridan Mall, 46
Novartis, 271
Novell, 376
Novo Nordisk, 42, 298

O

Oasis Centre for Problem
    Gamblers, 367
Ohio State University, 192
Omega, 251–252
1% for the Planet, 22
OneSight, 369
Ontario Securities Commission, 162
Organic Valley, 298
Outdoor Industry Association, 23

P

Patagonia, 362
Patek Philippe, 297
PayPal, 60, 363, 365, 369
PepsiCo, 293
Perot Systems, 345–346
Pfizer Inc., 341–342
Philippine Children's Medical Center, 58
Pinterest, 366
Polartec LLC, 133
Portus, 69
PricewaterhouseCoopers Canada, 153
Princess Margaret Hospital, 217
Princeton University, 360
PROFIT, 373
Prospectors and Developers Association
    of Canada, 371
PUMA, 57
Puma Energy, 344

Q

Quaker Oats, 320
The Quarterly Journal of Economics, 174n
Queen's University, 60

R

Rakuten, 338
Reddit, 289–290

Reell Precision Manufacturing
    Corporation, 321
REI, 301
Research In Motion (RIM), 118, 126–127
Rogers Communications, 76, 154, 227
Room 9 Entertainment, 363
R.W. Beckett Corporation, 106

S

SAI Global, 73
Saks Fifth Avenue, 238
Salvador's Coffee House, 296
The Salvation Army, 367
Sam's Club, 327
Samsung, 69
SAP, 279
SAS Institute, 310
Schulich School of Business, 218
Scotiabank, 242
Scouts, 119–120
Semco, 260, 269, 271, 273–274, 277–278, 281,
    295, 301, 321, 341
Sequoia Capital, 375
ServiceMaster, 195, 362
Shell, 277
Sherwin-Williams, 320
Shockley Semiconductor Laboratory, 365
Shoebox, 154
Siemens, 218
Sino-Forest, 69
Slide, 363
SNC-Lavalin, 69, 74
Société Générale, 130
Society of Human Resource
    Management, 247
SolarCity, 60
Southwest Airlines, 288, 325
SpaceX, 60
Specialisterne, 264, 279
Sport Chek, 4, 266, 324
Sports Mart, 4
Square, Inc., 68
Stanford University, 18, 60, 310–311, 375
Staples, 298–299
Starbucks, 92–93, 95, 268, 269, 364
Statistics Canada, 147
Statoil, 42
Steeped Tea, 373
Sun Microsystems, 375
Sustainable Apparel Coalition, 23
Swiss Chalet, 7

T

Tangerine Bank, 242
Target, 360
Tata Consultancy Services, 179
The Tata Group, 179
Tata Motors, 298
Tata Steel, 179
Tech Data Corporation, 302
TED Talk, 279
TELUS International, 58
Temple and Temple Tours, 199–200
Tennessee Valley Authority
    (TVA), 27
TerraCycle, 34, 360–361
Tesla Motors, 60, 301
Textile Exchange, 23
The Leadership Quarterly, 158n
3M, 154, 241, 301, 361
Timberland, 15, 324, 362
Tim Hortons, 49, 127, 287
Tim's Place, 49
Tomasso Corporation, 31
Tom's of Maine, 367
TOMS Shoes, 350
Topshop, 238
Toronto-Dominion Bank
    (TD), 48
Toronto French School, 154
Toronto Raptors, 265–266
Toyota, 114, 119, 264, 301
Trash Tycoon, 360
Treasury Board of Canada, 320
Trees for the Future, 369
Twitter, 68, 247

U

U2, 378
Umpqua Bank, 317
United Airlines, 344
United Nations (UN), 34, 68
University of British Columbia, 122
University of Michigan, 192
University of Pennsylvania, 60
University of Waterloo, 244
University of Western Ontario, 154
U.S. Environmental Protection
    Agency, 32
U.S. National Highway Traffic Safety
    Administration, 114
U.S. Postal Service, 294

V

Vermilion Energy Inc., 100
VF Corporation, 15
Village Progress, 296
Virgin Airlines, 189
Virgin Galactic, 189
Virgin Group, 189
Virgin Mobile, 189
Virgin Records, 189
VisionSpring, 276
Volkswagen, 114
Voluptuous Clothing, 46

W

Walmart, 6, 32, 46, 266, 287, 297, 303, 326–327, 360
Warby Parker, 276
Washington Post, 249
WD-40, 318
Wegmans Food Markets, 301
Western Electric Company, 25
WestJet Airlines, 106, 212, 262, 287
Westward Industries, 250
Whataburger, 323
Whole Foods Market, 34, 190, 360
Willamette Industries, 32
Windigo Catering Limited Partnership, 370–371
Windigo First Nations Council, 371
Windigo Ventures General Partner Ltd., 371
WIPNET (Women in Peacebuilding Network), 84
W.L. Gore & Associates, Inc., 227
Women's Business Enterprise Council, 329
World Bank, 34, 372
World Business Council for Sustainable
    Development (WBCSD), 28
World Cocoa Foundation, 39
World Resources Institute, 374
World Values Survey (WVS), 35
WorldCom, 138, 149, 188
WrightWay Training, 353

X

X.com, 60

Y

Yahoo! Inc., 346, 349, 375
Yelp, 369
York University, 122, 218, 279
YouTube, 29, 65, 363, 365, 369

subject index

Note: Page numbers with "*f*" indicate figures; those with "*t*" indicate tables

A

ABC framework, 76
abilities, 50
absenteeism, 223
accommodating style, 178
accommodation approach, 32
accounting fraud, 69
achievement, desire for, 96, 97–103
acquired needs theory, 96
acquisition, 344
active listening, 249, 249*t*
actor-observer bias, 80–81
adaptability, 263
adhocracy culture, 291–292, 291*f*, 293, 293*f*
adjourning, 215
adjustment, 79
administrative appraisals, 317
administrative inertia, 127–128
administrative method, 121
administrative model method, 121
affect, 76
affective commitment, 77–78
affiliation, desire for, 96, 106
affinity groups, 48
agreeableness, 51, 52
alternative responses, 117–119
alternatives, 119–124, 119*f*
  available knowledge, 120–124
  ethical decisions, 124
  goal consensus, 119–120
ambiguity, 343
ambiguous words, 243
Analyzer type, 299*f*, 302
anchoring, 79
anchoring and adjustment bias, 121*t*
appraisal systems. *See* performance appraisals
appreciative inquiry (AI), 346
Aristotle's virtue theory, 8, 10, 72, 96
artifacts, 265–266
aspiration point, 174
assumptions, 146
at-risk pay, 320

The Attentional and Interpersonal Style (TAIS), 51
attitudes, 75–77, 349–350
attraction-selection-attrition framework, 288–289
attributes
  abilities, 50
  beliefs, 55–59
  core self-evaluation, 53–55
  personality, 50–53
attributions, 79
authentic leadership, 139–140, 140*f*
authenticity, 139
authority, 36*f*, 272
autonomy, 153, 313
availability, 80
availability bias, 121*t*
available knowledge, 120–124
avoidance learning, 315
avoiding style, 177

B

B corporations, 298
behaviour modification, 315
behavioural intentions, 76
behavioural science, 339
behaviours, 191
beliefs, 55–56, 56, 146
beliefs era, 26–27
benefits, 319
best alternative to a negotiated agreement
  (BATNA), 175
bias
  actor-observer bias, 80–81
  anchoring and adjustment bias, 121*t*
  availability bias, 121*t*
  employee appraisals, 121*t*
  halo/horn bias, 121*t*
  perceptual biases, 79–80, 81
  self-serving bias, 142
Big Five personality traits, 51, 53*f*, 293, 364
bonuses, 319
bottom-up approach, 342
bounded rationality, 121

brainstorming, 176, 224, 225
Braveheart, 190
breaks, 151
bribery, 74
burning platform, 342–343
burnout, 147, 149
business plan, 368–372

C

calling, 146–147
career development, 323–324
case studies
    About Face at Interface, 303
    A Bay Worthy of the 21st Century, 238
    The Bittersweet Story of Chocolate, 38–39
    Brewing Motivation at Starbucks, 92–93
    Calming the Waters, 353
    Conrad Black Guilty of Fraud, 162
    Creating an Unparalleled Customer
      Experience, 4–5
    Creating Happiness: Passion and Purpose at G
      Adventures, 186–187
    Finding Strength in Community, 22–23
    Following a Different Voice, 138
    The Forest and the Trees at Timberland, 15
    The Fundamentals of Organizing at Semco, 260
    Getting Paid to Have Fun, 154–155
    Googling Google, 375–376
    High-Tech Loyalty at SAS Institute, 310
    How Decisions Can Lead to a $7 Billion Loss, 130
    Indigo Bookmarked Values, 108
    Jack Dorsey, 68
    Learning from the Journey, 336
    LEGO Mindstorms, 229–230
    Lessons in Teaching Abroad, 253–254
    Life in the Fast Lane—Elon Musk, 60–61
    Managing a Smile Factory, 286
    New Ways of Organizing for New Needs, 279
    One Person's Trash is Another Person's Treasure,
      360
    People, the Planet, and Profits at Herman Miller,
      328–329
    The Power of the Powerless, 84–85
    Recalling a Classic Example of Decision Making,
      114
    Sustainable Leadership at Work in the Philippines,
      205–206
    Taking WestJet to New Heights, 212
    Transformational Relationships at Tata, 179
    Understanding Angela Samuels, 46
    WorldCom, 138

centralization, 272–274, 272*f*
CEOs, and stress, 149
change agent, 347
change process, 339*f*, 340–347
channel, 247–248
character, 166
charisma, 188
clan culture, 290–291, 291*f*, 300
closed system, 26
coaching, 198, 202*t*
coalition tactics, 172*t*
code of ethics, 73
coercive power, 107*f*
cognitions, 76
cognitive abilities, 50
cognitive dissonance, 80, 289–290
collaborating style, 178
collateral, 372
collective decoding, 250
collectivism, 36*f*
commitment
    affective commitment, 77–78
    to change, 347–350, 348*f*
    escalation of commitment, 125–127, 126*f*
    limited alternatives, effect of, 77
    normative commitment, 78
    obligations, 77
    organizational commitment, 77–78
commitments, 77–78
communication, 239
    across cultures, 243–244
    challenges of, 240
    channels, 244–248
    communication barriers, 242–244
    computer-mediated communication, 246
    confirmation of message, 250–252
    decoding, 248–250
    encoding, 242–248
    feedback, 250–252
    feedforward communication, 251–252
    four-step communication process, 239–240, 239*f*
    identification of message, 240–242
    media, 244–248
    organizational change, 349
    receiving, 248–250
    transmission, 242–248
compatibility, 123
compensation, 319–321
competence, 166
competing style, 178
Competing Values Framework (CVF), 263–264,
    290, 294

competitors, 33
compromising style, 178
computer-mediated communication, 246
conceptual skills, 6
concession, 174
conditional contributors, 224
conflict
  causes and cures, 220*t*
  culture, and conflict style, 178
  role conflict, 148–149
  styles of, 177–178, 177*f*
  team conflict, 219–222
  work–family conflict, 148, 148*f*
  work–life conflict, 148, 148*f*
conflict styles, 177–178, 177*f*
conscientiousness, 51
consequentialist theory, 71
conservation of resources theory, 150
consideration, 192, 194
consistent contributors, 224
constructive criticism, 251
constructive thought patterns, 146
consultation, 172*t*
contingency theories, 195–198
  Fiedler's contingency theory of leadership, 195–196
  House's path-goal theory, 196–197
  Leader-Member Exchange (LMX), 197–198
Conventional Analyzer type, 302
Conventional Defender type, 300
conventional delegation, 168–169
conventional moral development, 71
conventional OB, 7
  adhocracy culture, 292
  affiliation, 106
  bottom line, 9
  career development, 323–324
  clan culture, 290
  commitment to change, 348*f*
  communication, 240
  contingencies, 197
  Conventional Analyzer type, 302
  Conventional Defender type, 300
  Conventional Prospector type, 301
  Conventional Simple type, 300
  decision, implementation of, 128
  decoding, 250
  described, 7–8
  directing, 202
  entrepreneurship, 362, 363–364, 366, 370
  ethics, approach to, 74
  ethnocentrism, 35
  fairness, 105, 172

  feedback, 143
  hierarchy culture, 291
  implementation of decision, 125
  implications of, 9–11
  instrumentality, 102
  job analysis and design, 313
  justice, 172
  key priorities, 8, 8*f,* 9*f*
  leadership, 202*t,* 203–204
  leading, 12
  market culture, 292
  messages, 241
  moral point of view, 71–72
  organization-specific responsibility (OSR), 30, 31*f*
  organizational change, 338, 340, 342, 351
  organizational structure, 294–295, 294*f*
  organizing, 12
  personality traits, 52, 53*f*
  planning, 11
  polycentrism, 35
  power, 107
  research designs, 29–30
  resistance to change, 344
  specialization, 270
  stakeholders, 31
  standardization, 268
  strategy, 297–298
  stress management, 150
  training, 322
  trust, 168
  values, 11, 264
  vision statements, 326
Conventional Prospector type, 301
Conventional Simple type, 300
convergent thinking, 152
core self-evaluation, 53–55
corporate social responsibility (CSR), 30
correlation, 28–29
cost leadership strategy, 297
counter-cultural decisions, 129
country club style, 193
courage, 12, 96
craft technology, 297, 300
creative process, 152
creativity, 151
  creative individuals, characteristics of, 152–153
  creative process, 152
  deadlines, 154
  goal setting, 154
  in organizations, improvement of, 153–154
  positive reinforcement, 154
  resource support, 154

creativity-relevant skills, 152
critical thinking, 10
cross-functional teams, 214
cultural artifacts, 265
cultural differences, 37
cultural "scripts," 26
culture
    appraisal systems, 318
    as communication barrier, 243–244
    and conflict styles, 178
    and decision making, 127
    ethical culture, 73
    national culture, 35, 36*f*
    and organizational change, 344
    organizational culture. *See* organizational
        culture
    and perceptual biases, 81
    in the workplace, 292

D

debt financing, 372
decision, 115
    counter-cultural decisions, 129
    ethical decisions, 124
    nonprogrammed decisions, 118
    programmed decisions, 118
    routine decisions, 118
decision making
    alternative choice, making, 119–124
    alternative responses, development
        of, 117–119
    counter-cultural decisions, 129
    and culture, 127
    four-step model, 115*f*
    identify need for decision, 115–117
    implementation of decision, 125–129
    and neuroscience, 116
    participation level, 125*f*
decoding, 239, 248–250
deep knowledge, 152
Defender type, 299*f,* 300–301
defensive strategy, 32
delegating, 199, 202*t*
delegation, 168–170
deliberative dialogue, 248
delightful organizations, 27
Delphi technique, 224, 225
departmentalization, 274–278, 275*f*
dependent variables, 28
depersonalization, 147
desire for achievement, 96, 97–103

desire for affiliation, 96, 106
desire for fairness, 96, 104–105
desire for power, 96, 107
desire to lead, 188
development, 321, 323–324
developmental appraisals, 317
dialectical inquiry, 222
differentiation strategy, 297, 301
dignification, 273–274
directing, 198, 202*t*
directive leadership, 196
discipline, 152
distress, 147
distributive bargaining, 173
distributive justice, 171
divergent thinking, 152
diversity, 47–50, 153, 290
divisional departmentalization,
    274, 275*f*
dominating style, 178
downwardly mobile, 366–367
drive, 188
dysfunctional cultures, 290

E

ecological sustainability, 27–28
economies of scale, 275
effective behaviour, 6
egalicentrism, 35
egoism, 71–72
emotional appeals, 349
emotional awareness, 142
emotional exhaustion, 147
emotional intelligence (EI), 82–83,
    190–191
emotional labour, 82
emotional stability, 51
emotions, 81–83, 346
empathy, 83, 191, 367
employee appraisal, 121*t*
employee candidacy tests, 51
employment contract, 324
empowering, 202*t,* 203–204
empowerment, 204
enabling, 202, 202*t*
encoding, 242–248
engaging, 202*t,* 203
engineering culture, 302
engineering technology, 296–297
entrepreneurial spirit, 204
entrepreneurs, 361

see also entrepreneurship
    Big Five personality traits, 364
    conventional *vs.* sustainable, 363–364
    lone entrepreneur, myth of, 365
entrepreneurship, 361
    see also entrepreneurs
    entrepreneurial process, 362, 362*f*
    hobbies, 366
    identification of opportunities, 363–364
    initiative, 364–367, 365*f*
    plans, development of, 368–372
    resources, mobilization of, 372–374
environmentally friendly products and technology,
    301–302
equipping, 202*t*, 203
equitably rewarded, 104
equity financing, 372
equity theory, 104–105, 104*f*
ERG theory, 94–95
escalation of commitment, 125–127, 126*f*
esteem needs, 94*f*
ethical behaviour. *See* ethics
ethical climate, 73
ethical culture, 73
ethics, 69–75
    code of ethics, 73
    ethical climate, 73
    ethical culture, 73
    ethical decisions, 124
    honesty, personal standards of, 75
    individual characteristics affecting
        ethical behaviour, 70–72
    leadership traits, 188
    organizational characteristics affecting ethical
        behaviour, 73–75
    unethical behaviour, contributions to, 70*f*
ethnocentrism, 35
eustress, 147
exchange, 106, 172*t*
executive summary, 368, 369
existence needs, 94
expectancy, 101–102
expectancy theory, 101–103, 101*f*
experimentation, 268–269
expert power, 107*f*
explicit knowledge, 122
external focus, 264
external locus of control, 55
extinction, 315
extraversion, 51, 52
extrinsic incentives, 349
extrinsic motivation, 103

F

fairness, 170–172
fairness, desire for, 96, 104–105
family business management, 361
feedback, 250–252
    challenge in delivering, 318
    and job design, 313
    self-assessments, 142–143
    360-degree feedback, 317
feedback-seeking behaviour, 143
feedforward communication, 251–252
Fiedler's contingency theory of leadership, 195–196
filtering, 240–241
financing sources, 370
First, Break All the Rules (Buckingham and
    Coffman), 196
first impressions, 81
First Nations culture, 36
FIT (Feelings, Issues, Techniques), 216*t*
fixed-interval schedules, 315
fixed-ratio schedules, 315
focus, 274
focus strategy, 297–298, 300
forming, 215, 216–219
framing, 121
free riders, 224
free riding, 223
front-line managers, 228, 241
frustration-regression principle, 95
functional departmentalization, 274, 275*f*
functional teams, 214
fundamental attribution error, 80

G

gain-sharing plans, 320
gender, and leadership, 194
generalized self-efficacy, 54
generational differences, 49
geographic differences, and political values, 59
glass ceiling, 48
global environment, 34–38
    ethnocentrism, 35
    individualism, 35–36
    materialism, 36
    multinational company (MNC), 34
    national culture, 35
    polycentrism, 35
    power distance, 37
    time orientation, 36
    uncertainty avoidance, 37

global marketplace, 296
globalization, 34
GLOBE project, 35
goal consensus, 119–120
goal displacement, 99, 271
goal-setting theory, 97–100
goal-sharing plans, 320
goodwill, 166
government incubators, 373
grapevine, 248
graphic rating scales, 317
group efficacy, 102
groups, 213
    see also teams
    characteristics of, 213*f*
    interest groups, 213
    vs. teams, 213–216
groupthink, 222, 223, 290
growth needs, 94

H

halo/horn bias, 121*t*
halo/horn effects, 80
happiness, 7, 8, 96
Hawthorne effect, 25–26
hierarchical teams, 214
hierarchy culture, 291, 291*f*, 301
hierarchy of needs, 94, 94*f*
history of organizational behaviour, 23–28
    human relations era, 25–26
    scientific management era, 24–25
    sustainability era, 27–28
    systems era, 26
Hofstede's five dimensions of national culture, 36*f*
Hofstede's materialism/individualism dimensions, 38*f*
holistic concerns, 28
honesty, 75, 188
House's path-goal theory, 196–197
hubris, 142
human relations, 25–26
human relations era, 25–26
human resource management (HRM), 311
humility, 142
hybrid departmentalization, 275–276, 275*f*
hybrid structure, 302
hygiene factors, 95

I

"I can do it" view, 102
idea champions, 347

ideal types, 9
identify and reply approach, 241
image theory, 123
imitation, 338, 338*f*
implementation of decision, 125–129
impoverished style, 192
impression management, 79
incentive pay, 320
incremental change, 338, 338*f*
incremental trial-and-error method, 120
incubation, 152
independent variables, 28
individual behaviour
    beliefs, 55
    potential influences on, 47*f*
    values, 55–59
individual states
    attitudes, 75–77
    commitments, 77–78
    emotions, 81–83
    ethics, 69–75
    key individual states, 69*f*
    perceptions, 78–81
individualism, 35–36, 36*f*, 38*f*
Industrial Revolution, 23
influence tactics, 172–173, 172*f*
informal expectations, 74
information distortion, 126
infrastructural behaviour, 193–194
ingratiation, 172*t*
initiating structure, 192, 194
initiative, 364–367, 365*f*
innate needs, 94–96
innovation, 151, 301, 338, 338*f*
insider trading, 69
inspiration, 152
inspirational appeal, 172*t*
institutionalization, 27
instrumental values, 57
instrumentality, 102
integrated conventional leadership model,
    199–201, 200*f*
integrated sustainable leadership model,
    201–204, 201*f*
integrating style, 178
integrative models, 198
    integrated conventional leadership model,
        199–201, 200*f*
    integrated sustainable leadership model,
        201–204, 201*f*
    situational leadership models, 198–199
integrative negotiation, 175–177, 175*f*

integrity, 188
integrity survey, 163
intelligence, 188, 190
intentional living, 144–147, 152
    behavioural strategies, 145–146
    constructive thought patterns, 146
    natural rewards, 146
intentions, 166
interactional justice, 171
interdepartmental communication, 153
interest groups, 213
internal focus, 264
internal locus of control, 55
internal motivation, 191
interorganizational politics, 165
interpersonal trust, 165
interventions, 345
intrapreneurship, 361
intrinsic motivation, 103, 153, 349–350
intuition, 121, 122–123
invisible hand, 7, 8, 72
invisible infrastructural behaviour, 194
invisible socioemotional behaviour, 194
inward-facing structure, 294, 295–296, 295*f*,
    300, 301, 302
iron cage, 7

J

job analysis, 312
Job Analysis at the Speed of Reality
    (JASR), 312
job-based pay, 320
job characteristics model, 312–314, 312*f*
job design, 312–314
job dissatisfaction, 95
job involvement, 76
job satisfaction, 76, 95, 293, 320
Johari Window, 142, 143*f*
joint diagnosis, 341
Journey to the East (Hesse), 195
justice, 13, 96, 171

K

kibbutzim, 37
*Know-How: The 8 Skills that Separate People
    Who Perform from Those Who Don't*
    (Charan), 190
knowing self, 141–144
knowledge, 188
KSAOs, 312, 314, 317

L

Larry Crowne, 170
layoffs, 167
Leader-Member Exchange (LMX), 197–198
leader-member relations, 196
leadership, 187
    see also leadership behaviour
    achievement-oriented leadership, 197
    authentic leadership, 139–140, 140*f*
    behaviours of, 191–195
    contingency theories, 195–198
    desire to lead, 188
    directive leadership, 196
    and gender, 194
    integrated models, 198–204
    job satisfaction, role in, 77
    Leadership Grid, 192–194
    leading yourself, 140*f*
    organizational culture, creation of, 288
    participative leadership, 196
    self-leadership practices, 144, 145*f*
    self-sacrificing leadership behaviour, 54
    servant leadership, 194–195, 339–340
    supportive leadership, 196
    techniques, 226
    traits, 188–191
    transactional leaders, 187
    transformational leaders, 187
    women and, 194
leadership behaviour, 191–195
    see also leadership; leadership traits
    dimensions of, 192
    Leadership Grid, 192–194, 193*f*
    servant leadership, 194–195
Leadership Grid, 192–194, 193*f*
leadership traits, 188–191
leading, 12–13
leading yourself, 140*f*, 141*f*
    authentic leadership, 139–140
    creativity. *See* creativity
    intentional living, 144–147
    knowing self, 141–144
    stress management. *See* stress management
legal approach, 32
legitimate power, 107*f*
legitimizing tactics, 172*t*
Level 5 leaders, 189
limitation, 338
Limitless, 116
listening, 249, 249*t*
listening posture, 117

living intentionally. *See* intentional living
locus of control, 53–54, 55
lone entrepreneur, 365
long-term orientation, 36*f*

M

Machiavellian personality, 51
Machiavellianism, 164
make the first offer, 173
management, 11
   and controlling, 13
   front-line managers, 228
   and leading, 12–13
   management 2.0, 12
   mid-level managers, and stress, 149
   open-book management, 341
   and organizing, 12
   and planning, 11
Management, 83
management-by-objectives (MBO), 317–318
Managerial Grid, 192
market approach, 32
market culture, 291*f,* 292–293
Maslow's hierarchy of needs, 94, 94*f*
materialism, 36, 36*f,* 38*f*
matrix departmentalization, 275*f,* 276
MBA oath, 123
McClelland's acquired needs theory, 96
meaningfulness, 312–313
mechanistic-organic structure, 294
mechanistic structure, 294
media richness, 245
medium, 244–245
membership, 274, 276
merger, 344
message, 240
   see also communication
   channel choice, 244–248
   confirmation, 250–252
   decoding, 248–250
   encoding of, 242–248
   impersonal delivery, 246
   media choice, 244–248
   receiving, 248–250
   transmission of, 242–248
meta-analysis, 29
The Michigan studies, 192
mid-level managers, and stress, 149
middle-of-the-road style, 193
minimizer strategy, 298, 301, 302
mission driven organizations, 298

mission statement, 325
money, 7
mood, 82
moral development, 70–71, 70*f*
moral point of view, 71
motivation, 94
   see also motivational systems
   desire for achievement, 97–103
   desire for affiliation, 106
   desire for fairness, 104–105
   ERG theory, 94
   expectancy theory, 101–103
   extrinsic motivation, 103
   goal-setting theory, 97–100
   innate needs, 94–97
   internal motivation, 191
   intrinsic motivation, 103, 153, 349–350
   Maslow's hierarchy of needs, 94, 94*f*
motivational systems
   career development, 321, 323–324
   job design, 312–314
   mission, 325–328
   and outcomes, 311*f*
   performance management, 314–321
   training, 321, 322–323
   vision, 325–328
motivator factors, 95
multiculturalism, 290
multinational company (MNC), 34
mutual discernment, 278
Myers–Briggs Type Indicator (MBTI), 52–53, 53*f*

N

national culture, 35, 36*f*
   see also culture
natural environment, 32–34, 32*f*
natural rewards, 146
negative affect, 51–52
negative correlation, 29
negative reinforcement, 315
negotiation, 172
   approaches to, 173–177
   conflict styles, 177–178
   and culture, 178
   influence tactics, 172–173, 172*f*
   integrative negotiation, 175–177, 175*f*
nepotism, 171
network structure, 276
noise, 242
nominal group technique, 224, 225
non-routine technology, 297

nonconformists, 153
nonprogrammed decisions, 118
normative commitment, 78
norming, 215, 223–226
norms, 223

O

obligations, 77
obliging style, 178
obstructionist stance, 32
Ohio State studies, 192
Olympic athletes, 98
on-site teams, 214
on-the-job training (OJT), 322
1001 Ways to Reward Employees (Nelson), 321
open-book management, 341
open system, 26
openness to experience, 51, 52
operant conditioning, 315
opportunity, 342, 363–364, 365
organic structure, 294, 300
organization-specific responsibility (OSR), 30
organizational behaviour (OB), 5
    see also conventional OB; sustainable OB
    effective approaches, 6–11
    effective organizational behaviour, 6–11
    global environment, 34–38
    history of, 23–28
    integration of concepts, 14*f*
    and management, 11–13
    perceptions of individuals, effect of, 78–81
    science of, 28–30
    study of, 5–6, 6*f*
organizational change, 337–340
    change process, four steps in, 339*f*, 340–347
    change stage, 345–350
    commitment to change, 347–350, 348*f*
    emotions, 346
    failure to change, 351*f*
    incremental change, 338, 338*f*
    intentionality, 337, 337*f*, 338
    members' attitudes toward change, 349–350
    need for change, recognition of, 340–341
    physical settings, 346
    planned change, 338, 338*f*
    refreezing, 350–352
    resistance to change, 343, 344–345
    scope, 337, 337*f*, 338
    source, 337, 337*f*
    structural change, 345–346
    transformational change, 338, 338*f*

types of, 337–338, 337*f*
    unfreeze, 341–345
    unplanned change, 338, 338*f*
organizational chart, 272
organizational citizenship behaviour (OCB), 51
organizational commitment, 77–78
organizational culture, 261, 287
    adhocracy culture, 291–293
    alignment of, 293–299
    artifacts, 265–266
    basic assumptions, 262–263
    clan culture, 290–291, 291*f*, 300
    Competing Values Framework (CVF), 263–265
    creating, 287–290
    elements of, 261, 262*f*
    engineering culture, 302
    forms of, 290–293, 291*f*
    hierarchy culture, 291, 291*f*, 301
    inward-facing structure, 294, 295–296, 295*f*
    key values, 263–265
    market culture, 291*f*, 292–293
    organizational structure, 294–296
    rewards, 289–290
    selection, 288–289
    socialization, 289
    strategy, 293*f*, 297–299
    structure, 293*f*
    technology, 293*f*, 296–297
    weak cultures, 290
organizational development (OD), 339–340
organizational politics, 163–165, 163*f*
organizational relationships
    fairness, 170–172
    negotiation, 172–178
    organizational politics, 163–165, 163*f*
    self-interest, 163–165
    trust, 165–170
organizational structure, 261–262
    see also organizational types
    centralization *vs.* dignification, 272–274
    departmentalization *vs.* participation,
        274–278
    elements of, 262*f*
    fundamentals of, 266–278, 267*f*
    in global marketplace, 296
    hybrid structure, 302
    inward-facing structure, 300, 301, 302
    mechanistic structure, 294
    organic structure, 294, 300
    and organizational culture, 293*f*
    organizational types, 299–302, 299*f*
    outward-facing structure, 294, 295, 295*f*, 302

specialization *vs.* sensitization, 269–271
standardization *vs.* experimentation, 267–269
organizational types, 299, 299*f*
    see also organizational structure
    Analyzer type, 299*f,* 302
    Defender type, 299*f,* 300–301
    Prospector type, 299*f,* 301–302
    Simple type, 299*f,* 300
organizations, 5
organizing, 12
outsourcing, 276
outward-facing structure, 294, 295, 295*f,* 302
over-rewarded, 105

P

partial goal consensus, 121
participation, 277–278
participative leadership, 196
path-goal theory, 196–197
pay-for-performance (PFP), 320
perceptions, 78–81
perceptual biases, 79–80, 81
perceptual errors, 79–80, 81
performance appraisals, 316–319
    delivery of appraisal, 317–318
    design of appraisal system, 317
    reinforcement of process, 318–319
    review of process, 318–319
performance management, 314–321
    compensation, 319–321
    performance appraisal, 316–319
performing, 215, 226–228
permanent teams, 214
persistence, 153
personal appeal, 172*t*
personality, 50–53
    agreeableness, 51, 52
    Big Five personality traits, 51, 53*f,* 293, 364
    conscientiousness, 51
    emotional stability, 51
    entrepreneurs, 364–365
    extraversion, 51, 52
    Machiavellian personality, 51
    negative affect, 51–52
    neurotic personality, 51–52
    openness to experience, 51, 52
    positive affect, 51–52
physical abilities, 50
physiological needs, 94*f*
planned change, 338, 338*f*
planning, 11

political method, 120
political values, 59
politics, organizational, 163–165, 163*f*
polycentrism, 35
Ponzi schemes, 69
position power, 196
positive affect, 52
positive correlation, 28–29
positive pulls, 367
positive reinforcement, 315
positive self-talk, 146
positivistic orientation, 29–30
postconventional moral development, 71
power, 107*f*
power, desire for, 96, 107
power distance, 36*f*
practical wisdom, 11, 96
preconventional moral development, 71
predictability, 263
preparation, 152
pressure, 172*t*
Principles of Responsible Management
    Education, 122
proactive approach, 34
procedural justice, 171
profit-sharing plans, 320
profitability (pro-fit-ability) test, 123
programmed decisions, 118
project teams, 214
Prospector type, 299*f,* 301–302
proxemics, 243
prudence, 11
psychological contract, 165–166
punishment, 315

Q

qualitative research, 30
quality of life, 36*f*
quantitative orientation, 29–30
quantitative research, 30

R

rank-and-yank, 319
rational choice, 120
rational persuasion, 172*t*
re-slush, 351
reality TV, 143
referent power, 107*f*
refreezing, 350–352
reinforcement, 314–315

reinforcement theory, 315
relatedness needs, 94
relational skills, 6
relationship
    negotiation, 172–178
relationship-oriented, 196
relationships
    fairness, 170–172
    politics and self-interest, 163–165
    stakeholder relationships, 30–34
    trust, 165–170
representativeness, 79, 121*f*
reservation point, 174
resistance to change, 343, 344–345
resources, 369–370, 372–374
reward power, 107*f*
rituals, 266
role conflict, 148–149
round tables, 243
routine decisions, 118
routine response, 118
routine technology, 296, 301

S

safety needs, 94*f*
salaries, 319
satisficing, 121
schedules of reinforcement, 315–316
science of organizational behaviour, 28–30
scientific management, 24–25, 313
scientific management era, 24–25
scripts, 116
selection, 288–289
selective perception, 80
self-actualization, 94, 94*f*
self-awareness, 83, 141, 142–144, 143*f*, 190
self-confidence, 188
self-control, 13, 96
self-cueing, 145
self-discipline, 144
self-efficacy, 54
self-esteem, 54, 94
self-evaluation, 53–55
self-fulfilling prophecy effect, 102
self-goal setting, 145
self-influence, 144
self-interest, 72
self-knowledge, 141–142
self-leadership practices, 144, 145*f*
self-managed teams, 214
self-management, 83, 190–191

self-observation, 145
self-reinforcement, 145–146
self-sacrificing leadership behaviour, 54
self-serving bias, 142
semantic problems, 244
Sense and Sensibility (Austen), 79
sensitization, 271
servant leadership, 194–195, 339–340
seven blunders of the world, 101
The 7 Habits of Highly Effective People
        (Covey), 176
shared stories, 266
shared vision, 345
short-term orientation, 36*f*
Simple type, 299*f*
Situational Leadership II, 198–199
situational leadership models, 198–199
skill variety, 312–313
sleep test, 124
slushing, 352
small business management, 361
SMART goals, 97–99, 99*f*
SMART2 goals, 99–100, 99*f*
social categorization theory, 47
social cohesion, 217
social construction of reality, 27
social entrepreneurship, 361
social needs, 94*f*
social networks, 166
social "scripts," 26
social skills, 191
societal well-being, 28
socioemotional behaviour, 193–194
span of control, 272
specialization, 269–271, 270*f*
spray and pray approach, 240
stakeholder, 30
    assumptions about responsibilities to, 31*f*
    competitors as, 33
    conventional *vs.* sustainable approach, 31
    relationships, 30–34
    suppliers as, 33
    trusting relationships, establishing, 167
stakeholder approach, 32
stakeholder relationships, 30–34
standardization, 267–268, 268*f*
start-up plan, 368–372
states, 69
    see also individual states
stereotypes, 48
stock options, 320
storming, 215, 219–222

strategy, 293f, 297–299
    see also specific strategies
stress, 147
    and CEOs, 149
    dealing with. See stress management
    and mid-level managers, 149
stress management
    conservation of resources theory, 150
    dealing with stress, 149–151
    simple approach to, 150
    taking a break, 151
    whole person, 149–150
    workplace stress, 147–148
stressors, 147
stretch goal, 98–99
structure. See organizational structure
structured self-reflection, 144
subject matter experts (SMEs), 312
subjective method, 121
substitutes-for-leadership theory, 200
sucker effect, 223–224
superordinate goal, 221
suppliers, 33, 369
supporting, 199, 202t
supportive leadership, 196
supreme good, 8
surface characteristics, 47–50
sustainability era, 27–28
Sustainable Analyzer type, 302
Sustainable Defender type, 301
sustainable development, 34
sustainable entrepreneurs
    entrepreneurship, 373–374
    non-financial resources, 373–374
sustainable entrepreneurship, 361–362
sustainable OB, 7
    adhocracy culture, 291–292
    affiliation, 106
    alternatives, choice of, 122
    appraisal system, 318–319
    business plan, 369–371
    career development, 324
    clan culture, 291
    commitment to change, 349–350
    communication, 240, 242
    contingencies, 197
    controlling, 13
    corporate social responsibility (CSR),
        30–31, 31f
    courage, 12
    decision, implementation of, 128–129
    decision making, 117, 118–119, 123

decoding, 248–250
delegation, 169–170
departmentalization, 277
described, 7–8
dignification, 273
diversity, 49
egalicentric, 35
emotions, 83
employment contract, 324
enabling, 202
entrepreneurship, 362f, 363–364,
    366–367, 370
ethics, approach to, 74–75
experimentation, 268–269
explicit knowledge, 122
fairness, 105, 171–172
feedback, 141–143
hierarchy culture, 291
implications of, 9–11
information sharing, 225–226
instrumentality, 102
integrative negotiations, 176–177
interorganizational politics, 165
inward-facing structure, 295–296, 295f
job analysis and design, 313–314
justice, 13, 171–172
key priorities, 8, 8f, 9f
leadership, 189–190, 202t, 203–204,
    347–348
leading, 12–13
market culture, 292–293
membership, 277
messages, 241
mission statement, 327–328
moral point of view, 72
motivation, 95–96
organizational change, 338–340, 340–341, 342,
    351–352
organizational commitment, 78
organizational culture, 288
organizational politics, 165
organizational structure, 294
organizing, 12
outward-facing structure, 295–296, 295f
participation, 277
performance management, 321
personality traits, 52, 53f
planning, 11
power, 107–108
prudence, 11
research designs, 30
resistance to change, 344–345

resources, 370
sensitization, 271
and SMART2 goals, 99–100
stakeholders, 31
standardization, 268
strategy, 298–299
stress management, 150–151
surface characteristics, 49
Sustainable Analyzer type, 302
Sustainable Defender type, 301
Sustainable Prospector type, 301–302
team-level rewards, 227
training, 322–323
triple bottom line approach, 9
trust, 167, 168, 242
valence, 102–103
values, 11, 264
vision statement, 327–328
Voluntary Simplicity type, 300
Sustainable Prospector type, 301–302
sustaincentrism, 72
SWOT (Strength, Weakness, Opportunity, Threat)
    analysis, 324
symbols, 243
systems analysis, 26
systems era, 26
systems theory, 26

T

tacit knowledge, 121
task analyzability, 296
task cohesion, 217
task identity, 313
task management style, 193
task-oriented, 196
task significance, 313
task structure, 196
task variety, 296
team conflict, 219–222, 220*t*
team diversity, 216
team identity, 214, 218
team style, 193
team task interdependence, 220
teams, 213
    characteristics of, 213*f*
    conflict, 219–222
    cross-functional teams, 214
    developmental categories, 215, 215*f*
    see also specific developmental categories
    FIT (Feelings, Issues, Techniques), 216*t*
    functional teams, 214

hierarchical teams, 214
on-site teams, 214
permanent teams, 214
project teams, 214
self-managed teams, 214
size and social cohesion, 218
student teams, 218
task-oriented, 213
team diversity, 216
team identity, 214, 218
types of, 214
virtual teams, 214
vs. groups, 213–216
technical skills, 6
technology, 293*f*, 296–297, 301–302, 345
teleopathy, 75
tell and sell approach, 241
temperance, 13
terminal values, 57
texting, 247
The Theory of Moral Sentiments (Smith), 8
Theory X, 56
Theory Y, 56
thinking, 153
threat, 342
threat-rigidity response, 341
360-degree feedback, 317
time, 243
time orientation, 36
top-down approach, 342
total quality management (TQM), 26
training, 321, 322–323
traits, 188
transactional leaders, 187
transformational change, 338, 338*f*
transformational leaders, 187
transformer strategy, 298, 302
triple bottom line approach, 9, 362,
    362*f*, 371
trust, 165–170, 166*f*, 168*f*, 347
tweeting, 247
Type A personality, 51

U

uncertainty, 36*f*, 120, 343
uncertainty avoidance, 36*f*
under-rewarded, 104–105
underscore and explore approach, 241
understanding others, 176
unplanned change, 338, 338*f*
utilitarianism, 71

V

valence, 102–103
validation, 152
values, 56–59, 58*f*
    Competing Values Framework (CVF),
        263–265
    conventional OB *vs.* sustainable
        OB, 57*f*
    influence on organizational culture,
        263–265
    instrumental values, 57
    political values, 59
    terminal values, 57
variable-interval schedules, 316
variable-ratio schedules, 316
venture capitalist, 369
venture concept, 368, 369
virtual organization, 276–277, 277
virtual teams, 214
virtues, 8, 72, 96
virtue theory, 8
virtuous arm, 8
visible infrastructural behaviour, 194
visible socioemotional behaviour, 193–194
vision statement, 326
visualization of performance, 146
Voluntary Simplicity type, 300

W

wages, 319
"we can do it" view, 102
weak cultures, 290
Wealth of Nations (Smith), 24
"What Great Managers Do" (Buckingham, Marcus), 198
willpower, 29
withhold and uphold approach, 241
women, and leadership, 194
work–family conflict, 148, 148*f*
work–life conflict, 148
workplace stress, 147–148
World Values Survey, 35

Y

yanking, 73

Z

zone of possible agreements (ZOPA), 174, 174*f*